Murakami Haruki

STUDIES OF MODERN JAPAN

Series Editor: Edward R. Beauchamp, University of Hawaii

Studies of Modern Japan is a multidisciplinary series that consists primarily of original studies on a broad spectrum of topics dealing with Japan since the Meiji restoration of 1868. Additionally, the series aims to bring back into print classic works that shed new light on contemporary Japan. In all cases, the goal is to publish the best scholarship available, by both established and rising scholars in the field, in order to better understand Japan and the Japanese during the modern period and into the future.

Titles in the Series

Murakami Haruki

The Simulacrum in Contemporary Japanese Culture

Michael Seats

LEXINGTON BOOKS

A division of
ROWMAN & LITTLEFIELD PUBLISHERS, INC.
Lanham • Boulder • New York • Toronto • Plymouth, UK

LEXINGTON BOOKS

A division of Rowman & Littlefield Publishers, Inc.
A wholly owned subsidiary of The Rowman & Littlefield Publishing Group, Inc.
4501 Forbes Boulevard, Suite 200
Lanham, MD 20706

Estover Road
Plymouth PL6 7PY
United Kingdom

British Library Cataloguing in Publication Information Available

Library of Congress Cataloging-in-Publication Data

Seats, Michael, 1958–
  Murakami Haruki : the simulacrum in contemporary Japanese culture / Michael Seats.
      p. cm.— (Studies of modern Japan)
  Includes bibliographical references and index.
1. Murakami, Haruki, (1949–)—Criticism and interpretation. I. Title. II. Series.
PL856.U673Z85 2006
895.6'35—dc22   2006010346

  ISBN: 978-0-7391-0785-0 (cloth : alk. paper)
  ISBN: 978-0-7391-2725-4 (pbk. : alk. paper)
  ISBN: 978-0-7391-4044-4 (electronic)

Printed in the United States of America

For Anton and Aisha

Contents

Preface

In January 2005, an essay by the contemporary novelist Murakami Haruki appeared in a special section of the Japanese newspaper *Asahi shinbun* commemorating the Great Hanshin Earthquake of a decade earlier.[1] In the article, Murakami reveals his own emotional responses to the catastrophe, and links the very personal experience of horror with the more collectively suffered dimensions of warfare, natural calamities and acts of terror. The author recalls his visit to the scene of the disastrous routing of Japanese troops at Nomonhan (Mongolia) in 1939. At night he is awakened by what he imagines to be an earthquake—soon realizing, however, that he has experienced some kind of 'violent personal convulsion'. He surmises that this has been brought on by an acute and initially unconscious realization of the fear and pain of the thousands who lost their lives—apparently without purpose—on this barren stretch of land.

Murakami's trip to the battlefield graveyard of Nomonhan had already been depicted in detail some years earlier in the essays and photos of the book *Henkyô—Kinkyô*.[2] The short commemorative piece in the newspaper revisits that 'incident' and its representation in *Nejimakidori kuronikuru*[3] (*The Wind-up Bird Chronicle*[4]). This is juxtaposed with an account of the shock that overcame him as he gradually learned of the catastrophic consequences of the earthquake in his hometown. Later in the essay, Murakami offers another comparison. He recalls how the English edition of *Kami no kodomotachi wa minna odoru*[5] (short stories around the theme of the Hanshin Earthquake) entitled *After the Quake*,[6] which was published after the September 11 2001 terrorist attacks in the United States, prompted recently traumatized Americans to convey to him their profound empathy with the devastated lives depicted in these stories. From this, Murakami concludes that in terms of the tremendous challenge of emotional recovery, human acts of terror and large-scale natural disasters seem to have a lot in common.

In recent years, it is not only journalists and writers of fiction who have undertaken to explore the politics of terror. Philosophers, too, have shown their interest. Like Murakami, Jean Baudrillard finds a resemblance between the terrorist act and the natural catastrophe—albeit for different reasons.[7] Obviously, there is a great deal of difference in the experiences of the victims of terror and natural catastrophe, and those who 'witness' these 'events' through the media. As Baudrillard points out, most people experience such calamities as the simulation of an object world where agency seems to have vanished and the real become indifferent to difference—and where terror and nature are viewed as malevolent and arbitrary.[8]

Yet, paradoxically, in the simulation of such an object world the real appears to return all the more forcefully as an idea. Here, simulation reveals itself as a kind of 'seduction': it is 'an ironic, alternative form . . . which provides a space, not of desire, but of play or defiance.'[9] Such a provocation should not be dismissed as mere solipsism. Rather, as one critic points out, in proposing a 'mischievous version of appearances', (Baudrillard's) theory of seduction 'suggests that there is a real world to be fought over and defined, even if we never know the world itself'. What is at stake, however, is the 'mastering of the reign of appearances' which 'opposes power as a mastery of the universe of meaning'.[10]

The extended reflections by Jurgen Habermas and Jacques Derrida on the September 11 attacks demonstrate just how far the philosophical discussion of terror can and should be taken.[11] Habermas views them as evidence of extreme reactions to modernization, as manifestations of 'striking cognitive dissonances',[12] while Derrida asks us to distinguish between two kinds of 'impressions' arising from the catastrophic events. On the one hand, compassion and indignation over the killings in an 'event' which was 'beyond all simulacra and all possible virtualization'. On the other hand, the need to understand the 'interpreted, interpretive, informed impression . . . that makes us *believe* that this is a "major event".'[13] For Derrida, this belief is signified in the repeated invocation of the event as a date, 'September 11', '9/11'—'this act of naming: a date and nothing more.' Something took place which cannot be named, and yet it is perpetually 'constituted . . . circulated through the media by means of a prodigious techno-social-political machine'.[14]

Baudrillard's concern with the 'reign of appearances' and Derrida's notion of the 'interpretative impression' help illuminate how we experience certain phenomena in contemporary culture. As such, they can be said to resonate with some of the representational strategies which are the hallmark of Murakami's literary experimentation, but which are not strictly limited to his fiction. For example, in his perspectives on the Tokyo subway gas attack of 1995, both the perpetrators and the killed or injured can be considered as victims, although in very different ways. Echoing Baudrillard, Murakami seems to be implying that the argument in favor of moral complexity acknowledges that in a system (the State, the Global) plagued by resistances which sometimes erupt in the form of 'attacks', terror is inexorably complicit with the processes of its representation in mediatized forms. Yet such a claim is not necessarily meant to imply that without the support of the media and its 'audiences' (both part of one, seamless process) terror, in its present manifestations, would disappear. Certainly, for Baudrillard, the facile lament that 'terrorism would be nothing without the media', is borne of an illusion: 'There is no "good" use of the media; the media are part of the event, they are part of the terror, and they work in both directions'.[15]

The often misunderstood writings of Baudrillard—as increasingly unsystematic and aphoristic as they are—contribute significantly to our understanding of the complex theory of the simulacrum. Although they do not provide the whole picture, perhaps the general *effect* of their presence is to continually provoke us into reexamining the ways in which we read culture. If there is any validity to Baudrillard's fundamental claim that the greater the simulation, the greater the sense of the real, then we have at least one plausible reason why Murakami's writings have been so consistently popular. That is to say, the more his works ostensibly move away from the real through experimentation with various modalities of the simulacrum, the stronger is the sense that the referent, the real, is somehow closer at hand, easier to grasp.

But why should this be important or even interesting? And for that matter, in Japan—arguably the most 'informationalized' and 'mediatized' of post-industrial societies—how can the real be theorized in a satisfactory way? Murakami's most recent long novel, *Afutâ dâku*[16] (*After Dark*), is the latest example of his writing that takes up the challenge of this question. By presenting the characters, setting and available reading positions of the narrative in terms of the voyeuristic and simulated modalities of the 'reality television' set, and by establishing the narrative, as one critic puts it,[17] as a kind of 'membrane' through which we experience the real, it suggests, like many of his previous works, that perhaps the real can be 'theorized' through fiction in more comprehensive ways than the discourses of history and philosophy may allow. Nevertheless, (and quite typically) there is a sense of contradiction in some of Murakami's claims. On the one hand, he acknowledges that in writing what he calls 'actual' and 'active' fiction, he is showing his determination not to 'lose out' to the popular virtual modalities of video games and the Internet.[18] Elsewhere, however, he admits to being fascinated by the 'virtual' narrative perspectives established in *Afutâ dâku* and insists that he has no interest in cinematic techniques which employ realism.[19]

Murakami's short essay on the anniversary of the Kobe earthquake (which would have been read by millions on that day of national commemoration), can be described as a recent snapshot of the multi-dimensionality of an author who continues to both delight and perplex his readers. The overt concern with recovery (*kaifuku*), and such a publicly declared personal sense of social engagement and 'commitment' would have been unthinkable in the first decade of his career as a writer, when he used very different methods for carrying out his project of cultural critique. During that period Murakami did not have (and arguably has not yet found) a suitable method for writing more *directly* about how postwar Japanese culture understands itself—although to some extent, his venture into 'non-fiction' writing in the form of interviews with the survivors and perpetrators of the 1995 Tokyo subway gas attack could be described as an exception. Instead, he has opted to approach problems of the representation of human experience in ways which provide ongoing opportunities for his explorations in literary method, language and subjectivity. Murakami's recourse to what may be called 'doubled structures' or, as shall be discussed later, versions of the simulacrum, has its origins in a period well before his apparent turn to 'social engagement' (or entry into the so-called *shakai-ha*) with the publication of his later trilogy. It also extends well beyond this phase, into his most recent novels *Umibe no kafuka*, 2002[20] (*Kafka on the Shore* 2005[21]), and *Afutâ dâku* (2004), and in both of these works, is manifested in surprising and complex ways.

Over the past few decades Murakami has emerged as one of the most significant literary figures in Japan. Having produced more than ninety original works and translations, he has recast the format of the novel, helped to reformulate the parameters of contemporary literary style and ventured into non-fiction writing and social commentary. Furthermore, he is now a thoroughly 'globalized' writer, with works translated into numerous languages and read in at least thirty-five countries. While some of the critical literature on Murakami in Japanese has recently become more sophisticated, works in English have remained largely bound to the conventional analyses applied to earlier forms of modern Japanese fiction. In particular, the nexus in Murakami's writing between modernity, subjectivity and representation has been poorly theorized.

This book offers a new approach to dealing with Murakami's radical narrative project by demonstrating how his first and later trilogies utilize the structure of the simulacrum, a second-order representation, to develop a complex critique of contemporary Japanese culture. It aims to make a contribution to the field of Japanese Studies, and, more generally, will also be of interest to those researching in critical theory, cultural studies and comparative literature. More specifically, it is intended that this book will make a philosophical intervention in the discussion about the significance of Murakami's fiction in contemporary Japanese culture.

To date there have been only two full-length English language monographs on this author. Jay Rubin's *Haruki Murakami and the Music of Words* (2002) makes for an informative and entertaining read, and although not intended as a 'scholarly work', is an essential text for anyone interested in both the biographical details and writing processes surrounding most of the works in Murakami's oeuvre. On the other hand, Matthew Strecher's *Dances with Sheep: The Quest for Identity in the Fiction of Haruki Murakami* (2001, 2002) is a more explicitly theoretical study, which posits a series of interpretative strategies for understanding Murakami's unique contribution to contemporary writing. As will be shown later, however, in its idealized conceptualizations of terms such as 'identity' and 'meaning', Strecher's book fails to adequately problematize certain presuppositions about the subject in/of Japanese literary modernity, which, as is argued here, Murakami is at pains to critique.

Unlike both of these works, the arguments presented in this book are not based on any personal interviews of Murakami by myself, nor do they include many references to the background details of his life, influences or interests.

This difference indicates a deliberate critical strategy and should by no means be construed as a lack of interest in Murakami's remarkable career and prodigious publishing achievements. On the contrary, it reflects, firstly, a respect for and empathy with Murakami's own tendency to shy away from discussion about the 'interpretation' of his writing. His highly intelligent and consciously asserted 'anti-critical' stance is an implicit recognition of the need to counter the tendency for ready-made, superficial characterizations of his works largely driven by advertising and commercial imperatives. Secondly, it serves to temper the cultism surrounding the popular author and literary star—which, in contemporary Japan, inevitably tends to obscure the value of the works themselves amidst a barrage of media attention.

It needs to be acknowledged that Murakami continues to give generously of his time to those who wish to interview him, and that such interviews form an important part of the body of critical literature on his works. Also, that although he may not offer interpretations himself, where possible, Murakami is happy to help facilitate the task of those who make it their business to do so. Furthermore, I would hope that this book be seen as a ringing endorsement of Murakami's courage in provoking his contemporaries to extend the boundaries of their thought in ways which are philosophically (and therefore socially) significant. His strategy of exploring various forms of the simulacrum in his writing is neither naïve nor imitative. On the contrary, it reflects the skill of a literary craftsman whose work has finally come to be recognized for its radicality and innovation. Hopefully, this book will also help redirect debate about the status of contemporary literature back to more fundamental questions concerning Japanese modernity, which have been neither resolved nor 'overcome' with the supposed advent of postmodernity.

After outlining the critical-fictional contours of the 'Murakami Phenomenon', the discussion addresses the vexed question of Japanese modernity within the contexts of the national-cultural imaginary, globalized artistic discourses and the idea of the Japanese novel. Some competing perspectives on the theory of the simulacrum are then presented as a way of demonstrating the wide applicability of a syncretic model of the simulacrum. Murakami's first trilogy is analyzed in terms of its use of the tropes of parody, pastiche, metafiction, allegory and 'landscape'—all of which are shown to be modalities of the simulacrum. Indicating a tentative 'return' of the referent, the second and much later trilogy is then investigated in terms of the way in which it uses the structure of the simulacrum to problematize the distinction between the discourses of 'fiction' and 'history' via the aesthetic modalities of the sublime. The book concludes by demonstrating that within the context of current media-entertainment technologies and the competing discursive regimes of contemporary Japanese culture, Murakami's destabilization of hitherto clearly defined genres of writing is also indicative of a new politics of representation, the limits of which have yet to clearly emerge.

Notes

1. Murakami Haruki, "Jishin no ato de," in 'Tokushû: hanshin daishinsai jûnen,' *Asahi Shinbun,* 17 January 2005, 12 (N).

2. Murakami Haruki, *Henkyô—Kinkyô* (Shinchôsha, 1998).

3. Murakami Haruki, *Nejimakidori kuronikuru* (Shinchôsha, 1994-95).

4. Murakami Haruki, *The Wind-Up Bird Chronicle.* trans. Jay Rubin (London: Harvill 1997).

5. Murakami Haruki, *Kami no kodomotachi wa minna odoru* (Shinchôsha, 2000).

6. Murakami Haruki, *After the Quake,* trans. Jay Rubin (London: Harvill, 2002).

7. Baudrillard writes: 'It may even be argued that natural catastrophes are a form of terrorism. The characteristic of irrational events is that they can be imputed to anyone or anything.' For Baudrillard, this is made possible by the extreme vulnerability of a system as it approaches perfection: 'In a system as integrated as our own, everything has the same destabilizing effect. Everything conspires towards the failure of a system that sees itself as infallible.' See Jean Baudrillard, *The Spirit of Terrorism,* trans. Chris Turner (London: Verso, 2003), 98-99(fn).

8. See Jean Baudrillard, *The Illusion of the End,* trans. Chris Turner (Cambridge: Polity Press, 1994), 81, 119.

9. Jean Buadrillard, *Seduction,* trans. Brian Singer (London: Macmillan, 1990), 21, 38.

10. Paul Hegarty, *Jean Baudrillard: Live Theory* (London: Continuum, 2004), 71. Here Hegarty is citing Baudrillard's *The Ecstasy of Communication,* trans. Bernard & Caroline Schutze (New York: Semiotext(e), 1988), 55, 62.

11. See Giovanna Borradori, *Philosophy in a Time of Terror: Dialogues with Jurgen Habermas and Jacques Derrida* (Chicago: The University of Chicago Press, 2003).

12. Borradori, *Philosophy in a Time of Terror,* 32.

13. Borradori, *Philosophy in a Time of Terror,* 89.

14. Borradori, *Philosophy in a Time of Terror,* 85-86.

15. Baudrillard, *The Spirit of Terrorism,* 31.

16. Murakami Haruki, *Afutâdâku,* (Kôdansha, 2004).

17. Koike Masayo, "Dokusho—Afutâdâku," *Asahi shinbun,* 19 September 2004, 10 (N).

18. Murakami Haruki in conversation with Shibata Motoyuki, cited in "Fuan to kibô no fuhensei," *Aera* 17, no. 44 (11 October 2004): 47.

19. See "Murakami Haruki—rongu intabyû: 'Afutâdâku' o megutte," *Bungakkai* 59, no. 4 (April 2005): 174.

20. Murakami Haruki, *Umibe no kafuka* (Shinchosha, 2002)

21. Murakami Haruki, *Kafka on the Shore,* trans. by Philip Gabriel (London: Vintage Harvill), 2005.

Acknowledgements

This book originated as a doctoral dissertation submitted in 2002 to the Division of Social Sciences, Humanities and Education at Murdoch University, Western Australia. As such, it has been revised and rewritten to incorporate some of the suggestions of my dissertation examiners, and updated to include discussion of Murakami's most recent fictional works and recently published critical literature. Various drafts of the book accompanied me while I moved between teaching positions at universities in Australia, Japan and Hong Kong.

I am very grateful to Professor Stephen Snyder of Middlebury College, Professor Toshiko Ellis of the University of Tokyo, and Professor Leith Morton of the University of Newcastle for their constructive and incisive criticism, invaluable suggestions and encouragement of the project. The shortcomings of the book are not from want of careful consideration of suggested improvements. Rather, they are the inevitable result of a decision to attempt a difficult balance between an overall interdisciplinary approach and specific textual focus.

Special thanks are due to Professor Leith Morton for recommending the project to Lexington Books. Also, I would like to thank former Acquisitions Editor at Lexington, Rebekka Brooks, for her patience and guidance in the earlier stages of the project; and more recently, MacDuff Stewart and Patricia Stevenson for their commitment to getting the book through the final stages of production. Patrick Dillon was also of great assistance.

Over a period of many years, numerous people have contributed to the production of this book. Thanks to Professor David George for initially sparking my interest in Japan through his stimulating lectures on Japanese aesthetics. I am very grateful to Professor Orie Muta for assistance in the early stages of research, and her ongoing advice and encouragement. I must express my deep gratitude to Professor Atsuko Suga, formerly of the Department of Comparative Culture at Sophia University. Her generosity of spirit made this project possible, even though she is not able to witness its fruition in published form.

Members of the Japanese Studies Department at Murdoch University, including Radha Krishnan, Takeshi Moriyama and Sandra Wilson, offered great encouragement and support. Thanks also to Yoko Imai and Shigeki Nomoto for their assistance in collecting materials. I greatly appreciate the help of Helen Trenos for her intelligent comments on the argument and structure of the book as well as invaluable assistance in the proof-reading of earlier drafts.

Gratitude is due to Murdoch University for financial support in the form of a Postgraduate Research Scholarship, and to the Australian Vice-Chancellors' Committee for a generous grant which enabled me to carry out research at Sophia University.

I am indebted to Dr. George Watt, Dean of the Faculty of Foreign Languages and Asian Studies at the Nagoya University of Commerce and Business, for granting me research time for the preparation of a later draft. Thanks also to Professor Michael Kindler for his encouragement, and to Dr. Michael Brennan for some lively discussion of Murakami's writing. I am also greatly appreciative of the help of Dr. Charles Taylor for his enthusiastic assistance in editing.

Heartfelt thanks go to my wife, Haruko Nomoto, who helped in ways too numerous to list. Not only did she provide invaluable advice on linguistic matters, but her emotional support has sustained me throughout the entire project.

I am forever grateful to my son, Anton, for his forbearance in putting up with a too often absent father. In many ways, of all those who have helped, his love, understanding and encouragement have perhaps sustained me the most. The arrival of Aisha has also been a tremendous blessing which has renewed my energy and enthusiasm for this and all future projects.

It is impossible to adequately thank one's parents, however I would like to acknowledge Shirley and Michael for their generosity of spirit in encouraging my endeavours over the years.

I recall how the seminal idea of the project was born of a happy conjunction of circumstances: engaging conversation over a glass of local Australian wine, made all the more pleasant by a late spring zephyr filtering through the eucalypts. Finally, then, I must express my deepest gratitude to my former supervisor, mentor and friend, Emeritus Professor Horst Ruthrof, for his intelligence, unwavering enthusiasm, encouragement and guidance throughout this project.

Abbreviations

In order to assist those readers who wish to locate quoted passages in either the Japanese or translated versions of the main fictional texts referred to, the following abbreviations have been used. For passages in the first trilogy, chapter numbers precede page numbers; for example: KUK 2; 11. Passages from *Nejimakidori/The Wind-Up Bird Chronicle* are referenced by book/volume number, chapter number, and page number; for example: NDK 3: 37; 449 denotes *Nejimakidori kuronikuru*, Book 3, Chapter 37, page 449. All other of Murakami's texts are cited using standard referencing conventions.

Japanese texts

KUK *Kaze no uta o kike*

PIN *1973 nen no pinbôru*

HMB *Hitsuji o meguru bôken*

NDK *Nejimakidori kuronikuru*

English texts

HWS *Hear the Wind Sing*

P73 *Pinball, 1973*

WSC *A Wild Sheep Chase*

WBC *The Wind-Up Bird Chronicle*

Conventions

Throughout this discussion the plural personal pronoun 'we' has often been used in place of 'I' or the more indirect passive sentence construction. This is part of a strategy to develop an argument which reflects the inherently dialogic relations established between the writer of this book, the reader and the numerous critics whose views are considered.

Unless otherwise stated, the place of publication for all references in Japanese is Tokyo. The name of the Japanese literary journal *Kokubungaku kaishaku to kyôzai no kenkyû*, is given in the abbreviated form of *Kokubungaku* whenever referred to in the endnotes.

All quotations from Murakami's writing have been given first in Japanese, then either in an English version from the published translations of the text, or, where this is not available, translations by myself. This inclusion of the original Japanese text along with its translation is based on the need to allow the full range of stylistic nuances to be conveyed for those who can read Japanese, while providing access to the texts for all other readers. Unless otherwise stated, all unspecified translations are mine.

The Hepburn system of romanisation has been followed — except that the macrons indicating long vowels have been replaced by circumflex accents. In some proper nouns which have become conventionalized and anglicised, the accent has normally been omitted. Japanese names in the main text and notes are given in the conventional Japanese order of surname followed by first name. Other Japanese words and phrases used in the course of the discussion are usually given in romanized form in italics, and in brackets.

To facilitate ease of reference, the bibliography has been divided into 'Bibliography of Works in Japanese', 'Bibliography of works in English' and 'Selected Bibliography of Works by Murakami Haruki' (both in Japanese and in English translation). Unless otherwise stated, all Japanese works listed in the bibliography are published in Tokyo.

Introduction

The simulacrum is the instance which includes a difference with itself. . . . All resemblance abolished so that one can no longer point to the existence of an original and a copy.

—Gilles Deleuze, *Difference and Repetition*[1]

The room is dimly lit, but our eyes gradually adjust. A woman is asleep in the bed. A beautiful young woman . . . with black hair, spilling like dark water over the pillow. Staring at her form, we merge into one line of sight—or perhaps we should say that we are *secretly observing* her. Our gaze becomes a camera, floating in space, able to move freely about the room. The camera shifts to a position directly above the bed, and takes in her sleeping face. . . .

—Murakami Haruki, *After Dark*[2]

This book demonstrates how selected texts of Murakami Haruki's oeuvre utilize the structure of the simulacrum to develop a complex critique of contemporary Japanese culture. It also shows how this critique is mirrored in the practices of current media-entertainment technologies which allow Murakami's works, and their critical/promotional meta-texts, to cohere under the rubric of the so-called 'Murakami Phenomenon'.

Broadly, the simulacrum can be understood as a second order (re)presentation of reality. The argument supposes that although the simulacrum reflects the fundamental condition of all representation, this is not necessarily apparent to those engaged in its performance. It assumes that art does not explicitly acknowledge its own discourse *with* itself—even if such a discourse is the condition, paradoxically, of its very existence as art.[3]

The discussion suggests, as well, that the operation of the simulacrum can be interpreted in numerous ways: in inter or intracultural contexts, across genres and in translated forms. It becomes clear, however, that despite this plethora of trajectories, the narrative conventions of a given literary text usually prescribe a limited range of its possible forms of expression. With regard to Murakami's two fictional 'trilogies' (*sanbusaku*[4]) which are considered at length, several forms of the simulacrum are identified as being deployed in quite original ways: specifically, the literary tropes of parody, pastiche, metafiction, allegory and 'landscape' (*fûkei*), and the aesthetic modalities of the sublime.

In a truly global sense, there is no doubt that Murakami's popularity and influence continue to expand unabated. The English edition of *Umibe no kafuka*, published in January 2005 as *Kafka on the Shore*, quickly appeared on many bestseller lists in Europe, Australia and the United States.[5] It has been reported that young British writers are 'copying' his style, and that the author is developing a 'cult following' in Australia.[6] Not only have his works become very popular in the Anglophone countries of the West, they have also attracted an 'enormous readership' across much of Europe,[7]—and there has even been speculation that one day Murakami may be awarded the Nobel Prize for Literature.[8] It is also highly significant that *Umibe no kafuka* (first published in September 2002) had, as early as May 2003, entered the Chinese top ten fiction best seller list.[9] No doubt this indicates a major shift from the tendency to view Japan predominantly in 'economic' terms, to a heightened awareness of 'cultural' dimensions. This is evidenced, according to the Chinese translator of *Umibe no kafuka*, in the way in which the 'urban sensibilities' of Murakami's works are directly influencing contemporary Chinese writing.[10]

Murakami's fiction (in the form of *Hitsuji o meguru bôken* (*A Wild Sheep Chase*) first appeared in Russian in 1995 on an Internet home page covering Japanese culture. The novel was finally published in book form at the end of 1998, and between 2000 and 2002 several more of Murakami's works made the bestseller lists in Moscow book stores. The article detailing this information is included in a special number of the Japanese journal *Gaiko fuôramu*, (discussing the theme of 'Japan as Brand'), and is part of the section which examines several key examples of the 'world's' fondness for 'Japanese cool' (*kûrusa*).[11] Russian interest in Murakami's fiction is thus juxtaposed to the craze for Japanese *manga* in Thailand, a boom in Japanese television dramas, animation and electronic games in China, and strong interest in traditional Japanese architecture within Australia.

How is it that Murakami's writing has come to figure so prominently in these globalizing waves of the consumption of Japanese 'art' and 'culture'? And why is it desirable for non-Japanese writers to imitate the style of works already translated from Japanese? Aren't these authors merely 'copying' the idiom and register adopted by Murakami's translators, thus feigning an originality which cannot withstand even the most cursory of scrutiny? Such questions notwithstanding, it is surprising that even Nobel laureate Ôe Kenzaburô has predicted that a young Chinese writer who is very similar to Murakami will soon emerge, and suggests that something very significant is happening in terms of the global literary 'influence' of Murakami's fiction.[12]

As a writer, Murakami's output has been as prolific as it has been diverse. Today he is perhaps more visible than ever, he pops up everywhere, he is peripatetic. His January 2005 essay commemorating the 1995 Kobe earthquake (discussed in the Preface) is just one recent example of this. Between September

12 and November 21 2002, Murakami participated in an interactive forum with readers aged between thirteen and seventy from all walks of life and from all around the world. In this forum, he personally responded, via email, to thousands of readers of *Umibe no kafuka* who had questions about, and comments on the novel. More than 1,200 of these email messages, along with Murakami's personalized response to each and every one of them, have been published in 'Shônen Kafuka: Kafka on the Shore—Official Magazine'. As well as reproducing the email correspondence, this remarkable text (of almost 500 pages) documents the lead up to the publication of the novel, with its marketing activities focused around an 'Umibe no kafuka' Home Page, consisting of a 'mail box', 'house rules', 'keywords' and a 'latest news' section as well as a long interview with the author. The magazine also contains a glossy 'Kafka on the Shore Special Goods' section, which effectively advertises merchandise linked to Murakami's personal preferences: an Apple Mac laptop computer, Smirnoff Vodka, classical music CDs and so on.[13]

In March, 2001, an edition of *Spirit*, the Qantas Airways inflight magazine in Japanese, featured as the main text on its cover an excerpt from Murakami Haruki's anthology of Australian travel essays entitled 'Sydney!'. This was a marketing strategy which brought together two important media 'events': the highly successful and spectacularly staged Sydney 2000 Olympic Games, and the publication of a book by one of the most popular Japanese writers in recent times.[14] The cover simply combines the peaks of the Opera House roof set against a blue sky, with the author's name. Such is the marketer's dream: two perfectly branded and iconic products whose simultaneous presentation ensure instant publishing success.[15]

There is no denying that as a marketing phenomenon Murakami's case has been quite astonishing. But this commercial success tends to conceal the highly complex nature of the 'Murakami Phenomenon': the advent and rise to fame of a writer who has tended to distance himself from Japanese literary circles, and whose radicality (in fictional writing and more recently as a 'social commentator') defies classification or genre.

Indeed, it will be argued here that Murakami's works represent much more than a case-study in successful marketing. The ensuing discussion seeks to illuminate what might be called the 'conditions of exteriority' which have *enabled* this phenomenon to emerge in the first place.[16] This book is about Murakami's writing, but its scope extends well beyond a purely 'literary' discussion. Broadly speaking, the question is posed: what does Murakami's fiction tell as about writing, representation and the status of the referent in contemporary Japanese culture?

The basic argument proposed is that in developing a critique of contemporary society both Murakami's first and later trilogies deploy various versions of the figure of the simulacrum in original and compelling ways. However, it is concluded that rather than indicating a 'fall' from authenticity, a loss or lack (in the Platonic sense, as a 'copy of a copy'), these works suggest an experimentation with the forms of the simulacrum which are much closer to the descriptions offered by Nietzsche and Deleuze, as arising from a repetition and a 'forgetting' of origins—a celebration of *difference* for its own sake, and on its own terms.

Undoubtedly, the 'Murakami Phenomenon' can be said to have emerged within the cultural context(s) of the rather extreme conditions of modes of 'postmodern' representation in contemporary Japan, where Baudrillard's melancholic claim of the complete loss of 'the referent' (or reference to anything but the signifier itself) seems all too evident. So, perhaps somewhat paradoxically, this book also contends that Murakami's ostensibly 'liberating' version of the simulacrum unfolds within the hegemonic constraints of a massive and complex system of media-entertainment technologies/discourses, wherein commodified image-forms are shifting so continuously, so restlessly, as to almost defy description.

Rationale and Methodology

What follows is a brief survey of the more important critical literature on Murakami's fiction. A more comprehensive 'literature review' is not offered in this Introduction for two reasons. Firstly, because the critical-fictional concerns of the 'Murakami Phenomenon' are more properly the province of Chapter 1. Secondly, in order to provide the reader with cogent evidence of the shortcomings and gaps in the critical works as they relate to each specific text, the critical literature is comprehensively reviewed and critiqued *throughout* the subsequent discussion.

Around a quarter of a century after Murakami's debut in Japan, and fifteen years after the first translations of his third novel appeared in the West, full length studies of Murakami in English have only appeared relatively recently. Matthew Strecher's *Dances with Sheep: The Quest for Identity in the Fiction of Murakami Haruki* (2002),[17] sets out to use Murakami's novels, as the author puts it, to 'outline Murakami's large(r) projects of probing the nature of identity, the unconscious, latemodel capitalism, and the tropes of postmodernism'.[18]

Strecher emphasizes that he has aimed to produce a 'study sophisticated enough to do justice to the complexities of Murakami's fictional world' while keeping discussion at a level which remains 'accessible to general readers'.[19] While this is indeed a noble goal, his analysis often seems to be walking a tightrope between sophisticated theory (Baudrillard, Hutcheon, Lacan) and quite bland literary criticism (the 'search'/'quest' for 'identity' and 'meaning'). In this sense, the argument proceeds somewhat haltingly as it meanders over the entire range of Murakami's long fiction, ostensibly in the interests of avoiding both a 'chronological approach' and reading Murakami's works in a 'deterministic way'.[20] Each of the four chapters in the book offers discussion of Murakami's works arranged around formulae and themes, but the various arguments seeking to explain an underlying authorial methodology are often unconvincing. Perhaps this is precisely because (despite Strecher's early declaration) such literary models, if not applied carefully, do tend to operate in rather prescriptive and deterministic ways—especially when applied to such a wide range of very different novels.

Each chapter of *Dances with Sheep* adopts a specific approach to some of Murakami's major works: the use of 'formula' (read: 'popular') vis-à-vis 'mimesis' (read: 'serious'); an elaboration of some conventions of magical realism; a lengthy introduction to Lacanian psychoanalytic theory and analysis of texts in terms of the 'Symbolic Order' and 'the Other'; and a discussion of language, historiography and the politics of representation. While acknowledging Murakami's use of radical narrative formats, unfortunately Strecher's central concern (to illuminate the quest for 'identity' in Murakami's fiction) is hermeneutically trapped in precisely those conventions of the 'I-novel' paradigm ('meaning', 'truth' and 'identity') which Murakami's writing is (as is argued in this book) so obviously at pains to critique. Furthermore, by positing these important works of contemporary Japanese fiction as indicative of a generalized or 'universal' malaise in late capitalism, his approach fails to more fully elaborate the nexus between specifically *Japanese* questions of subjectivity, modernity and representation in a rigorous way. It simply imposes conventional tropes of interpretation which do not allow the texts to sufficiently 'speak for themselves' in terms of the literary modalities in which they are cast.

Furthermore, it denies the specificity of Murakami's engagement with and interrogation of the unique cultural forms of Japanese modernity. Indeed the entire question of modernity is given only cursory reference by Strecher, and mainly in relation to the Habermas/Lyotard debate about whether or not modernity remains an 'unfinished project'.[21] Despite this paucity in the discussion about Japanese modernity, Strecher has no reservations in using the term 'postmodernism' in ways which seem not only relatively unproblematic, but which perhaps also imply a failure to distinguish between 'modernity' as a philosophical concept, and 'modernism' (and therefore 'postmodernism') as a description of tendencies in art and aesthetics.

A major premise of Strecher's argument is that Murakami's narrative project explores the loss of some prior, more stable 'identity'. There is, however, no suggestion that perhaps such an 'identity' is at best phantasmal and putative no more than a necessary construction which enables the stipulation of Japanese literary modernity as an object of enquiry. To be sure, Japanese literary modernity does need to be understood, however, perhaps more from a perspective which entails the natural corollary of the term 'identity'—that of 'difference'. Certainly, it is tempting to agree with Ann Sherif's suspicion of Strecher's repeated and unproblematic invocation of the terms 'selfhood' and 'identity', as 'reified concepts that loom as utopian goals rather than social and psychological processes'.[22] Undoubtedly, one of the key philosophical problems with *Dances with Sheep* is that it uses these terms ('self' and 'identity') almost interchangeably, and the reader is left unsure as to which version of 'self' is implied: the Western 'unified' subject so vigorously contested by poststructuralist theory, or the Japanese *jiga* or *shutai*—still trying to find an appropriate place in the discourses of modernity.

Some of these shortcomings are carried over into Stechers's short reader's guide to *Nejimakidori kuronukuru* entitled *Murakami Haruki's 'The Windup Bird Chronicle'*. Again, Strecher emphasizes Murakami's ostensible concern with elaborating the structures and process which constitute the 'solid identity', or the 'core identity'/'core consciousness' of the individual.[23]

Other substantial works in English which have given varying emphasis to the issues raised by Strecher include doctoral dissertations by Storey (1993),[24] who offers a comparative study of Murakami taking the fictional representation of the 'madwoman' as allegorical of the problems of defining the self in Japanese literature, and Fisher (1997),[25] who compares Murakami with Anglo-American author Russell Hoban, proposing that both authors enlist the generic devices of the Menippean Satire (given as fantasy, crudity, philosophical dialogues, inserted languages and invented languages) and that this is indicative of a genre which is apt for the 'postmodern' tenor of the times. Both dissertations are important for the ways in which they offer comparative literary contextualizations of Murakami's writing.

Apart from his accomplished and compelling translations of Murakami's fiction, Jay Rubin makes a significant contribution to the area of Murakami studies in what has been to date the only other full length monograph in English about Murakami.[26] Although Rubin acknowledges in the preface that his 'approach may call into question (his) 'scholarly objectivity' (a somewhat ironic claim given his distinguished academic career) there can be no doubt that the cornucopia of biographical detail provides very useful background to illuminating discussions of Murakami's fictional and non-fictional writing. Rubin is also to be applauded for his treatment, in an appendix entitled 'Translating Murakami', of the topics of Murakami and globalization, and the role of (and sometimes not so felicitous relations between) translators, editors and publishers.[27] As a major translator of Murakami's fiction, Rubin has usually tended to adopt a quasi biographical approach to the discussion of his writing, focusing mostly on themes and motifs.[28] However, in one important essay, he does offer a close textual analysis of Murakami's use of the trope of metafiction in a short story.[29]

Apart from these major contributions to the study of Murakami in the West, other critiques in English have been limited to chapters in anthologies, journal articles and 'nonscholarly' reviews in magazines. Strecher offers discussions of Magical Realism[30] and the nexus between the mimetic and the formulaic[31] in Murakami's writing which are clearly related to discussions developed in his lengthier works, while issues of 'influence' and intertextuality in regard to contemporary American fiction have been explored by Matsuoka.[32]

On the question of Murakami's treatment of subjectivity (*shutaisei*)—despite acknowledging that this is a highly problematic area for Japanese literary modernity—Iwamoto identifies, in the 'thinness' of the protagonist Boku's subjectivity, an 'absence of interiority' rather than a deliberate strategy by the author to achieve just such a narrative effect. This argument is undermined somewhat by Iwamoto's unproblematic acceptance of the label 'postmodern' to describe both contemporary Japan and Murakami's fictional endeavours.[33] In contrast, Loughman provides an interesting discussion of subjectivity and the poetics of the city in Murakami's fiction, which implies not only the 'emptiness' of a regime of monotonous, commodified sign-images, but also the suggestion of emptiness in Buddhist terms as an epiphanic instance of 'primal memory'—as oneness and harmony.[34]

A more recent discussion of Murakami appears in Leith Morton's *Modern Japanese Culture*.[35] Morton offers a highly readable biographical sketch of the author along with an outline of his first three novels (and the later *Dansu, Dansu, Dansu*, which completes the tetralogy). Furthermore, in this book Murakami's works are usefully situated in relation to those of other modern and contemporary writers. Significantly, Morton introduces to the reader who may not have access to the Japanese original, the essay by Karatani Kôjin which offers an important critique of Murakami's first two novels. He highlights Karatani's characterization of the novels as forms of pastiche—lacking historicity and experimenting with a new kind of 'transcendental' narrative subjectivity. (These issues will be addressed in detail in Chapters 4 and 5.)

It would be tempting to conclude that most of the English language studies of Murakami to date do not envisage many of the key perspectives developed in this book. There are, however, at least three analyses whose approaches necessitate a caveat to any such claim. One of the most refreshing discussions of Murakami in English comes from an independent Japanese researcher. Chiyoko Kawami's 'The Unfinished Cartography: Murakami and the Postmodern Cognitive Map', is clearly an analysis whose critical assumptions regarding Murakami's treatment of Japanese modernity resonate with those presented here.[36] Focusing mainly on the fourth novel *Sekai no owari to hâdoboirudo wandarando* (*Hardboiled Wonderland and the End of the World*), it represents one of the more sophisticated English language critiques in the area. Significantly, Kawakami assumes as a necessary premise of her discussion what she describes as a 'Jamesonian cognitive map of urban space' entailing, in this novel,

> a situational representation on the part of the individual subject [of a vast] and properly unrepresentable totality.[37]

By invoking Jameson she goes to the heart of Murakami's clever and radical narrative endeavours—but not in a naïve way. Her analysis stays close to the text and does not rely on the mere description of the double-world structures so popular in many discussions of that novel. Both her recognition of Murakami's concern with representing the 'unrepresentable', and description of his narrative project (especially in *Sekai no owari*) as some kind of 'unfinished cartography', acknowledge that Murakami has indeed been laying out a new 'cognitive' map for literary modernity in Japan. Moreover, (and as will be suggested towards the end of this discussion), two decades later, that map remains as incomplete and tentative as ever. The unknown and unimaginable terrain purported to be represented by such a map is limited only by the projected cultural fantasies entailed in our reading of Murakami. This is nowhere more clearly demonstrated than in the general sense of critical confusion (some might say exasperation) over Murakami's recent long novel *Umibe no kafuka* (*Kafka on the Shore*).[38] And Murakami himself continues to stubbornly resist the calls for his assistance in guiding us in our 'interpretation' of his works.[39]

Kawakami's contribution is to use the idea of the simulacrum to explicate Murakami's apocalyptic/utopian narrative in several important ways. Firstly, she borrows Gelfant's idea of the urban novel as 'synoptic study', to describe Murakami's approach which 'makes the city itself the protagonist'. With

> its contrasting and contiguous social worlds . . . its multifarious scenes, its rapid tempos and changing seasons, its tenuous system of social relationships, meetings and separation . . . the massive material of city life must be ordered and condensed to fit within a formal framework.[40]

This description characterizes the city as the epistemological matrix of the simulacrum (further explored in chapter three of this book) which, as Kawakami implies, can also be expressed as the 'limited fantasy' (*gentei gensō*) discussed in Imai's important 1990 work on Murakami.[41] Kawakami also recognizes Murakami's almost incessant deployment of what may be called the *deja vu* or 'nostalgia' simulacrum, with its endlessly playing screen of visual memory, patterns of representation and attendant sense of ennui and disillusionment:

> he (Watashi) has already seen his own experience represented somewhere—in movies, paintings, lyrics for popular songs, or literature.[42]

Significantly, however, Kawakami urges that the 'parade of trivia' in Murakami's novels requires 'a new reading'. Such a reading needs to acknowledge Murakami's critique of the complacent sense of 'consensus' of postwar so-called *Junbungaku (High Literature)*, showing that 'the cognition of reality, textualized in the image of all-visible things, is (according to Murakami) 'decisively different from its blind acceptance'.[43] And with a somewhat more explicit theoretical reference, Kawakami sees in the protagonist's arrival at the 'End of the World', (with 'his own inner world fabricated by a pastiche of fictional images') an indication of Baudrillard's 'fourth stage' of the simulacrum, where the image itself   no longer bears a relation to any recognizable 'reality' or referent.[44]

Indeed, according to Kawakami, the entire representation of the place simply called Town (with its Watchtower, Clock-tower and canal) is a fantasized simulacrum—cobbled together from advertising images 'the identical copy for which no original has ever existed'.[45] And although this fantasy is described as part of the 'program error' in which Watashi is confined to a 'consciousness' existing as no more than an 'artificial cognitive circuit' we can detect in Kawakami's description of the 'utopia of simulacra',[46] a sense of lost community equivalent to what Ivy describes as 'modernity's losses', and which is discussed here in a later chapter.

Given the similarities in its theoretical approach, it is somewhat surprising that Kawakami's paper makes no reference to an essay published six years earlier by Stephen Snyder in an anthology on contemporary East Asian Culture.[47] In his succinct and well crafted comparative discussion, Snyder takes on critical heavyweights like Miyoshi Masao and Ôe Kenzaburo, whom, he claims, dismiss Murakami as 'the ultimate postmodern fabulist, manufacturer of a glib, highly marketable . . . disposable literary product representative of his degenerating cultural milieu.'[48] Like Kawakami, he shows that they have entirely missed the point about the significance of Murakami's work in contemporary Japanese culture.

Snyder's description of his own bid to counter such limited readings of Murakami as 'recuperative' and 'counterintuitive', clearly resonates with one important aim of this book: to present new ways of discussing an important cultural phenomenon, which are not constrained by redundant characterizations of Japanese literary modernity as a struggle with 'truth', 'identity' and 'meaning'. Indeed, Snyder is astute in recognizing that such typifications evade altogether the question of the ethical status of much of modern Japanese fiction, in a way which 'turns memory into a form of creative forgetfulness, an elaborate exercise in slate wiping'.[49] Snyder's important theoretical intervention reverses the terms of the discussion about memory as something related to a collectively accessible past. In Murakami's *Sekai no owari*, it is claimed, something quite radical is being proposed:

> by reversing its trajectory, by taking the future as its proper object, memory becomes a kind of simple affirmation, an acknowledgement that, at the very least, narrative consciousness (or the novel itself) will persist.[50]

Of course, it can be claimed that all science fiction does this to a greater or lesser extent, but what is remarkable about the Murakami narrative is its assault on one of the central pillars of Japanese literary modernity. Snyder goes so far as to say that Murakami is both deconstructing and reinventing the 'I-novel' by 'dramatizing the fragility and friability of its central preoccupation, the modern 'subject'.[51]

This is precisely what will be demonstrated later in the discussion: that in place of the 'confessional' narrator or 'witness/recorder' narrator, Murakami has installed, in his fiction, a narrative subject which self-reflexively acknowledges its difference with itself. A subject, according to Karatani's designation, which occupies the position of a kind of 'transcendental narrator'. Snyder's argument, like Kawakami's, draws partly on Jameson's writing on postmodernism for theoretical support, and provides further evidence of the growing relevance of perspectives drawn from critical theory and Cultural Studies, to the study of contemporary Japan.

In this vein, Murakami Fuminobu's 2005 essay on Murakami's writing is one of the most recent examples of works written in English which offer critical perspectives not unsympathetic to the aims of this book.[52] Indeed, Murakami's essay 'Murakami Haruki's Postmodern World' has perhaps greater critical import because of its publication alongside insightful discussions on the thought of Yoshimoto Takaaki, Karatani Kôjin and the fiction of Yoshimoto Banana. Entitled *Postmodern, Feminist and Postcolonial Currents in Contemporary Japanese Culture*, the book is testament to the efficacy (and difficulty) of approaching Japanese writing through the prism of contemporary Western theory, and its argument has the perhaps unintended effect of deconstructing itself as it proceeds. Possibly this is because, as Murakami explains, not only does the book aim to examine Japanese writing in the light of Euro-American theory, it also seeks, in a strategy of reversal, to interrogate this body of theory 'from the perspective of Japanese literary work'. The rationale for this aim is clearly stated:

> So far, there has been little theorization of the relationship between Japanese
> critics studying literature and Western writers who have been interested in
> Japanese literary works.[53]

If the overall theoretical concern of the book is to explore the ways in which some prominent Japanese thinkers and writers have dealt with issues of rationality, knowledge and power, the section on Murakami Haruki is certainly in step with this. It is implied that precisely because Murakami's narrator is able to establish a psychological distance between the 'objectifying self' and the 'objectified self', the narrative situations developed support a pluralism of *utopias* and *heterotopias*, thereby suggesting 'the collapse of a single correct mode of representation.'[54] Such a claim is in accord with the analysis of narrative strategies in the subsequent chapters of this book, where it is suggested that above all, Murakami's fiction is grappling with the epistemological difficulties of representation itself by experimenting with a range of literary and aesthetic modalities.

Another noteworthy aspect of Murakami Fuminobu's essay is the recognition of a particular trajectory of narrative concerns emerging between Murakami's early and later work. The earlier fiction, it is claimed, evinces a 'comfortable and cosy, yet mindless and anti-evolutionary (postmodern) world'. This gives way, in later novels, to a 'space for mutual understanding, sex, incestuous empathy and the desire for violence' in works such as *The Wind-Up Bird Chronicle*, *Sputnik Sweetheart* and *Kafka on the Shore*. Such claims are not done justice by presenting them in passing reference here, and carry greater critical force when read in light of the detailed discussions of other writers in Murakami Fuminobu's study: Yoshimoto Takaaki's concerns with rationality and collective fantasy, Karatani Kôjin's theories of interiority/exteriority and the Other, and what Murakami describes as Yoshimoto Banana's longing for the 'feminist family' and 'subversion of modernist binary oppositions'.

Compared to the relative dearth of rigorous critical literature in English, amidst the growing body of Murakami criticism in Japanese which has emerged over the past two decades, there is a growing number of essays and monographs which are worthy of serious attention. Many of the individually published papers have been compiled in the *Murakami Haruki stadeizu* series brought out by Wakakusa Shobo —a multi-volume collection of essays most of which were previously published separately.[55]

One short but noteworthy publication, *Murakami Haruki ga wakaru*,[56] not only gives an account of the massive extent of the globalization of the 'Murakami Phenomenon', but also details numerous books (both original works and translations) by Murakami, as well as offering thoughtful short essays on some of the major works. Long-time Murakami commentator Katô Norihiro notes here that the more he reads Murakami, the sense that he is a writer of 'great depth' only gets stronger and he acknowledges that Murakami is now the Japanese writer who attracts, by far, the greatest *range* of readers.[57] This stylishly presented publication is just one example of the current, highly sophisticated marketing of Murakami criticism in Japanese.

Despite the enormous amount of material published under the category of *Murakami ron*, there are, nevertheless, several critics whose theoretical rigor and imaginative explication of Murakami's writing sets them apart. This book enters into an extended dialogue with the work of these critics, attempting to integrate many of their important insights into its broader argument. Although they do not *directly* propose the application of the structure of the simulacrum as a way of understanding Murakami's writing and situating it within a larger discursive context, it is important to acknowledge that many of their critical insights— often attracting special terminology and detailed discussion—have been important touchstones for the overall argument developed here.

The essays on Murakami Haruki by Karatani Kôjin must be acknowledged for their rigorous consideration of issues such as modernity, subjectivity, 'landscape' and aesthetics. In particular, Karatani's essays on the *fûkei* ('scene'/ 'landscape') which apply his earlier research on the literary 'discovery' of interiority to Murakami's 'inverted' urban landscape and transcendental narrative perspective, are pertinent to our argument about the manifestation of certain tropes of the simulacrum in Murakami's earlier writing.[58]

Maeda Ai provides a fascinating insight into the 'digital' arrangement of speech acts and the problematization of the 'private/public' opposition in Murakami's first novel, *Kaze no uta o kike* (*Hear the Wind Sing*),[59] as well as a useful discussion of the semiotics of urban space.[60]

Both of these reflect the importance of the poetics of the city as fundamental to our analysis of the presentation of the simulacrum. Suzumura extends Maeda's approach to speech act analysis by invoking the notion of 'telephone writing' as encapsulating the curtailed modalities and digital arrangement of presented dialogue in Murakami's fiction, and highlights the use of the 'fragment' as the minimal unit of narrative discourse in the earlier novels.[61] As far as monographs are concerned, in his *Ierôpêji: Murakami Haruki* (Volumes I and II), Katô Norihiro has offered compelling analyses of Murakami's long fictional works which are both eclectic in approach and rewarding in their extrapolation of the textual features of Murakami's fiction in terms of other novels and genres.[62] Yoshida Haruo's *Murakami Haruki, tenkan suru*, charts the development of Murakami's narrative endeavours and identifies two major 'turning points' in his career. His analysis of *Nejimakidori kuronikuru* (*The Wind-Up Bird Chronicle*) is especially useful for the way in which it relates the representation of 'personal' violence and 'historical' violence in this novel, and thus draws attention to the destabilization of the boundaries between the discourses of 'fiction' and 'history'.[63]

A psychoanalytic study by Kobayashi Masaaki which presents Murakami's use of the topoi of 'the sea' (*umi*), 'the well' (*ido*) and 'the tower'(*tô*), in terms of Freudian/Lacanian structures of the Oedipal configuration and the Symbolic, is also useful in that it broaches issues which have relevance to our later discussion of the aesthetic of the sublime and the representation of the abject in *Nejimakidori kuronikuru*.[64] Another noteworthy critique which utilizes a psychoanalytic approach is Saito Tamaki's discussion of the structure of dissociation (*kairi*), which analyses the figuratively presented trauma of unresolved 'historical wounds' in *Nejimakidori kuronikuru*, as a function of a disjunctive modality of representation which is ultimately about ethics. This insight is crucial because it lends weight to our argument in the Conclusion about the politics of representation (and the contestation of 'fiction' and 'history') in terms of competing discursive regimes.[65]

These are only some examples of the important observations made by Japanese critics which have been placed in a dialogue with the argument as it unfolds in this book. As outlined above, most of the English language studies have fallen short of presenting a theoretically rigorous account of Murakami's fiction, failing to *systematically* engage with the Japanese critical material in order to develop a discussion of the nexus between subjectivity and representation in Murakami's writings in terms of the broader theme of Japanese modernity. Mostly, these critiques remain, as it were, fixated on the textual irruptions or symptoms, the surface play of the texts—and with a few notable exceptions, fail to examine the complex process of the texts as both produced by and productive of the conditions of their exteriority. More than a decade ago Fujii made an observation which, to a large extent, still rings true: modern Japanese literature continues to be approached largely by way of European realist conventions by both Western-ers and Japanese alike.[66] The treatment of Murakami's fiction has been, gener-ally speaking, no exception to this tendency.

Most of the critical literature in English, and many more contributions in the Japanese language critiques, remain piecemeal and somewhat disparate in their approach. And even though some doctoral research in English has employed the themes of 'identity', 'madness' and 'satire' in approaching Murakami's fiction, it has remained largely thematic and merely addressed textual features which require explanation at a broader inter-discursive level. By recognizing, however, that the multivalent structure of the simulacrum is at the heart of the discursive construction of modernity, this book allows Murakami's fiction to be contextual-ized, in a new way, within Japan's 'narrating' of its own experience of moder-nity. Furthermore, it demonstrates that tropes of the simulacrum which are os-tensibly limited to the immediate 'textual' level, can and indeed should be extrapolated to a larger discursive arena.

In this way, the argument presented here proposes a way out of the hermeneu-tic treadmill which tends to invoke interpretative forms serving only to *reinforce those schema*, rather than helping to illuminate the possibilities suggested by the modes of *presentation* of the texts themselves (and not just their apparent the-matic concerns). It does so by projecting an overarching analytical paradigm of the simulacrum which, nevertheless, allows for the application of more specific theoretical approaches. And it aims to do so whilst not denying alternative mul-tiple readings and the possibility of the texts' radically cast modalities to 'speak for themselves' and to suggest the parameters of their own critique.

By showing how, in selected Murakami novels, the structures of the simula-crum problematize relations between ostensibly 'prior', 'original' and 'authen-tic' representations of the real, and their second-order or simulacral representa-tion, this book aims to contribute substantially to debate in an important area of contemporary critical Japanese Studies. In this sense, it offers the first system-atic account in English of the underlying *methodologies* of Murakami's radical project of critique.

In doing so, the book adopts a range of perspectives which are outlined in Part I. These perspectives are informed by (but not limited to) some of the central ideas of post-structuralist literary and critical theory which have emerged over the last several decades. Specifically, they assume that literary discourse only derives its generic status in relation to the other discursive formations which it excludes; that the literary text is produced and reproduced by acts of reading; that the 'conditions of exteriority' of a text powerfully inform its production. It is also assumed that the subject of literary discourse is a construction arising from the centrality of the 'name of the author', and that this subject is inherently unstable and only ever provisionally postulated in the act of reading. With regard to the theory of the simulacrum, not only is it used to explicate Mura-kami's specific narrative strategies and use of tropes in the fictional texts them-selves, but also to demonstrate the complex intertextuality which prevails between these texts and the critical discourses and broader discursive regimes of contemporary Japanese culture.

In demonstrating Murakami's critique of literary orthodoxy in both of these trilogies, the argument proceeds on the basis of a crucial assumption: in Japanese literary modernity conventionalized 'narrating' and 'reading' subject positions have been and continue to be largely prescribed by the 'I-novel' (*shishôsetsu*) tradition, which utilizes what Fowler describes as the 'recorder/witness paradigm', and in which the narrator is 'a happily non-transcendent figure, anchored in the narrative he both acts in and produces'.[67] This is all about the struggle toward 'truth', 'sincerity' and 'meaning', which is 'recorded' by the narrator and subsequently 'witnessed' by the reader. The argument presented here shows that Murakami's literary method actively subverts this kind of 'immanent' narrator-centred paradigm, and indeed, posits a transcendental narrative perspective which liberates the range of subject positions available to the reader.

Usually, a full-length author study examines most or all of the major works of a writer in order to make a particular point about their work. However, although it refers to a wide range of Murakami's texts, this book undertakes a close analysis of only the six novels of the first and later trilogies in order to demonstrate the veracity of its fundamental claim. There are important reasons for this restricted focus. Firstly, because this discussion is about Murakami's fiction as both produced by and productive of contemporary Japanese culture(s), and because it aims to offer a precise textual/critical analysis, it is important not to paint, so to speak, with too broad a brush. This has been the shortcoming of those analyses which attempt to deal with *all* the major novels, and so end up offering an impressionistic reading based mainly on the explication of certain repeated motifs.

Because the aim is to demonstrate, in the clearest possible way, the originality of Murakami's narrative experimentation, we have focused on the textual analysis of only those works which utilize innovative or radical narrative modalities. This focus is in no way meant to imply a dismissal of the 'double-world' novels of *Sekai no owari to hâdoboirudo wandârando* (*Hardboiled Wonderland and the End of the World*) and *Dansu, dansu, dansu* (*Dance, Dance, Dance*) or the 'psychological romance' novels (*renai shôsetsu*) of *Noruei no mori* (*Norwegian Wood*), *Kokkyô no minami, taiyô no nishi* (*South of the Border, West of the Sun*) and *Supâtoniku no koibito* (*Sputnik Sweetheart*). Rather, it is based on the view that the first three novels of the so called 'Rat Trilogy' and the later *Nejimaki-dori kuronikuru* (*Windup Bird Chronicle*) trilogy are important examples of new forms of fiction in Japan. If the narratives of the first trilogy imply a 'retreat' of the referent amid the play of the simulacral literary modalities of parody, pastiche, metafiction, allegory and 'landscape', then the second trilogy reverses this process: it reintroduces the referent in a phantasmal and highly complex way. And it does so with powerful effect, by problematizing the discursive division between 'fiction' and 'history' through a questioning of the boundaries of the subject as defined in the aesthetic of the sublime.

Dimensions of this Study

Chapter 1 discusses the so called 'Murakami Phenomenon' in terms of critical and reader responses both inside and outside Japan. It argues that this media/marketing 'phenomenon' is itself indicative of the simulacral typification of cultural forms in contemporary Japan both in terms of a *perceived* poetics of nostalgia and a privileging of the aesthetic of daily life in the post-industrial city. The chapter proposes that these are clearly manifested in the unusual narrative format and linguistic style of the early novels, which indicate a radically different approach to the conventions and limitations of much modern fictional writing in Japanese.

Chapter 2 begins with a definition and clarification of some important theoretical terms, and goes on to broaden the parameters of the contextualization established in the first chapter by considering the idea of the modern state of Japan as an entity constructed in terms of a national-cultural imaginary. Some of the key issues surrounding the complex debate about Japanese modernity are then outlined and given historical perspective. Uncertainty about the problems of defining subjectivity and the comparative theorization of modernity are shown to indicate the need for ongoing research. Furthermore, it is proposed that Japanese modernity has by no means been 'overcome' or even sidestepped merely by application of the label 'postmodernity'—a term which is itself fraught with definitional ambiguity.

The discussion then turns to a consideration of the meanings of the adjective 'contemporary' in the appellation 'contemporary Japanese novel'. The general question of periodization is addressed by way of the claim that the labels of periodization—especially 'contemporary' and 'modern'—imply imagined cultural unities which do not necessarily correspond, in any consistent or demonstrable manner, to the texts they purport to designate. The question of how to situate contemporary Japanese artistic discourses and Murakami's fiction specifically in global or transnational terms is then shown to be symptomatic of the persistence of the opposition 'Japanese/non-Japanese' (as a version of the opposition 'particular/universal') which still informs much critical debate. The possibility that writers such as Murakami are consciously writing with the ease of translation of their works in mind, suggests an even more complex intertextuality at play in the popular reception of their works. The final section of the chapter deals with the idea of 'the Japanese novel', which is discussed in terms of both the poetics of the *shôsetsu* genre and the modern European novel, and found to be indicative of a hybrid blending the narrative voice conventions of the former with certain realist conventions of the latter.

Chapter 3 comprises the final stage of the theoretical Part I of the book, by

presenting a detailed consideration of some competing perspectives on the theory of the simulacrum. It begins by way of questioning representation and the
status of the referent in the context of media representations of recent 'extreme
events' in Japan. After sketching the semantic latitude of the word 'simulacrum',
the discussion goes on to examine various theoretical dimensions of its use, by
firstly positing the city as the social and imaginary locus of its operation. This is
followed by a brief survey of the idea or figure of the simulacrum as treated in
the writings of Nietzsche, Foucault, Deleuze and Baudrillard. The chapter concludes by urging the efficacy of an eclectic definition of the simulacrum
which can be applied across a range of approaches to the textual analysis of narrative.

Part II, comprising Chapters 4, 5, 6 and 7, presents a detailed discussion of
Murakami's first trilogy as a generalized critique of modern fictional orthodoxy
exemplified in the dominant paradigm of the *shishôsetsu* or 'I-novel' form. After
addressing some of the critical responses to Murakami's maiden work *Kaze no
uta o kike* (*Hear the Wind Sing*), the discussion in Chapter 4 examines the
novel's use of the simulacral, double-order literary strategies of parody, pastiche
and metafiction as highly effective tools in destabilizing certain reading conventions which had developed around the supposition and projection of the modern
self (*jiga*) in fictional writing. It is also proposed that this first novel initiated a
critique of the language of media and advertising discourses as being irrevocably
productive of, and produced by, speech and writing in everyday contemporary
life.

Chapter 5 details Murakami's next move in *1973 nen no pinbôru* (*Pinball,
1973*), as a brilliant yet disarmingly simple strategy of foregrounding the *modality* of the established literary device of allegory to say something important
about the nature of writing and representation in general. After discussing the
theory of allegory in relation to contemporary or 'postmodern' fiction, it goes on
to outline Benjamin's theory of the commodity form as being the modern embodiment of the allegorical. The argument demonstrates Murakami's utilization
of the *form* of allegory to be allegorical about the status of the real—an approach
which in itself is a deployment of the simulacrum, as an allegory about allegory.
This chapter clearly shows that *1973 nen no pinbôru* continues the task set by
the previous novel, of disrupting the conventionalized tendency to equate the
narrative voice(s) of the text, with the 'life'of the author.

Chapters 6 and 7 undertake an analysis of the ways in which the third part of
the trilogy, *Hitsuji o meguru bôken* (*A Wild Sheep Chase*), extends the largely
temporal focus of the presented, deictic world of *1973 nen no pinbôru*. By applying the more 'spatial' trope of 'landscape' (*fûkei*) in order to better understand both the 'micro' and 'macro' level of presented worlds of the narrative, the
argument demonstrates Murakami's radical use of yet another allegorical, double-order, simulacral structure in his ongoing critique of and engagement with
literary orthodoxy and modernity. Indeed, in both these chapters an 'archeology'

of landscapes at both the immediate level of the deictic and the broader level of the national-cultural imaginary is presented.

After sketching the parameters of *fûkei* as discourse in Japanese modernity, and outlining early critical responses to the text, the argument in Chapter 6 turns to stylistic aspects of the presentation of the 'micro' landscape in *Hitsuji o meguru bôken*. Apparently straightforward stylistic 'imitation' evident in this novel, is argued to be indicative of a more complex artistic complicity and simulacral circle of intertextuality not fully appreciated by most critics. This lends support to the proposition that by adopting a style that *appears* to be imitative of the hard-boiled American detective story genre set within a Japanese urban context, Murakami is establishing a 'scene' which is at once both strange and familiar to the Japanese reader. Finally, by analyzing the idiosyncratic use of numbers, names and proper nouns in this text, it is shown that the deictic centre of this kind of narrative is destabilized, and that this accords with Karatani's claim for a 'transcendental' (*vis-à-vis* 'experiential') subject/narrator as a distinguishing feature of the Murakami narrative. Chapter 7 goes on to describe the deployment of a further dimension of *fûkei* in *Hitsuji o meguru bôken* in terms of the tropes of 'history' and 'nature' which are engaged as simulacra, at the 'macro' level of the national-cultural imaginary. Both of these tropes are shown to be transformations of one another as part of an implicit treatment in the novel of the repression of modernity's losses. It is argued that this repression irrupts through the protagonist's acts of viewing which range from 'realist' descriptions to the transcendental perspectives entailed in a kind of 'pseudo-sublime' within the shifting parameters of a provisionally defined self and subjectivity; and it is suggested that this fictional elaboration of *fûkei* ultimately relies on a particular construction of interiority/subjectivity.

The concluding part of the chapter posits the contiguous landscapes of self and world in *Hitsuji o meguru bôken*, and Murakami's inverted literary interiority is described as a simulacrum, a shadow of the interior 'discovered' in the Meiji era—itself modeled on European and Christian representations of self and world. The projected idea of the self in this novel is shown to reflect a conjunction of critical perspectives on *fûkei*, described in terms of a set of 'plural hypotheses', coextensive with certain 'contours of the world' and part of the broader 'collaborative fantasy' necessary for modern fiction. The analysis in this chapter effectively traces a path from the 'micro-landscape' presented in Chapter 6, through to the idea of *fûkei* writ large at the level of the national-cultural imaginary—only to arrive, once more, at the threshold of the vexed question of how to stipulate and situate the subject of/in Japanese modernity.

Far from being dispensed with, this question of the subject is shown to be couched in radically different terms in Murakami's second trilogy. The analysis of *Nejimakidori kuronikuru* (*The Wind-up Bird Chronicle*) is based upon the supposition of a cautious gesturing towards a 'return of the referent' indicated by the versions of self and world played out in this long narrative. Amidst the momentum of the critique of literary orthodoxy undertaken in the first trilogy, this 'referent' — as the putative object of fictional/historical discourse — is shown to have been essentially sidelined, as it gives way to the focus on presentational processes via the simulacral modalities of pastiche, metafiction, allegory and landscape.

Part III of the discussion begins, in Chapter 8, with the stated aim of demonstrating the phantasmal 'return' of the referent arising from a blurring of the boundaries between fictional and historical discourse in the text of *Nejimakidori kuronikuru*, and goes on to provide a brief outline of some of the conditions of exteriority of its publication. Translated versions of two alternative plot synopses are then offered as a way of foregrounding the radical arrangement and presentation of the major story lines of the novel, and in which the narrative format of the chapter order itself is shown to be indicative of its discontinuous, disjunctive treatment of time, space and action. The significance of the term 'chronicle' in the title is discussed in generic terms, and this is followed by an overview of some critical responses to the novel.

Chapter 9 outlines the theoretical parameters necessary for the task of proceeding with a close textual analysis of the novel in the following chapter. By positing the focus of such analysis in terms of an 'aesthetic function' of the text, the discussion reintroduces the generalized question of the subject in Japanese modernity, by describing it in terms of the aesthetic of the sublime. It is argued that the contradictory modalities of the Kantian theory of the sublime discussed in earlier chapters, could best be applied to our reading of *Nejimakidori kuronikuru* through consideration of their psychoanalytic, historical and political dimensions. It is also shown that discussion of the theory of the sublime has been taken up in recent critical debate regarding conventions of presentation and representation in 'postmodern' artistic discourses.

Assuming that the problem of history has to emerge as a crucial issue in any intelligent reading of *Nejimakidori kuronikuru*, the next section of the chapter considers competing perspectives on what *kinds* of history are at play in the text. It is argued that by blending the narrative tendencies of the fictional and the historical, Murakami has demonstrated a preference for history described as a kind of phantasmal *effect* — which, nevertheless, does not necessarily disengage its production, as cultural practice, from the social. On the contrary, it is shown that this simulacral form of presentation favours neither totalization, nor the collapse into the solipsism of extreme differentiation. Rather, it demonstrates a desire to explicate the possibilities of history's own self-critique, regardless of the narrative modalities which such a critique might entail.

In the final part of the chapter, the apparent privileging of the auditory image/register in *Nejimakidori kuronikuru* is claimed to imply a heightened sense of corporeality in the presented worlds of the narrative. This, the chapter contends, denotes a subversion of the primacy of the visual in contemporary Japanese society, and is also redolent of a 'splitting' of the semiotically condensed sign (as a combination of audio/visual image) which maintains the subject's instantiation in the symbolic order.

Chapter 10 proceeds with a textual analysis of several of the main narrative lines of *Nejimakidori kuronikuru*, in order to demonstrate displaced and uncertain subjectivities in the literary presentation of the aesthetic of the sublime. Firstly, the central motif of Boku's quest to retrieve his missing wife is linked to her physical absence as necessitating a subjective displacement by a universalized feminine other, in which her disembodied presence is 'virtually' substituted by the figures of other women. The 'masculinized' reading positions prescribed by the figure of Boku-as-narrator, are interpreted as regulated by the binary structure of freedom and constraint, within the modalities of the double movement of an encroaching and receding threat to Boku's sense of his own subjective unity. This 'quest', then, is nothing other than a device in which he plays out the uncertainties of his own struggle to maintain the borders of this fragile unity-as-subject.

The discussion then moves to the topic of the subject in/of history in terms of the dichotomy between personal memory and official history emerging in the wartime stories retold by Nutmeg and later 'chronicled' by Cinnamon. Here, the origins and veracity of these fragmented narratives are described as elusive and indeterminable, inhering only in the complex weave of memory, thought, speech and writing. By invoking the trope of 'landscape' as a version of the sublime, and connotative of a quasi-amnesic sense of stupefaction, this multiplex narrative is read as positioning history as a 'presupposition'—implying that it can only be grasped as a phantasmal effect. It is concluded that in *Nejimakidori kuronikuru* the subject of the narration of the past can only be cast in terms of the difference arising from history's discourse with itself, and that this demonstrates Murakami's radical recasting of history as a version of narrative discourse.

By this stage of the argument the status of the subject in terms of an aesthetic of the sublime in *Nejimakidori kuronikuru* has been well and truly problematized, yet it receives its most radical treatment in the presented episodes depicting the limits of the subject's encounter with itself. By applying the Kristevan theory of abjection, the analysis considers the depiction of the extreme experiences of revulsion and horror in this novel.

The process whereby the subject breaches the limits of its own self-definition and flirts with the possibility of the total collapse of meaning, is suggested to be not dissimilar to the violent disjunction, the inability to present the contents of the imagination, and the admixture of pleasure and pain central to the Kantian aesthetic of the sublime. Also, that the implied dissolution of the subject in the experience of the abject represents a threatened negation and unraveling of the Symbolic. The significant conclusion to be drawn is that the representation of such 'extreme phenomena' implies an aesthetic of dissociation which does not arise directly from the detailed graphic depictions themselves. Rather, that through the presentation of the sublime and the abject in this novel, the referents imagined in our reading require reformulation: specifically, these are described as the referent of the historical 'event' as a residual *eventivity*, 'the body' as the site (however tenuous) of an individuated *subjectivity* and 'the state' as the referent of an imagined *nationality*.

Having detailed various trajectories of the aesthetic of the sublime in *Nejimakidori kuronikuru*, the concluding part of the final chapter seeks to integrate and extrapolate these at a broader discursive level in terms of a generalized motif of dissociation. This is described as a kind of 'splitting' of the subject, in which the manifestation of the abject is shown to be synonymous with the appearance of that which is *not* the self, as well as indicating a division in which the alienated historical subject becomes 'fleshed-out' or *embodied* in the violence of history.

The discussion then outlines the way in which one critic has sought to make the important link between the psychoanalytic subject and the subject of history, by proposing the disjunctive effect of bringing the conventionally separated narrative modalities of fiction and history into a state of juxtaposition or contestation. It is also argued that the loss of spacio-temporal continuity in the pathology of dissociation can be transposed to the plane of history or the social, in order to give symptomatic form to the trauma of repressed, collective historical wounds or losses. Such symptoms as 'affects' arising from a collapse of meaning at the level of metaphor and the sign can become manifested in historical 'forgetfulness' and the displacement of, or resistance to, proper nouns. In *Nejimakidori kuronikuru*, these are given literary form in various examples of the shifting proper nouns and the 'splitting' of the auditory and visual registers signified particularly by the demise of the 'aural' in favour of 'written' historical transmission, in the final committal of the 'chronicles' to the graphic representation of the computer screen and storage in digital archives.

Finally, the chapter claims that the literary presentation of the abject and the sublime in *Nejimakidori kuronikuru* manifested in the motifs of psychoanalytic and historical dissociation, indicates a repression of the violence and trauma of Japan's encounter with modernity. In other words, it suggests an inability to present to the processes of rational understanding the abject/sublime contents of the imagination proscribed by the discourses of the state, but necessary to the modern subject's encounter with itself, with its 'history'. Ultimately, then, Murakami's attempt to reinstate the referent (however tangentially) in the discontinuous narratives of *Nejimakidori kuronikuru*, is an attempt to re-inscribe the political and historical into the narrative modalities of the fictional. This attempt to call forth the trauma of history in the deliberate clash of heterogeneous discourses, is shown to be indicative of Murakami's implicit demand that the representational possibilities of fictional art be reconsidered in terms of their capacity to engage with the social and political 'effects' of the discourses which they both enable and are enabled by.

The Conclusion begins by retracing, at an abstract level, the trajectories of presentation of the simulacrum from the first to the later trilogy, noting the emergence of an increasing sophistication in the deployment of its literary tropes. In the *Nejimakidori kuronikuru* trilogy, the simulacrum is described as having reached its limits, being transformed into a presentation of the confrontation between the competing discourses of 'fiction' and 'history', a form of discursive incommensurability best defined by Lyotard's notion of the 'differend'. Having shown that in terms of the aesthetic problem of 'presenting the unpresentable', the sublime and the differend have much in common (indeed that the sublime itself *is* a kind of differend), the discussion identifies the 'sublime violence' at the heart of *Nejimakidori kuronikuru* as inexorably linked to Murakami's endeavour to locate the subject, as the 'warp', the 'vertical thread' (*tateito*) of history. Murakami's attempt in this narrative to 'punch a hole in time', is thus seen to represent a critical engagement with the causal, temporal construction of modernity, which is somehow at odds with what Kawai describes as the traditional Japanese view of history as an amorphously defined 'lump' of phenomena.

The discussion then moves to a reflection on how these versions of the simulacrum and the differend are currently being played out in the broader discursive arenas of contemporary Japanese culture. Juxtaposing Murakami's recent ventures into overtly 'socially engaged' writing with the remarkable phenomenon of a controversial history textbook's rise to bestseller status, the Conclusion suggests that these developments indicate a dramatic change in the available paradigms of writing and representation in Japan—as well as, perhaps, in the possible future trajectories of the project of Japanese modernity.

Finally, it is shown how such trajectories have continued to be explored in Murakami's recent long novel *Umibe no kafuka* (*Kafka on the Shore*). The work is characterized as perhaps Murakami's most strident attempt yet to present a set of narrative possibilities which are deliberately *outside* the realm of 'interpretation' or readily generated sets of universalized 'meanings'. And yet, in being so, it is suggested that the semantic possibilities of these narrative worlds are greatly enriched. Indeed, it is argued that in this text can be found most of the literary tropes of the simulacrum deployed in the previous long fictional works: parody, pastiche, allegory, landscape, the sublime and 'history' as a signifier which invokes, more than ever, the struggle for the contested terrain of 'the real' as that which marks its difference with itself.

Notes

1. Gilles Deleuze, *Difference and Repetition*, trans. Paul Patton (London: The Athlone Press, 1994), 69.

2. Murakami Haruki, *Afutâdâku*, (Kôdansha, 2004), 35.

3. Karatani Kôjin, cited in Alexandra Munroe, *Japanese Art After 1945: Scream Against the Sky* (New York: H.N. Abrams, 1994), 33.

4. These are the so-called 'Rat-Trilogy' (*Nezumi no sanbusaku*, 1979-83) and 'Nejimakidori Chronicle' trilogy (*Nejimakidori kuronikuru*, 1994-95), both of which (as will

be discussed in subsequent chapters) were not originally envisaged by the author as developing into extended, tripartite forms.

5. Murakami Haruki, *Kafka on the Shore*, trans. Philip Gabriel (London: Vintage Harvill, 2005).

6. Matthew Spencer, "Ah, So Surreal," The Weekend Australian Book Review, *The Weekend Australian*, July 78, 2001.

7. This is the observation of Philip Hensher, in a review of the recently published translation of *Umibe no kafuka* (*Kafka on the Shore*). See 'Curiouser and Curiouser', (originally published in *The Spectator*,) reproduced in *The Weekend Australian,* January 22-23, 2005, R10-R11.

8. Spencer, "Ah, So Surreal," 78.

9. Wan Min and Rin Shaowa, "Chûgoku no Murakami bûmu," *Sekaishûho* 84, no. 28 (July 29 2003): 52-55.

10. Wan Min and Rin Shaowa, "Chûgoku no Murakami bûmu," 54.

11. Dmitry Viktorovich Kovalenin, "Murakami Haruki wandârando in Mosukuwa," in 'Tokushu: [NihonBurando]—Kokka no miryoku o kangaeru', *Gaikoku fuôramu,* 174, (January 2003): 45.

12. Xu Jinlong, "Murakami Haruki wa 'meido in chyaina' no haruki teki sakuhin o umu ka," in *Murakami Haruki ga wakaru*, Aera Mook, Asahi Shinbun Extra Report & Analysis, Special Number 75 (December 2001): 122-24.

13. Murakami Haruki, ed. *'Shônen kafuka—Kafuka on the Shore—Official Magazine'*, (Shinchôsha, 2003).

14. *Spirit* (Sydney: Fairfax Custom Magazines, March April, 2001).

15. Murakami Haruki, *Sydney!* (Bungeishunjûsha, 2001).

16. Murakami has been very much actively 'engaged' with the world for some time. This is evidenced, not only in the email forum of the 'Kafuka on the Shore—Official Magazine' of 2003, discussed above. Five years earlier, the book/CD package entitled *Yume no sâfushitei* (Asahi Shinbunsha, 1998) published alternating essays/stories with fully reproduced e-mail dialogues conducted with readers and fans. In October 2001, *Newsweek* magazine sought Murakami's opinion on the September terrorist attacks in America, ostensibly because of his investigation of the human dimensions of the Tokyo Subway Sarin Gas Attack, presented in the books *Andâguraundo I & II*. See *Murakami Haruki ga wakaru,* p. 171.

17. Matthew Strecher, *Dances with Sheep: The Quest for Identity in the Fiction of Murakami Haruki*, (Michigan: Centre for Japanese Studies, University of Michigan Press, 2002).

18. Strecher, *Dances with Sheep*, xii.

19. Strecher, *Dances with Sheep*, ix.

20. Strecher, *Dances with Sheep*, xii.

21. Strecher, *Dances with Sheep*, 162.

22. See Ann Sherif's review of *Dances with Sheep* in *Journal of Japanese Studies* 29, no.2 (Summer 2003): 368-72.

23. Matthew Strecher, *Haruki Murakami's 'The Windup Bird Chronicle': A Reader's Guide*, (New York and London: Continuum Contemporaries, 2002), 4247.

24. Donna Storey, *Speaking the Unspeakable: Images of Madwomen in the Works of Furui Yoshikichi, Murakami Haruki, and Yamamoto Michiko* (PhD dissertation, Stanford University, 1993).

25. Susan Fisher, *The Genre for Our Times: The Menippean Satires of Russell Hoban and Murakami Haruki* (PhD dissertation, The University of British Columbia, 1997).

Fisher also offers a short discussion of *Nejimakidori kuronikuru*, in which, in somewhat simplistic terms, she describes the hapless protagonist's descent into the well as 'allegorical of Murakami's own return to Japan' where he must do battle with Japan's recent past. See 'An Allegory of Return: Murakami Haruki's *The WindUp Bird Chronicle*', *Comparative Literature Studies*, 37, no. 2 (2000): 155-69.

26. Jay Rubin, *Haruki Murakami and the Music of Words*, (London: Harvill Press, 2002).

27. Rubin, *Haruki Murakami and the Music of Words*, 273-89.

28. See, for example, Jay Rubin, "The Other World of Haruki Murakami," *Japan Quarterly* 39, no. 4 (Oct.Dec.,1992), 490-500; "Murakami Haruki," in *Modern Japanese Writers*, ed. Jay Rubin (New York: Charles Scribner's, Sons, 2001), 227-43.

29. Jay Rubin, "Murakami Haruki's Two Poor Aunts Tell Everything they Know about Sheep, Wells, Unicorns, Proust, Elephants and Magpies," in *Ôe and Beyond: Fiction in Contemporary Japan*, ed. Stephen Snyder and Philip Gabriel (Honolulu: University of Hawaii Press, 1999), 185.

30. Matthew Strecher, "Magical Realism and the Search for Identity in the Fiction of Murakami Haruki," *Journal of Japanese Studies* 25, no. 2 (Summer 1999): 263-98.

31. Matthew Strecher, "Beyond 'pure' literature: Mimesis, formula, and the Postmodern in the Fiction of Murakami Haruki," *Journal of Asian Studies* 57, no.2 (May 1998): 354-78.

32. Matsuoka Naomi, "Murakami Haruki and Raymond Carver: The American Scene," *Comparative Literature Studies* 30, no. 4 (1993): 423-28.

33. Yoshio Iwamoto, "A Voice From Postmodern Japan: Haruki Murakami," *World Literature Today* 67, no. 2 (Spring 1993): 295-300.

34. Celeste Loughman, "No Place I was Meant to Be: Contemporary Japan in the Short Fiction of Haruki Murakami," *World Literature Today* 71, no.1 (Winter 1997): 87-94.

35. Leith Morton, *Modern Japanese Culture*, (South Melbourne: Oxford University Press, 2003), 178-185.

36. Kawakami Chiyoko, "The Unfinished Cartography: Murakami Haruki and the Postmodern Cognitive Map," *Monumenta Nipponica* 57, no. 3 (Autumn 2002): 309–37.

37. Kawakami, "The Unfinished Cartography," 310. Kawakami is citing Jameson, *Postmodernism, or the Cultural Logic of Late Capitalism* (Durham: Duke University Press, 1995), 51.

38. This claim will be discussed in more detail in the concluding chapter.

39. Responding to questions about the 'interpretation' of *Umibe no kafuka*, Murakami rejoinders that interpretations using words are more or less 'lies' and therefore 'meaningless'. See Murakami Haruki, "Umibe no kafuka ni tsuite," *Nami*, (September 2002), 52-57.

40. Kawakami, "The Unfinished Cartography," 321. Kawakami cites Blanche Housman Gelfant, *The American City Novel* (Oklahoma: University of Oklahoma Press, 1954), 14.

41. Imai Kyoto, *Murakami Haruki: Off no kankaku* (Kokken Shuppan, 1990),13. Imai's book is referred to at several stages during this discussion.

42. Kawakami, "The Unfinished Cartography," 325.

43. Kawakami, "The Unfinished Cartography," 323.

44. Kawakami, "The Unfinished Cartography," 326.

45. Kawakami, "The Unfinished Cartography," 327. Here she is citing Fukami's critique which will be referred to later in this discussion.

24   *Introduction*

46. Kawami actually uses the singular form 'simulacrum' in the heading of the penultimate section of her essay.

47. Stephen Snyder "Two Murakamis and Marcel Proust: Memory as Form in Contemporary Japanese Fiction," in *In Pursuit of Contemporary East Asian Culture*, ed. Xiaobing Tang and Stephen Snyder (Boulder, Colarado: Westview Press, 1996), 69-83.

48. Snyder, "Two Murakamis," 70.

49. Snyder, "Two Murakamis," 81.

50. Snyder, "Two Murakamis," 81.

51. Snyder, "Two Murakamis," 76.

52. Murakami Fuminobu, "Murakami Haruki's Postmodern World" in *Postmodern, Feminist and Postcolonial Currents in Contemporary Japanese Culture*, (London: Routledge, 2005), 20-57.

53. Murakami Fuminobu, "Introduction: Western Ideologies and Japan" in *Postmodern, Feminist and Postcolonial Currents in Contemporary Japanese Culture*, (London: Routledge, 2005), 16.

54. Murakami Fuminobu, "Murakami Haruki's Postmodern World," 45.

55. *Murakami Haruki Sutadeizu*, Vols. 1-4 (Wakakusa shobo, 1999).

56. *Murakami Haruki ga wakaru*, op.cit.

57. Katô Norihiro, "Seichô to henbô o kasaneru shôsetsuka" in *Murakami Haruki ga wakaru*, 5.

58. Karatani Kôjin, "Murakami Haruki no 'fûkei' (1)," *Kaien* (November 1989): 296-306; 301. And "Murakami Haruki no 'fûkei' (2)," *Kaien* (December 1989): 236-250.

59. Maeda Ai, "Boku to nezumi no kigoron," *Kokubungaku* (March 1985): 96-106.

60. Maeda Ai, "'Toshikûkan' kara no yomi," in *Gendai bungaku kenkyû: jôhô to shiryô*, ed. Hasegawa Izumi (Shibundo, 1985), 46-52.

61. Suzumura Kazunari, *Terefuon* (Yôsensha, 1987); *Murakami Haruki kuronikuru 1983-1995* (Yôsensha, 1994).

62. Katô Norihiro, *Ierôpêji Murakami Haruki* (Kôchi Shuppansha, 1996), and *Ierôpêji Murakami Haruki, Part 2*, (Kôchi Shuppansha, 2004)

63. Yoshida Haruo, *Murakami Haruki, tenkan suru* (Sairyûsha, 1997).

64. Kobayashi Masaaki, *Murakami Haruki: tô to umi no kanata ni* (Shinwasha, 1998).

65. Saito Tamaki, "Kairi no gihô to rekishiteki gaishô," *Yurîka*, Sangatsu rinjizôkan 32, no. 4 (March 2000): 62-71.

66. James Fujii, "Introduction," *Complicit Fictions* (Los Angeles: University of California Press, 1993).

67. Edward Fowler, *The Rhetoric of Confession: Shishôsetsu in Early Twentieth Century Fiction* (Berkely and London: University of California Press, 1988), 39.

Chapter One

The Murakami Phenomenon: Critical/Fictional Thematics

The publishing success of Murakami Haruki is well known, and yet perhaps just as noteworthy as the number of Murakami's books sold is the amount and astonishing speed with which critical literature (*Murakami ron*) follows their publication.[1] This is all part and parcel of the so called 'Murakami Phenomenon' (*Murakami genshô*) which, in terms of the sheer range of discursive forms in which it emerges, is deserving of a special study in itself. Such an observation can be partly justified by the fact that even though Murakami is now accepted in Japan as a writer of 'pure literature'(*junbungaku*), the critique of his writing appears not only in scholarly books and journals, but also across a range of 'popular' literary/culture magazines and newspapers.[2] In the West, however, for some time he was perceived as a popular writer whose stylistic and thematic concerns had little in common with the conventionally accepted canonic texts of modern Japanese literature. Yet, as Strecher reminds us, 'once borders are crossed, [such literary] categories can so easily change'.[3]

Of course, not all critics are agreed on the status of this 'phenomenon', and whereas some would prefer to approach it as a 'puzzle' (*nazo*) to be solved by looking for the image of its reflection in critical writing,[4] others reject the claim that it is a 'special *Murakami Haruki-like* phenomenon', preferring to explain it away as merely one example of the literature of the eighties which had freed itself from the relatively closed post-war literary world.[5] For critics such as Nakano, Murakami's early works were subject to the same media blitzing as Tawara's *Sarada kinnenbi* (*Salad Anniversary*)—although it is noted that their appearance marked a new trend in the consumption of 'literary information' (*bungakuteki jôhô*).[6] Another important critic accepts the existence of the 'Haruki—Banana Phenomenon', but concedes that criticism which really engages with Murakami's works is surprisingly rare.[7] One commentator has drawn attention to Murakami's indifference to Japanese literary circles, by suggesting that his story *Tongari-yaki no seisui* (*The Rise and Fall of Tongari-yaki*) is a critique of the *bundan* or 'literary world' in Japan which presides over the process of assigning literary worth or value.[8]

'Phenomenon' or not, Murakami has been widely characterized as representing something new in contemporary Japanese writing. However, whether his writing is symptomatic of the 'death' of modern Japanese literature (as Karatani maintains) is a more complex issue—especially with regard to the extent to which it subverts the *shishôsetsu* ('I-novel') form commonly acknowledged as paradigmatic of the modern novel.

The sales figures for Murakami's works are nothing short of astounding. *Noruei no mori* (*Norwegian Wood*) stayed in the top ten best-seller list for three years running (1987-89),[9] and had sold 4.3 million copies as at early 1996.[10] By November 2004, this figure had nearly doubled to 8.26 million.[11] In 1992, the editor of the Japanese journal *Litteraire* named Murakami's *Sekai no owari to hâdoboirudo wandârando* (*Hard-Boiled Wonderland and the End of the World*) as his personal favourite among contemporary Japanese novels,[12] and sales of that novel have continued steadily to reach the more 'modest' figure of 1.62 million by the end of 2004.[13]

Clearly, the spectacular publishing success of Murakami's fiction over two and a half decades needs to be accounted for as more than just a passing fad.[14] As Katô Norihiro (who has offered intelligent perspectives on Murakami's works over an extended period) reminds us, in the world of Japanese 'pure literature' it is highly unusual for a novelist to attract attention with the publication of each new work *and* be continuously supported by huge numbers of readers over a twenty-five year period.[15] A recent Japanese magazine article claims that Murakami is now being read in thirty-five countries worldwide, and suggests that it is the universality of human experiences of uneasiness (*fuan*) and hope (*kibô*) dealt with in his books, which may account for this popularity without borders.[16] In the light of such claims, we should hardly be surprised by Toshiko Ellis' observation that 'Murakami's case seems to represent many of the critical issues related to Japanese culture today'.[17]

In the United States, Murakami's earlier work was described as 'a presentiment of fresh outlooks and impulses' for the Japanese novel,[18] and writing of *Hard-Boiled Wonderland and the End of the World*, one critic urged that it should be part of 'every substantial collection of Japanese fiction'.[19] The major translator of Murakami, American scholar Jay Rubin, has drawn parallels between Murakami and Sôseki.[20] Another translator, Alfred Birnbaum, is adamant that the publication of Murakami's first novel marked a 'significant turning point': 'Mostly overnight—and single-handedly, Murakami Haruki brought about a revolutionary change in Japanese literature.'[21] At the other end of the critical spectrum, Miyoshi Masao's notorious characterization of Murakami and Mishima as 'nothing but stylists, lacking intellectual content', who sought to cultivate international audiences (albeit in radically different ways) has been dismissed by Hirata as a form of 'bitter Haruki bashing'.[22]

Murakami's reception in Germany was described as confronting the reading public with a completely different image of the Japan that has conventionally been represented in translations of Japanese literature, with one review of *Hitsuji o meguru bôken* (*A Wild Sheep Chase*) hailing Murakami as the 'star of postmodern Japanese literature'. Postmodern or otherwise, a German translation of

Sekai no owari to hâdoboirudo wandârando has found a place in the 'Japan Library' Series by publisher Insel (alongside such literary luminaries as Nagai Kafû and Tanizaki Junichirô) and even rates an entry in *Kindlers Neues Literatur Lexicon*.[xxiii]

More recently, Murakami's fiction appearing in German has been the subject of considerable controversy amongst scholars and publishers. In his book on Murakami, Rubin documents the trouble surrounding the German publication of *Nejimakidori kuronikuru*. The problem revolved around the German translation having been produced directly from the English version of the text, rather than from the original Japanese.[xxiv] This controversy highlights the implicit 'global imperatives' facing many contemporary Japanese artists, and will be discussed in more detail in the next chapter. It is also relates to an issue explored in subsequent chapters concerning the so-called 'translation style' adopted by Murakami.

Moving to eastern Europe, we have noted, in the Introduction, the relatively recent popularity of Murakami's fiction in Russia. However, in 1995, Anna Zielinska-Elliot's translation of *Hitsiji o meguru bôken* became the first Murakami novel to appear in Polish. It is testament to the 'universal' style of Murakami's writing that the translator felt the satisfaction of being able to directly render the 'atmosphere' (*fun'iki*) of his sentences, 'as they were' (*sono mama*), directly into Polish.[xxv] Although Murakami's success in Italy has been part of a larger 'boom' in contemporary Japanese literature in that country incorporating Murakami Ryû and Yoshimoto Banana, his works have, according to Okamoto, set themselves apart because of their 'mood-making detail', 'characteristic style' (*dokutoku no buntai*) and the strong sense of connectivity (*kanrensei*) established between characters in the stories.[xxvi]

We also noted in the Introduction, that by May 2003, a Chinese translation of Murakami's *Umibe no kafuka* (*Kafka on the Shore*) had entered the top ten bestseller list in China. However, the Murakami boom in that country is nothing new. A decade ago, Den Ken Shin claimed that through Murakami's fiction, young Chinese writers had recognized the opportunity to 'view the world through Japan' (*Nihon o tsûjite sekai o miru*). Furthermore, the popularity of Murakami (and contemporary Japanese literature generally in China) had meant that the notions of the 'love novel' (*ren'ai shôsetsu*) 'youth novel' (*seishun shôsetsu*) and 'urban novel' (*toshi shôsetsu*) had gained more credence in the Chinese literary world.[xxvii] Den also points out that in the year (1989) when the Japanese reading public had become intoxicated with Murakami's works, Chinese readers had tasted the setback for democracy in the Tiananmen 'incident', by sampling the 'reality' (*genjitsu*) of Murakami's writing: they were able to maintain a certain kind of silence 'from another perspective'. Also, from that time onwards, while young Chinese writers refrained from directly stating their opinions, they offered them to readers through their fiction. Interestingly, according to Den, this was a result not only of the general rejection of Social Realism, but also could be attributed specifically to the influence of Murakami's literature on contemporary writers.[xxviii]

In Korea, Murakami's popularity has been part of a strong interest from young Koreans in Japanese language, literature and culture, coupled with the general rule of thumb that many books which are well received in Japan will also sell well in Korea. In the case of Murakami's fiction, there has been a scramble amongst publishers who rely on 'in-house' translations (often done by general staff with Japanese language abilities), in a highly competitive race to prepare translations for publication at the expense of, according to Kim Sokuza, any perceived necessity to maintain the quality of the original work in the translated version. For example, *Kaze no uta o kike* (*Hear the Wind Sing*) was published in Korean in July 1991 by one publisher, and a month later by as many as three.[xxix] Kim cites as the reasons for Murakami's popularity: his fiction being 'easy to read'/'easy to grasp' (*yomiyasui/toritsukiyasui*), its marked difference to earlier forms of Japanese literature, and the fact that readers relate to his fiction's sense of 'emptiness' and 'loss' amidst the materialistic hyper-consumer culture of their daily lives, in a way not dissimilar to reader responses in the Japanese cultural context.[xxx]

The above discussion indicates that there are at least two important aspects of the reception of Murakami's literary works which support the proposition that they are indicative of the simulacral operation of cultural typifications in contemporary Japan. Firstly, that they represent some kind of departure from other contemporary Japanese fictional works in terms of their linguistic and narrative 'style', resulting in an extraordinary response from readers and critics alike, and thus justifying, in part, the label 'Murakami Phenomenon'. This phenomenon is simulacrul to the extent that all phenomena can be described as 'things that appear or are perceived',[xxxi] bearing in mind that 'a phenomenon is different from a substance'.[xxxii] Furthermore, it conforms to the definition presented later, which characterizes the simulacrum as 'mediating between human thought and inaccessible originals'. Secondly, that Murakami's works lend themselves to ready appropriation and assimilation into a universalized paradigm of 'global' writing which reflects both the foregrounding of the 'presentational process' vis-a-vis the 'presented world' of the narrative,[xxxiii] as well as a common concern with a poetics of nostalgia/loss (typical of modernity) alongside a privileging of the aesthetic of the post-industrial city. Both such features will later be shown to be indicative of a multitude of simulacral dimensions in the practices and discourses of contemporary Japanese culture.

Murakami criticism (*Murakami ron*) indeed covers a vast body of styles and formats. In terms of the more significant academic criticism, we can identify well over twenty monographs (*tankô hon*) in Japanese devoted exclusively to Murakami, as well as numerous essays in critical anthologies (*tankôhon shoshûronbun*), and at least ten special issues (*zasshi tokushû*) of major literary/critical journals. There are also hundreds of noteworthy essays/articles in journals, magazines and newspapers. This is not to mention, of course, the vast number of articles, essays, and interviews whose level of critical engagement with their subject appears not to be immediately worthy of scholarly attention, but which nevertheless constitute a rich storehouse of materials for Japanese cultural studies.

The Murakami Phenomenon positions the name of a literary star as the central signifier in a massively inter-textual system of genres (literary, academic, journalistic, musical, photographic). This system is informed by the discourses of Japanese literary modernity (with motifs of 'self', 'world', 'meaning' and 'truth'), the ideas/conventions of European Romanticism and Naturalism (as explored by the earlier Japanese translators of European fiction) and the paradigm of Japanese literary classicism (*koten, kanbun*), as contested in the *genbunitchi* policies of the Meiji state which attempted to 'unify' the classical forms of writing with the colloquial idioms of speech.[34] It is also informed by the paradigm of literary 'postmodernity', which Karatani equates with the 'setting free' or foregrounding of language.[35] In short, it is reasonable to conclude that all of these conditions of 'exteriority' attendant upon the category of the Murakami novel constitute a simulacral system of inter-textuality and meta-textuality which can be represented, in abbreviated form, in the following way (with notes providing details of selected examples):

The *'Murakami Phenomenon': Inter-textual & Meta-textual Relations*

'PRIMARY' NARRATIVE TEXTS   **'META'TEXTS/NARRATIVES**

long novels[36]   'non-fiction' works[37]
(*chôhen shôsetsu*)   essays[38]

short stories[39]   scholarly critiques[40]
(*tanpen shôsetsu*)

                                                                                            journalistic
                                                                                             critiques[41]

                                                                                    photo-essay works[42]

                                    'Murakami Haruki'
                                    (name of the author)

                                                                                  discussion (*tairon*)[43]
                                                                    travel accounts (*kikôshû*)[44]

                                                                                      musical reference
                                                                                             guide[45]

                                                                                          miscellaneous
                                                                                             texts[46]

The 'Murakami Phenomenon': Inter-textual & Meta-textual Relations

'PRIMARY' NARRATIVE TEXTS	'META' TEXTS/NARRATIVES
long novels	translation into other languages[47] (English, Polish, German, Italian, Korean, Chinese Russian)
short stories	
'Murakami Haruki' (name of the author)	Murakami's translation of American fiction[48]
	other contemporary Japanese fiction[49]
	Internet Murakami[50]

Of course, a more complex meta-textual chart than the one offered above would indicate relations between the themes, tropes, characters and figures of Murakami's narratives, but the purpose of this simple list is to demonstrate the sheer diversity and scale of the meta-narrative items comprising the Murakami Phenomenon. These meta-texts mediate and are mediated by the signifier 'Murakami Haruki', within the generalized reading regimes of Murakami's readers. To be sure, there are numerous examples of voluminous critical writing on canonical Japanese literature, but it is the range of forms made possible by the media, marketing and publishing technologies of contemporary Japan which assure that the 'name of the author' can be sufficiently reified to the extent that it functions efficiently amidst what Baudrillard called, in his early writing, the 'system of objects'.[51] It will be argued later that such a structuralist critique (which has been ostensibly displaced by the 'reign of simulacra' and the virtual) remains useful in explicating certain practices of consumption and commodification.

Within the context of such practices, the 'name of the author' is at once suggestive of a clearly discernible 'style' of contemporary daily life: an ideology, a sexuality, a taste in music and food, in speech and human relations—indeed an entire aesthetic sensibility is built upon the second order, simulacral enactment of the Murakami Phenomenon. In the final analysis, it is the operation of these modalities of style (related to, but also beyond the semiotic constraints of mere linguistic style or *buntai*) which enables the formation and ensures the persistence of the Murakami Phenomenon. Furthermore, a case could be made that the ubiquitous use of the list or table (*ichiranhyô*) and chart (*zu*) in Murakami criticism to express even the most trivial and far fetched imagined connections, information and both inter and intra-textual relations, also indicates the highly simulacral nature of the Murakami Phenomenon.

For example, Ishikura's 'Murakami Metatext Chart' distinguishes between a 'metatext' (*metatekusto*) and a sequel (*zokuhen*) as a way of describing connections between narrative worlds which are ordered 'historically' (in terms of order of publication) and thematically, depending on their plots and the characters which appear in them. Interestingly, in this scheme, there are two kinds of narrative (*monogatari*): those dealing with the 'interior of the self' (*jiko no naibu*) and those concerned with the self and its 'relationality to others' (*tasha to no kankeisei*). According to Ishikura, the novels of the first trilogy and *Dansu dansu dansu* (*Dance, Dance, Dance*) comprise the first type, and all other narratives following these, up to and including *Nejimakidori kuronikuru* (*The Wind-Up Bord Chronicle*), belong in the latter group.[52]

A more striking example of the use of tables, lists and charts as a means of explicating the macro-structural relations between, and internal characteristics of Murakami's narratives, is evident in Katô Norihiro's *Murakami Haruki—ierôpêji* (*Murakami Haruki—Yellow Pages*). The text is just that, a mock 'yellow-page' directory—covered in a striking yellow dust cover. In the first volume, published in 1996, it substitutes the usual alphabetical ordering of the commercial telephone directory, for a strict chronological treatment (in order of year of publication) of Murakami's novels (*chôhen shôsetsu*) from 1979 to 1995.

It is not only the macro structure of the index-style of presenting information which is interesting here, but also the tables, lists and charts interspersing the twenty-three 'columns' (written by other critics, as well as the editor) offering exegesis and critique of the novels. These range from a 'day chart' (*nissû keisanhyô*) linking action, character and scene in the context of three sub-narratives in *Kaze no uta o kike* (*Hear the Wind Sing*),[53] to a table which compares two female characters of *Nejimakidori kuronikuru* (namely Kumiko and Kanô Kureta) in terms of the mysterious 'figure of a baby' which is said to represent something curse-like carried within and expelled by the women (who are described as *bunshin dôshi*, or 'partners in birth'). The table compares the characters in terms of year of birth and family backgrounds, the dates of their first sexual experiences and their individual sexual sensibilities and experiences after the event of their 'rape' (*ryôjoku*) by the sinister Wataya Noboru.[54] The second volume of Kato's 'Yellow Pages', published in 2004, utilizes basically the same format as Volume One (minus the guest contributors), with an array of charts, columns and tables relating to works from *Andâguraundo* (*Underground*, 1997) to *Umibe no kafuka* (*Kafka on the Shore*, 2002).[55]

While the use of the charts, lists, tables and other numerical and diagrammatic forms of representing various textual features and relations reflects some interesting approaches to the novels, the actual task of writing about, or 'interpreting'

Murakami has become more like an exercise in hermeneutic endeavour. Like the sheep which is the subject of a search or quest in *Hitsuji o meguru bôken* (*A Wild Sheep Chase*), the deeply embedded, intertwining threads of inter and meta-textuality of Murakami's ouevre are teased out and exposed through a process of 'discovery'. We are dealing here with a kind of forensic sifting which yields correspondences and contiguities, as well as textual aporia and discontinuities, and which sustains the investigative momentum for the more serious critic/reader who has the inclination to grope along the faintly illumined contours of the ubiquitous 'maze' (*meiro*) or 'puzzle' (*nazo*) often said to be at the centre of all Murakami's texts.[56]

Underlying this process are at least two assumptions about the nature of contemporary Japanese narrative which lie firmly within the conventions of critical practice in Japanese literary modernity. Firstly, that the text ultimately has a referent and in that sense must 'mean' something, and secondly, that the cult of the writer (*sakka*) as expressed in the 'I-novel' (*shishôsetsu*) paradigm, requires the reader/critic to search for possible connections between the 'real' life of the author and the presented narrative worlds of the texts he/she presents.

It would be fair to say that until relatively recently, the interpretative strategies available to the modern Japanese reader had been broadly prescribed by the realist conventions of the nineteenth-century European novel (which provided the initial model for Japanese narrative modernity)—especially in the assumption that language is a 'transparent' medium through which the truth of immediate experience must be conveyed.

The problem is, however, that when we come to 'postmodern' writers like Murakami, Shimada, Yoshimoto and so on, the 'transparency' assumption no longer holds; the conventionalized available reading modalities are subverted, and language itself (not its 'referential' equivalences), as well as the processes of syntactic experimentation, become crucial to the construction of meaning. On the question of 'mediation' both Suzuki and Koschmann refer to Maruyama Masao's 1949 essay 'Literature and Carnal Politics' in discussion of the problematic nature of the mediation of the real, of experience, in the context of an 'indigenous linguistic and epistemological tradition' which valued only 'immediate, lived experience'. Suzuki also cites Fowler, who writes: 'In a culture that views 'reality' only as immediate experience of the natural world, literature not surprisingly becomes a chronicling or transcribing of that experience rather than an imaginative reconstruction of it.'[57]

Returning to our consideration of the more striking examples of simulacral forms of critical practice (and here we are not describing these examples of critical discourse as merely parasitic, but simulacral in the broader sense that they re-present the 'primary' texts and re-enact their narrative performance), there seems little doubt that over time, the burgeoning corpus of Murakami criticism resorted more and more to the use of charts, tables and diagrams for two reasons. Partly, no doubt, in order to handle the growing body of narratives to which it had to direct its hermeneutic effort, but also, it could be argued, as part of a general trend for critical discourse spanning the eighties and nineties to develop, parallel with forms of media and communication at large, a tendency towards a 'digital' arrangement of content. That is to say, as part of the larger discursive formations of artistic/aesthetic knowledge, critical discourse—as merely one more form of information in the 'information society'—was subject to the subtle but inexorable pressures of providing easy accessibility to a reading public overwhelmed by innumerable demands on their limited reading time.

Earlier, more 'analogical' critical writing relied on a simpler but perhaps more inaccessible metaphoric critical style. This has given way, over time, to the extreme format of the 'yellow pages' critical anthology. Interestingly, in precisely this way, one of the oft-cited features of Murakami's style has been made homologous to the critical practices which reflect it. The ready 'availability' of the text to be 'taken up at any point' (*doko kara mitemo ii*) is noted by Tsuge who goes so far as to describe Murakami as a 'digital writer/novelist' (*dejitaru na sakka*). He has in mind the digital format of Murakami's non-fiction *Andâguraundo* (*Underground*) which presents the narrative of each individual victim's experience of the Sarin gas attack as a series of flashbacks in space and time which move back and forth readily between the frames of 'the present' and that of 'the event'. However, it is not only because of the format of his latest non-fiction work that Murakami is described as being 'digital' (as well as very 'contemporary'—*gendaiteki*). Rather, it is the fact that he has a home page on the Internet which confirms his status as a 'digital' writer. According to Tsuge, although this home page allows two-way traffic (it is not a truly interactive 'chat' format), it only allows for the sending and receiving of messages 'one by one'. Tsuge is convinced that Murakami was a 'digital' writer from his very first work—in the sense that his style was 'dry and computer like'—but concedes that such a style existed long before the advent of digital technology, citing Akutagawa's *Yabu no naka* (*The Grove*) as one such example.[58]

Ishikura has also noted that the fact that Murakami is now 'on-line' represents a new era for writers, scholars and general readers alike,[59] although it could also be claimed that the February 1998 special edition of *Kokubungaku* functions much like an Internet 'home page' since it offers a comprehensive 'database' on Murakami's works, and research in the area. This development of the 'virtual writer' is interestingly parallel to the final part of *Nejimakidori kuronikuru*, in which the representation of speech acts conducted via the computer form a significant part of one chapter. With regard to this point about the digital, Ruthrof has noted that 'shelvability' and 'availability' are (among other features) indicative of a digital modality of narrative syntax.[60] In another context, Maeda has also highlighted the digital (i.e 'on/off' and 'either/or') format of communication in the 'disc-jockey' scene of *Kaze no uta o kike* (*Hear the Wind Sing*) which will be discussed in more detail later.

The broadly 'digitalized' appearance of the Murakami Phenomenon is also evident in another way. By the time of Murakami's movement into non-fiction, the 'meta-narrative' of his literary career had been fully constructed and retroactively applied to his fictional ouevre (specifically, the eight long novels, four of which are the focus of this book). Because the unity of this ouevre has by now been established, each text can then be accessed at any point—depending on the proclivities of the reader—without threatening the authority of the signifying function of the name of the author.

For example, a reader who is seeking the nostalgic evocation of a particular era (*jidai*) will be guided by the appropriate critical sign-posting in various anthologies and essays. One chasing information on the musical motifs and references of particular novels can check the Murakami musical guide book, and a reader interested in the sexual activities/personality types and relations between specific characters of the novels can access the range of charts and tables in more recent critical works. The reader feeling inclined toward a more investigative approach can follow the clues and references to 'real' geographical locations as specified in the critical text entitled *Nejimakidori no sagashikata* ('How to Search for the Wind-up Bird') which even goes so far as establishing latitudinal correspondences between locations in both the Mediterranean region (which are referred to in the testimonies of certain characters in *Nejimakidori kuronikuru*) as well as, more locally, in Japan.[61] Armed with an array of 'information' about the texts themselves, the reader is encouraged (in the way that Baudrillard describes) to 'sketch' the details and 'fill in' the appropriate colors of the text in a way pre-ordained by the various codes of 'interpretation' already provided by the voluminous critical writings. In such a context, the operation of Baudrillard's 'third order' or 'simulation' simulacrum is complete: the distinction between the referent and its forms of typification/representation in language is largely abolished.

All of this is related to the argument in the following chapter which proposes that the significance of periodization and the reification of 'the contemporary' confers a particular contextual dimension on the status of certain literary works which, once established, remains inexorably associated with a specific era, style or sensibility, and this in turn more or less establishes the parameters and limits of prescribed reading practices. Thus the advent of the 'Murakami Phenomenon' can be explained partly as a function of the emergence of a broad web of interrelated discourses on 'society', 'economy', 'media', 'technology' and 'history', which began to emerge in the high-growth sixties and which have become the standard fare of 'popular' debate (*tairon, giron, ronsô*) amongst public commentators and intellectuals in the diverse forms of contemporary media.

What is striking about many instances of these discourses is that they suggest a kind of self-reflexive, popular ongoing engagement with the 'political' in the public arena which is not, however, corroborated by trends such as poor voter turn-out at election time, apparent indifference to political scandal and the seeming mismanagement of the economy. There is no shortage of examples of these ostensibly 'self-reflexive' discourses, and it is worth considering a few of them here—particularly since they resonate with issues to be raised in the discussion, in the next chapter, of the Japanese modernity/postmodernity debate.

They are also important because they indicate some of the critical parameters for our later analysis of Murakami's texts.

In a three-way discussion in the late eighties entitled 'Owari no jidai' and later published in the journal *Kaien,* three prominent critics raised the connection between a new kind of writing, and the palpable sense that a particular era was drawing to a close.[62] Fukuoka remarked generally, that from a range of novels (including those by Murakami Haruki, Murakami Ryû and Ôe Kenzaburô) came the distinct feeling that something had finished,[63] and this was evident, according to Kanno, in the impression generated by the novels of 1988 as being 'thin/sparse' (*kihaku de aru*) and 'diffuse' or 'scattered' (*kakusan shite iru*).[64] The critics highlighted the conversational style of Murakami's *Dansu, dansu, dansu* and concurred that this style was a kind of 'fashionable language' (*ryûkôgo*) which symbolized the state of contemporary literature from the 're-verse side' (*urogawa*). It was also noted that the sense of something having ended was emphasized by Murakami's habit of always noting the precise date/year of the narrative.[65] Kanno was in no doubt that *Dansu, dansu, dansu* was an attempt at a critique of 'late capitalism' (*kôdôshihonshugi*).[66]

For other commentators, the new kind of literary language was something which 'reflected' the city, and was intimately tied to the image of the narrating 'I' in such an urban context. Taguchi and Kawanashi stress the importance of marketing in the success of a novel, but note that an 'easy-reading' (*yomiyasui*) style and 'special atmosphere' (*doku toku no fun'iki*) have also been crucial to the remarkable reception of novels like Murakami's *Noruei no mori* (*Norwegian Wood*). Judging from the broad-ranging nature of their discussion, however, there is no doubt that both these critics do not bestow upon the novel a special status as a consumable commodity. Indeed, there approach suggests that the novel takes its place along with the merchandising of other consumable art forms (such as movies, music and *manga*) in the marketing of culture in contemporary Japan.[67]

Kuroko characterizes Murakami and the literature of his era as the narrative of 'fear' (*kyôfu*) and 'crisis' (*kiki*), singling out Murakami for his 'cool, penetrating understanding' (*reitetsu na ninshiki*) in a barren age (*kawaita jidai*) in which 'love' (*ren'ai*) and human relations are akin to a kind of 'complicit fantasy' (*dôkyôgensô*).[68] Singling out Murakami's short stories 'T.V. People' and 'Zombie' as representative of the 'transmogrified subject' (*henyô suru shutai*), Kuroko sees such writing as indicative of a postmodern 'unsettled transition period' (*futeikei na katoki*).[69] However, he also suggests that a decade of Murakami's writing (namely, the 1980's) had shown that there was still a strong sense of the 'shishôsetsu/I-novel' method (*shishôsetsuteki hôhô*) in contemporary literature. Acknowledging the role of American writers such as Capote, Fitzgerald and Irving in shaping Murakami's 'literary world', Kuroko points to the *avant-garde* nature of his writing in that it takes up the latest, most advanced urban art.[70] But this is not as radical as Shimada's 'dystopian' writing, which for Kuroko, represents by far the greatest 'spirit of denial of the contemporary age'.[71]

It is clear that Murakami's novels are representative of a wider boom in the so-called 'youth-novel' (*seishun shôsetsu*), and that this is a product of the demographic configuration of the 'baby-boomer' generation (*dankai sedai*). Otuska, (writing in 1988) gives as prime examples of this two best-selling novels published in 1987, namely Murakami Ryû's *'69'* and Murakami Haruki's *Noruei no mori* (*Norwegian Wood*).[72] The appeal to nostalgic impulses is paramount here, and Otsuka is right in pointing out that both authors were teenagers in the late sixties/early seventies and that their popularity reflected a 'retro-boom' in the Japan of the late eighties. Fortuitously, many editors from the major publishing companies were also 'baby-boomers' — and they enthusiastically enacted highly successful marketing strategies for these texts.

Other critics like Kawamoto Saburô (who has written at length on Murakami) expressed the view, as early as 1983, that what he terms the 'youth-quake' of the sixties took America as its symbol, and coalesced into a singular identity of counter-culture. Kawamoto is gratified that writers like Murakami Ryû and Murakami Haruki persisted through their novels in addressing many of the issues of that period.[73]

It is worth noting, however, that despite being made a cult-figure for the iconoclastic and hedonistic themes of his earlier novels, Murakami Ryû himself, writing in 1995, reflected on the advent in the nineties of a 'bleak and dreary age' (*samuzamushii jidai*) — the era of the 'high yen', the stark realization of the limited nature of world resources and the Gulf War. We are told that these hallmarks of this age had their origins in the early seventies, and it was the early works of, for example, the popular writer Yoshimoto Banana, which (far from springing from the culture of school-girl comics or *shôjo manga*) actually reflected this.[74] In contrast to this, the approach taken by Ono seeks to capture the essence of Murakami Haruki's literary method through the analogy of jazz (which is a kind of euphemism for 'America'), and it is the more structured so-called 'West Coast' jazz clearly preferred and often referred to in his works, which differs markedly from the 'free jazz' style of a writer like Nakagami Kenji.[75]

'America', 'sub-culture', 'the youth-novel' — most of these suggest an over reliance on labels and clichés to describe the 'background' of Murakami's works, but there is very little genuinely insightful and self-reflexive sociological critique which attempts to relate the rise of a certain kind of writing to the epistemological and ontological matrices of the urban space, the representational logic and limits of the city, which have played a crucially determining role in the production of all manner of artistic discourses in the era of Japanese modernity.

Maeda Ai is one notable exception here, and he attempts a 'reading' prompted by the urban space (or *toshikûkan*) itself.[76] Maeda claims that the kinds of concepts (*hassô*) which utilized the notion of 'urban space' (*toshikûkan*) as a form of mediation in the re-reading of the literary text are fairly recent, and emerged in the early seventies.[77] This was related to the emergence and development of the field of urban studies (specifically the disciplines of urban engineering, urban policy planning and urban sociology) and along with these came the distinct notions of 'public space' (*kôkyô kûkan*), 'residential space' (*kyojû kûkan*) and 'productive space' (*seisan kûkan*). In terms of the literary representation of the projection of the modern 'self' into the urban space, Maeda finds early examples in the protagonists of Futabatei's *Ukigumo* and Ogai's *Maihime*.[78] He also cites the examples of Sôseki's *Sanshirô* and Ogai's *Seinen* as representative of the theme in later Meiji literature. In these kinds of works, there appears a structural differentiation in terms of an 'exterior space' (*gaibukûkan*) and 'interior space' (*naibukûkan*) in a way which concurs with Karatani Kôjin's insistence on the discovery of interiority in early modern literature.[79]

In *Maihime*, for example, there is said to be in operation the double structure of a transparent system of a public space based on the visual, and a private, intangible space (*shitekikûkan*) which provides a basic model and is typically repeated in modern urban novels.[80] The crucial point made by Maeda is that within the context of the contemporary urban space (*gendai no toshi*), this double structure is increasingly concealed/suppressed (*inpei sareru*), and it is 'signs' (*kigô*) and information (*jôhô*) which work to effectively blur, if not eradicate this distinction. Understandably, such a view has big implications for how we go about analyzing the contemporary urban novel (*toshi shôsetsu*).[81] And as will be argued later, it is the urban space which so powerfully informs the operation of the simulacrum.

It is clear that what can be called the overall 'critical-fictional thematics' of the Murakami Phenomenon are concerned principally with the following: firstly, a focus on the city or 'urban space'; secondly, a concentration on the changing language of the novel which becomes more closely correlated with an imagined 'colloquial' style; thirdly, an emphasis on 'era' (*jidai*) as being something which ultimately recuperates meaning through reference to semiotically configured codes of 'style' and 'nostalgia'. What is common to all of these is their simulacral dimension as typifications of modernity. This notwithstanding, and despite the undoubted value of Maeda's method in developing a semiotic approach to the urban contextualization of the novel, it has been noted that this kind of analysis does not attempt to fully consider the political implications of the urban 'scene' and the interiority/exteriority opposition. What needs to be considered is the extent to which the urban narrative (*toshi shôsetsu*) more generally, and Murakami's fiction in particular, constitutes a critique of the late capitalist Japanese state, as well as suggesting new forms of narrativity and subjectivity.

Having outlined some of the conditions of exteriority entailed in the emergence of the Murakami text and traced some of the contours of the so called 'Murakami Phenomenon', we will later undertake an examination of Murakami's first three novelistic works which constitute the so-called 'Rat Trilogy'. We will be particularly interested in establishing the political/historical dimensions of these texts as not only an experiment with the formal aspects of language and narrative structure, but also as an incipient critique of the state which was to be developed, in different ways, in later novels. However, before doing so, in the two chapters which follow, it is necessary to define terminology and clarify some important theoretical and methodological issues.

Notes

1. See Saitô Michiko, "Murakami Haruki ron kuesto," *Bungakkai* 50, no. 8 (August 1996): 162-75.

2. As far back as 1994, the popular book magazine *Da buinchi* , in a survey of reader's favourites, placed Murakami Haruki at the top of the *junbungaku* category. See *Da buinchi* 7 (November 1994): 16.

3. See Mathew C. Strecher, "Translators Note" to Aoki Tamotsu's "Murakami Haruki and Contemporary Japan," John Whittier Treat ed., *Contemporary Japan and Popular Culture*, (Honolulu: University of Hawaii Press, 1996), 265.

4. For example, Saitô, "Murakami Haruki ron kuesto," 162.

5. See Nakano Osamu, "Naze Murakami Haruki genshô wa okita no ka," *Yurîka—rinjizôkan* (June 1989): 39.

6. Nakano, "Naze Murakami Haruki genshô wa okita no ka," 45.

7. Yokô Kazuhiro, *Murakami Haruki no nigen teki sekai* (Chôeisha, 1992), 13.

8. Fukami Haruka, *Murakami Haruki no uta* (Seikyûsha, 1990), 8. The story 'Tongari-yaki no seisui' is published in *Murakami Haruki zensakuhin 1979-1989, Tanpen-shû II* (Kodansha, 1991).

9. *Nô saido—tokushû: besutoserâ saidoku* 6, no.3 (March 1996), 102-3.

10. *Da buinchi—kaitai zensho: ninki sakka no jinsei to sakuhin*, (February 1996), 20.

11. See "Murakami Haruki—25 nen," *Asahi shinbun*, 12 November 2004, 15.

12. Yasuhara Ken, "Toriaezu no nihon bungaku hen'ai besuto 10," *Litteraire* 2 (Fall 1992): 94-95.

13. "Murakami Haruki—25 nen," 15.

14. The sales success of his fiction alone has continued from 1979 through to the present, and his non-fiction works, including *Andâguraundo* (*Underground*) have also been top sellers.

15. See Katô Norihiro, " 'Ido no kabe' ushinatta jidai," *Asahi shinbun,* 12 November, 2004, 15.

16. See Ishikawa Masahiko, "35 ka kuni de yomareru ryû—fuan to kibo no fuhensei" in *Aera*, no. 44, 11 October 2004, 46-47.

17. Toshiko Ellis, "Questioning Modernism and Postmodernism in Japanese Literature," in *Japanese Encounters with Postmodernity*, ed. J.P. Arnason & Y. Sugimoto (London & New York: Kegan Paul International, 1995), 143.

18. Brad Leithhauser, "A Hook Somewhere," *The New Yorker* 65 (4 December 1989): 187.

19. J.M. Ditsky, "Hard-boiled Wonderland and the End of the World," *Choice* 29 (29 January 1992): 752.

20. Rubin compares *Hard-boiled Wonderland* with Sôseki's *Kokoro* and *Kôfu*, specifically with regard to these novels' 'exploration of the human psyche'. See Jay Rubin, "The Other World of Murakami Haruki," *Japan Quarterly* 39, 4 (Oct.-Dec.1992): 497.

21. Alfred Birnbaum, 'Murakami Haruki—oinaru hokotenkan', *Shincho* (January 1990): 266-69.

22. Miyoshi is taken to task by Hosea Hirata, in "Amerika de yomareru Murakami Haruki," *Kokubungaku* 40, no. 4 (March 1995): 102.

23. See Jurgen Stalph, "Doitsu no Murakami Haruki," *Kokubungaku* 40, 4 (March 1995): 105-8.

24. See Rubin, *Haruki Murakami and the Music of Words*, 273-89.

25. Anna Zielinska-Elliot, "Pôrando no Murakami Haruki," *Kokubungaku* 40, no. 4 (March 1995): 109-12.

26. Okamoto Tarô, 'Murakami Haruki to Itaria', *Kokubungaku* 40, no. 4 (March 1995): 120-23.

27. Den Kenshin, "Chûgoku no Murakami Haruki—shinsen ketsueki," *Kokubungaku* 40, no. 4 (March 1995): 113-16.

28. Den, "Chûgoku no Murakami Haruki—shinsen ketsueki," 115.

29. Kim Sokuza, "Kankoku no Murakami Haruki," *Kokubungaku* 40, no. 4 (March 1995): 116-18.

30. Kim , "Kankoku no Murakami Haruki," 118.

31. See *Concise Oxford Dictionary of Current English* (Oxford: Oxford University Press, 1982), 769.

32. On the Japanese definition of *genshô* (phenomenon), one dictionary gives the illustrative example: 'Genshô to jitsuzai to wa koto naru' ('A phenomenon is different from a substance'); See Kenkyusha's *New Japanese-English Dictionary* (Tokyo: Kenkyusha, 1987), 331. It is also worth bearing in mind that the Japanese term *genshô* may carry a slightly different sense than the English 'phenomenon' in that the character *gen* suggests 'present', 'existing', 'actual' *as well as* 'indicate', 'appear', 'express'; the second character in the term shô, indicates 'image', 'pattern after', 'imitate'. See Mark Spahn & Wolfgand Hadamitsky, *Japanese Character Dictionary* (Tokyo: Nichigai Associates, 1989), 1116 and 388 respectively.

33. According to Ruthrof, these are the twin dimensions of all narratives. See Horst Ruthrof, *The Reader's Construction of Narrative* (London: Routledge & Kegan Paul, 1981), 1-21.

34. For an authoritative study of this, see Nannette Twine, *The Genbunitchi Movement: A Study of the Development of the Modern Colloquial Style in Japan* (Ph.D dissertation, University of Queensland, 1975).

35. Karatani Kôjin, *The Origins of Modern Japanese Literature*, trans. Brett de Barry et.al (Durham: Duke University Press, 1993), 187.

36. See bibliography for details of the major novels.

37. For example, *Andâguraundo* (Kodansha, 1997).

38. For example, extending from such texts as *Murakami asahidô—haihô* (Bunka Shuppankyoku, 1984), to *Wakai dokusha no tame no tanpen shôsetsu an'nai* (Bungeishunjû, 1997).

39. See for example, Volumes 3 & 5 of *Murakami Haruki zen sakuhin (1979-1989)* (Kodansha, 1990-1991).

40. In the form of monographs, journal articles and essays referred to throughout this book.

41. Reviews and other articles appearing in newspapers and magazines, referred to in this discussion.

42. For example *Nami no e, nami no hanashi* (Bungeishunjû, 1984 and 1989); photos by Inakoshi Koichi, text by Murakami Haruki.

43. Including discussions between journalists, critics and other writers. For example, see *Murakami Haruki, Kawai Hayao ni ai ni iku* (Iwanami shoten, 1997).

44. For example, *Toi taiko* (Kodansha, 1990); *Uten—enten* (Kodansha, 1990).

45. See *Murakami Haruki no ongakuzukan* (Japan mikksu, 1995).

46. For example,"Bungaku karuto kurosu dai jûhachi kai"—Murakami Haruki', *Da buinchi* (November 1995): 170. The puzzle asks about thirty questions of readers concerning Murakami's works, background, likes/dislikes, etc. See also *Murakami Haruki—ierô jiten* (Koara bukksu, 1999).

47. See "Sekai kara—honyaku to hankyô," *Kokubungaku* 40, no. 4 (March 1995): 100-123. This article outlines the state of the translation of Murakami's works up until 1995 and his reception in the English-speaking world, as well as in Poland, Germany, Italy, Korea and China up until that year.

For more recent discussion of Chinese, Russian and German translations, see relevant references in the Introduction and Chapter One.

48. These include translations of Scott Fitzgerald (1981, 1996), Raymond Carver (1983, 1984, 1990, 1991, 1992, 1994, 1997), John Updike (1986), Paul Theroux (1987), C.D.B. Brian (1987), Truman Capote (1988,1989, 1990), Tim O'Brien (1989, 1990), Michael Gilmore (1996), Ursula Le Guin (1996). For precise publishing information see Ishikura Michiko's 'Murakami Haruki Dêtâbase' *Kokubungaku* (February 1998) 182-207. One of the more recent important translations by Murakami is J.D. Salinger's *Catcher in the Rye*, Shinchosha, April, 2003.

49. Of course, particular characteristics of Murakami's narrative style come to the fore in relation to the styles of other significant contemporary writers. These would include, for example, such authors as Murakami Ryû, Shimada Masahiko, Yoshimoto Banana, Takahashi Genichirô, Matsumoto Seichô, Shinna Makoto, Yamada Eimi, Watanabe Junichi, Itsuki Hiroyuki, Miyamoto Teru and Ôe Kenzaburô.

50. See Ishikura Michiko's article on "Netto no naka no murakami" in *Kokubungaku* (February 1998); also, Murakami's e-mail correspondence with fans in *Yume no sâfu shitei* (Asahi shinbunsha, 1998). And the open electronic forum (of 1220 e-mail letters and Murakami's replies to each of them) reproduced in *Shônen kafuka: Kafka on the Shore—Official Magazine (*Shinchôsha, 2003).

51. The relevance of Baudrillard's *System of Objects* will be discussed more fully in Chapter 5.

52. Ishikura "Murakami Haruki dêtabêsu," 208-9.

53. See Katô Norihirô, ed., *Murakami Haruki—ierôpêiji* (Kôchi Shuppansha, 1996), 10-11.

54. Katô, ed., *Murakami Haruki—ierôpêiji* 206.

55. See Katô Norihirô, ed., *Murakami Haruki—ierôpêiji Part 2*, (Kôchi Shuppansha, 2004).

56. For example, see Hisai Tsubaki, *Nejimakidori no sagashikata* (Ôta Publishing, 1994). This is a remarkable text which even employs maps and photographs of actual locations in order to establish connections between characters and themes in this long narrative trilogy.

57. Tomi Suzuki, *Narrating the Self: Fictions of Japanese Modernity* (Stanford: Stanford Univ. Press, 1996), 4. Suzuki is quoting from Edward Fowler's *The Rhetoric of Confession* (Berkeley: University of California Press, 1988), 12.

58. See Tsuge Mitsuhiko, "Dejitaru na sakka," *Kokubungaku* (February,1998): 37-40.

59. Ishikura, "Netto no naka no Murakami Haruki," 210.

60. See Horst Ruthrof, "Narrative and the Digital: On the Syntax of the Postmodern," *Aumla—Journal of the Australasian Universities Language & Literature Association* 74 (November 1990): 185-200; 193.

61. See Hisai, *Nejimakidori no sagashikata*, 44, 86.

62. See Kanno Shôsei, Akiyama Shun & Fukuoka Kôichirô, "Owari no jidai—1988 nen no bungaku kaiko', *Kaien* 8, no.1 (February 1989): 208-36.

63. Kanno et.al., "Owari no jidai," 209.

64. Kanno et.al., "Owari no jidai," 209.

65. Kanno et.al., "Owari no jidai," 211-12.

66. Kanno et.al., "Owari no jidai," 13.

67. Kawanishi Ran & Taguchi Kenji, "Toshi o utsusu kotoba, 'boku' o gataru eizô,"*Waseda Bungaku* 154 (March 1989): 18-35. See especially pages 22-23.

68. See Kuroko Kazuo, "Murakami Haruki to dôjidao no bungaku—kyôfu arui wa kiki no monogatari," in *Murakami Haruki to dôjidai no bungaku* (Kawai Shuppan, 1990), 40-74.

69. Kuroko, "Murakami Haruki to dôjidao no bungaku," 41-43.

70. Kuroko, "Murakami Haruki to dôjidao no bungaku," 45.

71. Kuroko, "Murakami Haruki to dôjidao no bungaku," 61, 65.

72. Otsuka Eishi, "Dankai no sedai gurafuitei," *Hon no zasshi* 13, no. 1-3 (May 1998): 46-48.

73. Kawamoto Saburô, "Rokujûnendai no shôchô toshite no Amerika," *Gunzo*, 38, no. 2 (April 1983): 230-33.

74. Murakami Ryû, "Samuzamushii jidai," *Gunzô* 5 (May 1995): 164-68.

75. Ono Yoshie, "Futatsu no JAZZ—futatsu no Amerika," *Kokubungaku* 3 (March 1985): 79-86; 83.

76. Maeda Ai, "'Toshikûkan' kara no yomi," in Hasegawa Izumi, ed., *Gendai bungaku kenkyû: jôhô to shiryô*, ed. Hasegawa Izumi (Shibundo 1985): 46-52.

77. Maeda, "'Toshikûkan' kara no yomi," 46.

78. Maeda, "'Toshikûkan' kara no yomi," 47.

79. Maeda, "'Toshikûkan' kara no yomi," 51.

80. Maeda, "'Toshikûkan' kara no yomi," 52.

81. Maeda, "'Toshikûkan' kara no yomi," 52.

Chapter Two

Simulacral Sutures:
Modernity, the Global and the Idea of the Japanese Novel

> Literature and ethnography (in Japan, in modernity) are always in ghostly complicity with one another. And this complicity is unthinkable outside the inter linked struggles about literary authority, speech and writing, and the status of representable reality in twentieth-century Japan.
>
> Marilyn Ivy, *Discourses of the Vanishing: Modernity, Phantasm, Japan* [1]

This chapter will establish a critical context for the analysis of Murakami's trilogies by setting some theoretical parameters within which the discussion will proceed. It will clarify certain terms denoting the object of this hermeneutic endeavour, because in the broadest possible sense we are seeking to illuminate what Murakami's fiction means in contemporary Japanese culture. In keeping with Ivy's claim that within the context of Japanese modernity, literature and ethnography remain inseparable, it is clear from the outset that this enquiry also constitutes a kind of ethnography. It is the category of 'the Murakami novel' which occupies the positions of both valorized cultural object (as a bearer of difference, in the structuralist sense[2]), and subject—to the extent that it operates partially as an effect of being *subjected to* hermeneutic method, and stands always in a dialogical relation with the available subjectivities of its interlocutor.[3] Throughout the subsequent discussion, this multi-dimensionality of the category 'the Murakami novel' will be variously invoked and interrogated, and it will be shown that as well as the literary motifs and styles of the novels themselves, it is also the conditions of 'exteriority' necessary to the category (i.e. everything deemed extraneous to or 'outside' the texts themselves) which help constitute the unities of meaning cohering around the author's name and his oeuvre.[4]

This chapter functions as a preparation for asking the larger questions of how the novels of Murakami's trilogies relate to other discourses and discursive formations of contemporary Japan.[5] To put it another way, how are these novels constituted, in the broadest sense, inter-textually? [6] How we are able to respond to such a question will depend, in turn, upon the argument that Murakami's literary 'style' forms an aesthetic code or poetics of the simulacrum, which makes an important contribution to contemporary Japanese fiction. This chapter will also consider what might be called the 'global imperative' characteristic of contemporary Japanese artistic production, as well as touch on the parameters of the modernity/postmodernity debate as it has found form in the Japanese context.

What's in a Name?

Aphorisms, like proper nouns, mark out boundaries (aphorism: from the Greek *aphorismos*, meaning 'definition'; *aphorizô* from *horos*, meaning 'boundary'[7]) and in asking the question 'what is Japan?', we cannot deny that the signifier 'Japan' may just as well be called an aphorism. In an essay on aphorism and naming Derrida writes:

1. Aphorism is the name.

2. As its name indicates, aphorism separates, it marks dissociation (*apo*), it terminates, delimits, arrests (*horizo*); it brings to an end by separating, it separates in order to end— and to define (*finir—et definir*).

3. An aphorism is a name but every name can take on the figure of aphorism.

22. Aphorism: separation in language, and, in it, through the name which closes the horizon.

25. Aphorism is at once necessary and impossible.

26. The name would only be a "title," and the title is not the thing which it names. . . .

35. Changing names: the dance, the substitution, the masks, the simulacrum. . . .

39. The absolute aphorism: a proper name. Without genealogy, without the least copula.[8]

Taking Derrida's approach, we might conclude that the proper name 'Japan' is absolutely nominalized and in its materiality, immutably given—outside genealogy and beyond the reach of agency or verbal process. We might also note that that which bears a name usually does not name itself: the name is bestowed from the outside in the play of difference. Accordingly, it can be said that in the discursive arena of the nation-state, the name of the 'nation' emerges ultimately from the interstices of competing imperial and colonial discourses.

On the issue of genealogy we may depart slightly from Derrida, and although conceding that the signification of the name of a nation-state is always massively overdetermined ('it immediately says more than the name'), in the proper name 'Japan', can be sensed a genealogy which marks an acute and perpetual alterity. We see (in 35 above) the possibility of changing names: 'the dance, the substitution, the masks, the simulacrum. . .' — and in so doing, recognize this in Japan's history of naming itself and being named. 'Japan' is of course an anglicized version (with European variants) of the earlier *Jipangu*, which derived from Marco Polo's designation of the place as the land of *Cipangu* ('said to be an island, rich in gold, 1500 nautical miles to the east of China').[9] *Cipangu* itself was a romanization of the Chinese ideographic compound denoting the direction or origin of the (rising) sun (日本). This compound also collapses into the single idiom (with a minor alteration) indicating 'the east' (東). Thus, in all these designations, it remains a place of origins and otherness. When Japan speaks itself through this proper name bestowed from without (*jipangu, jyapan, nippon, nihon*) it also fixes itself as a kind of centre and origin which is inextricably delineated *aphoristically* (as in Marco Polo's description) as that which can only be imagined through the limit or the horizon (see 22 above).

Speaking itself via the proper name bestowed from *within* (through discourses which strive to impart the fullest sense of a national entity) might suggest a dilution of the sense of alterity. However, if we take into account the enunciative modalities (i.e. ask: who speaks and from which institutional sites?[10]) of each instantiation of such a name, we inevitably return to the limit or horizon. That is, the act of establishing a centre is predicated on the possibility of marking out a similarly imaginable periphery.

One of the most striking *textual* examples in the twentieth century of Japan's efforts to speak and name itself from 'within', can be seen in the *Kokutai no hongi* or *Cardinal Principals of the National Entity of Japan*.[11] Although the text commonly employs the contemporary designation *Nihon/Nippon*, it calls forth the various renderings of the more 'divine' and originary namings: *Yamato, Ôyashima no kuni, Toyoashihara no mizuho no kuni*, to name a few.[12] The significance of the least obscure and most commonly used *yamato* (in its capacity as adjectival prefix) is evidenced by the fact that the *Kôjien* lexicon devotes more than a page of entries to examples illustrating its use.[13] Not surprisingly, it is the designation *yamato-kotoba* ('Japanese word/language') which should be of most relevance to this question of the naming of a 'nation' and its forms of cultural artifice, because it is at the very site of language that the problematic evincing of the meaning(s) of the proper noun 'Japan' is most acutely brought into relief.

Sakai has argued that the parameters of the task of thinking and imagining 'Japan' are to a large extent historically prescribed by discourses about the nature of 'the' Japanese language, and that 'the Japanese language and its "culture" were born in the eighteenth century'.[14] The argument that during this period the positivities of 'interior' and 'exterior' emerged and became valorized components of the discourses of 'national learning' (*Kokugaku*), is no more clearly evident than in Aizawa Yasushi's 1825 *New Theses* (*Shinron*) which employs terms such as 'homeland' (*naichi*) to dramatically depict the penetration of a newly imagined Japanese sovereign space.[15] Furthermore, as Wakabayashi has pointed out, although Aizawa was certainly not the only Tokugawa thinker to claim that Japan, rather than China, was the 'middle kingdom' (*Chûgoku*), he was able to achieve the 'ultimate synthesis of Confucian and na- tivist rationales for claiming Japanese superiority' and he was able to make 'the crucially important shift in world view from universal empire (*tenka*) to nation state (*kokka*), a perceptual shift that would take decades longer in China'.[16]

All of this demonstrates just how crucial language and the power of naming is to national self identity, and 'Japan', like other modern nation states, has had to painstakingly construct its identity through designating itself as an entity whose defining features are above all, linguistic and 'cultural' unity. The establishment of one, authoritative name for Japan (*Nihon/Nippon/Japan—and the variants on the latter*) in the Meiji era, put an end to the semiotic slippage entailed in the multiple uses of previous more archaic designations, and was co-extensive with, as Maher puts it, an 'historicizing' of language through the standardization im- peratives of the Meiji state:

> From the philosophical view, standardization may be viewed as a historicizing
> process conferring history upon a linguistic object which in turn confers his-
> torical (sic archaic) legitimacy upon the user and the state.[17]

For those discourses which seek to name and thus identify the nation from 'within' (including the voluminous writings which form the genre of the so- called *Nihonjinron* or 'Theories of the Japanese'[18]), the immutability of what are considered to be linguistic elements of the 'original' Japanese language (*ya- mato-kotoba*) powerfully enables discourses of national identity.[19] What is sig- nificant to note here is that the term *yamato-kotoba* signifies 'Japan' specifically through a process of exclusion. From about the eighth century onwards, how- ever, as Pollack points out, such processes of signifying through exclusion dis- play a tendency to become partial, ambiguous and 'fractured'. In offering an exposition of what he calls 'a uniquely Japanese dialectic' (to which the Japa- nese gave the name *wakan*—'Japanese/Chinese') Pollack demonstrates that 'the notion of Japaneseness was meaningful only as it was considered against the background of the otherness of China' (a view vigorously challenged by Sa- kai).[20]

In the same way that Pollack's approach claims to be no longer using the sig- nifier 'Japan' in an essentializing way, in this discussion 'Japan' will be implic- itly suspended within a semiotic frame of co-extensivity with other discursive entities represented by the signifiers 'China', 'the West' and so on. Pollack out- lines the epistemological and metaphysical 'fracture' wrought by a kind of crisis in representation at the site of writing the national-cultural entity currently called 'Japan'—a writing only available in/through the disjunctive, dialectical processes entailed in the adoption and continual adaptation of the script and lexical plenitude of the Chinese language to the Japanese idiom. In the light of Sakai's critique of Pollack (which stresses that China too required an 'other' (Japan) against which to define itself) and even assuming only the partial verac- ity of Pollack's claim, it could be said that the process of 'fracture' applies just as forcefully to the kinds of writing exemplified by the category of the 'contemporary Japanese novel', as it does to the eighth-century classical Japanese text. Pollack writes:

> The fundamental paradigm that for centuries would govern Japan's adaptation of Chinese (and perhaps Western) culture is to be found in the complex adoption and final acceptance of, and a profound alienation from, outward alien form as necessary for the expression of otherwise ineffable Japanese meaning.[21]

At the risk of essentializing such notions as 'ineffable Japanese meaning' it will be shown in later chapters that it is the very struggle with form (or 'style') in all its facets, and the various modalities through which this struggle is represented, that determines the status of the signifier 'Japan' in Murakami's fiction.

Our initial concern here, however, was in attempting to clarify the vagaries associated with the use of the proper noun 'Japan', and before proceeding further it is necessary to justify removing the term from its state of parenthetical suspension. To this end it should be noted that 'Japan' should neither be privileged nor fetishized as somehow a special case in the discourses of the nation state.[22] In line with an approach articulated by Homi Bhabha, we should aim to 'explore the Janus-faced ambivalence of language itself in the construction of the Janus-faced discourse of the nation', with a view to 'understanding . . . the performativity of language in the narratives of the nation'.[23] It was suggested above that especially since the advent of modernity, the name of a nation signifies in the interstices—the in-between spaces—of antagonistic imperial and colonial discourses. Re-invoking Derrida's reminder that 'when a name comes, it immediately says more than the name' we are ineluctably drawn back, in the narration of the nation, to the triumph of the syntagm and aphorism—to the 'irreducible excess of the syntactic over the semantic'.[24]

Finally, within the discursive limits of the discipline(s) of Japanology, we must concede (using Anderson's terminology) that like any other 'nation' Japan is *imagined*—and imagined in various ways: imagined as 'limited', imagined as 'sovereign' and imagined as 'community'.[25] Ivy invokes several distinct configurations of this imaginary in her attempts to articulate what she calls the 'phantasm' of Japanese modernity.[26] More recent research has highlighted the 'invented traditions' of modern Japan detailed in the writings of nativist ethnology[27] which, along with an array of 'competing modernities',[28] have been variously marshaled in the service of imagining and performing the Japanese nation.

From without, Japan has been construed through the desiring gaze of the projected reader of Lafcadio Hearn's record of his encounter with an imaginary Japan, which, a century later, still resonates (with the incredulous wonderment of the Kantian sublime) as the longed for alterity of the Orient: 'in this Far East, so much read of, so long dreamed of, yet, as the eyes bear witness, heretofore all unknown.' Or imagined as an infinitely self-referential, a more or less closed semiotic constellation, by the critic Roland Barthes:

> If I want to imagine a fictive nation, I can give it an invented name, treat it de-
> claratively as a novelistic object . . . I can also . . . isolate somewhere in the
> world (faraway) a number of features . . . and out of those features deliberately
> form a system. It is this system which I shall call: Japan.[29]

It is worth noting that Barthes is able, from the very beginning of his treatise on
the 'empire of signs', to dispense with the parenthetic framing of the name of
'Japan'—confident in the knowledge that he can never in fact move *beyond* such
a frame. In the same way and for the same reasons, we may proceed in the subsequent discussion to write about Japan and things Japanese in the knowledge
that the connotations of the signifier 'Japan' are, depending on the context of its
use, given their fullest possible range of play—and will inevitably be informed
by Hearn's amorphous and desiring imaginary, and Barthe's evocatively postulated synchronic textual schema.

In briefly touching on some of the implicit epistemological, ideological and
historiographical assumptions embedded in the use of the proper noun 'Japan',
we have set certain semantic parameters for the use(s) of the word throughout
the subsequent discussion. To do so, is to acknowledge that even though the
ultimate subject of our enquiry is a more or less homogeneously imagined entity
or referent, we remain vigilant in our attempts to avoid valorizing the name 'Japan' and thus assigning monolithic or reified 'meanings' to the various contexts
of its use. Such vigilance is crucial to maintaining the word's multivalence (ability to interact), with other putative terms signifying the entities of 'the West',
'the subject', 'the novel', and so on.

Modernity's Misgivings

The aim of this section is to discuss ways in which the concept of Japanese
modernity stands in a simulacral relation to the West. This is by no means a new
or original claim[30] and, as such, does not necessarily attribute to Japanese modernity an inferior status vis-à-vis some version of the 'authentic' modernity of
the West. Rather, it merely recognizes that as the diversity of views amongst
critics has shown, the debate about the nature and extent of Japanese modernity
remains unresolved on several key issues. Firstly, whether Japan can/should
have its 'own' modernity (and indeed 'postmodernity'). Secondly, whether or
not the term itself is relevant to the Japanese (or indeed other non-Western nations') experience. Thirdly, that in its dimensions of postmodernity (from here
on the parentheses are omitted) it actually represents a unique version of modernity, precisely because it has displayed—at least since the politico-cultural consolidation of the Edo period—both 'pre-modern' *and* postmodern characteristics
simultaneously or perhaps interchangeably.[31]

Epistemologically speaking, we see that the problematic nature of a Japanese
modernity which can only be logically stipulated in relation to a concept

developed *outside* the discursive space of Japan, must, *ipso facto*, stand in a secondary or simulacral relation to a more primary or defining concept. As noted earlier, such a view has been argued eloquently in Sakai Naoki's seminal essay 'Modernity and its Critique'. Although this is not the place to stray too far into the labyrinth of the complex debate about Japanese modernity, a brief examination of some important contributions to the topic will assist in laying the foundations for arguments developed in later chapters.

As the Japanese philosopher Maruyama Masao has observed, the course that many Japanese intellectual disputes (*ronso*) take is to temporarily clarify issues, then fizzle out without being resolved—only to re-emerge at a later date where they start again from the very beginning.[32] If this is true, then it is hardly surprising that recent discussions of Japanese modernity seem to be re-runs of earlier debates. Even the theme of the famous Kyoto symposium of 1942 entitled 'Overcoming the Modern' (*Kindai no chôkoku*) was not, according to Karatani Kôjin, merely invented at the conference. Rather, it was representative of an extreme intellectual viewpoint which has been around since the Meiji era.[33] It has also been noted that the theme of 'overcoming the modern' came about by chance[34]—but this has turned out to be quite fortuitous because the 'overcoming the modern' debate of the forties, actually resurfaced in the form of the postmodern faddism of the eighties. The question arises: were they really any different in their ideological foundations? If not, then Maruyama's thesis about the cyclical nature of Japanese intellectual debates is all the more compelling.

First, we must briefly recount the views of some major Japanese theorists (those writing in Japanese and *from* the discursive position of Japan) and then those of some scholars writing in the West. By doing so we will touch on the general terms of the debate rather than search for its resolution. Doing the former will be important to the task of establishing the operation of the simulacrum, because whether it is immediately apparent or not, the philosophical concept of modernity (as distinct from its economic and aesthetic adjuncts, modernization and modernism) and its supplement, postmodernity, form a crucial part of the conditions of exteriority in the overall discursive operation of the simulacrum which finds its expression in the 'Murakami Phenomenon'.

Having taken into account various aspects of the debate, it will be concluded that it is possible for Japan to invoke its own modernity *outside* the universal parameters of the West's modernity, but it has yet to (or perhaps has not yet been allowed to) fully take up this challenge. This would account for the 'recycling' of the terms of the debate every few decades—depending on the economic and political conditions of the day—usually when Japan is forced into an introspection or re-gathering of its 'self-sufficient space' (*jisokutekina kûkan*) by a perceived lack in its own self-definable subjectivity.[35] Although such a tendency is somewhat difficult to prove, its veracity would partly account for the equivocal (if not outright ambiguous) stance of those Japanese artists (including Murakami) cited later in this chapter.

Some Japanese thinkers grappling with the philosophical dimensions of the idea of modernity have perceptively raised the question (however tangentially) of the need to identify a national 'subjectivity' (*shutaisei*) which goes beyond that which might be imagined as the natural adjunct to the formation of a nation-state. Writing in 1961, after Japan had entered its period of high growth and taken its first tentative steps outside the role of vanquished enemy (and importantly, as new American ally in the Cold War) Maruyama Masao acknowledged that a thought tradition which historically places the self at its core (*chûkaku*) has remained unformed in Japan.[36] Similarly, in his detailed discussion of the 'Overcoming the Modern' symposium, Hiromatsu cites Kobayashi's observation during the gathering, that it was not necessarily the case that the scholars in attendance considered modernity an undesirable (*warui*) thing—rather, they sought to realize a new social form, and for this reason saw the necessity for the modern to be 'overcome'. However, in the attempt to move beyond historicity in the 'now of eternity' (*eien no ima*) we (Japanese) come across, according to Kobayashi, something which seems to have no core (*kakushin*).[37]

Here, the lack of a core or centre (read subjectivity) explains a perceived inability to move beyond modernity. However, rather than envisage this as a kind of lack couched largely in *negative* terms, one possible solution can be found in imagining its obverse. That is to say, in the topos or 'place of nothingness' (*mu no bashô*) proposed by Nishida Kitarô, Japanese Being coheres on its own terms as an ostensibly empty subject position only when viewed from the Western stance of identity and presence as the hallmarks of subjectivity. Viewed, however, from the perfectly 'full' emptiness of a Japanese subjectivity based on a Buddhist ontology, the question of subjectivity never actually arises, because it is outside the ontological and epistemological parameters of Japanese experience. This radical dismissal of the stipulation of subjectivity (or at least subjectivity as a form of agency) as a condition of modernity is, to say the least, highly provocative, and will be taken up again in later chapters.

As Victor Koschmann notes, confusion surrounding the complexity of the term *shutaisei* in postwar Japanese culture has arisen from the multiple contexts of its uses. He cites psychologist Miyagi Otoya's identification of at least seven different usages/meanings of the term in postwar discourses—ranging from its invocation as a necessary complement to the overly 'objectivist' emphasis of Marxist materialism, to the ethical sense of the term as the basis for the Kantian moral imperative, extending to the extreme description offered by Nishida as the 'the conception of absolute indeterminacy' or *mu*.[38]

Koschmann's important and detailed study of the concept of *shutaisei* in postwar Japan highlights just how difficult it is to even formulate clear questions about the nexus between Japanese modernity and subjectivity, and some key findings of his analysis are germane to this discussion. Firstly, that

> the *shutaisei* theorists established subjective engagement as opposed to contemplation as the fundamental criterion of productive political discussion in the postwar era.[39]

By foregrounding the question of agency, these theorists came up against the conundrum that goes to the heart of the modernity debate in Japan. That is, according to Koschmann, even if *shutaisei* were seen as an essentialized property of individuals or social entities such as 'the working class'—which could be utilized in the struggle *for* democratic revolution—such a view fails to recognize that 'democratic revolution *is* the very process of subject-formation itself'.[40]

Secondly, Koschmann has noted the connection between Ernesto Laclau's (and, we might add, Kristeva's and Lacan's) description of subjectivity as constituted negatively, and the intuitive hunches that certain postwar theorists felt but were unable to more fully develop. Namely, that subjectivity arose as a practice, or as an event, but was not necessarily an hypostasized entity existing prior to or outside language or discourse in its broadest sense.[41]

In one sense, Laclau's description can be construed as coming very close to Nishida's topos of emptiness or nothingness, which itself may provide a kind of ontological vacuum to be filled in by reactionary or nationalist ideologies. And such a description of *shutaisei* further complicates the problem of being able to adequately respond to conservative proclamations that modernity has been overcome. Koschmann concludes that the concept of the modern subject in the Japanese modernity debate has always been implicitly tied to the idea of the nation-state, and has provided the 'moral' basis for nationalism. In this sense, he claims, the neoconservatism which has emerged in the U.S. and England is no different to that witnessed in Japan, and democratic revolution in these nations has not failed—it simply remains, as in Habermas' famous assertion, an 'incomplete project'.[42]

Despite this apparent ideological convergence, it seems that in Japan discussion about modernity has been played out within specific cultural paradigms which themselves are suggestive of a certain discursive closure and circularity. Karatani Kôjin's *Kotoba to higeki* offers a succinct discussion of some key aspects of the Japanese modernity/postmodernity debate, and it will be useful to recount some of its main claims here.[43] Wanting to demonstrate some differences between the West and Japan on the question of modernity, Karatani suggests, firstly, that in the concept of 'structure' (*kôzô*), the notion of God (*kami*) is hidden—and that even post-structuralism is a method designed to 'drag out' (*hipparidasu*) or uncover a concealed god. (By 'god', here Karatani presumably means a transcendental rather than an immanent deity).[44] However, for the Japanese, from the very beginning of the modern era in the fields of the natural and social sciences, the kind of god necessary to the concept of structure was absent. Because of this it is possible to say that Japanese philosophy since the Meiji period was already postmodern. For example, looking at the philosophy of Nishida and others, it is clear that through the notion of 'overcoming the modern', the modern was indeed 'overcome' (bypassed) very early—but such a process is of course very different to the meaning-content (*iminaiyo*) of the current postmodern.

What Karatani stresses is that in the overcoming (*koeru*) and rejection/denial (*hitei suru*) of the modern, compared to the West, the reaction to modernity took place very early. This can been seen in the example of the Japanese so called 'I-novel' or *shishôsetsu* (the quasi-autobiographical narrative which is arguably paradigmatic of the modern Japanese *shôsetsu*[45]) which, Karatani claims, has overcome the category of the modern novel (*kindai shôsetsu*) in that it lacks coherence (*suji*), plot (*purotto*) and the structure of introduction, development, turn and conclusion (*ki-shin-ten-setsu*). Another difference can be seen in Karatani's claim that in Japan both a transcendent god and a 'different' kind of god can coexist in the one system—with the important qualification that the latter manifests in the form of nature (*shizen*), rather than in a transcendent being (*chôetsusha*), *and* represents a process of becoming (*mono ga naru*)[46] which is presumably juxtaposed to the Western metaphysical privileging of Being.

With regard to the conditions of the present informationalized-consumer society (*jôhôkasareta shôhishakai*) Karatani makes the point that critics such as Baudrillard in the West have made much of the overturning of metaphysical principles in a postmodern context—but that in Japan, such principles have not been broken (*hakai suru mono ni natte orimasen*), presumably because they never really took hold in the first place. To be sure, for Karatani, Japan's way of denying the modern is through a form of deconstruction, but it constitutes merely one current (*chôryû*) in a series (*ichi-ren*) of currents, and without any kind of resistance is able to proceed unhindered. As a result of the infiltration/permeation (*shintô*) of postmodernism, Karatani claims that the discursive space of Japan is ensnared in a 'self-immune, disease like self-referential condition', from which it will eventually have to escape. Subsequently, rather than strive to be postmodern, moving beyond this paradox it will be necessary to live again in a new way and strive, first of all, to become modern.[47]

Karatani, of course, is not the only critic to hold the view that Japan has yet to experience a 'genuine' modernity, but what makes his argument all the more compelling is his ability to define the *historicity* of cultural phenomena which tend to upset Western hegemonic views of modernity's assumed universally applicable trajectories. In an important sense, the Japanese 'assimilation' and/or contestation of Western modernity plays havoc with questions of periodization, style, epistemology and subjectivity taken for granted in Western discourses on the topic.

As a concrete example of this, Karatani analyses the so-called 'Edo Boom' of recent times, and sees in it a strongly *ahistorical* dimension. He calls attention to the Edo boom of the 1930s which witnessed a great popularity for the *jidai-shôsetsu* (period novel), and *jidai-eiga* (period film)—not those of *any* period, but specifically the Edo period. However, such a trend was not the result of a renewed concern with history. Rather, the obverse was the case, and was not unrelated, according to Karatani, to the kind of thought represented by the slogan 'overcoming the modern'. For example, it is suggested that Kuki Shûzô's *Iki no kôzô* (*The Structure of Edo Aesthetic Style*), published in 1930, was an attempt to give a philosophical meaning to the sensitivity and life of post-Edo Japanese culture, yet for Karatani this too was the kind of 'Edo' which sought to displace or overcome the modern West.[48] Ultimately, for Karatani, the current

Edo boom reflects a 'closed historical consciousness' (*rekishiteki na ishiki ga tojizasareru koto*) which might even be called an awareness of the 'end of history'.[49]

Related to this is a tendency toward a feeling of self-sufficiency which, rather than suggesting an anti-foreign nationalism, is indicative of a view that there is nothing more to learn from the West. This phenomenon is in turn seen as a product of the consumer society which has been thoroughly permeated by the sense of history having 'finished' in a cultural context, where people don't produce 'substantial' things—rather, it seems, 'difference' (*sai*) which is equivalent to 'information' (*jôhô*) is the only thing that is produced. In such a social milieu, the Japanese feel that they are more advanced than, and have nothing to learn from the West (and Karatani notes that this was also a feature of the pre-war period). He warns, however, that unless the Japanese examine more closely what he calls the 'Edo thinkers' (including Kobayashi Hideo, Nishida Kintarô and Kuki Shûzô), they will simply step again into the same rut (*wadachi*) of the *Kindai no chôkoku* of the thirties.[50]

Sketching a general description of postmodernism, Karatani acknowledges that it is based on the Western metaphysical stance of deconstruction (*datsukôchiku*) (although he is perhaps a little lax in assuming too much of a direct link between post-structuralism and postmodernism) whereby the subject is eradicated, the centre is decentered or dispersed into many centers, deep layers are brought to the surface, originals become copies and creation is replaced by collage and pastiche. Taking into account, therefore, Karatani's views on Japanese modernity as outlined above, it is not surprising that he sees Japanese postmodernism as quite different to the Western version.[51] After entering Japan and generating a boom, Japanese post-structuralism and postmodernism began to function in the self-sufficient space (*jisokutekina kûkan*) of Japan, as if it did not exist anywhere else.[52]

Karatani's basic position vis-à-vis the modernity/postmodernity debate can be gleaned from his afterword to Hiromatsu's study on 'Overcoming the Modern' referred to above. According to this view, for Japan the theory of postmodernism goes hand in hand with the consciousness that Japan is the most advanced consumer/information society in the world, and is thus already beyond the modern. In other words, within the closed 'self-sufficient' discursive space of Japan, '*kindai no chôkoku*' simply changed its label to 'postmodernism'—and again, by implication, avoided confrontation with modernity. Karatani insists that the idea of '*kindai no chôkoku*' is relevant to contemporary Japan in two important senses: firstly, that Japan is still in the midst of a modernity (*kindai*)—and this must be recognized for what it is; and that secondly, it has not yet moved beyond the pre-war concern with *overcoming* modernity.[53] Not only does Karatani's view affirm the complexity of theorizing Japanese modernity, but it echoes a similar debate in the West (most notably between Habermas and Lyotard) as to whether modernity has given way to the 'postmodern condition'[54] or remains an 'incomplete project'.[55]

Hoping to broaden the epistemological horizons of the debate, Arnason has lamented the lack of *comparative* theorizing of modernity, and has gone so far as to describe the Japanese experience as a 'counter-paradigm of modernity', in that it has remained a 'configuration of economic, political and cultural patterns' sharing very little with those which had developed in the West.[56] He is also critical of what he calls the 'postmodernist attempt to annex Japan', and sees this as symptomatic of Western modernity's ongoing self-reflexivity as manifested in the practice of comparative cultural hermeneutics.[57] The challenge for the West, according to Arnason, is to develop a way of theorising a non-universal modernity accommodating the interplay of 'unifying and pluralising factors within Japanese patterns of culture and power', and with such interplay being indicative of an ongoing 'dialectic of dynamism and containment' which has been operating in Japan since around the *Kinsei* (or 'early modern') period beginning around three centuries prior to the Meiji era.[58]

Arnason is in effect arguing the case for a plurality of possible modernities, whereby particular Japanese forms of traditionalization would interact with more universally founded economic and political processes to produce a modernity capable of defining itself *outside* the hegemonic terms of the West (which, as has been noted above, are so strongly contested by critics such as Sakai).

The approach to the question of Japanese modernity taken by John Clammer in his *Difference and Modernity* resonates with that of Arnason in that it acknowledges that Japanese society 'directly challenges western epistemological hegemonism'. By implication, this concurs with Arnason's claim of the paucity of the comparative theorization of modernity, although Clammer does not necessarily see this as a problem for the Japanese because, as exemplified in the *Nihonjinron* writings, they have excelled at the process of 'cognitive mapping' (here he is quoting Jameson, 1988). Consequently, according to Clammer, the problem posed by Maruyama (1985; and others, including Karatani as discussed above) that Japan cannot be described as postmodern because it has yet to achieve a genuine modernity, should be recast:

> It is not that the periodization of Japanese history into premodern, modern and postmodern needs to be rejected, but rather that the content of each of these labels needs to be seriously re-examined.[59]

Another of Clammer's important insights is to do with the relationship between aestheticization and postmodernism in the Japanese context. The aestheticization of ethics could hardly be seen as something new for Japanese society, since the aesthetic and the good have long been intertwined as expressions of harmony. However, the downside here may be that the over aestheticization of cultural forms represents a kind of culturalism which in turn can mask relationships of power and control—an appeal to cultural particularity as ideology, which effectively silences any voices of critique and opposition.[60] Less convincing is Clammer's suggestion that 'Japan is not a Baudrillardian paradise (or nightmare) in which all is simulation'—and this is because, apparently, the

Japanese do not take the simulation seriously: 'it is known to be simulation, to be played with and then discarded.'[61] At this point Clammer is stretching the argument, failing to give due regard to the implications of Baudrillard's thesis that the operation of the simulacrum in the post-industrial hyper-real context has very much altered our fundamental relationship to the referent, the real—and by implication, our ways of relating to one another.

This notwithstanding, the strength of Clammer's approach can be seen in his acknowledgement that there are indeed 'some very different ways of organizing the cultural ecology of advanced capitalist societies'.[62] This fact alone lends credence to his view that perhaps Maruyama is closest to the mark on the vexed question of Japanese modernity:

> It may well be that the Japanese 'postmodern' is surprisingly close to the image of modernity envisaged by Maruyama: the unique incorporation of 'traditional' values (constantly revised and redefined) into their other—the western epistemological model, with the resulting transcending of both into a new synthesis that constitutes contemporary Japanese culture.[63]

Such a characterization of Japanese modernity is not dissimilar to Arnason's notion of a 'dialectic of dynamism and containment' referred to above. Furthermore, Clammer is not alone in seeing the value of Maruyama's approach. Koschmann's insightful reading of Maruyama's writing on the Meiji period publicist, Fukuzawa Yukichi, suggests that Maruyama was able to find justification for his urging of the unfinished venture of a Japanese modernity, in the form of Fukuzawa's 'relativism'.[64] The latter notion (which Maruyama was apparently able to glean from reading between the lines of Fukuzawa's writing), far from reflecting the complete relativization of values characteristic of the postmodern ethos, suggests the possibility of 'splitting the difference' between extreme positions on modernity and postmodernity in a way which is not dissimilar to the social pragmatist stance adopted by Richard Rorty.[65]

Koschmann also focuses on Maruyama's insight that one defining feature of the modern is its ability to evoke systems of *mediation* which function between the extremes of the ludic (playful) and the 'serious'. By doing so, Koschmann's reading of Maruyama goes right to the heart of the question of the role of the simulacral processes necessary to modernity. This is so in the sense that 'mediated' reality, which gives expression to inaccessible 'originals', is very different to pre-modern or anti-modern (and arguably postmodern) constructions of the real, which privilege a *direct* access to truth, and thus tend towards fetishism and absolutism.

In other words (and here Koshmann quotes Maruyama's 1949 essay 'From Carnal Literature to Carnal Politics'), when institutions (which are really only 'fictions' established for the convenience of human activity) become hypostatized, 'there is no mediation going on between ends and means, and so means quickly turn into ends themselves'. According to Koschmann, Fukuzawa would characterize such a process as fetishism (*wakudeki*).[66] In his view, then, Maruyama, like his mentor Fukuzawa, can be characterized as a thoroughgoing per-spectivist and pluralist, whose thought remains crucial to the Habermasian 'in-complete project of modernity'—which although assuming different institu-tional forms, is just as relevant to the Japanese context as it is to that of modernity's still problematic status in the West.

While accepting the veracity of Maruyama's *theorization* of an ideal form of Japanese modernity, it is indeed difficult to ascertain to what extent modernity is a socially verifiable process which works to undermine the fetishism or at least what might be called 'hyper-reification' common to many contemporary Japa-nese cultural practices. For example, it is in the 'phantasmal' moments of cul-tural recuperation that, as Ivy as shown, modernity is defined negatively, in terms of its *losses*. Whether it be in the form of the practices of summoning the voices of the dead (*kuchiyose* performed on the remote Mount Osore), popular local theatre (*taishûengeki* in urban areas) or massive advertising campaigns promoting the '(re)discovery of a once familiar 'Japan'—as well as an unfamil-iar, 'exotic' Japan (as a treasure-house/museum of Asian culture)—there is no denying, according to Ivy, that

> the very search to find authentic survivals of premodern, pre-Western Japanese authenticity is inescapably a modern endeavor, essentially enfolded within the historical condition that it would seek to escape.[67]

Ivy's view resonates powerfully with the conclusion reached by Harootunian in his comprehensive treatment of the topic in a monograph entitled *Overcome by Modernity*. Not only does this wide-ranging discussion establish a series of cultural and epistemological contexts for a detailed consideration of themes re-volving around the fantasizing of modern life and the development of a self-ensnaring historical consciousness, it elaborately and convincingly demonstrates that the fundamental contradiction implicit in the notion of 'overcoming mod-ernity' achieves its most perfect expression in a very inversion of the terms. Summing up the achievements of the *kindai no chôkoku* symposium, Harootu-nian concludes that

> It had narrativized precisely the eventfulness it wished to overcome and man-aged to reaffirm the historicity it proposed to eliminate. The only destination reached by the symposium on overcoming modernity was the place where Ja-pan itself had been overcome by modernity.[68]

In a similar way, it will be shown that the simulacral stipulation of an uncer-tain 'national' subjectivity at the heart of Murakami's narrative endeavours re-flects the kind of double bind condition of Japanese modernity—afflicted by a historicity which can be dispensed with neither by being denied or 'overcome'. The peculiarity of this dilemma finds powerful expression in a supplementary aspect of the signifier 'modernity' known as 'the contemporary' which, as will now be argued, reflects a tendency toward the fetishization of novelty and new-ness in the consumption of commodified culture in present day Japan.

The Conundrum of the Contemporary

It is important to realize that any periodization, insofar as it assigns a beginning and an end (telos), cannot escape a certain teleological arrangement.

Karatani Kôjin, "The Discursive Space of Modern Japan" [69]

The discussion now turns to a brief consideration of the significations brought into play in the use of the term 'contemporary'. What will *not* be attempted here is a comprehensive treatment of problems relating to periodization and genre. However, since the analysis is predicated on the use of the Murakami narrative as one exemplar of recent Japanese fiction, a further clarification of terms is called for.

The adjective 'contemporary' (*gendai* or *gendai no/teki*) used as a descriptor to further differentiate a sub-category within the larger category of modern Japanese literature, is immediately evocative of certain historical, thematic and stylistic limits—yet is by no means entirely unambiguous. This is probably due to the particular ways in which the term resonates in Japanese with the word 'modern' (*kindai* or *kindai no/teki*) as well as the fact that *gendai* may also be used in a negative way, to distinguish itself from that which more properly be-longs to *kindai*.[70] It should be noted here that invoking 'the modern', in turn, inevitably calls into play the kindred terms of 'modern times' (*kinsei*), 'premod-ern' (*zenkindai*), 'postmodern' (*posutomodan),* 'super-modern' (*chôkindai*) and 'anti-modern' (*hankindai*), all of which refer circuitously back to the central paradigm of 'the modern'.[71]

Since this discussion aims to demonstrate Murakami's narrative writings as particular modalities *of* 'the modern' in its aspect as simulacrum (thereby touch-ing on the question of Japanese modernity in general), it will become clear that the notion of 'the contemporary' (*gendai*) operates as a kind of *supplement*—both as an addition to, and sometimes substitute for, 'the modern' (*kindai*). Like all supplements it is both superfluous and necessary, and herein lies its essen-tially ambiguous nature. It is a term which can accommodate an extremely wide range of uses and contexts. How else could it be, for example, that such dispa-rate texts as Sôseki's *Kokoro* (*The Heart*, 1914) and Yamada Eimi's *Hizamazuite ashi o oname* (*Kneel Down and Lick my Feet*, 1988), could both be designated as works of 'contemporary literature' (*gendai bungaku*)?[72]

What needs to be stressed here is the proliferation of names which designate periods or eras (in themselves almost 'mini-epochs') and function implicitly as markers of particular styles, idioms and ideologies. These names either revolve around the central category of 'the modern' (*kindai*) and its variants—as does the term 'contemporary' (*gendai*)—or signify via the name of an era of rule of the Imperial House (that is, *Meiji, Taishô, Shôwa* or *Heisei*). As Karatani reminds us, however, 'divisions according to era names ... make one forget relations to the exterior and construct a single, autonomous discursive space'.[73] The fact that all nations engage in constructing epochs when writing their national histories does not, for Karatani, make up for the fact that all periodization is essentially arbitrary, and part of an illusory and communally imagined discursive space. Karatani's crucial insight here is that in fact a 'plurality of worlds (eras) exists simultaneously, maintaining relations with one another.'[74]

We could say that the designators *kindai* and *gendai* operate in an acute relation of co-extensivity—if not supplementarity—and cohere not only in terms of they way they denote 'historical period' or 'style', but in terms of their ability to resonate with a construction of time and subjectivity which is firmly grounded in (to use Foucault's terminology) the episteme of modernity. It is also the case that because era-names organize a vast and discontinuous array of discourses into imaginary unities, they operate, increasingly, as signs of signs, thus facilitating the simulacral and symbolic ordering of values and meanings within the highly 'commodified' systems of commercial publishing. It is probably only the signifier of the name of the author which has more signifying power than the era name attached to his/her oeuvre. This being the case, it is fair to claim that era-name signifiers play a vital role in the reception aesthetics of reading, since they encode, in a primary sense, the reader's projected reading strategy and 'forward reading dimension', and set certain parameters for the activation of the overall work-ideology of the text.

Increasingly, in current Japanese critical writing, eras are further sub-divided and delineated as particular decades, such as 'the sixties', 'eighties', 'nineties' (*rokujûnendai, hachijûnendai* and so on) all of which carry specific 'events' (*jiken*), 'crises' (*kiki*) or 'trends' (*keikô*) as their hallmarks. If the titles of some topical bestsellers (*wadaihon*) in Japan's bookshops in the mid to later nineties were any indication, the sense of crisis at the century's end (*seikimatsu*) or impending Armageddon (*Harumagedon*) had been setting the tone for the closing chapter of the second millennium on the Christian calendar.[75] (These characteristics of journalistic/critical writing are of course not unique to Japan, but arguably assume greater centrality within the urgencies of Japanese modernity's attempts at self-critique).

Furthermore, as will be seen in the titles of critical works to be cited later, Murakami's novels are often overtly characterized as keys to understanding what are imagined as the essential concerns of a particular decade, and might revolve around such metaphors as 'nostalgia' (*natsukashisa*), 'protest' (*kôgi*), 'nothingness' (*kyomu*), 'autism' (*jiheishô*), 'neurosis' (*noirôze*), 'suicide' (*jisatsu*), 'romantic love' (*ren'ai*), 'apocalypse' (*sekai no owari*), 'historical memory' (*rekishitekina kioku*) and so on.[76]

Even if a specific year or text cannot be identified as marking the beginning of the 'contemporary' (*gendai*) era in Japanese literature, it seems clear that

Murakami Haruki has sometimes been popularly perceived as being the most *recent* of those contemporary writers whose works attain the status of 'serious' or 'high' literature (*junbungaku*).[77] Oya et.al's survey of literary styles since the Meiji period, positions Murakami as the final entry in the section entitled 'Contemporary Style', which begins with Mishima Yukio, followed by Yoshi-yuki Junnosuke, Ôe Kenzaburô, Abe Kôbô and Nakagami Kenji. The section ends with a brief reference to the style of some contemporary women writers (in the manner of separating out 'women's literature' or *joryû bungaku*).[78] In this context, if Mishima's writing is considered exemplary of the early 'contempo-rary', then the beginning of the contemporary would have to be situated squarely in the middle of the Second World War.

This is inconsistent, however, with the claim made in *Dabuinchi* that Mura-kami is 'the standard of the world of contemporary Japanese literature'—if that world is said to incorporate writers as far back as Sôseki and Akutagawa (of the *Meiji* and *Taishô* eras respectively), which are included in the survey of the most popular writers among present day readers (*Heisei Nipponjin*) in Japan. From this example alone, we see ample evidence of the ambiguity of the term 'con-temporary' (*gendai*) in the context of Japanese literature. If applied very broadly, the category of the contemporary may be used to include all writing from the Meiji period onwards. If, however, it is thought of in terms of language 'style' (*buntai*), then it may only apply from about, or just after, the Second World War. As was noted above, the *Kôjien* lexicon confirms this semantic lati-tude in the application of the term *gendai*, and we can only surmise, therefore, that it is necessary to be aware of the specific *enunciative modalities* of its use: who speaks the term and when, and from which institutional sites (aca-demic/publishing/marketing etc.)?

Despite this ambiguity, we see in the supplementary relation of *gendai* ('the contemporary') to *kindai* ('the modern') also the possibility of a metonymic relation, in which the sense of immediacy arising from the signifier *gen* (現, the first character in the compound which carries connotations of 'present', 'exist-ing', 'actual'),[79] readily lends itself to a process of valorization, wherein *gendai* stands for all that is desirable, knowable, obtainable within the modern—but only within the context of the self-perpetuating promise of redundancy, and the incessant discarding of the old to make way for the new.

This is not the place to argue an aesthetics of commodification with regard to the specific uses of the term *gendai*. Suffice it to say, however, that within cer-tain contexts of its uses, the term resembles or enlists the semiotic processes of a myth. Indeed, it is plausible that *gendai* may often be found to operate within the discursive economy of what Suga has identified as the 'myth of contemporari-ness' (*gendaisei toiu shinwa*).[80] In the case of Murakami's writing, this is appar-ently realized in the peculiar double structure of 'boredom' (*taikutsusa*) and 'novelty' (*zanshinsa*).[81] Suga claims that although the contemporary age is de-fined by boredom (or what we may call *ennui*, with its connotation of mental weariness), such boredom can be recuperated stylistically through novelty in writing, thus invoking a sense of 'contemporariness' (*gendaisei*). While conceding that the 'message' (*messeji*) of Murakami's works is of course not limited to conveying (and simultaneously subverting, through the idiosyncrasies of his style) a languid world-weariness, Suga is convinced that the success of Murakami's novels lies in their peculiar ability to operate within the limits of the 'myth of the contemporary'. Despite (or perhaps because of) this, Suga plays with the idea that Murakami may not in fact be very 'contemporary' at all![82]

This assertion of the mythic nature of the contemporary—especially within the binary form of the *taikutsusa/zanshinsa* ('boredom'/'novelty') opposition suggested by Suga—is worth considering in the context of Barthes' well known exposition, which posits myth as a 'second-order semiological system':

> Myth is a peculiar system, in that it is constructed from a semiological chain which existed before it: it is a second-order semiological system. That which is a sign (namely the associative total of a concept and an image) in the first system, becomes a mere signifier in the second.'[83]

Schematically, Suga's 'myth of the contemporary' can be transposed onto the classic signifier/signified/sign triad, keeping in mind that the sign itself is always also a signifier bearing the possibility of new sets of signifieds which may further coalesce into new signs, and so on:

I Signifier	II Signified
new linguistic form(s)	'convention' versus 'novelty'
'style' (*buntai*)	(*taikutsusa* versus *zanshinsa*)

III SIGN
'contemporariness'
(*gendaisei*)

Therefore, theoretically, the 'contemporary' literary text would perpetually enlist the sign of 'contemporariness' at the level of continually changing signifiers (the 'new' or different linguistic forms themselves). In the context of such a scheme, the 'contemporary Japanese novel' would fall into place alongside other genres adumbrated by the general category of signs of 'the contemporary'. It would form part of the semiotic configuration of highly differentiated cultural practices (including, of course, the active 'production' of literary texts by writers and readers alike) which both display and generate the sensibility of the new, the authentically avant-garde.

The sense of the contemporary, therefore, as inevitably having something to do with a certain 'style', provides one important key in unraveling the conundrum of the category in the context of Japanese literary modernity. This is nowhere more strikingly so than in the case of Murakami's writing. Kuroko has noted that even in the face of the radicality of cult novels such as the 'sex and drug culture' evoked by Murakami Ryû in works such as *Kagirinaku tômei ni chikai burû (Almost Transparent Blue)* and the catalogue-like narrative idiom of Tanaka Yasuo's *Nantonaku kuristuru (Somehow Crystal)*, it was widely sensed that with the appearance of Murakami Haruki 'something different' (*chigau ishitsu na mono*) had arrived. For Kuroko, the 'nihilism' of Murakami's *Sekai no owari to hâdoboirudo wandarando (Hard-Boiled Wonderland and the End of the World)* bears no relation to the inane celebration of the cycle of desire/consumption/satiation of the age (the seventies and eighties).[84] Is this the 'sense of novelty' alluded to by Suga, as the pivotal signified in the discourses sustaining the myth of 'contemporariness'? If it is, then it must also be the case that such a sense arises from the variations in the *linguistic* cast of much recent writing, but is also very much a function of experimentation in the *narrative* formats of such texts.

Shibata has drawn attention to the preponderance in 'contemporary' (especially *junbungaku* or 'high') literature of fable (*gûwa*) and caricature (*giga*) in the writings of Ôe Kenzaburô, Takahashi Genichirô, Shimada Masahiko—and of course, Murakami Haruki.[85] Whether it is the protest/nihilism/consumption of the seventies and eighties, or, as Yokô has put it, the 'reconstruction' (*saikôchiku*) of the nineties,[86] the metaphors and images of 'the contemporary' resonate with the hallmarks of a crude negative/positive opposition scattered throughout Murakami criticism (*Murakami Haruki ron*)—and are often centered on the character *kyo* (虚) connoting that which is 'empty', 'vain', 'futile', 'hollow' and so on, and occurring in compounds such as *kyomu* (虚無) 'nothingness', *kyokô* (虚講) 'fabricated', and *kûkyo* (空虚) 'hollowness'.

Focusing on a broader kind of *zeitgeist* approach, Matsuzawa, in grappling with the limits of the contemporary, posits an alignment (what he calls a simultaneous awakening—*kyôkisei*) between contemporary thought (*gendaishisô*) and contemporary literature. The label *gendaishisô* is so vague as to be almost meaningless, but Matsuzawa specifically refers to the wave of 'new age' religiosity (with its central metaphors of happiness, relief and redemption, and which are embodied within the eschatologies of the countless 'new religions', *shinshûkyô*, which have emerged in Japan), and as one example, the Indian mystic Rajneesh's critique of the entrenched dominant discourses of 'culture', 'society', 'education' and 'morality'. Invoking a tripartite matrix of chaos (*kaosu*), cosmos (*kosumosu*) and nomos (*nomosu*), he interestingly suggests that in Murakami's writing, the tale or narrative (*monogatari*) emulates the contours of such a matrix, in that it is synthesized from a pre-narrative disorder and eventually folds back into a kind of dismantled chaos (*kaitaisareta kaosu*) which is nevertheless a 'different' chaos—altered by the narrative's trajectory. The metaphor here is for contemporary narrative (and narrative is always made 'contemporary' through the immediacy of each and every act of its performance) as alchemical, cyclical, syncretic. Matsuzawa's version is a very *contemporary* contemporary, and not surprisingly, Murakami Haruki, Yoshimoto Banana and Takahashi Genichirô are characterized as 'three signals shaking the sensibility of the times.[87]

For Takeda, trying to locate Murakami's writing within 'the contemporary' has occurred within the context of a broader attempt to define various forms of romanticism, and he challenges Karatani's critique of Murakami's oeuvre as exemplary of merely a contemporary, decadent form of literary romanticism (*romansushugi no gendaiteki na taihaikeitai*).[88] Still other critics have wanted to evaluate Murakami's longest narrative *Nejimakidori kuronikuru* (*The Wind-Up Bird Chronicle*) as a narrative form of contemporary historiography (*gendaishi toshite no monogatari*) with its reference to the infamous *Nomonhan jihen* during the Japanese occupation of China and 'Manchuria', and the recounting of a surviving soldier's experiences of quasi-divine premonition within what was for the Japanese of that epoch, the almost mythic space denoted by that geographical region.[89] In fact, more than any other, this narrative work raises complex questions in regard to the recuperation of 'the historical', as an attempt to recast 'the contemporary' as that which enables revisionism, and allows the use of ideological grounds for justifying the re-emergence of certain repressed renderings of recent Japanese history.

At the same time, philosophically speaking, 'the contemporary' also carries the sense of that which is too immediate to be thought—encroaching uncomfortably, violating our attempts to establish a distance from that which can be readily historically 'framed' within the text of 'the modern'. Politically, the notion of 'the contemporary' helps engender discourses of urgency around specific economic 'events' or imperatives ('oil-shock', *endaka*, etc.)—but cannot properly be called upon in the legitimizing or imagining of the national entity (*kokutai*); the latter discourse belonging more properly to the domain of modernity writ large.

If it makes sense at all to consider the idea of 'the contemporary' within the context of the debate about Japanese modernity then surely, as Harootunian has shown, Prime minister Ôhira's 1980 heralding of a new 'age of culture' (*bunka no jidai*) represents yet another version of the attempt to 'overcome modernity'. The crucial feature of this attempt though, was that unlike the former critique of modernity, which at its most radical represented a direct affront to instrumental reason, this new approach sought to install a powerful state sponsored 'managerial' ethic cloaked by newly recuperated aspects of Japanese 'culture' which emphasized the 'relationalism' (*aidagarashugi*), or human-to-human nexus as the defining feature of Japanese society.[90] Also vital to the new age of culture was Ôhira's urging of a more clearly defined opposition between the 'Western thing' and 'Japanese thing'[91]. Of course, such thinking takes its most potent form in the phrase 'we Japanese', whose utterance, as Harootunian notes, is now the indispensable condition for all discourse between Japan and the outside world.[92]

What makes Harootunian's analysis most relevant to our discussion of the notion of the contemporary is his linking of the new 'age of culture' and the 'information society' (*jôhôshakai*) under the rubric of the imperative for 'perpetual novelty'. In this dimension there can be little doubt about the suitability of the label 'postmodern' in describing the consumption of 'knowledge' in contemporary Japan:

> This proliferation of information, deemed necessary for carrying on daily life in contemporary Japan, marks the indeterminacy of knowledge and places a high valuation on perpetual novelty, the newest of the new, the latest and most recent bit of knowledge: this is the sign that is mobilized everywhere these days, in order to stave off the threat of the historical.[93]

In other words, for Harootunian, the consumption of knowledge is actually a function of Baudrillard's 'system of objects' which operates in place (or, it might be said, as a simulacrum) of the social. This vindicates the view outlined above, that novelty (*zanshinsa*) and contemporariness (*gendaisei*) are semiotically configured within the structure of a myth which operates to ensure a ceaseless quest for 'new' information, as a means of maintaining the indistinguishability between practices of consumption and the domains of the political and the social. The celebration of information as knowledge and power was confirmed, six years after Ôhira's proclamation, by Prime Minister Nakasone's 1986 speech on 'intellectual standards' (*chiteki suijin*), described by Ivy as a 'delirious sweep through historical time and cultural space' and which characterized contemporary Japan as 'high-level information society':

> [T]here is no other country which puts such diverse information so accurately into the ears of its people.[94]

If, for Ôhira, the year 1980 was to mark the advent of the new age of culture, then the decades preceding it had been witness to the 'conquest of the modern'[95] during the 'age of the economy'.[96] This is confirmed by the critic Yoshimoto's observation which detects somewhere between 1960 and 1980, a major turnabout/conversion (*daitenkan*) in Japanese society. Interestingly, as a cultural phenomenon, it was expressed in terms of popular culture in the appearance of more complete, enriched and 'fresh' forms (*jūjitsushita shinsen na sugata*) in the areas of literature, film, television, animation and music. What especially symbolized this 'freshness' was the CM (commercial) as a means of advertising commodities, and this 'lightened up' field was expressed by authors who insisted on individuality. Such authors went beyond the CM draft and approached the artistic sensibility of contemporary poetry, song and *Haiku*.

Also, Yoshimoto notes, during this period the term 'shinjinrui' or 'new man' appeared in many areas of popular culture, and before long, gradually began to infiltrate the 'pure' or high arts (*junbungei*). This new way of expression was evident in the mixing of the sensibilities of language (*kotoba*), scene (*fūkei*) and image (*eizô*), which was parallel to the 'extinction' (*danzetsu*) of traditional means of expression. The new mode of expression was 'light, bright and freeflowing', and 'dispersed softly over the surface of social phenomena'. In terms of its relevance to this discussion, it is significant that Yoshimoto claims that this development was seen as a kind of debate/discussion (*rongi*) about

'separating out the old and the new' (*shinkyû o nibun suru*). This affirms both
the primacy of 'the contemporary' in the validation and dissemination of information and the quest for novelty, as well as its role in constructing a discur-
sive/cultural space which fetishizes the historical 'now', by paradoxically denying the very historicity of its construction.[97]

Both the idea of 'the contemporary' in the Japanese context, and 'postmodernity' more universally, share the same tenuous and vexed relations with the
modern: supplementary, perhaps superfluous, yet clearly a necessary part of the
critical lexicon of writing preoccupied with modernity's ongoing exegesis. As
signs of signs, era names themselves circulate within the simulacral, second-
order mythic dimension of discourses which organize and ascribe aesthetic value
to specific literary texts.

Having fleshed-out the connotative latitude of the term 'the contemporary'
from several perspectives (as 'period', 'style', 'myth' and *Zeitgeist*), it is clear
that its ambiguity belies attempts to strictly categorize twentieth century Japanese literary works according to the parameters of period or era name divisions.
In exploring some meaning(s) of the term 'the contemporary' in order to better
understand the idea of the 'contemporary Japanese novel', we have noted
Karatani's claim that periodization inevitably implies teleology and imagined
unities in the ways in which cultures produce meanings about themselves. Furthermore, it seems that 'the contemporary' is merely supplementary to the modern, perhaps in the way that in one of its aspects, the postmodern is. However,
lest the phenomenon of the contemporary be seen in too narrow a context, it will
be necessary to touch on the issue of the globalization of culture in the next section.

Global Imperatives

> I have a worldwide style; I want to be free, not to have a narrow style. . . . All
> the world is my studio; all motifs on Earth can be the motifs I use in my crea-
> tion.
>
> Ishioka Eiko, designer[98]

> I don't understand why westerners classify artists working in Japan as a group.
> There isn't a common thread of 'Japaneseness' that links together artists work-
> ing here. Each artist expresses him or herself as an individual, not as a member
> of some sort of nation state.
>
> Miyajima Tetsuo,
> installation artist[99]

No matter how much of an independent individual I am, and even though I
think I live a life unrelated to Japanese literature, day after day I have to
squarely face up to the objective reality that I am a Japanese writer who writes
novels in Japanese.

> Murakami Haruki,
> *Wakai dokusha no tame*
> *no tanpenshôsetsu no*
> *annai*[100]

Not long after Ôe Kenzaburô had been awarded the Nobel Prize for Literature,
an article appearing in the Japanese journal, *Gengo*, lamented Ôe's use of English in delivering his acceptance speech.[101] However, in a curious twist, it was
claimed that by having chosen English, Ôe was ironically duping his de facto
partners in so called 'English language preferentialism' (*eigoyûsenshugi*) since,
according to another commentator (who uses the more strongly worded 'English
hegemony'), English was the preferred language of the speech precisely because
the Nobel Committee wanted to promote the translation of Ôe's writing into as
many *other* languages as possible.[102]

If such criticism is a reaction to the homogenizing of disparate cultural identities through language hegemony, then the real irony here stems from a much
larger question with which Ôe has concerned himself. Namely, the extent to
which Japanese literature is subject to processes of 'universalization' —
especially at the hands of writers like Murakami Haruki and Yoshimoto Banana.
In Ôe's scheme, which attempts to characterize modern Japanese literature
within the world in terms of three distinct 'lines', the two contemporary writers
are characterized thus:

> What's the third line? It is what I call the Murakami Haruki/Yoshimoto Banana
> line. There are only two in this line, but they're selling two hundred times
> more than the second line! I think that these are truly typical writers in an ep-
> och where the subcultures of the whole world have become one.[103]

The contradiction lies in the fact that elsewhere, Ôe praises Murakami for having achieved the status of being the only contemporary Japanese writer to be
widely read overseas.[104] As was detailed in the previous chapter, it is significant
that as well as being widely read in English translation, Murakami's works are
also translated and read in Italy, Germany, Poland, Russia, Korea and China.[105]
In the same vein, (in an otherwise superficial appraisal of Murakami's international status), Matsuoka points to the obvious parallels between Murakami and
the American writer Raymond Carver, noting that 'the similarities in style and
tone suggest that we may consider them contemporary fictions rather than classifying them by countries.'[106]

Ôe would no doubt concur with this comment, without undermining his fundamentally 'ambiguous' position regarding the role of the Japanese writer 'in
the world'. There is nothing new about the notion that literature can represent a

kind of distillation of national identities—or, for that matter, reflect differences in regional identities (for example, 'African literature', 'South Asian literature', 'Pacific Rim' literature and so on). In the 'globalized' contemporary milieu, it is not surprising that literary production/consumption straddles hemispheres and continents in the form of transactable and transnational cultural artifacts.

Within the Japanese context, questions about the 'universalizing' (or at the other end of the scale, 'essentializing') tendencies of modern Japanese literature, go right to the heart of the complexities of the debate around the nature of Japanese modernity. Also, as was shown earlier in this chapter, this debate in terms of literary history is further confused by the vagueness of the terms 'contemporary' (*gendai*) and 'modern' (*kindai*). Simply put, determining whether a literary work is 'universalizing' or 'essentializing' requires a continuum capable of gauging 'cultural authenticity', with an imperial form of cultural/linguistic hegemony at the one end, and a highly introverted nationalism at the other. Since both of these extremes can co-exist and mutually reinforce the other ideologically (as confirmed, for example, by Ôe's equivocal and ambiguous stance), the usefulness of such an opposition is, to say the least, quite doubtful.

The ironies of Ôe's positions may in fact offer a way out of the dilemma alluded to above. Specifically, the question arises: is there a way of avoiding the snare of the universalist/essentialist dichotomy by accepting the tentative status of Japanese literature within a global context, as a spur to engendering more eclectic approaches to the topic? For Ôe, the answer would appear to be in the affirmative. In somewhat contradictory fashion, he is able to applaud Murakami's international reputation and simultaneously deride his works as vacuous. Also, to aspire to be read widely overseas, while retaining his commitment to a Japanese readership. Consider the three following separate statements by Ôe:

> When I write my books, I write them for Japanese readers. It might be that I am a more Japanese author than Mishima. Naturally, I believe that a real novelist is international.[107]

Ishiguro Kazuo responds to such comments by offering a way out of Ôe's perceived dilemma: 'someone can be addressing a small group of people, but if that work is powerful and sincere, it has a universal audience.' In contrast to this, in an obvious reference to writers such as Murakami and Yoshimoto, Ishiguro continues: 'I know that there are many writers who are consciously trying to write the novel that is all ready for translation. And of course, nobody particularly wants to read these things.'[108]

Clearly, however, many people *do* want to read them—possibly for reasons that Ishiguro is unaware of, or chooses to overlook, in deference to his notion of what constitutes good writing. Whatever the case, Ôe's and Ishiguro's views confirm that literature is subject to the shifting currents of global taste and marketing in the circulation of artistic discourses. Furthermore, the comments of Ishioka (designer) and Miyajima (installation artist) cited above, hardly veil their annoyance at the possibility of being branded 'Japanese' rather than 'international' in the outlook and practice of their art, while Murakami's revelation that he continually has to *remind* himself that he is both Japanese *and* writing in the Japanese language, suggests an outright rejection of national-cultural particularity—the latter perceived as parochial and limited. Western critics confirm the advent of the global in the production and dissemination of Japanese 'culture'; Whittier Treat acknowledges that 'it is now impossible to write or even conceive of 'Japanese' popular culture without involving much of the rest of the world',[109] while Goossen situates the modern Japanese short story in an 'uncertain and 'unbounded world—the upside being that at least it can now be read 'free of the weight of Oriental mystique.'[110]

Amidst the shifting sands of the uncertain and unbounded 'global', is discernible a new array of terminology which although often uncritically adopted, masks (to reiterate Bhabha's highly evocative metaphor) the Janus-like operation of the national-cultural entity. The latter must now present as a reified, unified and irreducible discursive space to its citizens, in the face of a 'borderless', 'globalized' 'playing field', over which capital, culture and knowledge restlessly roam in search of new markets and trends—all of which is made eminently possible and even desirable via instantaneous telecommunications and the Internet. The ascendancy of IMF econo-speak is evident, as those with audible voices in the public domain (including critics of 'culture') scramble to update their lexical proficiency. This, however, tends to obscure the semantic slippage involved in the reworking of language to achieve undeclared epistemological and ideological ends—one of which may be, for example, to reaffirm the inevitable global supremacy of capitalist liberal democracy as suggested in Fukuyama's 'The End of History' thesis. It could be argued that 'the world' is to modernity as 'the global' is to postmodernity, and that by extension, any talk of global styles, trends and forces must account for the unresolvable yet persistent modernity/postmodernity debate.[111]

Furthermore, by briefly sketching the terms of this debate as it relates to Japan, we have garnered support for the thesis that Murakami's narrative paradigm points to the operation of a simulacral rendering of contemporary Japan's self-elaboration: a particularity and subjectivity perhaps longed for, but not yet fully bestowed or bestowable in its relation to the universal of the West. This discussion seeks, therefore, to contest the idea of an unbridled globalization of cultural production, and instead, argues for the semantics of cultural particularity in Murakami's narrative trajectories.

The Idea of the Japanese Novel

The *shôsetsu* is the expression not of order and suppression, as the novel is, but of space, decentralization and dispersal.

Miyoshi Masao,
'Against the Native Grain:
The Japanese Novel and the Postmodern West'[112]

Modern Japanese literature has been and continues to be assessed largely
through European realist textual conventions by Westerners and Japanese alike.

James Fujii,
Complicit Fictions[113]

On the face of it, locating the Japanese equivalent of the genre of the European
novel should be straightforward. Roughly defined, it might be described as a
longer prose fictional form elaborating action, narrative agents ('characters') and
world, through and against a prescribed format of represented time and space,
marked by a not always explicit (but more or less complex) relation between the
projected interiority of the narrative agents' and the narrator(s)' voice(s). Similarly, we would expect that the appearance of the Japanese novel should more or
less equate with other non-European examples, emerging parallel to the rise of
the nation-state, and thus partially as an effect of the competing colonial enterprises of the nineteenth century.

However, for a number of reasons (partly to do with the novel's antecedents in
the Japanese literary tradition, and partly because of the particular trajectories of
Japanese modernity), the case can be made for treating the genre of the Japanese
novel as a kind of hybrid literary form (only 'hybrid' of course, vis-à-vis an idealized European form); a recent invention, but not entirely new, and one born of
the political and epistemological struggles at the centre of Japan's responses to
the universalizing forces of European modernity.

In unequivocal manner, Miyoshi Masao has argued for the maintenance of a
clear distinction between the European novel form and its supposed Japanese
homologue, the native Japanese *shôsetsu*.[114] While the grounds for establishing
too rigid a distinction are, in part, contestable, it must be conceded that the par-
ticularities of the *shôsetsu* form cannot be simply eclipsed by a universalist (i.e.
Western) poetics of the novel. As Janet Walker demonstrates, each indigenous
form of narrative (including the Japanese) has responded idiosyncratically to the
lure of the Western novel and its subtle enticements—its assumed status as the
most highly developed, most universal literary form.[115]

Even a cursory treatment of the subject reveals an array of claims with regard
to the emergence, status and structure of the modern Japanese prose fictional
form. To be sure, as the *Kôjien*'s explication of the term *shôsetsu* reminds us,
several features of the Western novel form are recognizable in the native Japanese version, including (i) the *shôsetsu*'s distinction from (and in a sense,
'overcoming' of) the verse form; (ii) its self conscious genesis within certain
socio-historical matrices, and (iii) the relatively free hand given to the narrator—
which can perhaps be taken to mean that in discarding/adapting hitherto indispensable structural and thematic formulae, the narrator is able to give freer reign
to a more individual vision.[116]

It would be a mistake, however, to read into these more universal features a
wholesale 'succumbing' of the Japanese *shôsetsu* to the Western novel form. As
Walker reminds us, 'in both China and Japan, modern long fiction was not so

much a new form as a continuation of a powerful tradition of long prose fiction from the pre-modern period.'[117] What specifically are these often touted antecedents of the modern *shôsetsu*, and do they justify the use of the term 'novel' in relation to modern Japanese prose fiction?

The term *shôsetsu* (小説), which has been rendered by one critic as 'short account',[118] came into use, according to Walker, rather circuitously via Europe and China as a translation of the Chinese term *hsiao-shuo*—itself introduced in the mid-1880s as a translation of the terms *Roman* and novel.[119] The emphasis given to particular antecedents of the *shôsetsu* varies somewhat among critics, with general consensus that the tale (*setsuwa*), diary (*nikki*), essay (*zuihitsu*) and longer prose/verse 'narrative' (*monogatari*) all play a part in the genealogy of the *shôsetsu*. Miyoshi has emphasized *gesaku* ('playful writing') which emerged as a genre in the late 1600s,[120] while Melanowicz finds significance in the fusion of lyrical and epic factors in the *uta monogatari* to be of significance in the genesis of the later narrative form.[121]

While the above mentioned commentators have made some reference to the formative literary currents which enabled the emergence of the loosely defined *shôsetsu*, a more comprehensive approach focusing on the aesthetic and generic preconditions of the modern *shôsetsu* is beyond the parameters of this discussion.

Despite this, it is in the writings concerned with elaborating what might be called the 'theory' of the Japanese 'novel', that important issues regarding its structure and historical 'function' emerge. Ever since Tsubouchi Shôyô's impassioned plea in *Shôsetsu shinzui* (*The Essence of the Novel*), for a Japanese fiction which 'will finally surpass the European Novel',[122] writers and critics alike have debated the nature and role of the *shôsetsu*. Tsubouchi's voice is but one of the better known attempts at theorizing an indigenous narrative form, but as Melanowicz points out, the self-reflexive critique of fiction goes back as far as Murasaki Shikibu herself, who in Chapter 25 of *Genji Monogatari* makes oblique references to both the 'didactic' but more importantly 'entertaining' functions of the tale/novel.[123]

Whilst Tsubouchi's treatise speculates about the possible 'social functions' assigned to the genre of the *shôsetsu*, it also forms part of a wider debate which might be called the discourse of *kindai shôsetsu* ('modern prose fiction'). This discourse operates well beyond the bounds of a merely 'literary' debate. Rather, it engages in a significant way with the whole question of conditions enabling the emergence of what can be called, for want of a better term, the 'modern Japanese subject'. The articulation of such a subject is the necessary condition not only for the rise of the 'modern Japanese novel', but is also an indispensable condition of the rise of the modern Japanese state. Precisely because the stipulation of the modern subject could arise only from/at the site of struggle between 'speech' and 'writing' (a struggle officially characterized as the 'unification' of 'speech' and 'writing', in the term *genbun'itchi*), even a cursory awareness of the genesis of the 'modern Japanese novel' would be necessary to the task of attempting a critique of some of its more recent forms.[124]

Rather than be too dismissive of the critical observations of Tsubouchi, Bimyô,[125] Sôseki and others on the theory of the novel, in their writings we are able to find some important theoretical pointers. Tsubouchi, for example, in lambasting the readers of the late Tokugawa/early Meiji era for their insatiable appetite for *gesaku* style works of 'cruelty and violence or else pornography' (a depiction, by the way, of popular taste in fiction which would be perfectly applicable today), and lamenting the 'sorry state' of fiction, declares that it is 'the indiscriminate readers everywhere [who] must bear their share of the blame'. In so doing, Tsubouchi fortuitously shifts the focus of the debate to the reader, implying the need for a form of reception aesthetics. This is the kind of approach which is usefully taken up in Maeda Ai's *Kindaidokusha no seiritsu* with its analysis of the transition from the reading out aloud (*ondoku*), to silent reading (*mokudoku*) of fictional works.[126] In a similar vein, Yamada Bimyô's[127] frustration at the unavailability of a suitably developed colloquial *written* style for fictional art tells us something about the urgently felt need for a recasting of narrative possibilities in an idiom appropriate to the construction of a homogenized 'mass' reading subject.

In both the literary and critical writings of Sôseki, can be found implicit and explicit speculation on the institutional practices of 'literature' and the new styles of writing of the later Meiji period—and their role in the production of certain forms of subjectivity. From the polyphonic dispersal of the narrating subject in *Kôfu (The Miner)*, to the conflation of narrating subject and language in *Wagahai wa neko de aru (I am a Cat)*, Sôseki hoped to challenge the tendency toward a monologic and authoritative narrative voice which emerged as a natural concomitant to the newly developed idiom of *genbun'itchi* ('unification of spoken and written styles').[128] Furthermore, according to Karatani[129] many of Sôseki's observations in *Bungakuron (A Theory of Literature)* foreshadowed some important principles of Russian Formalism (especially the distinction/relation between metaphor and metonymy). As well, it is clear that his concerns about the status of the literary work as a relatively 'autonomous' entity (and thus not merely reducible to essentialist notions of 'the spirit of the age' or 'the author') have implications for understanding the status of what may be called 'the speaking subject' in twentieth century Japanese prose fiction. Indeed, it is with the notion of the speaking subject that we conclude this brief foray into the epistemology of the Japanese novel. The questions raised by this topic are numerous and complex, and although they cannot be given further attention here, will continue to inform the subsequent discussion of Murakami's writing.

It can be no coincidence that so many critics have distilled the central problem of accounting for the idea of the Japanese novel to a consideration of the speaking subject and its putative constitution in the matrices of speech and writing. Perhaps the celebrated critic Kobayashi was referring to the disappearance or suppression of the speaking subject in literature, when he remarked that upon reading contemporary historiographical works, he was overtaken by the strong sense that the human being (*ningen*) had disappeared from contemporary fiction (*gendai shôsetsu*).[130] Fujii is much clearer on the matter, and suggests that as numerous critics have shown (among them Barthes, Beneviste and White), 'the novel form has produced a narrative that suppresses the speaking subject', and that *genbun'itchi*—far from being merely a matter of stylistics—is crucial to the issue of subject expression.[131] For a literature that displays, fundamentally, the 'inscription of orality' in its writing,[132] the implications of the tendency towards the eclipse or negation of the speaking subject are profound. This is in no small part due to the fact that Japanese is very much a speaker-oriented language. How can such an orientation yield to the dictates of a singularly authoritative narrative voice essential to the conventions of the realist novelistic enterprise?

One way out of this dilemma may be, as the Japanese critic Komori has shown, to identify (through an ostensibly Bakhtinian approach) multiple voices arising from a single utterance or sentence. Fujii points out, however, that such refracted subjectivities ultimately yield to the relatively fixed subject positions suggested by the categories of character, narrator and author.[133]

Miyoshi's attempt at reading 'against the grain', and refusal to relegate the *shôsetsu* to the position of poor relation of the Western novel is noteworthy in its determination to refocus the prism through which an indigenous narrative form has been conventionally viewed. For Miyoshi, the distinctive features of the *shôsetsu* include its lack of 'formal coherence', its non 'consequential' chains of events, a reliance on 'types' or names for characterization, its shifting narrative points of view, its 'dense, rhetorical and formulaic nature', its extremely variable length.[134] But the really crucial distinction between the classic nineteenth century novel and the *shôsetsu* is the latter's tendency to 'orality'.[135] Once again, we see the focus on the status of the speaking subject in the Japanese narrative form. However, Miyoshi is quick to reject Derrida's blurring of the distinction between speech and writing, orality and literacy (which was really an attack on Levi-Strauss' insistence that cultures are either 'oral' *or* 'literate', but never both).[136] In the same way that Miyoshi is able to situate the *shôsetsu* in both the Third *and* First Worlds, he also allows for an indigenous literature to retain 're-sidual oral traits'.[137]

Returning to our earlier claim of the 'hybridity' of the *shôsetsu*, we can see in it not so much an artifice, as a rich set of narrative possibilities. If the *shôsetsu* can be taken as one significant and continuing experiment in narrative form, then we are certainly justified in reading it in oppositional ways. As Layoun points out in her compelling study *Travels of A Genre:*

> While the novel was not a particularly indigenous literary genre in the 'third' or non-Western world, it quickly predominated as a privileged narrative construct. And yet, on the site of that hegemonic narrative form, there emerged counter-hegemonic opposition as well.[138]

It remains to be seen to what extent Murakami's fiction bears any vestiges of such 'counter-hegemonic opposition', but we can say with certainty that the question of 'orality' will re-emerge in other contexts later in the discussion. In treating the Japanese novel, in the first instance, as an 'idea' existing in the

minds of both Japanese and non-Japanese readers and critics alike, we have created more possibilities in exploring the *shôsetsu* and what constitutes the particular aspects of its 'narrativity'. For as Hayden White reminds us, the peculiar
form of a text's narrativity functions very meaningfully as a kind of 'content' in
its own right.[139]

Notes

1. Marilyn Ivy, *Discourses of the Vanishing: Modernity, Phantasm, Japan* (Chicago &
London: The University of Chicago Press, 1995), 67.

2. The term 'difference' should be understood in the contexts of its uses in the broad
grouping of critical methodologies in the humanities known as structuralism/post-
structuralism. For example, in the area of linguistics it is linked to the writings of Saussure, in anthropology to Talcott Parsons and Levi-Strauss, in historiography, literary theory and metaphysics to the work of Barthes, Foucault, Derrida, Deleuze and Lyotard. It
carries a plethora of nuances including (i) its use as the classifying principle in mapping
the articulation of minimal linguistic units such as phonemes. See Ferdinand de Saussure
Course in General Linguistics, trans. Wade Baskin (London: McGraw-Hill, 1966); (ii) as
the lynchpin of Foucault's notion of 'archive', which 'establishes that we are difference,
that our reason is the difference of discourses, our history, the history of difference, our
selves the difference of masks'. See Michel Foucault, *The Archeology of Knowledge*
(London: Tavistok Publications, 1982); (iii) in the form of the term *differance*, as the
fundamental 'principle' of Derrida's poetics. See Jacques Derrida, 'Difference' in *Speech
and Phenomena* (Evanston: Northwest University Press, 1973). For Derrida it is that
which can be characterized only in negative terms, and presents merely as 'trace'; (iv) for
Lyotard as the 'differend', which designates the condition of absolute incommunicability,
whereby the incommensurable idiomatic frames of two competing discourses effectively
remain mute to one another. See Jean Francois Lyotard, *The Differend: Phrases in Dispute*, trans. G. Bennington & B. Massumi (Manchester: Manchester University Press,
1988). The term 'difference' will (unless otherwise specified) be used throughout the
argument as conveying the polysemy and connotative richness imparted to it in the above
descriptions. At its most fundamental, 'difference' accounts for the value/meaning of an
individual item within the context of a larger system (for example, language). It relates
the part to the whole, the particular to the universal (as in Saussure's classic
langue/parole distinction). That is to say, its value arises only from its relation—its difference—to other items, and is in this sense best characterized *negatively*, by what it is
not. Saussure's approach (although ostensibly concerned with the mechanics of a purely
linguistic classificatory method as in the following example) represented almost an epis-
temic shift, and heralded profound implications for the methodologies of the human sciences: 'In classifying phonemes, what constitutes them is of much less importance than
what distinguishes them from each other. A negative force can be more important in classifying a phoneme than a positive one'. (Saussure, *Course in General Linguistics,* 42.)

3. (i) The notion of a dialogue of voices/consciousness operating in a text represents a
version of Mikhail Bakhtin's idea of the polyphonic novel, and is perhaps most clearly
defined in the following way. The dialogical 'is not constructed as the entirety of a single
consciousness which absorbs other consciousnesses as objects, but rather as the entirety
of the interaction of several consciousnesses, of which no one fully becomes the object of
any other one. This interaction does not assist the viewer to objectify the entire event in

accordance with the ordinary monological pattern (thematically, lyrically, or cognitively), and as a consequence makes him a participant'. See Mikhail Bakhtin, *Problems of Dostoevsky's Poetics*, trans. R. W. Rotsel (Ann Arbor: Ardis, 1973), 14. (ii) With regard to the use of the terms 'subject' and 'subjectivities' here, they should be understood within the context of the general way in which for Foucault, they are positioned through and by *discourses* (a term which will be more precisely defined below): 'I shall abandon any attempt . . . to see discourse as a phenomenon of expression—the verbal translation of a previously established synthesis; indeed I shall look for a field of regularity for various positions of subjectivity. Thus conceived, discourse is not the majestically unfolding manifestation of a thinking, knowing, speaking subject, but, on the contrary, a totality, in which the dispersion of the subject and his discontinuity with himself may be determined'. (Foucault, *The Archeology of Knowledge*, 55)

4. Obviously Foucault's conception of 'exteriority' bears some relation to the notion of 'intertextuality' (to be explained below); however, we can perhaps glean its more specific nuances by citing Foucault's gesturing towards a clarification of the term at several points in *The Archeology of Knowledge*: 'Usually, the historical description of things said is shot through with the opposition of interior and exterior; and wholly directed by a desire to move from the exterior—towards the essential nucleus of interiority'. (120-21) It is important to note that Foucault's notion of exteriority must be understood within the terms of his definition of the statement. A statement cannot be identical with a sentence—because the same sentence can produce different statements under different conditions of exteriority—and theoretically at least, a statement can never be repeated (because the same exteriorities would have to operate co-extensively with its repetition). 'The analysis of statements operates without reference to a cogito . . . we must understand it by the totality of things said, the relations, the regulations and the transformations that may be observed in them, the domain of which certain figures, certain intersections indicate the unique place of a speaking subject and may be given the name of an author: "anyone who speaks," but what he says is not said from anywhere. It is necessarily caught up in the play of an exteriority.' (122) 'To describe a group of statements not with reference to the interiority of an intention, a thought, or a subject, but in accordance with the dispersion of an exteriority.'(125) '(Archeology) . . . is nothing more than a rewriting: that is, in the preserved form of exteriority, a regulated transformation of what has already been written.'(140)

5. Innumerable, unspecified nuances of the term 'discourse' now so widely permeate critical writings across a range of disciplines, that it is necessary to declare, from the outset, the sense(s) in which the use of the term is intended here. As used by Foucault, the term 'discourse' represents a complete rethinking of a concept elaborated by the traditional disciplines of linguistics, socio-linguistics and sociology. McHoul and Grace have divided the non-Foucauldian approaches into two groups: *formal* and *empirical*. See A. McHoul & W. Grace, *A Foucault Primer* (Melbourne: Melbourne University Press, 1993), 73. Frow sees the two groupings as representing a 'renewal of the traditional dichotomy between text and context'. See John Frow, "Discourse Genres," *Journal of Literary Semantics* 9, 2 (1980), 73. The formal approach basically treats discourse in terms of a *text*, and according to McHoul and Grace is indicated in the works of linguists (Harris, 1952; Mitchell, 1957), socio-linguists (Giglioli, 1982) and ethnographers of communication (Bauman and Sherzer, 1974; Gumperz and Hymes, 1972). In this approach, it is variously known as 'discourse analysis' or 'text linguistics'—as products of both Russian Formalism and French Structuralism (Saussure, Levi-Strauss and the early Barthes). In contrast to the linguistic emphasis of formal approaches, the so called 'empirical' approaches adopt what might be called *sociological* analyses. In this context, 'discourse'

often means human conversation or the commonsense knowledges which underly the rules of conversation. Referring neither to language nor social interaction, Foucault's approach (which can be called 'critical') characterizes a discourse as a more or less clearly demarcated area of social knowledge. McHoul and Grace put it succinctly: 'in any given historical period we can write, speak or think about a given social object or practice . . . only in certain specific ways and not others. "A Discourse" would then be *whatever* constrains—but also enables—writing, speaking and thinking within such specific historical limits'. See McHoul & Grace, *A Foucault Primer*, 27-31. In short, we could define discourses in the Foucauldian sense, as forms of representation which constitute historically specific bodies of social knowledge.

6. 'Intertextuality' is originally a Russian Formalist term revived by Kristeva and although used initially only in the context of literary 'texts', could now be said to be applicable in describing relations constituted through and by a wide range of cultural practices, 'texts' and semiolological systems. Conceptually, it could be seen as an extension of Bakhtin's 'polyphony'/dialogue of voices as outlined above, which greatly broadens the scope for being able to think texts in their aspects of exteriority as well as in terms of the structures of their internal relations. The usefulness of the conceptual apparatus of 'intertextuality' has been succinctly put by Sakai. This could be summarized as follows: (i) the plurality not only of different voices but of different *modes* of utterance is taken into account; (ii) a text can be viewed as containing texts; (iii) rather than stipulating 'history and society' as some kind of general environment in which texts are produced, the notion of 'intertextuality' posits both history and society as texts against which a new text is produced; (iv) the term, therefore, helps to theorize modes in which the subject may be constituted; (v) finally, and importantly 'intertextuality can be instrumental in historicizing discursive formations'. See Naoki Sakai, *Voices of the Past: The Status of Language in Eighteenth-Century Japanese Discourse* (Ithaca: Cornell University Press), 28-30.

7. *Concise Oxford Dictionary* (Oxford: Oxford University Press, 1982), 39.

8. Jacques Derrida, "Aphorism Countertime" in *On the Name*, ed. Thomas Dutoit (Stanford: Stanford University Press, 1995), 89-90.

9. *Kôjien*, 1169.

10. Foucault writes: 'Instead of referring back to *the* synthesis or *the* unifying function of *a* subject, the various enunciative modalities manifest his dispersion. To the various statuses, the various sites, the various positions that he can occupy or be given when making a discourse'. See *The Archeology of Knowledge*, 54.

11. The *Kokutai no hongi* was first published in 1937 by a compilation committee of experts. Its stated objectives—described as 'our grave cosmopolitan mission'—were 'to trace clearly the genesis of the nation's foundation, define its great spirit, to set forth clearly at the same time the features the national entity (*kokutai*) has manifested in history, and to provide the present generation with an elucidation of the matter'. This excerpt is quoted from John O. Gauntlett's 1949 translation of the *Kokutai no hongi*. See *Kokutai no hongi*, trans. J. O. Gauntlett, ed. Robert K. Hall (Newton, Mass.: Croft Publishing Corporation, 1974), 55. Hall interprets the stated aims of the text in the following way: 'Its avowed purpose was to combat the social unrest and intellectual conflicts which sprang from the "individualism" of the people and to substitute a devotion to the "national entity" which it identified with unswerving loyalty to the Imperial Family'. See *Kokutai no hongi*, v.

12. (i) *Yamato* is probably the most widely understood pseudonym or alias (*ishô*) of *Nihon/Nippon*. It is considered to be the 'former' name of Japan (*kyûkokumei*), and designated the geographical area of the current Nara Prefecture. It was originally written

using only one Chinese character (倭)—a practice which is still in use—but is also written in several other ways, including ideographic compounds suggestive of 'place of mountains' (山処) or 'great harmony' (大和). 'Clashes with nature such as are found in Western Mythologies do not appear in our legends, and this homeland is to the Japanese a very paradise in which to live. It is not by mere chance that Yamato has been written in Chinese Characters, "Great Harmony".' See *Kokutai no hongi*, 129. It also operates as the adjectival prefix in a large number of compound nouns. The latter function was primarily to distinguish (*kan-suru*: name, entitle) between things possessing distinctly national (i.e. 'Japanese') characteristics, in relation to those considered in some way originally or inherently 'Chinese' (*Kara ni taishite, wagakunitokuyû no jibutsu ni kan-suru kotoba*). In the same way, *Yamato* was used in Okinawa to refer to the 'mainland' (*hondo*). We see here the unmistakable gestures of an attempt to demarcate an imagined proto-national centre and mythic space vis-à-vis various peripheries. (See *Kôjien*, 2589.) Familiar examples of the adjectival use of *Yamato* are: *Yamato-e* (a medieval picture in Japanese rather than Chinese style); *Yamato-uta* (a thirty-one syllable poem or *tanka*); *Yamato-damashii* (the Japanese spirit); *Yamato-kotoba* ('Japanese word/language').

13. *Kôjien*, 2589-90.

14. See Sakai, *Voices of the Past,* 335. Sakai argues that 'in the eighteenth century several positivities came into being, thanks to which a rigid partition between the inside of the "interior" and its "exterior" was formed. This was the moment when the Japanese as a linguistic and cultural unity was born. But the birth of the Japanese was a loss because the imagining of the homogeneous "interior" became possible only when historical time was constructed through the new reading of the classics'.

15. Aizawa writes: 'Only after developing their strength to the fullest did barbarian nations come to spy on us. The Portuguese were the first to enter our homeland (*naichi*)'. See Aizawa Yasushi, "New Thesis," in Bob Tadashi Wakayabashi, *Anti-foreignism and Western Learning in Early Modern Japan: The New Theses of 1825* (Cambridge. Mass.: Harvard University Press, 1986), 149 - 277. especially p. 201.

16. Wakabayashi, *Anti-foreignism and Western learning*, 8-9.

17. John. C Maher, "The Right Stuff: Towards an Environmental Linguistics" in *Diversity in Japanese Culture and Language*, ed. John C. Maher and Gaynor MacDonald (London & New York: Kegan Paul International, 1995), 101. Maher points to the early linguistic diversity of Japan as entailing the continual mixing and re-mixing of Malayo-Polynesian as well as Altaic languages—not to mention the advent of Chinese or *kanbun* from the seventh century onwards.

18. One of the better known critiques in English of *Nihonjinron* is Peter N. Dale's *The Myth of Japanese Uniqueness* (New York: St. Martin's Press, 1986). While it could perhaps be considered a rather too scathing attack on the closure and ethnocentrism of *Nihonjinron* writing, it is nevertheless well researched and insightful. Taking a more eclectic approach is John Clammer's work entitled *Difference and Modernity: Social Theory and Contemporary Japanese Society* (New York: Keegan Paul International, 1995). The book attempts to cast a more 'positive' light on some aspects of *Nihonjinron* literature, and considers their potential applicability to the study of non-Japanese societies. Miyoshi and Harootunian dismiss *Nihonjinron* as 'an ideology of cultural exceptionalism that has sought to construct a national subjectivity devoid of class and gender divisions'. See M. Miyoshi & H. D. Harootunian, *Japan in the World* (Durham and London: Duke University Press, 1993), 3. Yoshino's *Cultural Nationalism in Contemporary Japan* represents a 'sociological' study of the attitudes of contemporary Japanese 'thinking elites' (from the areas of government, education and business) in relation to *Nihonjinron*. He claims to

have identified two kinds of nationalism: 'resurgent cultural nationalism', is said to have developed in the 1970s and 1980s within the milieu of the growing body of *Nihonjinron* writings. The other, 'prudent revivalist nationalism' is more related to the 'old nationalism' of the emperor system (*tennô-sei*) and its 'concomitant symbols and practices'. See Kosaku Yoshino, *Cultural Nationalism in Contemporary Japan* (London: Routledge, 1992), 203-206.

19. Of this immutability, Dale writes: 'Strictly speaking, the linguistic repository of Japaneseness is seen to reside in that pristine part of the vernacular that, putatively, predates foreign influence and thus constitutes the autochthonous linguistic garment of the archaic *kokutai*'. Dale, 56.

20. See David Pollack *The Fracture of Meaning: Japan's Synthesis of China from the Eighth through the Eighteenth Centuries* (Princeton: Princeton University Press, 1986), 3. It should be noted here that Sakai Naoki has launched a strong critique against Pollack's central thesis that Japan could only be defined through its otherness. He senses in Pollack's argument a universalising tendency in most Western discourses about the East. (See Sakai's "Modernity and its Critique: The Problem of Universalism and Particularism," in *Postmodernism and Japan* ed. M. Myoshi & H.D. Harootunian (Durham: Duke University press, 1989), 99-105.

21. Sakai, "Modernity and its Critique," 53.

22. The signifier 'Japan' has often functioned as a trope for 'art' or 'the aesthetic' in the imagination of the West. For a discussion of this see my "'Difference or Differend?': Constructing Meaning Across Japanese and European Discourses on the Aesthetic," in *Japanese Studies: Communities, Cultures, Critiques, Volume Three: Coloniality, Postcoloniality and Modernity in Japan*, ed. V. Mackie et.al., (Melbourne: Monash Asian Institute, Monash University, 2000): 41-68. Examples from the writing of Oscar Wilde, Isabella Bird, Lafcadio Hearn, Roland Barthes and others are quoted in illustration of this point.

23. See Homi Bhabha's essay "Introduction: Narrating the Nation," in *Narrating the Nation*, ed. Homi Bhabha (London: Routledge, 1990), 3.

24. Derrida, *Writing and Difference*, 221.

25. See Benedict Anderson, *Imagined Communities: Reflections on the Origin and Spread of Nationalism* (London: Verso, 1992), 6-7. Of course, Japan is both imagined and imagines itself in these ways. Therefore, while Japan as 'nation' is partly the imagined object arising from competing imperialist discourses of the nineteenth century, it also represents the fruition of deliberate and strident Japanese public policy. David Williams writes: 'The struggle to transform an apolitical peasantry into a modern nationalist-minded population capable of sustaining state goals has stood at the heart of the Japanese programme of nation building'. And 'the most singular achievement of Japanese public policy over the last twelve decades may have been the creation of the modern Japanese "nation" itself'. See David Williams, *Japan: Beyond the End of History* (London & New York: Routledge, 1994), 8.

26. See Ivy, *Discourses of the Vanishing*, 4. These configurations of the imaginary are given as: 'Benedict Anderson's "imagined communities" as the basis for the modern nation-state; Cornelius Castoriadis's "social imaginary," which operates almost as an analogue to culture . . . as the codified ground for the social production of meaning; Claude Lefort's "imaginary community," which he links with modern ideologies and the mass media; and Lacan's "imaginary" as the phantasmatic basis for the human subject's early, pre-symbolic identification with the image'. Furthermore, Ivy is convinced that 'Japan is literally unimaginable outside its positioning vis-à-vis the West' and, that based

on Sakai's research, 'It is arguable that there was no discursively unified notion of the "Japanese" before the eighteenth century, and that the articulation of a unified Japanese ethnos with the "nation" to produce "Japanese Culture" is entirely *modern*'. (See Sakai, *Voices of the Past*, 336.) Cumings claims that within the last century Japan has 'emerged' in the Western mind 'at three critical and incommensurable points: at the turn of the century when it was a British *wunderkind* (but a "yellow peril" to the Germans and the Russians) in the world depression of the 1930s, when it was an industrial monster to the British (but a *wunderkind* to the Germans and the Italians) and in the 1980s when it was a *wunderkind* to American internationalists and a monster to American protectionists'. See Cumings' essay in *Japan in the World*, 88.

27. For example, see H. D. Harootunian's discussion of the work of nativist ethnologists such as Yanagita Kunio and Orikuchi Shinobu in "Figuring the Folk: History, Poetics, and Representation" in *Mirror of Modernity: Invented Traditions of Modern Japan*, ed. Stephen Vlastos (Berkeley and Los Angeles: University of California Press, 1998), 144-159.

28. See *Japan's Competing Modernities: Issues in Culture and Democracy 1900-1930*, ed. Sharon A. Minichiello (Honolulu: University of Hawaii Press, 1998).

29. Roland Barthes, *Empire of Signs*, trans. Richard Howard (London: Jonathon Cape, 1983), 3. Among critics, it remains a moot point as to whether Barthes' classic semiotic expository work on Japan entitled *Empire of Signs*, constitutes in itself both a valuable critique of the methodologies of Japanology (which have tended to construct Japan as object through the relatively *discrete* disciplines of history, literature, etc.), as well as an incisive interpretation of the non-centric nature of representation in Japanese cultural practices—or, represents merely an example of overweening (albeit brilliantly written) 'orientalism'. Ivy is somewhat dismissive of Barthes' 'residual orientalist confidence'. (See Ivy, *Discourses of the Vanishing*, 232.) Burch, however, has described *Empire of Signs* as a 'pioneer text', since it is 'the first attempt by any Western writer to *read* the Japanese 'text' in the light of contemporary semiotics, a reading informed by a rejection of ethnocentricism'. See Noel Burch, *To the Distant Observer: Form and Meaning in the Japanese Cinema* (Berkeley: University of California Press, 1979), 13. Yet, Burch's attempt (ostensibly inspired by Barthes' approach) to apply Western critical theory to the artistic practices of Japanese film has been rejected by Yoshimoto who writes: 'Japan as the Other, is then conceived as mere supplement, safely contained within the epistemological limit of the West'. See Yoshimoto's essay in *Japan in the World*, 344. In an insightful attempt to situate Barthes' *Empire of Signs* within the larger context of his writing as a whole, Morris writes: 'Certainly a Japanologist will need some introduction to Barthes in order to know what is going on in *Empire of Signs*. Happiest will be the expert on Japan whose knowledge is held onto with the least proprietary anxiety'. See Mark Morris, 'Barthes/Japan: the Texture of Utopia', in *Japan's Impact on the World* (Nathan: Japanese Studies Association of Australia, 1984), p. 35.

30. In various ways, as has been argued throughout this chapter, the views of Sakai, Miyoshi and Karatani confirm this fundamental proposition.

31. Maruyama Masao asserts that the notions of the 'super-modern'(*chôkindai*) and 'pre-modern' (*zenkindai*), are peculiarly combined in the character (*seikaku*) of the Japanese modern. See Maruyama Masao, *Nihon no shisô* (Iwanami Shinsho, 1992), 5. However, as Karatani's argumentation shows, both appear as ways of avoiding confronting a 'genuine' modernity, whose character in the Japanese context, can only be surmised.

32. Maruyama, *Nihon no shisô*, 7.

33. See Karatani's *Kaisetsu* (commentary) in Hiromatsu Wataru, "*Kindai no chôkoku*" *ron* (Kôdansha, 1991), 265.

34. Hiromatsu, *"Kindai no Chôkoku" ron* (Kôdansha, 1991), p. 232.

35. (i) Karatani Kôjin uses the term 'self-sufficient space' (*jisokutekina kûkan*) in various contexts and basically in a pejorative sense, to imply a closure, or lack of exteriority in Japan. See for example his comments on Japanese postmodernism and post-structuralism in *Kotoba to higeki* (Kodansha, 1993) 171. (ii) The perception that Japan is lacking in a subjectivity defined on its own terms, appears most obviously in disputes about economic domination, which actually mask a deeper question about Japan's sovereignty as an independent, subjectively constituted entity. The re-affirmation and extension of Japan's dependence on U.S. dictated security arrangements, coupled with international (IMF, G8 and American) pressure for Japanese internal de-regulation and reform, represents the most recent version of the seemingly inevitable pattern of perception of Japan's future direction as being determined from *without*. Although the focus is on ostensibly 'economic' issues, the underlying tension is clearly about the continued hegemony of the West under the guise of 'globalization', and whether Japan should continue to accept this unquestioningly. This is clearly evident in the terms of debates which are played out in the Japanese media, in a tone strikingly reminiscent of earlier texts which considered it a matter of urgency to re-affirm the need for Japan to defend itself in a hostile world. (More notable examples of this would include Aizawa's 1825 *New Thesis* and the *Cardinal Principles of the National Entity of Japan* (*Kokutai no Hongi*) of the 1930s). The parameters of such a debate are laid out in classic form in the journal *Bungeishunjû* 76, 5 (May, 1998), 94-124; with the former co-author (Ishihara Shintarô) of the 1989 best-seller *The Japan that Can Say No*, reiterating his challenge to the tyranny of American standards as 'world standards'. This is followed by an article by Kanagawa University Professor Kitsugawa Mototada, which, arguing in a similar vein, rejects the rule of 'dollar imperialism' (*doru teikokushugi*) over the economies of Japan and Asia. This is countered, however, by Komori Yoshihisa, (writing interestingly from across the Pacific as special editorial writer in Washington for the *Sankei Shinbun*) who puts the blame for Japan's recession and financial crises squarely with Japan and its refusal to seriously address the need for reform. The binary terms of Japan versus the rest (or at least the West) evident in this argument are familiar enough.

36. Maruyama, *Nihon no shisô*, 5.

37. Hiromatsu, *"Kindai no chôkoku" ron*, 200.

38. Victor Koschmann, *Revolution and Subjectivity in Postwar Japan* (Chicago and London: The University of Chicago Press), 1996, 2.

39. Koschmann, *Revolution and Subjectivity in Postwar Japan*, 231.

40. Koschmann, *Revolution and Subjectivity in Postwar Japan*, 239.

41. Koschmann, *Revolution and Subjectivity in Postwar Japan*, 240. Koschmann describes Laclau's ideas as an 'approach to the dynamics of *shutaisei* whose fundamental insights were anticipated at certain points by Ara, Umemoto, Mashita, Takakuwa, Shimizu, and Takeuchi, among others.'

42. Koschmann, *Revolution and Subjectivity in Postwar Japan*, 48.

43. Karatani Kôjin, *Kotoba to higeki* (Kodansha, 1993).

44. Karatani, *Kotoba to higeki*, 35. Interestingly, Kamei Katsuichirô, another participant in the *Kindai no chôkoku* symposium, observed that since the Meiji era 'kindai' signified a kind of loss—that is, the Japanese people's losing sight (*mishinau*) of God. See Hiromatsu, *"Kindai no chôkoku" ron*, 235.

45. For a detailed account of the generic features of the *shishôsetsu*, see Edward Fowler, *The Rhetoric of Fiction: Shishôsetsu in Early Twentieth-Century Japanese Fiction* (Berkeley: University of California Press, 1988).

46. Karatani, *Kotoba to higeki*, 35-36.

47. Karatani, *Kotoba to higeki*, 36-38.

48. Karatani, *Kotoba to higeki*, 114.

49. Karatani, *Kotoba to higeki*, 114.

50. Karatani, *Kotoba to higeki*, 115.

51. Karatani, *Kotoba to higeki*, 170.

52. Karatani, *Kotoba to higeki*, 171.

53. Hiromatsu, *"Kindai no chôkoku" ron*, 270-72.

54. See Jean Francois Lyotard, *The Postmodern Condition: A Report on Knowledge* (Minneapolis: Minnesota Univiversity Press, 1984).

55. See Jurgen Habermas, "Modernity versus Postmodernity," *New German Critique* 22 (Winter), 1981.

56. Johann P. Arnason, "Theory: Modernity, Postmodernity and the Japanese Experience," in *Japanese Encounters with Postmodernity* ed. J. P. Arnason and Y. Sugimoto (London & New York: Kegan Paul International, 1995), 12-14.

57. Arnason, "Theory: Modernity, Postmodernity and the Japanese Experience," 27.

58. Arnason, "Theory: Modernity, Postmodernity and the Japanese Experience," 29.

59. John Clammer, "From Modernity to Postmodernity" in *Difference and Modernity: Social Theory and Contemporary Japanese Society* (New York: Kegan Paul International, 1995), 13-20.

60. Clammer, "From Modernity to Postmodernity," 20.

61. Clammer, "From Modernity to Postmodernity," 21.

62. Clammer, "From Modernity to Postmodernity," 29.

63. Clammer, "From Modernity to Postmodernity," 30.

64. See Victor Koschmann, "Maruyama Masao and the Incomplete Project of Modernity," in *Postmodernism and Japan*, ed. M. Miyoshi & H. D. Harootunian (Durham and London: Duke University Press, 1989), 123-41.

65. Koschmann, "Maruyama Masao and the Incomplete Project of Modernity," 139.

66. Koschmann, "Maruyama Masao and the Incomplete Project of Modernity," 135-136.

67. See Ivy, *Discourses of the Vanishing*, 241.

68. Harry Harootunian, *Overcome by Modernity: History, Culture, and Community in Interwar Japan* (Princeton: Princeton University Press, 2000), 94.

69. Karatani, "The Discursive Space of Modern Japan," in *Japan in the World*, 291.

70. See *Kôjien*, 833. The *Kôjien* confirms the polysemy of the term. It is suggested that as well as denoting 'the present time' (*genzai*), and 'the world now' (*ima no yo*), in terms of Japanese history, *gendai* may signify the period commencing after the loss of the Pacific War. In the context of world history, it may indicate the period of heightened imperialism at the end of the nineteenth century — or, the period commencing from the conclusion of the First and/or Second World War.

71. In the Introduction to *Postmodernism and Japan*, Miyoshi and Harootunian write: 'The talk of premodernism, modernism, non-modernism, and anti-modernism has been going on in Japan ever since the mid-nineteenth century. Like all other non-Western nations for which the encounter with the West had been disastrous and traumatic, Japan had to face up to the chronopolitical condition as an urgent national thematic. Of course there never was a unanimity, but the constant process of locating the insular society on the international map of progress has at least provided it with a scheme of disagreements'. The dominance in Japan, of the epistemological/historical paradigm of the modern (*kindai*) meant, according to Miyoshi Yukio (1972, 149), that even the 'anti-modern' was no more than another version of the modern. He suggests that the 'anti-modern' is a syno-

nym of denial arising from within 'the modern' of any particular age, and provides the grounds for confirming the inherent contradictions of the modern. See Miyoshi Yukio, *Nihonbungaku no kindai to hankindai* (Tokyo Shuppan Kai, 1972), 149.

72. The works of not only Sôseki, but also other well known figures of the earlier phase of Japanese literary modernity are often incorporated into 'Collected Works' (*Zenshû*) series. See for example, an edition of *Nihon gendaibungaku zenshû*, (Kôdansha 1962), suggesting that *gendai* can signify as far back as the early Meiji period. On the other hand, a paperback edition of Yamada Eimi's (1988) *Hizamazuite ashi o oname* published over seventy years later, explicitly depicting the sado-masochistic practices of a couple of prostitutes—in highly vernacular style—is also designated as a work of *gendai bungaku*. An example of the 'supplementary' use of *gendai* in relation to *kindai* can be seen in Yoshida Seiichi's (1981) *Gendaibungaku to koten*, which begins with a discussion of Nagai Kafu, whose first two books (*shôsetsu*) were published in 1902. In this work, *kindai* is considered the overarching paradigm which subsumes *gendai*—as *kindai* itself is cast in terms of another paradigm, *koten* ('the Classical') with the simultaneous 'continuity' (*renzoku*) and 'extinction' (*danzoku*) of the latter, in turn, given as a defining feature of *kindai*. (See the section entitled *Kindai ni okeru koten no enzoku to danzoku*, 9-73).

73. Karatani, "The Discursive Space of Modern Japan," 289.

74. Karatani, "The Discursive Space of Modern Japan," 290.

75. Karatani comments on the 'narrative punctuation' provided by the Christian Calendar, whose metric divisions themselves give rise to the notion of the *fin de siècle*. See "The Discursive Space of Modern Japan," 289. Interestingly, for Karatani, the dominance of the Christian world view in Japanese modernity is also apparent in the rise of modern Japanese literature, which requires a system of 'confession', as well as an interiorized, individualized subjectivity as its indispensable precondition. This is explored in Karatani's *Origins of Japanese Literature* (1993) which will be referred to in detail later.

76. Other specific instances of the use of such metaphors are too numerous to list here, but the extent of their use can be gleaned from a perusal of the titles of critical essays given in the bibliography of works in Japanese. These essays will be cited throughout the discussion.

77. As mentioned in the previous chapter, in the November 1994 (14-16) issue of the popular literary magazine *Da buinchi*, a special edition featuring the 'voice of Japanese readers', a reader survey of the most popular ('best-loved, talented'—*aisare jôzu no sakkatachi*) writers listed Murakami Haruki as the most popular in the 'genre' (*jyanru*) of *junbungaku* ('pure' or 'high' literature), followed by Natsume Sôseki, Dazai Osamu, Miyamoto Teru and Yamada Eimi. The other genres used in this survey were 'Essay' (*essei*), 'Non-Fiction' (*nonfuikushyon*), 'Historical/Period Novel' (*rekushishôsetsu/jidaishôsetsu*), 'Mystery' (*misuterî*) and 'Science Fiction' ('SF').

78. See *Sutairu no bungakushi*, ed. Oya Yukio et.al (Tôkyôdô Shuppan, 1995), 182-227. The section on contemporary style also touches on T.V. commercials, 'young women's' comics, and 'new music' lyrics.

79. See M. Spahn and W. Hadamitzky, *Japanese Character Dictionary*, (Tokyo: Nichigai Associates Inc., 1989), 116.

80. See Suga Shûmi, "Gendaisei toiu Shinwa," in *Happy Jack: nezumi no kokoro*, ed. Takahashi Teimiko (Hokusôsha, 1991), 87-98.

81. Suga, "Gendaisei toiu Shinwa," 90.

82. Suga, "Gendaisei toiu Shinwa," 89-92.

83. See Roland Barthes, "Myth Today," in *Mythologies,* trans. Annete Lavers (London: Granada, 1981), 109-159. This argument is elaborated on pages114-117 of the essay.

84. See Kuroko Kazuo, *Murakami Haruki: za rosuto wârudo* (Daisan Shokan, 1993), 194-198. This critical monograph surveys several of Murakami's major fictional works, and attempts to situate his writing within the larger context of 'the contemporary'—both in relation to other writers and the particular, more noteworthy 'concerns' of specific decades.

85. Shibata Shôji, *Tojirarenai shinwa* (Chûsekisha, 1990), 9.

86. Yokô Kazuhiro, *Murakami Haruki - kyûjûnendai: saisei no konkyô* (Daisan Shokan, 1994), 137.

87. Matsuzawa Masahiro, *Haruki, Banana, Genichirô: jidai no kanjussei o yurasu mitsu no shigunaru* (Seikyûsha, 1989), 188-196.

88. See Kasai et.al., *Murakami Haruki o meguru bôken* (Kawade Shobôshinsha, 1991), 151-152. Takeda's rejection of Karatani's and others' critiques of Murakami, is concomitant with his claim that the positions adopted by these critics are borne of an outdated radicalism.

89. See Kawamura Minato, "'Nejimakidori Kuronikuru' no bunseki: gendaishi toshite no monogatari—Nomonhan Jihen o megutte," *Kokubungaku* 40, no. 4 (March 1995): 57-63.

90. See H. D. Harootunian, "Visible Discourses/Invisible Ideologies," in *Postmodernism & Japan,* 63-92; especially pages78-81.

91. Harootunian, "Visible Discourses/Invisible Ideologies," 81

92. Harootunian, "Visible Discourses/Invisible Ideologies," 89.

93. Harootunian, "Visible Discourses/Invisible Ideologies," 90.

94. See Marilyn Ivy, "Critical Texts, Mass Artifacts: The Consumption of Knowledge in Postmodern Japan," in *Postmodernism and Japan,* 22-23. Ivy is quoting from Nakasone Yasuhiro, "Zensairoku: Nakasone shushô no 'chiteki suijun' kôen" ("The Complete Text: Prime Minister Nakasone's 'Intellectual Standard's Speech"), *Chûo kôron* 101 (November, 1986): 152.

95. Ivy, "Critical Texts, Mass Artifacts," 78. Here Harootunian is referring to the "Reports of the Policy Research Bureau of the Ôhira Cabinet". See footnote 15, page 91.

96. Ivy, "Critical Texts, Mass Artifacts," 79.

97. See Yoshimoto Takaaki, "Nijû seikimatsu no Nihonbunka o kangaeru," in *Miedashita shakai no genkai* (Kosumo no Hon, 1992), 126-127.

98. Ishioka Eiko, cited in Henry Steiner and Henry and Ken Haas, *Cross-Cultural Design: Communicating in the Global Market Place* (London: Thames and Hudson, 1995), 104.

99. See Robert J. Fouser, "Life Without Zero: An Interview with Miyajima Tatsuo" in *Art Asia Pacific* 17 (1998): 51. Miyajima's comments are taken from an interview conducted in July 1996. As well as staging his own solo exhibitions, Miyajima has been involved in numerous group exhibitions around the world, and his works utilize a wide range of media—with a particular focus on electronic objects, and especially 'LEDs' ('light-emitting diodes').

100. See Murakami Haruki, *Wakai dokusha no tame no tanpenshôsetsu annai (A Short Story Guide for Young Readers)* (Bungeishunjû, 1997), 14.

101. Nakamoto Nobuyuki, "Gaikokugokyôiku no meniyu," in *Gengo* 4 (April 1995): 6-7.

102. This comment came from Professor Kirschenreit of Berlin Free University. See Nakamoto, "Gaikokugokyôiku no meniyu," 6.

103. See Ôe Kenzaburô, "Sekai bungaku wa Nihonbungaku tariuru ka?," in _Aimai na Nihon no watashi_ (Iwanami Shinsho,1995), 208-211. According to Ôe, the first line is part of a 'North-Asian totality' (_Kita ajia no zentaisei_), represented by Tanizaki, Kawabata and Mishima, having already been accepted, (particularly by Kawabata's receipt of the Nobel Prize) by the world as legitimately constituting part of 'world literature' (_Sekai no bungaku_). The second line is comprised of those writers who have closely studied foreign literature, and in response to this, have turned world literature into Japanese literature, and then sought feedback from the world regarding their writing. Ôe includes Abe Kôbô as well as himself in this category.

104. See Kazuo Ishiguro and Ôe Kenzaburô, "The Novelist in Today's World: A Conversation," in _Japan in the World_, 163-176.

105. For articles about Murakami's reception in these countries, see _Kokubungaku_ 40, no. 4 (March, 1995): 100-120.

106. Matsuoka, Naomi, "Murakami Haruki and Raymond Carver: The American Scene," in _Comparative Literature Studies_ 30, no. 4 (1993): 436.

107. Ishiguro and Ôe, "The Novelist in Today's World," 166.

108. Ishiguro and Ôe, "The Novelist in Today's World," 172.

109. John Whittier Treat, "Introduction: Japanese Studies into Cultural Studies," in _Contemporary Japan and Popular Culture_ (Honolulu: University of Hawaii Press, 1996), 10.

110. Theodore Goossen, "Introduction," in _The Oxford Book of Japanese Short Stories_, ed. Theodore W. Goossen (Oxford: Oxford University Press, 1997), xii.

111. The debate is crystallized in the running dispute between Lyotard, who argues for the incredulity towards the metanarratives of modernity, and Habermas, basing his views on the Kantian _sensus communis,_ seeing the project of modernity as incomplete. Broadly speaking, Richard Rorty's 'pragmatism' could be said to be somewhere in between these two positions.

112. See Miyoshi Masao, "Against the Native Grain: The Japanese Novel and the Postmodern West," in _Off Centre: Power and Culture Relations between Japan and the United States_ (Cambridge, Mass.: Harvard University Press, 1991), 9-36.

113. See James Fujii, "Introduction," in _Complicit Fictions_ (Los Angeles: University of California Press, 1993).

114. In his essay "Against the Native Grain: The Japanese Novel and the 'Postmodern' West," Miyoshi seeks to 'contest' the novel 'against the _shôsetsu_ form' — within the larger context of 'de-centering' the West and its ethnocentric practices of establishing cultural and artistic norms against which all Third World and 'native' versions are evaluated.

115. See Janet A. Walker "On the Applicability of the term 'Novel' to modern Non-Western Long Fiction', in _Yearbook of Comparative and General Literature_ 37 (1988): 47-68. As Walker notes (p. 59), using the term 'novel' with regard to non-Western countries fosters, in the words of Miyoshi, 'native concurrence and confirmation of the first world hegemonic interpretation, often accompanied by the Orientalist verdict that the (native aesthetic creation) is underdeveloped'.

116. See _Kôjien_, 1272.

117. Walker, "On the Applicability of the term 'Novel' to modern Non-Western Long Fiction," 56.

118. See J. Thomas Rimer, _Modern Japanese Fiction and Its Traditions: An Introduction_ (Princeton: Princeton University Press, 1978), 62.

119. Walker, "On the Applicability of the term 'Novel' to modern Non-Western Long Fiction," 56.

120. Mioyshi, "Against the Native Grain," 18. For a more extended discussion on the antecedents of the novel form, see J. Thomas Rimer (1978), 62-81.

121. See Mikolaj Melanowicz, "Some Problems in the Theory of the Novel in Japanese Literature," in *Europe Interprets Japan*, ed. Gordon Daniels (Tenterden, Eng: Paul Norbury, 1984), 147.

122. See Tsubouchi Shôyô, "The Essence of the Novel," in Donald Keene, *Dawn to the West: Japanese Literature in the Modern Era—Fiction* (New York: Henry Holt & Co., 1987), 102. For an original Japanese version, see *Shôsetsushinzui* (Iwanami Bunko, 1955). For a discussion relating aspects of *Shôstesushinzui* to Futabatei's *Ukigumo*, see Janet Walker, *The Japanese Novel of the Meiji Period and the Idea of Individualism* (Princeton: Princeton University Press, 1979), 31-32; 39; 57.

123. Melanowicz, "Some Problems in the Theory of the Novel in Japanese Literature," 148.

124. Nanette Twine has noted of the *genbun'itchi* 'movement': '[It] was vital to the success of the new order, but many intellectuals and statesmen regarded it as a threat to the security of their long-cherished, rigid views of the nature of scholarship and literature'. See "The Genbunitchi Movement: its Origins, Development and Conclusion," in *Monumenta Nipponica* 33 (Autumn, 1979): 333.

125. See the preface to Yamada Bimyô's *Fûkin shirabe no hitofushi* ("A Note on the Organ"; 1887), quoted from Miyoshi Masao, *Accomplices of Silence: The Modern Japanese Novel* (Berkeley: University of California Press, 1974), 4.

126. See Maeda Ai, *Kindai dokusha no seiritsu* (Iwanami Shoten, 1993), especially 167-210.

127. Bimyô in Miyoshi, *Accomplices of Silence*, 4.

128. For an extended discussion of Sôseki's critique of naturalist conventions and subjectivity in *Wagahai wa neko de aru*, see "Between Style and Language," in James Fujii, *Complicit Fictions*, 103-125.

129. Karatani, *The Origins of Modern Japanese Literature*, 12-15.

130. See "Jiko nitsuite" in *Kobayashi Hideo shû*, ed. Yoshimoto Takaaki, Kindai Nihonshisô taikei, 29, (Chikuma Shobo, 1977), 70.

131. Fujii, *Complicit Fictions*, 109.

132. Fujii, *Complicit Fictions*, 39.

133. Fujii, *Complicit Fictions*, 37. Fujii refers to Komori's writings extensively here.

134. Miyoshi, "The 'Great Divide' Once Again," 45-50.

135. Miyoshi, "The 'Great Divide' Once Again," 50.

136. Miyoshi, "The 'Great Divide' Once Again," 54.

137. Miyoshi, "The 'Great Divide' Once Again," 61.

138. Mary N. Layoun, *Travels of A Genre* (Princeton: Princeton University Press, 1990), xii.

139. Hayden White, *The Content of the Form* (Baltimore: John Hopkins University Press, 1987), 30.

Chapter Three

The Theory of the Simulacrum: Trajectories and Limits

It is no longer possible to manufacture the unreal from the real, to create the imaginary from the data of reality. The process will be rather the reverse: to put in place 'decentred' situations, models of simulation, and then to strive to give them the colors of the real, the banal, the lived; to re-invent the real as fiction, precisely because the real has disappeared from our lives.

> Jean Baudrillard,
> 'Simulacra and Science Fiction'[1]

For the wretched young salary-man, a victim of double violence, the competing theories of bystanders as to whether this (the Sarin gas attack) originated in the everyday, 'normal' world—or some other extraordinary 'abnormal' world, are singularly unpersuasive.

> Murakami Haruki,
> Forward to *Andâguraundo*[2]

The year 1995—marking the midpoint of the final decade in Japan's busiest century—was highly significant for the nation, for all sorts of reasons. It opened with the virtual destruction of the cosmopolitan port city of Kobe, in a terrifying conflagration which called into question the competence of the state in being able to adequately predict, prepare for and manage natural disasters. Early spring witnessed the Tokyo Subway Sarin gas attack. Later, in mid-August, Japan commemorated the fiftieth anniversary of the end of hostilities in the Pacific War with a much debated address delivered by Prime Minister Murayama in a ceremony officiated over by the Emperor and attended by members of the National Parliament.[3]

The larger Tokyo bookstores carried a range of topical books speculating on what fate awaited Japan at the century's end and beyond. The impetus for political and economic reform in the face of a persistent recession gathered momentum and soon become a matter of increasing urgency in the wake of corporate failures, a stagnant equities market and unacceptably high levels of public sector debt.

Ten days after the Prime Minister's commemorative address, the third and final volume of Murakami Haruki's *Nejimakidori kuronikuru* (*The Wind-Up Bird
Chronicle*) was published. This was the longest of Murakami's novels to date,
and was characterized by a mixed reaction from critics. There was general
agreement, however, that it indicated some kind of attempted return to—or perhaps rediscovery of—'history' or 'politics'.[4] At the very least, it represented a
concerted attempt to restore the signifier 'Japan' to something beyond its functioning in terms of either a muted self parody, or, by its very elision in many
earlier works,[5] something which had marked a profound complicity with its undeclared other, 'the West'.

Almost coincidental with Murakami's newfound interest in modern Japanese
history was his emergence as a high profile social commentator on behalf of
victims of urban terrorism. This took the form of an anthology of interviews
with the victims of the Tokyo subway gas attack. Both these developments have
added further dimensions to the already complex 'Murakami Phenomenon', and
made even more compelling the need to account for the status of the author's
writing in the context of contemporary Japanese culture.

However tenuous it may at first appear, the link between the above cited cas-
ual comments of the onlookers in the subway gas attack and the broad narrative
idiosyncrasies of Murakami's literary endeavors is far from insignificant. Simply
put, the speech acts of the bystanders, and Murakami's linguistic and narrative
style share a concern with the question of assigning meanings about the real.
This concern is manifested within a post-industrial cultural configuration so
thoroughly mediated by 'informatics'[6] as to considerably undermine the perceived semantic 'distance' operating between the imaginable form of an 'original' object routinely instantiated as the referent of language, and its simulacral
'double' or 'image'.

Furthermore, this is suggestive of a problematization of the status of the referent, which by itself is certainly not unique to the post-industrial Japanese context, but when taken in its broader historical dimension, indicates for Japan the
most recent stage in the long development of unfolding structures of the simulacrum in modernity. Attempting to understand such structures is not simply a
question of applying the models (or more specifically 'orders') suggested by the
most well known contemporary theorist of the simulacrum, Jean Baudrillard,
whose approach is both evocative and persuasive, but not without its shortcomings.[7] Nevertheless, as will be shown, Baudrillard's theorization and ongoing
revision of the simulacrum goes far beyond its popularly conceived image as an
aphoristic quip or mantra of the postmodern apparent in some attempts to con-
dense his complex social theories into more easily digestible form.[8]

If, as this discussion will argue, the key to understanding Murakami's significance as in some way paradigmatic of contemporary Japanese culture lies in its
utilization of unique forms of simulacra, then the method for unraveling such
structures must proceed from an explication of the role/status of language and

representation in Japanese cultural modernity. Although this topic is implicitly treated at certain points of the discussion, it would be prudent to concede at the outset that a thorough explication (as Sakai's erudite research has shown[9]) of such an unwieldy and complex object is well beyond the parameters of this study.

On the other hand, since certain manifestations of the simulacrum are so closely connected to the idea of modernity, and since Japan has long tried to understand its own complex relationship to the latter, it will be demonstrated that clarifying the operation of the simulacrum in terms of its cultural typifications remains an important and relevant task. In this respect, therefore, the application of the theory of the simulacrum as a tool of analysis should seem neither surprising nor especially radical.[10] The approach adopted here is to focus on certain literary, cultural and semiotic configurations of contemporary Japan, and by interrogating some of their structural features, lay bare the tissue of discourses which constitute and enable their operation as versions of simulacra.

Before doing so, we need a more thorough grounding in the notion of the simulacrum, and proof that this originally Greek concept has some relevance to our attempts to understand contemporary Japanese culture. After outlining the semantic range of the term 'simulacrum', the discussion of its many-faceted theoretical dimensions will begin by positing the city as the political and imaginary locus within which it operates, and as that discursive space which is most immediate to us. This will be followed by a brief survey of the idea or figure of the simulacrum as it appears in its various forms in the writings of Nietzsche, Foucault, Deleuze and Baudrillard. The chapter will conclude by urging the need to adopt an eclectic and multi-dimensional view of the simulacrum, suggesting the possibility of its use as a figure or trope of interpretation which traverses the more specific meanings assigned to it by some of the major theorists.

Defining the term 'simulacrum'

It would be impossible to identify one single, comprehensive definition of the term simulacrum which would adequately encompass the rich array of connotations which it evokes. Similarly, as the following discussion will demonstrate, there exists no single, unified theory of the simulacrum. Rather, the particular instances of the term's usage cohere around conventionalized applications which are historically, that is to say, discursively constrained. In the dialogues of Plato, for example, *phantasma* (the Greek precursor of the Latin originating *simulacra*) suggests a kind of second order signifying system, one level removed from true speech and being, but nevertheless an inevitable component of the political life of the city.[11] In European religious discourses the term is related to the image of divinity, and resonates semantically with the opposition sacred/profane.[12] On the other hand, in the writings of contemporary social theorist Jean Baudrillard, the term simulacrum functions as a kind of master metaphor for the post-represent-ational paradigm, and the 'disappearance' of history, the referent, the real. In this sense, it constitutes a new 'metaphysics of the sign', which is either hegemonic or redemptive, depending on your point of view.[13]

In between the words 'simulacre' (from Old French) and the current English usage 'simulacrum', we can glean an approximate sense of what the word might mean in contemporary critical discourses. That is, if we distill the essence of these OED definitions, we come up with several connotations which serve to encompass the broad dimensions of its usage in this discussion: that is, *image* (as opposed to an original or model), *artifice* (as against that which is authentic or true), *form* (vis-à-vis content) and *representation* (in contrast to the 'thing-in-itself'). These four senses of the word—*image, artifice, form and representation*, belie the fact that although its usage has become over-extended (even clichéd) as a signifier, the word simulcarum *itself* masks a difficult and complex concept about the nature of language and representation in human cultures.

The discussion which follows confirms the complexity of the concept by plac-ing it firstly within the general context of a semiotics of the city, and then by examining its place in the writings of several prominent Western theorists: Nietzsche, Foucault, Deleuze and Baudrillard. Perhaps Rosen's definition (de-tailed below) of the simulacrum as anything which *mediates* between cultural (that is to say human) practices, and 'original' but inaccessible forms, allows the broadest possible scope to be given to the topic.

The City as Simulacrum

> The things of the city are peculiarly resistant to dichotomy.
>
> Seth Benardete,
> from a commentary
> on Plato's
> *Statesman*[14]

As already intimated, the idea of the simulacrum is inexorably linked to the no-tion of the city. This is not to suggest that in human groupings outside or prior to the *polis* or city state, simulacral processes are absent. Rather, to acknowledge that the city—even in its most rudimentary form—requires the significantly *ab-stracted* representation of human desires, values and actions based on the political organization of things and people, as well as processes of production and exchange. Such processes occur in such a way as to engender maximal con-trol of competing forces which would otherwise revert to the unmediated order or tendencies of the Hobbesian 'natural state'.

It is apt to begin with a brief reference to Plato, not necessarily out of desire to seek origins, but because his treatment of the topic both illuminates that which we invariably take for granted, and because it attempts to think the city in a way which we are, without prompting, barely capable of.[15] In the *Statesman*, one of Plato's later and lesser known dialogues, the interlocutor known as 'the Stranger' engages in a long, turgid exposition on the art of weaving as the central metaphor in describing the necessity for the Statesman to reconcile contradictory forces in the city (e.g. the slave with the freeman, the mild with the courageous disposition and so on). Throughout the stranger's dialogue with Socrates there is a fundamental tension invoked between talk about the science (*techne*) of politics and the rule of *phronesis* ('sound judgement'),[16] which is most clearly manifest in the imperative to enshrine an account (*logos*) of the operation of *phronesis* in law. The tension arises because *phronesis* lies, by its very nature, outside the scope of politics.

The 'royal art of weaving' is then, in the words of Stanley Rosen, really analogous to a 'web of politics',[17] whereby the statesman attempts to manage fundamentally self-destructive forces and impulses inimical to the city's continued existence. In his commentary on the *Statesman*, Rosen succinctly characterizes the status of the city in this text as a kind of simulacrum. He goes on to explain that his use of the term is really an expanded interpretation of what the Stranger, in Plato's the *Sophist,* calls a *fantasm* (*fantasma*):

> A fantasm is an image that alters the original proportions in such a way as to exhibit an inaccurate copy of the original, yet one that looks accurate to human vision.[18]

He acknowledges that such an image is employed primarily in the plastic and visual arts of architecture, sculpture and painting, but wants to extend the notion to indicate

> any construction that is intended to mediate between inaccessible originals and human existence.[19]

The key term here is 'inaccessible originals', and precisely because *phronesis* is one such original human faculty, by implication the simulacrum is that process which attempts to give it a fixed form and value (i.e. to 'set it down') despite its being something which is by definition, mutable. In the words of the Stranger:

> All the arts that craft any tool, large or small, throughout a city—all of them must be set down as being co-causes, for without them a city would never come to be, or a political (art) either.[20]

One further apparent problem for the Statesman is that all the arts and indeed objects of the city do not easily lend themselves to dichotomous classification: 'Do you know (says the Stranger to Socrates) that it's difficult to cut them in two'.[21] The seven classes of possessions specified by the Stranger cannot be hi-erarchically ordered—rather they are mutually dependant and coextensive with one another.

In fact the Stranger's idea of weaving is suggestive of a theory of intertextual-ity, which does not simply meaning that everything is connected, but that things only gain their pattern or strength (their veracity, meaning, efficacy) in relation to other elements. This view of the simulacrum suggests some kind of perspec-tivism not often attributed, in contemporary discussions, to Plato. Certainly Rosen seems to think so:

> Human existence is a life of simulacra or inaccurate images proportioned to our defective and perspectival vision. But the stranger is not a follower of Nietzsche or his contemporary French interpreters.[22]

Benardete concludes that Plato's statesman cannot overcome the fundamentally simulacral nature of the city which is characterized as 'highly artificial and without any traces of life in its possessions.'[23] Similarly, in Rosen's view, the *techne* of weaving is the means by which the intentions of the authentic states-man (who is the apotheosis of *phronesis*) are carried out—with the implication however, that politics can operate only through images and simulacra.[24] This glance at a classical treatment of the city as a form of simulacrum, relates inter-estingly with more contemporary approaches to the topic. The obvious question arises: how would the Platonic model relate to the post-industrial, 'global' city of today?

Theoretically at least, the basic *techne* of the art of politics, as well as *phrone-sis* are present, but their *mediation* is what makes all the difference. Two things in fact make a very big difference, for it is the dominance of the modality of electronic materiality in the communication process, coupled with the ascen-dancy of the modality of the visual which are the defining features of the present day city as simulacrum.

In postmodern discourses, the city is, above all, a field of vision. Robins char-acterizes the city as a primarily visual experience: it is a 'mode of seeing', a 'structure of visibility'.[25] Interestingly, much Japanese critical discourse on modernity in literature places the 'scene' or 'landscape' (perhaps even 'topogra-phy') or *fûkei* at the centre of its discussion of the city, as evidenced in terms such as 'city-scene'/'cityscape' (*toshifûkei*) and 'city-space'(*toshikûkan*).[26]

As Ivy points out, 'there has recently been an explosion of interest in the con-cept of the city in Japanese-language scholarship',[27] and attention has moved well beyond the standard dichotomy of rural/urban.[28] The focus has shifted to a different kind of imaginary, a double of light and dark—'the city of light' (*hikari no toshi*) versus the 'city of dark' (*yami no toshi*). Ivy notes that the anthropolo-gist Kurimoto sees the notion of *yami no toshi* as signifying the entrance to the 'other world'.[29] This is clearly the kind of metaphor which can be applied to Murakami's *Andâguraundo* (not to mention the 'double world structures' of

many of his narratives) and it also coheres with the imagery evoked by the innocent comments of the subway gas attack bystanders. It goes without saying,
however, that within the current prevailing regime or 'order' of the simulacrum
which undermines referentiality and the reality principle, such an apparently
simple binary structure requires careful theoretical elaboration.

In terms of the complex representation of the city, Murakami's most recent
novel *Afutâ dâku* (*After Dark*) is undoubtedly one of his most exemplary. The
ways in which it presents the accidental, phantasmal, dream-like trajectories of
characters through the night hours in a megalopolis (Tokyo) which never sleeps,
are highly suggestive of the binary dimensions of the imaginary of 'city of
light'/'city of dark'. Within the modalities of the screen and surveillance monitor, the specular, spectral play of images generates seductive, sometimes alarm-
ing viewing positions for the 'reader', and yet the typically ambiguous denouement of the narrative seems to suggest a recuperation of corporeality, and affirm
the extremely unstable nature of the binary pairing 'actual'/'virtual'. The uncertain figuration of the liminal zones of 'light' and 'dark' in this novel is strikingly
suggested in a series of photo-images accompanying a review of *Afutâ dâku* in
the Japanese weekly *Aera*.[30]

Karatani Kôjin's brilliant analysis of the 'discovery' of landscape in the late
Meiji period in Japan is also highly relevant to our discussion of the poetics of
the city-as-simulacrum.[31] In a later article, Karatani even describes Murakami's
work not as 'literature' but as pure 'scene' (*fûkei*).[32] It is also suggested that Murakami re-inverts the inversion in representation (connected with the interior-
ity/exteriority, *naibu/gaibu*) that occurred with the first real (rural) 'landscape'
depicted in Kunikida Doppo's *Musashino*.[33] Perhaps the first effective *urban*
landscape appeared with Futabatei Shimei's *Ukigumo*. But this is digressing. We
must broaden our general theoretical exploration of the nexus between the notion
of the city and the simulacrum, by touching on the role of the visual, the image,
surveillance and simulation at the heart of post-industrial societies.

In a provocative study relying primarily for its theoretical impetus on the work
of Foucault and Baudrillard, William Bogard attempts to develop a theory of the
'imaginary of control' as a way of understanding the nexus between surveillance
and simulation technologies in telematic societies.[34] 'Telematic' is a euphemism
for 'post-industrial', and Bogard uses the terms interchangeably.[35] His central
thesis is that surveillance in the modern period (exemplified, originally, in the
prison as 'panoptican') has developed to its current stage fundamentally unchanged in its aim of total knowledge and control. What distinguishes the operation of current technologies of 'hypersurveillant control', is that they effectively
operate at the level of the *simulation* of surveillance based on:

> a fantastic dream of seeing everything capable of being seen, recording every
> fact capable of being recorded, and accomplishing these things, whenever and
> wherever possible, prior to the event itself.[36]

In this regime of simulation the 'future-history' of an event is always already disclosed. Coupled with Baudrillard's idea that the simulated *is* the only real available, this way of characterizing present social formations has obvious implications for the way in which contemporary artistic discourses may be approached.

Bogard's approach is relevant here because it is fundamentally concerned with the 'imaginary' aspect or 'fantastic dream' of omniscience and control as a hallmark of the post-industrial urban space. To put it another way, contemporary simulacral processes necessarily operate at the level of the imaginary and their essence is not to be found in the mechanical/cybernetic interface of actual technical practices, but at the next level of abstraction as always present *potentialities* in the form of what Bogard has called the 'panoptic imaginary'.[37] The concept of simulation in the post-industrial social order suggests that the process of representation becomes, in the words of Deleuze, a 'process of signalization'[38] through 'codes' or 'models' of the real.[39] However, as Bogard concedes, 'the use of the term "real" here involves considerable slippage, because its very definition becomes just one more effect of a process of coding'.[40]

Leaving aside such indeterminacy, we can at least accept, along with Bogard, that the simulacrum is woven into the technical practices of post-industrial societies, and in so doing, confirm the convenience of the Platonic metaphor of weaving in characterizing abstract social processes.[41] Assuming the efficacy of the idea of the 'panoptic imaginary', we may return briefly and by way of conclusion to this section, to the notion of the city as a 'field of vision'.

It has been noted above that the city of antiquity was characterized by Plato as displaying a fundamental social tension. This of course is very much a feature of the city today. Lewis Mumford writes of 'the realities of human antagonism and enmity' at the heart of urban life, which give rise to a 'paranoid psychical structure'.[42] The city remains forever poised *potentially* over the abyss of chaos and darkness, but is redeemed, as Robins argues, because it privileges light, the visual:

> The city gives prominence to the activity of the eye. It is a place of visual encounter and experience: the City of Light. It is through its visibility that we know the city.[43]

The pairing 'city of light'/'city of darkness' represents an attempt by anthropologists and cultural critics to think through the politics of chaos versus order in metaphorical terms already very familiar to writers of fantastic literature (a group to which Murakami Haruki undeniably belongs). Technocrats and urban planners have enthusiastically championed visibility and transparency as the hallmark of order and harmony in designing urban environments and 'concept' cities, which are testimony more than ever to Bogard's notion of the 'panoptic imaginary'.

Along with Bogard, Robins identifies the peculiar almost paradoxical nexus between distance and clarity of vision in the 'telematic society', referring to the 'distanced perspective of the panorama and panoptican, the encompassing gaze of the survey and surveillance, through which the city is visually possessed.'[44] The notions of 'dystopia', 'utopia'—even 'computopia' and 'teletopia'[45]—are in the end connotative of light versus darkness, while the digital technologies of the 'computopia' function entirely on 'light' transmitted by *optical* fibre, confirming the centrality of the trope of 'transparency'.

Such claims notwithstanding, lest the ascendancy of vision be fetishized, paradoxically for Robins, the post-industrial urban space displays a 'loss of perspective, a loss from view'.[46] Human experience entails a phenomenological 'doubling' effect of both seeing and being seen (Robin's cites Merleau-Ponty here) which creates the double subject positions, the strangely double presence of subjectivity. This implies a flux of subjectivity between immersion and detachment which, as Robins rightly affirms, is very much the condition of dreaming and the dream state. But how does the dream figure in the 'imaginary' of the city? Since dreams generate 'auras' or 'atmospheres', they 'fill-in' and 'animate' the city spaces. Dream spaces and city spaces are contiguous, and according to Louis Sass, in the interstices of such spaces,

> we enter into a universe devoid of both objects and selves, where there is only a swarming of 'self-objects', images and simulacra, filling us without resistance.[47]

The 'loss from view' in the post-industrial city is thus modernity's loss: subjectivity *appears* to inhere in the warp and woof of the simulacrum and perspective assumes tentative refuge in the 'panoptic imaginary'. The undermining of perspective requires that both subjectivity and 'the real, the banal, the lived' (as Baudrillard puts it) be continuously 'sketched', 'put in place' or 'filled in' in a seemingly endless, non-representational process which itself constitutes the quasi-locus of meaning. It may be thought that the web of technological engagement is largely vicarious—distanced and thus somehow 'contained'—in its virtuality, no threat to the physical unity of the body.

By and large, it is true that until recent times corporeality has successfully resisted the ineluctable slide towards being typified, along with its apparent obverse, subjectivity, as a mere phantasm. However, as Timothy Druckrey declares, 'the body is unquestionably the next frontier'.[48] Here we face the possibility of the collapsing of one further hitherto almost inviolable opposition: the inside versus the outside of the body. Taken to its logical conclusion, the technological mediation of corporeality and subjectivity as 'enframing',[49] ultimately entails the overcoming of the body, and perhaps a turning of the body 'inside out' as suggested in the notion of abjection. In conclusion, it can be said that the city and all its processes, objects, systems and relations are, by their very nature, simulacral. Plato sensed this in the fundamental disjunction between the *techne* of politics and the rule of *phronesis* in the city. The city is a system of control, which masks, contains and disperses forces of aggression and chaos, 'telematically'(from a distance). The city is both this and other worldly, it emanates light and conceals darkness, it is both utopian and dystopian. The city represents a field of vision which coheres at the level of the imaginary, as well as a set of potentialities. It often constitutes a 'scene' or landscape, comprised of numerous discrete spaces denoting, in turn, a myriad of 'auras' or atmospheres. The city is even a dream-scene. The city is a metaphor of the body, and a virtual embodiment of its anatomy and processes, and within the city the limits, functions and meanings of the body are tested and re-formed.

Consideration of the city as simulacrum is the appropriate starting point for the kinds of readings of Murakami Haruki's fiction which are presented in the forthcoming chapters. But before further exploration of the structure of the simulacrum in this specific context, the idea of the simulacrum needs to be placed within a broader historical and theoretical setting. Doing so will allow a more rigorous discussion of questions of language, representation and modernity, vital to the elucidation of the major premises of the argument that unfolds in the later chapters. What follows is a brief critical survey of some of the major theorists whose work is deemed highly pertinent to the task at hand.

Nietzsche's 'Perspectivism'

We operate with things which do not exist: with lines, surfaces, bodies, divisible times and spaces.

Friedrich Nietzsche,
The Gay Science[50]

We have already touched upon Plato's role in the development of the idea of the simulacrum as an explanatory principle well beyond its significance as merely describing a supplementary 'effect' of art or language. Rather, it necessitates and enables the very matrices of power which constitute the city. With Rosen's ironic declaration that 'the Stranger (sic) 'is not a follower of Nietzsche', a clue to the latter philosopher's relevance to our understanding of the simulacrum is given, and it is via his characterization as a 'perspectivist' that Nietzsche's contribution here is most widely known. As a thinker, he arguably set the agenda for much twentieth century philosophy and the writings of his later 'French interpreters' are admirable testimony to this fact. It is in his almost quixotic pursuit of a 'perspectivist', 'relativist' or as one critic puts it 'radical textualist' stance[51] (often couched in a highly aphoristic fashion, whose very style resists 'interpretation') that Nietzsche's important contribution to the way we have come to think about the nexus between language and 'the world' is most clearly evident.

How might we relate Nietzsche's insights to the question of the simulacrum? The key to his thought lies in his uncompromising views on the nature of truth, interpretation and representation. To begin with, what is important for Nietzsche is not whether something is true or not, but in understanding what lies behind the impulse *for* truth. His well known aphorism 'truths are worn out metaphors . . . coins which have their obverse *effaced'*,[52] belies the radicality of his critique of the fallacious notion that 'things' or 'the world' actually exist outside their represented forms in language:

> If only one did not eternally hear the word 'world, world, world', that hyperbole of all hyperboles; when we should only speak, in a decent manner, of 'man, man, man'.[53]

Elsewhere, he quips that after 'subtract[ing] the perspectival' we could hardly expect to find a world remaining.[54] Nietzsche's so called 'perspectivism' is a direct attack on the common sense Correspondence Theory of Truth which posits that truth inheres in establishing a nexus or correspondence between a sentence and a fact.[55] This may seem an obvious, almost naive observation within the paradigms of contemporary critical theory, but such a view remains the often unacknowledged premise of much analytical philosophy, empirical scientific method and transcendental metaphysics—as well as informing the practical, everyday view that behind every representational form, there lies a 'reality' which can ultimately be 'got at'. Admittedly, the proliferation of simulacra in postmodern cultural practices proceeds unabated, but this tendency in no way necessitates, *ipso facto,* an undermining of the perceived veracity of the reality principle as powerfully informing the way we commonly think about the world.

It follows that Nietzsche was equally hostile to the Kantian notion of the 'thing in itself', which like 'the world', feigns to present us with a readily knowable reality:

> 'immediate certainty', as well as 'absolute knowledge' and the 'thing in itself,"
> involve a *contradictio in adjecto*, I shall repeat a hundred times; we really
> ought to free ourselves from the seduction of words![56]

Even if 'the world' and 'things' did exist in their own right, our language is hopelessly ill-equipped to say meaningful things about them, simply because, as Arthur Danto puts it, Nietzsche identifies a process of projection, whereby 'the grammatical subject of our sentences is converted, through the mytho-poetic working of the primitive mentality of man, into the substance of the world.'[57] If Nietzsche's point is valid here, and the operation of language actually proves the fallaciousness of the reality or correspondence principle, then how has it come about that we still appear to function (for example, through legal and scientific discourses) as though the contrary were the case?

Foucault: The Liberation of the Sign

Michel Foucault's early writing on the shift from 'resemblance' to 'representation' (in Europe, between the sixteenth and nineteenth centuries) is relevant here. 'Archeology' is an apt analogy for Foucault's work in this area, because it suggests that various layers or strata of semiological systems can be identified as relatively discrete, and yet still somehow present to or embedded in discursive forms operating today. Hayden White has suggested that Foucault took over where Nietzsche left off in *Ecce Homo*.[58] Interestingly, for Nietzsche, nineteenth century European 'man' had reached his fullest potential and represented something which now had to be overcome.[59] Especially within their understanding of modernity, there are indeed parallels in the way Nietzsche and Foucault thought about the designation 'man'.[60] At another level of description, however, both had in mind different referents in their use of the word. Yet, this very difference is instructive for our understanding of Foucault's ideas on representation. It is Foucault's view that 'man' and 'discourse' appeared at roughly the same time in the early eighteenth century.

While Nietzsche's comments were universally applicable instances of what Foucault himself would see as profound insights into the very nature of language, Foucault's 'archeological' analysis goes deeply and specifically into the problem of accounting for the shift from *language as resemblance* to *discourse as representation* between the sixteenth and eighteenth centuries in Europe. Foucault was of course using the term 'discourse' in a way very different to its commonly understood usage in the discipline of linguistics, and this difference was outlined in the previous chapter. For Foucault, a discourse is a body of social knowledge—relatively discrete and well-bounded—that does not merely represent the 'real', but is actually part of its construction.[61]

The relevance of Foucault's thought to our consideration of the theory of the simulacrum lies in his subtle analysis of certain orders of similitude dominant in the Renaissance period, which ultimately give way to different forms of representation during what he designates as the Classical and Modern periods.[62] An understanding of these dimensions of similitude will allow us to extend and enrich our idea of the simulacrum in the context of its critical application to narrative works. Moreover, Foucault's insights as well as those of other theorists, suggest that at best, theorizing the operation of the simulacrum is a difficult and nebulous process which requires considerable methodological latitude. Foucault's thoughts on the topic generously encourage such liberality of interpretation, while remaining highly rigorous and original.

Foucault argues that up to the end of the sixteenth century it was resemblance that actually constructed knowledge in Western culture:

> It was resemblance that largely guided exegesis and the interpretation of texts; it was resemblance that organized the play of symbols, made possible knowledge of things visible and invisible, and controlled the art of representing them.[63]

Resemblance was constituted by at least four dimensions of similitude. Firstly, *convenientia* suggested adjacency, proximity and juxtaposition. Things were 'convenient' in so far as they were close to one another, and thus *convenientia* denoted a 'resemblance connected with space in the form of a graduated scale of proximity'. The things of the world were similar to one another to the extent that they were linked together in space, like a chain.[64]

The second important aspect of similitude was that of *aemulatio* ('emulation'), which was a kind of 'convenience' that operated from a distance, linking together things scattered throughout the universe that could 'answer one another': for example, the human face, from a distance, emulated the sky; human eyes, reflected the 'vast illumination' of the sky by the sun and moon, and so on. As Foucault recognizes, this kind of similitude calls into question the exact relationship between the original form of an object and its image: 'Which is the reality and which the projection? It is often not possible to say, for emulation is a sort of natural twinship existing in things'.[65] In this aspect of resemblance can be seen the incipient conceptual kernel at the centre of Baudrillard's orders of simulacra.

The third form of similitude was designated as *analogy*, which Foucault recognizes was a familiar concept with a long history, possessing 'immense' power precisely because it could operate well beyond the merely visible, substantial relations between things. Rather, it allowed the more subtle resemblance of relations, and significantly, man figured prominently in the operation of this kind of similitude, which potentially connected all things in the universe: 'The space occupied by analogies is really a space of radiation. Man is surrounded by it on every side'. The most obvious analogy was that of the body to the universe, which could evoke an infinite number of correspondences.[66]

The fourth and final kind of resemblance was that inherent in the play of *sympathies*. It was perhaps more powerful a form of resemblance than *analogy* because it moved throughout the 'depths of the universe' in a completely unfettered state. The example is given of 'the great yellow disk of the sunflower turn[ing] to follow the curving path of the sun'. But sympathy threatens to swallow up and assimilate things—overcoming difference and rendering objects identical, so *antipathy* performs the task of maintaining the separateness and individuality of things. Indeed it is the interplay of sympathy and antipathy that supports and allows the operation of the other resemblances of convenience, emulation and analogy. In this pre-modern, pre-representational scheme of the universe:

> The whole volume of the world, [is] supported by this space governed by sympathy and antipathy, which are ceaselessly drawing things together and holding them apart. By means of this interplay, the world remains identical; resemblances continue to be what they are, and to resemble one another. The same remains the same, riveted onto itself.[67]

Despite being ostensibly an hermetically sealed system, the harmonious play of opposites resolved into identities so poetically depicted by Foucault, is nevertheless vulnerable to the imperative that 'buried similitudes must be indicated on the surface of things; there must be visible marks for the invisible analogies'.[68] In short, the world of resemblances requires signatures, signs, inscriptions, special marks which indicate the various similitudes. Foucault concedes that although the sign is yet *another* kind of resemblance, it does not stand in a relation of homology with that which it purports to denote. Instead there is, inevitably, evident in the operation of this sixteenth century system of resemblances a process of slippage, a 'tiny degree of displacement which causes the sign of sympathy to reside in an analogy, that of analogy in emulation, that of emulation in convenience, which in turn requires the mark of sympathy for its recognition'.[69]

The discovery of resemblances could only occur by an agreed process of making such marks or signs 'speak', and Foucault defines the totality of learning and skills entailed in such a process as *hermeneutics*. By extension, skills involved in locating signs, finding out what constitutes them, and how they are linked are labeled under the rubric of *semiology*. In short, for Foucault, in the sixteenth century *episteme* (overall world view), hermeneutics and semiology converged in the form of similitude. But it seems that the 'tiny' displacement between the two grids when superimposed on one another, coupled with the sheer stasis or 'poverty-stricken' nature of knowledge ultimately allowed language (or more specifically, writing) to overwhelm and destabilize the system of resemblances, paving the way for the advent of the age of representation.[70]

The need for brevity dictates that we curtail any further (already significantly abridged) tracing of the minutiae of Foucault's argument, which for illustrative purposes has been undertaken above. From now, it will suffice to summarize the elements of chapters of *The Order of Things* most germane to this discussion.

Firstly, it is perhaps possible to say that out of the slight disjunction between interpretation (*hermeneutics*) and signification (*semiology*) in the late sixteenth and early seventeenth centuries language was 'set free'—released from a system which, eternally folding back on itself through the play of resemblances, could only ever be identical with itself.

Secondly, this 'liberation' of language was borne of, (and indeed contributed to) the proliferation of interpretation in the form of the commentary—that is, language *about* language. As Montaigne put it: 'There is more work in interpreting interpretations, than in interpreting things.'[71]

Thirdly, in the seventeenth century, the arrangement of signs became binary. Prior to this was a ternary (tripartite) system wherein the signifier and signified were linked in verisimilitude by the 'conjuncture', that quality of resemblance existing 'behind' the visible mark.[72] This binarization of the sign indicated the final severing of the link between things and words, and necessitated an analysis of *representation* in place of the notion of resemblance. And so it was, according to Foucault, that from the early seventeenth century onwards, all language came to have value 'only as discourse'.[73]

Finally, it can be said that just as interpretation was essential to the Renaissance era, the notion of *order* was the defining feature of the Classical (eighteenth century) period.[74] In the classical age the sign was employed not as a confirmation of resemblance, but rather in the service of confirming the efficaciousness of empirical knowledge. Three features of the sign became evident. Firstly, that it located its area of relevance within knowledge.[75] Secondly, that it became characterized by its 'essential dispersion',[76] and finally, that it could be either given by nature or established by convention.[77]

Despite the ostensible binarization of the sign, when considered more closely, there *appears* to be a third element in operation in the new regime of signification, and that is the very idea of the *representative power* of the signifying idea itself. This indicates 'an inevitable displacement within the two- term figure, which moves backward in relation to itself and comes to reside entirely within the signifying element'.[78] This can be represented in the following way:

idea signified   signifying idea

                      the supplementary
                      idea of the signifying idea's
                      role as representation

Another way of putting this is to say that just as in the sixteenth century, in the new order of knowledge in the seventeenth century, 'hermeneutics' and 'semiology' remained superimposed, but they were no longer joined or mediated by the element of resemblance—rather, in 'their connection in that power proper to representation, of representing itself'.[79]

This over-weighting on the side of the signifier and its imagined power to represent, coupled with the impetus to *order* things via the advent of the table, which emerged in the seventeenth century, leads Foucault to posit that 'the table of the signs will be the *image* of things'.[80] The emergence of a 'pure science of signs',[81] enables the development of abstract theories of value and exchange, as well as ideology, culminating, according to Foucault, in Saussure's 'rediscovery' of the seventeenth century project of a general semiology which allowed the 'psychologistic' linking of a concept with an image.[82] These developments notwithstanding, Foucault is forced to concede that although similitude no longer figures directly in the construction of knowledge, it is nevertheless an 'indispensable border of knowledge': in the overdetermined representational power of the signified, resemblance is not completely done away with; rather, it is displaced, and comes to be 'imagined'.[83] This 'shadow of signification' which itself signified the representative power of the signifier, could perhaps be said to form the basis of the privileging of the signifier in the modern/postmodern semiotic milieu or 'order of things'. This of course has big implications for our understanding of the development of the simulacrum in cultural modernity in general.

Deleuze: Plato's Simulacrum and Nietzsche's ' Eternal Return'

If Foucault could be said to have charted the 'liberation' of the sign in the shift from resemblance to representation in the pre-modern period, and thus identified a form of signification which, by its very structure, is highly simulacral (or readily lends itself to this characterization), then it is the task of yet another of 'Nietzsche's interpreters' to link Plato and Nietzsche's insights on the nature of the simulacrum from another standpoint—that of identity and repetition. Before rounding off this outline of the theory of the simulacrum with a consideration of Baudrillard, we will briefly consider Deleuze's approach, which links Nietzsche's notion of 'eternal return' with ideas arising out of Plato's treatment of the *phantasma* in the *Sophist.*

The latter comprises the second part of Plato's trilogy of dialogues *The Being of the Beautiful,* and is antecedent but complementary to the *Statesman* in it's attempts to juxtapose the sophist (in the same way as the statesman is positioned) vis-à-vis the true or real philosopher. As in other of Plato's dialogues, the structured dialectical play of the positions put, acceded to or opposed, yields as much—if not more—meaningful insight into the ostensible theme(s) of the discussion.   In *The Sophist,* not only is the term *phantasma* (simulacrum) commonly employed, but also the play of position and counter position, a discourse of phantastics itself, is meant to demonstrate, according to Benardete, the ultimate triumph of being and true speech in the weaving of the philosopher's art. If, for Benardete, the *Sophist* is a riddle, then Plato gestures towards its key by implicitly asserting identity as the ground of truth:

> Platonic Phantastics is the art of making thinking manifest and therefore immanifest, but thinking is the soul's silent conversation with itself as question and answer. To know how phantastics is possible, is to know how thinking is possible, in which the soul is the same as itself when it is other and other when it is the same.[84]

Deleuze, however, senses another kind of riddle in Plato's the *Sophist*: that in providing an answer to itself, it actually deconstructs itself—in other words, it contains its own 'anti-Platonic' stance.[85] Just as we saw in the *Statesman*, that the city vindicates itself, ironically, via that which can never be true in order to ensure its ongoing truth (or existence) through the operation of a simulacral web of the *techne* of politics, so too, according to Deleuze, the *Sophist* ends on a note which hints at the inevitable triumph of the simulacrum: 'The sophist is . . . the one who raises everything to the level of simulacra and maintains them in that state'.[86] The vexed questions of being and non-being, and true versus false speech at the heart of the *Sophist*, are in Deleuze's view indicative of a glaring irony in Platonic thought which works to overturn the distinction usually taken to be at the very foundation of Platonism—that is, the distinction between the 'thing in itself' and the simulacra.[87]

This 'deconstructive' move on the part of Deleuze is hardly surprising, since he is attempting to characterize Nietzsche's theory of the eternal return as a theory of the simulacrum, and he needs to re-cast the notion of difference in a way which has nothing to do with dichotomous forms which privilege identity as 'truth';

> Overturning Platonism . . . means denying the primacy of original over copy, of model over image; glorifying the reign of simulacra.[88]

Having acknowledged that nowhere does Nietzsche attempt an 'exposition' of his notion of eternal return,[89] Deleuze nevertheless ventures his own:

> Taken in its strict sense, eternal return means that each thing exists only in returning, copy of an infinity of copies which allows neither original nor origin to subsist. That is why the eternal return is called 'parodic': it qualifies as simulacrum that which it causes to be (and return).[90]

In order to now make the connection between Plato, Nietzsche and Foucault's insights, it is worth quoting at some length from Deleuze:

> When eternal return is the power of (formless) Being, the simulacrum is the true character or form—the 'being' of that which is. When the identity of things dissolves, being escapes to attain univocity, and begins to revolve around the different. That which is or returns has no prior constituted identity: things are reduced to the difference which fragments them . . . . In this sense, the simulacrum and the symbol are one; in other words, the simulacrum is the sign in so far as the sign interiorises the conditions of its own repetition. The simulacrum seizes upon a constituent disparity in the thing from which it strips the rank of model.[91]

In this interpretation, the eternal return is a process of ungrounding, in that it undermines the grounds which might function as instances of difference between things and their simulacra. Foucault's 'displacement' in the representational process, resonates with Deleuze's 'disparity' in the simulacral process—but it is only the simulacrum, as 'pure presence', which fully draws attention to its own disparate nature. Deleuze is adamant that Plato was wrong to relegate the sophist to the level of contradiction or chaos solely because the latter relied on simulacra, and by implication falsehood, for his art.[92] On the contrary, in the Nietzschean scheme, simulacra are the only true things: 'simulacra are the superior forms, and the difficulty facing everything is to become its own simulacrum, to attain the status of a sign in the coherence of eternal return.'[93] It seems that this recognition of simulacra as the only 'true' things—that is, the only things that we have access to—is to accept signification as a totally arbitrary and unstable process, and to revel in the interminable dance of the perspectival.

The key term here is 'sign', and as Foucault recognizes, signs refer only to themselves and to other signs in the semiotic constellation of all cultural practices, thus functioning to deprive the 'thing in itself' of any form of self-referential certainty. Putting together the insights of Plato, Nietzsche, Foucalt and Deleuze, we have arrived, conceptually, at the description of a circular movement. Furthermore, we are prompted to ask: to what extent would such a movement itself signify, as it were, the range of possible modes of being and representation so far imaginable in the emergence of human cultures?

Summing up, we have seen how Plato's own dialectics assert the triumph of identity, and relegate the simulacrum to a second order semiological functioning which although not 'true' in itself, is the inevitable tool of 'statesmen' and 'sophists' in the discourse of phantastics which characterize the city. Further, it has been shown that the simulacrum is also the *sine qua non* of the discursive space or 'panoptic imaginary' of the post-industrial city. Finally, it has been suggested that Nietzsche, and 'his interpreters' Foucault and Deleuze, have in mind a characterization of the simulacrum as an indispensable feature and condition of language which comes to light under particular discursive conditions (for Foucault, in the shift from resemblance to representation) and underpins a more general theory of signification (Deleuze's reading of Plato and Nietzsche). What remains now is to examine the notion of the simulacrum from a 'non-structuralist' perspective, and to ask how (if at all), in the Baudrillardian scheme of things, the simulacrum might emerge as the triumphant figure of modernity's disclosure to itself.

Baudrillard: Beyond Representation or, The Sign as its Own Simulacrum

Whether to read Baudrillard's work as science fiction or social theory, as pata-
physics or metaphysics, is undecidable.

Douglas Kellner[94]

The discussion so far has proceeded partly on the implicit assumption that there
exists a generally agreed, relatively stable definition of the simulacrum which
could be universally applied to all cultural and historical contexts. While we can
say that the term, as a translation of Plato's *phantasma,* has a range of connotations suggestive of the sense of an image or copy of 'the real', from the standpoint of modernity (as the writings of Nietzsche, Foucault and Deleuze attest)
the *operation* of the simulacrum is more or less transparent, more or less significant, depending upon the particular *episteme* ('world view') within whose discursive limits it may function and indeed prescribe.

The polysemy and analytical efficacy of the term is perhaps no more evident
than in the multiple dimensions of its deployment in the celebrated (sometimes
reviled) writings of the contemporary 'king' of the simulacrum, Jean Baudrillard. Unfortunately, however, in the context of the terminology of the postmodern, it has perhaps lost much of its explanatory power and according to Robins,
now functions largely as a cliché.[95] Ironically, if the postmodern is about the
play of surfaces, then as Kellner reminds us, the critique of Baudrillard's work
itself often falls short of rigorous and incisive analysis: 'many studies of Baudrillard have themselves skimmed the surface of Baudrillard's texts, failing to
interrogate their use and abuse, or the contributions and limitations of his writings'.[96]

In the hope of avoiding such superficial treatment of Baudrillard's contribution to social theory, the ideas and concerns of his writing will be utilized here in
their broadest possible application, as constituting an important and original
approach to the thorny issues of mediation, representation and reference within
the post-industrial cultural milieu. Specifically, a broadly defined theory of the
simulacrum incorporating Baudrillard's contribution to the topic will be indispensable in rigorously interrogating the conditions of its functioning within contemporary Japanese culture. This, in turn, will be crucial to demonstrating a
form of simulacral process as pivotal to Murakami's writing in the two trilogies.

Because of the very eclecticism of Baudrillard's concerns, the entire corpus of
his writings, ranging from *The System of Objects* to later writings, can be relevant to our analysis.[97] *The System of Objects,* for example, will help elucidate the
status of the commodity and fetish, and the elaboration of 'atmosphere' (within a
frame of 'systems of reference')—especially in Murakami's earlier writing,
while his ideas on science fiction as simulacrum[98] relate usefully to the multiple-
world narratives of the later trilogy. And the attempt to 'return to history' in

Nejimakidori kuronikuru (*The Wind-Up Bird Chronicle*) and *Andâguraundo* (*Underground*) will be more clearly understood via Baudrillard's notion that the 'simulation of history', in the words of William Bogard 'is exactly what confirms the irreversability of history's disappearance and the impossibility of a genuine return.'[99] In short, Baudrillard's work is shot through with the idea of the simulacrum—even when the term itself is not specifically mentioned.

To this end, it would be useful to extend the use of the term in Baudrillard's writing to give it almost the status of a sign in its own right—or perhaps suggest that much of what passes for contemporary postmodern theory does so under the signifying sway of the 'sign' of the simulacrum. At the very least, it is certainly a highly evocative figure, a trope, which like Nietzsche's 'eternal return', if properly understood, can form the basis of a systematic historical-social as well as metaphysical way of viewing the world.

Furthermore, it is fair to claim that the term simulacrum is not just another item in the unfolding glossary of descriptive categories of the Baudrillardian trajectory of radical social theory, but the very style and hyperbole of Baudrillard's writing is, in a sense, analogous to the discourse of phantastics woven by Plato's sophist, which importantly draws attention to its own function as artful artifice (albeit with very different consequences for a theory of referentiality). Zurbrugg insists that 'Baudrillard commands attention in terms of his rhetorical excess—in terms of the register—rather than the substance, of his patter.'[100]

Undoubtedly, positioning Baudrillard's writing vis-à-vis other forms of radical social theory is highly problematic. His urging to 'forget Foucault' and his critique of French Feminism cast him as somewhat of a theoretical terrorist.[101] And if we were looking for a connection with Deleuze, for example, we might imagine that Baudrillard's later notion of 'seduction'[102] which emphasized reversibility and play, might correspond with Deleuze's reworking of Nietzsche's 'eternal return'. Any such perceived relation would appear to be largely superficial, since Baudrillard's attack on Deleuze seemed very much part of a larger effort to carve out his own discourse and territory in radical social critique that operated outside the domination of the neo-Marxist/Freudian/Structuralist perspectives of post-war French social theory,[103] even though his debt to Foucault's thought should not be underestimated.[104]

It is important, therefore, to emphasize from the outset that Baudrillard's central thesis about our changed relation to the real is much more than just a timely and fashionable foray into, and valorization of, fantasies of hyperreality to be expected of cultural practices so deeply embedded in the modalities of electronic technologies. Rather, it insists that our relation to the real has been fundamentally altered by such developments to the extent that a comprehensive rethinking of the question is not only called for—it is indeed, well and truly under way.

Although various of Baudrillard's writings will be referred to throughout the subsequent discussion, of more immediate concern in this comparative introduction to the theory of the simulacrum is the notion that its historical appearance or functioning has been comprised of three distinct dimensions or 'orders'. In a lesser known essay published in the journal *Science Fiction Studies*, Baudrillard restates his three orders of simulacra (originally outlined in his work *Simulations*), with a view to relating them to the genre of science fiction.[105] The first order of *'natural or naturalistic simulacra'* are concerned with image or imitation. The second order of *'productive or productionist simulacra'* is based on energy and force and embodied in the machine and the assumption of limitless expansion and growth. *'Simulation simulacra'* constitute the third order, which utilizes information and the cybernetic system, and whose ideal state is 'maximum operationality, hyperreality, total control.[106]

Interestingly, where we might expect that the genre of science fiction would correlate with the third order, according to Baudrillard it actually fits in with the second order of productionist simulacra. He explains this by pointing out that the notions of 'the real' and 'the imaginary' require, above all, a sense of 'distance'. In the utopian, transcendent world, such distance is at its greatest 'and the separation from the real world is maximal'. It is implied that the utopian imaginary belongs to the first order which is 'harmonious' and 'optimistic'. Such distance, however, is significantly diminished in the world proposed by science fiction, which is certainly a *projection of* but is not qualitatively different from the real world of production. Baudrillard is led to conclude that with the triumphant advent of the third order of simulacra we are dealing with a purely self-referential model of the real:

> Models no longer constitute an imaginary domain with reference to the real; they are, themselves, an apprehension of the real, and thus leave no room for any fictional extrapolation—they are immanent and therefore leave no room for any kind of transcendentalism.[107]

In this view, the traditional genre of science fiction inevitably gives way to a form wherein the distance between the imaginary and the real totally collapses, and each aspect effectively cancels out the other. Baudrillard is in fact arguing for a kind of reversal or reversion wherein 'it is the real which has become the pretext of the model'.[108] This 'death of fiction' in the literary context can be understood in another way as the model surpassing the original. Or, as Baudrillard illustrates by way of reference to a Borges story, analogous to a situation where cartographers draw an imperial map so perfectly that it covers the entire territory it is supposed to represent. Interestingly, such a map would be confined to the second order of productionist simulacra, since it would eventually become frayed and imperfect. The hyperreal version of the map would be however, subject to no such constraint—indeed it would dispense altogether with its referent: 'the territory no longer precedes the map, nor survives it. Henceforth it is the map that precedes the territory—*precession of simulacra*'.[109]

A compelling example of the direct application of the third order of simulacra to the critique of a literary text, is Baudrillard's analysis of J. G. Ballard's cyber-sexual novel, *Crash*, wherein the 'nonsensicalness, the brutality of this mixture of body and technology is totally immanent—it is the reversion of one into the other'.[110] In another literary application, Willcox describes Don DeLillo's *White Noise* as a 'grimly satiric allegory of the crisis of the sign in the order of the simulacrum'.[111] Both of these analyses point to the efficacy of Baudrillard's 'third order' as a key to approaching difficult questions about the status of fiction in 'postmodern' cultural contexts.

However, in conclusion it must be stated that while the notion of third order or 'simulation simulacra' will prove to be a useful analytical tool in the analysis which follows, as Schoonmaker suggests, it is by no means without its short-comings. She points out that the advent of the digital, (which typifies Baudrillard's third order) masks an order which is still fundamentally driven by a process of *production* (vis-à-vis purely 'symbolic' exchange)—it is just that this happens now within an altered, that is to say 'global' context.[112] This view is reinforced by Ruthrof's analysis which shows that the digital still requires an ultimate referent—that of international capital.[113]

Another problem with Baudrillard's third order: the risk of valorising the sign or the notion of sign value in an overly deterministic reading of Marx's notion of exchange value (or indeed other theories of value). Such foregrounding of the digital or binary code as the current dominant form of signification disallows the deployment of any historical referentiality in actual contemporary critical practices. While recognizing, therefore, some theoretical shortcomings, the subsequent discussion finds much in Baudrillar's thought which is useful, while at the same time, situating his important insights within a broader critical context.

A Syncretic Theory of the Simulacrum?

Kellner argues for an underlying continuity in Baudrillard's work, indicating a concern with a kind of 'metaphysical imaginary' (vis-à-vis a 'political imaginary' or 'imaginary of social theory and critique').[114] It is the possibility of such continuity in an extremely wide-ranging body of writings which suggests, first of all, that the simulacrum as an explanatory principle coheres at the interstices of multiple perspectives on the problem of representation and the real. Secondly, and perhaps more indirectly, it confirms that any one version of the simulacrum should not be valorized to the extent that it occludes or negates other valuable insights and approaches.

In other words, and more specifically, we need Plato's insights for setting the terms of the dialectical opposition of the 'thing in itself' and its modes of representation, as a fundamentally political question arising from the myriad processes of classifying, ordering and controlling men (sic) and things in the discursive space of the city. Equally, we require Nietzsche's revolutionary modernist critique of the Platonic (or, more accurately, Aristotlean) enterprise as an over-turning or 'ungrounding' of the being of truth as identity in favor of the differ-ence of difference. Foucault's 'archeological' approach functions to continually refine a prismatic view of the nexus between the particular sign and its universal semiological matrices, in a way which emphasizes the relative, unstable and *diachronic* dimensions of knowledge and the *episteme*. Deleuze's re-reading of Plato in the light of Nietzsche greatly enriches the explanatory power of the simulacrum, while Baudrillard provides a provocative and compelling running commentary on the simulacral embedding of a destabilized referentiality at the core of post-industrial societies.

Given the above, it is clear that a syncretic concept of the simulacrum would enable the richest possible array of readings of specific cultural forms, and that *ipso facto*, the over reliance on any one version would be all the less fruitful an exercise. Having acknowledged this, we can bring to a close this brief discussion of the theory of the simulacrum by suggesting that perhaps the most useful way of approaching Baudrillard's three orders would be to argue for some transi-tional place in between the second and third orders which would then raise the question as to where the simulacrum stands in relation to the moder-nity/postmodernity debate discussed in the previous chapter.

We are lead to pose the question: might it be that in between the 'productionist simulacra' of the modern, and the 'simulation simulacra' of the postmodern, lies a semantic displacement or 'slippage' which is neither fully apparent to our analysis of contemporary cultural practices (simply because we are too inti-mately entangled in them), or completely exhausted in its potential to offer new ways of constructing the real, which are, as yet unimaginable? How we might respond to such a question would, in an important sense, determine our view of Murakami's narratives of the simulacrum as either radical and prophetic social critique—or, the mere 'simulation' of already simulated orders of repre-sentation. Our answer to this question will emerge, in various forms, throughout the discussion which follows.

Notes

1. See Jean Baudrillard, "Simulacra and Science Fiction," *Science Fiction Studies* 18 (1991): 311.

2. See Murakami Haruki, *Andâguraundo* (Kôdansha, 1997), 16. These comments are taken from the Forward to this anthology of interviews personally conducted by Mura-kami with victims of the 1995 Tokyo Subway Sarin-gas attack. He was originally moti-vated to undertake the interviews after being moved by a letter appearing in a women's magazine, written by the wife of a victim of the attack (*Andâguraundo*, pp.14-15). Ac-cording to Murakami, the young salaried office worker had suffered the 'double vio-lence' (*nijû no bôryoku*) of having been exposed to the poisonous Sarin fumes, and then

subsequently being hounded from his job by superiors and colleagues who had little empathy for his inability to quickly return to normal duties. Interestingly, Murakami sees both forms of violence as springing from the 'normal world' (*seijô na sekai*). The comment is included here because it highlights the persistence of the tendency to divide 'the world' (*sekai*) along binary lines into the real, normal and everyday vis-à-vis the fantastic, unusual or aberrant—even within the representational limits made available by the increasingly 'hyperreal' and simulacral conditions of contemporary Japanese culture. Such divisions, it can be argued, bear little relevance to those dimensions of production, consumption and desire, technologically managed by the discourses of instrumental reason in the Japanese corporatist state.

3. The debate centered around such issues as to what extent the address would constitute an 'apology' for Japanese wartime aggression, and indeed whether Japan had actually undertaken acts of 'invasion'(*shinryaku*).

4. This claim is comprehensively discussed in Chapters 8, 9 &10.

5. This applies especially to the first two novels in the so-called 'Rat Trilogy': *Kaze no uta o kike* (*Hear the Wind Sing*) and *1973 nen no pinbôru* (*Pinball, 1973*).

6. The term 'informatics' and other related terms will be discussed later in this chapter.

7. As will be suggested later, Baudrillard's importance may well may lie in his manner rather than his method; his rhetorical style than his 'content'.

8. See, for example, the kind of popular definition offered in Richard Appignanesi & Chris Garrat, *Postmodernism for Beginners* (Cambridge: Icon Books, 1995), 54.

9. See Sakai, *Voices of the Past*.

10. It is worth noting here that Sakai staunchly defends the use of Western theory to analyze 'non-Western objects', and does so as a vigorous opponent of the closure spawned by what he terms 'cultural particularism'. See Sakai, *Voices of the Past*, 1-19.

11. This will become evident in the discussion of Plato's the *Sophist* and the *Statesman*, below.

12. See Oxford English Dictionary, (Oxford: Clarendon Press, 1933) Vol.15. p.502.

13. Baudrillard's view of the simulacrum is of course not limited to the context of the post-industrial and 'simulation simulacrum'. The latter indicates only the most recent development in the orders of simulacra which will be outlined later.

14. The *Statesman*, III.119 See Stanley Rosen, *Plato's 'Statesman': The Web of Politics* (New Haven and London: Yale University Press, 1995).

15. It should not be assumed, however, that the modern Japanese city cannot be approached through the prism of early Greek philosophy. To begin with, the modern Japanese city (in the post-Edo/Tokugawa era) displays all the signs of systems of rational, instrumental control, organization, cybernetic structuring and surveillance common to any post-industrial metropolis (in Bogard's terms, discussed later, it is both 'informatic' and 'telematic' in nature).

16. Rosen, *Plato's 'Statesman,'* 11. Here *phronesis* is also rendered as 'practical intelligence'.

17. 'The Web of Politics' is in fact the title of Rosen's critique of the *Statesman*.

18. Rosen, *Plato's 'Statesman'*, 169.

19. Rosen, *Plato's 'Statesman'*, 169.

20. Quoted from Plato, the *Statesman*, III. 39.

21. Quoted from Plato, the *Statesman*, III. 39.

22. Rosen, *Plato's 'Statesman'*, 168.

23. Quoted from Plato, the *Statesman*, III. 122.

24. Rosen, *Plato's 'Statesman'*, 190.

25. Kevin Robins, *Into the Image: Culture and Politics in the Field of Vision* (London and New York: Routledge, 1996), 129.

26. Yoshida notes the highly 'visual' or 'imagistic' nature of scenes in Murakami's novels, and relates them specifically to Western movies such as *Flashdance* and *2001 Space Odyssey*. See Yoshida Haruo, *Murakami Haruki: tenkan suru* (Sairyûsha, 1997), 7.

27. Ivy, *Discourses of the Vanishing*, 206.

28. Although, as Ivy points out elsewhere, this binary opposition still strongly informs the myth of 'home-town-ism'; see her analysis of the 'Discover Japan' campaigns, *Discourses of the Vanishing*, 34-40.

29. Ivy, *Discourses of the Vanishing*, 206.

30. See Ishikawa Masahiko (text) and Umaba Maki, in '"Afutâ dâku" o Meguro bôken', in 'Murakami Haruki—Atarashî kibô no bôken', *Aera*, no.4 (October 2004): 40-45.

31. Karatani, *Origins of Modern Japanese Literature*.

32. This article and its central claims will be discussed in later chapters.

33. Karatani, *Origins of Modern Japanese Literature*, 65-72.

34. William Bogard, *The Simulation of Surveillance: Hypercontrol in Telematic Societies* (Cambridge: Cambridge University Press, 1997), 5.

35. Bogard, *The Simulation of Surveillance*, 9. Bogard defines 'telematic' from the Greek word for 'distant'.

36. Bogard, *The Simulation of Surveillance*, 9.

37. Bogard, *The Simulation of Surveillance*, 19.

38. Bogard, *The Simulation of Surveillance*, 10.

39. Bogard, *The Simulation of Surveillance*, 10.

40. Bogard, *The Simulation of Surveillance*, 10.

41. Bogard, *The Simulation of Surveillance*, 8.

42. Mumford quoted in Robins, *Into the Image*, 130.

43. Robins, *Into the Image*, 130.

44. Robins, *Into the Image*, 131.

45. See Tessa Morris-Suzuki, *Beyond Computopia: Information, Automation and Democracy in Japan* (London & New York: Kegan Paul International, 1988), 8. This latter term is closely linked to the notion of *jôhôshakai* ('information society'), and is used to characterize Japanese technocrats' utopia described as 'a society with highly intellectual creativity where people may draw future designs on an invisible canvas and pursue and realize individual lives worth living'. See *The Plan for an Information Society: A National Goal Towards Year 2000*, English translation published in *Change* (July-Aug. 1972), 31. It is remarkable how closely this fits Baudrillard's notion of sketching a simulacral form, and then 'filling' it in with the contours of the real.

46. Robins, *Into the Image*, 134.

47. Robins, *Into the Image*, 134.

48. Timothy Druckrey "Introduction: Cultures on the Brink," in *Cultures on the Brink: Ideologies of Technology at the End of the Century*, ed. Gretchen Bender and Timothy Druckery (Seattle: Bay Press, 1994), 9.

49. Heidegger uses the term 'enframing' in his essay *The Question Concerning Technology*, to be discussed in Chapter 5.

50. The quote is from Nietzsche's *Gay Science*, cited by Arthur Danto, "Nietzsche's Perspectivism" in *Nietzsche: A Collection of Critical Essays*, ed. Robert C. Solomon (New York: Anchor Books, 1973), 46.

51. Horst Ruthrof, *Pandora and Occam: On the Limits of Language and Literature* (Bloomington and Indianapolis: Indiana University Press, 1992), 9.

52. Nietzsche writes: 'What then is truth? A mobile army of metaphors, metonymies, anthropomorphisms: in short, a sum of human relations which become poetically and rhetorically intensified.' See "On Truth and Falsity in their Ultramoral Sense," in *Complete Works of Nietzsche*, ed. D. Levy (London & Edinburgh) Vol. 2, p.180.

53. Friedrich Nietzsche, "The Use & Abuse of History," in *Thoughts Out of Season: Part II,* trans. Adrian Collins (Edinburgh: T.N. Foulis, 1909), 75-76.

54. Danto, "Nietzsche's Perspectivism," 37.

55. Danto, "Nietzsche's Perspectivism," 33 -35.

56. Friedrich Nietzsche, *Beyond Good and Evil*, trans. Walter Kaufmann (New York: Vintage Books, 1966), 23.

57. Danto, "Nietzsche's Perspectivism," p. 55. The quote is from *The Gay Science.*

58. Hayden White, "Michel Foucault," in John Stuirrock, ed., *Structuralism and Since,* (Oxford: Oxford University Press, 1984), 81.

59. Nietzsche writes, 'The most concerned ask today: '"How is man to be preserved?" But Zarathustra is the first and only one to ask: "How is man to be overcome?"'. See "On the Higher Man," in *Thus Spoke Zarathustra*, trans. Walter Kaufmann (New York: Penguin, 1980), 287.

60. Both Nietzsche and Foucault agree that the designation 'man' has not been an historical given, but is a relatively recent invention which either had to be 'overcome' (Nietzsche), or indeed according to Foucault, was capable of receding just as quickly as it had appeared.

61. For a simple yet lucid definition of the Foucault's sense of the term 'discourse', See McHoul et.al. *A Foucault Primer,* 31-35.

62. This analysis is undertaken in Chapters 2 and 3 of *The Order of Things*. See Michel Foucault, *The Order of Things: An Archeology of the Human Sciences* (London: Tavistock, 1970).

63. Foucault, *The Order of Things,* 17.

64. Foucault, *The Order of Things,* 18-19.

65. Foucault, *The Order of Things,* 19-20.

66. Foucault, *The Order of Things,* 21-23.

67. Foucault, *The Order of Things,* 25.

68. Foucault, *The Order of Things,* 26.

69. Foucault, *The Order of Things,* 29.

70. Foucault, *The Order of Things,* 30.

71. Montaigne, quoted from Foucault, *The Order of Things,* 40. We can naturally sense, in the notion of interpretation, the operation of the simulacrum, and are reminded that even at this by now thoroughly naturalized level of 'second order' discourse, the processes of reflection and projection at the heart of the commentary, problematize the status of the 'original' work vis-à-vis its image.

72. Foucault, *The Order of Things,* 64. In other words, the three distinct elements of the sign were: 'that which was marked, that which did the marking, and that which made it possible to see in the first the mark of the second'.

73. Foucault, *The Order of Things,* 42-43.

74. Foucault, *The Order of Things*, 57.

75. Foucault, *The Order of Things*, 59.

76. Foucault, *The Order of Things*, 60.

77. Foucault, *The Order of Things*, 61.

78. Foucault, *The Order of Things*, 64.

79. Foucault, *The Order of Things*, 66

80. Foucault, *The Order of Things*, 66

81. Foucault, *The Order of Things*, 67.

82. Foucault, *The Order of Things*, 67

83. Foucault, *The Order of Things*; see section five in Chapter Three: "The Imagination of Resemblance".

84. The *Sophist*, II.112; see Seth Benardete, *Plato's Sophist: Part II of the Being of the Beautiful* (Chicago and London: The University of Chicago Press, 1986).

85. See Gilles Deleuze, *Difference and Repetition,* trans. Paul Patton (London: The Athlone Press, 1994), 126. Deleuze writes that Nietzsche's notion of 'eternal return' is the 'touchstone of Platonism and anti-Platonism'.

86. Deleuze, *Difference and Repetition,* 68.

87. Deleuze, *Difference and Repetition,* 66.

88. Deleuze, *Difference and Repetition,* 66.

89. Deleuze, *Difference and Repetition,* 297.

90. Deleuze, *Difference and Repetition,* 66-67. Here Deleuze is referring to views put forward by Pierre Klossowski.

91. Deleuze, *Difference and Repetition,* 67.

92. Deleuze, *Difference and Repetition,* 68.

93. Deleuze, *Difference and Repetition,* 67.

94. Douglas Kellner, "Introduction," in *Baudrillard: A Critical Reader*, ed. Douglas Kellner (Oxford: Blackwell Publishers, 1994), 18.

95. See Robins, *Into the Image*, 44: 'We are already more than familiar with Jean Baudrillard's descriptions of simulacra and simulations, of a deterritorialized hyperreality, of images or models of a real without origin or reality. The idea has slipped almost effortlessly into the discourse of postmodernism, and we have actually come to feel rather comfortable with our new condition of derealization'.

96. Kellner, "Introduction," in *Baudrillard: A Critical Reader* 3; 18. Kellner describes many critiques of Baudrillard as 'one-dimensional dismissals of his work'.

97. *The System of Objects* originally published in 1968 (and which has recently been re-published) is a semiotic analysis of commodity, consumption and desire, heavily influenced by a Barthean structuralist approach, but yields fresh insights when read in conjunction with more recent works, because it lays the ground for the analysis of the commodity/fetish/sign nexus.

98. See Baudrillard, "Simulacra and Science Fiction," *Science Fiction Studies* 18, (1991): 309-313.

99. See Bogard's essay in *Baudrillard: A Critical Reader*, 314.

100. See Zurbrugg's essay in *Baudrillard: A Critical Reader,* 228.

101. See Kellner, *Baudrillard: A Critical Reader*, 131, 143. Kellner refers to *Jean Baudrillard: From Marxism To Postmodernism and Beyond* (1989) and suggests that here Baudrillard claims, along with Freud, that there is only *one* sexuality, and that it is 'masculine'—as opposed to seduction, which is primarily 'feminine'.

102. Kellner, *Baudrillard: A Critical Reader*, 145. Kellner writes that for Baudrillard, 'seduction is precisely that which subverts fixed dualities between masculine and feminine and eludes definition and differentiation'.

103. Ironically, though, Baudrillard's early work drew heavily on such approaches for theoretical support.

104. In some instances, Baudrillard's attack on Foucault seems quite unjustified. It is clear, for example, that Baudrillard's notion of the orders of simulacrum relies heavily on Foucault's insights in *The Order of Things*.

105. Baudrillard, "Simulacra and science Fiction". Note that the three orders are originally outlined in "The Orders of Simulcra," in *Simulations*, trans. Paul Foss, et.al. (New York: Semiotext(e), 1983), 83-159.

106. Baudrillard, "Simulacra and science Fiction," 309.

107. Baudrillard, "Simulacra and science Fiction," 310.

108. Baudrillard, "Simulacra and science Fiction," 310.

109. See "Simulacra and Simulations," in *Baudrillard: Selected Writings*, ed. Mark Poster (Cambridge: Polity, 1988), 166.

110. See "Ballard's Crash" in *Science Fiction Studies* 18 (1991): 313-320. Also see Katherine Hayle's response to this essay in the same journal, pp. 321-323.

111. Leonard Wilcox, "Baudrillard, DeLillo's *White Noise* and the End of Heroic Narrative," *Contemporary Literature* 32, no. 3 (1991): 346-364.

112. Sara Schoonmaker "Capitalism and the Code: A Critique of Baudrillard's Third Order Simulacrum," in *Baudrillard: A Critical Reader*, ed. Douglas Kellner, 168-188; especially 179.

113. See Horst Ruthrof, "Narrative and the Digital: On the Syntax of the Postmodern," *AUMLA* 74 (November 1990): 185-200.

114. Kellner, *Baudrillard: A Critical Reader*, 152-53.

Chapter Four

Parody, Pastiche, Metafiction:
'Kaze no uta o kike'
(Hear the Wind Sing)

Murakami's first three novels (published in 1979, 1980 and 1982)[1] have been described as the 'Rat Trilogy'[2] because their common feature is the way in which they position the figure of Nezumi ('the Rat') in a dialogic way with the narrating first person character Boku ('I'). This textual relation is both dialogic at the level of represented speech acts in the narrative, as well as in a more metaphoric sense, with Nezumi as the narrator's imagined alter-ego or narrative foil in terms of narrated space, time and action, and finally as the projected phantasmal double of Boku's non-corporeal existence or subjectivity. Furthermore, the three texts can be said to constitute a narrative unity which has been bestowed, 'retrospectively', by critics who recognize that in these works Murakami establishes the structural, stylistic and thematic idiosyncrasies of his narrative endeavour writ large.

For the purposes of ensuring critical conciseness as well as aiding the expository flow of the argument, selections of authoritative[3] narrative synopses of each of these three texts will be presented. These will take the form of an abridged translation of the *kôgai* (outline, summary) of each novel presented by Ishikura Michiko et.al., in the *Murakami Haruki zenshôsetsu jiten* ('Encyclopedia of Murakami's Complete Narrative Works').[4]

These kinds of 'official' readings of the narrative outlines actually function as forms of critique in their own right, and for this reason can usefully be compared to the alternative versions offered in a range of critical texts. Such a view is based not only on the assumption that literary texts are inherently highly polysemic, but also that certain dominant critical orthodoxies are usually implied in their reading. In terms of reception, these synoptic versions also allow readers to 'sample the menu' by tasting the flavor of the narrative before 'filling in the details'[5] through retro-active reading practices. In this sense, they are akin to the 'hypertext' of the Internet site, which allows a sampling 'at random', and in an order not related to a conventionalized temporal or spatial narrative ordering, but rather to a meta-order signified by the subtitle of the 1998 special Murakami edition of *Kokubungaku* as *Hypâtekusoto—Murakami* ('Hypertext Murakami').

Narrative Synopsis (kôgai) of *Kaze no uta o kike*

(*Hear the Wind Sing*—hereafter referred to as *Kaze*.)

Facing the final year of his twenties, and while acknowledging the 'difficulty of writing', the narrator Boku ('I'), begins his story. The narrative of forty 'fragmentary' chapters (*danshô*)—which includes the biography of a 'fictional writer, a radio-studio setting, illustrations, and the translated lyrics of Western music—is woven into an 'eccentric' (*fûgawari na*) text which is set against a backdrop of summer in Japan, 1970. Boku is a third year student in a Tokyo university, who has returned to his hometown and spends time drinking beer with his friend Nezumi ('the Rat') in the bar run by a Chinese immigrant. One night he carries home a drunk young woman, and they have a fleeting relationship which leads to nothing. Nezumi, a university dropout, seems to want to communicate with the troubled Boku but somehow is unable to. The story is not a form of 'production' (*seisan*). Rather it is an attempt to relate a system as incommunicable as 'elephant training'.[6]

Critical Contexts of Murakami's Debut

In Japan in the 1980s modern literature seems to have died once and for all. All the concepts which had been dominant until that time—those of the 'inner-self', of 'meaning', of 'the writer', and of 'depth'—were rejected, while language, what had been subordinated to them, was set free.

Karatani Kôjin,
*The Origins of Modern Japanese
Literature*[7]

What I am able to set down here is merely a list—not a novel, not literature, not art.

The Narrator, *Kaze no uta o kike*[8]

Certainly 'eccentric' for its time, *Kaze* represented a radical experiment in structure and style when viewed against the prevailing paradigms of modern Japanese literary orthodoxy. The following discussion of various critical responses to this novel will attempt to demonstrate the efficacy of typifying Murakami's narrative style in terms of a simulacral rendering of a form of subjectivity which challenges the idea of 'the self' (*jiga*) in Japanese literary modernity. Furthermore, it will be suggested that this subversion of 'the self' has become inscribed within the representational limits of a new idiom, a new way of using language.[9]

Flying in the face of most of the central concerns of the modern Japanese novel (as Karatani notes: 'the inner self', 'meaning', 'the writer' and so on), from the outset, the narrator of *Kaze* seeks to establish an ironic metafictional position ('What I am able to set down here.').

This strategic move undermines the implicit senses of 'transparency' and 'sincerity' so paradigmatic of Japanese literary modernity, and which have so permeated the 'I-novel' (*shishôsetsu*) form. Murakami was at such pains to avoid the 'confessional'[10] format of the latter, that after first completing *Kaze* in a 'realistic' style, (and being so dissatisfied with the result) he rewrote it chapter by chapter.[11] In so doing, he forged a linguistic idiom which was to become an instantly recognizable hallmark of his writing, and, as will be argued here, simultaneously established the possibility of a 'doubled' structure or inscription of 'the self' in contemporary Japanese culture. In effect, this represented a critique of the late nineteenth century 'discovery' of 'self' and 'interiority' via the construction of 'exteriority' or 'landscape' (*fûkei*) (so convincingly elaborated by Karatani) whose epistemological corollary was purported to be a commitment to realism.[12]

Murakami's attempt at rewriting the Japanese fictional subject *via* the idiom of an earlier, inverted structure (that is, the initial elaboration through point-of-view, of 'realistic' vis-à-vis 'transcendental' perspectives and depictions of 'landscapes' or *fûkei)* originally employed by Kunikada Doppo, represents a 'double' inversion, because as Karatani has suggested elsewhere, Murakami's first two works are not novels but 'landscapes'.[13] This double inversion positions the narrative as 'twice removed' from the 'original' copy—and in this sense, suggests the kind of simulacral process explored by Deleuze (via Nietzsche) in his 'Difference and Repetition'. It also enables the 'freeing up of language', and thus new possibilities for meanings generated at the syntactic, syntagmatic level of narrative discourse.

If we accept both Karatani's and Murakami's claims (that Murakami himself wanted to *bypass* realism) as more or less valid, it seems rather ironic that Murakami wrote *Kaze* first in English[14] precisely *because* he wanted to avoid a lapse into the kind of realism/naturalism which was introduced to the Meiji pioneers of the modern novel[15] through their translations of Russian, French and English literature.[16]

But Murakami himself was very clear on this point: realistic description had outlived itself, and was no longer able to convey the sensibilities of the era in which his texts were to find astonishing acceptance and popularity. His insistence that 'any style is valid' was qualified by the claim that writing must fulfill three important conditions relating to style: firstly 'intelligibility', secondly 'self-expression' and finally, 'universality'.[17] While there is in fact plenty of 'realistic' writing in Murakami, it tends to construct reading positions which are not necessarily 'narrator' centered (and if there is a dominant point of view, it is often subject to a kind of instability, which tends to overrun the boundaries of the 'viewing/speaking' subject). The condition of 'universality' is addressed through a highly 'visual/cinematic' construction of 'mood' and 'atmosphere' in an urban context—powerfully evoked through the tropes of analogy/nostalgia/*déjà vu* (the 'as if' structure of other writers of the eighties

—Yoshimoto, Tanaka, Tachiwara) and also a kind of strictly followed deictic
code clearly related to the styles of certain American writers.[18] In the laying out
of a 'scene', he lets the objects speak for themselves in purely semiotic terms (as
signs for their own sake) the way in which, in Baudrillard's 'system of objects',
strategically placed objects determine the functional space and mythic meanings
of the domestic scene, where they are 'consumed' as signs.[19] Moreover, the 'object world' of Murakami's novels (to be discussed in more detail later) is intri-
cately related to the 'language world' which is carefully fashioned within the
parameters of typically defined speech acts.

Insofar as the writing in *Kaze* is a kind of 'false Japanese', a form of shadow
writing, it drags the tortuous equivocation of the self in the more orthodox Japanese modern novel into the stark light of a strange, yet refreshingly new idiom.
Ostensibly, it was because of its 'lightness' or *karuisa* (which seems to be the
most commonly appearing adjective of the critics' reviews) that Murakami's
writing drew attention to itself. Furthermore, the extent and the kind of challenge which Murakami's new writing threw down to the critics is evident in the
wide range of interpretative approaches it provoked. The debates surrounding
the question of how to approach and critique Murakami relate, not surprisingly,
to both issues of critical methodology[20] and questions of genre.[21]

This is confirmed, for example, by Tsuge's 1987 review of the development
and direction of Murakami criticism (*Murakami ron*) in its first seven or eight
years. The influence of American writers like Vonnegut was noted by critics
such as Marutani, and *Kaze* was given labels such as 'growing-up novel' (*seichô
shôsetsu*) by Kanno, 'youth novel' (*seishun shôsetsu*), and 'urban novel' (*toshi
shôsetsu*) by Kawamoto. Tsuge also noted the important contribution of critics
such as Maeda who attempted semiotic (*kigôron*) analyses within the broader
context of 'urban theory/studies' (*toshiron*).[22]

Significantly, however, this review of the state of and prospects for research
on Murakami, recognized the dearth of studies on language, (*kotoba, hyôgen*)
and more specifically, analysis of the represented speech acts (*jinbutsu no
kaiwa*) of the novels. It was also suggested that more attention needed to be
given to the author's expressed views on novel writing. More than eighteen
years later, it is clear that there has developed a marked sophistication and diver-
sification of Murakami criticism (*Murakami ron*), which could be said to have
addressed some of Tsuge's concerns regarding perceived gaps in the research.

This notwithstanding, there is no doubt that the field of Murakami criticism
displays a remarkable array of irreconcilable approaches. Clear evidence for this
can be found in Takeda Seiji's essay in the 1995 *Kokubungaku* special Murakami edition which draws attention to Katô and Kasai's earlier (1991) observation[23] that with the publication of the million-selling *Noruei no mori* (*Norwegian
Wood*), Murakami had become a 'problematic' writer.[24] In other words, as Takeda puts it, the view that the 'Murakami Phenomenon' symbolized the
contemporary 'conventionalization' (*fûzokuka*) of 'high literature' (*junbungaku*)
represented one side of a debate which tended to divide along the lines of

approval or disapproval of Murakami. The 'disapproval' (*tsuyoku hihan*) came from such renowned critics as Hasumi Shigehiko, Karatani Kôjin and Sengoku Hideo, while those who considered Murakami's writing as worthy of serious critical attention included well established critics such as Takeda himself and the co-participants in the discussion (*taiwa*) later published as *Murakami o meguru bôken*.[25]

Takeda has identified several keywords around which the 'disapproving' commentators have built their critiques of Murakami's writing: 'self-closure' (*jihei*), 'narrative' (*monogatari*), 'community' (*kyôdôtai*), 'refusal/rejection/denial' (*kyôhi*), 'escape/evasion of other people' (*tasha kara no tôhi*), and 'novelistic irony' (*roman-teki ironî*). Underlying what Takeda sees as these critics' 'ostentatious' arguments, lies a simple critical standard (*hihankijun*) which takes the form of the following question: 'In relation to the reality/circumstances of its epoch, to what extent has a particular literature been self-conscious (*jikaku-teki*), critical (*hihan-teki*) and oppositional (*taikô-teki*)?' Put another way, according to Takeda, in this view 'the value of a literary work can be reduced to its literary "socialness" (*shakaisei*)' — that is to say, its purely political dimensions.[26]

Takeda sees Murakami as re-asserting the primacy of the 'individual' vis-à-vis 'society', simply because, as he rightly recognizes, 'socialness' is always *already* a feature of literature. However, this does not necessarily make it the essential and *only* dimension of literature.[27] The foregrounding of the ideological/political approach had been the obvious tendency within the milieu of postwar Japanese democracy, but for Takeda, the emphasis on the social adopted by quasi or neo-Marxist critics of the so-called *shakaiha* ('socially concerned group') overshadowed more fundamental ethical and moral questions which universally arise in the transition from traditional to modern societies.[28] Therefore, according to Takeda, in Murakami's novels, social and human relations are not represented in 'real' form. Rather, from the perspective of the protagonist, the question of how experiences of 'romanticism', 'eroticism' and 'nostalgia' are to be 'restored' (*kangen sarereu*) in the face of modern rationalism and atheism is addressed. Significantly, for Takeda, in the world of the Murakami novel, it is the *conditions* (*jôken*) enabling/disabling these sensibilities which are examined within the larger context of a perceived loss of balance between 'lyricism' and 'cynicism'.[29]

Takeda's comments have been highlighted at some length here because they point to a fundamental feature of Murakami's highly ambivalent critique of orthodoxy; on the one hand, affirmation of the late-capitalist orthodoxies of consumption and the celebration of desire, and on the other, the almost complete ascendancy of systems of social control based on technology, information and irredeemably corrupt political practices. The significant insight of Takeda is to suggest that Murakami's narrative endeavours investigate the *conditions* for the recuperation (*kangen*) and experiencing of certain sensibilities. It is no mere coincidence that this kind of structure of nostalgia (in its many dimensions), lies at the heart of what Marilyn Ivy has called 'modernity's losses'.[30] It is in this context that the simulacral operation which establishes (however putatively) the conditions for the 'experiencing' of certain sensibilities is engaged through the act of reading the Murakami text.

The clear demarcation between 'self' and 'society' which had been the cornerstone of European modernity, may have always been such an artificial structure in Japan's experience of modernity that it could not be sustained—especially within a 'postmodern' literary milieu which, as Karatani acknowledges, has set language free and undermined many previous (and apparently self evident) modernist truths. Murakami's critique of orthodoxy is therefore a complex and ambivalent one, and this is no better demonstrated than in his debut work.

It is reasonable to assert that in the first wave of critical responses to *Kaze*—as well as in the continuing revision and development of these responses—can be identified a range of critical concerns which have relevance beyond that first work, extending to Murakami's entire novelistic oeuvre. For this reason, and because of the novelty and stylistic richness of the text itself, this chapter gives somewhat greater emphasis to *Kaze* in its capacity as a 'critique of orthodoxy' than is attributed to the second and third parts of the 'Rat Trilogy' in following chapters.

Well known as Murakami's debut work, *Kaze*, (awarded the *Gunzô* journal New Writers Award) was first published in serial form in that journal in 1979.[31] However, as Tazaki points out, because the literary/arts journal *Gunzô* was by no means a mass-circulation publication, *Kaze* staged a fairly modest debut as a well written 'youth novel' (*seishun shôsetsu*) and initially, at least, was certainly not a media sensation. Nevertheless, the ground-swell of interest in Murakami soon gathered momentum, and readers such as Tazaki joined the chorus of critics proclaiming that something very different (*mattaku ishitsu na mono*) had arrived on the literary scene.[32]

For the American translator, Alfred Birnbaum, who re-rendered *Kaze* into English for the Kôdansha English Library (as was noted above, *Kaze* was first written by Murakami himself in English!), the novel was hailed as 'a significant turning point'.[33] Birnbaum situated *Kaze* squarely within the context of the 'failed revolution' of the sixties, and noted that its debut took place at a time when, 'as always, the tired old faces of the Japanese literary world crowded the bookshelves'. Such writers had not necessarily set out to write 'I-novels' (*shishôsetsu*), but they inevitably wrote descriptions of their surrounding circumstances and events, or else individual and emotional reminiscences.

Significantly, for Birnbaum, Murakami appeared in the literary world amidst the dying stages of the *shishôsetsu* tradition: 'mostly overnight—and single handedly, Murakami Haruki brought about a revolutionary change in Japanese literature'. This, despite the fact that at first glance, Murakami's works appeared to conform to the traditional lineage, because in text-book like formulae the narrative was presented in the first person voice, and was all about an inglorious past: the failed student, alienated youth and dropout. Yet, it was not the 'content' but rather the *style* which really set *Kaze* apart: 'The dry wit of Boku, was fresh compared to the serious and grave Watashi.'[34] For Birnbaum, the 'influence' of Fitzgerald and Chandler was clearly evident in the various methods of sentence construction employed by Murakami: the modulation of 'tone' as well as the subject (*shugo*) and predicate (*jutsugo*), combined with the 'programming-in' (*kumikomu*) of everyday Japanese, helped create an eclectic or blended style.[35] Birnbaum acknowledges that Murakami's writing is 'easily translatable into English' (by this he presumably means contemporary American idiom), and his success lay in the fact that he 'knew the market and the current trends'.[36]

Because they represent the standard translations into English of several of Murakami's earlier novels, Birnbaum's translations (as well as his critical writings) stand in a peculiarly complicit relation to the Japanese texts themselves.[37] For example, in so far as *Kaze* was first written in English and then wrought into an ostensibly new Japanese idiom by Murakami, Birnbaum's translation is in one sense, almost redundant. This is because rather than being a translation, it is a kind of *transposition* ('transpose': cause two or more things to change places) of the language of the text into something approximating its 'original' format. The translator is ensuring its 'authentic' recasting into English—and very importantly, *American* English—for ready consumption in overseas markets. We see at this very immediate level of the re-presentation of the Murakami text, the evidence of a double figuration/movement which is clearly simulacral in nature. The conventionalized idiom of contemporary American English, mirrors and produces the 'new' Japanese idiom of a 'light and easy' style.

Conversely, through his translations, Murakami himself has been instrumental in introducing the works of many American writers to the Japanese reading public. Karatani has argued that these American 'works' (*sakuhin*) exist in Japan through the 'Murakami-like scene' (*Murakami-teki fūkei*)—but further than this, and rather astonishingly, that 'the whole of American Literature and what Murakami's readers imagine *is* contemporary American literature have nothing in common'.[38] If this is the case, could not the following question also arise: because of the dominance of one translation style (i.e. the idiom of contemporary American English) is there a similar disjunction between what American readers imagine contemporary Japanese literature to be and the whole of modern Japanese literature?

Working from within the tradition, Japanese critics clearly adopt approaches to Murakami which situate them differently to those of American critics such as Birnbaum and Jay Rubin (one of Murakami's major translators), yet in the range of critical responses to *Kaze* there is clear evidence of common ground in respect to several issues. The most obvious area of agreement is that the language of the text broke new ground in terms of linguistic style (*buntai*), and this will be considered in more detail later in this chapter. Regarding the related but more vexing issue of what this new style might *mean* for Japanese literary modernity, there is less unanimity.

Other aspects of *Kaze* as a contemporary narrative which presents a critique of orthodoxy relate to what might be called its narrative format, and the extent to which it represents parody or even pastiche; the significance of its overt metafictionality, and its 'political/historical' treatment of an epoch deemed a significant turning point in the rise and consolidation of the modern Japanese nation-state. In the discussion which follows, it will be concluded that the significance of such issues in critical writing on *Kaze* lends considerable support to the idea of the simulacral operation of the Murakami text in contemporary Japan.

Kaze and Narrative Format: Parody or Pastiche? Fiction or Metafiction?

In a discussion with Kawamoto Saburô, Murakami claimed that everything he wanted to say in *Kaze* was said in the first chapter, 'after that, everything else was just tacked on'.[39] If the reader considers this admission in conjunction with the narrator's metafictional reflection that he was only capable of writing a 'list' ('not a novel, not literature, not art'),[40] a serious question as to the narrative 'status' of the text arises. Despite this—and even if the reader can accept the narrator's attempts at succinctness and the ironicizing of generic conventions—it remains quite clear that *Kaze* represents, after all, some kind of story, or fragments of a story, or fragments of stories within stories. In somewhat contradictory fashion, the narrator in the fragment which comprises Chapter Two, explicitly affirms the *narrativity* of the text by precisely marking out the narrative time of the *hanashi* ('talk', 'tale', 'story'):

「この話は1970年の8月8日に始まり、18日後、つまり同じ年の8月26日に終わる。」[41]

This story begins on the eighth of August, 1970, and finishes eighteen days later—that is, in the same year, on the twenty-sixth of August.[42]

What is important here is to acknowledge that even if the narrator of *Kaze* is merely listing, he is at least *telling* that list. As Martin reminds us, 'the narrowest definition of narration equates it with summary or telling'.[43] In the same vein, it can be said that even if the narrator claims to be merely *showing* a list, the list adheres to some kind of arrangement (even if that is a deliberate *dis*arrangement). More significantly, it uses language, and therefore as Rimmon-Kenan points out (referring to Genette, 1972): 'since all texts are made of language, and language signifies without imitating, the crucial distinction is not between telling and showing, but between different degrees and kinds of telling'.[44] The narrator's ironic insistence that he is simply drawing up a list which indicates things is at best a playful yet untenable ploy to negate the act of writing, of being 'literary'. Significantly, however, the narrator is from the very outset destabilizing the act of meaning by making the point that his writing is not necessarily attempting to indicate a world. Yet this move is also unconvincing if we keep in mind Culler's reminder that

> the basic convention which governs the novel and which *a fortiori*, governs those novels which set out to violate it—is our expectation that the novel will produce a world. Words must be composed in such a way that through the activity of reading there will emerge a model of the social world, models of the individual personality, of the relations between the individual and society . . . and, of the kind of significance which these aspects of the world can bear.[45]

As a narrative text therefore, *Kaze* utilizes a narrator who is clearly telling a story—and not simply an 'author' who is merely presenting a list. Much, therefore, that is interesting about *Kaze* stems not so much from *what* it tells but from the *way* it is told, that is, in terms of its narrative format. In Ruthrof's twofold scheme, this would suggest an emphasis on 'presentational process';[46] for the Russian Formalists, a foregrounding of the *syuzhet* ('the narratives as told or written—incorporating the procedures, devices . . . of the literary text') vis-à-vis the *fabula* ('story'/'subject'); for Genette, a focus on the 'narrative discourse' rather than the 'story', and so on.[47] Critics have rightly noted the significance of form in *Kaze*, and its fragmented narrative renderings have attracted every kind of response: from applause,[48] as a spur to detailed textual analysis,[49] as indicative of the 'myth of contemporariness' (*gendaisei*),[50] and to its outright dismissal as 'mere pastiche'.[51] There should be little surprise about this apparent emphasis on the formal, since according to Suga, (citing Kawamoto) Japanese writers who have studied Russian Formalism will attempt to revive (*sosei saseru*) through 'form' (*keishiki*), rather than 'content'(*naiyô*). For Suga, Murakami (who would presumably have been exposed to Formalist theory in the Drama department at Waseda University) may well have had, with the writing of *Kaze*, a kind of 'formalist' experiment in mind.[52]

If we accept Bal's three layered definition of narrative as 'text', 'story' and 'fabula',[53] then Murakami's experimentation with narrative format (comprising these three elements) could certainly be construed as a critique, perhaps parody of the 'I-novel'(*shishôsetsu*) orthodoxy, which relied on a 'sincere' and naturalistic recording of the lived world of the author.[54] That is to say, the dimension of *fabula* in the 'I-novel' as a conventionally arranged 'series of logically and chronologically related events' is certainly undermined in *Kaze*. If indeed parody is an apt description of *Kaze* in its 'postmodern' aspect, the idea posited by Jameson that in the postmodern milieu pastiche replaces parody deserves at least cursory consideration here.[55] This is especially so if we accept that implicit in Jameson's discussion is the issue of the valuing or privileging of modernist parody *over* postmodernist pastiche. Jameson's early and insightful argument on postmodernism is relevant to our consideration of *Kaze* specifically (as well as to other works by Murakami) because it deals succinctly with at least two of the Fundamental elements of narrative: space and time.

Other insights of Jameson which are relevant to the *Kaze* text include the idea of postmodernity as reaction to the orthodoxy of high modernity;[56] postmodernity as an erosion of the distinction between high and mass culture;[57] and postmodernity as both cultural style *and* periodizing concept.[58] Another important observation of Jameson's is that postmodern forms, as well as overtly blending styles and formats in the production of pastiche, also rely on a specific structuration of nostalgia which, in turn, is not unrelated to what he describes as the 'schizophrenic' experience of time.[59]

In the Japanese context, the texts comprising the 'canon' of modern literature (*kindai bungaku*) include all those of the 'I-novel' format which sought to explore the newly formed modern Japanese subject (*jiga*), breaking from the representational possibilities of pre-Meiji narrative. It is not so much the undermining of a regular chronology in Murakami's *Kaze* which is indicative of parody/pastiche (for as Miyoshi points out, one feature of indigenous Japanese narrative is its relative indifference to linear/sequential chronology[60]), but rather, the lack of commitment to the certainties of accurately relating experiences and deriving stable meanings from the latter.

Jameson explores the idea of schizophrenia (in the Lacanian sense of the term) where the symbolic order of language is only made possible through a certain engagement of the subject with time. He suggests that the abolition/disabling of the 'normal' unfolding of language over time (the past, present, future of the narrative representational matrix) creates a continuous present which generates a kind of 'hyper-real', intensely immediate experiential world, thereby effectively disallowing 'history'. These characteristics are evident in *Kaze*, in the early autism (manifested as the speechlessness, *mukuchi*) of the protagonist Boku, and the failed attempt at a 'cure' through psychoanalysis,[61] as well as in the inclusion of historical markers, and specific dates/periods which represent ultimately, a certain denial—if not outright parody—of history.[62]

Jameson's suggestion that pastiche is a kind of de-invigorated parody (a parody 'emptied out' of its 'humor' and ironic force), is questioned by Rose who does not necessarily agree that pastiche is something new. She proposes, instead, that pastiche is something which extends/augments the critical power of parody:

> In other words, parody does not degenerate into pastiche in all post-modernist works, but may, with pastiche, be given further reflexive powers by being directed towards a critique of modernism itself.[63]

In this view, parody and pastiche can be co-extensive with one another and serve to augment the complexity of a text. We will refer to a later argument by Rose towards the end of this section. It can be noted at this point, however, that parody is simulacral in that it refers to another 'original' or prior text, as is pastiche to the extent that it 'copies' then combines elements from a range of prior or other texts. *Kaze* parodies the sincerity of the 'I-novel' form and blends together a range of textual components (pop-songs, pictures, telephone conversations, monologue, dialogue, etc). It is certainly the case that pastiche remains as a 'postmodern' element in Murakami's writing until the final *Nejimaki-dorikuronikuru* (*The Wind-Up Bird Chronicle*) trilogy, although the more explicit use of parody is confined mostly to the first three novels.

Japanese critics have noted the pastiche-like nature of *Kaze*, but have tended to value it either negatively or positively rather than see it as an inevitable postmodern textual strategy. Suzumura, for example, identifies in *Kaze* various of what he calls Murakami's 'fetishisms' in the pastiche-like 'fragmentary remarks' which appear to be randomly inserted and often de-contextualized.[64] For example:

「僕たちは朝日新聞の日曜版の上で抱き合った。」[65]

We embraced one another lying on the Sunday edition of the Asahi
newspaper.[66]

「6本のコマーシャルが入った。ビールと生命保険とビタミン剤と航空
会社とポテトチップと生理用ナプキンのコマーシャルだった。」[67]

They ran six commercials. Beer and life insurance and vitamins, an airline,
potato chips, and sanitary napkins.[68]

More recently, Suzumura has dismissively characterized *Kaze* as a fragmentary accumulation of separate passages which, by adopting an 'aphoristic' style, has borrowed a particular form and filled it in with 'empty maxims'.[69] Komori has also written of the 'fragments' (*tanpen*) of language which are scattered throughout the text without overall coherence, not even amounting to a narrative (*monogatari*). However, he suggests that read by a perceptive reader, they may be arranged into an appropriate form—in the same way that iron filings can be re-arranged by an electro-magnet.[70] On the other hand, Takahashi views *Kaze*, somewhat approvingly, as a collage of telephone conversations, movie theme songs, LP songs, quotes and so on with a characteristically 'dry touch' (*kawaita tacchi*).[71]

We noted above that Karatani has described *Kaze* as a pastiche, and although he seems to concur with Jameson's view that in postmodern artistic discourses pastiche replaces parody, he also identifies some characteristics specific to the contemporary Japanese context. Karatani offers quite an extended analysis of Murakami's second novel, *1973 nen no pinbôru* (*Pinball, 1973*), which will be considered in the next chapter, and also sees in that text a narrative style not significantly different from that of *Kaze*, suggesting that in both novels what appears to be 'a contemporary portrayal of expressionless irony', actually conceals the intention of an 'inversion' (*tentô*).[72] Karatani's theory of an 'inversion' in the representation of scene/landscape (*fûkei*) in modern Japanese literature and its treatment in Murakami's writing will be dealt with in more detail later, where it will be related to the question of whether or not it is possible to posit a distinctly Japanese sublime. However, what is relevant here, is his claim that with regard to pastiche/parody in the context of Japanese postmodernism, we find a 'romantic irony' quite different to the kind which exists within a 'historical' form. In support of his argument Karatani reminds us of Hartman's view that in irony everything is at once false and true, hidden and revealed.[73] Such a view helps elucidate the intertextual function of irony in Murakami's early work, but Karatani does not elaborate further as to why the 'hidden motive' of an inversion cannot be found in other 'Murakami-like' writers.[74]

In deciding on the usefulness (or otherwise) of distinguishing between parody and pastiche in relation to Murakami's early writing, Rose's critique of Jameson's argument (particularly her inclusion of Baudrillard's views on parody) is worthy of mention:[75]

> What we have with Jameson is . . . not just a set of category errors in which something defined as modern parody has been projected onto something called post-modern pastiche . . . but also an artificial distinction between parody and pastiche which tries to argue that parody is modern and pastiche is post-modern.

In claiming that both parody and pastiche are actually 'devices', which having been used for centuries are not necessarily modern *or* postmodern, Rose is of course referring to European artistic discourses. However, it is also reasonable to assert that parody and pastiche were not entirely absent from pre-modern Japanese literature—especially in the works of the *Gesaku* writers—and therefore that parody and pastiche are not necessarily confined to the Japanese modern/postmodern context. If irony is indeed the very basis of parody (and by extension, pastiche) then perhaps what has changed is the *kind* of irony, which as Karatani suggested, is an inescapably *Romantic* irony that entails a different kind of critique of literary texts and the social formations that enable them to function.

Modernist irony is of course a function of what Ivy calls 'modernity's losses', and relies on structures of nostalgia and certain kinds of experience in the construction of time. Also, Jameson is correct to see in the so-called 'schizophrenic' construction of time (via Lacanian theory) a seemingly 'postmodern' phenomenon. And yet it is Baudrillard who provides the link between parody and the operation of the simulacrum in contemporary cultural practices. As Rose reminds us:

> In his Orders of Simulacra, prior to speaking of the non-intentional parody which 'hovers over everything', Baudrillard had referred to the growth of a hyperspace of representation where each is already technically in possession of the instantaneous reproduction of his own life.[76]

In his essay entitled 'The Ecstasy of Communication', Baudrillard spells out this parodic 'hyperspace' in more sinister form, as the madness and obscenity of schizophrenia:

> The schizo is bereft of every scene, open to everything in spite of himself, living in the greatest confusion. He is himself obscene, the obscene prey of the world's obscenity. He can no longer produce the limits of his own being . . . He is now only a pure screen, a switching centre for all the networks of influence.[77]

Granted, this rather chilling characterization seems a little extreme in suggesting the operation of parody/pastiche in postmodern writing. Nevertheless, if there can be said to be a continuum in the crisis of representation, then such a description reflects a question of degree or intensity, rather than a difference in kind. And as we have shown, in Rose's scheme, this would see pastiche as one version of parody, rather than its replacement.

Regardless of whether Murakami's *Kaze* is an inversion of the originally inverted *fūkei* (as claimed by Karatani), it functions intertextually in a simulacral way to the extent that it is parodic of the 'I-novel' form and is ostentatiously pastiche-like in its re-presentation of the daily 'narratives' of the life-world of contemporary Japan. We can say that Baudrillard's insight that a 'non-intentional parody hovers over everything' certainly applies to contemporary texts such as *Kaze*. Furthermore, evidence of this parodic dimension can also be found in the metafictional aspect of texts like *Kaze*.

Self-referential literature—or what is now known as 'metafiction'—lies very close to parody on the literary continuum. As Ruthrof notes:

> All literary parody points to the literariness, the interpretative rather than the representational qualities of works of literature. And perhaps it is no accident that the present trend of metafiction performs the same function.[78]

Like parody and pastiche, metafiction is also simulacral in that it provides a 'second order' narrative or commentary imposed over the primary narrative. However, it is important to note that claiming a special status for metafictional literature belies the fact that literariness, as a special mode of reference, is by virtue of its very mimetic or 'as if ' structure always already more or less metafictional. Critics such as Todorov, for example, claim that literature entails an 'imaginary reference', and Arrive has actually characterized the referent of the literary text as a simulacrum.[79] Furthermore, as Waugh has convincingly argued, although 'metafictional practice has become particularly prominent in the fiction of the last twenty years, metafiction is not a new phenomenon, but rather a 'tendency or function inherent in all novels'.[80] In one sense, this claim holds for much modern Japanese fictional writing, having as its basic paradigm the covenant of understanding between reader and narrator, at the core of the 'I-novel' tradition. This notwithstanding, it is hardly surprising that critics have rightly sensed the metafictional significance of the opening lines of *Kaze*:

「完璧な文章などといったものは存在しない。完璧な絶望が存在しない
ようにね。」 [81]

There's no such thing as perfect writing. Just like there's no such thing as
perfect despair.[82]

These sentences have also attracted critical attention for other reasons. Suzumura, for example, offers the philosophical observation that while Murakami
may genuinely be making a statement about the non-perfectibility of written
self-expression, in fact the qualities of 'absence' (*fuzai*) and 'fiction/fabrication'
(*kyokô*) as evident in the novel form are 'perfect in themselves'.[83] Kasai extends
the meaning of 'perfect writing' to include the notions of 'true meaning' (*hontô
no imi*) and 'correct writing' (*seikaku no bunsho*), which he claims are related to
Ôe Kenzaburô's 'deceptive concern' with 'the truth' in *Mannen gannen no futobôru*. He suggests that as the reader begins and continues reading, the 'truth'
(*hontô no koto*) unfolds gradually. In the end, however, *Kaze* fails in this endeavour at 'truthful' writing.[84]

Yet another critic, Katô, concurs with Kasai's view that Murakami is implying
that certain things must be written but *cannot be*—and in the place of 'important
things' (*daiji na koto*) 'trivial things' appear. For Katô, this oppositional structure of 'writing' (*kaku koto*) and 'not writing' (*kakanai koto*) resonates with the
author's personal experience at the end of the sixties. In support of this, he invokes Takeda Seiji's work on Nietzsche's reaction to the philosophy of his age.
Interestingly, he suggests that what Takeda saw in Nietzsche's critique of Rousseau (naive radicalism), Goethe's 'high-minded conservatism', and Schopen-
hauer's 'romanticism of the wolf', aptly describes the confused condition of the
competing ideologies in the Japan of the late sixties. In this sense, suggests
Katô, *Kaze* represents a commentary on various aspects of that particular configuration of contradictory and confused views of the world.[85]

Murakami's overt concern with the writing process itself occurs at numerous
places throughout the novel. In the first chapter alone can be seen the following
observations which point to the narrator's difficulties with, and views on writing. Compared to the opening passages from other comparable novels, the *overt*
metafictionality is quite striking.[86]

「今僕は語ろうと思う。」 [87]

Now I think I'm ready to talk.[88]

「結局のところ、文章を書くことは自己療養ではなく……。」 [89]

You get right down to it, writing is no means to self help.[90]

「僕は文章についての多くをデレク・ハートフィールドに学んだ。
殆ど全部、というべきかもしれない。」[91]

I've learned a lot about writing from Derek Hartfield. Perhaps almost every thing.[92]

「ハートフィールドが良い文章についてこんな風に書いている。『文章
を書くという作業は、とりもなおさず自分と自分をとりまく事物との
距離を確認することである。必要なものは感性ではなく、ものさし
だ。』」[93]

Hartfield has this to say about good writing: 'The task of writing consists primarily in recognizing the distance between oneself and the things around one. It is not sensitivity one needs, but a yardstick'.[94]

「もう一度文章について書く。これで最後だ。」[95]

One more point about writing. And this will be the last.[96]

From the outset, the reader is left in little doubt that the narrator is engaged in a vigorously ironic commentary on the nature of writing. Acknowledging that 'writing is hard work' but conceding that it can 'also be fun',[97] the narrator then expects the reader to accept that this particular writing amounts to no more than a 'list', a 'catalogue'[98] with the final claim that 'that mere humans are incapable of writing—and that includes me'.[99] But it is perhaps not only the general question of 'writing' itself which is under intense scrutiny here, but more importantly, the *shôsetsu* (or its European homologue, the novel). As was shown in Chapter 2, the exact parameters of the 'genre' of the Japanese *shôsetsu* have been relatively undefined, and for this reason alone it is hardly surprising that the appearance of overt metafictionality would do even more to undermine the stability of the category. Karatani's observations on the decline of what might be called the Japanese 'high modernist' novel, represent also an acknowledgement that the contemporary novel is indicative of what John Barth (as far back as 1967) called the 'literature of exhaustion'.[100] Barth's saw, however, in this apparent 'demise', the possibility of greater artistic vitality through experimental techniques—and it is certainly the case that metafictionality has emerged as one such important technique.

It is because Murakami's *Kaze* not only scrutinizes the issue of 'writing' in general, but more specifically the question of 'the novel' (*shôsetsu*),[101] that it is also an important affirmation of the fact that the novel (whatever its style and despite the ascendance of electronic audio/visual media) remained in Japan, in 1979, something which was still a viable artistic form which could be commercially successful. Broadly speaking, the same could be said of the status of the novel in Japan today. And while Murakami's more recent major fictional works generally make no *overt* use of metafictionality, their highly 'postmodern' narrative style suggests that the contemporary novel's experimentation with form continues to assure it a place in the textual cornucopia of the electronic age. If the metafictional element is another indicator of the 'simulacral' tendency of Murakami's writing, then it is perhaps 'repressed' or at least displaced in later writings where it operates by structural or thematic means rather than by explicit, ironic statement.[102]

Even in these forms, the irony/contradictions of the writing enterprise still powerfully inform Murakami's narrative endeavour. Unlike *Kaze, Nejimakidori kuronikuru (The Wind-Up Bird Chronicle)* could be said to belong to what Linda Hutcheon has designated as the category of 'historiographic metafiction':

> Postmodernism (as) a contradictory cultural enterprise . . . uses and abuses the very structures and values it takes to task. Historiographic metafiction, for example, keeps distinct its formal auto-representation and its historical context, and in so doing problematizes the very possibility of historical knowledge, because there is no reconciliation, no dialectic here — just unresolved contradiction.[103]

This will be taken up in more detail in the chapters dealing specifically with the second trilogy, but is mentioned here so as to highlight and contrast the use of metafictional 'perspectives' in both Murakami's first and more recent fictional works.

Undoubtedly, Murakami's *Kaze* was received as something new and fresh because its metafictionality offered a certain 'freedom' to the reader. According to Ommundsen, the reader becomes a 'character' in metafiction, and is thus freed from the 'tyranny of intentionality' of the 'author' (the latter being a significant and enduring feature of the 'I-novel' form.) Ommundsen rightly insists that metafiction is by its nature a more 'writerly' kind of text (i.e. in Barthes' scheme of 'readerly/writerly') and concurs with Hutcheon's view that

> by reminding the reader of the book's identity as artifice, the text parodies his (sic) expectations, his desire for verisimilitude, and forces him to an awareness of his role in creating the universe of fiction.[104]

Sarah Lauzen has extended Linda Hutcheon's[105] well known 'typology of textual narcissism' into a 'typology of metafictional devices', and when elements of this typology are applied to a text such as *Kaze*, the metafictionality of the latter is brought into stark relief. As Lauzen puts it, in terms of narrating or point of view, 'when the narrating — the telling-the-story — becomes a major part of the subject matter, we are in the realm of overt self-consciousness.'[106] Other elements of Lauzen's typology which are clearly evident in *Kaze* come under the category of structure. It is usually assumed, according to Lauzen, that the structure of the narrative is 'organically' determined and not arbitrarily imposed. Significantly, the use of numbers to designate the forty fragmentary chapters of *Kaze* does not strictly indicate a narrative unfolding conventionally through space and time. On the contrary, such numbering is suggestive of a kind of 'digital' arrangement in which the reader can switch at random from chapter to chapter and still be able to construct meaningful narrative units which are relatively discrete or autonomous. Similarly, an absence or reduction of structure is evident in the use of 'semi-disconnected short takes' or fragments,[107] which are typified, for example, by Chapters 2, 6, 14 and 21 of the *Kaze* text.

Kaze as a Critique of 'the System'

In his *69—Sixty Nine*, (first published in serial form in 1984-85[108]) Murakami Ryû attempts a double kind of parody. Firstly, in its presented world, the narrative offers an hilarious account of a group of rowdy final year students in a provincial high school in Kyûshû. The students' boisterous activities are meant to parallel the 'real' political struggle in 1969 undertaken by the *Zenkyôtô* (the Joint Campus Struggle movement). From the beginning, the quasi-historiographic orientation of the text is clear, and yet any overt ideological posturing is disallowed by the texts overall parodic tone. The effect is a purely 'retro'—the nostalgic recuperation of an era which could only ever be ironically rendered for the students of eighties Japan:

「だが、この頃は、受験勉強をする奴は**資本家の手先**だ、という便利な風潮があったのも事実である。」 [109]

It's true that in those days it was convenient to describe those who studied for university entrance exams as **pawns of the capitalists.**

As shown above, 'Pawns of the Capitalists' is rendered in large bold-type characters as are numerous other phrases and words, seemingly selected at random throughout the narrative. The text is replete with the names of rock groups ('Iron Butterfly') and famous foreign names (Arthur Rimbaud, Trotsky)—a characteristic not uncommon in Murakami Haruki's *Kaze* and other works of that era.[110] In some respects, as a quasi-autobiographical narrative, *69—Sixty Nine* appears not dissimilar to *Kaze*, although Strecher has suggested contrasting emphases in the two texts. He describes *69—Sixty Nine* as expressing 'the rage of an impotent counter-culture', yet detects in *Kaze*, a 'quiet melancholy and abstract references to the failure of *Zenkyôtô*'. For Strecher, the latter text is less about the failure of the student movement than the collapse of a 'sense of identity and self that it provided its participants'.[111] Of course, *69—Sixty Nine* also operates parodically as a critique of Murakami Haruki's *Kaze*. The latter (in its experimental capacity as a critique of Japanese literary modernity in 1979) could only thereafter be parodied in the manner in which important literary innovation inevitably establishes a kind of intertextual, auto-referentiality with the texts which follow it. The striking difference between the texts by the two famous

Murakamis lies in the following: *69—Sixty Nine* is really a kind of 'third-order' critique—that is to say, it is a critique of *Kaze*, which is itself a critique (commentary) on the 'failed' critique of the State: not only the failed student movement, nihilism and alienation arising out of the unsuccessful 'revolution' of the sixties, but also the inevitable *ennui* of the consumer society which developed thereafter.

A different perspective on this is offered by Kuroko, who sees significance in the fact that the narrative time of *Kaze* extends over a two week period in 1970. According to Kuroko, the year 1970 marked the end of the 'age of politics' (*seiji no kisetsu*) in Japan. Put another way, it marked the movement from a period of violence to one of peace and heralded the advent of what was to become the very real prosperity of the eighties. Kuroko notes that in 1970 the Japanese Red Army's airline hijacking and the highly staged ritual suicide of Mishima can be seen, in hindsight, as the final symbolic events of the age of protest. In particular, the 'Mishima Incident' as a domestic event was 'illuminated' (*shôsha shita*) by Japan shaking off the 'fantasies' (*gensô*) created by the success of post-war high growth policies and moving out as an advanced industrial nation to assume it place in the world amidst the new forms of imperialism.[112]

In a similar vein, Imai has sought to situate *Kaze* within the general context of the critique of the Japanese postwar 'system'.[113] He identifies, for example, in Chapter 32 of *Kaze* a 'metaphor' for the formation of contemporary 'self-consciousness'. In this chapter, the narrator refers to Derek Hartfield's the *Wells of Mars* which describes the swelling and explosion of the 'red star', and Imai argues (somewhat unconvincingly) how this process signifies the interplay between the 'contemporary self-consciousness' (*gendai no jiishiki*) and the 'modern self' (*kindaiteki jiga*).[114]

On much firmer ground, Imai goes on to sketch the broader context of the emergence of the post-war mass media system within which *Kaze* must be situated. He refers at length to the work of Konakawa,[115] who noted that the postwar period began with the establishment of the *Tamahon Hôsô* ('Treasured Sounds Broadcast') which, it is claimed, significantly influenced the direction of the media from that time on. According to Konakawa, the postwar mass media actually developed through the large scale 'rebirth' (*saiseisan*) of what he calls the 'foolishness' (*guretsusa*) and 'transcendentalism' (*chôetsusei*) that accompanied the pre-war 'existence of the emperor' (*tennô no sonzai*). Interestingly—and in a seemingly contradictory way—although the authority of the emperor ostensibly weakened substantially in the postwar period, the process of the permeation of what Konakawa calls the 'ruling apparatus' (*shihaisôchi*) among the people (*minshû*) functioned extremely effectively. Even now, according to Konakawa, it is fair to say that the latent aim of the mass media as 'ruling apparatus' is still in use.[116]

This view of a new form of postwar 'emperorism' is of course not unique,[117] but what follows in Konakawa's argument seems especially pertinent to our consideration of the presented world and representation of human relations in

Murakami's *Kaze*. Konakawa goes on to argue that through this process of permeation, the mass media possessed the function of inheriting, in the form of the ruling apparatus (*shihaisôchi*), the unconsciously constructed 'vertical society' (*tate shakai*) of a 'public' (*minshû*) which itself was constructed through the patriarchal household and emperor systems in the first fifty years of the Meiji era. Imai cites Konakawa directly:

> That side (*sokumen*), which is made up by the invisible thread of the 'circuit of capital' (*shihon no kairo*) and which is bound up with the public, external things (*gaibu no mono*) is strong. And recently, it is the individual's choice of channels (*chyaneru*) and the gaining of rights in the space occupied by the 'residential space' (*ijûkûkan*)—which itself has become individualized and atomized (*koshitsuka*)—which is the very basis of this development.[118]

According to Imai, Konakawa is claiming that the non-existence *as household* (*katei*) of the ultimate form of the 'noble individual' (or so called *dokushin kizoku*) lifestyle, itself represents a reified form of the 'vertical society' (*tate shakai*). In the continuous re-presentation of this 'new lifestyle' (based on the 'myth of the new' or *atarashisa no shinwa*) through the repeated slogans of the mass media, as 'the new family' or 'the new Mrs.' and the prefixes 'new'(*niyû*) 'post' (*posuto*) and 'neo' (*neo*), can be discerned the nexus between the mass media and the individual who has left the family, and who lives by 'information' (*jôhô*) received and consumed through various channels.[119] From this kind of perspective the mass media is seen to have *replaced* the family. Like other commentators Imai notes the significance of the 'Disc-Jockey scene' (Chapter 12)—and notes particularly the Disc Jockey's admonition of Boku in the following chapter, for reading a book instead of listening to the radio:

「君何してた。」
「本を読んでました。」
「チッチッチ、駄目だよ、そりゃ……。」
「ラジオを聴かなきゃ駄目さ。」
「孤独になるだけさ。そうだろ？」
「ええ。」[120]

Did I catch you in the midst of anything?
I was reading a book.
Tsk, tsk, tsk, shame on you. You've gotta listen to the radio.
Reading only isolates you. Admit it?
Yeah.[121]

Despite this represented 'invasion' or 'violation' (*shinpan*) of Boku's private space, Imai is of the view that within the overall structural context of *Kaze*, Murakami is not presenting a critique of the mass media as such. On the contrary, he claims that despite the possible reading of *Kaze* as a critique of mass media

technologies, the general direction of the text is one of 'liberation' (*kaihô*) from
'the system' (*seidô*)—the latter of course comprising much more than simply the
mass media. Rather than direct critique or resistance, this liberating quality is
related to the sense of 'off'—literally 'switching off' from the system.[122]

Imai also relates the fragmentary construction of the forty chapters of *Kaze* directly to this sense of liberation. Such a structure is said to certainly change the
conventional linear narrative time of the novel, but the use of these 'snippets' or
'cuttings' (*setsudan*) in itself is not a denial of continuity (*renzokusei*). Rather, it
is the strategy of a text which seeks to construct, in a separate story, liberation
(*kaihô*) and desire (*yokudô*) at a deep level. It does this by encroaching upon
(*shinpan suru*) and dissolving (*yôkai suru*) the framework comprising the limits
of time and space (*jikan/kûkan no genkai*), the arbitrariness and rigidity (*shiisei,
genmitsusei*) of the story (*monogatari*) inherent to the overall continuity of the
text.[123]

Earlier in this chapter the use of 'fragments' in a narrative text was described,
according to Lauzen's schema,[124] as being a structural indicator of the metafictional mode. Concomitant with this, it was acknowledged by Ommundsen that
with metafiction, the reader is put very much back into the centre of the action.
According to Imai, the 'liberating' effect of this positioning of the reader is very
much a feature of *Kaze*. This is so, he suggests, because despite the fact of having the outward appearance of an eccentric, 'fragmentary mosaic', *Kaze* for
most readers, is a text which feels light (*keimyô*) and 'easy to read' (*yomiyasui*).
The 'liberation' is supposed to occur for the reader in the following way:

> By moving from fragment to fragment, and experiencing the in-between 'blank
> spaces' before and after each fragment, and by linking the fragments together
> and projecting the fragments of the readings between a sense of 'affinity'
> (ruiensei) and 'difference' (sôisei)—the direction (hôkô) of the 'system feed-
> back' *of the self (jishin) is located by the* reader. However, when the direction
> of one moment (shunkan) is revealed by the next fragment and becomes the
> new horizon, the reader must find a new direction, a new space.[125]

In this perceptive passage on the aesthetics of reader response entailed in the
narrative structure of *Kaze*, Imai has (perhaps unwittingly) offered a phenomenological description of the reading process which is both in accord with Ingar-
den's theory of indeterminacy in the literary text and very close to Iser's theory
of blanks.[126] Iser proposes a theory of the 'blank' or gap in the process of actively constructing the narrative, which stimulates the continuity and 'connecta-
bility' in the act of reading. By overtly foregrounding and multiplying the
number of 'blanks', a text like Murakami's *Kaze* offers a much more *inclusive*
role for the reader and is thus 'liberating' (in the sense that it allows for a more
polysemic aesthetic response to the text) as well as being an implicit critique of
more conventionalized reading practices which inform the milieu of intertextuality available to the reader. According to Imai, the reader revels in the challenge
of reading a text such as *Kaze*:

> Despite the fact that for many readers of *Kaze*, in the blanks between the frag-
> ments a strong tension is produced which may lead to the exhaustion of the
> process of being 'steered' through the text and the resultant danger of 'running
> aground' (*zasshô no kiken*), the feeling of lightness and ease of reading contin-
> ues.

He goes on to suggest that while following this kind of narrative, the reader
himself/herself (visits) these new found directions, but abandons the process of
anchoring meanings there, and as a consequence is rewarded by a 'lightening-
up' of his/her own reading. Furthermore, what Imai throughout his analysis has
called the innocent, laid back 'sense of off' (*OFF no kankaku*), is said to permeate the text. Imai is correct to qualify this claim by pointing out, however, that
this kind of 'drifting voyage', which ostensibly involves the abandonment of
meaning, is actually impossible without what he calls a 'complementary form of
navigation'.[127] In other words, it is suggested that even though the kinds of social semiosis which are required in order for even tentative meanings to be constructed are much less explicit than they could be, they are nevertheless a requi-
site element of the reading process:

> In *Kaze no uta o kike* the 'communal interpretative code' (*kaishaku kyôdôteki
> kôdo*) arising from the textual strategy of the reader automatically navigating
> through the text . . . is made immanent to the text.[128]

What, indeed, might this immanent 'interpretative code' be? Perhaps we can say
that in very specific ways, Murakami's critique of orthodoxy demanded new
ways of reading which were prescribed and tempered by the all pervasive new
modes of electronic and digital communication. Suzumura has gone so far as to
designate the modalities of representing many of the speech acts in *Kaze* as
'telephone writing' (*denwa no ekurichuru*—after the French *ecriture*). He proposes that in the types of conversations found in *Kaze,* the participants are
somehow *disembodied* from the details of their speech. Even though such
speech traces out some kind of image or depiction, the actual sense of embodiment is weak, and the scenes lack any 'realistic description' (*shajitsuteki na
byosha*).[129] However, Suzumura also makes the important point that it is not
simply the case that the represented speech acts in *Kaze* seem similar to typical
telephone conversations—for that would require the kind of 'reality' (situation)
of an actual telephone conversation. Rather, as he puts it, the conversations
apply the 'logic' of the *medium* of the telephone. Furthermore, it is argued that
the style of 'telephone writing' is not limited to conversational exchanges. It
appears in other sentences which, on the surface at least, manifest the style of
speaking into the telephone mouth-piece to someone. Murakami's application of
a telephone 'logic' (*ronri*) to his conversations,[130] connotes the strictly binary
form of telephone communication (i.e. listen/respond/listen/respond) which is
unable to utilize the myriad of non-verbal semiotic processes available in face to
face communication. With Suzumura's notion of 'telephone writing', we are

reminded of such either/or structures as a significant feature of the syntax of the postmodern as elaborated by Ruthrof.[131]

Although writing before Suzumura, Maeda Ai took this kind of analysis one step further with his representation of the speech acts in the famous disc jockey scene of *Kaze,* by way of a simple digital circuit diagram.[132] The 'scene' comprises Chapters 11, 12 and 13 of the text, and is marked out by the switches 'ON' (which puts the DJ 'on-air') and 'OFF' (which takes him 'off-air'). The ON/OFF switches appear in other scenes as well (in Chapters 7 and 32[133]) and according to Maeda, lend the text a kind of 'digital' dimension. It is claimed that originally, readers of Japanese had become accustomed to reading the groupings of characters along the 'temporal axis' (*jikanjiku*) continuously, and in an analogic way, but have had to learn to respond to and deal with fragments of time in a *discontinuous* (and by implication 'digital') way.

Reading *Kaze,* therefore, is no different from 'reading' a television drama interspersed with commercials, or dividing time in order to perform various tasks within a work schedule. It is for this reason, Maeda remarks, that dealing with the scattered fragments of discontinuous time which characterize the forty chapters of the mosaic-like *Kaze* as one deals with a television program, would seem to be the obvious and most natural way of 'reading' the text.[134] The use of a simple digital circuit diagram by Maeda illustrates the flow of 'information' in this scene, and the relations can be represented in the table below, where 'D' represents disc jockey and 'R' record:

D	R
1	0
0	1

When the disc-jockey's 'input' (*nyûryoku*) has a value of '1' it is a logical necessity that the 'output' (*shutsuryoku*) of the record has a value of '0' and vice-versa. The excerpts presented below demonstrate this binary arrangement:

'ON'
「オーケー、一曲目。これを黙って聴いてくれ。本当に良い曲だ。暑さなんて忘れちまう。ブルック・ベントン、『レイニー・ナイト・イン・ジョージア』。」[135]

O.K., our first number. Just settle back nice and quiet and give this a listen. A real mellow song. Forget all about the heat. Brook Benton's 'Rainy Night in Georgia'.[136]

'OFF'

「ふう……、なんて暑さだい、……まったく……ねえ、クーラーもっと
きかないの？……地獄だよ、ここは……おい、よしてくれよ、俺はね、
汗っかきなんだ……そう、そんなもんだ……。」 [137]

What the . . . ? Sure is hot in here . . . . phew! . . . . C'mon, won't the air condi-
tioning get any cooler? . . . Hot as hell in here . . . hey, stop that, I'm sweating
all over. . . . Oh yeah, right there, that's good. . . . [138]

'ON'

「素晴らしいね、これが音楽だ。ブルック・ベントン、『雨のジョージ
ア』、少しは涼しくなったかい。ところで今日の最高気温、何度だと思
う？」 [139]

How about that, then? That's real music. Brook Benton's 'Rainy Night in
Georgia'. Bet you cooled down a bit, huh? And say, speaking of temperature,
what do you suppose today's high was? [140]

Because it foregrounds the compression of discrete and fragmented speech acts
(commercial/music/talk-back/DJ commentary etc.) within the discontinuous
times frames of the radio studio, the scene could be said to be paradigmatic of
Kaze as a whole. That is to say, the text as a whole defies any attempt at being
'analogically' read—disavowing itself as a narrative to be placed within an
overall continuum of meaning or reference *outside* its own modality of presentation. In the same way that for Suzumura, it is the *modality* of the 'telephone-
writing' which is significant (rather than the 'content' of any particular conversation) in the repressed interstices of the binary ON/OFF format, what the disc
jockey says, and which records he chooses to play are irrelevant. The disc-
jockey's 'speech' alternates between the task of presenting a 'public' self (a
speech ostensibly directed towards each 'individual' listener) and reconstituting
a 'private' self, which can never represent itself authentically 'on air'. Here we
are reminded of the theme of quasi-autistic *dis-communication*, raised in the
scene of the therapy session for the speechless Boku in Chapter 7 of *Kaze*. [141]

In a later essay, Maeda returns to the analysis of *Kaze* and his focus on the
significance of the disc jockey scene. [142] Despite the fact that the disc jockey 'appears' in only two segments of the novel, Maeda claims the disc jockey's
'speech' (which we can take as a represented 'speech act') serves as a model of
the entire 'language world' (*kotoba no sekai*) of the text. Such a view affirms the
claim made above, that the narrative of *Kaze* requires a discourse which constructs the implied social life-world in a different way. The signs (*kigô*) of 'on'
and 'off' are written in advance of the DJ scenes. In the 'on' scene, the DJ is
intimately engaged with his listener, only to have this cut short by the playing of
the record. In such scenes, according to Maeda, the DJ is directing his discourse
to only the single, individual listener (*tatta hitori no kikite ni mukatte*). This is a
'provisionally constructed' (*kako sareta*) 'private/secret' communication. Such

is the kind of 'I' (*watashi*) that is performing. Conversely, when the 'OFF' switch is engaged and the DJ's speech is off air, it becomes broken and discontinuous. All of this seems obvious, but Maeda asks: what kind of problem does this scene present us with?[143]

He suggests that for the reader, the narrator (*katarite*) of *Kaze* is situated as a special kind of listener (*kikite*) of the DJ's speech. The DJ's speech takes on an almost 'visual' quality for the narrator, but when the 'OFF' switch is engaged, it is implied that the putative listeners in 'radio land' are denied access to both the imagined 'corporeality' (*shintaisei*) and 'interiority' of the DJ, which nevertheless remain always on the verge of being 'exposed' (*roshutsu suru*). For Maeda, this reflects the context of contemporary language use, where individuals subjects 'give off' (*hassuru*) or 'speak out' (*hatsuwa*) various linguistic forms which, however, ultimately disallow the conveyance of the interior (*naimen*) to others.[144]

In such a model, the implied function of speech acts is to perpetuate a splitting (*bunretsu*) in which *dis*communication is the norm, and the DJ scene simply functions as a magnification (*kakudai*) or intensification, of the represented speech acts operating between the narrator and other characters in the text. This process is said to be evident in a range of social domains other than the presented worlds of *Kaze*.[145]

Maeda's approach is relevant because it seeks to 'read off' the social implications of the way language is used in *Kaze*. Drawing a parallel between the latter and the lyrics of pop-songs, he sees a powerful opposition established between the popular discourses of 'tradition' (represented for example, by the *enka* genre) in which the subject 'dissolves' into the narrative of the song—and the kinds of 'non-sense' (*nansensu*), non-meaning of pop lyrics.

In the contemporary Japanese urban context, language comes under the sway of the all pervasive advertising copy (*kopi*), which functions as a stylistic determinant of other kinds of discourse.[146] The language of a text like *Kaze*, like copy, generates a brief and powerful impression (*tankikan kyôretsu na inshô*), but will inevitably have to make way for new material. Advertising copy implicitly insists upon the urgency of a present 'now' (*genzai*), and the 'now' which must be consumed on the spot is the temporal structure (*jikan kôzô*) required of contemporary consumers. It is significant for Maeda that specific instances of the language of 'copy' (and thus the language used in some contemporary fiction such as *Kaze*), settle in the terminals (*tanshi*) of the unconscious domain of the consumers' memories, where they continue to stimulate dormant desires. However, it is ostensibly futile for consumers to attempt to grasp what lays *behind* such copy, simply because, through the signs which present themselves, consumers discover semiotic forms which are already emptied out of meaning (*karrapo no kigônaiyô*)—or at least requiring 'supplementary' semiotic input.[147]

In summary, Maeda argues the following. Formerly, through language (*kotoba*), it was possible for implicit presuppositions (*anmoku no zentei*) to be retrieved from the psyche or interior of speaking human beings. In more recent times, however, understanding (*ryôkai*) reflects not a process which moves from language to human beings (*kotoba kara ningen e dewanaku*), rather, this is the era of the 'figure/graph/diagram' (*zushiki*) in which figuratively, there is a reversal: the movement is from human beings to language. It should come as no surprise that the postmodern foregrounding of language (as acknowledged by Karatani) should appear to a critic of the stature of Maeda, as a central feature of Murakami's *Kaze*.

Nevertheless, even if we if we accept the thrust of Maeda's argument, questions remain: to what extent can we read *Kaze* ironically? Is it a critique of the contemporary 'degeneration' of language use? Is it complicit with or productive of this process? Is it a celebration of its release from the artifice of 'sincerity' which was and remains so much a part of the 'I-novel' orthodoxy? We will have further opportunity to consider these problems in a different context, when we look more closely at questions of language in the next chapter.

At a very specific level, the evidence suggests that much of the language of *Kaze* is 'simulacral' of advertising copy and other sign systems circulating in the domain of the mass media—even if it is proposing a partial critique of such discourses. At a more general level, however, what has been shown in this chapter is that through the devices of pastiche, metafiction and the overt subversion of patterns of represented speech acts, Murakami's first fictional work is indicative of the operation of a simulacral process in the representation of the Japanese self (*jiga*) in contemporary fiction. This is so because in 'turning on the lights of language' (that is, in drawing language's attention to itself, and usurping narrative conventions) he sent the nocturnal obsessions of the *shishôsetsu* ('confession' and 'sincerity') scurrying for cover.

In dealing with different versions of the more sinister aspects of the Japanese experience of modernity, Murakami's writing has done a kind of violence to the modern Japanese language. Critics such as Karatani, Miyoshi and Ôe seem disappointed that the 'big issues' ('self', 'truth', and 'meaning') have been avoided in texts such as *Kaze*. However, as has been argued here, Murakami's writing (unlike Tanaka's, Yoshimoto's or Tachiwara's, which rely mainly on the structuration of nostalgia in terms of a 'desire' for modernity's losses, as well as a desire for things, *objects* per se) clearly represents a new kind of critique. It does so by questioning the essential notion of 'Japaneseness' through the problematization of previously relatively stable and transparent notions of self and language at the heart of the 'I-novel' enterprise. These were in themselves constructs of Japanese modernity, and thus already irrevocably displaced elements of an imagined 'Japanese' essence which must strive to 'overcome' modernity (as was argued in Chapter 2) and which is either not acknowledged, or clearly subverted by Murakami's literary endeavours.

Notes

1. *Kaze no uta o kike* (*Hear the Wind Sing*), 1979; *1973 nen no pinbôru* (*Pinball, 1973*), 1980; *Hitsuji o meguru bôken (A Wild Sheep Chase)*, 1982. All published by Kôdansha.

2. The three works are recognized as a trilogy (or *sanbusaku*) by numerous Japanese critics.

3. These outlines are 'authoritative' in the sense that they are published in the re-nowned literary journal *Kokubungaku—kaishaku to kyôzai no kenkyû* (abbreviated as *Kokubungaku*).

4. See *Kokubungaku,* (February 1998).

5. Recall that in the previous chapter, reference was made by Baudrillard to this proc-ess of 'filling in' as indicative of a simulacral operation of meaning construction.

6. Ishikura, et.al., *Kokubungaku* (February 1998): 183.

7. Karatani, *The Origins of Modern Japanese Literature,* 183.

8. KUK1;10: 僕がここに書きしめすことができるのは、ただのリストだ。

9. Ishimaru, who writes of the emergence and travails of 'the self' in literary moder-nity, puts it this way. The struggle of the 'modern self' (*kindaiteki jiga*) was 'carved out' by works such as *Ukigumo* and *Maihime*. This notion of self (*jiga*) is defined in dic-tionaries (Ishimaru quotes, for example, from *Nihon kindaibungaku shôsetsu ji-ten,*(Yuikaku, 1981), as: 'the self consciousness borne of the process which established the authority of an ego (*jiko*) which refused to yield to the external authority (*gaitekikenni*) imposed by feudalism'. Even after the war this historical view continued for some time—but it was the new generation of best-seller authors such as Murakami and Yoshimoto, who did not understand this notion of *kindaiteki jiga* and who gathered together the common sensibilities of huge numbers of readers. Ishimaru points to Ya-nagida Kunio's view that the background to the struggle of the modern self was the fact that cities had been created out of a rural village sensibility (*nôsonsei*), but had lost their organic nature (*yûkisei*); Ishimaru also quotes Kawamoto's depiction of the city as 'the dwelling space for human beings displaced from the soil' (*tsuchi kara hanareta ningen no*). See Ishimaru Akiko, "Gendai toshi no naka no bungaku: Murakami Haruki *Kaze no Uta* o Chushin ni," in *Tokyo keizaidaigaku kaishi* 190 (January1995): 185-200.

10. See "Confession as a System" (Ch.3) in Karatani's *Origins of Modern Japanese Literature*. As far as 'confession' and the 'I-novel' is concerned, Edward Fowler's *The Rhetoric of Confession*, is important—especially his notion of the 'recorder-witness para-digm'.

11. See Murakami Haruki, "Kono jû nen" in Yukawa Yutaka, ed. Murakami Haruki Bukku *Bungakkai* 45, no. 5 (April Extra Number, 1991) *Bungei Shunjû*, 35-37.

12. As stated above, Karatani's 'discovery of landscape' thesis is elaborated early in *The Origins of Modern Japanese Literature*. Elsewhere, Karatani suggests that if Mura-kami's work is a reaction, ultimately, to 'realism', it is not simply through the 'influence' of the writing of certain American authors, but is related, ultimately to the writing of the English Romantic poets *through* the work of Kunkida Doppo. See Karatani Kôjin, "Mu-rakami Haruki no 'fûkei'—(I)," *Kaien* (November 1989): 296-306; especially 301.

13. Karatani, "Murakami Haruki no 'fûkei'—(I)," 300.

14. Murakami defended his so-called 'translation style' in a 1985 interview with Ka-wamoto Saburô, claiming that 'any style is valid, as long as the writer's intention is made known to the readers'. See Murakami Haruki, "Tokubetsu intabyû—monogatari no tame no bôken," *Bungakkai* 39 (August 1985): 49-50.

15. For example, writers such as Futabatei Shimei and Mori Ôgai.

16. Here we are reminded of Ôe Kenzaburo's use of English in his Nobel Prize acceptance speech, precisely because he wanted it to be translated into as many *other* languages as possible.

17. Murakami Haruki, "Tokubetsu intabyû," 50.

18. For example, Raymond Carver and Raymond Chandler.

19. See Baudrillard's *The System of Objects*.

20. Modern Japanese literary criticism identifies two main approaches, which are either 'author-focused' (*sakkaron*) or 'work-focused' (*sakuhinron*).

21. Tsuge Teruhiko attempts to link the author (*sakka*) with the critique of a work's structure (*sakuhin no kôzô*). In his view, the author is nothing more than the 'subject' (*shutai*) expressed as 'an awareness of the world', and while there is a text which is definable as a 'novel' (*shôsetsu*) it effectively occurs across a vast array of genres—for example, 'novel' 'roman' 'tale', 'fantasy', 'mystery', 'SF' as well as 'history' (*rekishi*), 'myth' (*shinwa*) 'epic or long narrative' (*monogatari*) and 'fable' (*setsuwa*). See "Sakuhin no kôzô kara —Murakami Haruki," *Kokubungaku* 35, no. 7 (1990): 117.

22. The writings of most of these critics are variously referred to throughout this discussion. For specific reference details in Tsuge's overview article see Tsuge Mitsuhiko, "Murakami Haruki—Kaze no uta o kike," *Kokubungaku* (Special Number) 32 (July1988): 223.

23. Takeda is referring to comments contained in the Forward of Kasai Kyoshi et. al.'s *Murakami o meguro bôken*, (Kawade Shobô Shinsha, 1991), 6.

24. Takeda Seiji, "Ririshizumu no jôken o tou," *Kokubungaku* 40, no. 4 (March 1995): 32.

25. Takeda, "Ririshizumu no jôken o tou," 32.

26. Takeda, "Ririshizumu no jôken o tou," 32-33.

27. Takeda, "Ririshizumu no jôken o tou," 32.

28. Takeda, "Ririshizumu no jôken o tou," 34-35.

29. Takeda, "Ririshizumu no jôken o tou," 34-35.

30. See Marylin Ivy, *Discourses of the Vanishing,* Chapters 1 & 2.

31. Takahashi Seori, "Murakami Haruki nenpu," *Kokubungaku* 30 (March 1985): 134.

32. See Tazaki Hiroshi , "Murakami Haruki 'Kaze no uta o kike' o yomu," *Sasebo Kôgyô Kôkô Senmon Gakko Kenkyû Kôkoku* 32 (February1996): 2.

33. Alfred Birnbaum, 'Murakami Haruki—oinaru hokotenkan', *Shinchô* (January 1990): 266-69.

34. Birnbaum, "Murakami Haruki—oinaru hokotenkan," 267.

35. Birnbaum, "Murakami Haruki—oinaru hokotenkan," 267.

36. Birnbaum, "Murakami Haruki—oinaru hokotenkan," 269.

37. Birnbaum has translated all three novels of the first trilogy.

38. Karatani, "Murakami Haruki no 'fûkei' —(I)," 301.

39. See Yokô Kazuhiro, *Murakami Haruki to kyûjûnendai* (Daisanshokan 1994), 159.

40. See fn. 9, above.

41. KUK 2; 11.

42. See HWS 2; 11. In "Kiete yuku mono e no manazashi," Katô suggests that in fact there are three narratives in *Kaze*—the story of 'Boku', the story of 'Boku' and 'Nezumi', and the story of the 'girl with the missing finger' (*koyubi no nai onna no ko*) which cover nineteen (not eighteen) days. Furthermore, in what seems to be a rather pointless exer-

cise, Katô claims that in order for the DJ radio program scene to occur twice, three weeks are necessary. See Katô Norihiro (ed.), *Ierôpêji*, 8-9.

43. Wallace Martin, *Recent Theories of Narrative* (Ithaca: Cornell University Press, 1986), 148.

44. Shlomith Rimmon-Kenan, *Narrative Fiction: Contemporary Poetics* (New York: Methuen, 1983), 108.

45. Jonathon Culler, *Structuralist Poetics: Structuralism, Linguistics and the Study of Literature* (London: Routledge and Kegan Paul, 1980), 189.

46. See Ruthrof, *The Reader's Construction of Narrative*.

47. Martin, *Recent Theories of Narrative*, 108. It must be noted that these categories by no means represent simple unproblematic divisions—but the complexities of their relations are not directly pertinent to this discussion.

48. Birnbaum, "Murakami Haruki—oinaru hokotenkan".

49. See for example, Suzumura Kazunari, *Terefuon—Murakami, Derrida, Yasunari, Prûsuto,* (Tokyo: Yôsensha, 1987), 103; and *Murakami Haruki kuronikuru—1983-1995,* 14; 25.

50. Suga , *Happy Jack—Nezumi no kokoro*, 87-88.

51. See Karatani Kôjin, "Murakami Haruki no 'fûkei'—(II)" *Kaien* (December 1989): 242.

52. Suga, *Happy Jack—Nezumi no kokoro*, 87-88.

53. See Mieke Bal, *Narratology: Introduction to the Theory of Narrativei* (Toronto: University of Toronto Press, 1997), 5. Bal draws on a wide range of theories and approaches in the field of narratology in order to come up with the following succinct and useful definitions: (i) 'A *narrative text* is a text in which an agent relates ("tells") a story in a particular medium, such as language, imagery, sound, buildings or a combination thereof'; (ii) 'A story is a *fabula* that is presented in a certain manner'; (iii) A *fabula* is a series of logically and chronologically related events that are caused or experienced by actors.

54. Sincerity—or at least the *appearance* of sincerity—is crucial to what Fowler has called the 'recorder-witness' paradigm of the Japanese 'I-novel'.

55. See Frederic Jameson, 'Postmodernism and Consumer Society', in *The Anti-Aesthetic—Essays on Postmodern Culture*, ed. Hal Foster (Seattle: Bay Press, 1993), 111-125.

56. Jameson, "Postmodernism and Consumer Society," 111.

57. Jameson, "Postmodernism and Consumer Society," 112.

58. Jameson, "Postmodernism and Consumer Society," 113.

59. Jameson, "Postmodernism and Consumer Society," 116.

60. See Miyoshi Masao, "Against the Native Grain," in *Off Centre*.

61. See KUK 7; 30-35.

62. See for example, KUK 1; 2; 19.

63. Margaret A. Rose, "Parody/Post-Modernism," *Poetics* 17 (1988): 49 -56; 53.

64. Suzumura Kazunari, *Terefuon* (Yôsensha, 1987), 103.

65. KUK 19; 91.

66. HWS 19; 61.

67. KUK 10; 56.

68. HWS 10; 40.

69. Suzumura Kazunari, *Murakami Haruki kuronikuru: 1983-1995* (Yôsensha, 1994), 25.

70. Komori Yoichi, "Tekusto ron no tachiba kara—jitsu rei: Murakami Haruki no *Kaze no uta o kike,*" *Kokubungaku* (July 1989): 88.

71. Takahashi Yoshiki, 'Murakami Haruki sakuhin annai', *Kokubungaku* (March 1985): 132.

72. See Karatani Kôjin, "Murakami Haruki no 'fûkei'—(II)," 242.

73. Karatani, "Murakami Haruki no 'fûkei'—(II)," 244.

74. Karatani, "Murakami Haruki no 'fûkei'—(II)," 242.

75. Margaret A. Rose, "Post-Modern Pastiche," *British Journal of Aesthetics* 31, no. 1 (January 1991): 26-38.

76. Rose, "Post-Modern Pastiche," 33. Rose is quoting from Baudrillard's "The Orders of Simulacra" in *Simulations*, trans. Philip Beitchmann (New York, 1983), 150 ff.

77. Jean Baudrillard, "The Ecstasy of Communication," in *The Anti - Aesthetic: Essays on Postmodern Culture,* ed. Hal Foster (Seattle: Bay Press, 1983), 133.

78. Horst Ruthrof, *The Reader's Construction of Narrative* (London: Routledge & Kegan Paul, 1981), 142.

79. See Winfried Noth, *Handbook of Semiotics* (Bloomington & Indiana: Indiana University Press, 1990), 350.

80. Patricia Waugh, "What is Metafiction and Why are They Saying Such Awful Things About It?," in *Metafiction,* ed. Mark Currie (New York: Longman, 1995), 42.

81. KUK 1; 3.

82. HWS 1; 5.

83. Suzumura Kazunari, *Mada/sude ni* (Yôsensha,1990), 239-40.

84. Kasai Kyoshi et.al., *Murakami Haruki o meguru bôken,* 22-26.

85. Kasai Kyoshi et.al., *Murakami Haruki o meguru bôken,* 27-29.

86. Fictional writing which refers to writing in more tangential ways can still be described as metafictional in that it calls attention to its own status as a literary work. For example, Inoue Hisashi's *Bun to fun* (Shinkobunko, 1970, Chapter One: "Bun to wa nani mono ka") parodies the life of an ageing and not so successful novelist; Takahashi Genichiro's *Jeimusu jiyoisu o yonda nekko* (Kodanshabunko, 1990) opens with a description of the narrator scribbling his travel diary in the taxi on the way to the airport. Such references are all metafictional markers, but not as overt as the narrator's treatment of the issue of writing as in *Kaze*. In Murakami Ryu's *69—Sixty Nine,* a 1987 text which, it must be said, is either an attempt at emulation (or perhaps parody) of Murakami's *Kaze*, the narrator eschews overtly metafictional devices—except in the closing lines of the novel, with a classic conflation of narrator with author (so typical of the 'I-novel' convention) : *'But even now, as a thirty-two-year-old novelist, I get the sense that I seem to forever be chasing the next party.'* (*69—Sixty Nine,* Shûeisha, 1987, 214) and *'I debuted as a novelist nine years ago, and after my first work became a million seller.'* (p.223) *'After becoming a novelist I received a few letters and one phone call from her'.* (*69—Sixty Nine,* 227.)

87. KUK 1; 4.

88. HWS 1; 6.

89. KUK 1; 4-5.

90. HWS 1; 6.

91. KUK 1; 5.

92. HWS 1; 7.

93. KUK 1; 7.

94. HWS 1; 8.

95. KUK 1; 9.

96. HWS 1; 9.

97. KUK 1; 9.

98. KUK 1; 10.

99. KUK 1; 11.

100. See John Barth, "The Literature of Exhaustion" first published in 1967, but more recently published in *Metafiction*, ed. Mark Currie (London: Longman, 1995), 161-171.

101. Overt references to novel writing can be found in the following Chapters in *Kaze*: 5 (25-26); 6 (28); 23 117); 39 (191); Postscript, 199.

102. Towards the end of *Nejimakidori kuronikuru (The Wind-Up Bird Chronicle)*, for example, the represented speech act which takes place between the protagonist and his estranged wife is in the form of an Internet e-mail chat format, complete with computer commands reproduced throughout the dialogue. This is highly metafictional in the sense that even though it does not appear overtly self-referential, the radicality of its inclusion in the midst of a conventional narrative flow, draws attention to its interpretative (or as was noted above, as Ruthrof puts it, 'presentational') rather than its re-presentational dimension.

103. See Linda Hutcheon, *Narcissistic Narrative: The Metafictional Paradox* (New York: Methuen, 1984), 52.

104. Ommundsen offers an insightful discussion of the role of the reader in metafiction. See "The Reader in Contemporary Metafiction: Freedom or Constraint?," *AUMLA* 74 (November 1990): 169-83; esp. 173-175.

105. See Linda Hutcheon, *Narcissistic Narrative: The Metafictional Paradox*. Her typology has two axes: along one axis are diegetic ('narrative') self-awareness and linguistic self awareness, which are further divided on the vertical axis by 'covert' and 'overt' or 'thematized' self-consciousness.

106. Sarah E. Lauzen, "Notes on Metafiction: Every Essay Has a Title," in *Postmodern Fiction—A Bio-Bibliographical Guide*, ed. Larry McCaffrey (Connecticut: Greenwood Press, 1986), 98.

107. Lauzen, "Notes on Metafiction," 102-3. Lauzen offers an extended discussion of structure in metafictional texts over pages 102-6.

108. The novel was first published in serial form in the magazine *MORE* (between July 1984 and October 1995) and later in hardcover by Shuheisha, 1987.

109. Murakami Ryu, *69—Sixty Nine*, 7.

110. See for example Tanaka Yasuo's notorious *Nantonaku kurisutaru*, 1981, (Shincho Bunko, 1992), which lists in great detail the fashionable brand names and commodities of daily consumer life in early eighties Japan.

111. See Matthew Strecher, "Magical realism and the Search for Identity in the Fiction of Murakami Haruki," 264. Strecher's paper is important for other insights, particularly on the Lacanian 'Other' and subjectivity, which are discussed later.

112. See Kuroko Kazuo, *Murakami Haruki—za rosuto wârudo* (Daisanshokan, 1993), 8-9.

113. Imai Kyoto, *Murakami Haruki—OFF no Kankaku* (Seiunsha, 1990), especially. 65-76.

114. Imai, *Murakami Haruki—OFF no Kankaku*, 65.

115. Imai, *Murakami Haruki—OFF no Kankaku*, 68-69. Imai is referring to Konakawa Tetsuo's "Masu medeia jidai no kazoku to kojin," in *Medeia no Sôgoku* (Shobunsha, 1982). Unfortunately Imai does not offer specific page numbers for these references to the Konakawa text.

116. Imai, *Murakami Haruki—OFF no Kankaku*, 68.

117. See for example Miyoshi & Harootunian's Introduction to *Japan in the World.*

118. Imai, *Murakami Haruki—OFF no Kankaku*, 68-69.

119. Imai, *Murakami Haruki—OFF no Kankaku*, 69-70.

120. KUK 12; 69.

121. HWS 12: 48.

122. Imai, *Murakami Haruki—OFF no Kankaku*, 70-71.

123. Imai, *Murakami Haruki—OFF no Kankaku*, 72.

124. Lauzen, "Notes on Metafiction," 102-3.

125. Imai, *Murakami Haruki—OFF no Kankaku*, 71.

126. See "How Acts of Constitution are Stimulated," in Wolfgang Iser, *The Act of Reading: A Theory of Aesthetic Response* (London: Routledge and Kegan Paul, 1978), 180-203.

127. Imai, *Murakami Haruki— OFF no Kankaku*, 76.

128. Imai Kyoto, *Murakami Haruki—OFF no Kankaku*, 76.

129. See Suzumura Kazunari, *Terefuon* (Yôsensha, 1987), 59.

130. Suzumura, *Terefuon,* 59-60.

131. See Ruthrof's essay "Narrative and the Digital: On the Syntax of the Postmodern."

132. Maeda Ai, "Boku to nezumi no kigoron," *Kokubungaku* 3 (March 1985): 96-106.

133. See KUK 7; 35 and KUK: 32; 136 respectively.

134. KUK, 100.

135. KUK 11; 63.

136. HWS 11; 45.

137. KUK 11; 63-64.

138. HWS 11; 45.

139. KUK 11; 65.

140. HWS 11; 46.

141. See KUK 7; 30-35. It is noteworthy that Kawamoto has characterized the narrative speech acts in *Kaze* in terms of the English prefix *dis*—and its use in words such as 'disappoint', 'disillusion', 'discourage', etc. Using the corresponding Japanese negative prefixes (*hi/mu/bu*), he suggests that "Murakami prefers being immersed in the empty world of 'hi', 'mu' and 'bu'". See "'dis' no kyorikan," *Kokubungaku* 3 (March, 1985): 112-17. For an example of such negation in speech, see the conversation between the girl and Boku (KUK 9; 44), about whether she had spoken during her drunken sleep.

142. See Maeda Ai, "Kaku koto to kataru koto," in *Bungaku tekisto nyûmon* (Chikuma Shobo, 1988).

143. Maeda, "Kaku koto to kataru koto," 28.

144. Maeda, "Kaku koto to kataru koto," 29.

145. Maeda, "Kaku koto to kataru koto," 130.

146. Here, Maeda offers examples of advertising copy, presumably drawn from instances around him: 'Don't look at the naked body, *be* naked!' (*hadaka o miruna, hadaka ni nare*); 'delicious daily life' (*oishii seikatsu*); 'you're happy aren't you sâchan!' (*ureshii ne, sâchan*). "Kaku koto to kataru koto," 30-31.

147. Maeda, "Kaku koto to kataru koto," 30-32.

Chapter Five

Allegory as Modality: 1973 nen no pinbôru
—Pinball, 1973

The previous chapter demonstrated several ways in which Murakami's debut fictional work presented a challenge to some conventional aspects of the modern Japanese novel by employing devices such as parody, pastiche and metafiction in ways which were, for the time, quite radical. This chapter will examine the second book in the 'Rat Trilogy', *1973 nen no pinbôru (Pinball, 1973)*, with the aim of demonstrating the further establishment by Murakami of the parameters of a discourse of the simulacrum. As well as considering the broad allegorical modalities indicated by the idea of 'the game', the analysis will explicate a number of specific linguistic devices and tropes which have become a hallmark of Murakami's narrative styles—many of which, however, have been ignored or only partly dealt with in the critical literature emerging around the Murakami oeuvre.

Allegory is Beyond Genre

If it were not for the theoretical ambiguity currently surrounding the notion of allegory, (with the rash of ostensibly 'fresh' insights into genre theory and the taxonomic classification of literary texts implied therein) it would be tempting to see in the recent revival of critical interest in the term a relatively straightforward way of explicating all 'postmodern' narratives. However, it is precisely because allegory persistently fails to constitute any sort of quasi-coherent genre, that it remains at once a compelling if not somewhat elusive feature of narratives which declare that they have something significant to say about the world, but employ relatively indirect methods for doing so.

While some earlier critics (despite conceding that several features of allegory could be seen as generic[1]) deny allegory the status of a genre *per se*, more recent theorists such as Kelley are prepared to concede that it persists as an 'historically contingent genre'.[2] Her point is that allegory is re-visited and re-worked in different ways, contingent upon the dominant tropes and reading conventions of specific time and place. Madsen argues that 'allegory is one of many genres in which a text might participate',[3] while Clifford insists that 'essentially, allegory is, like irony, a mode, and capable of subsuming many different genres and forms'.[4] Van Dyke foregrounds the etymology of the word as highly indicative of a sense of 'otherness': 'The term clearly derives from *allos* and was defined by rhetoricians as *inversio* or *alieniloquium*.'[5] 'Inverse', 'reverse', 'alien', 'other'; all such connotations are appropriate to a broad definition of allegory.

Also pertinent to the concerns of this discussion is the observation that while the definitions of allegory may change, the assumption that 'allegory is a secondary mode, logically or chronologically' persists.[6] It is precisely allegory in its dimension as a 'secondary' way of telling, which provides theoretical impetus for our central claim about the simulacral or 'double order' nature of Murakami's narratives.

But allegory is more complex than the terms 'second order', 'double' or 'other' may suggest. As was shown by reference to Foucault in Chapter 3, in the transformations from the medieval to the modern systems of constructing knowledge in the West, the forms of the sign and representation within which allegory could be expressed have been transformed. It is even more so the case that the so called 'return to allegory' in postmodern fiction is operating under a very different regime of representation dictated by, as Baudrillard argues, the modalities of simulation and the simulacrum.

We noted Foucault's claim that even though in modernity similitude no longer figured directly in the construction of knowledge, it was nevertheless an 'indispensable border of knowledge': in the overdetermined representational power of the signified, resemblance is not completely done away with—rather, it is displaced and comes to be 'imagined'. It was concluded that, assuming the validity of Foucault's argumentation, this new kind of 'shadow of signification' (which itself signified the representative power of the signifier) formed the basis of a semiotic process which allowed the privileging of the signifier in the modern/postmodern 'order of things'. Assuming the veracity of Baudrillard's three orders of simulacra,[7] such privileged signifiers can be said to operate within the semiotic matrix of the 'second order' of productivist simulacra (based on production and the expansion of energy and the machine) and the third order of 'simulation simulacra' (based on the model and the cybernetic game)—or, in terms of their paradigmatic forms of cultural typification, modernity and post-modernity respectively.

The place of allegory in the Japanese literary tradition needs to be examined, but at this point it is worth noting that in a universal sense (recalling Derrida's question 'what would be the metaphor of metaphor?'[8]) it is clear that in the same way all language is 'figurative', it is also allegorical:

> Allegory . . . acquires the status of trope of tropes, representative of the figurality of all language, of the distance between signifier and signified, and, correlatively, the response to allegory becomes representative of critical activity per se.[9]

We are aware, however, that unlike metaphor, allegory entails an *extended* system of reference, and that it usually forms the basis for an entire narrative. Murakami's texts utilize allegory as one amongst a range of simulacral narrative *modalities* which are typically part and parcel of the 'estrangement' function of a literary text. The allegorical master trope serves Murakami well, since 'making strange' is undoubtedly something he has put to good use in his fiction. As Clifford notes:

> Allegory is . . . a natural language for visionary strangeness and intensity, and its moral and intellectual preoccupations strengthen rather than diminish this visionary power.[10]

In the post-structuralist critical milieu it seems odd that while the ostensibly ideological function of allegory may have receded, it has perhaps given way to an 'individualist' and 'moral' tenor which, nevertheless, seems entirely 'modern' in its overtones. In Murakami's case the 'moral core' of his texts has been characterized by one Western critic as 'individual' rather than 'ideological'[11] — although this apparent post-Cold War aversion to the term 'ideology' is not especially useful. If the attempt at the writing of fiction or history (allegorically or otherwise) is in any way 'ideological', then of course Murakami's texts cannot be said to operate 'outside' of ideology.

Debate about the political/ideological status of allegory in contemporary writing appears to be related to another kind of argument about genre; while some critics have argued that recent post-structuralist discussion does not represent a substantial reformulation of allegory,[12] another approach has noted, by extension, that the apparent foregrounding of the *modality* of allegory in much contemporary fiction is significant. For example, the 'magical realism' claimed by Strecher for Murakami's work, suggests not that it has tried to emulate the magical realism of South America, but merely its format or modality:

> The literature of Murakami Haruki merely uses the techniques of magical realism without necessarily involving itself in (its) various political attachments.[13]

In a somewhat contradictory manner, Strecher goes on to acknowledge that although Murakami's fiction partakes in the worldwide movement of postmodern fiction in eliminating the barriers between 'art' and 'entertainment',[14] the author 'uses magical realist techniques, in order to advance his own agenda, political, cultural or otherwise'.[15] It is argued throughout this discussion that Murakami's fiction does have a political 'agenda', but it is often less explicit than may at first appear.

Perhaps the most succinct characterization of the significance of allegory in postmodern fiction comes from Kelley, who recognizes its meta-textual function in a wide ranging legitimization of the ludic, experimental and critically self-reflexive tendencies for which contemporary writing is known:

> As the metafigure of irony and invention, allegory hovers playfully and seriously over late modernity's turn from realism toward something else whose

hybrid nature is one sign of its resilience . . . . call it Latin American magical
realism, philosophical or science fiction, postmodern or postcolonial political
fable, or critical theory. In all these modes allegory authorizes 'metacommen-
tary' and improvisation.[16]

Japanese Allegory

Some of the metafictional aspects of Murakami's novels were noted in the previous chapter, and it was suggested that both structural and stylistic improvisation are common in his works. Despite the fact that Murakami's fiction as a literature of 'defamiliarization' [17] has much in common with other major
contemporary exemplars of 'world literature' (for example De Lillo, Pynchon,
Rushdie, Marquez), it is necessary to consider how it stands more specifically as
allegorical experimentation within the context of the modern Japanese literary
milieu. But first a brief digression. In the Western tradition, stories which depict
events in a narrated 'concrete' world in order to extrapolate abstract ideas about
how things could or should be in an 'imaginary' world, are variously known as
allegory, fable and parable, and are exemplified canonically by texts based on
the symbolic modes of Platonic idealism and, as is more well known, medieval
Christian theology.

In the Japanese context, literary discourses which have utilized the device of
allegory have been a feature of several 'genres' such as *monogatari*, *setsuwa*,
gûwa and *tatoebanashi*. However, attempting a more definitive explication of
these forms in terms of Western corollaries is complicated by the fact that each
of these words relies on one or more of the other terms for its definition. Naturally, under the broad rubric of 'narrative', it is reasonable to claim that allegory
is subsumed by the 'master genre', *monogatari*, which is defined by the *Kôjien*
as 'a literary work of narrated prose (*jojutsu shita sanbun*) about people and
events based on an author's knowledge, experience (*kenbun*) and imagination
(*sôzô*)'.[18] Nevertheless, as generally spoken of, it is thought to have been an historically limited literary form properly belonging to a period extending approximately eight centuries, from the *Heian* (794-893) to the *Muromachi* (1334-1573)
eras.[19]

The term *setsuwa* is variously given as *hanashi* ('talk', 'story') and *monogatari* (defined above). More specifically, it has also been described as 'myth'
(*shinwa*) 'legend' (*densetsu*) and 'fairy tale' (*dowa*).[20] With *tatoebanashi*, we
sense something more akin to our usual understanding of allegory, since the term
is derived from the transitive verb *tatoeru*, meaning 'to compare or liken'.[21] Indeed this term is also defined as *gûwa*, the Japanese term most often translated
as fable or allegory.[22]

Notwithstanding the fact that the term 'allegory' has officially entered the
Japanese language in its katakana form as *aregori*,[23] the definition of *gûwa* is
given as a *tatoebanashi* which may incorporate a 'lesson' (*kyôkun*), or 'satire'
(*fûshi*). Moreover, it is said to often involve a process of anthropomorphisization

or personification (*gijinka*). Remarkably, the *Kôjien* gives the Greek storyteller, Aesop, as its only illustrative example.[24] This is more than a little surprising, since, as in the European context, some of the more striking examples of allegory are to be found in the context of religious literature, and as in the West, it is the medieval period in Japan which offers some of the most engaging examples. We will refer more specifically to the medieval Japanese use of allegory later in the chapter, and suggest a parallel to Murakami's efficacious use of the device as a key narrative strategy.

If reading a Murakami text is indeed liberating from the conventional tropes of 'sincerity' and 'truth' evident in the reading practices implied in more orthodox works of modern Japanese fiction, it is not necessarily because Murakami alone has had a monopoly on allegorical fiction. In an important comparative work on contemporary Japanese narrative, Shibata has noted that texts utilizing allegory (*gûwa*) and caricature (*giga*) seem to have become, in recent years, an increasingly common feature of the literary landscape.[25] In Shibata's list of texts which are described as challenging the orthodox sense of 'imitation' (*mozô*) of 'real society' (*genjitsushakai*), Ôe Kenzaburô features prominently. However, Shibata's analysis rightly cites authors such as Tsutsui Yasutaka, Abe Kôbô, Nakagami Kenji, Murakami Ryû, Takahashi Genichirô, Shimada Masahiko and Murakami Haruki as key figures in contemporary 'allegorical' (*gûwa*) writing. Of course, a genealogy of 'allegorical' texts in Japanese literary modernism should probably commence with Sôseki's *Yume jûya* (*Ten Night's of Dream*);[26] one critic has even drawn a parallel between Sôseki's 'Dream of the Sixth Night' and Murakami's *Sekai no owari to hâdoboirudo wandârando* (*Hard-boiled Wonderland and the End of the World*).[27]

In such a view, Murakami's works could be described as among the more recent instances of the literary topos of interrogating 'the real' in a way which is not dissimilar to conventions deeply entrenched in the Japanese literary tradition. The sheer range in style of twentieth century Japanese writers who have used allegory as a key narrative strategy is indeed impressive, although the use of allegory extends far back into the Japanese medieval and classical literary traditions.[28]

What is compelling about Murakami's narratives is that by employing allegory in terms of a generalized *modality*, they are able to fashion more overtly meta-fictional and self-reflexive texts. In other words, they are texts which rely not so much on their apparent 'propositional content' to make certain points about the world, but draw attention more to their *modes* of delivery. According to Ruthrof, the theory of modality in language, (and especially in literary language) has been sorely under-theorized, and he urges that we not shy away from the task of elucidating modal processes in our haste to elicit more readily recoverable meanings:

> One (important) function of the text can be seen to be a complex concealment of multiple modalities: the text as hermeneutic challenge.[29]

Attempting such 'unconcealment' is precisely the way in which Murakami's texts will be approached in this chapter—but not in the quasi 'forensic' way in which some critics have sought the 'truth' of the texts by identifying parallels in the 'real' world, and by way of distilling obscure 'clues' and 'symbols' to solve riddles or puzzles (*nazo*).[30] Rather, before returning to develop broader aesthetic and philosophical questions in later chapters, the task in this chapter will be to examine the specific uses of allegorical tropes as modal signifiers in the text of *1973 nen no pinbôru* (*Pinball, 1973*). This will occur specifically with reference to the industrial/political matrices of post-war Japanese culture, and more generally, as a further step in continuing the interrogation of Japanese modernity undertaken in the second chapter.

Narrative Synopsis (kôgai) of *1973 nen no pinbôru*

(*Pinball, 1973*—hereafter referred to as *Pinbôru.*)

The parallel or 'double series'(nikeiretsu) story of 'Boku' (I) and 'Nezumi'('the Rat') established in the first novel, proceeds. Boku, who jointly runs a small translation office in Tokyo, becomes increasingly preoccupied with an eerie feeling that he should be somewhere else. By making a connection with the hometown of his dead college girlfriend, and an old style electrical switchboard, he is confronted with his longing for a certain pinball machine. He played this machine in his home town at a time in the early seventies, when he was at a loss as to what else to do with his life. After descending into an 'underworld' search of disused pinball machines, he eventually finds the particular machine that he had formerly used, and through this process, is able to return to 'reality' (genjitsu). Meanwhile Nezumi, who has remained in his hometown, is also overtaken by a strange sensation that whatever the cost, he will have to start a process of self-transformation. He confesses this to Jay (the owner of their regular drinking bar) and decides to leave town. However, as he is about to leave on his journey he is overtaken by a longing to sleep at the bottom of the ocean.[31]

In keeping with the practice adopted in the previous chapter (and for the purpose of achieving consistency in presenting the synoptic version of the text to readers unfamiliar with it) a translation of the narrative outline presented in the *Murakami zen shôsetsu jiten*[32] is offered above. Despite being a highly abridged form of the story, the editor has mentioned aspects of the narrative which also feature quite centrally in the analysis which follows.

The Critical Reception of *1973 nen no pinbôru*

As with all of Murakami's published work, there has arisen alongside this text a plethora of critical literature clamoring for attention in the over-crowded market of the 'criticism' industry in Japan. As was shown earlier, the 'Murakami Phenomenon' is above all a successful *publishing* phenomenon and as such attracts a wide range of responses, especially in mass circulation magazines. Nevertheless, amidst the surfeit of commentary several critics stand out. Their work is important because it contributes to the difficult enterprise of attempting to situate Murakami's texts in relation to a clearly defined canon of literary/critical orthodoxy, whose parameters are dictated by the authority vested in the relatively closed critical milieu of the enduring *bundan* ('literary world') in Tokyo. Our discussion of these more sophisticated analyses is preceded by a brief survey of some of the less scholarly responses to the text which are, nevertheless, deserving of mention.

One of the very first critical reviews of *Pinbôru*, written in September 1980, characterized the work as a form of 'kindhearted nihilism' (*yasashii kyomukan*), concerned with 'loss' and a sort of 'decadent nostalgia' in its depiction of feelings directed towards a machine, rather than a human being.[33] This response typifies the kind of reading which seeks to impute a stock of themes apparently directly inferable from a process which 'identifies' (or perhaps constructs) homologous patterns of action and meaning, connecting the author's (*sakka*) life with the voice of the narrator (*katarite*). Such an approach is an exemplary instance of the 'I-novel methodology' (*shishôsetsuron*) underlying much modern Japanese literary-critical practice.

Other examples of this methodology include an approach which sees in the protagonist's search for the lost pinball machine a search for his own 'identity',[34] and another perspective which attributes Boku's obsession with pinball and his sense of despair to the lingering grief over his dead girlfriend Naoko.[35] Of course, as many commentators have noted, the overarching motif of the *Kaze* and *Pinbôru* texts which ostensibly connects the protagonist with the 'real life' of the author is the deep sense of despair engendered by the failure of the student protest movement (*zenkyôtô*) in the late sixties.[36]

Some critics have tended to focus more on linguistic features such as nomenclature and the tenor and register of represented speech-acts in the text, drawing various implications from the use of such stylistic devices. For instance, in noting the special role of personal pronouns (*ninshô daimeishi*) in place of proper names (*koyûmeishi*) in *Pinbôru*, Hayashi observes that the peculiar naming of Boku ('I') and Nezumi ('the Rat') signifies a process of perpetual alterity or the interchangeability of the roles of the characters, which, by denying the attribution of idiosyncratic personality traits to either of the figures, is suggestive of the motif of 'the loss of identity'.[37] In a similar vein, Kanno describes a process of the muted expression of 'background emotions', signified through the formulaic use of set phrases in the narrator's reflections, while acknowledging the problematic nature of attempting to contextualize what appears to be an 'Americanized' and 'hardboiled' narrative idiom.[38] Linguistic features constitute an important aspect of our analysis of Murakami's narratives, and will be considered in some detail in this and subsequent chapters.

In order to substantiate the claim that in *Pinbôru*, the structure of allegory itself—rather than its 'content'—is being used as a modal device to signify the problematic nature of representation, we will demonstrate that the text develops an overall work ideology in two stages. Firstly, by building up a rhetoric of commodified sign-fetishes in the first part of the narrative (within the presented world of the post-industrial cityscape), the text establishes a discourse of nostalgia by extrapolating the idea of 'individual' loss into the generalized yearning for 'modernity's losses' typified in the analyses articulated by Ivy.[39] This discourse establishes a system of symbolic equivalences in which the sign-fetishes are allocated appropriate 'exchange-values', and the protagonist is free to manipulate/substitute them in ways which reflect his feelings and emotions. Importantly, in order for these exchange-values to have been established, all of the sign fetishes are assigned the quality of absolute substitutability.

The author's second move is surprising yet disarmingly simple. Here we take our theoretical lead from Iser, and note that through expectations established in the process of activating 'blanks' in the forward reading dimension,[40] the reader's anticipation of narrative outcomes has become more or less firmly established. Such certainty precedes the unexpected move of the narrator effectively 'cashing in' the sign-fetish values in a final clean sweep of meaning entailing existential illumination: an apparent realization that if all things are of absolutely the same value, then they are also of absolutely equal valuelessness. This is realized in a moment of epiphany, in which the narrator proclaims his feeling of wonderment at the day 'shining brightly through each and every thing'.

The narrative requires these two distinct stages because from the outset it needs to speak in the language of familiarity: the ostensibly nostalgic sense of loss signified through an object-world typified by the late-capitalist order of production, consumption and obsolescence. The established narrative order is then abruptly 'de-familiarized' in the denial of a closure at the end the novel, signified by the loss of *all* things. The 'allegorical' elements are used to engage the reader in preparation for a demonstration of the negation of the very validity of such elements in being able to represent the 'truth' of the world. By relating some critical perspectives directly to the language and structures of the text, we can substantiate our claim for the status of allegory as modality in *Pinbôru*.

Allegory, Game, History

Given the title of the novel, there can be no more obvious starting point than a consideration of the allegorical rendering of the idea of 'the game'. In so doing, it is necessary to think about the implications of such a metaphor, both in terms of the construction of individual subjectivity, as well as in the broader context of a literary/historical trope whose referent is constructed by the prevailing discourses and systems of production and knowledge in post-war Japanese society. As a point of entry into the topic, we begin by juxtaposing *Pinbôru* with a novel by Japan's most recent Nobel laureate.

Having noted Shibata's observation that allegory (*gûwa*) has become a prominent feature of much contemporary Japanese writing, it should come as no surprise that narratives which utilize the metaphor of 'the game' exemplify this tendency. Arguably, the most well known recent example of this can be seen in Ôe Kenzaburô's *Mannen gannen no futobôru*.[41] Although translated by John Bester as *The Silent Cry*,[42] a more literal rendering of the title might be *Football Match in the First Year of Eternity*. The work is a complex expression of modernist anguish, and if there is any 'game' metaphor to be read from the narrative, it is the rivalry of two brothers played out in a remote rural valley formerly inhabited by their ancestors. Among other things, the text interrogates the role of myth, place, history and collective memory in the formation of contemporary identity. We noted in Chapter 2 that in terms of its theorization, Japan's experience of modernity remains highly problematic, and Ôe's text deals with many of the major themes about loss, identity and authenticity dominating debate on the topic.

Karatani Kôjin's suggestion that Murakami's *Pinbôru* is a kind of parody of Ôe's *Mannen gannen no futobôru* is worth noting.[43] Despite the fact that Murakami has denied that he intended to present a parody of the content of Ôe's work,[44] there is little doubt that the regime of intertextuality operating in the world of contemporary Japanese fiction implies that the parodic *effect* of the text's reception must at least be allowed for.

In any event, Karatani's point about the commonality of the game motif is well made, especially in the light of his comments on its sociological dimensions. He cites Levi-Strauss' analysis of the game as 'structure', noting that it provides both a dividing *and* a connecting function. In the context of a symmetry which is pre-established, all participants are initially viewed as being equal. Following the game, despite the fact that a winner and loser are identifiable (as the result of a combination of will, luck and ability manifested through acting and performance (*engi*) in the execution of the game), *all* participants are ultimately allowed to enter the side of the winners. In short, rather than dividing and separating, the game functions to affirm social union and (comm)union, by continually reasserting symmetry and harmony through the structure of the *performance* of rivalry and opposition.[45]

It is noteworthy that Karatani has chosen to apply some of Levi-Strauss' anthropological insights on the structural analysis of gaming in his approach to *Pinbôru*, because as will be detailed later, a structuralist typification is also crucial to Baudrillard's sociological method in *The System of Objects*. And although Karatani doesn't embrace Levis Strauss' method completely, his reference to a structuralist orientation forms the basis of some interesting insights into the *Pinbôru* text.

Karatani notes the enduring nature of 'the contest' and 'the game' in contemporary industrial society, as well as its variation in the form of 'the hobby'. Of course, these phenomena do allow for the formation of social groupings and structures of social cohesion through contestation. On the other hand, there are different *kinds* of contestation, and in the case of the Ôe and Murakami texts, it is clear that any inter-textual parodic resonance is undermined by the fact that *as* games, 'football' and 'pinball' are highly dissimilar.

Indeed, such heterogeneity informs Karatani's comparative observations. Firstly, that Ôe's 'Football' is synonymous with Levi-Strauss' 'contest' (*kyôgi*), and that this allegory of 'the game' makes possible a view which sees the creation of history 'from structure' (*kôzô kara*). Without such a perspective it seems that Ôe's text would have been written up as an 'ordinary historical novel' (*arifureta rekishi shôsetsu*). However, according to Karatani, if this novel had been written *only* from 'structure', history itself would have vanished. His point is that since history is 'outside' structure, and emerges from the traffic (*kôtsû*) of asymmetrical relations, the 'eventivity' (*dekigotosei*) of history can never be reduced solely to structure. In other words, by juxtaposing the terms 'the first year of eternity' (*mannen gannen*) with 'football' (*futobôru*), Ôe was attempting to interrogate the notion of history in terms of structure, and the idea of structure in terms of history.[46]

Secondly, in contrast to the above, the nexus between '1973' and 'Pinball' in the title of the Murakami text is purely arbitrary. That is to say, the term '1973' is nothing other than a sign (*kigô*), which functions purely as a marker of difference (*sai*). Superficially, it appears that the games of football and pinball are similar in-so-far as they both result in the emergence of winners and losers. However, Karatani characterizes victory on the part of the pinball machine as implausible and suggests that strictly speaking, in this game 'winning' and 'losing' do not occur—or if they do, then surely it is the player who is always the loser. But such loss does not constitute an 'event', because the player has the option of a 'replay' and attempts, as far as possible, to become familiar with the constraints and rules established by the machine. Out of such observations, Karatani sums up by claiming the following: in using the pinball metaphor, Murakami is implying not that history is created from structure (i.e. a system of rules), but that history, *per se*, does not exist.[47]

If indeed Murakami's resort to the use of allegory represents a kind of philosophical move to dis-engage from 'history', then there is also much in the presented world and structure of the *Pinbôru* text which might just as well function to undermine the subversive sway of such a position. The value of the signifier 'history' in this text is very much a function of the available readings which are brought to it. For instance, a parodic reading would at least suggest an engagement with the kind of diachrony not necessarily precluding history, while a 'nostalgic' and quasi-realist reading would trivialize and fetishize any recuperable historicity.

Karatani's point about the status of history in the *Pinbôru* text resonates with several issues to be explored in this chapter. However, it seems fair to argue that the 'use and abuse of history'[48] in the novel is but one of many examples of the deployment of the sign-fetish or commodity which serve merely to signify difference *for its own sake*, and which are metonymically arrayed throughout the text in order to establish an allegorical discourse.

The link between allegory and the commodity was established through Walter Benjamin's depiction of the commodity as the modern embodiment of the allegorical. And it is clear that the discourse of *Pinbôru* weaves its incantation of 'ruination' precisely through a self-reflexive adherence to a semiotic process of the 'hollowing-out of meaning', as indispensable to its status as modern allegory. Although we will return to Benjamin's theory of allegory and ruination later, we may note here a clear exposition of these relations in the following succinct description:

> For Benjamin, the commodity both exhibits characteristics similar to the allegorical — it is 'hollow' — and is the object of the allegorical gaze — as a result of which, it becomes a ruin.[49]

It seems that it is precisely the self-conscious and highly metafictional use of 'history' in the prologue of *Pinbôru* which establishes the ground rules for reading the entire chain of metonymy and fragmentation extending throughout the narrative. This is evident in the following excerpt, in which the narrator relates details of the involvement of 'a guy from Saturn' in the campus protest activities (*Zenkyôtô*) of Japanese college students in late 1969:

> 「彼はある政治的なグループに所属しそのグループは大学の九号館を占拠していた。『行動が思想を決定する。逆は不可。』というのが彼らのモットーだった。何が行動を決定するのかについては誰も教えてくれなかった。ところで九号館にはウォーター・クーラーと電話と給湯設備があり、二階には二千枚のレコード・コレクションとアルテックA5を備えた小奇麗な音楽室まであった……それは天国だった……。
> 気持ち良く晴れわたった１１月の午後、第三機動隊が九号館に突入した時にはヴィヴァルディの『調和の幻想』がフルボリュームで流れていたということだが真偽のほどはわからない。６９年をめぐる心暖まる伝説のひとつだ。」[50]

> He belonged to a political group that had staged a take-over of Building 9 in the university. Their motto was 'Action Determines Ideology — Not the Reverse'. No one would tell him what determined action. No matter, Building 9 had a water cooler, a telephone, and boiler facilities; and upstairs they had a nice little music lounge with Altec A-5 speakers and a collection of two thousand records. It was paradise . . . .

> Then one beautifully clear November afternoon, riot police forced their way into Building 9 while Vivaldi's L'Estro Armonico was blaring away full blast. I don't know how true all this is, but it remains one of the more heartwarming stories of 1969.[51]

Apart from the more obvious sense of parody invoked by the conjunction of the Vivaldi music and the climactic, abrupt end to the students' occupation, the passage is replete with signifiers that fetishize the presented retro-world of the narrative. The term 'Building 9' occurs three times in the short passage. Although it is common for Japanese institutions to designate buildings by number, this instance is typical of Murakami's proclivity not only to avoid the use of proper nouns (*koyûmeishi*), but also to append arbitrary numerical values to the description of objects.

The possibility that the Marxist political slogan might be connotative of 'history' itself, is immediately foreclosed by its being trivialized through juxtaposition with the detailed list of generically given objects. The 'water cooler', 'telephone', 'boiler facilities' and 'record collection' bespeak the mundane and familiar comforts of modern urban existence—and the 'farce' of revolutionary action is further compounded by the narrator offering specific details of the audio-speaker model/serial number 'A5'. This reminds us of Baudrillard's analysis of the importance of the phenomena of the 'model' and 'series' as crucial to our understanding of the role and formation of the modern object:

> The psycho-sociological dynamic of model and series . . . [operates] at the level of an object grounded simultaneously in individual requirements and in that system of differences which is, properly speaking, the cultural system itself.[52]

It is precisely in relation to the 'cultural system' of advanced capitalism—and the thorough-going differentiation and commodification of daily life within it—that the presented object-world of Murakami's early narratives poses the question of the representation of 'history' and the possibility of critique. The feigned banishment of the referent in *Pinbôru* is in stark contrast to the narrative processes which will be described in later chapters, where the term 'the use of history' assumes entirely different connotations.

What is evoked in the references to the political slogan, the objects and the classical music piece is a presented world defined entirely on the basis of the possibility of different 'styles'—of systems of thought, audio speakers, musical melodies—signified by reference to marginally differentiated objects, which 'stand in for' meanings which might otherwise be made possible through such devices as non-ironical historical reference, or the represented speech-acts of characters.

But the array of presented possible styles does not function, in terms of the text's overall work ideology, in a 'nostalgic' way (i.e. nostalgia as an attempted recuperation of loss). Rather, the prologue establishes the rules for reading which will be called upon in order for the reader to substantiate the metonymic links and substitution of signs later in the narrative. This is the prelude to the effective banishment of allegorical signification at the conclusion of the novel. The narrator must set up the system—that is, the *modality* of allegory—as a way of allegorizing the *impossibility* of allegorical representation, and signifiers such as 'history' and those of 'the commodity' are part of his tool kit in this task. Without such a strategy, the narrative would be hampered in its task of critique, and unable to escape the tyranny of the 'I-novel' conventions. In short, this text treads the precarious path between being read as an 'historical allegory', or perhaps even worse, 'nostalgically'.

On the face of it, further evidence for the apparent denial of 'history' might be seen in the quasi-documentary sketch on the origins of the pinball machine, which is said, surprisingly, to parallel Hitler's rise in the new Weimar Republic:

> 「もっともピンボールの史上第1号機が1934年にこの人物の手によっ
> てテクノロジーの黄金の雲の間からこの汚れ多き地上にもたらされたと
> いうのはひとつの歴史的事実である。そしてそれはまたアドルフ・ヒッ
> トラーが大西洋という巨大な水たまりを隔てて、ワイマールの梯子の一
> 段目に手をかけようとしていた年でもあった。」 [53]

> To be sure, it's a historical fact that by this man's very hands the first prototype of the pinball machine was brought unto this realm of defilement in 1934 from out of the great, golden cloud of technology. Which is again the very year that, across that giant puddle called the Atlantic, one Adolf Hitler was getting his hands on the Weimar ladder.[54]

However, the 'historical fact' (*rekishiteki jijitsu*) of Raymond Maloney's invention is brought into sharp contrast with a process much less clearly defined: the mysterious, almost alchemical emergence of the machine 'from the golden cloud of technology' (*tekunorogî no kogane no kumo no aida kara*). Here, 'fact' and 'myth' stand in an uneasy conjunction, the purpose of which becomes clear further on in the same section:

> 「ピンボール・マシーンとヒットラーの歩みはある共通点を有している。
> 彼らの双方がある種のいかがわしさと共に時代の泡としてこの世に生じ、
> そしてその存在自体よりは進化のスピードによって神話的オーラを獲得
> したという点で。進化はもちろん三つの車輪、すなわちテクノロジーと
> 資本投下、それに人々の根源的希望によって支えられていた。」 [55]

> The progress of the pinball machine and of Hitler exhibit certain similarities. Both have dubious beginnings, coming on the scene as mere bubbles on the froth of the times; it is through their evolutionary speed rather than any physical stature per se that they acquire their mythic aura. And of course, that evolution came riding in on three wheels: to wit, technology, capital investment, and last but not least, people's basic desires.[56]

Far from *denying* history, at this point the narrator is actually making a concise statement about issues at the core of historiography: 'historical facts' as truth, the 'eventivity' of historical process, continuity versus discontinuity, and so on. Indeed, the narrator's comments are actually much closer to establishing a kind of historical-materialist perspective, signified by the suggestion of a nexus between technology, capital and desire. Perhaps more importantly, we also see the narrator's treatment of 'myth' in the sense that Barthes has typified it: not only as a 'meta-language'—a second-order signifying system—but also in its capacity as 'de-politicized speech'. In other words, the narrator of *Pinbôru*, is actually describing the *historical* process whereby myth assumes its fullest expression *vis-à-vis* history:

What the world supplies to myth is an historical reality; . . . and what myth
gives in return is a natural image of this reality. Myth is constituted by the loss
of the historical quality of things: in it, things lose the memory that they were
once made.[57]

But this 'forgetting' of the material conditions of historical production (signified
by reference to the 'mythic aura' surrounding both Hitler and the pinball machine) is ironically undermined by the provision of details of the rapid development of the technical capabilities of the pinball machine. Subsequent to this the
narrator goes on, finally, to assuage any doubt the reader may have about the
'real' topic of the novel, by way of the following curt, metafictional flourish:

「これはピンボールについての小説である。」[58]

This is a novel about pinball. [59]

In *Pinbôru*, history is not simply 'absent', as Karatani would have it. Rather, the
narrator is intimating that perhaps history is just too complex a topic to be dealt
with in an unproblematic way—and certainly not in a too transparently 'allegorical' fashion. The narrator's commentary actually destabilizes the status of the
referent (thus broaching the intractable problem of representation in historical
discourse) in a way quite different and more urgently compelling) than the
method adopted by Ôe in his more overtly allegorical tale. Interestingly, this
move occurs relatively early in Murakami's novelistic enterprise, and is really
only subject to significant qualification and revision in the long trilogy appearing
more than a decade later.

Despite the possibility of operating by default, the centrality of the signifier of
an ironicized 'history' in *Pinbôru* cannot be discounted. Instead, its relative importance is actually a function of the extent to which it supports a process of
seemingly disparate and incoherent narrative strands being woven around various fragments and sign-fetishes. It will be shown that this dimension of the text
operates synchronically and metonymically, and provides further evidence of the
use of allegory in an unusual way. It establishes a system for the symbolic exchange or substitution of signs, which actually functions as a 'modal' operation
of semantic significance in its own right. Such a system—although indispensable
to the narrative momentum of the text—derives its usefulness from the fact that
it is established precisely in order to be, in the end, completely dissolved.

The Poetics of the Machine

If the narrator's version of 'history' is indeed germane to our understanding of
Pinbôru, the question arises as to the metaphorical significance of the 'pinball
machine'. If the allegory of the game relates to the formation of social structures,
is there anything about the *machine* game that might indicate or preclude certain

kinds of social structures? Is the choice of a pinball machine as one of the central tropes of the narrative a flippant or arbitrary selection? If not, to what extent can an understanding of the aesthetics and format of the machine game be relevant to our analysis of the text?

We may respond to such questions by noting, first of all, Orita's observations about the advent of the first modern 'flipper machine' in 1947. Whereas the earlier machines had a 'payout' hole and were a form of gambling based largely on chance, the new models did away with monetary reward, and placed much greater emphasis on player technique. The new machine itself became screened off from the outside world and came to operate in a highly 'privatized' space, and because no material prize was offered, playing it became, effectively, a perfectly 'useless' activity.[60] The question arises: what were the implications for subjectivity entailed in playing this new kind of a machine?

The issue of the apparent aimlessness and redundancy of such an activity is taken up by the narrator of *Pinbôru* in the final passages of the prologue:

「しかしピンボール・マシーンはあなたを何処にも連れて行きはしない。リプレイ（再試合）のランプを灯すだけ。リプレイ、リプレイ、リプレイ……、まるでピンボール・ゲームそのものがある永劫性を目指しているようにさえ思える。

永劫性について我々は多くを知らぬ。しかしこの影を推し測ることはできる。ピンボールの目的は自己表現にあるのではなく、自己革命にある。エゴの拡大にではなく、縮小にある。分析にではなく、包括にある。もしあなたが自己表現やエゴの拡大や分析を目指せば、あなたは反則ランプによって容赦なき報復を受けるだろう。良きゲームを祈る。」[61]

Pinball machines . . . won't lead you anywhere. Just the replay light. Replay, replay, replay . . . so persistently you'd swear a game of pinball aspired to perpetuity. We ourselves will never know much of perpetuity. But we can get a faint inkling of what it's like. The object of pinball lies not in self-expression, but in self-revolt. Not in the expansion of the ego, but in its compression. Not in extractive analysis, but in inclusive subsumption. So if it's self-expression or ego-expansion or analysis you're after, you'll only be subjected to the merciless retaliation of the tilt lamps. Have a nice game.[62]

In this candid account by the narrator, some very important issues about subjectivity and the machine as aesthetic 'object' are being implicitly addressed. One critic has seen in the above passage, confirmation that the 'inclusive subsumption' (*hôkatsu*) into which the player must enter is a kind of 'compensation' (*daishô*) for the failed revolution of the sixties.[63] This view resonates with another perspective which ascribes to the protagonist, Boku, the appearance of 'entrusting' the pinball machine with the memory of the game-like 'season of rebellion'—that is, the leftover (albeit benign) radical student consciousness of the early 1970s.[64]

Karatani, on the other hand, deals more directly with the question of the transformation of individual subjectivity. Not only does the possibility of 'the replay' provide the player with a 'sense of eternity' (*eigôsei*), but the closed world of the game comes to depend on the player's arbitrariness. A new form of the subject (*shutai*) is made to appear through the game, and this is none other than the player as 'transcendental subject/ego' (*chôetsuron teki shukan*). In short, when deeply immersed in the playing of the game, the 'experiential self' (*keikenteki na jiko*) is reduced, while conversely, the 'transcendental self' which is observing that process of reduction, becomes augmented — 'corpulent' or 'fleshed out'.[65]

The physical setting in which the player 'operates' the game—the highly privatized world of player and machine—is carved out from within a space allocated as 'game centre/arcade' deep within the urban-industrial labyrinth. It is a contradictory space, characterized by functionality and utility and the playing out of desire, to which 'players' regularly commute, and within which the 're-duction of the experiential self' proceeds in a way not unlike the kind of alienation which derives from the mundane and repetitive work practices of the industrial /post industrial age.

Shibata has noted that most protagonists in Murakami's narratives are urban workers more attuned to leading a highly regulated daily life than being preoccupied with revolution.[66] Certainly, Boku's job as a translator is described as a kind of process or piece-work, involving little more than the transfer of documents from the in-tray to the out-tray. And to what extent, it might be asked, does the accumulation of a numerical score on the pinball machine, parallel the accumulation of the small sums of 'surplus value' resulting from the aggregation of the worker's daily labor?[67] About midway through *Pinbôru*, the narrator reflects on his brief but obsessive encounter with the 'three-flipper "Space-ship" machine':

> 「僕が本当にピンボールの呪術の世界に入り込んだのは1970年の冬のことだった。その半年ばかりを僕は暗い穴の中で過ごしたような気がする……。限りのない硬貨が機械に放り込まれ、ちょうど一ヶ月後……僕のスコアは……6桁を越えた……。僕は……スコア・ボードに表示されたままの105220という6個の数字を長い間じっと眺めていた。」
> [68]

It was the winter of 1970 when I slipped into the enchanted kingdom of pinball. I might as well have been living in a dark hole those six months. An endless stream of coins fed into the machine, until one month later, my score soared to six-figures . . . I stared for the longest time at those six digits registered on the scoreboard—105,220.[69]

The fetishized 'six-figure' score reads like a substantial bank balance, achieved only after considerable effort and thrift. Herein lies a metaphor of the promise of accumulation for those with the required dedication, single-mindedness and skillful development of technique. How tellingly does this kind of fleeting, gratifying sensation reflect that experienced by countless individual workers—and through whose labor, the postwar Japanese 'miracle' was built? And how much closer is the following image to accurately evoking the largely unacknowledged story of postwar Japanese labor, buried within the exponentially rising national production statistics of the high growth period of the sixties and seventies?:

「ハギング、パス、トラップ、ストップ・ショット……大抵のテクニックを習熟した……。スコアが１５万を越えるころに本当の冬がやってきた。僕は冷えきって人影もまばらなゲーム・センターで、ダッフル・コートにくるまり、マフラーを耳までひっぱりあげたままピンボール・マシーンを抱き続けた。便所の鏡の中に時折見かける僕の顔はやせて骨ばり……。」 [70]

I became practiced in most techniques—hugging, passing, trapping, the stop shot. . . . By the time I broke 150,000 winter had really set in. There I'd be, alone in the freezing, deserted game centre, bundled up in my duffel coat, muffler wrapped around my neck up to my ears, grappling with the machine. The face I'd encounter from time to time in the restroom mirror looked lean and haggard. [71]

It is hard to imagine a more stark image of the lone and alienated worker, laboring to perfect prescribed and repetitive physical, manipulative techniques in a harsh environment and without apparent gratification. Indeed this 'lean and haggard' visage represents precisely the reflection of Karatani's 'reduced experiential self'—arising spectrally and momentarily in between bouts of compulsive and incessant engagement 'with the machine'. Here is a clear example of the process described by Adorno where, despite the fact that the worker's 'free time' has become strictly divided from 'work time', internalized work habits have been smuggled into leisure activities expressed through the simulation of work in hobbies. Stallabrass, taking his lead from Benjamin's analysis of the nineteenth century Parisian arcade, notes that 'the arcade, while evoking gambling and sex, is actually a furtive simulacrum of the sweatshop.' [72] This contradictory yet symbiotic coupling of work and leisure is also described by Adorno:

While in their structure work and amusement are becoming increasingly alike, they are at the same time being divided ever more rigorously by invisible demarcation lines. Joy and mind have been expelled equally from both. In each, blank-faced seriousness and pseudo-activity hold sway. [73]

But of course Murakami's 'Boku' is very different from Baudelaire's *Flanier*, the stroller who loves nothing more than the anonymity of the crowd. Although we can see some glimpse of earlier industrial manipulation of the machine which might involve 'sliding a mechanism home, depositing a token or triggering an apparatus'[74] in the analogic operation of the pinball machine, Boku's responses are essentially autistic and narcissistic in nature. Benjamin's notion of the 'shock' felt in the midst of an urban crowd, is reduced to a very different kind of experience. Surprisingly, according to Jameson, the kind of analysis of the machine offered by Benjamin is not about a theory of causality, but is best explained by Benjamin's notion of the aura which is actually 'the opposite of allegorical perception'. This is so because with the aura of the work of art in the precommodified world, the 'mysterious wholeness of objects' is contrasted with the 'broken fragments of allegory.'[75] The aura of pre-commodified perception thus becomes Utopian and the pinball machine is able to momentarily take on the aura of a whole, non-fragmented object.

Periodically, however, as if in compensation for the experience of the 'reduced experiential self' in alienated labor, the gambler's playing out of desire yields brief episodes of intense intoxication, and the significance of Karatani's expanded and 'corpulent' transcendental ego in the game becomes apparent:

> 「僕がプレイ・ボタンを押すたびに彼女は小気味の良い音を立ててボードに６個のゼロをはじき出し、それから僕に微笑みかけた。１ミリの狂いもない位置にプランジャーを引き、キラキラと光る銀色のボールをレーンからフィールドにはじき出す。ボールが彼女のフィールドを駆けめぐる間、僕の心はちょうど良質のハッシシを吸う時のようにどこまでも解き放たれた。様々な想いが僕の頭に脈絡もなく浮かんでは消えていった……。ガラス板は夢を映し出す二重の鏡のように僕の心を映し、そしてバンパーやボーナス・ライトの光にあわせて点滅した。」[76]

Whenever I pressed her replay button, she'd perk up with a little hum, click the six digits on the board to zero, then smile at me. I'd pull her plunger into position—not a fraction of an inch off—and let that gleaming silver ball fly up the lane onto the field. And while the ball was racing about, it was as if I were smoking potent hashish: my mind was set free. All sorts of disconnected ideas floated into my head and disappeared. Like a two-way mirror to my dreams, the glass top reflected my own mind as it flickered in unison with the bumper and bonus lights.[77]

In this passage, the embodiment ascribed to the alter-ego of the player appears to extend to the personified, feminized machine-object. Apart from the more phallic image connoted by the plunger, we noted earlier how the engagement of the 'replay' button brings with it the promise of infinity—or infinite plenitude/pleasure—signified by the theoretically limitless score to which the player may aspire. This reminds us of Kant's notion of the 'mathematical sublime', in which numerical magnitude is sensed as being so vast as to be incapable of (re)presentation to the imagination.[78] However, since the mathematically sublime is contingent upon magnitude (and thus ultimately, a numerical concept), the more the mind strives to represent this magnitude to reason, the more the mind is perceived to be 'aesthetically confined within bounds'.[79] This means that the experience of the sublime is ultimately a pleasure that must be mediated by a *displeasure*—or, indeed, that the pleasure of the sublime derives from the tension established between chaos and form, freedom and constraint, overload and the capacity to judge.

The means by which the sublime experience actually 'hangs together' is through its teleology or purposiveness, and the latter is crucial to Kant's entire theory of aesthetic judgment, which, as Adorno claims, 'is so subjectively conceived that an interior of the aesthetic object is not even mentioned, [rather] . . . this interiority is . . . implicitly presupposed by the concept of teleology'.[80] We are aware, however, that Kant was writing at a time prior to the advent of 'the object' (in the semiotic and functional sense of the term given to it by Baudrillard[81]) and the 'commodity-fetish' (as described by Marx and Benjamin), and we can assume that the operation of the condition of purposiveness had been undermined by shifts in the nature and status of the aesthetic object in the era of the machine, and the age of the 'reproducible work of art'.

If we accept Jameson's reading of Benjamin, then the protagonist's psychological state might also be explained as a sort of momentary experience of 'the aura', which as the 'single, unrepeatable experience of distance, is the 'opposite of allegorical perception.'[82] And if, in the Kantian aesthetic scheme, the purposiveness of aesthetic judgement (and especially of the sublime) is ultimately a function of 'the moral' (*das sittlichkeit*)[83] — which in turn, is mediated by a common or universal sense (*sensus communis*)[84] — then it is hardly surprising that with the advent of the object and commodity, a different social and metaphysical description of aesthetic experience should be required.

Although the experience of the sublime was described by Kant as being a fundamentally *negative* experience, its contradictions were nevertheless 'available' to the transcendental subjective apperception, and were not meant to be subjected to occlusion or suppression.

However, with the reification of the art work into the fetishized forms of 'machine', 'object' and 'commodity', we might expect an inevitable shift in the conditions and description of aesthetic experience from an extraneous subjectivity to one of immanent objectivity. Adorno recognized the emergence of a kind of 'phony sublime', in which the contradictions inherent to the 'genuinely' sublime experience are passed over, or 'reconciled', and the sublime becomes 'latent'. Accordingly, this kind of art 'is not capable of the positivity of negation that animated the traditional concept of the sublime as the presence of the infinite.'[85]

As the protagonist of *Pinbôru* shows, prowess in the manipulation of the fetishized and sexualized machine-object produces only a momentary and attenuated 'pseudo sublime'. And the endless playing out of processes expressed in the following unconsummated discourse with the machine/dead lover Naoko, which are mimetic of repetitive labor in the engagement of an embodied alterego, are ultimately frustrating and unproductive:

「<u>あなたのせいじゃない</u>、と彼女は言った。そして何度も首を振った。<u>あなたはわるくないのよ、精いっぱいやったじゃない</u>。違う、と僕は言う。左のフリッパー、タップ・トランスファー、9番ターゲット。<u>違うんだ。僕は何ひとつできなかった。指一本動かせなかった。でもやろうと思えばできたんだ。人にできることはとても限られたことなのよ</u>、と彼女は言う。<u>そうかもしれない</u>、と僕は言う、<u>でも何ひとつ終わっちゃ</u>

いない、いつまでもきっと同じなんだ。リターン・レーン、トラップ、
キック・アウト・ホール、リバウンド、ハギング、６番ターゲット……
ボーナス・ライト。１２１１５０、終わったのよ、何もかも、と彼女は
言う。」⁸⁶

It's not your fault, she said. To which I only kept shaking my head.
You're not to blame, you gave it your all, didn't you?
No way, said I. Left flipper, tap transfer, ninth target. *Not even close. I
didn't get a single thing right. I hardly moved a finger. But I could have,
if I'd been on the ball.*
There's only so much a person can do, she said.
Maybe so, said I, *but that doesn't change a thing. It'll always be that
way.*
Return lane, trap, kick out hole, rebound, hugging, sixth target . . . bo-
nus light: 121,150.
It's over, she said, *it's all over.*[87]

After several decades of postmodern fiction, it is perhaps understandable that the
form of presentation of this dialogue hardly seems radical. However, for the
Japanese literary world of 1980,[88] it undoubtedly represented a curious, if not
outrageous transgression of the conventional reader expectations of a typical
literary speech-act.[89] It is not so much that an interior monologue is formed by
two voices in dialogic engagement, but that this represented speech-act is entangled with the precise description of the movements of a machine (actually determined by the player) as a form of 'speech', and the inclusion of this dimension in the speech-act has a powerful effect: the machine movements enact
something very unsettling in the overall *effect* of the speech-act.[90]

It is well known that a speech-act implies a particular dimension of agency; it
has, in Searlian terminology, 'illocutionary force'—it actually *does* something.
In the case of the above passage, the illocutionary act could be described as 'for-
giveness' or 'the absolving of blame' on the part of Naoko 'embodied' in the
machine. And the perlocutionary *effect* might be described as creating feelings
of guilt, shame and regret on the part of Boku.[91]

However, because it is difficult to determine 'who' is actually speaking (the
pinball machine or Naoko), and because each of the speaking positions is perfectly capable of substitution,[92] the only common idiom which they share is the
technical, foreign machine language of the 'flippers', 'holes', 'traps', 'springs',
'magnets' and so on. In a sense, they both *potentially* occupy the speaking position of the machine. The event is represented as a perfectly closed, narcissistic,
even autistic 'speech-act' which displays elements of conflict and incommensurability. 'Communication' is performed through the speaking positions as man-
dated by the machine, and the discourse is limited and perfectly prescribed by
the number of moves that the ball and machine can make. In short, the two par-
ties to the speech-act are actually involved in a process whereby the possibility

that communication actually *does not* take place is distinctly plausible. As Pratt has noted, conventional speech-act theory assumes that the participants cooperate—or at least imagine that they *are able to* cooperate.[93] It is therefore the incommensurability described in Lyotard's notion of the 'differend' which perhaps more aptly characterizes the machine speech-act scene of *Pinbôru*.[94]

And what is at the centre of this—what prevents or 'interferes' with the normal expectation of the speech-act—is the inclusion of the English foreign-loan words in *katakana*, as speaking *on behalf* of Boku, as well as being some kind of 'static' in the communication process. Indeed, cannot this highly unusual literary speech event (which is mediated by the poetics of a kind of machine language) powerfully represent the loss to speech, the silence, the inability to communicate 'modernity's losses'—or be indicative of, as Katô puts it, the 'impossibility of recovery' (*kaifuku no fukanôsei*)?[95]

Certainly, the way in which items of Western (and especially English) vocabulary have become so thoroughly naturalized in the discourses of contemporary Japanese daily life, indicates a remarkable hybridity in Japanese thought and language which itself has ramifications far beyond the totalizing effects and authoritarian tendencies of the language standardization process (*genbun-ichi*) instigated by the Meiji modernizers. Perhaps in a way not dissimilar to Pollack's description of the 'fracture of meaning' entailed in Japan's encounter with China, the massive and ongoing adoption of foreign loan words via the *katakana* alphabet has helped to inscribe yet another dimension of alterity indicative of the simulacral and tentative nature of Japan's versions of its own modernity. Ono is at once both stating the obvious and expressing dismay when he writes:

> Each Western word is loaded with cultural and historical meanings, associations. . . . Thus Western words as such are not appropriate for describing non-Western reality.[96]

The crude assumption of this observation is of course that the cross-fertilization of 'distinct' languages either does not or indeed should not occur—an idea which is completely at odds with the evidence provided by the procedures of the discipline of philology. Of course in the machine speech-act, the Japanese reader has little sense of the semantic embeddedness or indeed etymology of these 'foreign' words, but vaguely recognizes the lexicon of gaming and the techno-industrial terminology which litters the discourse of daily life in contemporary Japan: in sports journalism, technical manuals, economic reviews and machine operating instructions. Even though there exist perfectly functional and acceptable equivalents for these words in Japanese using Chinese ideographs, their rendering into foreign loan/katakana form conveys semiotic economy and expediency, as well as a sense of disjunction and otherness.

Overall, therefore, this speech-act represents both a glorification *and* critique of the ideology of modernity. Here it seems, the signification of loss and regret is only re-presentable through the fleeting and spectral 'simulation' of work, in the act of playing the game-centre machine. It is the pervasive ideology of modernity in the modern Japanese state which actually allows this machine speech-act to become normalized. As is the case with myth, ideology functions, above all, to normalize and naturalize:

> Ideology always appears as the overblown discourse of some great theme, con-
> tent or value (patriotism, morality . . . happiness, consumption, the family)
> whose allegorical power somehow insinuates itself into consciousness . . . in
> order to integrate them. These become, in turn, the contents of thought that
> come into play in real situations.[97]

The 'great theme' here is of course the unspoken and as yet apparently unspeak-able allegory of Japanese modernity as discussed in the second chapter. Alle-gorical, in the sense that it cannot be spoken *directly*, but also in that it cannot be spoken in a conventionally allegorical way. Rather, in the above quoted speech-act from *Pinbôru*, it is the formal *modal* determinants of the event whose aber-rant form functions ideologically. As Baudrillard affirms (after Marx), the ob-jectivity of ideology 'does not reside in its "ideality", that is, in a realist meta-physic of thought-contents, but in its form.'[98] It is the formal play of the substitution of signs as commodities which functions allegorically to permit the weaving of the three narrative strands of the *Pinbôru* text. But what is the pre-cise status of the 'commodity' here, and how does it function apparently 'alle-gorically'? That is to say, how does the commodity in its form as sign-fetish come to be recuperated by the reader in an 'allegorical' way?

The Commodity as Allegory

As Benjamin has so eloquently shown, it is the qualities of 'ruination' and 'fragmentation' typified in the representational trajectories of modernity which allow the commodity to emerge as the modern embodiment of the allegorical.[99] This enables readers of *Pinbôru* to 'read-off' the sign-fetishes in a predictably 'allegorical' way. However, because the narrator effectively abolishes the ideal-ized meaning-contents of these commodities in a final gesture of narrative closure or denouement, it becomes apparent that it is the *process* of allegorizing which has in fact been under scrutiny—and since it has been found to be want-ing, actually self-deconstructs, devolves or diminishes its own explicatory or symbolic force. In *Pinbôru*, it seems, allegory has been highlighted as a prob-lematic method, and as an exploration of issues of representation in 'his-tory'(*shi*) and in 'narrative' (*monogatari*).

To demonstrate this point let us consider more closely the substitution of sign-fetishes, and specifically examine the function of the electrical switch-panel (*haidenban*) in the narrative. There can be no better example of Benjamin's no-tion of 'ruination' than in the example of industrial garbage represented by the function of the redundant electrical switch-panel in *Pinbôru*. Boku is disturbed one Sunday morning by the telephone company repairman wanting to upgrade the switch-panel in his apartment. The repairman offers the following reflection on the value of switch-panels:

「でもね、みんな配電盤をひどく邪魔者扱いするんですよ。普段は使わないもんだし、かさばるからね……。」
「まるで宝探しなんだ。そのくせ部屋には馬鹿でかいピアノを置いて人形ケースを飾ったりするんだ。おかしいよ。」 [100]

Most people seem to find switchboards a real nuisance. They're nothing you'd generally have much use for. They just get in the way. . . . A regular treasure hunt. Switch-panels get stashed away in the most unbelievable places. It's a crime. And then what do people do? They turn around and fill their apartments with mammoth pianos and dolls in glass cases and what have you. It just doesn't make sense. [101]

In its unseen, occult state, the switch-panel has a latent value which is only brought to light through a process of exposure whereby, paradoxically, its use-value comes to be *re-valued* precisely because of its sudden redundancy. Put another way, in order to function allegorically, it first must be objectified—or in Benjamin's terminology, commodified.

Although we sense in the image of the switchboard an initially ambivalent status somewhere between 'use-value' and 'exchange-value', it is only when the transition to a fully fledged 'object' appears to be complete, that this ambivalence recedes. As Baudrillard notes, even though ambivalence 'haunts the sphere of value every where', in the trinomial system of symbolic exchange, (i.e. use-value/exchange-value/sign-exchange-value) value is ultimately, always totalitarian:

The value process is equivalent to a phantasmic organization, in which desire is fulfilled and lack resolved; in which desire is achieved and performed; and in which the symbolic dimension and all difference are abolished. [102]

Accepting Baudrillard's perspective on the birth of the object following Bauhaus, and the 'universal semanticization of the environment', it can be argued that the electrical switch-panel in *Pinbôru* (like 'the coffee spoon' or 'the entire city') becomes the object of and participates in, a 'calculus of function and signification'. [103] Nevertherless, the narrator of *Pinbôru* describes a *phantasmic* or *simulacral* system of symbolic exchange in which the switch-board effectively maintains its ambivalent status as both 'work of art' and mass-produced industrial 'object'. As a work of art, however, it would exist in a non-objectified way, which is perhaps best explained by Benjamin's theory of the 'aura':

The experience of aura is based on the transposition of a social reaction onto the relationship of the lifeless or of nature to man. The person we look at, the person who believes himself looked at, looks back at us in return. To experience the aura of a phenomenon means to endow it with the power to look back in return. [104]

Although Boku actually tries to attribute some value to the switchboard, he is unable to rise above its meaninglessness since the system of exchange has attributed to it a value of precisely zero: not an absence of value, but a relative *valuelessness* which functions positively within a graded system of differentiated values:

> 「僕は流しの脇に立てかけられた配電盤を手に取り、しげしげと眺めてみた。どれだけひっくり返してみても、それはただの薄汚れた意味のないボードにすぎなかった。僕はあきらめてそれをもとの場所に戻して手についたほこりを払い、 煙草の煙を吸い込んだ。月の光の下では何もかもが青ざめて見える。どんなものにも価値も意味も方向もないように思える。影さえもが不確かだ。」 [105]

> I picked up the switch-panel the twins had stood by the side of the sink, and looked it over. No matter how you turned the thing over, front or back, it was nothing but a meaningless piece of fiberboard. I gave up and put it back where I'd found it, brushed the dust off my hands, took a puff on my cigarette. Everything took on a blue cast in the moonlight. It made everything look worthless, meaningless, I couldn't even be sure of the shadows.[106]

To be sure, the switch-panel takes its place within a universe of ruined and worthless things, all equally incapable of returning the knowing and intelligent look entailed in the experience of distance established by the 'aura' of a phenomenon.

But because it has been completely emptied out of all value, hollowed out and become, in effect, 'a broken fragment of allegory (representing) a thing-world of destructive forces',[107] Boku then decides precisely because of its redundancy (it has neither use-value nor exchange-value) to bestow upon it a significance tentatively beyond commodity and object (that is beyond the allegorical) in the form of a sign-exchange value woven into the seemingly disparate narrative strands of *Pinbôru*. In an unusual signification of the interplay between nostalgia (*kishikan*) and the sense of loss (*sôshitsukan*), the narrator sets up a system of substitution and symbolic, metonymic exchange, which seemingly parallels the system of commodity production, and is peculiarly *beyond* and simulacral of it. The solemnly performed parody of 'last rites' in the funeral service for the switch-panel effectively takes the forlorn object out of 'circulation' and re-establishes its distance, as well as, therefore, its ability to return Boku's loving gaze in the form of the gaze of his lost beloved, Naoko.

> 「『哲学の義務は、』と僕はカントを引用した。『誤解によって生じた幻想を除去することにある……。』配電盤よ、貯水池の底に安らかに眠れ……。
> 　僕は右腕を思い切りバック・スイングさせてから、配電盤を４５度の角度で力いっぱい放り投げた。配電盤は雨の中を見事な弧を描いて飛び、

水面を打った。そして波紋がゆっくりと広がり、僕たちの足もとにまで
やってきた。」

'The obligation of philosophy', I drew on my Kant, 'is to eradicate illusions
born of misunderstanding'. . . . Oh, switch-panel! Rest ye at the bottom of the
reservoir . . . I went into a windup, and hurled it up at a forty-five-degree angle
with all my might. The switchboard traced a beautiful arc through the rain, and
struck the water. The ripples slowly spread, finally reaching our feet.[108]

This timely rescue from the industrial scrap heap and the ritualistic laying to rest
of the obsolete switch-panel, paradoxically restores to it the possibility of new
life, and in so doing subverts the very basis of the system of production and circulation of objects in which, under the tyranny of the perpetual cycle of 'the
model' and 'the series', as Baudrillard puts it, 'the object cannot be allowed to
escape death.'[109]

Although the narrative threads of *Pinbôru* appear to be as fragmentary and
disconnected as those of the previous novel, *Kaze*, it is not in the more obviously
metaphorical devices which demand to be read allegorically in isolation that
make the text interesting. Rather, it is, as one critic writes, 'the line of association connecting all the fragments and images' and the deployment of a series of
'physical metaphors', which suggests an exploration of the idea that no distinction can be drawn between fiction (*kyokô*) and reality (*genjitsu*).[110] Such an observation indeed supports the central claim being made in this discussion about
the dominance of the *modal* determination of meaning in the text, and in the
closing section of this chapter, we will demonstrate the operation of a kind of
narrative matrix which functions metaphorically *in its own right* and not merely
in support of some more typically 'direct' allegorical signification.

An Economy of Metonymic Exchange

Strecher has undertaken an analysis of what he calls 'metonymic substitution' in
Pinbôru, but unfortunately, his discussion remains over-simplistic—proposing a
direct 'allegorical' reading of the metaphors presented. For instance, the pinball
machine is described merely as 'a metonymical image of nostalgic desire'. Strecher also misses the possible significance of Boku's 'somewhat incongruous'
quoting of Kant in the switch-panel funeral scene.[111] Katô, however, draws our
attention to an observation in the critic Starobinski's discussion of the concept of
nostalgia, in which he notes that it was Kant who was indirectly responsible for
the European shift from tending to think nostalgia spatially, to a more temporal
orientation, which forms the Romantic basis of nostalgia found in the major
themes of modern literature.[112]

Certainly, it is the case that in his 'Transcendental Aesthetic of Time', Kant
actually argued for the 'empirical' (rather than 'absolute') reality of time, in the
sense of 'its objective validity in reference to all objects which can ever be

presented to our senses'.[113] And the importance attributed to time vis-à-vis space, is clearly stated in Section 7(c):

> Time is the formal condition a priori of all phenomena whatsoever. Space, as the pure form of external intuition, is limited as a condition a priori to external phenomena alone.

It is precisely the idea that time forms the *a priori* ground of cognition, and thus the imagination, that gives the Romantics what they require to counter the hegemony of pure and abstract logic entailed in the assumption of time as an absolute value in Natural Philosophy prior to Kant's *Critique of Pure Reason*. Not surprisingly, the European Romantic conception of subjectivity also forms the basis of what Karatani has shown to be the Japanese discovery of 'interiority' and the temporal projection of subjectivity entailed in such a conception of the self.

Significantly, in *Pinbôru*, the substitution of various objects as metonymic sign-fetishes, may *appear* to suggest that the narrator is actually playing with spatial elements—or in Kantian terminology—'external phenomena'. On the contrary, however, the narrator is manipulating time in the truly modern and nostalgic sense given to it: that is, the Romantic conception of nostalgia as a sense of loss expressed in terms of the ideas of 'then' and 'now'. The unquestionably Romantic substitution of signs along the 'temporal' axis engages the semiotic process whereby 'Naoko' can signify 'Nezumi', and the switchboard and pinball machine stand in for 'Naoko'. These signifiers are, in somewhat contradictory fashion, variously imagined to be anthropomorphized machine-objects, which nevertheless *are* capable of returning the knowing and intelligent gaze of Boku as described in Benjamin's conception of the auratic revelation of wholeness of the pre-commodified object.

However—and this is crucial to our argument—although Kant's transcendental aesthetic *made possible* the development of the Romantic notion of nostalgia in terms of a privileging of time vis-à-vis space in the latter, Kant's analysis did not *directly* propose what was to become a Romantic conception of the individualized and subjectified experience of time. Rather, the discussion of time proposed in Kant's Transcendental Aesthetic also allows the kind of Buddhistic epiphany experienced by Boku in the closing scene of *Pinbôru*. The Romantic construction of nostalgia temporally expressed in terms of presence and absence, gain and loss, relies on a metaphysics of time which is, of course, culturally and historically constructed by modernity. It was not Kant who was directly responsible for the artistic manifestation of such a metaphysics in Romantic literature.

Kant's purpose was to show that our conception of time is merely a representation of the 'internal sense . . . of the intuitions of self and of our internal state'.[114] By drawing the firm distinction between our common conception of time, and the nature of the cognition of time on a cosmic scale, Kant was merely demonstrating that the individual subject requires time as a representation of its internal sense of change and motion in order to mediate contradictory or opposing predicates.[115]

Although Kant's purpose was to clarify and establish the limits and processes of the synthetic *a priori* grounds of cognition, it is certainly the case that a non-Romantic conception of time is allowed for in Kant's transcendental scheme:

> Different times are merely parts of one and the same thing. . . .The infinity of time signifies nothing more than that every determined quantity of time is possible only through limitations of one time lying at the foundation.[116]

Boku's statement that Kant's mission is to 'eradicate illusions born of misunderstanding' is therefore not only ironic in the context of the ritual of funeral (in terms of the parodic element of 'burying' a switch-panel), it also smacks of a very Buddhistic statement that suffering is a function of limited understanding and the reliance on false and unverifiable conceptions presented to cognition. Furthermore, it implicitly supports the notion that in a Buddhist aesthetics of time, different times and different worlds are described as co-existing.

Boku's conception of time, therefore, while ostensibly nostalgic, in the end becomes the opposite—it is anti-Romantic and anti-nostalgic. It is the interwoven narrative threads of substitution, memory and loss which (because they are integrated and ultimately dissolved) operate ultimately as modal signifiers of the contemporaneous nature of time, and the co-existence of phenomena as representations *in* time.

In the same way that the discussion in Chapter 3 demonstrated a multiplicity of versions of the simulacrum, our discussion of the modal functioning of allegory in *Pinbôru* suggests an alternative response to the operation of a predominantly Romantic poetics of nostalgia in literary modernity. The latter, which elevates to truth status merely one aspect of the Kantian understanding of time, and posits a corresponding subjectivity/self and sense of loss expressed historically and in referential terms, is different to the kind of model proposed by Murakami's narrative.

Frow has drawn the distinction between what he calls the 'melancholic vision' of Baudrillard's simulacrum, and the celebration of difference and the 'reign of simulacra' proposed by Delueze in his *Difference and Repetition*. Although it would be a mistake to be overly dismissive of Baudrillard's brilliant and wide ranging analyses, Frow's point about the loss of the historical referent is important, in that it suggests Baudrillard concurs with the Platonic version of the simulacrum (stressing the priority of the original over the copy) as a form of loss, and a kind of 'moral fall'.[117]

For Murakami, however, there is no such 'moral fall'—simply an extended reflection on the lapse in an alternative poetics of representation which existed prior to the litany of 'discoveries' elaborated by Karatani. That is to say, 'landscape', 'interiority', 'confession' and so on, suggest nothing more than the imposition of a Romantic version of subjectivity and representation perceived as somehow necessary to the Japanese project of modernity. It is not simply that reading the Murakami text does not require the invocation of such conventions, but that they are used in order to dismantle and problematize them. In this sense they are used in a de-constructive way.

What then, is the bigger picture, the larger referent behind the use of allegory as modality in *Pinbôru*? The answer may well lie not in the 'individual' loss seemingly apparent in the novel, but in a 'collective' sense of 'loss', or as Katô has put it, the collective sense of the 'impossibility of recovery' (*kaifuku no fukanosei*). Certainly, Murakami has been playing with the referent, but he is perhaps playing not with a 'lost' referent, rather a 'repressed' referent—since, as Karatani has shown, memory of the origins of an inversion (*tentô*) is repressed as soon it is formed.[118]

Most critics identify several distinct narrative lines in *Pinbôru* and they differ only in how they think these are linked, integrated or 'resolved'. For instance, Suzumura thinks that in between *Kaze* and *Pinbôru*, Murakami was faced with the problem of the 'romanesque'.[119] Allowing for the full connotative play of 'romanesque' (*romanesuku*), the sense of a relatively unrefined style in medieval architecture and the concomitant image of the medieval labyrinth is signified in the image arising from what Suzumura calls the 'tubificid worm-space' (*ito-mimizu uchû*).[120] This signifies not only the labyrinth of feelings and emotions,[121] but is also the generalized metaphor of the 'seek and find' structure in *Pinbôru*.

But of course, Suzumura's main concern is with the *roman*-like or 'novel-like' qualities of this narrative, because he rightly suspects that it is precisely the form of the Japanese novel (*shôsetsu*) itself which is under interrogation in this and other of Murakami's texts. With a novel taking up a self conscious relationship with the *idea* of the novel, it is as though Murakami is, as Suzumura avers, able to express his irony through this metafictional concern with the roman-esque, rather than through the more conventional device of the hero seeking justice. Presumably, the larger problem of avoiding the oxymoronic pitfall of a novel adopting a 'non-novelistic' exploration of the novel, is solved, according to Suzumura's approach, by the juxtaposition of 'romanesque' and 'unromanesque' story lines within the one text. Thus the character and emplotment of the figure of Boku, is 'unromanesque' in relation to that of the distinctly 'romanesque' figure of Nezumi. The three narrative lines are given as that of Boku, Nezumi and a third one which incoprorates *both* of them.[122]

In acknowledging that the reader is capable of occupying a plurality of positions anywhere within these three lines, Suzumura is affirming the relevance of Iser's phenomenological notion of the reader's 'wandering viewpoint'.[123] He is also identifying an attempt to address the problem of the novel *through* the novel. However, the crux of Suzumura's argument lies in a discussion of the forms of subjectivity arising from the deployment of grammatical person (*ninshô*) in *Pinbôru*. It is suggested that by limiting the romanesque or novel-like attributes of the text to the narrative strand concerning Nezumi (which is always narrated in the third person or *sannin shôtai*), Murakami is effectively undermining the dominance and gravity of the first person *watashi* voice, which is the lynch-pin of the conventional 'I-novel' form.[124] For Suzumura, this subversion of the expectation of 'sincerity' built around the narrative perspective of Boku is augmented by the presentation of the novel as 'situation'—a narrative without apparent direction and conclusion.[125] At work is a process of 'denovelization' (*hishôsetsuka*) where the text's narrativity (*monogatarisei*) becomes merely a function of the accumulation of fragments.[126]

Despite Suzumura's insights, it is clear that the questions of grammatical person, fragmentation and lack of closure alone cannot explain entirely the processes of symbolic exchange and substitution in the *Pinbôru* narrative. Although this discussion has attempted to avoid a directly allegorical reading in the attempt to demonstrate the *modal* significance of the text's deployment of allegory, it remains, finally, to speculate more definitively as to what the referent or 'meaning contents' of such a narrative strategy might be.

Of the plethora of critical responses to *Pinbôru*, it is the approach taken by an acknowledged Murakami 'expert' (some would even say Murakami apologist) which supports our argument here. Katô Norihiro's analysis goes further than the simplistic gesturing towards 'nostalgic' readings of the text. While acknowledging the existence of three or four seemingly disconnected stories in *Pinbôru*, he is nevertheless led to pose the question: why is it that after reading the text, there is a strong sense of lyricism (*ririshizumu*) related to the impression that the apparently isolated narrative threads actually cohere in the form of a single composite narrative?[127]

Katô suggests that it is the unspoken story of Nezumi's suicide which integrates the narrative fragments and that this is coupled with the 'seek and find' structure of the search for the lost pinball machine. In so doing, the narrative takes things which cannot be recovered and places them within a *mode of recovery* (*kaifukukanô na taiyô*).[128] The term 'mode' is obviously important here, and the original Japanese *taiyô*, which is defined simply as 'mode', is also a synonym for *arisama* which suggests 'state', 'condition' or 'circumstances'.[129]

Katô's point affirms the argument developed in this chapter about the *modal* deployment of the allegorical figure as a vehicle for semantic content and a system of reference *for its own sake*. It is claimed that in *Pinbôru,* Boku substitutes (*okikaeru*) Nezumi's death with the disappearance of the pinball machine. In the first half of Boku's narrative line, the death of the electrical switch-panel replaces Nezumi's death. In the latter half of this story, the 'dead' switch-panel becomes the vanished pinball machine which is eventually recovered. Regarding this point in the narrative, Katô asks: what does the shift from the 'impossibility of recovery' (*kaifuku no fukanô*) to the 'possibility of recovery' (*kaifuku no kanô*) imply for the reader?

We have noted above Katô's reference to Starobsinki's claim that Kant's critical philosophy effectively allowed a shift in the primary orientation of the concept of nostalgia from a spatial to a temporal one and thus indirectly influenced the themes of Romantic literature. Accordingly, the notion of nostalgia shifted from the desire for healing by returning home (physically, spatially) to one's native village, to a kind of 'literary illness' (*bungaku no byôki*) expressed temporally in the idea of 'lost youth' and the incurable grief of not being able to return to one's childhood.[130] As already noted, Karatani has argued persuasively that in incipient Japanese modernity 'the child' was discovered through a process of semiotic 'inversion' in the same way as 'landscape' and 'interiority', and that the origins of this process were immediately repressed from memory. The implications for modern Japanese fiction were self evident:

> Many modern writers look back on childhood, as if they could find their true origins. The only result of this is the construction of a narrative of the 'self'. At times, such stories take the form of psychoanalytic narratives. . . .What has been hidden from us is the system that produces psychoanalysis itself.[131]

The 'system' that produces this construction of 'the child' is the entire paradigm of Japanese modernity, which requires a cohesive notion of the individual subject primarily for the purpose of attempting to engender the idea of civil society crucial to the acceptance of an ideology of modern statehood.

The narrator of *Pinbôru*, however, deflects or transfers the romanesque attribute of psychological maturation (essential to Romanticism), which is usually reserved for the first-person narrator, to the figure of the third-person, Nezumi, and thus subverts a typified reading of the *seishun shôsetsu* or youth novel within the conventionalized parameters of subjectivity prescribed by the 'I-novel' form. Katô notes that according to Starobinski, Kant had already given notice of the 'impossibility of return' long before Rimbaud, Baudealire and Poe took up these themes in the so called 'literature of banishment' (*tsuihô no bungaku*), signifying that the literary age of the 'impossibility of recovery had arrived.'[132]

Katô then shifts his focus to the more immediate context of modern Japanese history in claiming that through the experience of large-scale death in World War II, the basis for the idea of the possibility of recovery, along with the basis for the possibility of an 'individual, dignified death' has for 'us' (*watashitachi*) been taken away. 'Death', in its capacity to represent the *possibility* of recovery (this important and meaningful kind of death) has in fact become impossible. By replacing the story of Nezumi's death with the tale of the search for the pinball machine, the narrator of *Pinbôru*, according to Kato, is alluding to the profound grief of the second half of the twentieth century, which, it is claimed, has denied individuals even the 'ability to lose something' (*ushinau koto sura dekinai*).[133]

In Katô's scheme of metonymic substitution, Boku seeks Nezumi in the form of the '3 Flipper Space-Ship' pinball machine, but instead, finds Naoko. We have discussed above the unusual nature of the ensuing 'machine speech-acts', and noted the sense of the 'loss of speech' in the fervent, mechanical, jerking movements of the metallic apparatus signified by the foreign loan words. It comes as somewhat of a surprise therefore to note that Katô argues for what he calls a 'deep sense of lyricism' (*aru shu no fukai ririshizumu*) in this scene.[134] Could this be synonymous with a kind of intoxicating sense of alterity, projected by the already naturalized techno-discourse alluded to above?

Katô does acknowledge that *Pinbôru* is very much a narrative of substitution (*daichi*) and metonymy (*kan'yu*) and argues that Nezumi's death is effectively replaced by his *second* departure. But he insists that the latter should by no means be read as metaphoric of Nezumi's death. Rather, the effect of such sub-stitution here indicates a further act of substitution: that is, the replacement of 'despair' (*zetsubô*) with 'hope' (*kibô*). Paradoxically, for Katô, a deeply felt de-spair is close to a sense of genuine hope, and when the reader discovers that the pinball machine represents not *Nezumi* but the dead lover, Naoko, the 'lyricism' experienced in this realization derives from a new sense of loss — in losing the motif of the sense of loss *itself* originally derived from the perceived sense of the impossibility of recovery.

With such a claim, Katô is presumably referring to a 'loss' in terms of a cast-ing off of the old form of nostalgia for modernity's losses, which was somehow artificially and violently imposed by the imperatives of nurturing a nation and a national literature within the simulacral shadow of European Romantic literary orthodoxy, and the contours of subjectivity which the latter entailed. In the final scene, Boku has effectively been separated from the pinball machine, Nezumi and the twins, finding himself completely alone. The 'lyricism' which Katô as-cribes to this presented situation indicates both a reference to and restoration towards a different ontology. For the reader to be moved by this overwhelming feeling of 'nothingness' (*nanimonai koto*) is to experience a 'fresh, absent sense of existence' (*shinsen na fuzai no sonzaikan*):[135]

> 「何もかもが繰り返される……。僕は一人同じ道を戻り、秋の光が溢れ
> る部屋の中で……コーヒーを立てた。そして一日、窓の外を通り過ぎて
> いく１１月の日曜日を眺めた。何もかもが透き通ってしまいそうなほど
> の１１月の静かな日曜日だった。」[136]

> Everything was repeating itself. I retraced my steps by the exact same route,
> and sat in the apartment awash with autumn light. . . .I brewed coffee. And the
> whole day through I watched that Sunday pass by my window. A tranquil No-
> vember Sunday of rare clarity shining through each and every thing.[137]

The dreamlike quality in this recollection of epiphany and realization, represents the narrator's final annulment of the metonymic system of substitution estab-lished in order to make a point about allegory (that it should not be taken alle-gorically at all) and the unsustainable illusion of the divide between 'fiction' and 'reality'.

Loughman has noted an instance of Buddhist epiphany in other of Murakami's texts, and offers the example of a narrative excerpt in which the excitement and irritation, coupled with resignation and despair of daily urban life, can only be apprehended by a Zen aesthetic of nothingness:

> And everywhere, infinite options, infinite possibilities. An infinity, and at the
> same time, zero. We try to scoop it all up in our hands, and what we get is a
> handful of zero. That's the city.[138]

Surprisingly, further evidence for the use of the idea of modality to make a point about representation can be seen in a much earlier Japanese text. William La

Fleur's illuminating explication of the nexus between Buddhist thought and literature in medieval Japan provides us with a convincing example of how the device of allegory as modality could be precisely employed within a metaphysical frame in order to say something about the nature and representation of knowledge and 'truth' under the sway of a particular episteme.[139] It matters little whether that episteme be labeled 'Japanese Medieval Buddhist' or 'Japanese Postmodern'. What is important about La Fleur's proposition is that it identifies a textual process through which allegory draws overt attention to its status *as* allegory—and most significantly, not to some 'transcendent' truth. Rather, it points to the problematic nature of attempting to represent and talk *about* truth.

In this sense, both the *Tendai* Buddhist metaphysic and apparent postmodern 'anti-metaphysic' in Murakami's writing have something in common. It could be argued that this is why contemporary Japanese readers have so enthusiastically embraced the peculiar tenor and style of Murakami's writing. That is to say, perhaps Japanese reading/subject positions under the broad sway of Buddhist thought, have long been implicitly attuned to the problematic nature of representation and truth in language, in a way which has become apparent in the West only recently in post-structuralist theory. In modernity, Japan inevitably embraced the models of representation and subjectivity necessary for the modern novel form, but such paradigms remained alien within the context of a highly developed Buddhist aesthetic, which by definition was incommensurate with the transcendentalism implicit in Western (i.e. Platonic) idealism.

La Fleur's analysis is directly relevant to our discussion of Murakami's *Pinbôru*, in that it provides a clear example of the textual use of allegory as a self reflexive exercise which is symbolic of itself—that is to say, of allegory *as* modality. It does so by proposing that we think allegory as a means of destabilizing the hierarchies of immanence and transcendence, means and ends. In his reading of the Buddhist *Lotus Sutra (Hokke-kyô)*, La Fleur proposes the following:

> The sutra radically relativizes our customary projection of an implicit hierarchy
> of value onto the relationship of means to ends.[140]

The evidence for this ostensibly 'allegorical' text functioning primarily as a self reflexive mode or way of viewing the world lies in the fact that its most fundamental proposition is predicated on an exposition of the problem of the one to the many; in other words, the relationship of unity to diversity. The crucial term appearing early in the text is the Japanese *hôben* (from Sanskrit *upaya*, Chinese *fang pien*) which although usually translated as 'expedient means', may, according to La Fleur, also be rendered as 'modes', largely because 'the point about a single message mediated through a variety of modes, is made again and again in the text'.[141]

In a similar manner, if Murakami's *Pinbôru* can aptly be described as a postmodern allegory, it is because the narrative trajectories of most of his novels are never played out or indeed 'resolved' in ways which rely on a firm ontological distinction between 'the concrete' and 'the abstract', or the oppositional structures of 'means versus ends', 'real versus imaginary', and 'copy versus original'. Instead, within the ambivalent and tentative context of an 'incomplete' Japanese modernity, the ontological and epistemological conditions required for their construction as an inter-subjectively constituted system of reference, function to *prescribe* or *precede*[142] the forms of subjectivity and narrativity possible in contemporary Japanese culture. This is entirely consistent with Baudrillard's claim that such texts are in fact their own simulacra, and that within such a semiotic order, the simulacra *themselves* are indeed perceived as being 'true'.[143]

The discussion in this chapter has attempted to demonstrate that Murakami's *Pinbôru* is 'allegorical' only of itself, and for this reason alone is worthy of careful critical attention. Of course it has been read (and no doubt will continue to be) simply as a 'nostalgic' text, lamenting wasted youth and lost revolutionary fervor. However, it has been shown that the text builds on and expands the experimental narrative horizons explored in *Kaze*, and establishes a paradigm of reading necessary for the third text in the 'Rat Trilogy'. Through its metafictionality and deployment of parallel narrative strands, as well as its systems of exchange and substitution established around the sign-exchange-value of the represented commodity-object, the narrative momentum of the text works towards a deconstruction of the possibility of overtly established referential meaning.

Indeed, the fact that the redundant electrical switch-panel and outdated pinball machine figure as the central fetishized signs of affection in the text provides a curious, contradictory and quite startling reflection on the status of the modern commodity-object in contemporary Japan. The narrator's auratic and epiphanic experience of a 'rare clarity shining through each and every thing', effectively counters the aspect of morbid inevitability in Benjamin's notion of the experience of ruination in the form of commodity-as-allegory.

On the other hand, the veracity of this kind of ecstatic epiphany is no doubt partly undermined by Heidegger's claim that the essential nature of technology as exemplified in the modern machine can be expressed as a kind of 'challenging forth', and an enframing (*Ge-stell*) which configures the unrealized energies of nature for the instrumental purpose of establishing a 'standing reserve' to be called upon when necessary.[144] Importantly, it has been noted that the instrumental functionality of such 'standing reserve' (*Bestand*) is predicated not so much on the notion of permanency, but rather on the 'orderability' and 'substitutability' of objects.[145]

It may well be that Katô's 'impossibility of recovery' is emblematic of the perfect substitutability of objects as played out in the narrative matrix of *Pinbôru*: the object as commodity; the commodity as allegory; the allegorical exchange of signs; the banishment of all signs and signification. But it may also be suggestive of a much more sinister process of the pre-determined plight of individual human beings as the 'standing reserve' of the modern capitalist Japanese state. This possibility is further explored in the discussion of the third and final part of the 'Rat Trilogy' undertaken in the following two chapters.

Notes

1. Clifford, for example, sees a form of allegory in the kind of text which projects 'the extended and extensive use of personification and personified abstractions . . . into the action.' And, it could be argued, this also applies to the reverse of personification, namely 'objectification', which is apparent in many of Murakami's narratives. See Gay Clifford, *The Transformations of Allegory* (London: Routledge & Kegan Paul, 1974), 5.

2. Theresa M. Kelley, *Re-inventing Allegory* (Cambridge: Cambridge University Press, 1997), 13.

3. Deborah L. Madsen, *Rereading Allegory: A Narrative Approach to Genre* (London: Macmillan, 1995), 25.

4. Clifford, *The Transformation of Allegory*, 5.

5. Carolyn Van Dyke, *The Fiction of Truth: Structures of Meaning in Narrative and Dramatic Allegory*, (Ithaca: Cornell University Press, 1985), 27.

6. Van Dyke, *The Fiction of Truth*, 16.

7. See Baudrillard, "Simulacra and Science Fiction," in *Simulacra and Simulation*, trans. Sheila Faria Glaser (Anne Arbor: University of Michigan Press, 1997), 121-127.

8. Jacques Derrida, "White Mythology: Metaphor in the Text of Philosophy," in *Margins of Philosophy*, trans. Alan Bass (Brighton: Harvester Press, 1982), 220.

9. Van Dyke, *The Fiction of Truth*, 27. Here Van Dyke is quoting from Joel Fineman, "The Structure of Allegorical Desire" in *Allegory and Representation*, ed. Stephen J. Greenblatt (Baltimore: John Hopkins University Press, 1981), 27.

10. Clifford, *The Transformations of Allegory*, 4.

11. See Susan Napier, *The Fantastic in Modern Japanese Literature: The Subversion of Modernity* (London: Routledge, 1996), 207.

12. Napier, *The Fantastic in Modern Japanese Literature*, 27.

13. Matthew C. Strecher, "Magical Realism and the Search for Identity in the Fiction of Murakami Haruki," *Journal of Japanese Studies* 25, no. 2 (1999): 269.

14. Strecher, "Magical Realism and the Search for Identity," 269.

15. Strecher, "Magical Realism and the Search for Identity," 269-70.

16. Kelley, *Re-inventing Allegory*, 249.

17. Strecher sees the term 'defamiliarization' (the English equivalent of Viktor Sklovsky's *ostranenie*) as a corollary of Alejo Carpentier's 'marvellous'. See Strecher, "Magical Realism and the Search for Identity," 268.

18. *Kôjien*, 2547.

19. *Kôjien*, 2547.

20. *Kôjien*, 1448.

21. *Kenkyusha's New Japanese English Dictionary, Fourth Edition*, ed. Koh Masuda, (Kenkyûsha, 1987), 1752.

22. *Kôjien*, 1602.

23. *Kenkyûsha's New Japanese English Dictionary*, 38.

24. *Kôjien*, 719.

25. See Shibata Shôji, *Tojirarenai gûwa* (Chusekisha, 1991), 9.

26. For an English version of the text see *Ten Night's of Dream* (Tokyo: Charles E. Tuttle, 1974). Napier notes a comment by Oka Yasuo et.al., that 'Modern Japanese fantasy begins with Ten Nights of Dream'. See Napier, *The Fantastic in Modern Japanese Literature*, 2. Also, see Oka Yasuo, et.al., 'Gensô bungaku sono honshitsu to hirogari', *Kokubungaku* 44, no. 10 (1979): 14-38.

27. Napier writes: 'While Soseki's "Dream of the Sixth Night" is an appropriate representative for Meiji Japan, perhaps the archetypal fantasy for contemporary Japan is Murakami's *Sekai no owari to hadoboirudo wandarando*' [*Hard-boiled Wonderland and the End of the World*]. See *The Fantastic in Modern Japanese Literature*, 4.

28. See William La Fleur, *The Karma of Words—Buddhism and the Literary Arts in Medieval Japan* (Berkeley & Los Angeles: University of California Press, 1983). Apart from challenges to the 'real/unreal' opposition in orthodox Bhuddhist texts, La Fleur also notes Ivan Morris' assertion that the supplementary Buddhist notion of *mujô* (impermanence) had a significant influence on the literature of the Heian period and beyond. Examples of the representation of Buddhist epiphany in Murakami's writing have been noted by Ploughman, and as will be shown, the double world structures, abjection and the sublime are all examples of a simulacral structuring of the experience of 'reality' which are not unrelated to a Buddhist understanding of the world. See Celeste Loughman, "No Place I was Meant to Be: Contemporary Japan in the Short Fiction of Haruki Murakami," 91.

29. See Horst Ruthrof, "Language and the Dominance of Modality," in *Language & Style: An International Journal* 21, no. 3 (1988): 315-326; especially 321.

30. For a critical text which partly employs this kind of 'riddle solving' approach, see for example Hisai Tsubaki, *Nejimakidori no sagashikata* (Ôta Shuppan, 1994). On the other hand, another well known Murakami commentator suggests that everything is always 'already known' in the Murakami's texts. See Suzumura Kazunari, *Murakami Haruki kuronikuru*, 14.

31. See Ishikura Michiko, et.al. "Murakami dêtabêsu" in *Kokubungaku* (Feb. 1998), Special Edition.

32. Ishikura, et.al. "Murakami dêtabêsu".

33. Ueda Miyôji, "Yasashii kyomukan," *Gunzô* 35, nos. 7-9 (September 1980): 298-99.

34. Matsumoto Ken'ichi, 'Shudai toshite no "toshi"', *Bungei* 21, no. 1 (1982): 281.

35. Kuroko Kazuo, *Murakami Haruki: za rosuto wârudo* (Daisan Shokan, 1993), 49.

36. These commentators were referred to in the previous chapter.

37. Hayashi Yoshii, "Boku wa nezumi de, nezumi wa boku de," in *Showa bungaku kenkyû Vol. 19* (1987), 48-60.

38. See Kanno Akimasa, "Ukai sakusen shindorômu—gendai shôsetsuko" in *Kokubungaku* 33, nos. 9-12 (August 1988), *Tokushû: Gendai shosetsu no hôhô teki seiha*, 7. Kanno gives as his examples: 'taishita koto jyanain da' and 'tada sore dake no koto da'. Translatable as: 'It's no big deal.' ; 'That's the way it is.'

39. Ivy, *Discourses of the Vanishing*.

40. Here we will rely on Wolfgang Iser's theories of 'negations' and 'blanks' as elaborated in *The Act of Reading*.

41. Ôe Kenzaburô, *Mannen gannen no futtobôru* (Kôdansha Bungeibunko, 1994).

42. Ôe Kenzaburô, *The Silent Cry,* trans. John Bester (Tokyo: Kôdansha, 1990).

43. Karatani, "Murakami Haruki no 'fûkei' — (II)," 236.

44. Matthew Strecher claims that Murakami made this denial during an interview in 1994. See Strecher, 'Magical Realism and the Search for Identity in the Fiction of Murakami Haruki', 276, fn. 20.

45. Karatani, "Murakami Haruki no 'fûkei' — (II)," 237.

46. Karatani, "Murakami Haruki no 'fûkei' — (II)," 237.

47. Karatani, "Murakami Haruki no 'fûkei' — (II)," 238.

48. In his essay "The Uses and Abuse of History," Nietzsche writes: 'The fact that life does not need the service of history must be as clearly grasped as that an excess of history

hurts it. . . . History is necessary to the living man in three ways: in relation to his action and struggle, his conservatism and reverence, his suffering and his desire for deliverance. See Nietzsche *Thoughts Out of Season Part II,* trans. Adrian Collins (Edinburgh & London: T. N. Foulis, 1909), 16.

49. Graeme Gilloch, *Myth and Metropolis: Walter Benjamin and the City* (Cambridge: Polity Press, 1996), 135.

50. PIN: 5.

51. P73: 7

52. Jean Baudrillard, *The System of Objects* (London: Verso, 1996), 140.

53. PIN: 28.

54. P73: 25-26.

55. PIN: 29.

56. P73: 26-27.

57. See Roland Barthes, *Mythologies,* trans. Annette Lavers (London: Granada, 1981), 142.

58. PIN: 30.

59. P73: 27.

60. See Orita Yûko's "Column" in *Ierôpêji—Murakami Haruki,* 33.

61. PIN: 32.

62. P73: 28-29.

63. See Ueda, "Yasashi kyomukan," 299.

64. See Yokô, *Murakami Haruki—kyûjûnendai,* 165.

65. Karatani, "Murakami Haruki no 'fûkei'—(II)," 238.

66. Shibata, *Tojirarenai Gûwa,* 130-31.

67. See PIN: 1; 36;   P73: 1; 33.

68. PIN: 15; 133-134.

69. P73: 15; 117-118.

70. PIN: 15; 134-135.

71. P73: 15; 118.

72. See Julian Stallabrass, *Gargantua: Manufactured Mass Culture* (London: Verso, 1996), 100.

73. Stallabrass, *Gargantua,* 101. The quote is from Adorno's *Minima Moralia,* 130-31.

74. Frederic Jameson, "Walter Benjamin; Or, Nostalgia," in *Marxism and Form* (Princeton: Princeton University Press, 1974), 75.

75. Jameson, "Walter Benjamin; Or, Nostalgia," 77.

76. PIN: 15; 135-136.

77. P73: 15; 118-119.

78. See Immanuel Kant, *The Critique of Judgement,* trans. J. C. Meredith (London: Oxford University Press, 1973), 109.

79. Kant, *The Critique of Judgement,* 109.

80. Theodor Adorno, *Aesthetic Theory,* ed. Gretel Adorno & Rolf Tiedemann, trans. R. Hullot-Kentor (Minneapolis: University of Minnesota Press, 1997), 100.

81. See Baudrillard, *The System of Objects.*

82. Jameson, "Walter Benjamin; Or, Nostalgia," 77.

83. Kant, *The Critique of Judgement.* Kant discusses the issue of the moral foundations of taste in the "Appendix to the Dialectic of Aesthetic Judgment" (Section 60).

84. Kant, *The Critique of Judgement,* 51. Kant emphasizes here that the word 'common' (*gemein*) has wide connotative scope, and it is used here in the sense of its being 'public' or 'universal'.

85. See Adorno, *Aesthetic Theory*, 197.

86. PIN: 15; 136.

87. P73: 15; 119.

88. For example in Ueda's 1980 article, "Yasashii kyomukan," (cited above) which speaks of the nihilism inherent in the protagonist's propensity to have better communication with a machine than a human being.

89. This notwithstanding, it is the case that radical instances of interior monologue are evident in the 'stream of consciousness' format in a much earlier modern works such as Soseki's *Kôfu*.

90. But these effects, *perlocutionary effects*, constitute a form of Lyotard's 'differend', in that they reflect the incommensurability, the talking at odds, in Japanese, the '*kui chigai*' of the former lovers.

91. John R. Searle and Daniel Vanderveken, *Foundations of Illocutionary Logic* (Cambridge: Cambridge University Press, 1989), 11.

92. Naoko is the machine speaking 'normal discourse' 'It's not your fault'; or perhaps Boku also becomes the machine, but speaks through the movements and sounds of the machine — the kinetic force, so to speak.

93. Mary Louise Pratt, "Ideology and Speech-Act Theory," *Poetics Today* 7, no.1 (1986): 59-72; especially 64-5. In response to what she sees as Grice's somewhat limited notion of the 'Cooperative Principle', Pratt argues that we must also be able to account for 'speech events that are principled ways, not cooperative, not exchanges, not efficient, and where truthfulness, proportion, relevance, and informativeness are systematically absent or mitigated.'(64)

94. Lyotard's 'differend' corresponds to a 'state'which suggests an 'unstable . . . instant of language wherein something which must be able to be put into phrases cannot yet be.' See Jean-Francois Lyotard, *The Differend: Phrases in Dispute,* trans. G. Van Den Abbeele (Manchester: Manchester University Press, 1988), 13.

95. We will return to Katô's argument at the end of the chapter.

96. In citing Ono (1976:26) Florian Coulmus was not necessarily agreeing with this proposition, rather she was using Ono's observation as a point of departure in order to demonstrate an argument about the non-universal nature of speech-acts. See "'Poison to Your Soul': Thanks and Apologies Contrastively Viewed," in *Conversational Routine: Explorations in Standardized Communication Situations and Prepatterned Speech,* ed. Florian Coulmus (The Hague: 1981), 80.

97. Jean Baudrillard, *For a Critique of the Political Economy of the Sign,* trans. C. Levin (New York: Telos Press, 1981), 144.

98. Baudrillard, *For a Critique of the Political Economy of the Sign*, 144.

99. See Gilloch, *Myth and Metropolis: Walter Benjamin and the City,* 136.

100. PIN: 3; 53.

101. P73: 3; 47.

102. Baudrillard, *For a Critique of the Political Economy of the Sign*, 206.

103. Ibid., p.185.

104. Quoted in Frederic Jameson, *Marxism and Form*, 77. Jameson is quoting a translated passage from Walter Benjamin's *Schriften, (Vol. I),* ed. T.W. Adorno & G. Adorno (Frankfurt: Suhrkamp Verlag,1955), 461.

105. PIN: 5; 76-77.

106. P73: 5; 68.

107. See Frederic Jameson, *Marxism and Form*, 77.

108. P73:11; 102.

109. Baudrillard, *The System of Objects,* 146.

110. See Nakamura Miharu, "'Kaze no uta o kike', '1973 nen no pinbôru', 'Hitsuji o meguru bôken', 'Dansu, dansu, dansu' yonbusaku no sekai: enkan no sonshô to Kaifuku," *Kokubungaku* 40, no. 4 (March 1995): 72.

111. Strecher, "Magical Realism and the Search for Identity," 278.

112. See Katô, "1973 nen no Pinbôru" in *Ierôpêji—Murakami Haruki*, 44-45. Katô is referring to an article entitled "Nosutarujî no gainen" trans. Matsumoto in *Deiogenesu*, No. 2 No further publication details are given, although it is worth noting that Karatani Kôjin also refers to Starobinski in regard to the latter critic's discussion of Rousseau's forging of a new kind of unified interiority in which 'writer, language and emotion cannot be distinguished.' For Karatani, Rousseau is crucial to Meiji ideology as a kind of polysemic signifier deployed in support of the People's Rights movement. See Karatani, *The Origins of Japanese Literature*, 67-68.

113. See Immanuel Kant, "Transcendental Aesthetic of Time," in "Transcendental Doctrine of Elements," *Critique of Pure Reason*, trans. J. M. D. Meiklejohn (London: Dent, 1984), 50.

114. Kant, "Transcendental Aesthetic of Time," 49.

115. Kant, "Transcendental Aesthetic of Time," 49.

116. Kant, "Transcendental Aesthetic of Time," 48.

117. See John Frow, "Tourism and the Semiotics of Nostalgia," *October* 57 (1990-91): 123-15; 126.

118. Karatani *The Origins of Modern Japanese Literature*, 34.

119. Suzumura, "Atarashii kyokô no tanjô," 17.

120. Suzumura, "Atarashii kyokô no tanjô," 17-20.

121. Suzumura, "Atarashii kyokô no tanjô," 20.

122. Suzumura, "Atarashii kyokô no tanjô," 18.

123. See Iser, *The Act of Reading*, 109. Iser describes the reader's wandering viewpoint as a process of apperception, with the important caveat that the aesthetic object itself 'cannot be identified with any of its manifestations during the time flow of the reading.' This wandering viewpoint engaged in multiple narrative strands adds a further dimension of metafictionality to the text.

124. Suzumura, "Atarashii kyokô no tanjô," 19.

125. Suzumura, "Atarashii kyokô no tanjô," 19. As one example, Suzumura gives Murakami's short story *Mekurayanagi to neru onna*. According to Suzumura, this strange drama 'doesn't lead anywhere' (*doko e mo ikitsukanai*).

126. Suzumura, "Atarashii kyokô no tanjô," 19.

127. Katô Norihiro, "Atarashii sôshitsukan" in *Ierôpêji—Murakami Haruki*, 39.

128. Katô, *Ierôpêji*, 44.

129. *Kenkyûsha's New Japanese English Dictionary*, 1718; 40, respectively.

130. Katô, *Ierôpêji*, 44-45. Of course, nostalgia is still to be recuperated in a contemporary Japanese context in terms of the 'spatial' metaphor of the division between city and hometown (*furusato*) as Ivy has discussed in *Discourse of the Vanishing*, Chapters 2, 3 & 4.

131. Karatani, *The Origins of Modern Japanese Literature*, 128.

132. Katô, *Ierôpêji*, 47.

133. Katô, *Ierôpêji*, 47.

134. Katô, *Ierôpêji*, 50.

135. Katô, *Ierôpêji*, 51.

136. PIN: 25; 207.

137. P73: 25; 179.

138. See Loughman, "No Place I was Meant to Be: Contemporary Japan in the Short Fiction of Murakami Haruki," 90. These words are actually the narrator's recollection of a conversation with a Chinese girl in "Slow Boat to China"—see the short story anthology *The Elephant Vanishes,* trans. Alfred Birnbaum & Jay Rubin (New York: Knopf, 1993), 238.

139. See La Fleur, *The Karma of Words*, Chapter Four; especially pages 84-89.

140. La Fleur, *The Karma of Words*, 87.

141. La Fleur, *The Karma of Words*, 84-85.

142. See Jean Baudrillard, "The Precession of Simulacra," in *Simulacra and Simulation*, trans. Shiela Faria Glaser (Ann Arbor: The University of Michigan Press, 1997), 1-42.

143. Baudrillard, "The Precession of Simulacra," 1. As an epigraph to the essay "The Precession of Simulacra," Baudrillard cites *Ecclesiastes* to dramatic effect: 'The simulacrum is never what hides the truth—it is truth that hides the fact that there is none. The simulacrum is true.' (no textual reference is provided.)

144. See Martin Heidegger, *The Question Concerning Technology and Other Essays,* trans. William Lovitt (New York and London: Garland Publishing Inc., 1977), 19-30.

145. Heidegger, *The Question Concerning Technology*, 17, (fn.16).

Chapter Six

Allegory as Landscape I: Hitsuji o meguru bôken
—A Wild Sheep Chase

「僕らの中に残っているいくつかの風景、いくつかの鮮烈な風景、でも
それらの風景の使い道を僕らは知らない。」

There are scenes—some really vivid scenes—that remain within us, yet we
have no idea how to make use of them.

Murakami Haruki,
Tsukaimichi no nai fûkei[1]

Murakami offers the above reflection on 'landscape' or 'scene' (*fûkei*)[2] in a 1994
photo/essay anthology on a journey through Greece by himself and photographer
Inakoshi Kôichi, entitled *Tsukaimichi no nai fûkei* (*Useless Landscapes*). Born
of his quite extensive periods of overseas travel and residence, the essay is an
extended discussion of the themes of travel, landscape, memory and loss, and
concludes with the observation by the author that poring over old photographs
gives rise to the sense that something is decisively missing or lost from the
'original' experience of the scene. He muses, however, that one of the most
wonderful things about life (*jinsei ni oite mottomo subarashii mono*) is that we
can never really return to that which has passed. For example, staring intently at
the photographic depiction of two anteaters at the Frankfurt Zoo, or of the eyes
of a young Greek sailor gazing at the horizon, Murakami recounts how inspiration for a story suggested by these photos remained so elusive. Certainly, in this
restricted sense, such images may be deemed largely useless. Their real value
lies, he concludes, in their role in conveying to us the marvelous sense that the
things of the past can never return.

In the previous chapter, it was argued that this view of time does not necessarily represent, as many commentators would have it, a Romantic view of loss
based on a linear and one-dimensional projection of temporality exemplified in
the clichéd view of the nostalgic loss of childhood, youth, innocence and grace
in accordance with the Kantian description of the *human* construction of time.
Rather, it is much closer to a notion of time as *simultaneous, synchronistic*—a

phenomenological clarity and perhaps epiphany—reflecting the unity of the imagined *cosmic* scale of time which in no way depends on its human construction or perspective.

It will be argued in this chapter, that simultaneously apprehended landscapes exist in a very compressed way in the cultural practices and artifacts of Japanese modernity. It is not as though each is simply overturned and then its origins repressed, as Karatani claims, but in the 'postmodern' worlds of Murakami's texts, can be found an archeology of landscapes—a kaleidoscope or cornucopia of 'scenes'—reflecting the tremendous compression of the Japanese experience of modernity.

These scenes or *fūkei* exist at two fundamental levels: the micro level, exemplified by the term 'urban scene' (*toshi fūkei*), and at the macro level of the signifier 'modern Japanese history' (*Nihon gendaishi*), exemplified as the amorphously defined contemporary 'national-cultural imaginary'. Both these levels of *fūkei* are mediated by the problematic idea of 'the self' (*jiko, jiga*)—which, it will be shown, is inscribed in the privatized narrative of Boku's 'quest' as allegorical of a phantasmal construction or 'collaborative fantasy' at the kernel of literary modernity and those texts (such as Murakami's) which form part of its critique.

In *Tsukaimichi no nai fūkei*, Murakami reflects on something he had viewed from the window of a country inn while traveling in Germany: an unremarkable vignette of a bridge over a canal, and a passing boat. He photographed the scene thinking that it may be of some use in the future. Years later, with the photograph on his desk, he set out to write a story with that very scene as the starting point for a new tale, yet as he recalls, inspiration was not readily forthcoming. Instead, Murakami writes that the image triggered the experience of a prior or more fundamental scene, and we can only wonder to what extent the author may have been referring to the faint memory of pre-modern 'transcendental landscape', or the inkling of a repressed childhood memory.[3] Whatever the case, it is precisely this idea of 'useless scenes' (*tsukaimichi no nai fūkei*) which seems to corresponds with Kunikada Doppo's view of landscape implicit in 'Unforgettable People'. Here, people functioning merely as objects of viewing remain nameless, but the *conscious self-reflection* of the fact that 'now I am viewing a scene' is given prominence.

In the previous chapter we demonstrated Murakami's use of allegory as a narrative modality in exploring the nature and limits of metaphor and representation in a fictional work. It also became clear that the focus on modality, in turn, indicated a concern with a different and more philosophical trajectory regarding the nature of being and non-being.

In this chapter, the terms of the equation, 'allegory as modality', will be turned inside out: we will interrogate the conventional use of allegory as employing a metaphor (in terms of a journey, pilgrimage or 'landscape') to indicate something 'propositional' about the world. In particular, we will be responding to Karatani's claim that 'Murakami's writing in his first two novels represents nothing but a 'landscape' or 'scene' (*fûkei*) but in the third novel, *Hitsuji o me-guru bôken* (*A Wild Sheep Chase*), apparently becomes something else.

It will be demonstrated that *Hitsuji o meguru bôken* presents an allegorical form (and this is crucial—it is simulacral, phantasmal) of the pre-modern, transcendental landscape and is also partly constructed as a national-cultural imaginary produced by the Meiji modern state, as well as the semiotics of tourism and 'discovery' constructed by postwar advertising—but not strictly along the lines defined by Karatani as a discovery of 'interiority'. What will be argued is that as a new form of 'landscape' which once again shifts the focus *from* 'interiority' as defined by Karatani, back to a kind of 'exteriority' (this time reflected in the 'aesthetic of the city' or, what many critics have called the *toshigensô*) it suggests partly a phantasm of 'interiority' based not on the search for individual, subjective truth, but on the 'living out' of a lifestyle based on numerous 'choices'.

Here can be discerned a multi-layered genealogy of 'landscape' and the attendant notions of interiority/exteriority/subjectivity implied therein, ranging from 'transcendence to immanence', from exteriority to interiority. Murakami has basically mixed 'pre-modern' and 'modern' versions of landscape in a 'postmodern' pastiche of the two, and in which each becomes simulacral of the other. This is no doubt one important reason why his fictional style has been perceived to be so different. 'Landscape', here, is also allegorical of the national-cultural imaginary and the imaginary of 'the self', and in the latter we see an especially interesting example of the peculiar tension between 'self' and 'other' inscribed in the linguistic foundations of the Japanese language. Thus we arrive at a description of 'landscape' in *Hitsuji o meguru bôken* as a set of discourses marking the *intersection* of different forms of the national-cultural imaginary— overlapping with the imaginary of the 'self' (*jiko, jiga*) also postulated, but never fully elaborated in modernity.

'Fûkei' as Discourse in Japanese Modernity

It is well known that Karatani gave recent critical prominence to the concept of 'fûkei' ('landscape') through his radical claim of the 'discovery of landscape' in the literature of the third decade of the Meiji era. Needless to say, however, the idea of landscape has existed apart from this particular moment of epistemological 'inversion' (*tentô*), and it is clear that there has existed a tension between heterogeneous versions of landscape in the elaboration of Japanese modernity. It is the aim of this chapter to show how Murakami has used some of these competing versions of landscape to reveal the complex archeology of Japanese modernity in terms of the nexus between a national-cultural imaginary and the contradictory and phantasmal 'self' of novelistic convention. This self is elaborated by and through the interplay of the discourses of 'history', 'nation' and 'city' — and *Hitsuji o meguru bôken* can be described as a complex allegorical tale which utilizes a multi-layered theory of 'landscape' to explore this interplay.

All versions of landscape imply a visually elaborated scheme of the spatio-temporal world. In the Japanese case, the most archaic representation of this world is evident in the mytho-poetic imagery of early texts such as the *Nihon-shoki* and *Kojiki*. By necessity, such representations require the attribution of divinity to an imagined, yet materially definable topography of land and sea. In such a mythic depiction, the process of making firm the land is the first step in giving form to the amorphous domains of heaven and earth. This primal narrative was useful in the later construction of a national ideology in the 1930s, and was deemed so important as to be given special reference by the authors of the ultra-Nationalist *Kokutai no hongi (Cardinal Principals of the National Entity of Japan)*, who emphasize the *Nihon-shoki's* depiction of the 'floating and drifting of the Land'—a land which, according to the *Kojiki,* is ordered to be 'made', 'consolidated' and 'brought into being' by the two deities assigned the task.[4]

The issue of determinate form is not directly addressed in a more recent and polemical text marking a significant epistemological shift in the schematization of 'Japan' vis-à-vis 'the world'. In the language of an officially commissioned dissertation aimed at shoring up the fading political power of the Edo *Bakufu*, we see an example of how the idea of 'landscape' writ large was indirectly informed by an incipient concept of 'nation' in early Japanese modernity. As we have noted in an earlier chapter, Wakabayashi has argued that Aizawa's *New Theses (Shinron)* of 1825, projected a 'proto-nationalist' representation of Japan by its use of the terms 'Divine Realm' (*tenka*) and 'Middle Kingdom' (*chûgoku*). The use of this latter term in particular, indicated the deliberate formation of a new ideology of 'nation' (*kokka*) and the designation of 'Japan as Middle Kingdom' (rather than China) enabled *Bakufu* leaders to 'extricate Japan from subservience to a China-dominated diplomatic world order of universal empire and culture.'[5]

However, agreement on which land masses constituted precisely the borders of this realm was continually mediated by the descriptive opposition between 'Japan proper' (*naichi*) and those islands both to the north and south which were subject to incessant incursion and invasion by foreigners. Aizawa writes:

> It [Russia] utilized Christianity to seduce the Ezo tribes into submission and to capture island after island (to our North). Now (it) has turned its predatory eyes on Japan proper (naichi).[6]

Even prior to this, there were attempts at fixing the idea of 'Japan proper', through such terms as *Nihon no sankei* ('Three Views of Japan'). Although it is now a tourist industry cliché designating the three most famous 'views' of Japan, this nomenclature originally specified the geographic constellation of a national-cultural imaginary whose dimensions and scale could be readily evoked in the popular imagination.

According to Unno, the invention of the 'Three Views of Japan' can be explained in several ways. The number three was a both a logical necessity based on the fact that the binary form of two always implies a third—and it was also indicative of the Chinese proclivity for tripartite forms: heaven, earth and man; sun, moon and star, and so on. But more importantly, the three places formed one 'set', whose locations were well known long previously but only legitimized in the seventeenth century in Hayashi Shunsai's *Nihon jisekiko*, where this particular triad is said to have been first described.[7]

Undoubtedly, this set functioned 'politically' by placing Edo at the centre of a newly emerging national-cultural imaginary. Earlier, well known scenic 'sets' incorporating eight famous locations in China were arranged in such a way as to realistically allow the visiting of all sites within a reasonable time. This was clearly not possible in the Japanese case, with the *sankei* consisting of Miyajima in the far west (near Hiroshima), Matsushima in the north (near Sendai) and Amanohashidate (on the Japan Sea coast, north of Kyoto). According to Unno, tracing a line on the map between these three points delineated an area broadly covering what may described as the middle of the Japanese archipelago, and thus gave to Edo a central position equidistant to all. Such a constellation provided a unitary perspective and image of a united Japan for a government which relied heavily on control and political order covering a determinate and clearly specifiable domain.[8]

In a fundamental sense, therefore, the notion of *fûkei* or 'landscape' prior to and concurrent with Japanese modernity has been part of the larger discourse of the 'imagined community' of the nation much more so than the associated term 'scenic and historic places' (*meisho kyûseki*) might suggest. While there is no doubt that Karatani's persuasively argued proposition that the 'discovery' of landscape towards the end of the nineteenth century corresponded with the formation of a new form of subjectivity and 'interiority', it is also clear that in the proto-modern and early modern contexts the idea of landscape had implications beyond its function of merely providing the typical means for representing a transcendental world alluded to in Chinese landscape painting.

Comprising discursive layers of mytho-poetic, political-historical and religious-aesthetic significance, the Japanese term *fûkei* is therefore highly polysemic, and thus able to be deployed in quite elaborately allegorical terms by writers such as Murakami. It is one amongst a number of narrative topoi, enabling complex themes of historical, aesthetic and linguistic import to be explored. In functional terms there is no doubt that *fûkei* (as a form of allegory) is simulacral and phantasmal in its operation, and herein lies its obvious appeal to a writer who has tended to reject the conventions of available narrative orthodoxy.

If the pre-modern 'landscape' in literature was devoid of unitary perspective and detailed description, it relied instead on the poetic and auratic invocation of well established sensibilities of association. For instance, the simple elegance and lucidity of the eighteenth century poet Bashô's writing, is in no way diminished by the characterization of his masterpiece 'The Narrow Road of Oku' (*Oku no hosomichi*) as the record of an old man on a well journeyed trail visiting places of note that he had already imagined well *before* departure. This is clear when we consider, for example, his expectation and response to visiting the site of arguably the most famous of the 'three views of Japan' at Matsushima Bay. He acknowledges that prior to the journey,

> The thought of the moon at Matsushima began to occupy my thoughts.

Upon visiting the site and taking in the view:

> No matter how often it has been said, it is none the less true that Matsushima is the most beautiful place in Japan.

Later upon reflection, after the viewing:

> I lay down without composing any poem, but I could not sleep. I remembered that when I left my old cottage, I was presented with a poem in Chinese about Matsushima and with a Japanese one on Matsugaura Island. I opened my knapsack and made the poems my companion for the night.[9]

As an act of seeing, Bashô's writing indicates a process of what may described as similar to that of the tourist taking a photograph: 'not an empirical act of seeing but the congruence of the sight with the idea of the sight.'[10] Unno observes that before departure, Bashô already had an image of Matsushima Bay—and the literary/visual figures of pine tree, sea and moon in the quintessential arrangement of Japanese aesthetic sensibility. He also confirms the phenomenological aspect of what is brought to the viewing of a natural scene: it takes the form of a predetermined language and grammar for reading that scene—and when confronted with a nameless place or view, it is clear that the viewer quite naturally uses the interpretative code of the already 'known' and 'named' site in order to complete the act of interpretation.[11]

Bashô apparently had little interest in the detailed recording of what he 'saw'. On the contrary, as Keene notes, for the purpose of writing excellent poetry, he often 'changed the order of places visited, or turned rainy days into sunny ones, and as the literal truth was of little interest to him, he did not hesitate to embroider.'[12] In a similar vein, Oketani affirms that upon reading certain passages of *Oku no hosomichi*, he has the strange impression of an almost complete lack of description in the text (*'koko ni wa fûkei no byôsha rashii mono wa hotondo nai'*).[13]

Rather than provide realistic 'description' from the position of a single viewing point, Bashô's writing exemplified the transcendental and non-representational envisioning of the world in the form of what Karatani has called the pre-modern 'weave of language'.[14] This is a non-representational, transcendental envisioning of *fûkei* in language which has no use for mundane physical description and the kinds of perspective and subjectivity implying the position of the viewer.

Japan's great modern writer Natsume Sôseki (an ardent admirer of Bashô's poetry) was perhaps caught in between the pre-modern and modern versions of landscape, standing on the cusp of a new version of representation—acutely aware of certain contradictions, and somewhat dubious of his position. As an author steeped in the conventions of classical Chinese writing (*kanbun*) and its visual equivalent in landscape painting, he sometimes explored the Romantic confluence of interiority and natural landscape to striking effect, and at other times, lamented the loss of disinterested 'distance' from the classical text. In a remarkable passage in *Kusamakura*,[15] the narrator reflects on the possibility, on his short journey, of regarding events 'as though they were part of the action of a Noh play, and the people I meet, merely as if they were actors'.[16] In a somewhat contradictory blending of the Chinese classical landscape motifs with the Western Christian view of Nature, and acknowledging that 'the "Southern Hills," the "bamboo grove," the skylark and the rape-blossom possess a character all their own, which is vastly different to humanity', the narrator hopes to regard all the people that he meets—'farmer, tradesman, village clerk, old man' and so on—as 'no more than a component feature of the overall canvas of Nature.'[17]

Just when the narrator has completed this extended meditation on his resolve to maintain a distant and strictly 'classical' observation and aesthetic sensibility of 'what is and what is not beautiful', Romantic 'Nature' suddenly impinges— and with full psychological effect—'turning the whole sky as far as I could see into a rolling, awe-inspiring see of cloud'. Lost in a wandering and sublime reverie amidst the rain and mist, the narrator muses:

> Whether it was the rain or the trees that was moving, or whether the whole thing was merely the unreal wavering of a dream, I did not know. Whatever it was, it struck me as most unusual and wonderful.[18]

In another of Sôseki's fictional works *Kôfu* (*The Miner*)—a novel striking for its use of stream-of-consciousness narration—the narrator moves his gaze from providing a detailed description of shade and colour, to being absorbed in a much grander vision:

> When I shifted my eyes from the mountain to the sky, I lost any conscious sense of their having left the mountain and saw the sky as a continuation of the mountain. And the sky was huge.[19]

Notwithstanding the veracity of this description of the experience of the sublime in the face of Nature, we should note Karatani's claim that Sôseki's unique position enabled him to 'maintain within himself a certain attitude toward life that had existed prior to "landscape" and "modern Japanese literature"', quite simply because he 'lived through' the discovery of 'landscape'. Significantly, for Karatani, the move to a non-transcendental form of representation was an acutely condensed process in Japan—unlike that which occurred in the West, evolving as it did over centuries. The crucial insight of Karatani is his claim that 'once landscape has been established, its origins are repressed from memory'.[20] This is certainly true of the various tropes of landscape deployed in Murakami's

Hitsuji o meguru bôken, which rely on firmly established conventions of reading the represented world being effectively unavailable for ready recuperation. As with the operation of myth, historical referentiality masks the multi-layered discourse of landscape which is at play in the text.

This repression of the historicity of forms of representation is clearly evident in the circle of intertextuality (if not 'complicity') characterizing the way in which the depiction of Mt. Fuji (a fetishized site which is now iconic of 'Japan') moved from 'transcendental' to 'realistic' representation. Shiba Kôkan (an important exponent of Western painting in late eighteenth century Japan) insisted that only a 'realistic' rendering of *Fujisan* could capture its true beauty:

> If one follows only the orthodox Chinese methods of painting, one's picture will not resemble Fuji, and there will be none of the magical quality in it which painting possesses. The way to depict Fuji accurately is by means of Dutch painting.

As has been noted elsewhere, Shiba played a significant role in the burgeoning 'intertextuality' of Japanese and European painting, and was important, according to Keene 'because of his influence on many later Japanese artists including Hokusai—who in turn influenced the French impressionists to make the circle of borrowing complete.'[21]

If Sôseki possessed an acute awareness of the competing and contradictory versions of the 'landscape' of his time, the same cannot be said of Kunikida Doppo. It is in Doppo's texts that, according to Karatani, the first examples of realistic depiction are evident, and it is Doppo who first presents what Karatani has described as 'people-as-landscape'.[22] These are nameless individuals, whose physical characteristics and perhaps occupation are detailed, but who remain anonymous and simply a part of the depiction of the 'scene' in which they appear. Karatani notes that at the conclusion of Doppo's *Wasureenu hito bito* ('Unforgettable People'), the protagonist Otsu's former acquaintance Akayama is referred to merely as 'The Inkeeper of Kameya' rather than 'Akayama'.[23]

Another of Doppo's stories, *The Bonfire*, is peopled by 'old men', 'young men' and 'boys' who all remain nameless. There are also 'a traveler', 'a boatmen' and 'a farmer'. All seem almost superfluous, significant only insofar as they 'appear' in the scene, providing a locus of consciousness as a foil to the depiction of the overall scene:

> A child of the seashore waits alone. The north wind at his back. He sits on the white, withered grass of a sandy slope, watching the dim glow of the sun sinking behind the Izu mountains. His father's ship is long overdue.

And the anonymous man, his occupation uncertain, who

> only looks, says not a word, nor laughs nor sings, this man, this fisherman or farmer who plies his oar in loneliness.

There is also a direct reference to the idea of similitude, and the scene as 'art':

> Here one sees at times, as in a picture, a pair of young men astride bareback
> horses, walking them quietly through the shallows of the river mouth as the last
> rays of the setting sun linger on the slope above.[24]

Karatani's notion of an epistemological 'inversion' exemplified in Doppo's stories, describes, therefore, an elevation of the solitary and introverted Romantic
locus of consciousness , as well as clearly establishing the dominance of the
point of view of the narrator through detailed, realistic description. Doppo, of
course, imitated the style of Turgenev in his attempt to show, as Donald Keene
suggests, 'that quite ordinary landscapes and the unremarkable people who
moved through them were as worthy of being commemorated as the traditional
utamakura, the "famous places" that had attracted Japanese travelers of the
past.'[25]

How does all this relate to Murakami? If Karatani's description of Murakami's novels as merely 'landscapes' has any validity, then it is reasonable to
assume that the two conditions of his theory (i.e. 'introversion'/'interiority' and
'detailed description') should be readily identifiable. In one sense, we can concede to agree that Murakami does use the trope of 'landscape' very differently in
his third novel. That is, he uses it allegorically and in a simulacral, phantasmal
way, in order to partially restore the 'transcendental' dimension to the text. On
the other hand, we can suggest that he is also playing with a polymorphous and
loosely defined notion of landscape (in this sense, vastly extending its scope)
and in so doing, is very much demonstrating a concern with the politi-
cal/historical dimensions of the term.

The central proposition of this chapter is, therefore, that the novel *Hitsuji o
meguru bôken* extends the idea of landscape *allegorically*, with the unspoken
referent of this allegory inhering in the signifier 'modern Japanese history' (*kindai nihonshi*). This idea incorporates pre-modern, modern and therefore *post-*
modern elements of Japanese *fûkei ron*. By arguing thus, we have not foreclosed
the debate about Japanese modernity as discussed in Chapter 2. Rather, we are
acknowledging that the distinction 'modern'/'postmodern' can usefully underpin
some theoretical parameters we are attempting to establish, and that Murakami's
texts respond to the core issues of the modernity debate without, of course, necessarily 'resolving' any of them.

For all its originality, Karatani's theory does not adequately address two aspects of landscape as discourse in Japanese modernity. One of these is the theory
of the sublime (although this is indirectly referred to in the after-note to the essay entitled 'The Discovery of Landscape' and related to the 'discovery' and
depiction of Hokkaido[26]). The other inadequacy is that Karatani's argumentation
does not fully theorize the poetics of the *urban* landscape.

In *Hitsuji o meguru bôken*, the sublime depiction of Hokkaido and Manchuria,
and implicit reference to 'emperorism', is in fact the first use of what can be
called Murakami's 'historical sublime': within the apocalyptic frame of post-

Edo Japanese 'history' ('forced opening', imperial 'restoration', industrializa-
tion, military defeat, nuclear devastation and the postmodern disintegration of
'the social'), Murakami's radically de-centered subject engages in a schizophrenic experience of the spatio-temporal matrix. This 'historical sublime' is
further developed in later novels to such an extent, that it can be said to powerfully underpin the recurring trope of the 'double/multiple world' structure of
these texts. Just as the origins of the discovery of *fûkei* became submerged in the
self-absorption and narrowly prescribed deictic possibilities of the 'I-novel', it
was only natural that a radical overturning of such conventions and a concomitant 'freeing up' of language came to be crucial to Murakami's experiments
with fictional form.

'*Fûkei*', therefore, as a discourse central to Japanese modernity, is ascribed an
allegorical (and thus simulacral) role in the development of Murakami's narrative oeuvre. 'Landscape' as utilized here is thus a 'discourse' in the fullest sense
of the word: a body of social knowledge, an array of possible statements about
place and time, and not simply a unified concept available for ready interpretation. As a discourse, it displays all the semiotic slippage entailed in the processes
of representation as outlined in our prior discussion of the shift from 'resemblance' to 'representation' (Foucault), and the theory of the simulacrum
(Nietzsche and Deleuze), as well as enabling a generalized poetics of allegory as
described in the previous chapter.

Narrative Synopsis (kôgai) of *Hitsuji o meguru bôken*

(*A Wild Sheep Chase*—hereafter referred to as *Hitsuji*.)

Separated from his wife, and feeling a little like an orphan, the protagonist
Boku is put under considerable pressure from the private secretary of a right-
wing magnate, for having used in an advertisement, a certain photo which was
sent to him by his friend Nezumi, whose whereabouts are unknown. Together
with the woman possessing 'mysteriously powerful' ears, he sets out to search
for the place where the photo of the sheep with the distinctive star shaped mark
on its coat was taken. It seems that the sheep is the source of some kind of su-
per-human powers. In the 'Iruka' Hotel in Sapporo, the couple meet the 'Sheep
Professor' who had brought the sheep from Manchuria, and get to know of Nezumi, who is at the former country house of the sheep professor. After arriving
there, the woman mysteriously disappears. Wearing a sheep skin, the 'Sheep
Man' shows himself. In order to dispense with the sheep once and for all, Nezumi, still in the state of being possessed by the sheep and having appeared
before Boku as the 'Sheep Man', kills himself. The final request of Nezumi's
ghost, is that Boku arm the time bomb for the destruction of the house.[27]

Critical Responses to *Hitsuji o meguru bôken*

In conversation with Nakagami Kenji in 1985, Murakami intimated that when approaching the writing of *Hitsuji*, he desired to 'dismantle' (*kaitai suru*) and then attempt to 'reconstruct' (*saikôchiku*) the novel form—not deliberately and from the beginning, but rather through the 'spontaneous' development of a story (*sutôrî*).[28] Nevertheless, as Yokô notes, in the trend towards the 'return to story' (*monogatari kaiki*) of the eighties, Murakami's approach differed from comparable writers such as Takahashi Genichirô. The latter was described as attempting to disassemble the framework of the novel *itself*, while Murakami is cast in the light of a writer who, in terms of the novel-as-system (*shôsetsuseido*), sought to retain the 'hardware' while changing the 'software' of that system.[29]

In one of the more important monographs on Murakami, Yoshida Haruo charts what he sees as this author's literary 'conversions' (*tenkan*), with the first turning point being represented by *Kokkyô no minami, taiyô no nishi* (*South of the Border, West of the Sun*, 1992) and the second in the form of *Nejimakidori kuronikuru* (*The Wind-Up Bird Chronicle*, 1994-95).[30] However, Yoshida also describes a dramatic change well before these novels of the nineties, with the 'rapid progress' (*hiyaku*) and 'opportunity' (*keiki*) presented in *Hitsuji o meguru bôken*. Interestingly, as Yokô notes, it is the completeness of the 'storiness' (*sutôrîsei*) of the text, which sets it apart from the 'fragmentary' nature of the previous two works in the trilogy.[31] Whether it is the 'narrativity' of the text, or the clearer exposition of plot and action that Yokô is referring to here, is unclear. Also problematic, is the unspecified extent to which the terms *monogatarisei* and *sutôrisei* are supposed to differ as descriptors.

Regardless of the vagueness of such terminology, the question arises that if *Hitsuji* is indeed qualitatively different to Murakami's first two novels, to what extent does this have something to do with Karatani's claim that in fact the latter are not novels (*shôsetsu*) at all, but merely 'landscapes' (*fûkei*)?[32] If *Hitsuji* really is a 'novel', then on what basis is this so? We will have cause to question aspects of Karatani's claim, partly because there are dimensions of *Hitsuj* which are in concord with the previous two novels. On the other hand, to accept that the work-ideology of the text appears have to changed to the extent that it has become *allegorical of* landscape (rather than a version of landscape itself) at both the 'micro-level' of language and the deictic, as well as the 'macro-level' of the national-cultural imaginary.

The very early reviews of *Hitsuji* highlight some of the themes which were to be taken up in subsequent years in critical essays. Naturally, over time, each reading has been tempered by the accretion of previous critical approaches, to the extent that later critiques (for example Katô 1996, Tamaki 1996, Yoshida 1997) are able to situate the novel within a broader discursive context, and offer more compelling and thoroughgoing readings based on critical theory and cultural studies (the latter only recently being taken up in earnest by sections of Japanese literary academia). Immediately following the publication of *Hitsuji* by Kôdansha in October 1982, came Ayukawa's description of it as an 'occult style thriller', 'rich in allegory' and addressing aspects of postwar Japanese religion, politics and culture.[33] Aono wrote of a 'fairy story', a 'white novel', a 'pure white blank'—with the stance of the narrator oscillating between 'boldness' and 'stupidity'.[34] Kawamura bluntly characterized the story as 'entertainment' (vis-à-vis 'pure literature'), yet noted its treatment of the theme of corruption in the postwar Japanese state.[35]

In 1989, Murakami effectively made his debut in the West with the publication of *Hitsuji* in English. A novel stylistically and thematically divergent to the stereotypical images of modern Japanese literature, it made a strong impression on American readers. Most were no doubt unaware of the text's status as the final part of a trilogy, even though Kôdansha paperback translations had appeared in Japan in 1985 (*Pinball, 1973*) and 1987 (*Hear the Wind Sing*).

Early responses in English were restricted to brief reviews in magazines. This 'strikingly original novel'[36] was seen as 'interesting as an example of current Japanese writing',[37] 'displaying few of the traditional adornments of specifically Japanese fiction'[38] and 'a presentiment of fresh outlooks and impulses'.[39] As well as the usual comparisons to Chandler, Carver, Irving and Pynchon, the novel, according to Leithauser, 'quietly exchanges the hard-packed ground of naturalism, for the boggy, fog-wrapped surrealism'.[40] What seems to have been most striking for the reviewers is the fact that the 'detail is strictly non Japanese',[41] lacking in the list of exotic items such as 'tea ceremonies, moss gardens and painted screens.'[42]

The publication of *Hitsuji* in English corresponded with the zenith of American awe (if not suspicion) of Japanese economic power, and the rhetoric of 'Japan as Number One' sweeping America in the mid to late eighties.[43] It is somewhat of a contradiction, therefore, that these reviewers delighted in Murakami's abandonment of exotic Japanese items in his narrative. Despite this, the fundamentally Orientalist caricature of the 'inscrutable Japanese' was readily recuperable from their undisguised dismay at the systemic corruption alluded to in the text, as a product of 'modern Japan's frantic addiction to alien ideals of power and money'[44]—as if to suggest that home grown authoritarianism and greed had their origins somewhere *outside* Japan.

And it is ironic that, as Tsuboi notes, neo-Marxist critics such as Miyoshi Masao berated Murakami for aiming his books at the American market, while it is clear that for Japanese readers, Murakami's books were admired precisely *because of* their 'internationalism', (*kokusaisei*) 'exoticisim' (*ekizochishizumu*) and 'un-nationality-like flavour' (*mukokuseki teki na fûmi*).[45]

This apparent complicity of the Orientalism/Occidentalism pairing indicates a play of tropes which points to the simulacral structure of the Murakami enterprise. In the mirror-like reflection of the image of the exoticized or de-exoticized Other, inheres a multi-layered semiosis, wherein distinctions between 'original' and 'copy' become meaningless. As Ryckmans has argued, complicity and borrowing are in fact the *very conditions* of culture,[46] and it would be simplistic to emphasize notions of 'authenticity' within the inter-textual circle of borrowing of the mega-genre known as 'world literature'. The operation of this circle in fact confirms the efficacy of Baudrillard's idea of the 'precession of simulacra', wherein the elaboration of the copy *precedes* the production of a new 'original' which is merely a 'filling in' of the prescribed model of the text. It also confirms the veracity of the Deleuzean play of difference through repetition —and since we are arguing that this is the hallmark of Murakami's critique of modernity, it remains a central concern of our discussion of the novels of his trilogies. Rather than inter-cultural complicity, what is perhaps more pertinent to our discussion of *Hitsuji* is what Takami describes as the *intra-cultural* phenomenon of the 'collaborative fantasy' (*kyôdô gensô*) which in turn lies at the heart of the 'urban phantasm' (*toshi gensô*).

The Complicity of 'Style'

The observation that Murakami's fiction has been 'influenced' by that of Raymond Chandler has been noted above. The term 'influence', however, is very different in connotation to the idea of 'imitation', and there are even more divergences if the 'original' and the 'copy' are rendered in different languages. The most common comparison of *Hitsuji* is with Chandler's *The Long Goodbye*.[47] Not surprisingly, *Hitsuji* has been translated in accordance with the American idiom of the 'hardboiled', laconic, detective novel. This style was chosen even though there is no absolutely compelling evidence in the original Japanese to do so, except for the fact that as was the case with the two previous novels, Murakami wrote in a terse and unambiguous style which was readily able to be reformed into the language of a prescribed idiom. This required the uniform application of such an idiom, and it is from such necessity that our method of analysis is indicated.[48]

The question arises, therefore, about the implicit reference to the structure and style of language in the *Hitsuji* text. Perhaps Murakami's use of Japanese might be said to approximate the status of an 'inter-language' (described by linguists as the kind of hybridized version used by beginner learners who have not fully mastered the codes of the new language). Yet to describe it as 'imitation is another matter altogether. Also to be considered is the uniquely hybrid nature of the Japanese language—which utilizes a combination of phonetic alphabet and ideographic script—and the effect that this might have on translation.[49]

Attempting to test the efficacy of the assertion by mystery writer, James Ellroy, that 'Chandler is a very easy writer to imitate', American researchers Sigelman and Jacoby undertook a detailed, statistical and quantitative/qualitative stylistic analysis of Raymond Chandler's fiction, using four broad parameters of 'simplicity', 'action', 'dialogue' and 'vivid language'. Their results were remarkable: all but two of the twenty five works by authors who were reputed 'imitators' of Chandler showed, according to the study, significant linguist variation to those of the Chandler texts—proving the point that certain kinds of literary style may indeed be very difficult to reproduce.[50]

If anything, it is one of Murakami's American translators, Alfred Birnbaum, who has done the 'imitating'—forced as he is to work within a consistent idiom and mood, or risk incoherence and the production of a cumbersome text. Anglophone readers are not getting a Chandleresque version of Murakami. Rather, they are getting Alfred Birnbaum's *interpretation* of Chandler. And although Birnbaum's text was not part of the Sigelman study, given the definitive results of the latter, it seems highly unlikely that it more closely approximates the ostensibly difficult-to-imitate Chandler style.

When journalist Murray Sayle quipped that 'Murakami writes much as private eye Philip Marlowe talked, as no one has ever written Japanese before',[51] he was unwittingly implying that, whereas twenty five purported 'imitators' of Chandler (all native English writers) had failed, Murakami—writing in Japanese and in conjunction with his English translator—had somehow succeeded. This is clearly inconsistent with Sigelman's conclusion that 'no pastiche has penetrated close to the stylistic core of Chandler's oeuvre'.[52] Moreover, Sayles' observation is blind to the specific illocutionary/perlocutionary effects of the represented literary speech act vis-à-vis the narrative voice of the text.

The evidence of a prescribed 'complicity' in matters of style, is clear even from the translation of the very first passage of the novel. The Japanese text reads as follows:

> 「新聞で偶然彼女の死を知った友人が電話で僕にそれを教えてくれた。
> 彼は電話口で朝刊の一般記事をゆっくりと読み上げた。平凡な記事だ。
> 大学を出たばかりの駆け出しの記者が練習のために書かされたような文
> 章だった。」[53]

And Birnbaum's translation:

> It was a short one paragraph item in the morning edition. A friend rang me up
> and read it to me. Nothing special. Something a rookie reporter fresh out of col-
> lege might've written for practice. The date, a street corner, a person driving a
> truck, a pedestrian, a casualty, an investigation of possible negligence.[54]

Admittedly, the matter of the listing of these events of a violent death in such a nonchalant way is typical of the terse, laconic Chandleresque narration. However, translating it by following the same sentence order (which in no way alters the propositional/informational content) alters the overall sense of the narrator's attitude to the events described. Coupled with a more direct or literal rendering into a British-like idiom, for example, a variant translation might appear as follows:

> I learned of her death by telephone from a friend who had, by chance, happened
> upon its reporting in the newspaper. He read the article, from the morning edi-
> tion, slowly over the phone. It was a standard report—as if written as a practice
> exercise by a newly graduated novice reporter: the date, a street corner, a truck

running into somebody. And a police investigation of possible negligence was under way.

The Birnbaum translation has reversed the order.[55] The first sentence in English is actually the third sentence in Japanese. Yet Birnbaum has aimed for and successfully achieved the 'hardboiled' effect by starting out: 'It was a short one paragraph item. . . .', substituting the subject at the start of the sentence with the pronoun 'it', and beginning the novel *in medias res*, a device typical of, but of course not exclusive to, the detective genre.[56]

However, there actually is no imperative to choose this particular style of translation—except for the fact that Birnbaum, having translated Murakami's first two works in this way, is fulfilling the expectation that Murakami's is, without doubt, a 'hardboiled' style. The *Los Angeles Times Book Review* put it this way:

> In a staccato, hardboiled American style, he tattoos out short, snappy sentences
> of world-weary deadpan. . . . Alfred Birnbaum's excellent translation has got-
> ten his sentences down exactly right. [57]

The problem is that this reviewer (assuming he/she knows no Japanese) is incapable of judging whether Birnbaum has got it 'just right'. Indeed he has only 'got it right' in confirming that Murakami's texts *should* read like Chandler or Carver or Fitzgerald or one of the other authors whom Murakami avidly read before writing his own fiction. Here we get a picture of artistic complicity and inter-textuality which can be expressed in the following way:

1. Murakami reads a lot of Chandler.
2. Murakami writes an apparently 'Chandleresque' style novel, based on his knowledge of Chandler's style.
3. With the knowledge of Murakami's boyhood reading and influence, Birnbaum translates Murakami into his imagined equivalent of the Chandleresesque style in Japanese.
4. Critics say that Murakami has imitated Chandler.
5. Americans read Murakami as 'Chandleresque'.
6. Japanese read Murakami as a 'Japanese Chandler', under the critic's paradigm of the 'hardboiled'novel.
7. The simulacral precession—the 'filling in' of the prescribed style is accomplished, and the circle of inter-textuality is complete.

At this point any distinction between imitation, copy and original becomes blurred, for as Karatani notes, Japanese are reading American literature *through* Murakami, who has invented an entire idiom based on *his interpretation* of American English. Equally, Americans are reading Murakami through Alfred Birnbaum and Jay Rubin (a translator of some later Murakami texts) as well as Philip Gabriel. Therefore, the only thing in common here is the 'urban' context of the novels—and this enables, it would seem, the 'urban fantasy' as a 'collaborative fantasy', which will be discussed later.

Instead of engaging in the somewhat fruitless practice of searching for evidence of 'imitation', it is only by examining some specific linguistic devices (the use of nouns, numbers, and simile) that we are able to support our claim that although Murakami's style *appears* to have imitated the idiom and register of Chandler, it has actually been establishing a 'landscape' which is at once both strange and familiar to the Japanese reader. 'Strange', in the sense that it uses names, numbers and simile in an unusual and idiosyncratic way. 'Familiar', to the extent that it is elaborated within the context of an urbanized 'presented world' or 'landscape', the origins of which although perhaps partially 'repressed' or 'forgotten', are also the referent which constitutes the immediate and experiential matrix of lived daily urban life.

Tamaki is close to the mark by honing in on the theme of language, and proposes that the question: 'Where are words of substance to be found?' is the central 'allegory' of the *Hitsuji* text, while acknowledging that this ostensibly represents a common 'linguistic' view (*gengokan*) of language.[58] He notes, however, that without explicitly stating so, this view of Murakami's sense of language is accepted by many critics, and cites the example of Sakurai Tetsuo's depiction of Murakami's 'linguistic contempt' (*gengo besshi*): a dismantling of meaning based on a 'despairing emptiness' (*zetsubôteki na munashisa*).[59]

Nevertheless, Tamaki insists that there is no need to direct this criticism toward Murakami, because the author is in fact taking up an 'extremely logical position towards language', and 'hypocritically' and tangentially offering a critique of the flood of advertising copy in the mass media. More importantly, Tamaki notes that Murakami acutely feels the difficulty of writing a novel in the circumstances whereby 'language' is far removed from 'substance' (*jitai*).[60] In short, Tamaki claims, Murakami's position is that rather than focus on the fact of language being empty of substance, we should face the paradox that *in spite of having no substance, such language still carries meaning.*[61]

This is the crux of our discussion of the use of language—what we have called landscape at the 'micro' narrative level in *Hitsuji*. We will suggest that Murakami is 'playing' with language and uses the various devices relating to names, nouns and numbers as part of his multi-dimensional construction of landscape. Many critics take this literally and without seeing his parodic, ludic treatment of language. However, this is only part of the story, because as we have already proposed, *Hitsuji* is allegorical of landscape at many levels. It will be suggested that this use of language helps generate the micro-landscape of the 'urban phantasm' or *toshi gensô*, which is an integral aspect of Murakami's multi-layered archeology of landscape, and is indicative of, as we shall conclude at the end of this chapter, 'the plural hypotheses of which the city is constructed.'[62]

Systems of Reference: Numbers, Names and Nouns

As is the case with regard to all signifying systems (texts), it is possible to construct a simple semiotic grid of the items which constitute processes of 'intra' and 'inter' textuality in a novel such as *Hitsuji*. Such a grid would indicate what may be called the broad 'systems of reference' of the presented world of the text: the patterns of signification generated by specific categories of single signifiers (or clusters of signifiers) which are deployed in order to evoke signifieds such as 'Westernness', 'conspicuous consumption', 'city life', 'rural landscape' and so on. Implicit in such grids is the operation of a series of binary oppositions, such as 'Western/Japanese', 'urban/rural', 'named/unnamed', 'counted/uncounted', 'past/present' and so on. From such a series we can make general statements about the system of signs which constitutes the Murakami *fūkei* at a more immediate level of reference, or what may be called the 'micro-landscape', and which includes some discussion of the deictic processes of locating, naming, describing and the represented acts of speaking. These statements can then be added to and integrated with (at the level of the allegorically construed narrative of 'nation') more general statements describing the contours of the 'macro-landscape' or 'national-cultural imaginary', in order to validate our argument about the allegorical use of the trope of 'landscape' in *Hitsuji*.

Many of the features of the 'micro landscape' of *Hitsuji* are of course not limited to that text alone, and appear more or less consistently across Murakami's oeuvre, forming the linguistic mosaic of his distinct narrative style. However, those that are discussed below, are interesting in so far as they constitute an imagined and presented world providing a foil and a context for the narrative *writ large*. What is discussed here, is the use of numbers, and perhaps most importantly, the idiosyncratic use of names and proper nouns.

Numbers

The plethora of seemingly arbitrarily chosen numbers has been noted as one of the most distinctive aspects of Murakami's unique style. There are approximately twenty-five overt and noteworthy numerical references[63] in *Hitsuji*, with the first significant example in the 'sixteen steps' (*jūroppo*) episode of Chapter 2:

> 「エレベーターのドアが閉まるシュウッというコンプレッサー音を確かめてから、おもむろに目を閉じる。そして意識の断片をかき集め、アパートの廊下をドアに向かって16歩歩いた。目を閉じたまま正確に16歩、それ以上でもそれ以下でもない。」 [64]

I waited for the compressed-air hiss of the elevator doors shutting behind me. Then gathering up the pieces of my mind, I started off on the sixteen steps down the hall to my apartment door. Eyes closed, exactly sixteen steps. No more, no less.[65]

Karatani has used this passage to make a point about what he calls the 'flood of numbers' (*sûji*) in Murakami's works. When Dostoyevsky writes 'exactly three steps', he claims the excessive accuracy (*kajô na seikakusa*) lends a dreamlike sense of unreality (*higenjitsusei*) to the event. In contrast to this, Murakami's 'exactly sixteen steps' seems purely optional and lends a sense of arbitrariness to the description of the action. The numbering of the identical twins as '208' and '209', and the reference to a former girlfriend as 'the third women I slept with' seems similarly arbitrary.[66]

Iguchi sees in the scene of Boku as the well-mannered drunk boasting about his exact measuring of the 'sixteen steps', the image of the rational idea of the 'model citizen' who is both controlling and controlled, and 'the self' (*jiko*) is unable to escape from the place which exists somewhere between the Boku who can count (*kazoeru boku*) and the Boku who can be counted (*kazoerareru boku*). In support of his thesis that the role of numbers in Murakami's fiction is to 'convey' (*dentatsu suru*) in order *not to convey*, Iguchi places Kurimoto's theory of exchange (which discusses the fundamental complicity of giving and receiving) within the framework of giving and receiving and the continuous payment and repayment of social obligation as debt (*fusai*) in Japanese society. Extending this model to language, transmission/communication (*dentetsu*) as a gift entails an endless process of expectation and obligation in the form of linguistic exchange.[67]

The most overt and meta-fictional reflection on the value of numbers can be found in Chapter 23 of *Kaze*, when Boku's admission of an obsession with counting things (and his precise recording of, in a six-month period, attendance at 358 classes, 54 acts of sexual intercourse, and the smoking of 6,921cigarettes) is said to reflect a belief that 'putting a numerical value on everything would enable [him] to transmit something to others.'[68]

However, Karatani claims that in this context, numerals represent an extreme manifestation of the meaning of language which has been reduced to the highly differentiated level of the sign (*kigô*), and concludes that up to and including the sixth of Murakami's novels, *Dansu, dansu, dansu* (1988), the prolific use of numbers and specific dates in his narratives signifies merely 'difference' and 'sequence' (*junjo*), and that this repeated use of numbers is a denial of 'singularity' (*tandokusei*) because it assigns a numerical value in place of names and descriptions and therefore, a denial of 'historicity' (*rekishisei*).[69] This view is somewhat in variance to Wada's observation that the use of Arabic numerals (*sanyô sûji*) used in counting items/events, and the specification of dates using the Western calendar, actually connotes a dimension of 'historical meaning' (*rekishiteki na imi*). Wada clearly rejects Maeda's view that this use of numbers is meaningless.[70]

In focusing on the much discussed passage in Chapter 23 of *Kaze*, critics are in fact searching for a way of accounting for the rhetorical basis of this profusion of numerical references, and the way in which it allocates relative values in the presented world of the narrative. Kasai is correct in noting that Boku's apparent equation of the 'serious' event of learning of his former girlfriend's death with the banality of the fact of smoking cigarette 'number 6,922' appears to be a 'rhetorical' attempt to dispel the gravity of the topic by way of trivial observation as a form of 'urban lyricism' (*tokaiteki na jojô*).[71] This is echoed in Nagashima's suggestion that replacing the event of the death with numbers is a way of establishing a position of distance from the overt awareness of human relations which accompanies the event of death.[72]

However, it is Watanabe's assertion--of the irony that this apparent device of 'postmodern lightness' (*posutomodan no keikaisa*) actually *foregrounds* the gravity of the previously more direct ways that fiction dealt with these themes— that is suggestive here.[73] Tanaka's essay 'Identity in Numbers' points out that the narrative of *Kaze* implies that 'participation in civilization' requires the surrendering of subjectivity, and that numbers are used in Murakami's fiction as a way of acknowledging this.[74] However, he also recognizes that this use of numbers may be symptomatic of a deeper issue that stems from a fundamental clash between the Western 'logos' and Japanese 'kotoba'—where the former has required, in the form of modernity in Japan, a kind of subjectivity not necessarily found in the pre-modern structures of self and world. It is implied that if indeed numerical value (*sûchi*) becomes the yardstick/ruler (*monosashi*) of meaning and representation, then perhaps tentative subjectivity can be stabilized, and the contours of the presented world more convincingly maintained.[75]

Fukami rejects what he sees as the over-simplistic idea that the flood of details and numbers in Murakami's fiction is simply an expression of the 'empty interior' and easy going (*karui*) 'urban sensibility' of people in contemporary advanced capitalist society. Behind the scattered appearance of this apparent emptiness and urban sensibility lies a hidden structure, the allusion to which provides the most fascinating aspect of Murakami's fiction.

It should be said that Murakami's style displays that he is fully aware of the 'conceptual illness' in which people are inevitably engulfed, and his skill, according to Fukami, is in assisting in the attempt to pull back and rise above this enveloping 'conceptual delusion'.[76] We can conclude, therefore, that Murakami's use of numbers in *Hitsuji* is not merely symptomatic of the 'hard-boiled' style (notwithstanding the fact that Chandler makes considerable use of this[77]) but that it also represents a subversion of conventional deictic process, which usually relies on an appropriate mix of verbal process, nouns and proper names to establish a predictable and acceptable presented world.

Names and nouns

Of all the idiosyncrasies of Murakami's apparently new style, it is the issue of names and naming which has attracted some of the most interesting (and contradictory) critical commentary. Hatanaka suggests that following the seminal passage of the discussion of the role of names in *Hitsuji*, proper names gradually begin to reappear in Murakami's narrative. (For example 'the girl with the beautiful ears' assumes the name 'Kiki' in *Dansu, dansu, dansu*.) The unnamed objects/people of the world are soon lost to memory, so the restoration of names is seen by Hatanaka as a way of restoring to memory—and thus to the world—a sense of connectedness to 'the real' (*genjitsusekai*).[78] Hatanaka's hunch is, in part, in the right direction, but it is unable to go beyond the idea of the omission of proper nouns as some kind of 'lack' or 'shortfall' which is later redressed.

On the question of personal names, we have already noted in a previous chapter Hayashi's claim that Murakami's use of personal pronouns (*ninshô daimeishi*) in place of proper names (*koyûmeishi*) indicated a perpetual alterity, for example, between the figures of 'Boku' and 'Nezumi', which disallowed a stable and individualized identity.

From another perspective, as Tamaki notes, not only does the fact that the characters who appear (including Boku) do not have names indicate the metafictionality of this novel, but the name of, for example, 'Boku', or 'taxi driver' is also a kind of compensation. As such, it suggests the abandonment of consciousness and signifies a kind if 'death' (*shi*) of the subject. In order to live, Tamaki writes, 'Boku has to forget his own name'.[79]

Of the many references (both direct and indirect) to the issue of naming in *Hitsuji*, some point more directly than others to the issue of the presence, or lack of a proper name. The first and most glaringly dramatic instance occurs in the opening pages of the novel in the form of 'the girl who would sleep with anyone'.[80] Other examples include the anonymous 'Boss' (*sensei*),[81] the Hokkaido pioneers refusing to officially name their new settlement,[82] and the repeated reference to the ear model (Boku's companion/girlfriend) merely as 'she'.[83]

Iwamoto attributes to the narrator's implied attitude toward naming, a form of exteriority which suggests aloofness and detachment: 'the wife', 'the girlfriend with the beautiful ears', 'the secretary', 'the business partner', 'the hotel clerk' become, in this view, mere signifiers of 'functional categories'.[84] He also notes the meta-fictional self-reflexivity in what is clearly the most overt reference to the issue of naming in the text: the extended dialogue between Boku and the chauffeur on the philosophical problem of naming, where Boku insists on an explanation of 'principle' rather than one at the 'purposive' (*mokuteki teki*) level.[85] The chauffeur concludes that the principle of 'non-interchangeability' justifies the need for proper names, but when Boku counters by asking whether this implies merely a focus on role and or function, the chauffeur shifts the analogy to the idea of 'fixity' (for example, in regard to parks, streets, movie theatres and so on) whereby *Boku* muses on the possibility that if he were to completely 'obliterate his consciousness' and become 'totally fixed' (*kichinto koteika sareru*), that this would be sufficient cause for him being able to assume a marvelous name.

This particular dialogue in *Hitsuji* can be described as a condensed reflection on the question of whether or not proper names have qualitative criteria of identity attached to them. This seems a reasonable way to approach the question of meaning with regard to proper names; however, as Harrison notes, the common-place view of a name denoting an individual does not indicate a logical neces-sity—rather, it is merely a *convention* of logic or logical grammar.[86] He suggests that as well as this convention, we must also consider the use of partial criteria of identity which are used to single out an individual. More importantly, we must take into account 'the general considerations of coherence of discourse and action within a community' which enable members of that community to keep a continuous check on the accuracy of the established criteria for the identification of individuals.

This acknowledges the fact that a name signifies with the addition of knowl-edge established *beyond* the parameters of formal or merely 'linguistic' knowl-edge, and that we need these other forms of knowledge to 'make sense' of a name. The requirement for these supplementary forms supports the observation that 'any "sense" which we can attribute to proper names is a "sense" which varies indefinitely from context of use to context of use'.[87] This seems a contra-diction in light of Foucault's claim that 'a noun is defined by its possibility of recurrence'.[88] However, we know that especially if a noun is a *proper* noun, then we must acknowledge the level of instantiation of that proper noun as part of a 'statement'—the latter being able to exist 'outside any possibility of its reappear-ing' except, according to Foucault, under strictly limited conditions.[89] Using the terminology of Frege's basic distinction between 'sense' and 'reference',[90] it would be reasonable to conclude, therefore, that although all proper names can be said to usually have readily identifiable referents, they do not necessarily give rise to a single determinate 'sense' which can be universally agreed upon.

It is this idea of the pluralities of 'sense' which is relevant here, and whilst not wishing to delve further into the labyrinthine debate about meaning which still animates language philosophers, the point can be made that Murakami's omis-sion of proper names (in his first two works and part of *Hitsuji*) in deference to, for example, personal, species or occupation specific pronouns, is an important element of his narrative strategy.

In other words, by destabilizing the naturalized process of the deployment of proper names in the modern Japanese fictional context, Murakami's narrator is in fact undermining the relatively stable system of reference which revolves around the personal pronoun 'I' (*Waga, Boku, Watashi,*) as the deictic centre in the conventional 'I-novel' narrative. In order to signify *beyond* the normalized parameters of reference in such narrative, Murakami's repression or temporary occlusion of the proper name, can perhaps be described as an overt acknow-ledgement of Derrida's assertion that 'when the name comes, it immediately says more than the name: the other of the name and quite simply the other, whose irruption the name announces.'[91]

The system of naming in *Hitsuji* is, therefore, about challenging the deictic centre, and positing a transcendental, self-reflexive site of subjectivity—an 'other' of the conventionalized 'self' (*jiga, jiko*). Karatani is able to recognize this and tie Murakami's approach to proper names into his theory of landscape. If, according to Karatani, the earlier of Murakami's novels are little more than 'scenes' (*fûkei*), and if indeed *Hitsuji* signals a return to a more orthodox narrative format, we can claim that this is not necessarily because in the third part of the trilogy the author had finished with the process of constructing 'scenes'. Rather, it seems possible that he moved towards the deployment of *fûkei* itself as a second order or allegorical discourse as part of the pre-empting of a 'return' of the referent in his later fiction.

Because of the effective repression of the signifier 'modern Japanese history' in much of the publicly sanctioned discourse of postwar Japan, Murakami perhaps attempted to deal subsequently with *fûkei* mimetically or allegorically — and in this way, much more powerfully. Imai implicitly acknowledges this indirect rendering when he describes *Hitsuji* as the 'tale which is imitated' (*mime-ishisu sareru monogatari*).[92] However, it is Karatani's insights which once again provide the most compelling argument in relation to this. What could the expression 'the girl who would sleep with anyone', in *Hitsuji*, possibly have in common with that of the equally nameless innkeeper of Kunikida Doppo's *Waser-eenu hito bito*?

For Karatani, the kinds of *fûkei* constructed by Doppo and Murakami were not dissimilar in so far as the 'inversion' (*tentô*) hidden in Murakmi's *fûkei* and that which is to be found in Doppo's (and by extension, in modern Japanese literature) are of the same form.[93] In Karatani's view, Murakami is not attempting a description of the post-industrial consumer society, rather, like Doppo he is constructing *fûkei* as a form of 'writing' (*ecriture*).[94] According to Karatani, we need to acknowledge Murakami's 'newness' as evident from the structure of his finding a new form of *fûkei*. Although it appears that Murakami has abandoned the interiority (*naimen*) developed by Doppo, he has actually *added a new dimension* to the narrative processes which construct interiority and landscape.

We might conclude, in fact, that Murakami has added the Kantian dimension of the transcendental, self-reflexive subject, and that whereas this form of subjectivity appears to be operating more explicitly in *Kaze* and *Pinbôru*, it is alluded to only allegorically in *Hitsuji*. This is because the operation of the metaphor of *fûkei* develops in a multidimensional way (via the codes of 'history', the 'urban phantasm', the 'phantasm of self') and paradoxically, within an apparently conventional narrative format of emplotment and deixis.

Exploring this point a little further, we have also noted, in the previous chapter, Karatani's distinction between the narrative or signifying function of the first person pronominal Boku in Murakami's early fiction vis-à-vis that which appears in the fiction of Ôe Kenzaburo. While in the texts of the latter, Boku is said to belong to the world (i.e. the presented world of the novel) the narrating subject in Murakami works is, at best, given tentative status. Boku continues to narrate 'the world situation' (*sekai jôkyô*) as if it were optional — neither judging, nor insisting upon anything. However, this does not, according to Karatani, preclude the signifier *Boku* from signifying the possibility of arriving at a place where both 'judgement' (*handan*) and 'insistence' (*shuchô*) are possible.[95]

At this point of the argument we must work back through the dense, philosophical Japanese of Karatani's reading of Kant. Karatani incisively observes that although these possibilities of 'judgement' and 'insistence' are explicitly addressed in Kant's *Critique of Judgement*, apparently as extensions of the earlier transcendental critique of metaphysical dogma (*keijijôgaku teki na dokudan*), the word 'critique' (*hihan*) actually originated in the domain (*ryôiki*) of the 'judgement of taste' (*shumi hihan*). And since in the realm of taste, there are no firm or definite standards (*kakutaru kijun*), all views can be described as prejudiced and biased (*dokudan to henken*). Because Kant regarded 'truth' (*shinri*) and 'good' (*zen*) as part of the larger domain of the judgement of taste, he considered all judgements to be, ultimately, judgements of taste.

It comes as no surprise to Karatani, therefore, that the German Romantic movement seemingly subordinated everything to judgements of taste. This being the case, Karatani is led to conclude, Murakami's *Boku* is reading Kant's *Critique of Pure Reason* 'correctly' (*'seikaku ni'*)—and is justified in regarding all judgements as judgements of taste which are subject to dogma and prejudice. The figure of *Boku* clearly signifies, therefore, the 'transcendental subject' (*chôetsu shukan*) rather than the 'experiential self' (*keiken teki na jiko*).[96]

By staging such a relatively complex defense of Murakami's *Boku*, Karatani is able to explain the apparent paradox that although Murakami's novels give the impression of being intensely personal and private (*kiwamete shiteki*), they are most definitively not forms of the 'I-novel' (*shishôsetsu*)—precisely because the experiential 'I' on which this form is based is denied throughout his writing. Even though the 'I' (*watashi*) is dispersed (*sanran shite iru*), there remains a transcendental self 'staring coldly' at this dispersed 'I'. Karatani is able to conclude, therefore, that compared to Ôe's *Boku*—which is a device which brings about an 'allegorical traversing' (*aregori teki na ôdan*) of the 'gap' (*zure*) between the subject and language—in Murakami's works, language is *always already* controlled (*tôgyo sarete iru*) by the transcendental subject.[97]

This is not the first time that such a protagonist is portrayed in modern Japanese fiction. As Komori Yôichi notes, Bunzô of Futabatei's *Ukigumo*, and Dostoyevsky's 'underground man' share an acute form of 'self consciousness' (*jiko ishiki*), which is described by Bakhtin as the depiction not of the ordinary person, but the subject (*shutai*) of consciousness (*ishiki*) and fancy (*kûsô*) dreaming.[98] Komori is, however, quick to point out that Futabatei does not consciously 'intend' to portray the kind of Dostoyevskian subject as described by Bhaktin, but to apply the already known notion of the 'analysis of human emotions' (*ninjô kaibogaku*) as a version of 'self consciousness' (*jiko ishiki*) in a deliberate attempt to develop an awareness of the notions of 'self' (*jibun*) and 'world' (*sekai*) as distinct and separate functions in the literary text.[99]

One further noteworthy aspect of Komori's analysis of *Ukigumo* is its highlighting of the purportedly 'uninteresting' content of the narrative. Dostoyevsky's 'I' could be Bunzô, and the basement could substituted for the second floor attic, but both narratives display a pronounced sense of banality. Following criticism in the wake of the publication of Part II of *Ukigumo*, Futabatei responded by claiming that, being fully aware of his portrayal of the trivia of people and their affairs, the attempt to write in such a way actually presented an interesting challenge to the author.[100] This notwithstanding, we should be aware that Futabatei was faced with the task of constructing a new idiom using the so called *Genbun itchi*, (a proposition, which by the way, is supported by Donald Keene yet rejected by Karatani Kojin[101]). In a not dissimilar fashion, Murakami was also attempting the construction of a new form of writing.

Despite the convincing nature of Karatani's discussion of the significance of the omission of proper names (*koyûmei*) in Murakami's fiction, there is a short-fall in his analysis of Kant's judgements of taste which is deserving of mention. Karatani has neglected to consider Kant's crucial condition of the *sensus communis* as the inter-subjectively and socially constructed judgement of taste which would ultimately be mediated by reference to 'the moral' (*Das Sittlichkeit*). It is this implied *social* dimension of the Kantian scheme which suggests that we should be able to read the novel *Hitsuji* genealogically and as a plurality of *fûkei* (landscapes). Postmodern fiction is replete with examples of this kind of play of multiple perspectives.

Karatani is most definitely correct in insisting that Murakami's works are not *shishôsetsu*, but perhaps a little off the mark in claiming that only the first two works are *fûkei*. To put it another way, we can say that *Hitsuji* engages *fûkei* allegorically (that is, as a sustaining master metaphor) in the way that it gener-ates a multi-layered plurality of *fûkei* which is typically postmodern in char-acter—offering a range of viewing perspectives without necessarily privileging any of them. This is perfectly in keeping with the argument developed by Deleuze around the idea of difference and repetition, and thus suggests a form of the simulacrum which celebrates difference and repetition.

Karatani is also certainly correct to claim that with the novel *Hitsuji*, there is a return to a more orthodox narrative structure following the experimentation of the first two texts of the trilogy.[102] However, this apparent return to orthodoxy does not, *ipso facto*, negate the use of *fûkei*—it simply requires the shift to the second order, allegorical or simulacral and polysemic/multi-layered trope of 'landscape'. Some critics might be shocked to see Karatani's use of such pio-neers of modern fiction as Futabatei Shimei and Kunikida Doppo to support an argument about Murakami, but the comparison is, in the end, efficacious.

Reference to one more critical perspective will serve to further clarify the point made about the metafictional self-referentiality evident in the treatment of proper names in *Hitsuji*. Focusing on the above cited dialogue on the issue of naming, Tamaki cites linguist Maruyama Keizaburô's observation of a twofold process in name calling: 'Name calling (*nazuke*) has the fundamental effect of giving birth to an object which did not previously exist, as well as the secondary function of attaching a label to things and concepts that already existed.'[103] In other words, claims Tamaki, through 'purposiveness' (*mokutekisei*), the act of naming is the deed which distinguishes one thing from another thing—and nam-ing which is for this purpose only, is nothing but a secondary effect or function.

When the cat with no name is tentatively named 'iwashi' ('kipper'/'sardine') by Boku's driver, apart from the obvious level of humour, it is evident that Mu-rakami is signaling an interest in names as signs (*kigô*). At a linguistic level, calling the cat 'iwashi' is almost meaningless. However, the choice of hiragana letters which are given emphasis is quite significant. The name is written in hiragana letters as いわし. These letters are given emphasis by the addition of *bôten*—the side dots written alongside each letter. Alternatively, the name could have been written in *kanji* as 鰯 or in *katakana* as イワシ. In Japanese, the choice of script (*hiragana, kanji or katakana*) affects, in a fundamental way, the semantic value and orientation of a word or expression. The choice of the use of *hiragana* with the added emphasis of the *bôten* signifies, according to Tamaki, that Murakami is actually proclaiming or 'blessing the birth' of this proper noun (*koyûmeishi*) and that this indicates that the author is extremely sensitive to the use of proper nouns.[104]

Tamaki extends his discussion of Murakami's use of the proper name to a consideration of meaning at the broad level of 'the sign' (*kigô*). Boku's reverie as he is transported by limousine to the Boss's mansion is on the theme of the circular and seemingly endless semiosis played out across the domains of what he calls 'symbolic dreams' and 'symbolic realities'.[105] If Boku despises what he calls the *itomimizu uchû* (translated by Birnbaum as 'the worm universe'), this is because, according to Tamaki, it 'represents the ruling world of the symbol' (*shôchô*).

Suzumura also highlights this tendency when he notes that Murakami's literary adventure can be described not as one of language (*kotoba*), but of 'signs' (*kigô*), and furthermore, that the mode of representation of the word 'sheep' (*'hitsuji'*: in Kanji, as 羊) allows a huge connotative range of meanings to be played out throughout the text.[106]

Tamaki argues that within the ruling world of the symbol (*shôchô*), the symbol is never completely arbitrary. It is neither free from the taint of experience nor the transcendental *a priori* (*senken teki kiban*). Rather, it exists within a highly determinate framework, a 'system of symbols' (*shôchô taikei*), a 'collaborative, conceptual and cumulative' structural system comprised of the intersecting discourses of 'religion' (*shûkyô*), 'law' (*hô*) and 'nation' (*kokka*), which regulate individual thought and action. Despite this seemingly totalizing and controlling structure, Tamaki notes Kristeva's observation of an inevitable and contradictory tendency of the sign: even though the sign evokes and requires unified mental images and concepts, by virtue of its abundant and excessive signifying power, it always implicitly threatens to secede from the system which sustains it.[107] Each enunciation of the sign *'hitsuji'* (羊) in this novel, therefore, allows for a process of 'conspicuous connotation' (*sugureta shisa*), and Tamaki is led to conclude that Murakami is a writer who recognizes the dynamism of the original movement (*honrai no ugoki*) of linguistic expression in its 'original effect' (*kongenteki sayô*)[108] —or, what can be taken as the process of endless semiosis.

In a sense, Murakami's overt attention to the issue of naming and numerical values effects a kind of incursion into language, and teases out the occluded syntactic and semantic aspects of a typified and somewhat ossified narrative weaving of thought, place and action which are embedded in naturalized ways of reading the modern Japanese novel. The stark, parodic and overly reductive (often seemingly inappropriate) resort to the assignation of arbitrary numerical values, and the omission of proper names, are instrumental in the meta-fictional and allegorical construction of *fûkei* at the 'micro-level' in the text of *Hitsuji*.

Notes

1. Murakami Haruki, *Tsukaimichi no nai fûkei* (Asahi Shuppansha, 1994), 82. The title comes from an old song by Antonio Carlos Jobin, the words of which, Murakami could not recall. Nonetheless, the idea of 'useless landscapes' attracted his attention, and he claims that it seemed a highly appropriate title for the anthology.

2. The Japanese term *fûkei* carries the connotations of 'scene', 'scenery', 'landscape' or 'view', but in the tremendous range of connotation of its use, can also be found the idea of 'atmosphere' and 'image'. The term as understood in its context as a central trope in the discourses of Japanese modernity will be explored in this and the following chapter.

3. Murakami, *Tsukaimichi no nai fûkei*, 86-96.

4. See *Kokutai no Hongi—Cardinal Principals of the National Entity of Japan*, 60-61.

5. Wakabayshi, "Prologue: Looking Backward," in *Anti-Foreignism and Western learning in Early Modern Japan*, 3-16; 8-10.

6. Aizawa, "The Barbarian's Nature" from *New Theses (Shinron): Six*, 204.

7. See Unno Hiroshi, "Nihon Sankei" in *Fûkei gekijô: rekishishôsetsu no toporoji* (Rokyô Shuppan, 1992), 9-10.

8. Unno Hiroshi, "Nihon Sankei," 10-11.

9. See Bashô Matsuo, "The Narrow Road of Oku" (*Oku no Hosomichi*), in *Anthology of Japanese Literature*, ed. Donald Keene (Hammondsworth: Penguin, 1978) 347; 351-2.

10. See John Frow: "Tourism and the Semiotics of Nostalgia," *October* 57 (1990-91), 125.

11. Unno, "Nihon Sankei," 7-8.

12. Quoted in Nina Cornyetz, "Tracing Origins: Landscape and Interiority," in *Dangerous Women, Deadly Word* (Stanford: Stanford University Press, 1999), 168.

13. See Oketani Hideaki, *Fûkei to kioku* (Yayoi Shobô, 1987), 81-82.

14. Quoted in Cornyetz, "Tracing Origins: Landscape and Interiority," 168.

15. This title translates literally as "The Grass Pillow" and immediately signifies the idea of a journey. However the passages quoted here are taken from the Alan Turney translation which gives the title as "The Three Cornered World". See Natsume Sôseki, *The Three Cornered World*, trans. Alan Turney (London: Arena, 1984).

16. Sôseki, *The Three Cornered World*, 23.

17. Sôseki, *The Three Cornered World*, 23.

18. Sôseki, *The Three Cornered World*, 24.

19. See Natsume Sôseki, *The Miner*, trans. Jay Rubin (Tokyo: Charles E. Tuttle, 1988) 36.

20. Karatani, *Origins of Modern Japanese Literature*, 34.

21. See Michael Seats, "'Differânce' or 'Differend': Constructing Meaning Across Japanese & European Discourse on the Aesthetic," 41-68; 47. Also, See Donald Keene, *The Japanese Discovery of Europe* (London: Routledge and Kegan Paul, 1952), 84.

22. Karatani, *Origins of Modern Japanese Literature*, 24.

23. Karatani, *Origins of Modern Japanese Literature*, 24.

24. See Kunikida Doppo, "The Bonfire," in *The Oxford Book of Japanese Short Stories*, trans. Jay Rubin, ed. Theodore W. Goossen (Oxford: Oxford University Press), 31-35.

25. See Donald Keene, *Dawn to the West: Japanese Literature in the Modern Era - Fiction* (New York: Henry Holt and Co., 1987), 234.

26. Karatani, *Origins of Modern Japanese Literature*, 40-41.

27. See Ishikura Michiko, et.al., *Kokubungaku* (February, 1998).

28. See the text of a conversation with Nakagami Kenji in *Kokubungaku* (March 1985). Quoted in Yokô Kazuhiro, *Murakami Haruki no nigenteki sekai* (Chôeisha, 1992), 25.

29. Yokô, *Murakami Haruki no nigenteki sekai*, 26.

30. Yoshida Haruo, *Murakami Haruki: tenkan suru* (Sairyûsha, 1997).

31. Yoshida, *Murakami Haruki: tenkan suru*, 57.

32. See Karatani Kôjin , "Murakami Haruki no 'fûkei' — (1)," *Kaien* (November 1989), 300-301.

33. Ayukawa Shinô, "Jidai o yomu (5): wakai sedai no kansei — Murakami Haruki: hitsuji o meguru bôken," *Shûkan bunshû* 24, nos. 43-46 (25 November 1982): 152.

34. Aono Satoshi, "Sutekina otogibanashi," *Gunzô* 37 (December 1982): 360-61.

35. Kawamura Jirô, "82 Bungei jihyô," *Bungei* 21, nos. 7-9 (September 1982): 20-25.

36. J. M. Ditsky, *Choice* 27, no. 2 (May 1990): 1510.

37. Mark Woodhouse, *Library Journal* 114, no. 2 (October 1989).

38. Ditsky, *Choice*, 1510.

39. Leithauser, "Books," *The New Yorker* 65, nos. 42-52 (4 December 1989): 186.

40. Leithauser, "Books," 183.

41. Phoebe-Lou Adams, "A Wild Sheep Chase," *The Atlantic*, 264 (December 1989): 128.

42. Leithauser, "Books," 184.

43. This was exemplified by Vogel's *Japan as Number One*, and Michael Chricton's *Rising Sun*.

44. Phoebe-Lou Adams, "A Wild Sheep Chase," 128.

45. See Tsuboi Hideo, "Puroguramu sareta monogatari," *Kokubungaku* (February1998): 69.

46. See Pierre Ryckmans, *The View from the Bridge: Aspects of Culture—The 1996 Boyer Lectures* (Sydney: ABC Books, 1997).

47. See, for example, Tamaki Kunio "Murakami Haruki 'Hitsuji o meguru bôken' ron (1): "Toshi shôsetsu e no Shikô," 27-40; esp. page 28. *The Long Goodbye* was first published by Hamish Hamilton in England in 1953. For a more recent edition, see *The Long Goodbye* (Oxford: Clio Press, 1993).

48. We also noted above Miyoshi Masao's complaint that Murakami is writing primarily for the foreign Western market—although, the fact that his fiction has been successfully translated into non-Western European languages (Korean, Chinese, Polish and Russian) diminishes, in part, the veracity of this claim.

49. Saussure's assertion (*Course in General Linguistics*, 25-26) that there are only two systems of language: the ideographic and the phonetic, is limited in many ways. Not least because of the problem of translation arising when Chinese characters are chosen to translate non-Chinese words, whereby they are often chosen for the phonetic value alone (and the 'semantic' content becomes a secondary or connotative effect). Japanese, however, uses both the ideographic and phonetic to represent words originally 'Japanese', but often a separate phonetic alphabet for foreign-loan words. So, if we take a translated passage

from *Hitsuji*, and examine how it is composed, we get a mixture of the three signifying components of *Kanji, Hiragana* and *Katakana*. The question arises: in what specific ways does this combination affect the complex interplay of deixis, speech acts and meaning construction?

50. Lee Sigelman & William Jacoby, "The Not-So-Simple Art of Imitation: Pastiche, Literary Style, and Raymond Chandler," *Computers and the Humanities* 30, 11-28 (1996), 11-28.

51. See Murray Sayles, "Tunnel Vision," in "The Australian Review of Books," *The Australian,* 13 December, 2000, 12(N).

52. Sigelman & Jacoby, "The Not-So-Simple Art of Imitation," 24.

53. HMB: 1; 11.

54. WSC: 1; 3.

55. Although the reversal of word order within a sentence is always indicated by the difference in the placement of verbs in Japanese and English, there is no linguistic/grammatical imperative *per se* to change the order of sentences within a passage or paragraph. The method chosen for doing so will be a function of the stylistic constraints of the idiom chosen by the translator at the outset.

56. Chandler's fiction abounds with such examples of the use of the pronoun 'it'. For example, in the opening scene of *The Little Sister,* 'It is a reasonably shabby door'; 'It was one of those clear, bright summer mornings'. See Raymond Chandler, *The Little Sister* (London: Pan Books, 1979), 5.

57. Quoted from the dust cover of the 1991 Kodansha International hardcover edition of *Hard-boiled Wonderland and the End of the World.*

58. Tamaki, "Toshi shôsetsu e no shiko—(I)," 27-28.

59. Tamaki, "Toshi shôsetsu e no shiko—(I)," 27-28. Tamaki is referring to Sakurai Tetsuo's ' "Omoi ire" no tôsô', *Chûô kôron* (September 1983).

60. Here we recall Karatani's claim that in the eighties, 'language [had] been set free'.

61. Tamaki, "Toshi shôsetsu e no shiko—(I)," 28.

62. Tamaki, "Toshi shôsetsu e no shiko—(I)," 29.

63. Of the numerous overt references to numbers in *Hitsuji*, the following examples are listed (all taken from the English edition): 'sixteen steps', p. 13; 'counting fish', p. 125; 'the value of pi to 32 places'; 'three scrub brushes, one box of paperclips, a six can pack of beer', and 270,00 sheep, 5,000 sheep, p. 133; 'giant cookie would take three hundred kids, 2 weeks to eat.' p. 150; 'eight people in the audience', p. 161; 'forty names in yellow pages', 'forty percent less than I had expected', Dolphin Hotel located three blocks West, One block South of the movie theatre', 'building five stories tall' p. 163; 'the clock was seven minutes off' p. 164; 'number of times we'd had sex in our four years or married life', 'eight notebooks', p. 167; 'drank seven cups of coffee per day', 'took a leak every other hour', p. 172; 'three line notice in the morning edition of four newspapers', 'next two days, three calls', p. 173; '5 books, 6 cassettes etc.', pp. 193-194; 'three bedrooms on the second floor', 'second drawer', 'third drawer', 'three boxes of cartridges', 'fifteen inch neck', 'twenty nine inch waist', p. 239; 'two hundred old records', 'four six foot double hung windows', 'eight by twelve foot carpet', p. 241; 'two puffs of the cigarette', p. 242; 'two glasses of cold water', 'two cloves' p. 243; 'three glasses of wine', 'one in twenty five chance', 'three tries', p. 244; 'ten hand towels', p. 246; 'three packs of larks', 'the clock struck nine', p. 247; 'knock two times', 'a three-breath pause, then three times', 'two yards away', 'six inches from the sill', p. 249; 'three bottles of whiskey', 'one bottle of brandy', 'twelve cases of canned beer', p. 258; 'morning of the tenth day', 'thirty minute soak in the tub', 'the next two hours', 'listened to "White

Christmas" 26 times', p. 267; 'eight times', 'Eight O'clock'; 'Eight at night', 'the clock struck nine', pp. 274-275; '7.35 am', 'fifteen minutes', '8.30', '2 glasses of grape juice, a large Hershey bar, and two more apples', p. 289; '12 O' clock sharp', p. 293.

64. HMB: 2; 25.

65. WSC: 2; 14.

66. Karatani, "Murakami Haruki no 'Fûkei' — (I)," 301.

67. See Iguchi Tokio, "Dentetsu toiu dekigoto — Murakami haruki ron," *Gunzô* (October 1983), 152-163; 153-155.

68. KUK: 23; 117; and HWS: 23; 77.

69. Karatani, "Murakami Haruki no 'fûkei' — (I)," 302.

70. Wada Masahide, "Murakami Haruki ni okeru aishô sôshitsu no bungaku," *Waseda Bungaku* 147 (August 1988): 60-73; 62.

71. See Kasai Kyoshi, "Nezumi no sôshitsu — Murakami Haruki ron," *Waseda Bungaku* 160 (September 1989): 80-96; 83.

72. Nagashima Kiyoshi, "Hitsuji o meguru bôken," *Kokubungaku — kaishaku to kansho* 54, nos. 696-699 (June 1989): 178-181; 179.

73. See Watanabe Naomi, "'Chi' no Murakamika," in *Kami omutsu shindorômu — Heisei Gannen e no barizôgen kuriteikku* (Kawade Shobô Shinsha, 1989): 19-20.

74. See Tanaka Minoru, "Sûchi no naka no aidenteitei" in *Nihon no bungaku* 17 (June 1990): 143-171; 157.

75. Tanaka, "Sûchi no naka no aidenteitei," 166.

76. Fukami Haruka, *Murakami Haruki no uta* (Seikyûsha, 1990): 10-11.

77. For example the hotel rooms 214 and 215, and the phone number '13572' in chapters 4 & 5 of Chandler's *Little Sister,* 22-27.

78. Hatanaka Yoshiki, "Murakami Haruki no namae o meguru bôken," *Yurîka — Sôtokushu: Murakami Haruki no sekai* 21, no. 8 (1989): 138-139.

79. See Tamaki Kunio: "Murakami Haruki: 'Hitsuji o meguru bôken' ron — II: toshi shôsetsu e no shikô," *Jinbunronkyû — Kansai Gakuin Daigaku Jinbun Gakkai* 46, no. 2 (September 1996): 2.

80. HMB: 1; 14

81. HMB: 6; 158-161 and 4; 85-87.

82. HMB: 8; 272

83. HMB: 8; 300, 303, 308.

84. See Iwamoto, "A Voice from Postmodern Japan: Haruki Murakami," 298.

85. HMB: 6; 208-209 and WSC: 6: 152-154.

86. See Bernard Harrison, *An Introduction to the Philosophy of Language* (London: Macmillan, 1979), 152-3.

87. Harrison, *An Introduction to the Philosophy of Language,* 154.

88. Foucault, *The Archeology of Knowledge,* 89.

89. Foucault, *The Archeology of Knowledge,* 105.

90. In simple terms, the referent of an object is the imagined object itself, and the sense is determined by the modality of the delivery of the word or expression, and range of connotations which the word or expression gives rise to. For a basic outline of Frege's distinction between 'sense' and 'reference', see Harrison, *An Introduction to the Philosophy of Language,* 55-58. This basic distinction is by no means unproblematic, but further discussion of this topic in the context of language philosophy is well beyond the parameters of this discussion.

91. Derrida, "Aphorism — Countertime," 6.

92. See Imai Kyoto, "Hitsuji o meguru bôken: mimeishisu sareru 'monogatari'," in *Murakami Haruki — OFF no kankaku* (Kokken Shuppan, 1990), 165-200; 178.

93. Karatani, "Murakami Haruki no 'fûkei'—(I)," 300.

94. Karatani, "Murakami Haruki no 'fûkei'—(I)," 301.

95. Karatani, "Murakami Haruki no 'fûkei'—(I)," 298.

96. Karatani, "Murakami Haruki no 'fûkei'—(I)," 298.

97. Karatani, "Murakami Haruki no 'fûkei'—(I)," 298.

98. See Komori Yôichi, *Buntai toshite no monogatari* (Chikuma Shobo, 1988), 44.

99. Komori , *Buntai toshite no monogatari*, 44-45.

100. Komori, *Buntai toshite no monogatari* 42-43.

101. Keene asserts that *Ukigumo* was 'the first novel written almost entirely in the colloquial'. See Donald Keene, *Dawn to the West*, 112. However, Karatani claims that *Ukigumo* is 'permeated with stylistic elements drawn from the comic fiction of Shikitei Samba . . . and cannot be considered a *genbun itchi* work.' See *Origins of Modern Japanese Literature*, 50-51.

102. Karatani, "Murakami Haruki no 'fûkei'—(1)," 301.

103. See Tamaki Kunio, "Murakami Haruki: 'Hitsuji o meguru bôken' ron—II: toshi shôsetsu e no shikô," *Jinbunronkyû—Kansai Gakuin Daigaku Jinbun Gakkai* 46 no. 2 (September 1996): 1-2. Tamaki gives the Maruyama reference as *Bunka kigogaku no kanosei* (Nihon Hôsô Shuppan Kyôkai). No publication date is given.

104. Tamaki, "Murakami Haruki: 'Hitsuji o meguru bôken' ron—II: toshi shôsetsu e no shikô," 3.

105. HMB:4; 98-99 and WSC: 4; 67-68.

106. Suzumura Kazunari, *Murakami Haruki kuronikuru, 1983-1995*, 18-19. Suzumura notes that this view of the ambiguity did not dissuade many critics for searching for a whole range of possible 'meanings' of the symbol 'Hitsuji'—despite the fact that Murakami himself denied the attribution of any special meaning to the word.

107. Tamaki, "Murakami Haruki: 'Hitsuji o meguru bôken' ron—II: toshi shôsetsu e no shikô," 3-4. Tamaki gives his reference as Julia Kristeva, *Tekusuto toshite no shôsetsu*, published by Kokubunsha (no publication year of this translation is provided).

108. Tamaki, "Murakami Haruki: 'Hitsuji o meguru bôken' ron—II: toshi shôsetsu e no shikô," 4.

Chapter Seven

Allegory as Landscape II: Hitsuji o meguru bôken —A Wild Sheep Chase

'History' and 'Nature' in the National-Cultural Imaginary

Kawamura has written of the 'new world' exemplified in Murakami's *Hitsuji* (*A Wild Sheep Chase*) and *Dansu, dansu, dansu* (*Dance, Dance, Dance*) noting especially what he describes as the 'Hollywood-film-like scale' of *Hitsuji*. What is more specifically relevant to our discussion is that he highlights the deployment, in *Hitsuji*, of Hokkaido and Manchuria as two 'model cases' of Japan's 'new world' which are described as phantoms of Japanese modernity.[1] The sub-narratives within *Hitsuji*, which clearly invoke an allegorical rendering of the geo-historical contours of these two phantoms in terms of the national-cultural imaginary, are the narrator's re-telling of an episode from an authoritative history of the pioneer settling of a remote region in Hokkaido[2], the Sheep Professor's recounting of his colonial service in Manchuria and Mongolia, and Boku's account of the life and rise to power of *Sensei*, the A-Class war criminal who becomes the invisible and all powerful postwar underworld figure.[3]

Within these sub-narratives we can identify the signifier 'history' as the central trope, but unlike Basho's poetic pilgrimage several centuries earlier, Boku's investigative journey to the North represents a trip 'back into' a history which has been, in a broad sense, negated or repressed. And although his journey entails an allegorical filling-in of the pre-imagined landscape—the kind of travel that fulfills the promise of the simulacral congruence of the physical 'viewing' of the site with the preconceived idea of that site—its larger paradigm is that of the officially sanctioned 'modern Japanese history' (*Nihon kindaishi*) of textbooks and mainstream academic publishing.

And unlike Bashô, instead of the poetic fragments and images of earlier aesthetes, Boku has in his possession two very different kinds of texts. One is the 'artificially' constructed photo of the clichéd mountain-pasture scenery with the grazing sheep, the use of which in an advertisement has visited upon Boku the wrath of the underworld leader.[4] The other is an authoritative history of the pioneer settlement of the township of Junitaki in Hokkaido.[5] Boku's is both a journey through the 'exterior' and 'physical' landscape, as well as representing an 'interior' quest which culminates in the confrontation with his alter-ego or unfathomable 'other' in the form of Nezumi's ghost.

The visual text of the Hokkaido landscape clearly signifies a constructed and contained 'Nature' (*shizen*), while the written text represents the enactment of 'history' as a forging of meaningful and purposeful narrative from the anecdotal portrayal of the desperate bid for survival and independence undertaken by itinerant farmers in the uncharted and hostile wilds of Hokkaido.

These tropes of 'nature' and 'history' are legitimized by the generalized discourses of 'modernity' and 'nation' *writ large*, which themselves are enabled by the rendering of *fûkei* as both rhetorical figure in the national-cultural imaginary, and the geographical 'referent' of the Japanese archipelago (*Nihon rettô*), whose limits are politically prescribed and continuously reasserted by the enactment of Edo as the mythic and indisputable centre of Japanese political power.[6]

Yet, as a landscape or *fûkei*, the photograph is also an 'artificial representation', an image which stands in opposition to the function assigned to the premodern transcendental landscape painting. Despite his admission that something about the photograph was not quite right, Boku confirms a realist 'reading' of the photo:

「どれだけ考えてみても羊の群れが意味するものは羊の群れであり、白樺林の意味するものは白樺林であり、白い雲の意味するものは白い雲だった。それだけだ。」[7]

All things considered, the flock of sheep could only be taken for a flock of sheep, the birch wood only for a birch wood, the white clouds only for white clouds. Simply that and nothing more.[8]

In other words, the copy of the artificially constructed photograph of the pastoral idyll is synonymous with 'the real', and the modalities of the camera lens and xerox machine are implicitly confirmed as the basis of a way of seeing which faithfully and accurately reproduces the object seen. Even though the image can be reproduced endlessly,[9] the conventional composition and perspective of this scene of the pastoral idyll is thoroughly European in form, and derives its meaning only in opposition to the image of nature untamed—an opposition reflected in the Kantian distinction between the beautiful and the sublime. We have noted that Karatani acknowledged the characterization of Hokkaido as the terrifying wilderness 'and in order to grasp this territory as sublime it was necessary . . . to take on the Christian attitude which regards Nature as the handiwork of God'. Yet this attitude prevails, and the origins of this emergence of a way of seeing 'which was not previously continuous with Japanese thought'[10] have been occluded by the thoroughly conventionalized depictions of Hokkaido in the advertising of the contemporary travel industry.

For instance, the Japan Travel Bureau (JTB)'s Internet web page divides Hokkaido as tourist destination along the lines of clearly defined modernist divisions of nature versus culture, the naturally occurring and the human made: 'nature and natural features' (*fûdo*), 'climate and plant life' (*kikô to shokusei*), 'geographic features' (*chiriteki tokuchô*), 'people and history' (*jinbutsu, rekishi*), 'culture, festivals' (*bunka to matsuri*) and 'industry' (*sangyô*). There is no doubt, however, that its general description of Hokkaido's most compelling features is clearly cast in terms of the sublime: 'mighty nature on a vast scale' (*yûdai na sukêru no daishizen*) and a 'tourist treasure trove' (*kankô no hôko*) of 'grand nature'.[11]

Murakami's *Hitsuji* entered mass circulation in Japan at a time when the 'Discover Japan' travel advertising campaign of the 1970s had already conventionalized the quest for recuperation of lost 'history' and lost 'self' by embarking on nostalgic journeying, and the first two editions (1982 and 1983) preceded the 1984 launch of the 'Exotic Japan' campaign. As Ivy points out, the key to the first campaign was the idea of 'discover myself',[12] and through this linkage of 'landscape' and 'self', we see an attempt at recovering something which was construed as an inevitable loss brought about by modernity, rather than by the repression of the signifier 'history' in the educational discourses of postwar Japan.

More than twenty years later, urging the rediscovery of a 'lost' Japan would seem almost absurd, at best naïve. The quest for authenticity has more recently assumed new and highly differentiated forms as exemplified, for instance, in the NHK guidebook *Rekishi michi* (*Historical Trail*). The cover urges readers to

「歴史にまつわる道を訪ねイメージを膨らませながら歩いてめぐる小さ
な旅心も体も軽く……。」

Follow the winding historical trails and, enlarging the image as you wander, experience the lightness of the traveler's mind and body.

The 'images' to be enlarged are formed from the color photographs, detailed maps, sketches and travelogues of the established walking trails presented in the magazine to be read *before* departure. The text is in fact a pastiche of landscape painting, poetry, essay and diary entry as well as a manual providing detailed practical information on clothes, shoes, walking style, health matters and so on. It is interspersed with advertisements for a range of personalized equipment from art supplies (for sketching) to miniature electronic devices for measuring exact distances walked and calories consumed. The projected experience of the journey is prescribed in such detail *prior to* departure, that all that is required for the successful 'transaction' to be completed is the participation of the walker. The circular process of the simulacral 'filling-in' is achieved not simply by the act of establishing the congruence of the act of seeing the site with the idea of the site, but also through the purchase of equipment, and the careful following of instructions—and in doing so, the promise implicit in the act of consumption is fulfilled.[13]

But perhaps what is most striking is that the guide is not concerned with the earnest search for the discovery of a lost 'self' in travel. On the contrary, the keywords are *raku raku* (comfortably/easily) and *karuku* (lightly/softly), and the commercial gain is to be made from the provision of detailed local information and the sale of a myriad of personal goods necessary for such travel—not through the attempt at selling the idea of a 'lost Japan' (entailing the consumption of railway/hotel/guided tour packages). This is arguably so because the origins of any loss are now so thoroughly repressed and lost from view, that they are presumably no longer meaningful or saleable. This kind of travel is meant to be light, enjoyable and non-confronting—a diversion and a health giving hobby-like activity designed for members of an aging, and perhaps somewhat jaded post-industrial society.

What is the point of showing the 'landscape' of Japan, which was in pre-modern times traversed for religious and political reasons (and is described as formerly the number one 'travel kingdom of the world'[14]), now becoming the stage for a highly individualized and innocuous free-time leisure activity? It is to highlight the fact that the treatment of landscape at the macro level in *Hitsuji* in the Japan of the early eighties depended upon the fact that the view of lost nature was really a metaphor for a repressed 'history' of Japanese modernity. We can say that the signifier 'history' is itself occluded by the signifier 'nature' in *Hitsuji*: the two are indeed interwoven, each referring allegorically to the other, via the master trope of 'landscape'. If the figure of Hokkaido is a contradictory one, it is because the destruction of 'nature' suggests both a loss and a promise. Its incorporation into the discourse of landscape functions ideologically and precisely to *maintain* the forces of industrial production—but these forces must be continually transformed into systems of representation which themselves are contingent upon the conspicuous 'consumption' of nature. Baudrillard writes:

> With Nature, at the same time as with the urban world, it is necessary to recreate communication by means of a multitude of signs. . . . All of this only aims at the better and better alignment of the participant nature . . . along the norms of a rational hyperproductivity.[15]

As the flipside of 'nature', 'history' informs the narrator's retelling of the 'authoritative' account of the settlement, the rise and fall of the Junitaki village in a remote and inhospitable area of Hokkaido—referring only indirectly to the crucial ideological role which the containment of Hokkaido played in the formation of the modern Meiji state. Apart from the initiative taken to develop a self-sufficient wool industry in preparation for upcoming military campaigns, and other practical agricultural developments, this historical account does not allude to the crucial ideological role which the construction of Ainu identity played in the formation of a unitary national-cultural imaginary underpinned by a theory of racial homogeneity. Howell notes the development of a mutual dependency based on economic factors for the Ainu, but on purely political factors on the part of the Japanese:

> The emergence of the Ainu as a unitary, yet dependent culture, [allowed] . . .
> the Japanese in northern Honshu and southern Hokkaido to redefine their own
> identity during the process of ethnic contact.[16]

The perpetuation of reference to a distinct Ainu culture in the service of promoting interest in travel to Hokkaido belies the fact that, as Howell notes, 'today the
Ainu language is dead, the culture is moribund and the Ainu people themselves
are on the verge of a sort of extinction'.[17]

This suggests a 'double loss' in the Japanese experience of modernity in a
highly compressed time scale. The move to the urban environment as well as the
adoption of an alien aesthetic (an 'interiority' and 'immanence') could be said to
form a large part of Murakami's attempt to re-establish a transcendental subject-
position (even if only tentatively) in response to this legacy of modernity's 'double loss'.

There are numerous examples in the *Hitsuji* narrative in which Boku is given
over to gazing at landscapes—but these episodes do not necessarily conform
steadfastly to any one particular or conventional way of seeing. For example, a
realist and modern perspective is confirmed in Boku's reading of the book *The
Mountains of Hokkaido*, in a description which lacks any reference to religious
or transcendental significance, and in which photographs of mountains appear in
nauseating profusion. What stands out is the author's assertion that mountains
can effectively change their appearance according to a myriad of factors influencing the conditions of their viewing:

> 「従って我々は常に山の一部分、ほんのひとかけらしか把握してはい
> ないのだという確認をもつことが肝要でありましょう。」[18]

> Thus it is essential to recognize that we can never know more than one side,
> one small aspect of a mountain.[19]

Other examples suggest that the scene described is more or less a direct projection of the interior state of the observer, climbing ever higher into the mountains:

> 「見晴らしとしては素晴らしいものだったが、どれだけ眺めていても
> 楽しい気分にはなれなかった。全てがよそよそしく、そしてどこかし
> ら異境的だった。」[20]

> A breathtaking panorama, but it made me feel no better. Everything seemed so
> remote, so . . . alien.[21]

And here at the periphery of the imaginable Japanese nation, comes an inkling
of the terror of the un-chartered and hostile domain of the Other:

「その下を黒い雲の塊が低く流れていた。手を伸ばせば指先が触れそ
うな気がするくらいだ。彼らは信じ難いスピードで東へと向かってい
た。中国大陸から日本海を越えて北海道を横切りオホーツクへ抜ける
重い雲だ。」[22]

Below, lumps of dense black cloud matter blew by, almost within touching distance. The clouds raced eastward from the direction of the Asian continent, cut-
ting across the Japan Sea to Hokkaido on their way to the Sea of Ohotsk with
remarkable speed.[23]

Elsewhere, the narrator subverts what appears at first to be a conventionalized
'Doppo-like' detailed rural landscape inhabited by anonymous figures, through
the parodic use of similitude to represent the ironic witnessing of an act of witnessing:

「川の向こう岸には水田が広がり、見渡す限りに実った稲の穂が不規
則な朝の風に奇妙な波の線を描き出していた。コンクリートの橋の上
をトラクターが山に向かって渡っていった。トラクターのトクトクト
クというエンジン音が風に乗っていつまでも小さく聞こえていた。三
羽のからすが紅葉した白樺林のあいだから現れ、川の上でぐるりと輪
を描いてから欄干にとまった。欄干にとまったからすたちは前衛劇に
出てくる傍観者のように見えた。」

Rice fields spread out on the opposite bank, where irregular morning breezes
traced random waves through the ripened, tall grassiness, as far as the eye
could see. A tractor crossed the concrete bridge, heading towards the hills, its
puttering engine faintly audible in the wind. Three crows flew out of the now-
golden birch woods. Making a full circle above the river and landing on a rail-
ing of the building. Perched there, the crows acted the perfect bystanders from
an avant-garde drama.[24]

Precisely because Murakami's writing tends to install a transcendental subject as
narrator there remains, paradoxically, in the range of representations of the
viewing of landscape throughout the *Hitsuji* text,[25] the logical necessity of an
implied interiority which enables in the narrative point of view the experience of
the sublime sentiments of, for example, awe and wonder. This is clear in descriptions such as the following:

「ぶ厚い雲が粘度のようにところどころでちぎられ、そこから差し込
む陽光が壮大な光の柱となって草原のあちこちを移動した。素晴らし
い眺めだった。」[26]

The thick clouds tore off in places as grand columns of sunlight thrust down to
play in the pasture. It was magnificent.[27]

Even though the sublime, as it is known in the Western sense, is fundamentally absent from the pre-modern traditions of Japanese artistic representation, as these examples from *Hitsuji* demonstrate, it has certainly become a conventionalized trope arising from a transformed view of nature in Japanese modernity. On the other hand, versions of the pre-modern 'quasi-transcendental' landscapes are, of course, also still observable in many contemporary cultural practices; for example, in the supernatural imagery of the desolate environs of Mt. Osore,[28] or in Nakagami Kenji's invocation of the otherworldly landscape of Kumano.[29]

On this basis we can reiterate what was demonstrated in the previous chapter. The contemporary Japanese 'sublime' is a true simulacrum. And because it is a central proposition of this book that Murakami's texts do not constitute a quest for 'identity' and 'the self' — and do not struggle to 'overcome' modernity — we see also in *Hitsuji* an exploration of the Deleuzean simulacrum which foregrounds difference and the 'reign of simulacra' in a way which is closer to the pre-modern Japanese construction of 'the world': employing amorphous versions of self and subjectivity, non-perspectival and non-realist art, and a relativism of thought strongly influenced by a Buddhist aesthetic.

The Japanese pseudo-sublime (and here 'pseudo' is used with no intended deprecatory connotation) can also be characterized — in a way which will be explored in detail in the following chapters — as what may be called the trope of the 'historical sublime'. This trope does carry both aspects of Kant's 'dynamical sublime' (the power of destruction in natural calamities) and 'mathematical sublime' (the number of Japanese killed in WWII) in terms of scale (the vastness of Hokkaido and Manchuria) and finds its apotheosis in the unspeakable horror of the nuclear destruction of Nagasaki and Hiroshima. This Japanese 'historical sublime' lends itself to apocalyptic vision, but it is also apocryphal in that it requires a cohesive, self-reflexive subject (the Kantian subject of modernity), which has yet to be convincingly 'located' in fictional or critical discourses.

The contrasting scenes of utopia and nuclear devastation in Kurosawa's film sequences *Yume*, bespeak the mediation of the sublime as negation — of all that the world *cannot* be — and the dubious 'negative pleasure' arising from such a realization. Yet the form of subjectivity implied in such experience remains, according to the tenor of the debate around the idea of 'the self', elusive. This has not, however, precluded the 'historical sublime' from being endlessly connoted in popular discourses converging around signifiers such as 'America', 'Hiroshima', *'Harumagedon'*, 'Manchuria' and so on.

We have demonstrated that in the text of *Hitsuji*, the signifiers or tropes 'nature' and 'history' are artfully woven together as an expression of a tentative modernity inexorably linked to an unstable and indefinable notion of 'self'. And we can also conclude that in *Hitsuji*, the signifier 'history' itself is subsumed by the overarching discourse of *fûkei*, both at a micro, deictic level, and at the level of the imagined national community. However, it is necessary to qualify this conclusion with the recognition that because this process of subsumption is effectively concealed, the repressed 'history' takes the form, ultimately, of a confrontation with the self (*jiga*). Nevertheless, it be must conceded that it is also highly paradoxical that this problem of the self can only really be mediated *historically*, as itself a function of the idea of modernity—and it is to a consideration of this circular movement, this mutuality, that we turn in the concluding part of this chapter.

Contiguous Landscapes—The Contours of 'self' and 'world' in *Hitsuji*

At the outset of her 1995 discussion of Murakami's *Kaze* as exemplary of the contemporary urban novel, Ishimaru makes the observation that ever since the publication of novels such as *Ukigumo* and *Maihime*, accepted critical theories have concurred that most modern works of fiction have been preoccupied with the literary representation of the struggle of the 'modern self' (*kindai jiga*).[30] She notes, however, that in the last twenty years, amidst the increasingly audible lamentation of the 'decline of literature' emanating from the literary establishment (*bundan*), writers such as Murakami Haruki and Yoshimoto Banana, who seemingly have no understanding of this 'struggle', have become best-selling stars. This is said to be the result of rapid economic growth, prosperity and the transfiguration of urban areas which (as Yanagita Kunio notes) were previously rural villages. As a result, in the view of Kawamato, the modern city has lost its 'organicism', and become a 'space inhabited by beings separated from the soil' (*tsuchi kara hanareta ningen no sumu kûkan*).[31]

While it is clearly the case that this characterization applied especially to the earlier works of narrative which emerged from within the new social configurations of modernity in the Meiji era, recent fiction is more a product of the 'vicarious experience' (*dairitaiken*) produced by the consumption of information, and meaning has become a function of 'symbolization' (*shôchôka*) and 'signification' (*kigôka*).[32] In short, this is indicative of the so called 'Baudrillard Syndrome' whereby, according to Ishimaru, Japan (and not the West) has experienced the adoption of the most complete form of the Baudrillardian 'consumer society'.[33]

As was demonstrated in the argument presented in the previous three chapters, Murakami has indeed sidestepped the modernist preoccupation with the search for the self—preferring, instead, to implicitly articulate a new set of questions. The choice to do so has apparently not proceeded from a belief that the issue of subjectivity has been successfully resolved, or that modernity has been somehow 'overcome'. Rather, it indicates a recognition that perhaps the wrong kinds of questions were being posed from the outset. Murakami's fiction is marked by its refusal to engage in the conventional presentation of the structure of the modern 'self' (*jiga*) as exemplified by the conventions of the 'I-novel'. And its apparent preference for what may be described as subjective dispersal and discontinuity is not a failure but a redeeming feature which, as Karatani has noted, ironically connects it with the aversion towards logo-centrism evident in pre-modern Japan.[34]

As a qualification to this, we have already noted (in Chapter 2) the difficulty of the debate centered around the assumption that Japan could 'avoid' the experience of modernity—merely because it had already seemingly displayed some features of *post* modernity in the pre-Meiji era. The challenge is to avoid a narrow definition of 'the self' (*jiga, jiko, etc.*) as variously imagined in modern Japanese fiction, while at the same time attempting to clarify how subjectivity is broadly integral to the discourses which constitute the Japanese experience of modernity—one of which is fictional writing. Although a comprehensive attempt at undertaking this task is well beyond the scope of this discussion,[35] we will at least be able to interrogate some aspects of the issue of subjectivity in order to demonstrate that a text such as *Hitsuji* is interesting precisely because it reverses the terms of the ontological equation, which usually proceeds *from* subject *to* world. Conversely, Murakami's writing tends to locate possible subject positions at the nodal points of intersecting representations of the world, which indicate the constitution of a phantasmal 'self' as both point of departure and narrative destination. The uniqueness of Murakami's style could be said to inhere in just such a deliberate strategy.

In his essay 'A Voice from Postmodern Japan', Iwamoto notes that some Japanese critics have been very uneasy about the lack of subjectivity (*shutaisei*) in Murakami's characters—and Iwamoto himself acknowledges an impression of the 'thinness of Boku's *shutaisei*'.[36] Yet, paradoxically, while acknowledging the great difficulty of applying the European idea of subjectivity to Japanese culture, Iwamoto does not move beyond a very limited view of subjectivity in his claim that Boku's 'own subjective self is wanting in depth.'[37] He also fails to give due credence to those Japanese critics who are only too aware of the historically contingent nature of terms such as 'self' (*jiga*) and 'subject' (*shutai*) in the discourses of Japanese modernity.[38]

The common and uncritical use of the Japanese terms *jiga* and *shutai* to designate 'self' and 'subject', proceeds on the assumption that these entities are naturally and universally occurring. This is a point which is vigorously contested by Lydia Liu in her study *Translingual Practice*:

> Serious methodological problems arise when a cross-cultural comparative theory is built upon the basis of an essential category, such as 'self' or 'individual' whose linguistic identity transcends the history of translation and imposes its own discursive priority on a different culture.[39]

Whilst the tenor of Liu's assertion is perhaps a little over-emphatic, her point is well made. Perhaps we should accept her description of the 'trope of equivalence' of meaning which is established by bilingual dictionaries as the best we can hope for. To do so would be to partly acknowledge that cultural genesis emerges entirely from difference and borrowing, and also to accept that the experience of modernity is, if nothing else, a globally disseminated phenomenon where culturally hegemonic practices and boundaries tend to become less distinct over time.

This notwithstanding, what is beyond dispute is the fact that even monolingual dictionaries have to grope for the sense of meaning in the *already* translated forms of foreign words. The *Kôjien*, for example, acknowledges both the Latin *ego* and English 'self' in defining 自我 (*jiga*): 'the word which distinguishes the subject (*shutai*) of understanding, emotions, will and deed from the external world and other people'. The key terms here are 'world' and 'other'—in juxtaposition to which the self becomes apparent. But the definition goes on to develop an even more essentialist tone: 'Through the passage of time and change, the self (*jiga*) brings with it the consciousness of self-identity (*jiko doitsu*)'.[40]

Naturally, we also require clarification of the term *shutai*, which we are told derives from the Greek *hypokeimenon* and English 'subject'—and ignoring the fact that the Chinese characters 主体 (literally 'main body') formerly designated 'the emperor' (which itself was also previously signified by the term 天子 *tenshi*—literally, 'son of heaven'), the definition goes on to confirm semantic aspects similar to that of *jiga*. It indicates an entity which undertakes acts of 'awareness' (*ninshiki suru*), 'doing' (*kôi suru*) and 'judging' (*hyôka suru*) and unlike the more nominalized *jiga*, the emphasis in *shutai* appears to be rather on verbal, transitive process and agency.[41]

While acknowledging that the ideas of 'self' and 'subject' must be used with some qualification, there is no imperative to make them the central concerns of our analysis. And if we have allowed 'modernity' and a number of other provisionally defined terms to be employed, it is clear that we must permit use of a tentative notion of 'self'. This is because the discourses of modernity and postmodernity have brought about stupendous changes in social relations—about which debate (in Japan no less than elsewhere) is both necessary and desirable.

Perhaps Murakami's 'transcendental', 'attenuated' or 'dispersed' subject actually provides us with a new opportunity to interrogate certain fundamental issues central to modernity in ways more interesting than the conventional idea of the so called 'struggle with the self' in modern Japanese fiction has hitherto allowed. We might respond to Liu's querulous interjection 'why should the self be an analytical category in the first place?'[42] with an observation by Kondô that 'perhaps in the end, resistance or a resisting subject should not be the starting point for a politics of meaning.'[43] Surprisingly, this observation is the result not of idle philosophical speculation, but results directly from carefully implemented case-studies of contemporary Japanese socio-linguistic practices. The deictic peculiarities of everyday Japanese discourse naturally tend to disperse meaning *away from* any identifiable subjective 'centre' and the enactment of what Quinn describes as 'person as evidential cline' is not only based on a 'mutual indexing with reference to *uchi/soto* ('inside/outside') parameters', it in fact amounts to a description of 'how people, together, create their selves'.[44]

The narrating subject of *Hitsuji* can be said to be constituted both by a dispersal (in Foucault's sense) and a kind of transcendental distance (in Derrida's sense), which is away from positivities and more about empty relations as pure differentiation. Murakami's use of the trope 'landscape' in *Hitsuji* enables the construction of subjectivities which are open ended, and not co-extensive with any kind of unified 'self'. The inserted 'discontinuous histories' which supplement the narration of the lives of Boku, The Ear Model, Nezumi, The Hokkaido Settlers, the Sheep Professor, Sensei and Nezumi, function genealogically to undermine, as Foucault puts it, 'the sovereignty of the subject'.[45] Any putatively established subjectivities emerge merely as a 'tangle of contradictions, ambiguities and ironies . . . within shifting fields of power'.[46]

However, the narrating subject in *Hitsuji* is also 'transcendental' (as argued in a previous chapter) and it is important to note that this is so in terms of the Derridean *difference* of 'empty relations', and negatively defined. If some critics are irritated by Murakami's treatment of subjectivity, it may be precisely because he has attempted to constitute it *negatively* by focusing the narrative perspective *outward* to the world, and adopting a position of observation whereby the narrator's presented consciousness merely reflects the 'eventivity'of history. Here the subject is tentatively, phantasmally established as a set of correspondences and mutualities *with* the world.

Clearly the idea of 'the subject' was crucial to the ideology of the emerging modern Japanese state. However, Murakami demonstrates its apparent redundancy within the postwar milieu of a vast system of political and economic relations which has shadowed and effectively negated the ostensibly democratic institutional processes established under the American-imposed constitution. Two key figures in the narrative of *Hitsuji*, namely Sensei ('The Boss') and the Sheep Professor (*Hitsuji Hakushi*), both begin their careers in the service of Japanese imperialist aggression on the Asian Continent in the twenties and thirties, and Sensei—who goes on to become the all powerful but largely 'invisible' power broker—is clearly modeled on the figure of the Rightist Kodama Yoshio who was also implicated along with Tanaka in the Lockheed scandal.[47] Within the context of attempting to represent this almost phantasmal world of postwar Japanese power (what Miyoshi and Harootunian have called 'emperorism'[48]) it seems clear that the trope of the modernist struggle with 'the self' is of little value, and Murakami has enlisted other methods. These methods have been described in various ways by some of the more astute commentators on *Hitsuji*, yet they all more or less support the main proposition of this chapter, by identifying the fundamental nexus between 'interiority' and 'landscape' as the most useful hermeneutic touchstone for locating and explicating the text.

Prior to detailed discussion of the works of both Murakami and Shimada Masahiko, the critic Takeda Seiji in his *Sekai no rinkaku* offers a succinct and compelling account of some recurring signifiers identified as key concepts (*gainen*) in contemporary fiction. His introductory remarks also pre-empt a brief critique of *Hitsuji* which is notable for its attempt at offering a synthetic account of the symbiotic nexus between politics and the mass media in postwar Japan.[49]

Takeda's focus is on the notion of 'world' (*sekai*), and he takes his lead from Yoshimoto Takaaki's *Masu-imêji ron*. He goes on to discuss Kobayashi Kyôji's allegorical novel *Shôsetsuden* and its ironic questioning of the possibility of novel writing in the contemporary era.[50] Takeda's argument follows a clearly outlined trajectory which begins by examining how we construct the idea of 'contours of the world' (*sekai no rinkaku*), and then traces the rise of notions of 'blood', 'nation', 'race', and 'ideology' and the subsequent collapse of the power of these signifiers. In recent times, what constructs the contours of the world are the tropes of 'the festival' (*shukusai*) 'the game' (*gêmu*) and 'the narrative' (*monogatari*). The world image which is depicted through these events (*dekigoto*) and remarks (*gensetsu*) is thoroughly simulacral. His discussion ends with reference to the Baudrillardian description of the endless circulation of images in the mass media which only ever exchange with themselves.[51]

Takeda notes that it cannot be said that this 'line of contours' of the image of the world was 'original' in the sense that it was created by Japan. Rather, the 'ideology of the system' (*taiseijô no rinen*) in postwar Japan can be regarded merely as constituting the process *itself* of the relativization of the idea that *monogatari* (narrative) equals *gensô* (phantasm/fantasy/illusion). It should come as no surprise that, according to Takeda, the collapse of the key signifiers of the grand national narrative coincided with the importation of the Western critical/metaphysical systems of structuralism, cultural anthropology (*bunkajinrui gaku*) and post-structuralism.

What is most interesting about Takeda's analysis is that it identifies key aspects of Yoshimoto's argument in *Masu imêji ron,* which deal with the idea of 'grasping the world'. He notes Yoshimoto's claim that formerly our inference (*suiri*) consisted of the supposition of the belief in the existence of a 'united perspective' which could 'press up hard against reality itself'; however, belief in the method and concept of holistically grasping the world has fallen away, and because of this, nobody possesses a clear image of how to 'take even one step towards reaching the world'.[52]

This 'united perspective'—the loss of which is bemoaned by Yoshimoto—is presumably meant to indicate that which itself was the product of a new form of 'unified subject' brought by modernity. Proof for the loss of this 'united perspective' can be seen, according to Takeda, in the radical transformation of the 'literary interior' (*bungakuteki naimen*). Formerly, the literary interior was more or less opposed to the criteria of worldly things—for example 'household' (*ie*) and 'sex' (*sei*)—and writers keeping the lid on repressed feelings (*yokuatsukan*) intuitively perceived that they could outwardly reflect, within the work, the essential contradictions played out between the individual (*kojin*) and society (*shakai*).[53]

The relentless dismantling of these criteria of 'household' and 'sex' in the contemporary daily life in the city has meant the reduction of the problem of the reflection of social relations in the text, to merely a question of the deliberate choices of individuals. The 'literary interior' (and the once daring resistance to the conditions of daily life) has been transformed, as it were, into a false or 'phantasmal' (*gensôteki*) viewpoint, and no longer provides a method for 'reading' images of society. The fiction of contemporary writers such as Murakami, clearly displays this fundamental change in method (*hôhôjô no henyô*).

In this way, the inverted 'literary interiority' indicated by Murakami's *Boku* operates as a simulacrum in the original, Platonic sense. That is to say, it is a copy of a copy in so far as it shadows an interior, 'discovered' in the Meiji era, which in turn, was 'copied' from conventions of European and Christian representations of self and world. The way in which this is manifested in the text of *Hitsuji* as a genealogy of landscape, requires further clarification.

Tamaki suggests that the meta-textual status of Chandler's *The Long Goodbye* and *Hitsuji* compels the reader to attempt an interpretation of the exterior (*gaibu*) of the world of the novel.[54] The compulsion towards a focus on such exteriority is clearly consistent with Murakami's stated aim of the 'reconstruction' of the novel[55] in terms of his declared intention to restore its fictionality (*kyokôsei*) and to re-assert the independence (*jiritsu*) of fiction outside the frame of 'everyday reality'.[56] Tamaki observes that it is significant that Murakami looks to Chandler's 'hardboiled style', not for its own sake, but because it presents a particularly unique aesthetic of the city. Murakami himself puts it this way:

> Marlowe's role is in verifying the plural hypotheses (*fukusû no kasetsu*) of which the city is constructed.[57]

Towards a particular hypothesis, Murakami observes, Marlowe becomes either cynical or sentimental—this is his 'yes' or 'no', his standard of recognition (*nintei kijun*), his 'moral' or 'complex hypothesis'—and what makes Chandler's fiction fascinating is precisely its endless hypothesizing. The hypotheticality of a hypothesis is clarified by means of a separate hypothesis![58] The *toshi shôsetsu* as *meta shôsetsu* depicts the city, and through the verification of the hypothesis of the city we come to know, claims Tamaki, how the 'phantom nature' (*gensôsei*) of the hope of self fulfillment is expressed. The formation of the urban hypothesis (*toshi kasetsu*) finds its equivalence, according to Tamaki, in the 'urban phantasm' (*toshi gensô*). Murakami describes this in the following way:

> The limited phantasm of the city is a phantasm of choice (*sentaku gensô*). It is, in other words, the phantasm of all of us subjectively choosing something. The choice of the limited style of a fashionable brand name, the choice of multiple channels on the mass media, the choice of a 3LDK or 2DK living space, choice

of university, choice of transport, of restaurant, of magazine. . . .Through these choices we are convinced that we live subjectively one possibility of the countless permutations of lifestyle available.[59]

For Tamaki, Boku's living city vividly informs the narrative space (*monogatari kûkan*) of a novel such as *Hitsuji*, and Boku, as one individual hypothesis, 'verifies' the multitude of hypotheses existing in the city of this novel. The historical subtext of the loss of national consciousness and identity embedded in these multiple hypotheses of the city of Tokyo is, interestingly, of the kind explored by Wim Wenders in his *Tokyo-Ga*. Nora Alter identifies these losses as 'linked to, and coterminous with, the dissolution of the nuclear family', in place of which arises, paradoxically, an 'unmediated vision' borne of the obsession with the 'production and reproduction of images'.[60] These multiple hypotheses are thus endlessly re-affirmed and played out in the simulacral precession of images for which there are no meanings or referents.

But the hypotheses of the post-industrial city inevitably spill over into the discursive arena of all that which the city is not—'history' and 'nature', the province of terrible landscapes and the pseudo-sublime, which we have suggested are the twin tropes of *fûkei* 'writ large' in the text of *Hitsuji*. The 'verification' of hypotheses is radically destabilized once the city limits have been breached, and Boku's journey to the North threatens to usurp the already phantasmal and transcendental subjectivity of the narrator.[61] Ultimately, however, for the reader, the allegorical journey does not *negate* this subjectivity—on the contrary, it simply augments its scope. In *Hitsuji*, therefore, relations between the two levels of ('micro' and 'macro') *fûkei* can be characterized as contiguous, with neither one being privileged.

In his 1996 essay, *Jidai no monogatari kara jiga no monogatari e*, Katô demonstrates this contiguity in terms of the integration of not two but four levels of *fûkei*, which he characterizes as 'atmospheres' (*yotsu no kiken*). These layers cohere synchronically in the text of *Hitsuji*—that is to say, without the conventional diachronic scope or limitations in terms of narrative development and denouement. Katô's main inter-textual reference is Coppola's film *Apocalypse Now* (which, of course, refers to Conrad's *Heart of Darkness*) where all possible histories, all hypotheses, become realized simultaneously in the context of a confrontation with a projected version of the self in the form of absolute horror or evil.[62]

The attempt to validate his claim for the movement in *Hitsuji* from a 'period narrative' to a 'narrative of the self', moves Katô's compelling analysis in an interesting direction, and takes its lead from Murakami's reading of the formal features of Coppola's *Apocalypse Now*:

> It is my judgement that *Apocalypse Now* (*Jigoku no mokushiroku*) is a huge 'private film' . . . I would go so far as to say that this 70mm large scale movie can be thought of as being no different to a 16mm student film produced by amateurs on a low budget. The quality is high but the lens is narrow . . . and it

is in the very narrowness of the lens that there is a reality . . . this is my definition of a private film . . . and *Apocalypse Now*, so to speak, represents the zenith of this kind of film.[63]

Murakami observes that the first two hours of the film depict as spectacle the
fear and madness of war, but in the final thirty minutes, following the hero's
arrival at Kurtz's 'Kingdom', the essence of the novel's 'meaning' or work ideology emerges. In the same way, Katô observes, the final section of *Hitsuji* appears to be mysteriously 'idling'. For Murakami, Coppola's ostensibly 'Vietnam
War' movie becomes, in the final analysis, a giant 'private film' — and the many
criticisms of the film for its lack of thought and 'historical grasp' of the Vietnam
War are completely vindicated, precisely because, according to Murakami, it has
dropped 'thought' altogether and become a film which is completely unrelated
to the Vietnam War.[64]

Both *Apocalypse Now* and *Hitsuji* share, according to Katô, the sensibility of a
new epoch, a new generation of the Hollywood film. Beginning with Coppola
and continuing with Lucas and Spielberg, there was a shift in focus from 'minor'
to 'major' concerns, and these directors created narratives on a grand scale.
Paradoxically, however, such narrative edifices worked to fuse, neutralize, and
effectively eliminate the twin tropes of 'thought' and 'history', and in such an
epistemological scheme the metaphor of the continuously open shutter constructs the dominant narrative subject position of an observer who is strangely
distant — even powerfully transcendent.

The central idea of the heretic who cannot be repatriated home in *Heart of
Darkness*, *The Long Goodbye* and *Apocalypse Now*, takes its special significance in *Hitsuji* in the figure of Nezumi, and in juxtaposition to the presentation
of the multi-layered and contiguous landscapes through which the figure of
Boku moves. For Katô, the hero of *Hitsuji* comes and goes amidst the 'four levels of atmosphere' (*yotsu no kiken*) of the text-as-landscape in a vain and empty
(*munashii*) narrative whose spatio-temporal matrix extends from the provincial
city of Ashiya (as in *Kaze*) to the Tokyo metropolis (the setting of *Pinbôru*) and
on to Hokkaido, only to be completed full circle by its return to the original
scene of 'Jay's Bar' in urban Ashiya. Here, 'contradiction' is substituted for
thought,[65] and in a situation of being able to believe in nothing, the contours of
the world are piled upon the contours of 'the self'. The world becomes the interior world of the self [66] and accordingly, for Murakami, in the language of film
of the new directors, 'anarchism' and 'privatism' become linked.[67]

But how is this specifically manifested in the structure of the self as postulated
in *Hitsuji*? Despite years of critical commentary more or less repeating the
theme in different ways, even the more recent articles[68] on *Hitsuji* persist in
offering simplistic, quasi-Jungian interpretations of Nezumi as the shadow or
alter-ego of Boku, representing the negative, primitive side of Boku's self. However, these critiques fail to account for Murakami's demonstrated refusal to take
up the conventional trope of the modern 'self' struggling *with* and *against* itself.

Any convincing attempt to account for the transcendental subject position of the narrator in *Hitsuji* must offer a description of 'the world' *and* 'self' in Japanese modernity as complicit, simulacral and inexorable functions, each of the other. In the final meeting with Nezumi, Boku is confronted with the stark originality of his friend's thought.[69] When the sheep's demand for the possession of Nezumi's entire personality was rejected through the act of Nezumi's suicide, Nezumi claimed and even celebrated his own weakness (*yowasa*) as something personal and in defiance to the world:

「……本当の弱さというものは本当の強さと同じくらい稀なものなんだ。絶え間なく暗闇に引きずり込まれていく弱さというものを君は知らないんだ。」[70]

Real weakness is as rare as real strength. You don't know the weakness that is ceaselessly dragging you under into darkness. You don't know that such a thing actually exists in the world.[71]

According to Tamaki, it is the phantasmal concept of the world (*sekai*) which is crucial here, precisely because it is stands in *opposition to* the self fantasy (*jiko gensô*) and oppresses it. The 'contours of the world' proposed by Takeda and the 'revolutionary thought' discussed by Kawamoto, present, as implied in Tamaki's argument, both the threat and the very sustaining principle of 'the self' in Japanese modernity, and to this extent can be said to comprise a double structure which is 'mutually fantastic', or what Tamaki terms a 'collaborative fantasy' (*kyôdô gensô*).[72]

Tamaki acknowledges Nezumi's description of his 'rare weakness' as a condition both 'spellbindingly beautiful' and 'hideously evil'—but one which in the end, is no more than a radical 'self fantasy' (*jiko gensô*).[73] Nezumi refers, in his first letter, to the fantasy that if born in the nineteenth century (whilst not attaining the literary achievements of a Dostoyevsky) he would at least have been able to have 'written better novels'. This foregrounds the metafictional function of an allegorical deployment of the narrative within a narrative, as a kind of reflection on what Tamaki calls the 'problematization of the framework of consciousness in nineteenth century Russia'. Tamaki notes that what Dostoyevsky called 'atheism' can be described, in modernist terms (in the words of Takeda Seiji), as 'the pathology of self-consciousness' (*jiishiki no byôri*)—and the 'evil' (*aku*) of the 'accumulation of the self-fantasy', perfectly characterizes the essence of Nezumi's stated 'problem'.[74]

Through a conceptual inversion in which it is acknowledged that the acceptance of weakness is in itself a strength, the freeing up of the morally bound, unified self-struggling subject is inevitable—as is the acceptance of all phenomena as being, in the end, equally contingent and ephemeral. This is expressed in Nezumi's declaration of his fondness for his weakness, suffering and pain, in the same way that he is fond of the 'light of summer' and the 'fragrance of the breeze'.[75] Nezumi chooses his weakness over the totalizing momentum of the Japanese experience of modernity (allegorically rendered in the figure of the sheep-possessed right-wing Boss), which was leading only to a 'kingdom of total conceptual anarchy' within a scheme which would attempt to 'resolve all opposites'.[76] And the characterization of weakness, suffering and pain as being just as desirable as the ephemeral experiences of the senses, corresponds, according to Tamaki, with the 'vision' or epileptic fit of Dostoyevsky's hero, totally absorbed in the transcendental moment or epiphany.[77]

Boku's brush with this experience of transcendence suggests only two options: death, or return through the circuitous landscapes that he has already traversed. He chooses the latter, and thus re-affirms that engagement with the contiguous, mutually dependant and fantastically constructed 'landscapes' of 'self' and 'world' as emblematic of a contrived dualism at the heart of modernity, is more apposite to the task of coping with modernity's contradictions, than feigning a 'struggle *with* the self', which never quite rings true. In this sense, Murakami's detractors are as justified in their critique of the unconvincing 'thinness' of Boku's subjectivity, as they are in construing his linguistic anarchism as evidence of literary banality.

We can conclude, therefore, that whether it is in the form of Takeda's 'contours of the world', Murakami's 'plural hypotheses', Katô's 'four atmospheres' or Tamaki's 'collaborative fantasies', we have arrived at a consideration of definitions of 'self' and 'presented world' which, via the trope of 'landscape', are both disseminated and provisional—but which subvert the idea of a prescribed literary response to the conundrum of Japanese modernity. What remains to be discussed is how this is further played out in the narratives of the later trilogy.

The difference between Coppola's representation of the confrontation with 'the self' and Murakami's in *Hitsuji*, is that the self of the latter has always only been tentatively presented. We will need a different term to describe this, and perhaps Tamaki's 'collaborative fantasy' is the best alternative here. It suggests an archeology of contours of the tentative 'world' of modernity, laid upon the putative layers of 'the self'. As such, the categories of 'world' and 'self' are not arrayed chronologically or in a way in which either one is prior (ontologically or epistemologically).

Instead, they take the form of contiguous landscapes or presentations, whose mutual dependence and co-relationality form the 'sub-text' or perhaps even the repressed master trope of most modern Japanese fiction, which can only be allegorically or elliptically constructed in writing such as Murakami's. *Hitsuji* shows very clearly that there are no neat solutions or correspondences—indeed, that 'modernity' and 'self' are still very much negotiable categories in the context of contemporary Japanese culture. Such issues are taken up in more complex and compelling fashion in Murakami's fictional tour de force, the *Nejimakidori kuronikuru (The Wind-Up Bird Chronicle)* trilogy.

Notes

1. Kawamura Minato, "'Shinsekai' no owari to hâto bureiku wandârando," *Yurîka,* Sôtokushû 21, no. 8 (1989): 174-181; 174; 177; 180.

2. See HMB: 8; 269-298 and WSC: 8; 199-223.

3. See HMB: 7; 244-60 and WSC: 7; 179-189.

4. The picture is first described in Chapter 4 as: 'An ordinary photograph of an idyllic Hokkaido landscape—clouds and mountains and grassy pastures and sheep, superimposed with lines of an undistinguished pastoral verse. That was all.' See WSC: 4; 54; and for a more detailed description WSC: 4; 62. HMB: 4; 83-84, and 4: 93.

5. The narrator relates parts of this text before arrival in Junitaki-cho itself. See HMB: 8; 269-298; WSC: 8; 201- 223.

6. This is all too clearly identifiable in the rhetoric of politicians such as former Prime Minister Mori, whose comments that 'Japan was a divine country with the emperor at its centre', and annoyance at the 'Communist party dominated Teachers Union of Okinawa which opposes every 'national' [read Tokyo-centric] issue' display an Edo-centered consciousness which needs to continually reassert the dominance of the centre over the peripheries in the maintenance of its hegemony (See the Weekly magazine *Aera,* Asahi Shinbun, 13, no. 22 (May 29 2000): 15.

7. HMB: 4; 93.

8. WSC: 4; 62.

9. A version of it even appears in the reception area of the Dolphin Hotel in Sapporo. See HMB: 7; 242 and WSC: 7; 177-8

10. Karatani, *Origns of Modern Japanese Literature,* 41.

11. See <http://www.jtb.co.jp/TJsite/Pref/Hokkaido/pr.html> (7 Jan. 2001)

12. See Ivy, *Discourses of the Vanishing,* Ch. 2.

13. See *Rekishi michi: raku raku uôkingu,* Tokyo: NHK, July, 2000.

14. *Rekishi michi,* 32.

15. Jean Baudrillard, *For a Critique of the Political Economy of the Sign,* trans. C. Levin (New York: Telos Press, 1981), 201.

16. See D. L. Howell, "Ainu Ethnicity and the Boundaries of the Early Modern Japanese State," in *Past and Present* 142 (February1994): 69-93; 77.

17. D. L. Howell, "Ainu Ethnicity," pp. 91-2.

18. HMB: 7; 230.

19. WSC: 7; 170.

20. HMB: 8; 312

21. WSC: 8; 233.

22. HMB: 8; 312.

23. WSC: 8; 233.

24. WSC: 8; 226.

25. See for example, the following: HMB: 8: 329, 343, 346, 347 and WSC: 8; 245, 256, 258, 259, 268, 290.

26. HMB: 8; 347.

27. WSC: 8; 259.

28. See Ivy, *Discourses of the Vanishing,* Ch.5.

29. See Cornyetz, "Tracing Origins: Landscape and Interiority," 168-70.

30. Ishimaru Akiko, "Gendai toshi no naka no Bungaku: Murakami Haruki 'Kaze no uta o kike' o chûshin ni," *Tôkyô Keizaidaigaku Kaishi* 190 (January1995): 185-200; 200.

31. Ishimaru, "Gendai toshi no naka no Bungaku," 199-200. This is quoted by Ishimaru from Kawamoto Saburo, *Toshi no kanjusei* (Chikuma Bunko, 1988).

32. Ishimaru, "Gendai toshi no naka no Bungaku," 198. Here Ishimaru is referring to claims by Imamura Ninshi in his "Bôdoriyaru shindorômu," *Tosho shinbun* 2, no. 11(1983).

33. Ishimaru, "Gendai toshi no naka no Bungaku," 199.

34. Karatani Kôjin, *Hihyô to posutomodan* (Fukutake Shoten, 1985), 9-49.

35. Monographs which address the topic from various perspectives include James Fujii's *Complicit Fictions* and Edward Fowler's *The Rhetoric of Confession*, both cited above.

36. See Iwamoto, "A Voice from Postmodern Japan: Haruki Murakami," 295-300. Iwamoto is referring to opinions expressed in the published seminar (*taiwa*) of Kasai Kyoshi, Katô Norihiro & Takada Seiji, entitled *Murakami Haruki o meguru bôken,* (Kawade Shobô Shinsha, 1991).

37. Iwamoto, "A Voice from Postmodern Japan," 297.

38. For example, even in regard to the *taiwa* entitled *Murakami Haruki o meguru bôken,* to which he critically refers in footnote 13 of his essay, he fails to acknowledge that Takeda Seiji offers an astute and succinct account of the dissolution of the modern subject as discussed by Baudrillard and Deleuze and Guattari, and the way the topic is addressed in the writings of contemporary critic Asada Akira, and 'postmodern' novelist, Shimada Masahiko.

39. See Lydia H. Liu, *Translingual Practice: Literature, National Culture, and Translated Modernity—China, 1900-1937* (Stanford: Stanford University Press, 1995), 9.

40. *Kôjien,* 1099.

41. *Kôjien,* 1235.

42. Liu, *Translingual Practice,* 9.

43. Korinne K. Kondô, "Uchi no Kaisha: Company as Family?" in *Situated Meaning: Inside and Outside in Japanese Self, Society and Language,* ed. J. M. Bachnik and C. J. Quinn, Jr. (Princeton: Princeton University Press, 1994), 190.

44. See Quinn, "Uchi/Soto: Tip of a Semiotic Iceberg?," 286.

45. Foucault, *The Archeology of Knowledge,* 12.

46. This description occurs in Dorinne K. Kondô, "Uchi no Kaisha: Company as family?" in *Situated Meaning,* 190.

47. For a brief historical outline of Kodama's life see Kurata's "Koramu 9—sensei no Moderu" in *Ierôpêji—Murakami Haruki,* 70. Kawamura also makes the connection between Sensei and Kodama in *Hitsuji,* suggesting that the sheep symbolizes the super-will of the Mongolian-like power of such a figure in subjugating and conquering the world. See Kawamura Jirô, "82 Bungei Jihyô 9," *Bungei* 21, nos. 7-9 (September 1982): 20-25; 21.

48. Miyoshi and Harootunian, *Japan in the World,* 'Introduction'.

49. Takeda Seiji, *'Sekai' no rinkaku,* (Kokubunsha, 1987), 7-14.

50. Kobayashi Kyôji's *Shôsetsuden,* (Fukutake Bonko, 1988). Set in the Tokyo of 2064, a floppy disk left by one Nonomure Yusuke is discovered in the goods bequeathed after his death. On the disc is stored an enormously long novel of 400,000 pages. Because of the extreme difficulty of being able to completely read through this text, it becomes highly topical and is taken up in a whirlwind of sensationalism by the media. The very few who are able to complete reading it receive the highest national honors, but a year later a previously unannounced 876 kilo movie reel is discovered, is taken up by the media, and the novel is soon forgotten.

51. Takeda, *'Sekai' no rinkaku*, 14. Takeda quotes from Baudrillard's *Simulation and Simulacra*, but gives no page number or reference details.

52. Takeda, *'Sekai' no rinkaku*, 7-8.

53. Takeda, *'Sekai' no rinkaku*, 8-9.

54. See Tamaki, "Toshi shôsetsu e no shiko—(I)," 28.

55. See Murakami Haruki, "Shigoto no genba kara: Nakagami kenji to no kaiwa," *Kokubungaku* 3 (March, 1985).

56. See Kawamoto Saburô & Murakami Haruki, "Watashi no bungaku o kataru—Interview," *Kaien* (August 1980).

57. Quoted in Tamaki, "Toshi shôsetsu e no shiko—(I)," 29.

58. Tamaki, "Toshi shôsetsu e no shiko—(I)," 29. Also, see Murakami Haruki, "Toshi shôsetsu no seiritsu to tenkai," *Umi* (May 1982).

59. Quoted in Tamaki, "Toshi shôsetsu e no shiko—(I)," 29. See Murakami Haruki "Toshi-shôsetsu no seiritsu to tenkai".

60. See Nora M. Alter, "Documentary as Simulacrum: *Tokyo-Ga*," in *The Cinema of Wim Wenders*, ed. Roger F. Cook and Gerd Gemunden (Detroit: Wayne State University Press, 1997), 136-162; 142.

61. Although, we note that Boku returns with his subjectivity in tact to his familiar world of Jay's bar.

62. Katô, "Jidai no monogatari kara iga no monogatari e," in *Murakami Haruki—Ierôpêij*, 54-78.

63. Katô, "Jidai no monogatari kara iga no monogatari e," 56-57. Katô notes that this excerpt comes from article number three in a series of six articles by Murakami appearing in the journal *Umi*. (Including discussion of Stephen King, John Updike, Raymond Chandler and other contemporary American literary figures.)

64. Katô, "Jidai no monogatari kara iga no monogatari e," 58-59.

65. Katô, "Jidai no monogatari kara iga no monogatari e," 75.

66. Katô, "Jidai no monogatari kara iga no monogatari e," 77.

67. This idea is expressed in Murakami's (*Hôhôron toshite no anâkizumu*) cited by Katô, "Jidai no monogatari kara iga no monogatari e," 78.

68. For example, see Shimizu Yoshinori, "Sakka nezumi no shi," *Yurîka*, Tokushû (May 2000), 96-103; 97.

69. See HMB: 8; 377-87 and WSC: 8; 280-86.

70. HMB: 8; 381.

71. WSC: 8; 282.

72. Tamaki, "Murakami Haruki: 'Hitsuji o meguru bôken' ron (2)," 5.

73. Tamaki, "Murakami Haruki: 'Hitsuji o meguru bôken' ron (2)," 7.

74. Tamaki, "Murakami Haruki: 'Hitsuji o meguru bôken' ron (2)," 6-7.

75. See HMB: 8; 383, and WSC: 8; 284.

76. HMB: 8; 383, and WSC: 8; 284.

77. Tamaki, "Murakami Haruki: 'Hitsuji o meguru bôken' ron (2)," 8.

Chapter Eight

Nejimakidori kuronikuru—The Wind-Up Bird Chronicle: Contexts

The argument in the third and final part of this book will demonstrate how one of the most compelling versions of the simulacrum in contemporary Japanese culture has taken the form of a semiotic structure of repression and absence, called forth by the signifier 'history'. In order to do this, the discussion will undertake a detailed analysis of how Murakami's *Nejimakidori kuronikuru (The Wind-up Bird Chronicle*—hereafter referred to as *Nejimakidori*) attempts to engage with and destabilize this structure, and will consider the implications of a subsequent re-casting of the discursive contours of the writing of 'fiction' and 'history', within the context of the current epistemological and epochal moment of Japanese modernity.

We begin by briefly revisiting the rationale for the choice of texts for this study, and by way of response to the question: what is the point of juxtaposing the first and later of Murakami's tripartite works (with their respective publications spanning one and a half decades) in order to say something about questions of representation in contemporary Japanese culture? The short answer is that these particular texts have challenged conventional modes of representation in postwar fiction in most interesting ways. As Rubin astutely notes, *Nejimakidori* takes up some unfinished business which was only intimated and amorphously sketched in *Hitsuji o meguru bôken (A Wild Sheep Chase)*. The 're-telling'[1] of which he writes, is even more than that: it is a radical re-contextualizing of the signifier 'history' in fictional terms (specifically in terms of what he describes as 'Japan's continental depredations'[2]) which, as we have demonstrated in previous chapters, was dealt with only tangentially in *Hitsuji* via the trope of the multi-dimensional *fûkei*.

The most obvious point of commonality is that both sets of novels came to be constructed as trilogies[3] within Murakami's oeuvre only *subsequent to* their publication and mass diffusion in the literary market in Japan, and their treatment by critics as more or less unitary textual entities belies the fact that this is not consistent with the original authorial 'intention'.[4]

The most significant difference between the two trilogies is what can be called the 'status of the referent' in the respective texts. At the level of formal description, it would appear that many of the elements of the first trilogy are present in the later one: the use of pastiche (as a 'postmodern' version of parody), as well as the allegorical deployment of the tropes of 'modality' and 'landscape'. Strecher goes so far as to claim that in *Nejimakidori*, 'every major and minor theme from [Murakami's] previous literature is present.'[5] As for meta-fictionality, it can be said to be a feature of *Nejimakidori* only to the extent that the novel incorporates such a variety of disparate texts (including poems, dream texts, business cards, narrated 'historical' events, newspaper articles, transcribed 'oral' histories and 'e-mail' dialogues) that the fiction writing process continually draws attention to itself—even if this no longer shocks or surprises the contemporary reader.

Yet, what neutralizes or diminishes the significance of all of these is the problematic treatment of the referent couched in terms of the massively over-determined signifier 'history'. Put another way, the representation of reality in the early trilogy was always qualified by the parenthetical suspension of the idea of 'literature' as a vehicle for relating a conventionalized, imaginable lived experience stipulated by the 'I-novel' orthodoxy. And this implicit critique, in an unstated yet *de facto* sense, meant that the category of 'history' or 'the real' was also, through association, under suspension.

However, in the *Nejimakidori* trilogy there appears to be a distinct attempt to 'resurrect' the referent, although by no means in an unproblematic way. On the contrary, it will be argued that the outcome of this attempt is to install a revised kind of referent as a 'phantasm' or second-order signifier of the empirically stipulated referent—one which draws attention more to the *processes of its re-presentation* than to the imagined 'event' as the 'object' of reference. And consequently, that this is a further example of the operation of the simulacrum as the central, structural and figurative device deployed in Murakami's early and later fiction.

In order to help justify our claim that the repression of 'history' is somehow synonymous with the as yet unspecifiable nature of the 'subject' of Japanese modernity, we will also offer a consideration of the nexus between 'history' and the 'subject' implicitly established through the operation of the tropes of abjection, versions of the sublime, and Lyotard's notion of the 'differend'.

Murakami's attempt at a redeployment of the status of the referent is indeed encouraging, if only because the residual semiotic effect of this is to reinforce the sense that although these texts deny the efficacy of the simple 'event' and 'fact' as the indisputable objects of reference, clearly the effect of this phantasmal stipulation of history as narrative (*monogatari*), recollection (*kioku*), dream (*yume*), phantasm (*gensô*) or revelation (*keiji*), is to confirm 'eventivity' and 'facticity' as forms of socially recuperable and verifiable meaning that are 'beyond' dispute. That is to say, they are outside the conventional empirical parameters central to processes of historical 'verification' and historiography, yet demand attention not *in spite of* the fact that they are woven into an ostensibly 'fictional' work, but precisely *because of* this fact.

It is the task of the first part of this chapter to outline some of the conditions of exteriority of, and versions of critical response to the *Nejimakidori* texts. Also, an *explication* of the various narrative strands of the work will illustrate some of its more important structural, formal and stylistic features and a range of critical responses to the text. This is in preparation for a consideration of the broader and more abstract *implications* of what this text may mean as a work of contemporary Japanese fiction. Specifically, over the next three chapters (and into the Conclusion), it will be argued that the 'revised' status of the referent as configured in *Nejimakidori* operates as a function of the simulacrum—of reference-as-phantasm, which inheres ultimately in the semiotic/semantic disjunction and cognitive incommensurability of what Lyotard has called the 'differend'. It will be concluded that (as Lyotard is at pains to point out), the differend of the Kantian sublime is to do with neither moral nor aesthetic universality, but simply a presentation of the terms of a discursive contestation.

The result of stipulating this operation of the differend in the reading of *Nejimakidori* as a 'fictional' text which stands in simulacral relation with the writing of a 'non-fiction' history text in contemporary Japanese culture is as follows. 'Reference' indicates a process best described as a phantasm of the struggle for a re-presentation of the real, yielding a trace of meaning which paradoxically leads the text squarely back into the vexed question of how to think Japanese modernity *outside* the tired and flawed rhetoric of either an under-theorized condition of postmodernity, or the 'overcoming' of a rejected and incomplete modernity. As arguably the most striking moment in the unfolding 'Murakami Phenomenon', the novel *Nejimakidori* (and the broadly stipulated conditions of its exteriority) do not offer concrete solutions as to how to step outside this circle, but they do recast the whole question of reference and the referent in a way which may allow for new trajectories of meaning within the ongoing conundrum of Japanese modernity.

Conditions of Exteriority

It is common knowledge among informed readers and critics that the opening chapter of Book One of *Nejimakidori* is comprised of the entire short story published eight years earlier entitled *Nejimakidori to kayôbi no onnatachi* (*The Wind-up Bird and Tuesday's Women*).[6] Despite the overall content remaining substantially unchanged in the novelistic version of the narrative, there are slight stylistic differences. Yoshida has noted the dropping of a few sentences towards the end of the original story in the novel as the mark of a more 'objective' style—important in the later novelistic development of the character Kumiko—which is established from the beginning.[7]

The original hardcover version of the Japanese publication of the *Nejimakidori* trilogy was comprised of the first two volumes appearing in April 1994 with the third volume available in bookstores in August 1995. It was unknown until well after the publication of the first two volumes that a third volume was imminent, and its publication became much anticipated. We have noted above that Murakami conceded that after finishing the second volume (and even though the text appeared to lack an unsatisfactory 'closure') he had no intention of writing a third volume. The first English translation appeared in 1997 and was a slightly abridged version of the original three volumes.[8]

What is evident about this publishing phenomenon—particularly since the rapid diffusion of the Internet[9] (and especially from the second half of the 1990s) —is an author whose commentary on his own publications becomes very much a determinant of their reception by general readers. And this possibility that readers are exposed to authorial guidance[10] *before* they purchase and read the 'original' text, is further evidence of the simulacral construction of textuality, where the boundaries between the text and its critique become blurred. This is no more evident than in 'The Making of Nejimakidori Chronicle' article (published in 1995), an edited version of an interview in which the author discusses a range of topics around the writing of *Nejimakidori*.[11] The 'making of' genre has become a common feature in Japanese popular discourses to the point where its rendition in *katakana* syllabary as メイキング・オブ (*meikingu obu*) is readily observable in a variety of media. This development has taken it well beyond its original most well known form as an aid in the promotion of new Hollywood movies, and it has become an almost essential component of the marketing of many kinds of texts.

This meta-textual phenomenon is consistent with the kind of simulacral 're-versal' (in which the copy precedes the original) of Baudrillard's 'precession' of simulacra, whereby the map exists *prior to* discovery of the territory ('it is the map that engenders the territory'[12]) or, as Frow points out, acts of imagining and *knowing about* the photograph *precede*, both cognitively and temporally, the visiting of the famous site.[13] Furthermore, in this kind of discourse, as we have shown in the previous chapters on the tropic modalities of landscape, 'historical knowledge' of a place (in formal 'histories', poems, travel guides, magazine articles and photographs) precedes the visiting and viewing of the site, where-upon the expected form is simply 'filled-in' with the already known 'content'.

We ought not, however, be too dismissive of this genre of 'the making of' simply because we seek to avoid accusation of a disguised search for some kind of authorial 'intentionality'. It has earlier been argued that Murakami's fiction must be situated *outside* the hermeneutic parameters of the *shishôsetsu* form and its narrow 'autobiographical' constraints. It follows that the critical/fictional conditions of exteriority surrounding his works may function as touchstones to the kinds of issues which are circulated (explicitly or otherwise) throughout the discursive domains of contemporary Japanese culture. Rather, we will be able to use the author's 'retrospective' commentary as a way of eliciting a dialogue with the novel itself, and in so doing, confirm the problematic and complex forms of intertextuality which Murakami's fictional works have both constructed, and been constructed by.

One noteworthy example of Murakami's meta-textual intervention in the reception and reading of his works is identified by Rubin in the short story *Binbô na obasan no hanashi* (*A Poor Aunt Story*), which is described as 'a rarity among Murakami's works, however common it may be in the modern *shôsetsu* in general: a story about a writer trying to write a story.' Murakami explains that 'the story has a double structure: it consists simultaneously of 'A "Poor Aunt" Story' and 'the Making of "A Poor Aunt Story".'[14] In this tale, Murakami once again demonstrates his preferred view of a 'reader response' aesthetic and a kind of 'anti-interpretation' view of language, literature and semiosis in which monolithic meanings are eschewed, and whereby meaning is described as an effect of the process of telling—what he calls a 'conceptual sign' (*gainen teki kigo*)—not a direct manifestation of some established 'real'.[15]

The same resistance to generalized 'interpretation' clearly emerges in the 'Making of Nejimakidori' interview, and it will be very useful to place excerpts from this text alongside other critical commentaries as we seek to explicate the main literary and structural features of this long and complex novel. In short, it seems the novel itself, critical commentaries, the 'making of' essay, and conversations with the psychoanalyst Kawai, all form part of the complex intertextuality of *Nejimakidori*, and we have little choice but to engage with all of these. This provides a contextual setting for our discussion of and engagement with the *New History Textbook* controversy of 2001 in Japan, which provides further and quite compelling evidence for the kinds of claim being made about the status of the referent in *Nejimakidori*.

Narrative Synopses

As with the synopses of novels examined in previous chapters, the following is provided as a translation of the narrative synopsis taken from 'Murakami Database' appearing in the Special Edition of *Kokubungaku* in February, 1998. Although it provides a succinct outline for the reader unfamiliar with the text, it is worth noting that what this particular summary elides is in some ways perhaps more significant than what it includes.

> When thirty-year-old 'Boku' (Okuda Tôru) quits his job as a clerk in a legal office, and takes charge of the housework at home, there begins a strange disruption of his peaceful daily life: starting with the disappearance of his cat and followed by an erotic phone call from a woman (who knows Boku but is unknown to him)—a clairvoyant who calls herself Kanô Malta.
>
> Boku is an acquaintance of the elderly man Honda, a spirit medium who also possesses the power of prophecy. The old man is a survivor of the 'Nomonhan Incident' (the routing of Japanese troops by the Russians in Outer Mongolia in 1938). The history of Japanese involvement in Continental Asia is woven throughout the narrative.
>
> While looking for his cat in the rear lane, Boku meets up with high school drop-out Kasahara Mei, and stumbles across a disused well. The well is near a house which was the site of the suicide of a high-ranking infantry officer, a suspected war criminal who had been recalled from Northern China.
>
> Boku learns by letter of the death of the old man, Honda, and visits retired Lieutenant Mamiya to chat about the wartime adventures that Mamiya and

Honda shared. One such episode occurred a year before the Nomonhan Incident, when the two men, together with two officers from a special services unit crossed over into Outer Mongolia. The group was captured by a Mongolian army unit led by a Russian officer, and only Mamiya and Honda survived.

Boku's wife, Kumiko, disappears, and although Boku is informed by Kumiko's elder brother Wataya Noboru that Kumiko is seeking a divorce, Boku refuses to agree, feeling a great sense of strained relations with Wataya. Boku decides to climb down into the disused well, and falling asleep, dreams of a darkened hotel room in which he engages sexually with the woman who had previously made the suggestive phone call. A strange black/blue bruise appears on his right cheek, and he soon becomes convinced that the woman in the dream is his estranged wife, Kumiko.

Boku realizes that the disused well is a point of connection, and deciding that he must buy the empty house in order to secure access to the well, goes to work for the fashion designer, Nutmeg.[16] Nutmeg offers treatment to the 'deformed interiors' of the wives of influential and powerful people. Boku is able to assist in this work after gaining special powers associated with the bruise on his cheek. With the aid of Nutmeg's son, Cinnamon, Boku continues this work at the vacant house with the well.

At the same time, Wataya Noboru attempts to adversely pressure Boku, but Boku decides to try and locate and bring home his wife Kumiko, and to this end he goes to the bottom of the unused well and gets in touch with the 'unreal' darkened room where Kumiko is. In that unreal place, he comes across a man resembling Wataya Noboru, and strikes him down with a baseball bat. It seems inevitable that Boku will perish at the bottom of the well, but he is eventually rescued by Cinnamon.

Back in the 'real world', Wataya Noboru collapses with what appears to be a brain hemorrhage (cerebral apoplexy). Kumiko sends an e-mail message claiming that it was her brother who was the cause of her leaving and that she is planning to murder her brother by disconnecting his life support machine.
The story concludes with Boku visiting Kasahara Mei at the wig factory in Niigata, and telling her that he plans to wait at home for Kumiko who is in police custody awaiting trial.[17]

Notably, this synopsis of the basic plot(s) lacks even a cursory reference to the wartime atrocities which are vividly detailed at various points of the text. Instead, the 'history of/on the continent' (*tairiku de no rekishi*), rather than the more specific 'history of Japanese involvement on the Asian continent', is characterized as being 'woven into the narrative' (*monogatari ni wa orikomarete iku*).[18]

In the following chapters, by extracting the episodes of 'history' (seemingly 'arbitrarily' punctuating the 'main' narrative of the search for the lost Kumiko) and placing them contiguously, we will be able to more thoroughly explicate those dimensions of the narrative which clearly fall under the rubric of 'historical fiction', and examine their functional significance in the trilogy *writ large*.

Katô has offered an alternative way of representing the plot synopsis which takes the form of a chronologically arranged table (*monogatari nenpyô*) of a daily summary of events (*dekigoto*).[19] The following translated excerpt of this table (excluding the *zenshi* or 'prehistory') offers, at a glance, the time frames of each of the three volumes, specified by numbered days and dates. Not only does this schematic layout of the narrative allow a clearer recognition of relations between contiguous narrative lines and the ordering of presented 'events', but perhaps more significantly, it conforms to the promise of the 'chronicle': to situate itself as a series of smaller units of 'narrative time', within the context of a larger, 'historical time'. This way of presenting the narrative is also given here because it gives a strong sense of the disjointed, random and 'anti-structure' like aspects of the novel, which is even augmented by the current Japanese critical proclivity for the use of charts and tables (*hyô* and *zu*) in making sense of the more radical examples of contemporary fictional writing. This theme is taken up by Shimamura in his '"Kuronos" to no Kôsô', which we will return to later.

BOOK ONE : Dorobô Kasasagi (The Thieving Magpie) June ~ July, 1984

June 26 Boku receives the sex-call from the mystery woman; meets Kasahara Mei.

June 27 Meets Kanô Maruta. Maruta tells how Noburu Wataya violated Kanô Kureta.

June 28 Meets Kasahara Mei in the vacant house; gets named Mr. Nejimaki-dori.

June 29 Kanô Kureta visits and tells of her pain.

June 30 Boku dreams of Kanô Kureta and Kanô Maruta; has a 'wet dream'.

July Three months have passed since Boku quit his job as a legal-office clerk. The letter from Lieutenant Mamiya arrives.

Day Three Boku discovers his wife's empty perfume box; Mamiya visits and offers his fearful tale of the Haruha River.

BOOK TWO: Yogen suru tori hen (Bird as Prophet) July ~ October, 1984

July:

Day Four Wife Kumiko disappears; Boku has the second dream about Kanô Kureta; in this dream Kanô Kureta turns into the mystery telephone woman; Boku ejaculates.

Day Five In the Shinagawa Hotel, Boku meets Kanô Maruta and Wataya Noboru; he hears the suggestion of divorce with Kumiko; reads Lieutenant Mamiya's letter.

Day Six   Boku descends into the well at the vacant house.

Day Seven Boku meets the mystery woman in the hotel room of the 'other world'; he passes through the wall and returns to the well; at 5am, Boku notices the well's ladder is missing.

Day Nine Kanô Kureta rescues Boku; upon returning home, Boku finds the letter from Kumiko; he receives a call from Kanô Maruta (and senses this is the last call from her); the bruise (*aza*) appears on Boku's cheek.

Day Ten   Upon waking, Boku finds the naked Kanô Kureta lying next to him; she invites Boku to the island of Crete; they have sex.

Day Eleven Kanô Kureta loses her name.

Day Fifteen Boku's uncle visits him with some advice.

Day Sixteen   In accordance with this advice, Boku goes to Shinjuku to search among passers by; he is beckoned by a woman.

Day Twenty Six This is the eleventh day of Boku's standing in Shinjuku; he spots a man he had previously met in Sapporo — follows him, attacks him, and beats him to death. He cancels his plans to travel to Crete.

August Kanô Kureta sets out for Greece by herself.

The End of August Boku receives a postcard from Kanô Kureta in Greece; Kasahara Mei visits Boku, informs him that the vacant house is being demolished; Kasahara Mei decides to go to back to school.

The Middle Ten Days of September The vacant house is demolished, and becomes vacant land.

The Middle of October Boku has a revelation while swimming in the local pool. He realizes that the mystery telephone woman is his wife, Kumiko.

BOOK THREE: Torisashi hen (The Bird Catcher) October 1984 ~ December 1985.

Spring 1985 Wataya Noboru is elected to the Japanese National Parliament.

The Middle of March Boku's 'bruise' becomes 'feverish'; Boku is convinced that he must take possession of the well on the vacant land. Through the act of being beckoned by the woman at Shinjuku Station a year earlier, and the ability gained as a result of passing through the wall, Boku commences works curing the pain of women; the 'prostitutes' of his consciousness. The missing cat Wataya Noboru returns, and is re-named Sawara. Akasaka Nutmeg purchases the vacant land and builds a new mansion—this becomes Boku's new work place. Boku descends into the well, and attempts to enter the other world.

One Day Mr. Ushikawa conveys Wataya Noboru's proposal.

Before Long Mr. Ushikawa suggests Boku corresopond with missing wife Kumiko via computer.

The Following Day Boku gains access to Cinnamon's computer.

Before Long Boku communicates with Kumiko via computer; prepares to return to the outside world.

Before Long Boku wonders why Kanô Maruta—who seems like a person from antiquity —is living now. Akasaka Nutmeg visits, and says that she will have to interrupt her work temporarily. Boku communicates with Wataya Noboru by computer. The computer calls Boku, and he accesses it using the appropriate password. Nobody visits the mansion. Akasaka Nutmeg and Mr. Ushikawa vanish. Boku tells of his dream that Kanô Maruta and Kanô Kureta named Corsica.

The Following Day (Near the year's end); Boku visits the local pool. He reads Captain Mamiya's letter which contains discussion of 'Boris the Skinner'.

The Second Day Before dawn, Boku goes to the mansion and descends into the well. He passes through the wall into the other world. In the hotel lobby of the other world, Noboru Wataya is attacked by someone resembling Boku. He meets the mystery woman—who is actually Kumiko—and confronts and knocks down somebody who comes to the room. Boku then passes back through the wall and into the well, which he finds is now filling up with water. He seeks the help of Kasahara Mei but is eventually rescued by Cinnamon.

The Fourth Day Boku sleeps for a full two days. Nutmeg says she will dispose of the mansion. Whilst in Nagasaki, Wataya Noboru collapses with a brain hemorrhage. Kanô Kureta appears in a dream to Boku, and says that she is actually in Japan, and has given birth to a child.

The Seventh Day The computer calls Boku, and he learns that the new version 'Number 17' has been entered. Kumiko murders Wataya Noboru (by disconnecting his life-support system). Boku goes to meet Kasahara Mei.

Of the two narrative summaries presented above, the former can be described as a précis or kind of synoptic plot overview, while the latter, giving priority to a different combination of action and description of psychological states, offers more of a 'list' or the diary-like presentation of a chronologically ordered format. Neither can be described as an integrated presentation of the key narrative threads which might be expected to provide for the reader, at certain points, consolidation of the overall narrative momentum for the convergence of meaning, closure and a sense of denouement.

Interestingly, many of the seventy chapters of the trilogy are headed-up by double or alternative titles,[20] and this feature is important for establishing the parameters of reader expectations. In her cogently argued discussion of the importance of applying speech-act theory to 'literary texts', Marie-Louise Pratt recasts the speaker/audience relations of oral narration in terms of a similar or parallel structure in literary/written texts. The 'layout' and marked divisions/stages of the written narrative should not be overlooked, because as Pratt notes, 'we knowingly and willingly enter a speech situation in which another speaker has unique access to the floor. . . .Titles, subtitles, chapter headings, and summaries, for example, perform the "request for the floor" role . . . and similarly correspond in function to . . . public speaking conventions.'[21]

Perhaps what is more interesting about the division of narrative units in *Nejimakidori* is the fact that because many of the chapters are marked by 'two-part' titles often signifying completely different ideas/events in the context of the unfolding narrative, the reader is given a sense of at least two alternative ways of proceeding. Such a feature does not offer a clearly prescribed and authorially guided 'interpretation' via the 'forward reading dimension'.[22] In fact, some chapters seem completely out of context, at odds with the expected teleological momentum of the narrative, and to some extent, function in a way similar to the 'anti-narrative' pastiche-like format of Murakami's first novel, *Kaze no uta o kike.*

The second reason that we should be interested in the formal narrative divisions of the books and chapters of *Nejimakidori* is that they tell us something about the projected narrative time(s) of the presented world(s) of the novel. As with other of Murakami's novels, *Kaze, Pinbôru* and *Hitsuji*, the 'narrative/fictional' time of the text is specified at the beginning of each Book (*Book One:* June and July, 1984; *Book Two*: July to October, 1984; *Book Three:* October, 1984 to December, 1985). And this time interacts in a complex way with other 'historical' times mediated by the meta-textual devices of oral-narration, dream texts, letters, newspaper articles and 'virtual' computer dialogue.

This obvious concern with the structuring and presentation of clearly definable units of duration/time in *Nejimakidori* is highlighted by Shimamura, who extracts the original Greek *kronos* (given in the title phonetically as *kuronos*) as the reading of the character 時 (*toki/ji*) from the title of the trilogy—*kuronikuru* ('chronicle')—and casts it as the central 'code' for reading the text.[23] Specifically, this narrative is described as a 'battle *with* time' (*toki to no kôsô*). What is perhaps more relevant is his musing on how Goya's *Figure of Kronos (kuronosu no zû*) thoroughly expresses 'wickedness' (*jaakusa*) and 'horror' (*ozomashisa*), and the subsequent suggestion that this implication derived from the title *kuronikuru* ('chronicle') is definitely not unrelated to the depicted scenes of wickedness and horror in *Nejimakidori*—with its implicit and explicit treatment of the tyranny of the 'rule' (*shihai*) of time. Shimamura also describes the sub-narratives of Cinnamon, Boku and Kumiko as 'battling' *with* the narrative of a more original, unified time (*ichigen teki na 'toki' no monogatari to kôsô*), and asserts that this once again confirms Murakami's belief in the power of narrative. He concludes with the speculation that whether this will move Murakami's readers to 'make/move' history themselves (*rekishi o ugokasu*) remains a function of the as yet un-narrated future lying beyond the horizon of their own 'chronicle'.[24]

If it is useful to highlight the fact that because the chapter headings mark out the battle with time (and indeed that the various narrative threads compete with larger and different 'times'), then Murakami's choice of the term 'chronicle', as noted by Hisai,[25] has even further significance. Hisai suggests two possible Japanese equivalents for the English word 'chronicle', (rendered in *katakana* in the title as クロニクル) as either *nendaiki* (年代記 : 'chronicle') or *hennenshi* (編年史 : 'chronicle', 'annals'). The former gives the sense of a 'diary/journal' of the times, while the latter term *hennenshi*—utilizing as it does the characters *hen/amu*—connotes 'to knit', 'compile', 'edit'; as well as the character *shi*, for history, implying a more orthodox and officially sanctioned selection, compiling and editing: a bringing-to-order of the stuff of history.

Both these senses—of a *personal* account of the times, as well as the idea of a more formally compiled 'history'—are contained in the term 'chronicle'. And precisely because it is a foreign loan word (deliberately selected in place of two perfectly acceptable terms in Japanese) it immediately invokes a sense of strangeness, a writing/witnessing/recording/ calling forth of a more explicit connotation of modernity and otherness than would be invoked by the use of the Japanese alternatives. In Chapter 29 of Book III, Boku speculates as to why Cinnamon has chosen the term 'chronicle' to narrate the stories of his mother, Nutmeg, and grandfather in Manchuria, and suggests that 'chronicle perhaps indicated a "chronological" ordering of the stories'.[26] We will have cause to revisit this reflection in the following chapters, when we consider the nexus between memory and history in Nutmeg's and Cinnamon's stories.

Hisai has argued that the main problem with the use of the term 'chronicle' in the title of this trilogy is the *length* of time it is ostensibly meant to 'narrate'. If it really is intended to present the record of Boku's 'life and times', then it would have to cover a considerably longer period. If it fails to do this, then the naming of the trilogy is in fact, according to Hisai, potentially 'fraudulent' (*meishôsagi*). We are aware that the presented narrative time frame of Books One and Two is between June and October, 1984—less than half a year. We are also aware that the wartime tales of Mr. Honda and Lieutenant Mamiya—of which Boku is a privileged listener—are selected from their own chronicles, and that these most definitely do not belong to the chronicle of Boku's life. Furthermore, even the tales of events from the childhood of his wife Kumiko, and her 'evil' brother Wataya Noboru, (notwithstanding the fact that they would overlap with the time-frame of Boku's) do not warrant being called 'chronicles'.

Perhaps the most interesting thing about Hisai's approach is evident in a much larger arena of intertextuality. In spite of the seeming inappropriateness of the title 'chronicle', it is suggested that perhaps something else is being hinted at. In terms of the larger hermeneutic grid for 'reading off' this text, Hisai claims that the average reader brings to *Nejimakidori* the following implicit cultural knowledge which strongly suggests an intertextual relation with the classical Japanese tale *Ise Monogatari*:

> (i) The reader is aware that the *Ise Monogatari* (*Tale of Ise*) is a kind of record of the   male hero Ariwara no Narihira's generation;
> (ii) The reader is aware that the 'central line' (*chûshinsen*) of the narrative of *Nejimakdori* is about a 'well' 「井戸」 (*ido*);
> (iii) The reader is also aware that a 'well' 「筒井」 (*tsutsui*) is the theme of a famous song in/from the *Ise Monogatari*;
> (iv) The reader implicitly recognizes that the story of the well in *Ise Monogatari* has some correspondence to the contents of the *Nejimakidori* narrative.[27]

Furnished with such information, argues Hisai, the reader realizes that along with the title of 'chronicle' (*kuronikuru*) comes an important 'hint' (*hinto*). At the very least, the title 'chronicle' cannot be taken as fraudulent (*meishôsagi*), and that it would be a 'misreading' (*yomichigai*) or even 'serious misunderstanding' (*hanahadashii gokai*) for readers to view the entire *Nejimakidori* trilogy as a fraudulent or 'phony' novel (*sagishôsetsu*) simply because its expected content in terms of genre, seems somewhat at odds with what is implicitly promised by the title 'chronicle'.[28]

But perhaps the most important thing about this concern with genre and the title of the text is that it foregrounds the importance of the treatment of time in *Nejimakidori*. The forms of constructing and representing the ideas of 'narrative' time and 'historical' time are implicated in the very construction of the paradigms of Japanese modernity and modern Japanese history, which this ostensibly 'fictional' text is at pains to interrogate. We will have cause to revisit these problems when we respond to Frow's claim that modernity is characterized by a very specific nexus between time and the rise of what he terms 'commodity culture'. We will also have the opportunity to demonstrate how this aspect of the construction of modernity relates to the 'false' epistemological moment of a phantasmal Japanese 'postmodernity', and how this relates to Murakami's self-acknowledged attempt, in the writing of *Nejimakidori*, 'to punch a hole in time'.

The trilogy contains three volumes each with a different title, and a total of seventy chapters covering 1156 pages in the hardcover edition. By any measure, this is a very long novel (*chôhen shôsetsu*), which mixes 'narrative' and 'historical' times and presents the kinds of difficulties for a readership which has come to expect (especially of a writer like Murakami) increasingly complex narrative forms. Indeed, the challenge of meaningfully engaging with this text is very much a function of being able to synchronically integrate three distinct time frames: mid-nineties Japan—the time of initial publication, characterized by a sense of economic, social and political decline; the spatio-temporal frame of the presented world of Boku, covering 1984-85—a period of unprecedented prosperity and confidence in post-Meiji Japan; and the time frame of the Japanese involvement on the Asian continent and the Pacific War (1930s to mid 1940s)—a period characterized by high hopes, wild imaginings of colonial expansion, false expectation, terror, grief and crushing despair.

Before examining in detail the interaction of these temporal frames, we will provide a general overview of some of the more important critical responses to this text as a way of identifying key issues which can be explored in depth in the subsequent chapters. This will be followed by an explication of the key narrative threads prior to a consideration of the implications, at a more abstract level, of their interaction.

Critical Responses

More than two decades have passed since the publication of Murakami's first trilogy incorporating *Kaze*, *Pinbôru* and *Hitsuji* (1979-83), and it is clear that a considerable volume of critical literature relating to these texts has developed. While much of it is undeserving of the label 'scholarly', there have emerged in recent years, many more sophisticated critiques which attempt integrated theoretical approaches with comparative textual analyses covering Murakami's entire oeuvre.[29]

In comparison, *Nejimakidori* has only been in the literary 'market place' since 1995, and the above-mentioned trend notwithstanding, the number of critical works on the text deserving of serious attention remains relatively small—although the analytical depth of some of them compensates for this. Clearly, the development of a body of comprehensive research on the complex structure and thematic concerns of a 'landmark' novel such as *Nejimakidori* requires the 'historical' and 'critical' perspectives gained with the passage of time, and more sophisticated and interesting analyses are sure to emerge with the new waves of younger Japanese scholars who are become increasingly at home with the approaches of cultural studies and European critical theory.

Many readers may not have been aware that Book One was published in serial form in the literary journal, *Shinchô*, between October 1992 and August 1993. In April 1994, Books One and Two were published as complete texts. In the Japanese 'paperback' (*bunkô*) form, the first two volumes alone amounted to more than 1250 pages—and with the addition of the third volume, the total was more than 2180 pages. Katô Norihiro notes that as very long novels, they quickly developed a reputation and became widely discussed, although not all responses were positive. Severe criticism came from Yasuhara in his 'Hon nado yomuna, baka ni naru', and in an article by Nakajô in the 1994 summer edition of the journal, *Riterêru*, which listed no less than seventeen 'unaddressed puzzles' (*hôchi sareta nazo*) in the novel.[30] Yet, in his capacity as a prominent and respected Murakami commentator, Katô dismisses these superficial concerns with the resolution of 'riddles' (*nazo*), seeing instead three main areas for consideration and research. Firstly, the relationship between Books One and Two as a complete novel, and Book Three; secondly, the issue of the new literary horizons which this work opens up; thirdly, the relation between this work and Murakami's previous works. Noting Murakami's insistence that the first two volumes should be treated as distinct from the third, Katô argues for a clear distinction between narrative (*monogatari*) and novel (*shôsetsu*), and concludes that what took place here was a 'splitting off' *bunretsu* of 'narrativity' (*monogatarisei*) from 'novelness' (*shôsetsusei*). In other words, with the publication of the first two volumes the novel was complete, but the *narrative* remained unfinished.[31]

Ishikura has also noted that amid the 'wild enthusiasm' and generally positive reception of *Nejimakidori*, some readers expressed anger and confusion at the unsolved puzzles and lack of development of the novels.[32] On this question of riddles/puzzles, Ôtsuka Eiji has written a lengthy paper entitled *Murakami Haruki wa naze 'nazohon' o yûhatsu suru no ka* ('Why does Murakami Haruki Give Rise to "Puzzle" Books?'), and lists several such texts.[33]

The impetus of some critics towards identifying and solving riddles is partly a function, suggests Ôtsuka, of the tendency for Murakami's presented fictional worlds to shift between narratorial perspectives identified as being peculiar to specific historical periods/epochs. The implication is that critics seek 'solutions' to riddles by attempting to construct 'equivalents' between the presented 'fictional' world of a novel, and the 'real' world of a particular imagined epoch. Compared to a writer such as Nakagami Kenji, who constructs narrative time and space in terms of what Ôtsuka calls 'mythical' and 'sub-cultural' dimensions, in *Nejimakdori,* the narrative perspective of Boku is a function more of the 'chronicle' (*nendaiki*) style. Initially, this takes the form of the 'moratorium-oriented' ideology of the late sixties and early seventies (as it clearly is throughout several earlier novels) until the sudden and unexpected insertion of the signifier 'Manchuria' (*Manshû*) into the story, which immediately re-contextualizes the dominant narrative perspective of the presented world of 1984 suburban Tokyo, in juxtaposition with the imagined 'episodes' of Japanese military involvement in 1930s continental Asia.[34]

In terms of responses to *Nejimakidori* in the West, we note Fujimoto-Keezing's observation that in recent times, apart from what he terms the 'pioneers of postmodern writing' (Abe Kôbô, Endo Shûsaku and Ôe Kenzaburô), there has been no equal to Murakami in terms of a successful Japanese novelist in America.[35] In his web-published 'America de yomu Murukami Haruki', Kazama notes that the dominant readings of modern Japanese literary giants such as Kawabata and Mishima—which were informed by an 'Exoticism' and 'Orientalism'—are still evident in the ongoing phenomena of best-selling Japanese-theme texts such as *Memoirs of a Geisha*.[36]

Although the magazine/newspaper reviews of *Nejimakidori* are little more than marketing aids, their titles and contents[37] tend to emphasize that the success of Murakami in America with *Hitsuji* (1989), and more recently *Nejimakidori*, is precisely because of the fact that (contrary to the expectations of an exoticised 'other' implicit in the above-mentioned conventionalized reading paradigms) readers are confronted with the surprisingly 'un-Japanese-literature-like' (*nihon-bungaku rashikunai*) work of Murakami's 'American pop-culture-like' style.[38]

Despite a number of journalistic book reviews of *Nejimakidori* in English,[39] only the more scholarly responses such as those offered by academics like Rubin and Strecher are of any real relevance to this discussion. In his capacity not only as the English translator of the text, but also as a modern Japanese literature expert, Rubin has written worthwhile articles published in Japanese[40] and English,[41] while Strecher has also discussed *Nejimakidori* in terms of the conventions of 'Magical Realism'.[42]

However, by far the more comprehensive body of critical writing is to be found in the monographs and journal essays in Japanese, by Japanese scholars. That is to say, the attempt at a critique *of* and *through* the discursive and subjective parameters of contemporary Japanese fictional/critical practices, ironically reveals much about the increasing possibilities of the self directed deconstruction of literary texts, in which the object of reference ('Japan' or 'Japanese life') has receded amidst the growing dominance of the 'precession' of simulacral cultural forms. And we see in this tendency further evidence of the growing hegemony of the operation of simulacral structures of signification, the limits of which have become increasingly difficult to specify.

It is clear that there are indeed many possible ways of approaching and organizing the critical literature on *Nejimakidori*. For example, it is possible to draw the following distinctions: those critiques responding to the publication of the first two volumes; those written after the publication of the third volume; those responding outside Japan to the 1997 English translation; those written after the publication of *Andâguraundo 1* (*Underground I*, 1997) and *Andâguraundo II* (*Underground II*, 1998) when Murakami's entry into the so called *shakaiha* ('socially concerned') writers cohort is 'confirmed' by some critics.

For the purpose of this discussion, however, it is deemed more useful to arrange the critical texts along the lines of theoretical approaches and thematic concerns falling under the following broad rubrics: (i) critiques concerned with broad literary contextualization and genre; (ii) critiques which focus on literary motifs and narrative structures including 'double-world' structures and the 'reality/unreality' opposition; (iii) critiques which focus on 'history', and issues relating to memory, representation and the writing of 'fiction' and 'history'; (iv) approaches concerned with the psychoanalytic dimensions of the novel, including the representation of sex and sexual violation, abjection, Oedipal configurations, gender relations, madness, therapy and recovery; (v) critiques which examine the nexus between power and authority, political structures, violence and the state. Apart from the first category of contextualization and genre, the other broad areas of critique will be considered in the next chapter.

Obviously, many of the above areas of enquiry are not mutually exclusive, and the more sophisticated analyses tend to touch on several of them. Apart from these broad categories, in the following chapter, some of the formal narrative features considered in earlier chapters (e.g. the devices of pastiche, allegory and *fûkei*) will be reviewed in terms of the extent to which they are utilized or developed in the *Nejimakidori* text.

We conclude this chapter by way of brief reference to some attempts to situate *Nejimakidori* in terms of genre, and have noted above the discussion by Shimamura and Hisai, of the significance of the use of the term 'chronicle' in the title as denoting: diary, personal account, historical record—and the sense of strangeness connoted by the choice of this foreign loan-word, rather than its Japanese equivalent. In contrast to this, Suzumura and Numano have described the text as perhaps an 'un-chronicle like' (*hinendaiki teki*) chronicle.[43] Like *Dansu, dansu, dansu* (*Dance, Dance, Dance*) the novel takes as its stage the year 1983-1984 as the 'peak' of the late capitalist Japanese economy and the 'bubble' (or *kûdô*—'hollow' or 'cavity'). Naturally, the 'present' (*kono genzai*) of the novel is around 1984; however there are many 'lags' or 'divergences' (*zure*) in this present—including the 'present' of the reader of 1995. Into the time-frame of the year 1984 in *Nejimakidori*, Suzumura argues, the author has programmed-in the 'real time' of his present in a 'twisted' or 'parodied' form (*nejireta katachi de*), and that this functions as a kind of prophetic deed or orientation (*yogen kôi*).[44] It is certainly the case that Murakami presents complex series of relations of historical and narrative times, and as will be discussed later, the text is playing with numerous conflicting and contiguous 'times'.

Taking a broader approach, Hatori attempts to situate *Nejimakidori* generically and historically by referring to a much larger schematization of the development and repetition of literary forms. According to this description, the forms of *joji bungaku* (narrative/descriptive writings), *jojôshi* (lyric poetry), *monogatari shôsetsu* (narratives/tales) and *gekibungaku* (dramatic literature) are variously in ascendance or decline, despite simultaneously existing in the one period. Hatori identifies at least six major cycles in the development of Japanese Literature, with the most recent postwar period in fact constituting several 'mini-cycles'.[45]

What especially interests Hatori is the emergence of an increasing 'realism'— especially in the third decade of the *Shôwa* period—within which (and despite being of 'realistic depiction') it is claimed that there was also an increasing tendency toward the depiction of abnormality and insanity in the midst of daily life. Around the end of the third decade of *Shôwa*, claims Hatori, there occurred a boom in the 'mystery novel' (*suiri shôsetsu*)—and soon came the 'ghost story' (*yûrei banashi*) figuring the ghosts of the *Genji monogatari*, and of the Noh drama, and so on. Following this was what in hindsight can be seen as the emergence of 'occultism' (*okaruteizumu*)—and although the idea of 'telepathy' was only under discussion in the early essays on the topic, the American 'occult boom' (especially in the form of movies), had already commenced in Japan.

Notwithstanding the fact that by the 1990s fortune telling (*uranai*) and telepathy (*shinrei genshô*) had become 'normalized', Hatori notes that its spread was not unrelated to the success of the fiction of writers such as Endô Shûsaku, Shôno Yoriko and Murakami Haruki—and that Murakami's *Hitsuji* was the Japanese version of 'The Exorcist'.[46] Hatori's focus on 'occultism' and *Nejimakidori* must be viewed within the context of the theme of the March 1995 Special Edition of *Kokubungaku* on Murakami Haruki, which was entitled 'Murakami Haruki: yo-chi suru bungaku' ('Murakami Haruki—The Literature of Prophecy'). And we note the description of clairvoyant, Honda, and the sisters Kanô Kureta and Kanô Maruta who are characterized as possessing 'super power' (*chônoryoku*) and the ability to enter the 'super-real world' (*chôgenjitsu sekai*).[47]

Despite its attempt at a generic contextualization of the novel, Hatori's discussion is quite unsophisticated, if only because it suggests that even Honda's relating of the Nomonhan incident is 'not a critique of war'.[48] Also, it gives itself over to a sense of inevitable resignation regarding the myriad of unresolved 'puzzles' of the text described as being merely a function of the age of puzzles and TV games, with the occult being a part of this broader tendency to foreground 'super-real' or 'occult-like' spaces.

Finally, it is worth noting that in terms of the question of 'influence', and the writing of *Nejimakidori*, Katô has noted Murakami's stated dissatisfaction with the American fiction of the nineties. In the age of the 'politically correct' spirit of regulation and control, Murakami claims that the 'trickster-like' power of fiction had been killed off. Katô describes Murakami's divergence from American literature in the nineties as a fundamentally new approach to the question of subjectivity: the individual (*kojin*) which had formed the basis of morality in literary modernity, had been subverted (largely through the pervasive influence of the horror movie and science fiction), and especially in *Nejimakidori*, Murakami had split the core (*kaku*) of the individual and brought a new technique and tendency to Japanese literature.[49] Yoshida has argued that aspects of *Nejimakidori* have been inspired by the American writer Tim O'Brien's 'Lets Talk About the Real War'—and claims that there are parallel scenes of 'skinning alive', with the caveat that while O'Brien's is a relatively 'realistic' depiction of the episode, Murakami's is more 'dream-like'.[50]

Leaving aside these questions of context, comparison and 'influence', the discussion now turns, in the following chapter, to an examination of some important theoretical issues which are crucial to our subsequent analysis of the *Nejimakidori* text in Chapter 10.

Notes

1. Rubin writes: 'In many ways, *The Wind Up Bird Chronicle* can be read as a retelling of *The Wild Sheep Chase*.' See Jay Rubin, "Murakami Haruki," in *Modern Japanese Writers,* ed. Jay Rubin (New York: Charles Scribner's Sons, 2001), 238.

2. Rubin, "Murakami Haruki," 238.

3. Some critics claim that *Dansu dansu dansu* makes it a tetralogy. See for example Rubin, "Murakami Haruki," 237.

4. We have previously noted that after writing *Kaze* Murakami intended to write no more. Similarly, after completing the first two volumes of *Nejimakidori*, Murakami claimed that he had no intention to write a third volume. See "Meikingu obu 'Nejimakidori kuronikuru'" ("The Making of Nejimakidori Chronicle"), *Shinchô* 92, no. 11(November 1995): 274. Interestingly, Suzumura Yasunari, in his 1994 commentary on the first Two Volumes, speculated that according to a 'rumor' surely there would be a third—and possibly even a fourth volume to follow. See Suzumura Kazunari, *Murakami Haruki kuronikuru 1983-1995,* (Yôsensha, 1994), 240.

5. Matthew C. Strecher, "Magical Realism and the Search for Identity in the Fiction of Murakami Haruki," *Journal of Japanese Studies* 25, no. 2 (1999): 286.

6. This story first appeared in *Shinchô*, January, 1986, and in April of the same year, in an anthology of short stories entitles *Panya saishûgeki* (Bungeishunjû, 1986): 157-203.

7. Yoshida notes that because the three sentences in the scene, occuring towards the end of the story where Boku speculates on Kumiko's inner thoughts are cut from the corresponding scene in the novel, the narratorial perspective in relation to Kumiko remains at that point, more of 'objective' description, than 'subjective' conjecture. See Yoshida Haruo, *Murakami Haruki, tenkan suru,* (Sairyûsha, 1997), 179. For the specific scene in the short story, see Murakami Haruki, "Nejimakidori to kayôbi no onnatachi" in *Panya saishûgeki,* (Bungeishunjû, 1990), 200. For the amended scene in the novel see NDK: 1; 40 and WBC: 1; 23.

8. Chapters 15 and 18 in Book Two of the original Japanese text are excluded entirely from the English translation. Chapter 17 of the original becomes Chapter 16 of the English text, and Chapter 16 of the original becomes Chapter 15 of the translation. See NJK: 2; 259-280, and 328-356. Also, Chapters 1, 2 & 26 of Book Three are excluded from the translated version. See NJK: 3: 11-21 and 290-99.

9. For example, in *Yume no sâfu shitei*, are published a selection of Murakami's e-mail dialogues with fans on topics ranging from his novels, to sports, movies, music and the changing nature of the novel in the electronic age. The text comes complete with CD Rom. See *Yume no sâfu shitei* (Asahi shinbunsha, 1998).

Furthermore, Ishikura Michiko discusses the inter-textual significance of Murakami's home page in "Netto no naka no Murakami Haruki," in 'Murakami dêtabêsu', *Kokubungaku*, Special Edition, (February 1998): 210.

10. This is not to suggest that Murakami offers specific guidance to readers on *how* to interpret the texts, but that the existence of his commentaries nevertheless forms part of the extra and inter-textuality of their readings, by subtly foreclosing certain readings and generating a series of plausible interpretations sanctioned by orthodox critical commentary.

11. Murakami Haruki, "Meikingu obu 'Nejimakidori kuronikuru'," 270-288.

12. See J. Baudrillard, "The Precession of Simulacra" in *Simulations* (New York: Semiotext(e), 1983), 2.

13. Frow is quoting from the episode in Don DeLillo's *White Noise* about a visit to 'the most photographed barn in America', where the visitors acknowledge that 'we're not here to capture an image, we're here to maintain one'. See John Frow, "Tourism and the Semiotics of Nostalgia" in *Time and Commodity Culture* (Oxford: Clarendon Press, 1997), 67.

14. Murakami Haruki, "Jisaku o kataru: tanpen shôsetsu e no kokoromi" in *Murakami Haruki Zenshû* supplement, pp.4-6. Cited in Jay Rubin, "Murakami Haruki's Two Poor Aunts Tell Everything they Know about Sheep, Wells, Unicorns, Proust, Elephants and Magpies," in *Oe and Beyond: Fiction in Contemporary Japan*, ed. Stephen Snyder and Philip Gabriel (Honolulu: University of Hawaii Press, 1999).

15. Murakami writes: A word is like an electrode connected to the mind. If you keep sending the same stimulus through it, there is bound to be some kind of response created, some effect that comes into being. Each individual's response will be entirely different, of course, and in my case the response is a kind of sense of independent existence. . . .What I have stuck to my back, finally, is the phrase 'poor aunt'—those very words, without meaning, without form. If I had to give it a label, I'd call it a 'conceptual sign' or something to that effect. Cited in Rubin, "Murakami Haruki's Two Poor Aunts Tell Everything they Know about Sheep, Wells, Unicorns, Proust, Elephants and Magpies," 185.

16. Note that the anglicized versions, 'Nutmeg' and 'Cinnamon' are used in preference to the original Japanese *Natomegu* and *Shinamon*.

17. See Ishikura, et.al., "Murakami Haruki Dêtabêsu," 186.

18. Ishikura, et.al., "Murakami Haruki Dêtabêsu," 186.

19. Katô Norihiro, "'Nejimakidori kuronikuru': ozomashisa to keiji," in *Ierôpêji: Murakami Haruki*, 198-199.

20. For example, in Book One, Chapter Four is entitled: *Takai tô to fukai idô, arui wa nomonhan o tôku hanarete (Tall Towers and Deep Wells, or Far from Nomonhan)*; See NDK: 1; 84 and WBC: 1; 46.

21. Mary Louise Pratt, "The Literary Speech Situation," in *Toward a Speech Act Theory of Literary Discourse* (Bloomington: Indiana University Press, 1977), 114.

22. The notion of the 'forward reading dimension' has been discussed in earlier chapters, as an important feature of Wolfgang Iser's theory of aesthetic reception in the reading of narrative texts.

23. See Shimamura Teru, "'Kuronos' to no kôso—'Nejimakidori Kuronikuru' no kôdo," in *Murakami Harukei Sutadeizu 04*, ed. Kuritsubo Ryôki & Tsuge Teruhiko (Wakakusa Shobô, 1999), 87-97; 87, 88.

24. Shimamura, "'Kuronos' to no kôso—'Nejimakidori Kuronikuru' no kôdo", 97.

25. See Hisai Tsubaki, *Nejimakidori no sagashikata* (Taida Shuppan, 1994), 133-136.

26. NDK 3: 29; 330-31; WBC 3: 27; 528-29.

27. Hisai, *Nejimakidori no sagashikata*, 134-5.

28. Hisai, *Nejimakidori no sagashikata*, 136.

29. For example, see the *Murakami Sutadeîzu (Murakami Studies)* series which is a multi-volume anthology of the more important critical papers of Murakami (Wakakusa shobô, 1999). See also Koboyashi Masaaki's *Murakami Haruki: Tô to Umi no Kanata ni* (Moriwasha, 1998).

30. Katô, "'Nejimakidori kuronikuru': ozomashisa to keiji," 192. Yasuhara's critique was published in *Toshoshinbun*, in 1994 (no dates provided).

31. Katô, "'Nejimakidori kuronikuru': ozomashisa to keiji," 193.

32. See Ishikura Michiko, "Murakami Haruki—'Nejimakidorikuronikuru' Nôto," *Bunkenronshû* (October 1994), Senshû Daigaku Daigakuin, 1-36; 1-2.

33. See Ôtsuka Eiji, 'Murakami Haruki wa naze 'nazohon' o yûhatsu suru no ka', *Bungakkai* 52, no. 10 (1998), 238-264. The list includes Takahashi's 1986 *Hitsuji no Resutoran—Murakami Haruki no shokutatsu kenkyû*, Katô's *Murakami Haruki— Ierôpêji* (1996), and Hisai Tsubaki's *Nejimakdori no sagashikata* (1994) and *Nonfuikushon to karei na kyogi* (1998).

34. Ôtsuka, "Murakami Haruki wa naze 'nazohon' o yûhatsu suru no ka," 245. Although the so-called 'Nomonhan Jihen' ('Monhan Incident/Battle') of 1939 is the central incident here, most readers will be much more sensitive to the 'signifier' 'Manshû Jihen' ('Manchurian Incident' of 1931) as the officially sanctioned justification for an escalation of Japanese military activity in the region.

35. See Michael Fujimoto-Keezing, "Naze kare wa sonna ni subarshii no ka: Murakami Haruki ga America de seikô suru ryû," trans. Okuji Hisayo, in *Yuriika* 32, No. 4, *sangatsu rinji zôkan* (March 2000): 72.

36. See Kazama Ken "Bokura wa ima doko ni iru no da?—Amerika de yomu 'Nejimakidorikuronkuru',"<http://www.asahinet.or.jp/~hf2tskym/neji/essays/america/1.html>, 2.

37. For example, in American journalistic reviews, consider the use of evocative phrases such as 'a surreal novel', 'Japan as a postmodern wasteland', Japan as a 'wannabe Prozac Nation' and 'a goofy sensibility shaped by American pop culture'. As exemplars of this see, for example Pico Iyer, 'Tales of the Living Dead' in 'The Arts Book Review', *Time*, 150, 18 (November 3, 1997); also Laura Miller, "Books: The Wind-up Bird Chronicle," *Salon* (November 24), 1997:
<http://www.salon.com/books/sneaks/1997/11/24review.html>.

38. Miller, "Books: The Wind-up Bird Chronicle".

39. For a list of 'non-scholarly' reviews of *Nejimakidori kronikuru*, see the website: <http://www.asahi-net.or.jp/~hf2t-skym/neji/bibliography/1.html> 2-3.

40. Jay Rubin, "Sekusu to rekishi to kioku: Murakami Haruki—Nejimakidori kuronikuru," trans. Sakai Yokuko, *Shinchô* (February 1995): 254-9.

41. Rubin, "Murakami Haruki," 227- 43.

42. Strecher, "Magical Realism and the Search for Identity in the Fiction of Murakami Haruki".

43. Suzumura Kazunari & Numano Mitsuyoshi, "'Nejimakidori' wa doke e tobu ka," *Bungakkai*, 49, no. 10 (October 1995): 100-123; 111, 112.

44. Suzumura & Numano, "'Nejimakidori' wa doke e tobu ka," 112.

45. See Hatori Tetsuya, '"Nejimakidori" no bunseki: chônôryoku no gendaiteki no imi," *Kokubungaku* 40, no. 4 (March 1995): 64-69. Hatori refers to Doi Mitsutomo's *Bungaku Josetsu* (no publication details offered). The six periods suggested are (i) from the *Kojiki* and *Manyôshu* to the *Heian Monogatari*; (ii) the period up to the completion of the *Noh*; (iii) the *Edo* period; (iv) the period from *Meiji* to *Taishô*; (v) from *Shôwa* to the middle of the Second World War; (vi) the post-war period, which itself is said to contain several smaller cycles.

46. Hatori, "'Nejimakidori' no bunseki," 65.

47. Hatori, "'Nejimakidori' no bunseki," 68.

48. Hatori, "'Nejimakidori' no bunseki," 68-69.

49. Katô is referring to Murakami's comments in the "Meikingu obu nejimakidori kuronikuru" interview. See Katô, "Dai hasshô: 'Nejimakidori kuronikuru'—ozomashisa to Keiji," in *Murakami Haruki—Ierôpêji*, 196-197.

50. See Yoshida Haruo, *Murakami Haruki, tenkan suru*, 196.

Chapter Nine

Nejimakidori kuronikuru—The Wind-Up Bird Chronicle: Subject and Text

The previous chapter presented an outline of the formal narrative features, and sketched the general conditions of exteriority (critical, inter-textual, generic) of *Nejimakidori* in order to contextualize the trilogy as an unusual and important work of contemporary Japanese fiction. In this chapter and the next, we will explore how *Nejimakidori* engages with contemporary Japanese culture by producing meanings across several broadly construed dimensions of narrative as discourse—that is, narrative as both productive of, and produced by the category of the social.

These dimensions appear as linguistic/artistic manifestations of the following: an unorthodox literary re-presentation of 'the real'; an attempted subversion of the opposition 'fiction'/'history'; a gesturing towards a more 'psychoanalytic' treatment of subjectivity and desire; and a synthesis of all of these in new kinds of propositions about 'individual subjectivity' (*kojin teki na shutai*), 'national' subjectivity (*kokutai*), and the postwar Japanese State. Implicit in these textual idiosyncrasies is an overall narrative momentum to present the 'return' of a previously repressed social and historical referent (albeit in a phantasmal way), one effect of which is to suggest new parameters for thinking about subjectivity and the subject of Japanese modernity.

As the final stage of an argument which attempts to validate the description of Murakami's narrative method as a cogent example of the operation of the simulacrum in contemporary Japan, it will be proposed that in *Nejimakidori* Murakami deals with history tangentially: he chooses a figurative, trope-like and allegorical method woven into the formal structural and stylistic dimensions of the text, and continues the function of the 'transcendental' narrative position as a refusal to engage with a form of an imagined, unproblematic 'modern' subjectivity he is clearly at pains to undermine.

Again, we pause to consider the question: what is the rationale for skipping from the first to the most recent trilogy of Murakami's oeuvre without considering, in detail, those major novels published in between? It is clear that although *Sekai no owari to hâdoboirudo wandârando* (*Hardboiled Wonderland and the End of the World*) published in 1985, considerably develops the double-world structure, it raises no new issues about 'history' and 'the System' which are not already alluded to in *Hitsuji*. And perhaps it is a little too simplistic to merely show (as many have done) that the double-world structure of the novel is, in itself, interesting. The novel *Dansu, dansu, dansu (Dance, Dance, Dance)* — considered by some to be the fourth novel which effectively completes a tetralogy — brings into relief and extends the treatment of many of the formal narrative features of *Hitsuji*. Furthermore, the two main 'romance novels', the mega-bestseller *Noruei no mori (Norwegian Wood,* 1987) and *Kokyô no minami, taiyô no nishi (South of the Border, West of the Sun,* 1992) have been subject to largely socio-psychological critical comment which is not directly pertinent to the aims of this discussion.

In terms of cinematic equivalents of *Sekai no owari to hâdoboirudo wandârando* and *Dansu, dansu, dansu,* films such as *Blade Runner* and *The Matrix* come to mind. In the cyborgian world of the replicant in the former we are reminded of the digital information processing brain of Boku, and in the 'double world' structures of *The Matrix* are to be found clear parallels of the kinds of narrative format employed by Murakami to explore questions of being and non-being, real versus non-real, the constitution of subjectivity and so on.

Via the incessant stream of narrative special 'effects' in *Nejimakidori* we are continually thinking about the status of the referent — which is 'the real' and which is 'the virtual'? Indeed, just as in *The Matrix,* in *Nejimakidori* this becomes a major theme, in the same way that it is central to novels such as *Sekai no owari to hâdoboirudo wandârando* and *Dansu, dansu, dansu.* What makes *Nejimakidori* different, however, is the inclusion of 'historiographic' material which foregrounds not necessarily history as such, but the *idea* of 'history'. And herein lies its simulacral dimension. *Nejimakidori* fuses and confuses 'narrative' and 'historical' discourse, and implicitly establishes a debate about the nature of history by using many of the strategies of the previous novels: pastiche, metafiction, modality and landscape — this time adding 'history', in its most overt form yet, to the narrative formula. The method chosen to do this is crucial, because it establishes a semiotic tension between the signifier 'history' and the *idea* of its signified — the imputed object or referent.

The Subject as Aesthetic Function

It was demonstrated in an earlier chapter that the vexed question of Japanese modernity turns on the problem of an inadequately defined subject and subjectivity. At this point of the discussion the question naturally arises as to how we can establish a nexus between the issue of subjectivity and the central proposition of this and the following chapter: the phantasmal 'return' of the referent in Murakami's longest and most ambitious narrative project. If we accept that one important aspect of the debate about Japanese modernity is essentially concerned with subjectivity, and furthermore, that issues about the real and referentiality revolve around difficulties in stipulating the 'object' of historiography, then we require an explanatory principle for mediating the dimensions of the subject (as the originator, agent and knower of history) and the referent, as the stipulated 'object' of such agency and knowing. However, since it is assumed that such an empiricist model of the subject/object is no longer a tenable way of approaching the real (because it mistakenly assumes that language is a transparent and un-problematic vehicle for accurately 're-presenting' the world) we must resort to a description of the apparent *processes* of subjectivity operating within and around the aesthetic parameters of modernity.

In short, we require an explanatory schema for teasing out the possibilities of the subject, and it will be demonstrated that the textual process employed by Murakami is a method which engages several dimensions of the representational possibilities of the aesthetic of the sublime. In *Nejimakidori*, Murakami has util-ized three versions or aspects of the sublime in order to deal with the complex issue of referentiality in such a way as to not foreclose new ways of thinking about the subject of/in Japanese modernity. These three versions can be de-scribed, in broad terms, as the 'psychoanalytic sublime', the 'historical sublime' and the 'political sublime', and it will be demonstrated that the major narrative strands of *Nejimakidori* variously employ one or more of these. Each of these versions of the sublime indicates an engagement with the problem of 'presenting the unpresentable' as a disjunctive modality of the simultaneous affirmation and negation of the subject, whereby the limits of such subjectivity remain uncertain and tentative.

In narrative terms, these aspects of the sublime are integrated through the dis-cursive trope of irony proposed by White,[1] and assume their apotheosis in the figure of Wataya Noboru, where their threat to subjectivity is expressed in terms of an incommensurability in the modalities of presentation of that which cannot be directly presented—ultimately, that is, in the form of what Lyotard has termed the 'differend'.

In a discussion of Maruyama Masao and the question of the subject in Japa-nese modernity, Sakamoto has drawn on critiques by Sakai and Kasai challeng-ing Maruyama's discursive dichotomy of 'the West' and 'Japan', suggesting that 'Asia' seemed to 'form a blind-spot for Maruyama'.[2] Sakamoto succinctly re-minds us of Maruyama's central thesis on the 'incomplete' nature of Japanese modernity:

> Arguing that the tragedy of Japanese fascism was caused by the lack of free, autonomous subjects with 'internalized ethics', Maruyama counterposed an idealized model of Western modernity to ultra-nationalism.[3]

While we now acknowledge the flawed nature of the argument in Maruyama's relativist proposition that in the context of an idealized Western modernity, Na-zism was the more 'rational' and 'modern' form of fascism,[4] we nevertheless cannot ignore the subject of Japanese modernity in terms of a tendency towards a system of pervasive, ongoing 'fascism' in the post-war system of political

and economic practices and structures, aptly described by Miyoshi and Harootunian under the rubric of the term 'emperorism'. *Nejimakidori* is implicitly concerned with all of these issues, and this fact is justification enough to make it a
text worthy of serious critical attention.

The general question of how to think concisely about this long and complex
novel suggests that we take as the foundation of our method an analysis of the
significant story lines which will form the following chapter. Within these, the
figure of Boku is presented as both the teller and listener, narrator and addressee
of stories. The narrative perspectives established are therefore multiple and
complex, yet these contradictory textual positions encapsulate and reflect the
lack of development towards monumental closure, and an avoidance of attempted resolution of the myriad 'riddles' which have been the bane of critics
and readers alike.

Throughout the analysis of the main narratives will be woven perspectives of
comments from Murakami's 'making of' interview, the views of various critics,
and Murakami's discussions with the psychoanalyst Kawai. The main narratives
discussed are the story-lines of Kumiko, Lieutenant Mamiya, the Kanô sisters,
Akasaka Nutmeg and Wataya Noboru. The figure of Boku as the protagonist is
of course not treated separately but by implication, as the dominant, overarching narratorial perspective guiding the reader's attempts at constructing
meanings. And although we will utilize the theory of the sublime, we acknowledge the need to be very specific about what *sort* of sublime we are referring to.
The aspects of the sublime with which we will be working in these chapters are
based primarily on Kant's discussion of the sublime which has already been outlined (in Chapters 5, 6 & 7), as well as on Hayden White's 'historical sublime'
and Lyotard's re-reading of the Kantian sublime and subsequent invocation of a
form of 'political sublime'.

The attempt to offer specific theoretical bases for these versions of the sublime
is in contrast to the somewhat loose application of the term 'sublime' by some
critics of contemporary Japanese fiction. Susan Napier, for example, citing Nobel laureate Ôe Kenzaburô's claim that 'we've reached this point where it is
crucial for the Japanese to think seriously about the question of the Japanese
sublime' (with the implication that the truly developed subject of modernity requires a version of the sublime in order to adequately define itself), proposes
three major paradigms of the sublime in Ôe's fiction: a vision of violence and
apocalypse; the notion of a 'human collectivity' tied to a natural setting; 'the
body, usually in its sexual aspect, but also in relation to violent action.'[5]

In short, Napier's 'three major paradigms' of the sublime in Ôe's fiction assume the three forms of 'apocalypse', 'collectivity', 'the body'. While these may
appear to have some correspondence to the three aspects of the sublime (the historical, the political and the psychoanalytic sublime) to be discussed in this chapter, they are sorely under-theorised and undeveloped in Napier's discussion. Despite referring to the *Kojien*'s definition of the term 'sublime' in Japanese (*kôsô*),
Napier makes no reference to Kant's extensive and foundational writing on the

theory of the sublime—let alone the work of more contemporary theorists such as White and Lyotard. In contrast to this methodological omission, the use of the sublime in this discussion will always make explicit which aspects of this complex theory are being referred to, because it is the specificity of such dimensions which help configure the very forms of subjectivity imaginable in Japanese modernity.

In an early and groundbreaking essay on postmodernism, Lyotard recognizes that the task of integrating and connecting Kant's three Critiques (of the 'passage which must be charted between the heterogeneous language games . . . of cognition, of ethics, of politics') needs to be submitted to rigorous re-examination in order to scrutinize the Enlightenment assumptions of a unitary end of history and a subject.[6] Lyotard takes up this challenge in his later works on the differend,[7] and his close reading of sections 23-29 of Kant's *Critique of Judgement*, in a book entitled *Lessons on the Analytic of the Sublime*.[8]

We will return to these texts later, but for now we make brief reference to Lyotard's proposition about the 'presentational' criteria which mark out an artistic work as 'postmodern'. Lyotard describes the difference between the modern and the postmodern in terms of what he designates as 'presenting the unpresentable', and the sublime:

> Modern aesthetics is an aesthetic of the sublime, though a nostalgic one. It allows the unpresentable to be put forward only as the missing contents; but the form, because of its recognizable consistency, continues to offer to the reader or viewer matter for solace and pleasure. Yet these sentiments do not constitute the real sublime sentiment, which is an intrinsic combination of pleasure and pain: the pleasure that reason should exceed all presentation, the pain that imagination or sensibility should not be equal to the concept.[9]

We have already noted the 'real sublime sentiment'—as an admixture of pleasure in pain—in earlier chapters which refer to Kantian aesthetics. In contrast to this, and in regard to the postmodern aesthetic, Lyotard proposes:

> The postmodern would be that which, in the modern, puts forward the unpresentable in presentation itself . . . that which searches for new presentations, not in order to enjoy them but in order to impart a stronger sense of the unpresentable.[10]

While it is the case that Lyotard's earlier depiction of the postmodern—as exemplary of the most recent in a series of recurrent epochal phases of an ever-beginning modernism—is open to criticism,[11] we can also say that the general orientation of his earlier hypothesis aptly describes the kind of radicality epitomized in *Nejimakidori*, where the writer-as-philosopher produces a text which is not governed by pre-established rules, and where the text cannot be judged according to familiar categories. On the contrary, writes Lyotard, 'those rules and categories *are what the work itself is looking for*' [my emphasis].[12] Lyotard's earlier writing about the question of 'presenting the unpresentable' in postmodern art takes on broader epistemological significance in his later work on the differend, and we will have cause to test the efficacy of this idea in relation to the over-arching 'work ideology' of *Nejimakidori*. However, before proceeding, we need to clarify the kinds of approach(es) to history which inform these discussions, and which are outlined briefly in the following section.

History as Text: Hermeneutic or Hyperbole?

There were no shameful episodes in modern Japanese history.
> Former Japanese Education Minister,
> Fujio Masayuki[13]

Some of the things we did, I could not bring myself to speak about.
> Lieutenant Mamiya, *Nejimakdori kuronikuru*[14]

Empirical and fictional are blended tendencies, rather than distinctive kinds; history and fantasy stand as the poles of a narrative spectrum.
> Barbara Foley,
> *Telling the Truth: The Theory and*
> *Practice of Documentary Fiction*[15]

The phantasm, rather than constituting the event, hovers over its surface like a cloud, as an effect of meaning not identifiable with anything in the event as such.
> Robert Young, *White Mythologies*[16]

Taking our cue for one trajectory of the argument in this chapter from the above quotations, in our discussion of *Nejimakidori* we are faced with a consideration of whether it is possible (or indeed desirable) to reconcile three seemingly irreconcilable perspectives on the nature of history:

(i)   History is a recuperable, representable reality which can be spoken and written.

(ii)   History is simulacral—it arises merely as an effect of speaking and writing, and is not co-extensive with any referent.

(iii)   History inheres only in the unutterable aporia of meaning/sense, arrayed between memory, thought, speech and writing.

Clearly, these competing views on the nature of history are related to the question of subjectivity and Japanese modernity, and turn on the possibility of being able to stipulate history-as-subject, or, alternatively, the subject in/of history. The first proposition incorporates what have been broadly described as 'reconstructionist' (empiricist) and 'constructionist' ('social theory') forms of history.[17] The second and third propositions are somewhat complementary, and indicative of what can be described as a 'post-structuralist' view of history.[18] The first suggests a method which has now undeniably assumed the status of pariah in progressive sections of contemporary Western academe: outdated, intellectually untenable and 'ideologically unsound', it is a method which Foucault describes as 'total history', and something which for Derrida is 'impossible and meaningless', keeping 'to the difference between totality and infinity'.[19] For Deleuze, it is the operation of difference in the endless simulacral repetition of 'bad copies',[20] and for Lyotard, it is the incommensurability of language games, built into the very project of history itself.[21] In his *White Mythologies*, Robert Young encapsulates this dilemma in a way which proposes moving beyond the disjunction between history and historicism as contradictory—preferring, instead, the description of history *as* difference. History

> is thus a contradictory (quasi) concept—a phantasm—in which neither the elements of totalization nor difference can be definitively achieved or dispatched. This means that history can be theorized not so much as a contradictory process but as a concept that must enact its own contradiction with itself.[22]

As indeterminate as the above propositions about history may appear, Murakami has set himself the task of confronting the question of history in *Nejimakidori* in a complex way which addresses all of these perspectives, without necessarily arriving at their synthesis or resolution in the form of a coherent theory. Rather, the text simply lays bare the terms of a debate which is related to the much earlier 'overcoming modernity' conundrum (discussed in Chapter 2), and the concomitant repression of the signifier 'history' in the discourses of post-war Japanese 'Emperorism' discussed by Miyoshi and Haratoonian.[23] For evidence of such repression we need look no further than the long-running Ineaga Saburô saga in which an aging history Professor has challenged, in the highest Japanese courts, the authority of the Ministry of Education to precisely control (and as Ienaga claims 'sanitize') the contents of text books approved for the high school history curriculum.[24]

In such books, 'history' appears in the form of timelines, dates and events (according to typical re-constructionist methods) with the most well known trope of the imagined defining 'event' of Japanese modernity signified by the proper noun 'Meiji Restoration', which, as Harootunian argues, 'from the early 1930s down to today has been employed to dramatize loyalties and to force men to make clear their ideological commitments'.[25] This is consistent with what Young describes as history's attempt to 'conceptualize the event, to wean it from its finitude'.[26]

In an earlier chapter, we described how Foucault identified the movement from resemblance to representation in the discursive domains of early European modernity, and noted that the semiotic slippage in the very 'idea' of representation became an essential condition of the epistemological contours of modernity. Similarly, we can observe in Murakami's work generally—and most specifically in *Nejimakidori*—a writing which self-reflexively foregrounds the processes of re-presentation, the signifier and the syntagmatic arrangement of the material at hand. If the postmodern suggests a new kind of syntax for narrative,[27] then in terms of White's well known 'tropology' of history as story-telling, it is clear that *Nejimakidori* prefers metonymy and synecdoche to metaphor and irony (although these latter two are also deployed in at least two of the main narrative lines: Nutmeg's telling of 'The Zoo Attack', and Wataya Noboru's story).[28] A fundamental concern of the discussion will therefore be the representation of the 'event' as a meaning-effect, a simulacral rendering of the chaotic contents of 'history'.

All of these claims will be clarified in the ensuing argument, but for now we can say that *Nejimakidori* is a precursor text which is augmented by Murakami's apparent return to the *shakaihai* ('socially concerned') evident in his implicit and explicit references to the issue of social commitment in later works such as *Andâguraundo* (*Underground*) and *Kami no kodomotachi wa minna odoru* (*After the Quake*). This re-introduction of at least the *signifier* is the first step towards recognizing the 'contents' (signified) of the history of Japanese modernity, which have been disturbingly absent in many post-war discourses. Murakami's has in fact been a multi-pronged attack on the illusion of the 'overcoming' or 'sidestepping' of Japanese modernity, by using the simulacrum (in the form of the tropes of pastiche, metafiction, modality, landscape and the sublime) to expose the phantasmal and elusive nature of Japanese modernity, at the heart of which lies the problem of how to write history.

Is Murakami's treatment of history in *Nejimakidori* 'postmodern'? As this and the next chapter will show, the answer to this question is both 'yes' and 'no'. 'Yes', to the extent that it blends ostensibly discrete genres of fiction (*shôsetsu*) and history (*shi*); 'no', in so far as it maintains a strong sense of overriding narratorial perspective (although as we will see, Yoshida points out that *Nejimakidori* is very different to the so-called 'historical novel' or *rekishi shôsetsu*). The answer to this question depends, ultimately, on one's view of what constitutes the postmodern. To the extent that it does attempt to 'present the unpresentable' in a new way by proposing new modalities for the delivery of narrative 'content', it does conform to Lyotard's view of the postmodern.

On the other hand, according to Frow's critique of the theory of postmodernism, the latter displays the artistic sensibilities of merely one more moment of modernism, which by no means fully excludes the category of 'tradition' which it is supposed to have replaced.[29] An instance of the conceptual complexity surrounding postmodernism and the assigning of literary value can be seen in the way in which Ôe Kenzaburô praised *Nejimakidori* when presenting Murakami with the prestigious Yomiuri Literary Prize in 1996,[30] even though he had been quite critical of his earlier writing. Presumably, Ôe sensed that *Nejimakidori* proposes news way of reading which, even more than a decade later, have not yet been fully comprehended or exhaustively discussed. When Baudrillard outrageously proposed that 'the Gulf-War did not take place',[31] he was doing something both dangerous and exciting—and although exposing himself to ridicule, he opened up debate about the epistemological status of the fetishized object of historiography, proposing that in the age of the hegemony of the tele-visual sound/image, the event-referent might need to be recast in different terms. Similarly, when the text of *Nejimakidori* relates the tale of a Japanese massacre of Chinese civilians, the skinning alive of Japanese prisoners by Russians, and the routing of the Japanese army at Nomonhan, it is drawing direct attention to the possibility of a certain kind of writing and re-writing of history—*not necessarily to the 'events' themselves.* This, too, is both dangerous and exciting, yet remains to be more fully debated in forums which declare the methodological and ideological assumptions informing their approaches to the narrating of modern Japanese history.

The following discussion will proceed by way of reference to several key narrative strands of the novel. The analysis of these strands assumes the validity of our first two propositions about history as a simulacral/phantasmal 'meaning-effect' that is arrayed in the aporia between memory, thought, speech and writing, as well as the fact that it arises discursively via the tropic tendencies of metaphor, metonymy, synecdoche and irony as proposed by White. Such assumptions support our central proposition that the overall work ideology of *Nejimakidori* is to affirm the 'historicity' of all discursive forms (history as 'narrative fiction' and 'fictional narrative'), including the genre known as the 'contemporary Japanese novel' as outlined in Chapter 2.

The Auditory over the Visual

「台所でスパゲッティーをゆでているときに、電話がかかってきた。僕はFM放送にあわせてロッシーニの『泥棒かささぎ』の序曲を口笛で吹いていた。それはスパゲッティーをゆでるにはまずうってつけの音楽だった。」 [32]

When the phone rang I was in the kitchen, boiling a pot full of spaghetti and whistling along with an FM broadcast of the overture to Rossini's 'The Thieving Magpie', which has to be the perfect music for cooking pasta.[33]

The opening passage of *Nejimakidori*, with its cacophony of sound-images—boiling water, whistling, ringing telephone, and radio broadcast—sets a remarkably 'auditory' mood for the presented world of the novel. It also helps establish the physicality, the marked corporeality of many of the protagonist's narrated experiences. In a general essay on Murakami's literary style, Koizumi Kôichirô has proposed that through the invocation of a strong sense of corporeality suggested by the emphasis of the sensory, through this foregrounding of 'the flesh' (*nikutai*), bridges are built between society (*shakai*) and history (*rekishi*), consciousness (*ishiki*) and collective consciousness (*shûgô ishiki*).[34] This purported correspondence reminds us of the relations between 'individual' and 'collective' memory, 'history' and 'historicity' as outlined in the above discussion on the competing methods of historiography. Perhaps more importantly, it offers a description of the literary dimension of what Ruthrof has argued is a fundamental feature of natural language: it establishes corporeality and the body as the primary integrative/referential ground for all human semiosis.[35]

In *Nejimakidori*, there is no doubt that the focus on the auditory sense broadens the range of interpretive possibilities of the work as fictional art. For Koizumi, this 'auditory style' (*chôkaku no buntai*) signals Murakami's originality in a significant way because, as he claims, it challenges the hegemony of the visual in contemporary Japanese culture. The central trope of the mysterious, screeching cry of the unseen 'wind-up' bird which marks out 'individual' and 'historical' time and is often heard by characters in the in-between state of dreaming and waking, consciousness and unconsciousness, is one of the most obvious examples here,[36] but there are various episodes throughout the novel in which specifically auditory hallucinations and images figure.[37]

The significance of the foregrounding of the auditory image has significance in broad social terms, as well as at the psychoanalytic level of individual consciousness and subjectivity. In terms of the social dimension, Koizumi suggests that in *Nejimakidori* Murakami is conducting an original and sustained critique of the hegemony of the visual in contemporary Japanese culture. The primacy of the visual, the scopic, the specular, is denied by the presented spatio-temporal matrix of *Nejimakidori*, which as Koizumi argues, is stridently 'anti-mass media', 'anti-televisual' — in short, anti-visual (*han shikakubunka*).[38]

But this is not because the visual image *itself* is repressed (*yokusei sareru*) or denied (*massatsu sareru*). Obviously the numerous retold narrative episodes (for example, Lieutenant Mamiya's, Nutmeg's) and Boku's dreamscapes are strongly visual. However, the narrative dimensions of 'phenomenon as phenomenon' (*jishô wa jishô toshite*) and 'visual sense as visual sense' (*shikaku wa shikaku toshite*) are not, according to Koizumi, in themselves conferred with fragmented meanings. Rather, there is a generalized 'imagization' (*imêjika*) of the symbolic spaces of the novel: in the calm spaces on the other side of Boku's back-lane,[39] the silent stone bird statue, the dried up well, and the detailed depiction of the physical appearance of various characters. In these senses, the novel is visual. Ultimately, however, for the reader living in the maelstrom (*kachû*) of visual culture, the visual image is *reversed*, and a strong sense of the *rejection* of the visual is said to permeate the novel.[40]

For Koizumi, a massive disjunction has arisen between the pervasive contemporary myth of being able to 'see all' (*subete o miru*) and the realization that our existence is marked by the cynicism and despair of knowing that we cannot actually do this. On the contrary, the primacy of the visual is actually disempowering because it dismantles (*kaitai suru*) meaning, fragments and scatters it: looking (*miru to wa*), is not an act of establishing harmony with another person — rather, it is a violation (*okasu*).[41] This critique of the visual exposes the myth of Japan as the 'information society' (*jôhô shakai*) which emerged in the eighties, and is clearly connoted in the figure of the thirty-year-old unemployed Boku whose life is effectively in moratorium mode — he neither watches television nor reads newspapers[42]—and is connected to the outside world only through the *auditory* modality of the telephone.

In stark contrast to this, claims Koizumi, the figure of Wataya Noboru, the consummate political performer and 'television man', violates Kanô Kureta through an 'act of seeing'—and this is part of a larger, generalized violence of the visual that permeates and controls every corner of contemporary daily Japanese life. Assuming that one of the key generative principles of modernity is reason, it is worth noting Koizumi's conclusion that because reason (*risei*) is synonymous with the visual sense (*shikaku*), with the ongoing belief in the supremacy of the visual, we ourselves are 'cut up' (*kirikizamu*), dismantled, fragmented and dispersed.[43]

Here, Koizumi is touching upon the dismantling of subjectivity through a challenge to the visual, but he does not further explore the psychoanalytic dimensions of this hunch. Nevertheless, extending this important insight, and taking as our starting point the basic fact of the sign as being comprised of an audio-image (signifier) and a visual-image (signified), we are left to ponder the implications of how the privileging of the auditory over the visual might prescribe the range of subject positions available to the reader of *Nejimakidori*. Put another way, we might ask: how are the primary configurations of subjectivity affected by such a 'splitting' of the inextricably linked components of signification?

Given the many instances in *Nejimakidori* of the characters' experience of alterity, dream states, other-worldliness and self/body alienation, it seems reasonable to think more carefully about the operation of the auditory and the visual in terms of the unconscious. Freud acknowledged that although in dreams we do 'make use of auditory images', in these non-waking states 'we think predominantly in visual images'.[44] So there is, in terms of the Freudian system, a clear distinction between the visual and audio in relation to the unconscious. However, in the light of Freud's assertion that 'dreams *hallucinate* . . . they replace thoughts with hallucinations', and of the subsequent implication that 'there is no distinction between visual and acoustic representations', we feel something of a contradiction:

> It has been observed that if one falls asleep with the memory of a series of musical notes in one's mind, the memory becomes transformed into an hallucination of the same memory.[45]

In his later work, *The Ego and the Id* (1923), Freud expands his earlier binary model of the subject comprising the unconscious and the preconscious/conscious, and analyses the specific functions of the auditory and visual senses in terms of the tripartite topographical scheme of id, ego and super ego—offering a diagrammatic representation of this which is relevant to our argument:

> Perhaps . . . the ego wears a 'cap of hearing'—on one side only, as we learn from cerebral anatomy. It might be said to wear it awry.[46]

This implies that the way in which the auditory sense is at once separated or even 'alienated' from the generalized structure of the ego (plus its mediating role in between the preconscious and the repressed), and the striking suggestion that perhaps the ego wears the cap of hearing 'awry', gives us a clue to the idea that a privileging of the auditory sense may *destabilize* the subjective configuration of the Oedipal triangulation, which, as proposed by Lacan, is founded on the primacy of the visual sense as the key dimension of the symbolic order.[47] The possibility of this subversion reflects the fragile nature of an already fractured subject, described by Silverman in the following way:

> The Freudian subject is above all a partitioned subject, incapable of exhaustive self-knowledge. Its parts do not exist harmoniously; they speak different languages and operate on the basis of conflicting imperatives.[48]

This partitioning and alienation extends to the subject's relation between the real and the social, and the visual image or the gaze is crucial to this relation. As Lemaire puts it, in the Lacanian scheme,

> Caught up in the symbolic, where he is simply represented, obliged to translate himself through the intermediary of a discourse of the symbolic, the subject will become lost, lured away from himself, *and will shape himself in accordance with the other's look.* [my emphasis][49]

Lacan likens this experience of the 'loss' of the subject to itself, to a kind of objectification: 'I identify myself in Language, but only by losing myself in it like an object.'[50]

Returning to the function of the auditory in the unconscious, it is noteworthy that in his discussion of memory traces and word-presentations, Freud notes that 'verbal residues are derived primarily from auditory perceptions' and concludes that 'in essence a word is after all a mnemic residue of a word that has been heard.'[51] We note that this corresponds to Saussure's assertion of the primacy of the phonemic unit of linguistic difference over the graphic.[52] We are also aware of the Derridean critique of this scheme as arising from the Platonic privileging of speech over writing and the necessary implication of a unified subject as presence; however, we need to consider how these claims are interpreted and developed by the approaches of Lacan and Kristeva.

In particular, we will demonstrate that it is the approach of Julia Kristeva in her analysis of the abject, which shows that through a process of 'dissociation' of the auditory from the visual, there is a threat to subjectivity in the form of a dissolution of the Oedipal configuration. If the phallic system of the-law-of-the-father, culture and reason is primarily the province of the hegemonic gaze (which is both the originator and maintainer of prescribed subject positions), the auditory always implicitly threatens to overrun the subject and confront it with the possibility of its own abjection. Freud argues that the 'demolition of the Oedipus complex' is a natural process of the subject's development,[53] and the implication of this for the Lacanian scheme is that the various players assume their roles in the social/symbolic order.

From this it can be surmised that if we could identify a strong opposition between the audio and the visual as dominant narrative tropes or modalities in *Nejimakidori*, we could extrapolate from the reading of that text an implied threat to the Lacanian symbolic order, which suggests a movement back to the pre-symbolic stage of the imaginary and the undifferentiated self-perception of the subject, in a way not dissimilar to—and even indicative of—the moment of the subject *just prior to* abjection. It will be argued later that this is perhaps one of the effects of the privileging of the auditory: to indicate a potential dissolution of the presented Oedipal configuration in *Nejimakidori*, constructed around the figure of Wataya Noboru.

Because one of our most common contemporary experiences of the visual is in film viewing, the obvious question of the relation of the 'literary' to the 'cinematic' representation of audio images arises. Building on Lacan's theory of lack, Silverman has argued that speech as sound in cinema produces absence rather than presence, and this means, therefore, that 'the discoursing voice is the agent of symbolic castration'.[54] Not satisfied with the equation of sound with speech, Shaviro has argued against this, suggesting that in the cinematic apparatus all sounds are freed from their discursive contexts and occur as events of 'visceral immediacy':

> The indiscernibility of initial and reproduced sounds points to (a) simulacral logic . . . it becomes impossible to identify definitively either the original or the copies.[55]

That is to say, claims Shaviro, 'their [the sounds'] *reproduction* cannot be equated with or reduced to their *representation*.'[56] Rather, they form part of a continuous and heterogeneous semiosis which does not conform to the classic structuralist opposition of *langue* and *parole*.[57] This is a complex debate which is really beyond the parameters of our present discussion, yet it will suffice for us to be aware that the privileging of the modality of the auditory in *Nejimakidori* indicates a further aspect of the multi-dimensional aesthetic of the sublime, and has implications for the kinds of subject positions recuperable from/in our reading of this text.

In conclusion, it is worth noting that in his essay *Freud and the Scene of Writing*, Derrida has described the Freudian project of understanding the unconscious and dreams as a kind of writing, as subversive of the phono-centric foundation of subjectivity-as-presence. The extent to which this describes a universal process applicable in even non-Western cultural contexts is a moot point, but we note that Derrida does gesture in this direction:

> Logo-phonocentrism is not a philosophical or historical error which the history of philosophy, of the West, that is, of the world, would have rushed into . . . but is rather a necessary, and necessarily finite movement and structure: the history of the possibility of symbolism in general.[58]

If the privileging of the auditory sense signals an undermining of the writerly/graphic nature of the dream contents and the unconscious in *Nejimak-dori,* this indicates a general possibility in the case of all natural human languages, and such subversion would apply equally in the case of artistic discourses generated in a Japanese context. In particular, if we assume that the broad social critique offered by *Nejimakidori* is implicitly also a critique of the undeveloped subject of modernity in its myriad discursive forms, then the refusal to privilege the visual in this novel (and by implication deny the hegemony of the symbolic order *writ large* in the various discourses of post-war Japan), is effectively a challenge to think Japanese modernity outside the dominant literary/cinematic conventions of representation—based on the undisputed primacy of the visual and the spectacle—which have come to prevail in the contemporary cultural setting.

Notes

1. White's 'tropics' of discourse are detailed later in this chapter.

2. See Sakamoto Rumi, "Dream of a Modern Subject: Maruyama Masao, Fukuzawa Yukichi, and 'Asia' as the Limit of Ideology Critique," *Japanese Studies*, 21, no. 2 (2001): 137-53; 138.

3. Sakamoto, "Dream of a Modern Subject," 137.

4. Sakamoto, "Dream of a Modern Subject," 138.

5. See Susan Napier, "Ôe Kenzaburô and the Search for the Sublime at the End of the Twentieth Century," in *Oe and Beyond: Fiction in Contemporary Japan,* ed. S. Snyder & P. Gabriel (Honolulu: University of Hawaii Press), 1999.

6. See Jean-Francois Lyotard, "Answering the Question: What is Postmodernism?," in *The Postmodern Condition: A Report on Knowledge,* trans. Geoff Bennington & Brian Massumi (Manchester University Press, 1991), 81.

7. See Jean-Francois Lyotard, *The Differend: Phrases in Dispute,* trans. Geoffrey Bennington and Brian Massumi, (Manchester: Manchester University Press, 1988).

8. See Jean-Francois Lyotard, *Lessons on the Analytic of the Sublime,* trans. Elizabeth Rottenberg (Stanford: Stanford University Press, 1994).

9. Lyotard, "Answering the Question: What is Postmodernism?," 81.

10. Lyotard, "Answering the Question: What is Postmodernism?," 81.

11. For example, consider Meagan Morris' critique of Lyotard's hypothesis that postmodernism is modernism not at its end—but at its very beginning, and this beginning is always recurrent. Morris characterizes this as 'quite banal, because it restores us to the paradox of a history driven by the *sole* and traditional imperative to break with tradition'. Cited in John Frow, *Time and Commodity Culture,* 54.

12. Lyotard, "Answering the Question: What is Postmodernism?," 81.

13. Quoted from Ian Buruma, *The Wages of Guilt: Memories of War in Germany and Japan* (New York: Meridian, 1994), 199.

14. NDK: 1 ; 12; 258, and WBC: 1; 12; 143.

15. Barbara Foley, *Telling the Truth: The Theory & Practice of Documentary Fiction* (Ithica & London: Cornell University Press, 1986), 29.

16. Robert Young, *White Mythologies: Writing History and the West* (London & New York: Routledge, 1995), 82. The 'phantasm' that Young is referring to is the Plato's 'bad copy'—*phantasma*— (of the 'good copy') which Deleuze actually validates, and a process which, as Young notes, 'breaks down all adequation between copy and model, appearance and essence, event and Idea'. Deleuze's theory of the simulacrum was discussed in detail in Chapter 3.

17. See Alan Munslow *Deconstructing History* (London & New York: Routledge, 1997).

18. The major proponents of these are Foucault, Deleuze, Derrida and Lyotard, and the texts where these are explored are *Archeology of Knowledge, Language, Counter-Memory, Practice, Difference and Repetition.*

19. Derrida writes: 'Perhaps one would have to show . . . that history is impossible, meaningless, in the finite totality, and that it is impossible, meaningless, in the positive and actual infinity; that history keeps to the difference between totality and infinity, and that history precisely is that which Levinas calls transcendence and eschatology'. See Derrida "Violence and Metaphysics: An Essay on the Thought of Emmanuel Levinas," in *Writing and Difference* trans. Alan Bass (London: Routledge and Kegan Paul, 1981), 123.

20. Deleuze, *The Logic of Sense.*

21. Lyotard, *The Differend: Phrases in Dispute.*

22. See Robert Young, *White Mythologies: Writing History and the West*, London: Routledge, 1990, 84.

23. This is not to say that 'history' has been entirely absent—but has appeared only in the marginalized discourses of resistance such as the postwar labour and socialist movement, Zenkyôtô, Red Army, the parliamentary presence of the Communist Party, and the textbook reform movements. Although, in recent years, there is evidence that incipient resistance at many levels is starting to appear over issues such as environmental concerns, justice for the so-called 'comfort-woman', and so on.

24. Buruma, *The Wages of Guilt,* 189-201.

25. H. Harootunian "From Principle to Principal: Restoration and Emperorship in Japan" in *The Uses of History; Essays in Intellectual and Social History*, ed. Hayden White (Detroit: Wayne State University Press, 1968), 221-245; 221.

26. Young, *White Mythologies,* 81.

27. Not only at the level of the syntagm and sentence, but also by way of reference to the macro-narrative features which relate metaphorically to the digital/binary modalities of computer re-presentation of knowledge and information. See Ruthrof's 'Narrative and the Digital'.

28. White proposes the four tropes of historical discourse as discursive transformations moving from metaphoric to metonymic and synechdocic representations, and finally, to the trope of irony. See "Introduction" in Hayden White, *Tropics of Discourse: Essays in Cultural Criticism* (Baltimore: John Hopkins University Press, 1978), 1-25.

29. Frow, "What was Postmodernism?," 54-55.

30. Rubin, "Murakami Haruki," 239.

31. See Jean Baudrillard, *The Gulf War Did Not Take Place,* trans. Paul Patton (Bloomington & Indianapolis: Indiana University Press, 1995).

32. NDK:1; 1; 7.

33. WBC:1; 1; 5.

34. See Koizumi Kôichirô, "Murakami Haruki no sutairu—'Nejimakidori kuronikuru' o chûshin ni," *Kokubungaku* 40, no. 4 (March 1995): 27-31; 29.

35. See Horst Ruthrof, *The Body in Language* (London & New York: Cassell, 2000), 1. Ruthrof argues, as part of his central claim, that 'when a meaning event occurs, the body enters language in the form of quasi-perceptual readings of the world'.

36. The cry of the wind-up bird first appears early in Chapter 1: 'Every day it would come to the stand of trees in our neighbourhood and wind the spring of our quiet little world.' See WBC: 1; 1; 9 and NDK: 1;1;14.

37. The most striking example of an auditory hallucination occurs in the form of the premonition which Boku has while swimming at the end of Book II. Boku pricks up his ears in order to hear 'words which were not quite words', a calling and beckoning voice, reverberating with the sound of water, piped music and the laughter of other swimmers. See NDK: 2; 18; 355-6. The young boy, Cinnamon's awakening to hear in the middle of the night the cry of the wind-up bird. See NDK: 3; 5; 46. WBC: 3; 3; 362. During the 'Zoo Massacre', the young soldier hears the cry of the unknown bird, the day before he will meet probable death at the hands of the Soviet troops. See WBC 3: 9; 407.

38. Koizumi, "Murakami Haruki no sutairu," 30.

39. Urazami cites the conversation between Murakami and Nakagami Kenji in which the 'Asian-style' lane (*roji*) of Nakagami's poor childhood is contrasted with the lanes of the Hanshin area of Murakami's childhood. The latter are layered with pre and post-Meiji, Japanese and Western artifacts and atmosphere. Urazami characterizes Nakagami's *roji* as signifying 'other worlds', but Murakami's as 'in-between' or transitional spaces. See Urazumi Akira, *Murakami Haruki o aruku* (Sairyûsha, 2000, 106-7).

40. Koizumi, "Murakami Haruki no sutairu," 31.

41. Koizumi, "Murakami Haruki no sutairu," 30.

42. Koizumi, "Murakami Haruki no sutairu," 30. Towards the end of the narrative, Boku recommences reading newspapers 'in order to begin getting in touch with the reality of the outside world'. See WBC 3: 23; 497 and NDK 3: 24; 266.

43. Koizumi, "Murakami Haruki no sutairu," 30.

44. See Sigmund Freud, "The Distinguishing Psychological Characteristics of Dreams," in *The Interpretation of Dreams*, trans. James Strachey (Harmondsworth: Penguin, 1982), 112.

45. Freud, "The Distinguishing Psychological Characteristics of Dreams," 112.

46. Sigmund Freud, *The Ego and the Id*, trans. Joan Riviere (London: The Hogarth Press, 1962), 15.

47. Lacan's idea of the 'mirror stage' and the child's subsequent entry in to the symbolic are the key theoretical premises of his writings, and they describe processes of *visual* identification and alienation. Lacan writes: 'The mirror stage is interesting in that it manifests the affective dynamism by which the subject originally identifies himself with the visual *Gestalt* of his own body . . . it represents an ideal unity, a salutory *imago*'. See Jacques Lacan "The Mirror Stage as Formative of the Function of the I as Revealed in Psychoanalytic Experience," cited in Anika Lemaire, *Jacques Lacan,* trans. David Macet (London: Routledge & Kegan Paul, 1997), 80. Furthermore, the subsequent entry into the symbolic order of language and the Oedipal configuration of identifications is also regulated by visual modalities of identification and alienation from the subject's 'self' and other(s).

48. Kaja Silverman "The Subject" in *The Subject of Semiotics* (New York: Oxford University Press, 1983), 132.

49. See "The Oedipal Phenomenon," in Anika Lemaire, *Jacques Lacan,* trans. David Macey (London: Routledge & Kegan Paul, 1981), 178.

50. Jacques Lacan, *The Language of the Self: The Function of Language in Psychoanalysis*, trans. Anthony Wilden (New York: Dell Publishing Co., 1968), 63.

51. Freud, *The Ego and the Id*, 9-10.

52. See Ferdinand de Saussure, *Course in General Linguistics*, trans. Wade Baskin (London: Fontana, 1974).

53. Freud, *The Ego & the Id*, 22.

54. Kaja Silverman, *The Acoustic Mirror; The Female Voice in Psychoanalysis and Cinema* (Bloomington: Indiana University Press, 1988), 43.

55. Steven Shaviro, "Film Theory and Visual Fascination," in *The Cinematic Body* (Minneapolis: University of Minnesota Press, 1993), 34.

56. Shaviro, "Film Theory and Visual Fascination," 35.

57. Shaviro, "Film Theory and Visual Fascination," 34.

58. See Jacques Derrida, "Freud and the Scene of Writing," in *Writing and Difference*, trans. Alan Bass (London: Routledge & Kegan Paul, 1981), 197.

Chapter Ten

Nejimakidori kuronikuru—The Wind-Up Bird Chronicle: The Stories

Not Being Kumiko: The Displaced Subject

The opening chapter of *Nejimakidori* is important not only because it establishes the primacy of the auditory sense in the novel. It is also the first episode in the central, integrative narrative line of the protagonist's quest for re-unification with his missing wife, Kumiko. Despite the fact that her disappearance is not revealed until the opening sentence of Book Two,[1] the estrangement between Boku and Kumiko is evident from the outset. Significantly, the mission for Kumiko's retrieval and return to the family home is homologous with another quest for the unattainable object of a more amorphous desire. That is, the sexual yearning of the imagined male subject is displaced to a hankering for subjective unity at the level of the historical subject's encounter with itself.

Several of the more prominent critics of the novel have preferred to focus on describing thematic aspects of the representation of male/female relations in the text. Jay Rubin (who has provided the excellent English translation of *Nejimaki-dori*) identifies the essence of the central narrative as a story about a sexually suppressed wife who leaves her husband for a lover, with the husband left floundering in a state of fear and confusion as to how to accomplish her return.[2] In a later discussion, he does, however, hint at a larger project for the protagonist: 'his search for her is more a search inside himself for the meaning of his marriage to her and the meaning of his life as a product of Japan's modern history'.[3] From another perspective, Strecher suggests that although the 'quest of the novel is the retrieval of Kumiko and the restoration of [Boku's] relationship with her', there is also the related theme of a nexus between the 'bodies of women' and the removal of their 'core identities'.[4]

Japanese critic Ishikura notes that there are numerous novels which deal with the misunderstandings (*kuichigai*) of couples in a 'minimalist' way, and as society has become more complex, the focus of contemporary fiction has tended to move from a macro to a micro level—and subsequently, the larger 'world-image' (*sekaizō*) has been lost. In *Nejimakidori*, however, Ishikura suggests that

Murakami offers both a view of human relations (especially of 'couples'—*fūfu*) *and* a 'new world-image' (*aratana sekaizō*).[5] Elsewhere, she characterizes the presented parallel structures of male/female relations in the novel in terms of a kind of pathological mix of pain (*kurō*), pleasure (*kairaku*) and release (*kaihō*).[6]

This approach approximates a kind of psychoanalytic explication of Kumiko's story as, fundamentally, an extended exploration of the male subject's projection of woman-as-other. Evidence of Boku's sex with this 'woman' who is both Kumiko and *not* Kumiko (but always the universalized, feminized object of his fantasy) runs throughout the text. And it is also clear that Boku's 'quest' is a displaced search for an *unattainable* other: the ostensible object of his emotional cathexis is constantly shifting (Kumiko, Kanō Kureta, Kasahara Mei, Kumiko) and he can only simulate union with a woman who is always the 'temporary substitute', an amorphous space in which his momentary transcendence is ensured, yet in which even his usually guaranteed ejaculation is delayed—or potentially denied:

> 「最初にクミコの中に入ったとき……そこには何か、奇妙に覚めたものがあった……そこには一種のかいりの感覚があった。自分が抱いているこの体はさっきまで隣に並んで親しく話していた女の体とはべつのものなんじゃないか、自分の気づかないうちにどこかでべつの誰かの肉体と入れ代わってしまったんじゃないかという不思議な思いに僕は捉われた。そして今僕が抱いているのは、一時的にここにあるかりそめの肉体であるようにさえ思えた。あるいはそのせいかもしれないけれど、性的に興奮していたにもかかわらず、射精をするまでにけっこう時間がかかった。」[7]

> The first time I went inside Kumiko . . . There was something oddly lucid there, a sense of separation . . . I was seized by the bizarre thought that the body I was holding in my arms was not the body of the woman I had had next to me until a few minutes earlier . . . a switch had been pulled without my noticing, and someone else's flesh had taken its place. . . . The body I was holding was nothing but a temporary substitute. This might have been the reason why, although I was fully aroused, it took me a very long time to come.[8]

Later, (and once again with the auditory image privileged over the visual) Boku fantasizes about Kumiko's sexual encounter with her unnamed secret lover, and in the same passage of text, moves to the FM Classical music station; in the dead of night he listens to Tchaikovsky's *Serenade for Strings*, and while enjoying 'the seventh of Schumann's *Forest Scenes*' ('Bird as Prophet') his imagination wanders:

> 「僕はクミコがその男の体の下で腰をくねらせたり、相手の背中に爪を立てたり、シーツの上によだれを垂らしたりしていたところを想像した。」[9]

I imagined Kumiko twisting her hips beneath the other man, raising her legs, planting her fingernails on his back, drooling on the sheets.[10]

This is followed, once again, by the ubiquitous telephone call ('The sound shot me out of the sofa'[11]) from Kanô Kureta, and the imagined object of Boku's generalized desire is once again transferred to the 'other woman' as the site of alterity.

Later, we will show how this act of semiotic 'dissociation'—this splitting off of the auditory image from the visual image—indicates (according to Kristeva's approach) a rupture in the Oedipal triangulation, and in *Nejmakidori* we see this rupture reach its apotheosis in the 'murdering' of the possessor of the Name of the Father/Phallus, Wataya Noboru. If there is a certain 'blindness' given over to a privileging of the auditory over the visual (recall the contrast between what marks the difference between the two Japanese soldiers who are skinned alive: one screams, the other remains completely silent—and a far greater sense of horror emanates from the latter), then in the semiotic interstices of the 'silent scream' lies the horror of the threat of abjection, since no voice marks out the possibility of a subject brought to presence.

It is clear from various examples that the masculinized reading positions prescribed by the figure of Boku-as-narrator indicated early in the text, revolve around the tropes of 'fantasy' and 'constraint'. Boku's first two conversations in the opening chapter are sexually charged dialogues with women previously unknown to him. When the telephone rings a second time he is drawn into a simulated 'telephone sex' dialogue, an encounter which feels tantalizingly 'real':

「声の調子から、彼女が嘘をついていないことはわかった。彼女は本当
に両脚を十時五分の角度に開き、性器をあたたかく湿らせているのだ。
『唇を撫でて。ゆっくりとよ。そして開くの。ゆっくりとね。指の腹で
ゆっくりと撫でるの……。』」[12]

I could tell from her voice that she was not faking it. She really did have her legs open to ten-oh five, her sex warm and moist.
'Touch the lips,' she said. 'Sloowly. Now open them. That's it. Slowly slowly. Let your fingers caress them.'[13]

Soon afterwards, meeting Mei Kasahara, (the Lolita-like figure who later writes him a string of unanswered letters) this originally 'auditory' image is repeated, and mingled with a visual form:

「十五か十六というところだろう。わずかにめくれあがった上唇が不思
議な角度宙につきだしていた。『撫でて』、という声が聞こえたような
気がした。それはあの電話の女の声だった。僕は手の甲で額の汗を拭っ
た。」[14]

She couldn't have been more than fifteen or sixteen. With its slight curl, her upper lip pointed up at a strange angle. I seemed to hear a voice saying 'Touch me'—the voice of the woman on the phone. I wiped the sweat from my forehead with the bank of my hand.[15]

In the second chapter, after a trivial argument with his wife Kumiko, he lays awake next to her sleeping figure in the dark, and casts her existence in terms of vast, dark and unknowable domain:

「何かもっと大きな、致命的なものごとの始まりに過ぎないかもしれないのだ。それはただの入り口なのかもしれない。そしてその奥には、僕のまだ知らないクミコだけの世界が広がっているのかもしれない。それは僕に真っ暗な巨大な部屋を想像させた。」[16]

I might be standing in the entrance of something big, and inside lay a world that belonged to Kumiko alone, a vast world that I had never known. I saw it as a big, dark room.[17]

In the kind of Feminist approach to narrative suggested by Gabriel Schwab, we note that in this passage woman is positioned as being both 'inside' the narrative (through grammatical association) and 'outside' the narrative (through gender affiliation). In this kind of text, the woman is cast as absolute Other, a stranger, an object, 'a dark shape on the bed'.[18] As we have shown above, the image of woman as unspecified, universalized quasi-subject, emerges after Boku's first two conversations with women. Firstly, with the telephone-sex girl, there unfolds an 'unconstrained relation' of fantasy. The second, with his wife Kumiko, is clearly of a constrained nature and synonymous with the socially sanctioned role of 'the wife'. Although both the implied exemplars of the 'unconstrained' and 'constrained' turn out to be the same woman, the reader may not become aware of this until much later in the narrative.

It is clear that this text (along with others of the Murakami oeuvre) lends itself strongly to a feminist critique, but we need to show what the implications of such a critique might be in regard to our claims, in this chapter, regarding the sublime. Although Boku's relations with the 'virtual' and 'real' women are being continuously displaced and transformed, a key point seems to be the notion of 'universal woman', a hint of which emerges from the following statement, once again, very early in the narrative:

「世界中の女が僕をびっくりさせるために電話をかけてきているみたいだ。」[19]

Had the women of the world chosen today to surprise me on the telephone? [20]

This idea of a ubiquitous, universalized woman compares very interestingly with a passage from Marguerite Duras' *The Malady of Death,* cited by Schwab in her work on otherness in literary language:

> You wouldn't have known her, you'd have seen her everywhere at once, in a hotel, in a street, in a train, in a bar, in a book, in a film, in yourself, your inmost self, when your sex grew erect in the night, seeking somewhere to put itself, somewhere to shed its load of tears.[21]

Although the text is scripted by a woman, Schwab's response to this could have been written for precisely the opening scene of *Nejimakidori,* as an invitation for the male reader to partake in a fantasy:

> Mediated by an abstract narrative voice—a fantasy about a man 's intimate encounter with a woman who is 'everywhere at once', every-woman, anonymous, yet pertaining to everyman's 'inmost self.'[22]

As we have shown in some selected examples, evidence of Boku's sex with this woman who is both Kumiko *and* not Kumiko (universal feminized object) runs throughout the text. From the beginning of the narrative, the scene is set for the projected desires of the male protagonist only ever occurring in the liminal/virtual/ phantasmic sites of telephone, dream-work or 'e-mail' message.

There is no doubt that the transference of Boku's desire from woman to woman, specified through the proper nouns 'Kumiko' and 'Kanô Kureta' is mediated by the general category/signifier 'Woman', and the impossibility of engaging with a present, 'real' and 'non-virtual' woman emerges from a matrix of unspecifiable intentionality and orientation, mingling both Oedipal and sublime dimensions of desire: simultaneously shoring up and breaking down the boundaries of subjectivity, in a way which forestalls abjection by the incessantly ambiguous and contradictory process of marking out presence/over-running the subject, performed in the periodic acts of ejaculation in the novel.[23]

In a fascinating twist, it is the elusive 'object' of Boku's erotic dreams, Kanô Kureta, who actually reveals to Boku, by recounting precisely the contents of his dreams, the nature of his deferred and displaced subjectivity as desire. Not only does Kanô Kureta often appear wearing the clothes of his missing wife, she reveals to him her clairvoyant knowledge that as an object of fantasy, her identity often alternates with that of 'another woman' who remains unknown to her:

> 「二度目に岡田様の夢に現れたときに、私は岡田様と交わっている途中で知らない女性と交代いたしました……。その女性が誰であったのか、私にはわかりません。でもその出来事は岡田様に何かを示唆しているはずです。」[24]

In your second dream, when I was in the midst of having relations with you, another woman took my place . . . I have no idea who she was. . . . But that event was probably meant to suggest something to you.[25]

Yet, the more profound revelation comes in the form of Kanô Kureta's lucid explanation of the closed circularity of Boku's own economy of desire:

「もちろん私たちは現実に交わっているわけではありません。岡田様が
射精なさるとき、それは私の体内にではなく、岡田様自身の意識の中に
射精なさるわけです。おわかりですか？それは作り上げられた意識なの
です。」[26]

Of course, we did not have relations in reality. When you ejaculated, it was not into me, physically, but in your own consciousness. Do you see? It was a fabricated consciousness.[27]

Boku is very often confronting boundaries, and engaging with limits: the boundaries of subjectivity, the boundaries of the body, the boundaries of social constraint and censure, the boundaries of sexual engagement (marital/extra-marital/dream-state). But the attempts at shoring up boundaries around corporeality and subjectivity are always tentative, and need to be continually renewed. At the bottom of the well 'with its moldy smell and its trace of dampness', he undertakes a strangely contradictory musing (utilizing woman as metaphor) on the tension between maintaining a discernable self and loss-of-self, the slide into an amorphous, undifferentiated state of non-being:

「僕は暗闇の中でそれらの物体が自分の身体にぴったりと密着している
ことを確認する。僕が自分から離れていないことを確認する。」[28]

I check to see in the darkness that these objects are in firm contact with myself. I check to see that I am not separated from myself.[29]

and only a few lines later,

「僕はまじり合っていく違った種類の暗闇の中で……。僕は『彼女た
ち』を相手にしてるときと同じように、自分から離れようとする。暗闇
の中にうずくまっている不器用な僕の肉体から逃れ出ようとする。僕は
今ではひとつの空き家に過ぎず、捨てられた井戸に過ぎないのだ。」[30]

In the two increasingly intermingled darknesses . . . I try to separate from myself, just as I do whenever I am with the women. I try to get out of this clumsy flesh of mine, which is crouching down here in the dark. Now I am nothing but a vacant house, an abandoned well.[31]

This ambiguous process of Boku's confirmation that he is *not* separated from himself—and yet wants to separate himself—is significant in two ways. Firstly, the attempted shoring up of his sense of a discrete, subjective cohesion is mediated by reference to his differentiation to woman as other, the *plural* form 'the women' (given in Japanese as *kanojotachi*): all women certainly—yet, also specifically, Kumiko, Kanô Kureta and the 'telephone-sex' girl who are, as we have shown above, the inter-changeable objects of an incessantly displaced desire.

Secondly, what is also interesting about this rejection of corporeality, the revulsion towards the body ('this clumsy flesh of mine'), and the figure of 'a vacant house', (an 'abandoned well') as signifying absence and an abject *lack* of subjectivity, is its equivalence with the lack of specific subjectivity of 'the women' indicated by the generalized signifier 'woman'. Boku's justification for going down into the well is to find access to the 'non-real', virtual space into which Kumiko has disappeared, but the price which must be paid is a surrendering of his sense of self: subjectivity here is at best confused, and in an extreme sense, under suspension.

In Boku's allegorical quest for Kumiko, the key metaphoric devices are 'the wall' (*kabe*) and the well (*ido*). In terms of the Freudian tripartite structure of Super-ego, Ego and Id, the well clearly signifies the Id, as the seat of dark passions, the death instinct and so on. The well is the position from which Boku launches himself into sex as well as unbridled acts of violence—attacking the guitar player and Wataya Noboru. In the Lacanian scheme, the Id is closer to the Imaginary, the pre-linguistic state of undifferentiated being in which the subject is yet to identify its separateness prior to entry into the order of the Symbolic, language and the Oedipal configuration.

As possibly the only attempt to offer, in Japanese, a sophisticated and extended critique of Murakami's fiction in terms of the psychoanalytic perspectives of Freud and Lacan, Kobayashi Masaaki's approach has recognized, in the central quest of *Nejimakidori* (the attempt to retrieve Kumiko) the crucial link between the tropes of the wall, the well and the question of the subject, language and the Symbolic. Kobayashi notes Lacan's claim that the relationality (*kankeisei*) of the small 'o' 'other', and the imaginary 'self'—that is, of the 'immature other' (*mijuku na tasha*) and the 'immature self' (*mijuku na jiga*)—is a fiction. The cause of the misunderstanding which supports the axis (*jiku*) of such a fiction, is the modification of 'empty or hollow language' (*kûkyo na kotoba*) into a 'wall of language' (*rangêji no kabe*).[32]

For the psychological subject (*shinteki na shutai*), the Other (*daimonji no tasha*) which is comprised of the objects of the real, is obstructed by this wall of language—and this difficult to attain phase is isolated/segregated (*kakuri sarete iru*). It is noted that Lacan implies that in order to break through (*tsukiyaburu*) this barrier, the psychological subject continually seeks to replenish and give substance to language *through* dialogue (*taiwa*). For Kobayashi, in Book Three of *Nejimakidori*, such a process is attempted as it traces the possibility of dialogue to the imagined room(s) (*heya*) of Boku's unconscious, and extends to the virtual correspondence (*tsûshin*) with Kumiko.[33] This ostensibly 'disembodied', and dematerialized discourse remains part of a broader ambiguous, problematic and unresolved process for the promised yet continually deferred reunion with Kumiko. Is the wall which Boku passes through in order to enter the disembodied realm synonymous with the 'wall of language'?

Our response to this can only be tentative, nevertheless it is clear that the 'wall of language' which Kobayashi refers to is crucial to this ambiguity—but precisely *because* Boku must give up or lose something in order to pass through it. On this point, Lacan makes two relevant observations on the nexus between language, subjectivity and the body:

> I identify myself in language, but only by losing myself in it, as an object.[34]

and

> The Word is in fact a gift of Language, and language is not immaterial. It is a subtle body, but body it is. Words are trapped in all the corporeal images which captivate the subject.[35]

In support of this, Lacan offers as examples, descriptions which seem highly apposite to Kristeva's later discussion of materials which exceed the boundaries of the body as signifying the threat of abjection: 'the flood of urine of urethral ambition . . . the retained faeces of avaricious *jouisannce*'.[36] To this, we might add the ejaculatory excesses of Boku's 'wet dreams', and the free-flowing blood of the acts of violence occurring on the other side of the wall—and the other side of time, history and memory.

Returning to our central proposition in this section, we can conclude that indeed Kumiko does not have a story—or, for that matter, subjectivity of her own. The story is Boku's; it 'stands in' for Kumiko's, and the latter is merely one aspect of the presented process of the protagonist's continually displaced libidinal desires, oriented toward the imagined object of woman-as-other. In so far as this narrative thread is no less than a story about Boku's desire, it is also a story about woman as elusive, phantasmal, without subjectivity—the cliched 'universal' woman defined through the imagined, displaced figure of Kumiko, whose disembodiment sees her recede into the virtual space of a series of digitally stored speech acts presented via the aesthetic modality of an illuminated computer monitor:

> 「この画面の向こう側に、東京の地下の暗闇を這う長いケーブルの延長
> 線のどこかに、おそらくクミコがいるのだ。そこで彼女は同じようにモ
> ニターの前に座り、キーボードに両手を置いているはずだ。でも僕がこ
> こで現実に目にできるのは、ちりちりというかすかな機械音を立てるモ
> ニターテレビのスクリーンだけだ。」[37]

Beyond this screen, at the far end of the cable that creeps through Tokyo's underground darkness, may be Kumiko. She, too, should be sitting before a monitor, with her hands on a keyboard. In reality all I can see is my monitor, which sits there making a faint electronic squeal.[38]

However, because human language is essentially never 'disembodied'[39] (despite a range of new modalities of its presentation), Boku senses the physical presence and nuances of Kumiko in the saved transcript of their dialogue which emphasizes the curtailed semantic economy of their virtual exchange :

「僕はコンピューターの前に戻り、椅子に腰を下ろし、青い画面の上で
のやりとりをもう一度始めから終わりまで注意深く読み返してみる。僕
が何を言ったか、彼女が何を言ったか。それについて僕が何を言ったか、
彼女が何を言ったか。」[40]

I go back to the computer and sit there, carefully rereading our entire exchange on the glowing tube from beginning to end: what I said, what she said, what I said to that, what she said to that.[41]

This purely graphic and 'verbal' exchange is nevertheless semantically regulated and presented via an imagined simulacrum of the auditory modalities of the embodied cadences of a human voice:

「我々の会話は画面の上にそのまま残されている。そこには不思議に
生々しいものがある。画面の上に並んだ字を目で追いながら、僕は彼女
の声を聞き取ることができる。その抑揚や、微妙な声のトーンや間の取
り方を、僕は知ることができる。カーソルは最後の行の上でまだ心臓の
鼓動のような規則的な点滅を続けている。次の言葉が発せられるのを息
を殺して待ち続けている。でもそこに続く言葉はない。」[42]

The whole thing is still there on the screen, with a certain graphic intensity. As my eyes follow the rows of characters she has made, I can hear her voice. I can recognize the rise and fall of her voice, the subtle tones and pauses. The cursor on the last line keeps up its blinking with all the regularity of a heartbeat, waiting with bated breath for the next word to be sent. But there is no next word.[43]

Ultimately, Boku's relation with Kumiko moves from a highly corporeal to an *auditory* one, conducted over the telephone—and then finally, to a 'disembodied' modality: a series of virtual dialogues conducted via the 'e-mail' format. The literary representation of this kind of speech act was quite revolutionary at the time of publication, because 'e-mail' was not nearly as common or widespread as it is now. The 'virtual relationship' is indicative of a new contemporary mode of communication, where the words on the screen mark out the phantasmal trace of subjectivity, which is, nevertheless, tentatively bestowed on the woman who is not Kumiko, in this story which does not belong to her, but rather to the position of the imagined male protagonist as reading and speaking subject.

Nutmeg's Stories: The Subject of History

There were no shameful episodes in modern Japanese history.

> Former Japanese Education
> Minister,
> Fujio Masayuki[44]

And the power of gradually losing all feelings of strangeness or astonishment, and finally being pleased at anything, is called the historical sense or historical culture.

> Friedrich Nietzsche,
> *The Use and Abuse of*
> *History*[45]

Writing at the end of the nineteenth century, Nietzsche expressed an instinctive revulsion towards the kind of historiography being practiced all around him. He saw it as a form of falsification indicating the descent into mass ennui. This was the great burden of the writing of history (and an apparent 'inability to forget') which characterized modern European society with its opinions, its newspapers —but most of all, its history.[46]

Nietzsche would be shocked to learn that in contemporary Japanese society, surveys repeatedly show that newspapers are considered to be by far the most 'trustworthy' sources of news and information. And of course, he would be dismayed (for very different reasons) at the astonishing disjunction between officially sanctioned information in the form of 'historical discourse' in textbooks and much scholarly writing, and the creeping hegemony of the visual image as the most authoritative purveyor of truth—not to mention the entropy of thought amidst the so called 'postmodern' circulation of images. Indeed 'postmodernism' is a characterization now almost laughable, in the sense that the minute it was invoked as a new label in Japan in the eighties, it became instantly redundant, in what Karatani has described as the 'closed discursive space of Japan'.[47]

A century later, Nietzsche's abhorrence of the 'abuse' of history still proves to be justified (but for the opposite reasons) in many contemporary cultural settings, where 'history' is almost entirely *lost from view*. Nietzsche's lament about the modern complacency of 'being pleased at anything' resonates perfectly with Jameson's observation of the postmodern tendency to 'seek history by way of our own pop images', through the mechanism of 'a vast collection of images, a multitudinous photographic simulacrum'.[48]

In his essay 'Repetition and Forgetting', Frow suggests that modernity has constructed history in terms of a 'temporal dichotomy between authentic historical memory and a debased and mediated relation to the past' which, he claims, is related to the Durkheimian concept of collective memory.[49] Frow notes that Pierre Nora's work on the 'loss of memory' in modernity distinguishes between memory and history, where 'memory is plural and concrete, reflecting the diversity of actual social groups', unlike history, which is described as abstract and unitary, belonging to everyone and no-one.[50]

Undoubtedly, this disjunction between memory and history is exemplified in an extreme sense in the context of the electronic media-entertainment regimes of contemporary Japanese society. When this totality of 'history' as signifier—as 'officially sanctioned memory'—becomes paramount in its authority to proclaim the 'truth' of the past (as in the Japanese Education Ministry's control over textbook publishing through the imprimatur system), the discursive vacuum of the specific *contents* of history is easily filled by discourses which have huge political stakes in crafting and shaping certain contemporary readings of the past.

We sense this dislocation between memory and history most acutely in artistic texts such as Kurosawa's film *Yume*. The haunting scene of the ghosts of dead soldiers emerging from the dark cave of memory in search of their missing platoon members. The disjunction between the personal memory of unspeakable loss and grief (echoing through generations of bereaved families) and the official government view, indirectly expressed in the strictly disciplined stance of the platoon leader, resonating with the statistics of troop deployments and casualties, campaign victories and losses.

An instance of Nietzsche's sense of 'losing all strangeness and astonishment' appears in Book Three of *Nejimakidori* in the figure of the exhausted Vet witnessing the slaughter of the zoo animals,[51] the atrocity of the massacre of Chinese Soldiers,[52] as well as Nutmeg's dream-like rendition of the 'escape' from the Asian Continent by ship,[53] all of which can be read as metaphors of stupefaction. These are equivalent to the intellectual stupor and quasi-amnesia induced by the vicarious 'witnessing' of violence amid the incessant parade of disparate images in contemporary Japanese tele-visual culture. But this literary rendition is also especially evocative of the visceral, the olfactory (with the smell and taste of blood), as well as the auditory—the 'dull crushing sound as the skull scattered', the bat striking down the Chinese prisoners.[54]

Nutmeg's are strangely alluring and fragmented narrative passages in *Nejimakidori*, which invoke the tropes of 'landscape' (Manchuria/*Manshû*, as both plenitude/pleasure and danger/threat) in a significant way. Her stories exemplify our third proposition of history as being arrayed between memory, thought, speech and writing. This is clear from her episodes of daydreaming, *déjà vu* and spontaneous recollection:

「彼女は目を閉じて新京の動物園のことを考えた……。彼女の意識は肉体を離れ、記憶と物語の狭間をさまよい、そして戻ってきた。」[55]

She closed her eyes and thought about the Hsing-Chin zoo. . . . Her consciousness left her body, wandered for a while in the spaces between memory and story, then came back.[56]

Nutmeg's stories also rely very much on second-hand telling and re-telling, clearly evoking the dimensions of metaphor (the 'zoo massacre') and metonymy/synecdoche (the individual 'events' of the killing of the Chinese prisoners), as well as irony (the reprieve for the fleeing passenger ship only to arrive back in a defeated, devastated Japan).

The figure of Nutmeg's father, the Japanese Veterinary officer, is witness to all of this in an exhausted and confused haze of revulsion, resignation, reluctant duty and disbelief. The narrative which he relays is both one of individual despair, yet also reflects the repository of a 'collective memory' (the memory of defeat, death and loss) as well as a rebuke to the 'total history' of the whitewashing mentality which flatly proposes that 'there were no shameful episodes in modern Japanese history'. After overseeing the killing of the zoo animals, he reflects:

> 「あるいは世界というのは、回転扉みたいにただそこをくるくるとまわるだけのものではないのだろうか、と薄れかける意識の中で彼はふと思った。その仕切りのどこに入るかというのは、ただ単に足の踏み出し方の問題に過ぎないのではないだろうか……。そこには論理的な連続性はほとんどないのだ。そして連続性がないからこそ、選択肢などといったものも実際には意味をなさないのだ。自分が世界と世界とのずれをうまく感じることができないのは、そのためではあるまいか……。」[57]

Maybe the world was like a revolving door, it occurred to him as his consciousness was fading way. . . . And which section you ended up in was just a matter of where your foot happened to fall. . . . And there was no logical continuity from one section to another. And it was precisely because of this lack of logical continuity that choices really didn't mean very much. Wasn't that why he couldn't feel the gap between one world and another?[58]

This contradictory attempt to think the chaotic 'contents' of history as *discontinuous* and *disparate* sections or worlds which nevertheless repeat and revolve, reminds us of the threat of the 'historical sublime' proposed by White and Nietzsche's idea of the 'eternal return'.

The kind of bewilderment expressed by the critic Hasumi towards the apparent 'absence' of history in a novel of over a thousand pages—in which a large portion is written as though it *were* history—reflects the problematic nature of the Japanese critical responses to the issues of memory, history and representation discussed above. More than just reflecting Murakami's 'eerie imaginative power' (*usukimiwarui sôzôryoku*), such a response fails to recognize that this apparent 'absence' is suggestive of a deliberate narrative strategy.[59]

Yoshida discerns such a strategy when he contrasts the writings of Yasuoka Shôtarô with Murakami's. As a 'historical novel' (*rekishi shôsetsu*) Yasuoka's *Ryûritan's* use of a 'retroactive method' (*sokyû no shikata*) does not betray what he calls the 'consistency of expression' of the author himself. But when Murakami mentions the word 'history', a difficult to accept 'severance' with the author's previous method becomes apparent. Yasuoka's text is depicted in a style in which a strong 'tension' (*kinchôkan*) accompanies the historical content (*rekishi ni tadori tsukereu*). However, in the case of *Nejimakidori* (and especially Book Three of the novel), 'history' is an arbitrarily taken up 'presupposition' (*zentei*) which makes an appearance in the work.[60] This notion of history as 'presupposition' is significant: it suggests a kind of produced *effect*, which necessarily arises from the conditions of exteriority of the text's production. However, it also implies that these events can never be directly or concisely represented *in* or *through* the text. In other words, in this kind of narrative 'history' can only function as a kind of phantasmal effect, yet in a way which powerfully enables the construction of a plurality of meanings outside the parameters of 'official' historical discourse. As to the question of why the atrocities are so graphically depicted, Yoshida's analysis proposes a plausible explanation which will be discussed later.

This mere 'presupposition' of history—that is, of history as a kind of 'effect'—is confirmed when, in the prologue to 'Nutmeg's Story', the narrator offers the caveat that historical 'accuracy' cannot be assured:

> 「それは果てしなく長く、無数の寄り道に満ちた物語だった。だから僕はそのごく簡単な……要約のようなものをここに示すわけだが、それが話の骨子をうまく伝えているのかどうか、正直いって自信が持てない。しかし少なくともそれは、彼女の人生の節々で起こった事件の概要を伝えているはずだ。」[61]

> It was a long, long story, with many detours, so that what I am recording here is a very simplified . . . summary of the whole. I cannot honestly claim with confidence that it contains the essence of her story, but it should at least convey the outline of important events that occurred at crucial points in her life.[62]

The original Japanese employs two terms which are of interest. Firstly, *jiken* (事件) which usually translates as 'event' but also carries the broader sense of 'incident', or 'affair', 'question', 'difficulty'—and in some contexts, even implies 'cause'.[63] Its semantic latitude is augmented by its use with the term *fushi-bushi* (節々), the corporeal metaphor of 'joints' connecting separate parts of the body or 'points' in a talk.[64]

The use of both terms gives a more precise sense of narrated memory as an 'outline' (*gaiyô*) as compared with the notion of the 'essence', gist or 'substance' (*koshi*,骨子) which the narrator lacks confidence in conveying. It also implies some continuity (*jiken*: 'occurrence' and/or 'cause'), connectivity (*fushi-bushi*: 'joints' or 'points') around which, whenever such a narration derived from 'personal memory' is attempted, meaning can at best be only tentatively surmised. Nutmeg confirms this when she recalls that before relating to her son Cinnamon the various wartime stories, she had 'wandered in silence through the gloomy labyrinth that spread out between illusion and truth'.[65]

Nutmeg's reflection on memory and truth is echoed in Suzumura and Numano's conclusion that as a novel, *Nejimakidori* has opened up the possibility of a different narrative stance and treatment of the real. They suggest that Murakami has discovered a new route for connecting the 'darkness of the world of the narrative' (*monogatarisekai no yami*), with the 'dark segments of actual history' (*jissai no rekishi no ankokububun*), and go on to applaud this as a great step forward on the author's part.[66]

It is Nutmeg's relating of Japanese atrocities on the continent which brings sharply into focus these specific questions, as well as the larger problem as to what extent we can characterize 'history as narrative', or indeed, 'narrative as history'. The problem here, as Foley reminds us, is the inherent instability of discursive boundaries: 'modes of discourse change . . . as much as do the modes of social and political representation in the worlds that they take as their referents'.[67] In this context of discourse analysis, Struever has divided the main contemporary approaches to history into three models: 'history as narrative', 'history as rhetorical style', and 'history as argument'.[68]

We now pause to briefly consider some of these instances of 'fiction as history'/'history as fiction' as narrated by the figure of Nutmeg. Firstly, it is clear that the zoo massacre episode is indicative of Whites trope of 'metaphor'. In the form of a security precaution in the face of an imminent assault on Japanese occupation troops by the Soviet army, it is allegorical of gratuitous violence and connotes the absurdity of war—in killing caged animals originally placed in captivity for peoples' pleasure:

「その八月の午後には、人も動物たちも、誰もが死ぬことを考えていた。
今日は彼らが動物たちを殺し、明日はソビエト兵たちが彼らを殺すのだ。
おそらく。」[69]

On that August afternoon, people, animals—everyone was thinking about death. Today the men would be killing animals; tomorrow Soviet troops would be killing the men. Probably.[70]

As a literary passage it is highly evocative, and once again employs the device of the auditory register to striking effect. Following the shooting of the tigers, the zoo descends into an uncanny silence:

「すべての動物たちははっと息をひそめた。蝉さえもなきやんだ。銃声
のこだまが引いてからも、あたりには物音一つ聞こえなかった。」[71]

The animals held their breath. Even the cicadas stopped crying. Long after the echo of gunfire faded into the distance, there was not a sound to be heard.[72]

Later, as the animals instinctively realize the fate that is about to befall each of them:

「猿たちがなにかを予測するように大声をあげ、空を切り裂き、そこに
いるすべての動物たちに激しく警告を与えた。動物たちはそれぞれのや
り方で、猿たちに唱和した。狼は天に向かって長く吠え、鳥たちは大き
く羽ばたき、どこかで何か大きな動物が威嚇するように檻に強く身体を
打ち付けた。」[73]

The monkeys . . . rent the air with ominous screams, sending frantic warnings
to the other animals in the zoo, who in turn joined the chorus in their own
distinctive ways. The wolves sent long howls skyward, the birds contributed a
wild flapping of wings, some large animal somewhere was slamming itself
against its cage.[74]

And in the title of the chapter, depicting the 'second massacre', we see 'the second clumsy massacre'—this time of human beings. However, this baseball bat
massacre of Chinese prisoners of war can be seen in terms of White's trope of
the synecdoche—of Japan's mounting of the so-called 'Fifteen-Year War' in
China, beginning with the 'Manchurian Incident' (*Manshû jihen*) and extending
to the invasion of the Asian continent, along with the various atrocities sometimes 'recorded' but certainly not over-emphasized in high school history text
books.

Perhaps one of the most important things about the status of the referent in *Nejimakidori* is the fact that it emerges from the *difference between* stated and well
known historical 'facts' *and* uncertain dream states and recollection:

「十五日の正午に、天皇の終戦の詔がラジオから流されていたのだ。七
日前に、長崎の街は一発の原子爆弾によって焼き尽くされていた。満州
国は数日のうちに、幻の国家として歴史の流砂の中に飲み込まれ、消え
去ろうとしていた。そしてその頬にあざのある獣医は、回転扉の別の仕
切りに入ったまま心ならずも満州国と運命をともにすることになっ
た。」[75]

At noon on August 15, the radio had broadcast the Emperor's announcement of
the war's end. Six days before that, the nearby city of Nagasaki had been incin-
erated by a single atomic bomb. The phantom empire of Manchukuo was dis-
appearing into history. And caught unawares in the wrong section of the re-
volving door, the veterinarian with the mark on his cheek would share the
fate of Manchukuo.[76]

Because it is deployed merely as a 'pre-supposition' throughout the text, the
specific use of the signifier 'history' has a special semantic force here, suggesting the possibility of the *difference* arising from history's discourse with itself,
as alluded to earlier. The appearance of the proper nouns 'Manchukuo' and
'Nagasaki' is highly significant, because these signifiers have become inscribed
in Japanese post-war memory as traces of an indefinable unease: the intimation
of a Japanese sublime—the contours of which, as we noted above, have not yet

been adequately defined. Not surprisingly, therefore, from between the interstitial spaces of Nutmeg's dreaming and recollection, we inevitably return to the question of subjectivity, and in the concluding sections of this chapter will show how this question relates to the problematized themes of 'history' and 'memory'

Abject Stories: The Subject in Retreat

> The subject never is. The subject is only the signifying process and appears only as a signifying practice, that is, only when absent within the position out of which social, historical, and signifying activity unfolds.
>
> Julia Kristeva,
> *Revolution in Poetic Language*[77]

If the narrative perspectives established around the stories of Kumiko and Nutmeg are made possible by a range of unstable, shifting subject positions in the presented worlds available to the reader, the stories told by several other characters can be said to radically broach the very question of even the *possibility* of maintaining any cohesive sense of subjectivity. In particular, Boku's narrated episodes of alienation from his own body, the acts of sexual violation recalled by Kanô Kureta and the horrific episodes of human skinning alive related by Lieutenant Mamiya, mark perhaps the most shocking and extreme condition of the sublime limits of the subject's encounter with itself. Indeed, it is arguably the graphic, 'horror-movie-like' scenes of the latter, which have made *Nejimakidori* such a landmark contemporary novel.

In the previous section we noted Lacan's comments that the subject is defined by a kind of *lack*—that it must 'lose' itself in order to enter language. We see this affirmed in Kristeva's comments that as a signifying practice, subjectivity 'appears', paradoxically, only by being *absent* from 'the position out of which social, historical and signifying activity unfolds'. It is well known that Kristeva transformed Lacan's categories of Imaginary and Symbolic into, respectively, the semiotic and the symbolic,[78] and it is also the case that she extended and explored the central idea of 'lack' in her studies in terms of the notion of abjection, the theory of which is outlined in her important essay *Powers of Horror*.[79] Put very simply, abjection describes that state the subject falls into when it is threatened within a return to the pre-Oedipal, pre-symbolic, maternal realm. Burgin describes the Kristevan sense of the abject as

> the means by which the subject is first impelled towards the possibility of constituting itself as such—in an act of revulsion, of expulsion of that which can no longer be contained. Significantly, the first object of abjection is the preoedipal mother—prefiguring that positioning of the woman in society which Kristeva locates, in the patriarchal scheme, as perpetually at the border line, the edge, the 'outer limit'.[80]

The putative subject's response to such a threat can manifest itself in the experience of revulsion or rejection of the body, or what it produces. We can characterize the episodes of Boku's alienating 'out of body' experiences as an intimation of the Kristevan notion of abjection, and as an important dimension of the aesthetic of the sublime in *Nejimakidori:*

> 「僕はその完璧な暗黒のそこにしゃがみこんでいた。目にすることのできるのは無だけだった。僕はその無の一部になっていた。僕は目を閉じて自分の心臓の音を聞き、血液が体内を循環する音を聞き、肺がふいごのように収縮する音を聞き、ぬめぬめとした内臓が食べ物を要求して身をくねらせる音を聞いた。深い暗闇の中ではすべての動きが、すべての振動が不自然に誇張されていた。これが僕の肉体なのだ。でも闇の中ではそれはあまりにも生々しく、あまりにも肉体でありすぎた。」[81]

> I was crouching down in the total darkness. All I could see was nothingness. And I was part of this nothingness. I closed my eyes and listened to the sound of my heart, to the sound of the blood circulating through my body, to the bellows-like contractions of my lungs, to the slippery undulations of my food-starved gut. In the deep darkness, every movement, every throb, was magnified enormously. This was my body: my flesh. But in the darkness, it was all too raw and physical. [82]

The original Japanese gives a much greater sense of the sheer viscerality of Boku's revulsion, of his sense of horror at the immediacy of his own corporeality: the onomatopoeic resonance (*gion*) of words like *nume nume toshita* ('slimy', from *numeri*: 'slime'; 'sliminess')[83] and *namanamashiku*, an adverbial form of the adjective connoting 'green', 'fresh', 'vivid', certainly of the sense of the word 'raw' which is used in the translation, but also 'vivid', 'graphic' or even 'reeking'.[84]

In the darkness at the bottom of the well, Boku's revulsion towards his own body is played out blindly—without vision—and relying on the auditory and haptic senses for perception. Boku as subject, moves closer to a state of undifferentiation, a state of abjection, where he is only flesh and no-subject, or where the borders of his subjectivity are at best elusive and tenuous. He tries to forestall this threatened abjection by imitating the sound of the wind-up bird, but fails. The cry of the wind-up bird as the central trope of the novel is the audio-image of that which 'winds the world's spring' and signifies the passage of contiguous as well as discontinuous time(s): generalized cosmic time, as well as the specific times of 'memory' and 'history', which take form in the narrative-as-chronicle. It is this sound which gives order to the chaos and horror of his threatened abjection by invoking the elements of the symbolic: language, conscious memory, history and articulated desire.

What is signified here is the liminal, the interstitial realm of the semiotic, which always 'feels the pressure' of the symbolic. In the Lacanian Imaginary or the Kristevan realm of the semiotic, where the auditory image of the phonemic unit is first modeled on the metabolic sounds of the body: the 'throbs' and 'undulations', the 'bellow-like' contractions, we sense a transitional state of subjectivity. Grosz describes it thus:

> The semiotic transfers its particular characteristics onto signifying elements: phonemic units are produced from the energies and impulses of the drives . . . creating the irreducibly material elements of representation.[85]

Here language is a 'breaking-through', an irruption of the semiotic into the pre-established social order of the symbolic. However, as we shall see, in the necessary unification of the different aspects of the signifier (that is to say, of the dimensions and modalities of the visual, the audio, the haptic, olfactory, etc.) there occurs a kind of unification, the origins of which are at once repressed. Kristeva characterizes the specific melding together of two aspects of these sensory modalities—the audio image and visual image—as a 'condensation', and we shall consider later her claim that not only does this function as an indispensable condition for the establishment of the Oedipal configuration, but also that any threat to its continuity represents a direct threat to the Oedipal.

In another vividly depicted episode at the bottom of the well, Boku describes his unrelenting efforts to confirm the existence of a body he cannot see, but that can only be surmised through the modalities of the audio and the haptic:

> 「暗闇の中でただじっとしていると、自分がそこに存在しているという事実がだんだんうまく呑み込めなくなってくるのだ。だから僕はときどき軽い咳払いをしたり、手のひらで自分の顔を撫でてみたりした。そうすることで僕の耳は僕の声の存在を確かめ、僕の手は僕の顔の存在を確かめ、僕の顔は僕の手の存在を確かめることができた。」[86]

> Staying very still in the darkness, I became less and less convinced of the fact that I actually existed. To cope with that, I would clear my throat now and then, or run my hand over my face. That way, my ears could check on the existence of my voice, my hand could check on the existence of my face, and my face could check on the existence of my hand.[87]

Here, the sheer redundancy of verbal language is made evident, and it must accede to the demands of a form of semiosis generated entirely in the matrix of the corporeal:

> 「まるで僕の中で無言の熾烈な綱引きのようなことが行われていて、僕の意識が少しずつ僕の肉体を自分の領域に引きずり込みつつあるようだった……。肉体などというものは結局のところ、意識のために染色体という記号を適当に並べかえて用意された、ただのかりそめの殻にすぎないのではないか、と僕はふと思った。」[88]

I felt as if a fierce and wordless tug-of-war were going on inside me, a contest in which my mind was slowly dragging my body into its own territory . . . The thought struck me that my own body was a mere provisional husk that had been prepared for my mind by a rearrangement of the signs known as chromosomes.[89]

We might wish to characterize Boku's imagining of and revulsion towards his own body in the darkness as evidence of the fact that, as Ruthrof puts it, generally speaking 'we do not feel at home in this body'. Citing Ackerman, Ruthrof notes that we all carry 'an exaggerated mental picture of our body' which is somehow frightening. He argues, however, that this is inevitable:

To say that this grotesque body is the wrong one would require a plane of meta-judgement which is denied us. All we can say is that ordinary perceptions of ourselves and the haptic body are in conflict. The signs responsible for the two Gestalten are in conflict.

It is inevitable, because this perceptual conflict is no more than an instance of 'sign conflict' or 'heterosemiosis'. This should not seem so surprising, since as Ruthrof reminds us, the heterosemiotic merely reflects what has been described, at a more abstract level, in the larger project of much contemporary theory's concern with signification *as* differentiation.[90]

What all these disjunctive notions such as 'sign conflict', 'heterosemiosis' and 'differentiation' have in common, is that they are to do with *dissociation*. And if we have difficulty in the context of our approach to *Nejimakidori* in linking the displaced subject, the retreating or the threatened subject with the subject of history, it is because we require an integrating principle—formed, paradoxically, from a process of dis-integration or incommensurability. We shall return to this idea of dissociation when we consider Kristeva's discussion of the splitting of 'condensation', and then examine how this might be transposed to the plane of what can be called the political sublime.

Let us now consider the process of abjection in Kanô Kureta's story. Before doing so, it is worth recalling some aspects of Kristeva's description of abjection which are particularly apposite to the cases of the sexual violation of Kanô Kureta (as well as Kumiko) at the hands of the 'evil figure' of Wataya Noboru. Expressions of the abject can be manifested in any number of happenings *to* the body, and its continued state of existence as a discrete entity. Two points about Kristeva's approach are important here: firstly, her claim that when the abject arises, there is neither subject nor object and secondly, that with the abject, there is the sense that one is put 'beside oneself'.[91]

Kristeva's insight certainly applies to our understanding of the episode where Kanô Kureta describes the final stages of the mysterious act of her violation/liberation at the hands of Wataya Noboru, entailing a sublime admixture of pleasure and pain, 'the two as a single entity':[92]

「自分が解剖される光景を目にしているような感じでした。自分の体が
切り裂かれて、内臓やら何やかやがずるずると引きずり出されていくの
をどこかから自分の目で見ているような気持ちなのです。私は体を痙攣
させながら、枕の上によだれを垂らし続けていました。失禁もしていま
した……。自分の肉からいろんなものがどんどんこぼれて抜けていきま
した。かたちのあるもの、かたちのないもの、すべてのものがよだれや
尿と同じように、液体になってだらだらと私の外に流れて出ていくので
す。こんなまま何もかもをこぼしてしまうわけにはいかないと私は思い
ました。このまま無駄にこぼして失ってしまうわけにはいかない……。
それがどれぐらいの時間続いたのか、私にはわかりません。なんだかす
べての記憶とすべての意識がすっかり抜け落ちてしまったみたいでし
た。」[93]

I felt as if I were watching from some vantage point as my body was being cut
open and one slimy organ after another was being pulled out of me . . . I continued to lie there, drooling on the pillow, my body racked with convulsions,
and incontinent . . . Everything came gushing out of me. Things both tangible
and intangible turned liquid and flowed out through my flesh like saliva or
urine. I knew that I should not let this happen, that I should not allow my very
self to spill out this way and be lost forever . . . How long this continued, I have
no idea. It seemed as if all memories, all my consciousness had just slipped
away.[94]

Not only those things 'like saliva and urine' as expelled objects, but also the
object of the phantom birth/abortion, the expelled thing, which was 'as wet and
slippery as a new born baby',[95] put her beside herself, 'watching from some vantage point'. It is from such a position, argues Kristeva, that the threat to the subject takes the form of the dissolution of meaning:

If the object . . . through its opposition, settles me within the fragile texture of a
desire for meaning . . . which makes me ceaselessly and infinitely homologous
to it, what is abject, on the contrary, the jettisoned object, is radically excluded
and draws me toward the place where meaning collapses.[96]

Ironically, the 'expelled' object—in this case, un-named and unspecified—
which might be thought to shore up subjectivity and identity, simultaneously
occurs as the dissolution of meaning; as the site of dissociation or difference, it
is also a dismantling of identity, and marks Kanô Kureta's personal transformation—a becoming someone *other* than herself:

「そして意識が戻ったとき、私はまた別の人間になっていました。」[97]

And when I regained consciousness, I was a different person.[98]

This loss of meaning and the experience of dissociated identity in the 'birth scene', is also highly paradoxical as a metaphor of pleasure and pain, liberation and constraint. Kristeva puts it this way:

> The scene of scenes is . . . the one of giving birth, incest turned inside out, flayed identity. Giving birth: the height of bloodshed and life, scorching moment of hesitation (between inside and outside, ego and other, life and death), horror and beauty, sexuality and the blunt negation of the sexual.[99]

Kristeva marks the connection of this expression of the abject with fascism. The 'libidinal surplus-value', the excesses of the act of birth which she writes of in relation to Celine, are clearly what is rationalized, distilled and 'made operative' by a politics of fascism, in a way highly apposite to *Nejimakidori*:

> At the doors of the feminine, at the doors of abjection . . . we are . . . given the most daring X-ray of the 'drive foundations' of fascism.[100]

Here, in the abject which occurs at the 'doors of the feminine' (and thus by extension, at the 'doors of the maternal') we have affirmation that the Oedipal configuration is at once confirmed and simultaneously exposed to threat. The symbolic birth and horror witnessed 'at the doors of the other', the site which must always be inferred but never directly seen (Kanô Kureta is denied watching her own act of giving birth: *'opening my eyes was an impossibility'*[101]) prepares the way for the later 'murdering of Wataya Noboru' and the implied destruction of the Oedipal relations. Wataya Noboru is, of course, the maintainer of the 'law of the father', the keeper of the 'emperorism' or neo-fascism at the heart of the transformed hierarchies of post-war Japan, which have reshaped the pre-modern and war-time discursive hegemonies into a seamless aesthetic where, amidst the image-parade of daily life, sex, economics and politics have become entirely interchangeable. The 'bringing of the inside to the outside' is one more version—a transformation of the confrontation with the pre-Oedipal maternal matrix—which must be repressed in order for the subject to hold its own coherent position in the Oedipal web of the Symbolic.

However, this repression is overturned, even disallowed, in most striking form in *Nejimakidori*, in the 'skinning' episodes to which we now turn—some of which are clearly allegories of the efficiency and mechanization, the aesthetic of fascist terror. Consider the Russian officer's unconcealed delight in the pure artistry maintained by the skilled handiwork of the Mongolian soldier with his razor-sharp knife:

> 「男はまず山本の右の肩にナイフですっと筋を入れました。そして上の方から右腕の皮を剥いでいきました。彼はまるで慈しむかのように、ゆっくりと丁寧に腕の皮を剥いでいきました。たしかに、ロシア人の将校が言ったように、それは芸術品と言ってもいいような腕前でした。」

The man started by slitting open Yamamoto's shoulder and proceeded to peel off the skin of his right arm from the top down—slowly, carefully, almost lovingly. As the Russian officer had said, it was something like a work of art.[102]

In *Nejimakidori* there are three main references to skinning: the skinning alive of Japanese war prisoners near the Mongolian border, Boku's dream about being covered by the flayed skin of a man he has bashed to death and the skinning of animals following the zoo massacre. It is the first two which concern us here. Towards the end of Book One, Mamiya relates to Boku the almost unspeakable horror of an episode he is forced to witness at the hands of his captors:

「熊のような蒙古人の将校は最後に、すっぽりときれいに剥いだ山本の胴体の皮を広げました。そこには乳首さえついていました。あんなに不気味なものを、私は後にも先にも見たことがありません……。あとには皮をすっかり剥ぎ取られ、赤い血だらけの肉のかたまりになってしまった山本の死体が、ごろんと転がっているだけでした。いちばんいたましいのはその顔でした。赤い肉の中に白い大きな眼球がきっと見開かれるように収まっていました。歯が剥き出しになった口は何かを叫ぶように大きく開いていました……。地面はまさに血の海でした。」[103]

At last, the bear-like Mongolian officer held up the skin of Yamamoto's torso, which he had so cleanly peeled off. Even the nipples were intact. Never to this day have I seen anything so horrible ... All that remained lying on the ground was Yamamoto's corpse, a bloody red lump of meat from which every trace of skin had been removed. The most painful sight was the face. Two large white eyeballs stared out from the red mass of flesh. Teeth bared, the mouth stretched wide open as if in a shout ... The ground was a sea of blood.[104]

The 'silent scream' of the lifeless lump that was Yamamoto (who, while alive, had screamed in horror throughout the process), resonates eerily as a mirror 'audio-image', with that of the other soldier, who, whilst undergoing a similarly horrific ordeal, had remained absolutely silent from the beginning. And this is clearly one further example of the how the evocative power of the auditory modality competes with the conventionalized expectation of the dominant narrative register of the visual in the horror movie-like scenes of *Nejimakidori*.

Later, in one of the many dream sequences narrated by Boku, during the episode of his brutal bashing of the guitar player, the trope of 'skinning' is deployed in a particularly striking manner. Once again, we see that the threat of 'the inside' coming to 'the outside', is indicative of the threatened loss of self: the man is reduced to a 'lump of raw flesh', and his flayed skin (peeled off with his own hands) gradually engulfs and covers the body of Boku:

「やがて……、その剥がれた皮膚が床を這って、ずるずると音を立てながらこちらに近づいてきた。僕は逃げようとしたのだが、足は動かなかった。その皮膚は僕の足もとにたどり着くと、ゆっくりと体を這い上が

ってきた。そして僕の皮膚を上からべっとりと覆っていった。僕の肌の
上に、男のぬめっとした血だらけの皮膚が少しずつ貼りつき、重なって
いった。血糊の匂いがあたりに満ちた。皮膚は薄い膜のように僕の脚を
覆い、体を覆い、顔を覆った。」[105]

Soon . . . the man's peeled skin began to slither across the floor towards me. I
tried to run away, but my legs would not move. The skin reached my feet and
began to crawl upward. It crept over my own skin, the man's blood-soaked skin
clinging to mine as an overlay. The heavy smell of blood was everywhere.
Soon my legs, my body, my face, were entirely covered by the thin membrane
of the man's skin.[106]

Again we note the debilitating fear that the abject potently brings with it: the loss
of self, and the entry into and broaching of the domain of the liminal heralds the
threat of dissolution of the subject—which is really an implied negation and unraveling of the symbolic order. Yet, this experience is also restorative and em-
powering for Boku, who upon waking from the nightmare, finds that the quest to
retrieve the object of his endlessly displaced desire (Kumiko, as the universalized feminine other) from the virtual world, is the very thing which will guarantee his continuity as subject:

「目を覚ましたとき、僕はどうしようもなく混乱し、そして怯えてい
た。しばらくの間、自分自身の存在をうまくつかむことさえできなかっ
た……。でもそれと同時に、僕はひとつの結論にたどり着いていた。僕
は逃げられないし、逃げるべきではないのだ。それが僕の得た結論だっ
た。たとえどこに行ったところで、それは必ず僕を追いかけてくるだろ
う。どこまでも。」[107]

Confusion and fear overtook me then. For a while, I even lost hold of my own
existence . . . But at the same time, I knew that I had reached a conclusion . . . I
had to get Kumiko back. With my own hands, I had to pull her back into this
world. Because if I didn't, that would be the end of me. This person, this self
that I thought of as 'me', would be lost.[108]

This is a clear example of the fact that, as Weiss reminds us, 'abjection is necessary to create the boundaries that will individuate the self'.[109] Although
the important point is, as Grosz notes, that this abjection is at the edge of limi-
nality, it also implies a negation and threatened unraveling of the Symbolic:

Abjection is the underside of the symbolic. It is what the symbolic must reject,
cover and contain. The symbolic requires that a border separate or protect the
subject from this abyss which beckons and haunts it: the abject entices and attracts the subject ever closer to its edge.[110]

In citing the importance of the skinning episodes in *Nejimakidori*, the question arises as to their relevance to the central argument of this chapter. At this point, and as we move towards bringing this part of the discussion to a close, it is worth noting that in *Powers of Horror*, Kristeva's comments on the metaphoric role of 'the skin' occur directly after her discussion on the sign as a form of semiotic 'condensation'—the description of which, is pivotal to the claims which will be made in our conclusion.

> The body's inside . . . shows up in order to compensate for the collapse of the border between inside and outside. It is as if the skin, a fragile container, no longer guaranteed the integrity of one's 'own and clean' self, but scraped or transparent, invisible or taut, gave way before the dejection of its contents.[111]

The vividly depicted scenes cited above, the clods of bloody flesh, the skinned bodies, the 'insides' which 'show up' as forms of what Baudrillard might designate as 'extreme phenomena',[112] perform a very different role in *Nejimakidori*, compared to scenes of violence and horror central to the fiction of a contemporary writer such as Murakami Ryû. In an insightful essay on the shock value, the guerilla tactics of Murakami Ryu's narrative presentation of instances of 'extreme imagination', Stephen Snyder argues that in the end, Ryû's radically disturbing fiction melds seamlessly into the simulacral economy of image-circulation it ostensibly aims to critique:

> Unfolding across dozens of works in various media, Murakami's 'virtual catastrophe', his ongoing paean to the extremes of sexual and political violence, his narrative virus, may, in the end, be yet another way of preserving the body politic it infects.[113]

This cannot be said of the presentation of sexual and political violence in the text of *Nejimakidori*, because the signifier 'history' and the implied status of the referent have been juxtaposed in an unusual and complex way. As has been shown, in the aesthetic matrices of the corporeal and the historical sublime, is indicated a *problematization* of the referent—rather than the mere assumption that in the so-called postmodern context, all simulacral images refer only to themselves.

On the contrary, through the literary mechanisms of the representation of the sublime and the abject in *Nejimakdori*, the referent is recast in new forms. To be more precise, these referents imagined in our reading are the 'historical event' as a residual *eventivity*, 'the body' as the site (however tenuous) of an individuated *subjectivity*, and 'the state' as the meta-referential and unseen referent of the hegemonic discourses of an imagined *nationality*.

Unlike Murakami Ryu's propensity to shock and revolt in a direct, almost instantaneous way, the unease arising from our reading of *Nejimakidori* is much harder to fathom, and the effects of its radicality will (as Murakami implicitly acknowledged more than a year after its complete publication) take time to be appreciated:

「ただ、僕の感じでは、非常に傲慢な言い方に聞こえるかもしれないけ
れど、『ねじまき鳥クロニクル』という小説が本当に理解されるには、
まだ少し時間がかかるのではないかという気がするのです。」 [114]

This probably sounds like a very arrogant way of putting it, but I have the feeling that a novel such as *Nejimakidori kuronikuru* will take a little more time to be really understood.

What Murakami is acknowledging is the kind of incommensurability, the disjunctive sense, which we will attempt to elucidate in the conclusion to this chapter.

The 'retreat' of the subject evident in the threat of abjection should not be surprising, since all of the disjunctive moments discussed so far seem to revolve around the crisis of not being able to stipulate and maintain the subject. It has been shown, in Part II of this book, that commencing with the debut novel of the first trilogy, Murakami refused to engage the subject of modernity which had emerged from modern Japanese fiction's modeling of itself on European naturalist and romantic notions of selfhood. Very few commentators have attempted to explicate how this refusal to privilege a discrete, fictional subject has been played out in the text of *Nejimakdori*—but the insights of those who have, are worth noting.

Katô, for example, in an essay sub-titled 'Ozomashisa to keiji' ('Horror and Revelation'), casts his discussion of the threat to the subject in terms of an aesthetic formulation not unfamiliar to Japanese readers: the dichotomy of being and non-being signified by the characters *yû/aru* (有) and *mu/nai* (無). [115] He refers to Kumiko's story of the 'thing' that was inserted into her (*jibun no naka ni ireta*) whereby she gained an extra 'unknown self' (*shiranai mô hitori no jibun*)—an experience described as the most wonderful thing to happen to her body. Was this re-gained 'thing' her own subjectivity, previously lost through the experiences of incestuous violation and abortion? Katô claims that this physically pleasurable experience is, paradoxically, later expressed in the episodes of skinning and appearance of the 'raw lumps of meat/the body' (*akamuke no nikkai*). Yet we are compelled to ask: why is this an experience of 'pleasure' (*kaikan*)? Katô argues that by using the horror movie-like form of the human being as depicted in *Nejimakidori*, Murakami has been able to substitute the depiction of 'nothing' (*nai*) with the depiction of the 'fact of the existence of nothing' (*nai ga aru koto*). And furthermore, that the substance of this novel is the 'narrative dynamic' (*monogatari teki rikigaku*) of having at its command the cinematic-like depiction of this 'fact of the existence of nothing'.

In explaining this, Katô notes that from within this dichotomy, two aspects of the 'non-self' (*jibun ga nai*) become apparent. His argument unfolds along the following lines. Looked at from the side of the self (*jibun no hô kara mirareba*), non-being can be seen as the dissolution of the ground of consciousness, and we sense the fact of the non-existence of being (*aru ga nai koto*). However, looked at from *outside* consciousness (*ishiki no soto kara mireba*), we get a reverse image, so to speak, of the fact of the existence of non-being (*nai ga aru koto*). The question arises for Katô: is the disappearance of the 'self' the disappearance of the united consciousness from within, *or* is it the appearance of that which is *not the self*?

His response is to suggest that earlier in *Nejimakidori*, we see the theme of the narrative enquiry into the drama of discovery of the exposure (*roshûtsu*) of the non-self *within* the self. However, later in the narrative, with the threatened loss of this self, and the subsequent non-appearance of something to replace it, Boku is visited by the revelation that he can no longer connect with that which is his *non-self*.[116] This is perhaps a rather long-winded way to say something relatively simple about the status of the subject and the figure of the abject in *Nejimakidori*. Nevertheless, it allows us to hone our argument by placing a kind of culturally contextualized caveat on the application of the theory, and despite this qualification, we can conclude that in the process of the awareness of the 'splitting' of the self with non-self, there arises, as Kristeva puts it, the situation of being *beside* oneself—a kind of trope of dissociation which we will now explore further.

Splitting the Difference: The Aesthetics of Dissociation

Interestingly, none of the Japanese commentators referred to here—most of whom are familiar with Western theory and the terminology of psychoanalysis—have used the term 'abject' (let alone 'sublime', *kôsô*) to describe the radical treatment of subjectivity in *Nejimakidori*. However, they have used approaches and terms which resonate with the idea of the transformation or subversion of an implied subject, a locus of consciousness expressed in terms of 'individual core' (*kojin no kaku*) or 'self' (*jibun*), which might undergo 'splitting' (*bunretsu*) or 'dissociation' (*kairi*).

For example, in his discussion of *Nejimakidori* in terms of the genre of 'horror' (*horâ*), Katô prefers the term *bunretsu* ('splitting') as a key explanatory principle used at a number of levels. Described as the application of a 'new literary method', the dismantled individual disappears in order to pass through the provisional structure of the narrative that lies ahead.[117] But the 'literary' application of movie-like images is a kind of 'reverse imitation' (*gyakuten sareta mohô*), which has the effect of doing away with the character's range of sight/view (*jinkakuteki shikai*) as in the genre of photo-realism. For Katô, the lump of red flesh which 'shows up' (to use Kristeva's phrase) in the episode of the Japanese soldier being skinned alive, indicates the original form (*genzô*: 'original figure', not a replica) of that which is not the self within the self,[118] and is synonymous with the *ozomashii mono* (the 'hideous thing') at the root of the suffering of characters in previous novels.[119]

Basically, however, Katô is attempting to describe his own version of abjection in terms of a splitting of the self with that which is *not* the self. In the world which Boku must descend into in order to 'rescue' Kumiko, he becomes that which is not himself (*jibun denai mono*), and commits acts of horrendous violence against the 'guitar player' and Wataya Noboru. Clearly this is the 'splitting' (*bunretsu*), the dissociation from the self, the 'being beside oneself' of abjection.

Yet, the contradiction arises, according to Katô, that with the loss of the basis (*konkyo*) of the self, and the becoming of the 'hideous thing' which is *not* the self, the subject (*shutai*) which is supposed to affect the rescue of Kumiko (or perhaps symbolic redemption of the dismantled 'self') is also dissolved. So we are faced with the basic problem of understanding the relation or nexus (*kankei*) between the fact of the loss of the basis of the self, and the fact of becoming something (*nanika*) which is *not* the self. We need consider Katô's observations no further here, except to note that on the plane of the literary, he claims that this disjunction appears as a 'splitting' between the 'large-scale narrative' (*ôki na monogatari*) and the 'small-scale 'novel' (*chîsana shôsetsu*).[120]

No matter how we rephrase the question of the abject, or the inexplicable appearance of the 'hideous thing' (*ozomashii mono*, that which is not the self)—and even if we attempt to explain this in terms of an explicit strategy to foreground the dissociative or disjunctive elements of this narrative—we inevitably return to the question of accounting for the vividly depicted representations of violence and horror in *Nejimakidori*. Are these merely devices of provocation? Or perhaps indicative of forms of authorially guided 'therapy' built into the reception possibilities of the text—a bringing to light of repressed memories?

Consistent with his characterization of Book Three of *Nejimakidori* as a 'second turning point or conversion' (*saitenkan*), Yoshida contextualizes his consideration of the function of violence (*bôryokusei*) in this novel, with a comment by Takeda Seiji. Takeda laments the fact that in the subsuming of the tale of the quest for the missing Kumiko within the narrative of evil played out by the figure of Wataya Noboru, the usual lyricism, the resonant charm characteristic of Murakami's fiction, is effectively destroyed.[121] There is no denying that the 'lighthearted' style of previous works is definitely absent from *Nejimakidori's* grave treatment of history and physical and psychological abuse, but this still does not fully explain the need for such graphic and direct representation of violent action.

In conversation with the Japanese psychiatrist Kawai Hayao, Murakami has stressed that in the imagined narrative of Boku's quest to retrieve his missing wife, the protagonist would have to 'turn something upside down' (*hikkuri kaeshi*), and this inevitably resulted in a resort to violence. In the section of the dialogue entitled 'The Violence in Japanese Society', he also concedes that although at a personal, authorial level, he is at a loss to explain his creation of such extreme images (the skinning episodes and the execution of Chinese prisoners), at a more abstract level, the nexus between the personal world of darkness and historical violence is clear:

「……闇の世界はなにかというと、そこにはえんえん積み重なった歴史的な暴力というのが存在しているのです。」[122]

If one asks 'what is the world of darkness?' — it is that place where far-reaching, accumulated historical violence exists.

Murakami goes on to reflect on the probability (*gaizensei*) that the personal violence which is used to return from the 'world of darkness' (*yami no sekai*) to the 'world of light' (*hikari no sekai*) at the end of Book Three, is in concert with historical violence — and this reflects his own particular sense of historical awareness (*rekishi ninshiki*).[123]

Remaining dissatisfied with Murakami's explanation, Yoshida suspects that the inclusion of this violence is arbitrary and unconvincing — adding that the author is attempting to depict a violence that he has no connection with.[124] Nevertheless, the concession is made that during his four and a half years in America, Murakami came to the realization of the idea that through violence, history is embodied/made flesh (*nikkuka suru*), and through the corresponding 'non-fictionalization of the interior', (a term which Yoshida borrows from Yamada Eimi) can be 'measured'. The extent to which this 'interior' (*naimen*) relates to the idea of the subject is unclear from Yoshida's analysis, although what is more apparent is that it suggests the stipulation of a certain 'historicity' (*rekishisei*) which can be gleaned in Murakami's much discussed move from 'detachment' (*kakawari no nasa*) to 'commitment' (*kakawari*).

What is interesting here is the shoring up of the subject (in the form of the 'non-fictionalized' interior) as a precondition for the acceptance of 'historicity' (*rekishisei*). In particular, it is in Book Three of *Nejimakidori* that, according to Yoshida's estimation, 'history' takes the form of an 'arbitrarily adopted presupposition' (*shiiteki ni toriagerareta zentei*). Rather than being a failing, this 'presupposition' is actually a symptom or indication of *Nejimakidori's* radical treatment of the problem of history. We have already shown that Yoshida recognized this when he drew a firm distinction between the genre of the conventional 'historical novel' (exemplified by Yasuoka's *Ryûritan*) and the *Nejimakidori* trilogy.

If Yoshida's hunch about history signified as a 'presupposition' in *Nejimakidori* is correct, his conclusion about the implications of this does not accord with the general thrust of the argument developed in this chapter. On the contrary, the idea of history as 'presupposition' casts it as a kind of secondary *effect* — which, it is implied, informs the conditions of exteriority of the text's production, which themselves can never be adequately presented *in* or *through* the text itself. Rather, such conditions entail the phantasmal presentation of a kind 'facticity' or 'eventivity', instead of the re-presentation of the 'facts' and 'events' usually associated with the methods of 'reconstructionist' historiography.

In other words, the lack of an emphatic insistence on 'the real' in *Nejimakidori* does not preclude the possibility of a referentiality which has 'reality effects'— and which is, therefore, also productive of the discourses to which it refers. As Yoshida concedes, however, the presupposition of history as historicity does reflect the complexity of the 'difficult themes' facing the protagonist of this novel. And such complexity is confirmed by Murakami's own admission of the apprehension which he felt about the extent to which his powers of logic and integration could adequately handle the materials he uncovered in his research on the Nomonhan Incident.[125]

If Katô's analysis unwittingly describes the split subject as a version of the Kristevan theory of abjection, and Yoshida's approach couches this division in terms of the subject 'fleshed-out' or embodied in the violence of history, Saito's perspective can be said to implicate both approaches in its foregrounding of the psychoanalytic theory of dissociation (*kairi*). As a psychiatrist himself, Saito immediately discerns the significance of Murakami's 'confession' (in dialogue with Kawai)[126] that he had no clear idea why certain actions were represented in the text and what meanings were generated by them. Acknowledging that Murakami's works in the nineties have achieved a 'high standard' in terms of being able to couple 'trauma and dissociation' (*torauma to kairi*), he enthusiastically declares that he has something to learn (in a professional sense) about the 'phenomenon of dissociation', by reading *Nejimakdori*.[127]

Here we see an indirect reference to the contradictory tension between the splitting of the subject (the discordant and conflicting modalities of the subject, directly linking the discursive power of the writing of history—the efficacy of its logic—to its power to synthesize and integrate the chaotic contents of history) and the command to bring-to-order the subject of history, and history as subject. But to what extent is this reflective of a more fundamental schism in the interstitial spaces of subjectivity (arrayed between memory and thought) implied by the dissociative effect of bringing together the conventionally perceived modalities of 'fiction' and 'history'? Or, to rephrase the question: in the context of their deployment in *Nejimakidori* and the critical texts surrounding it, are these narrative modalities fundamentally in conflict or not?

In terms of the contradictory, multiple meanings of *Nejimakidori* as contemporary fiction, our answer to this question is in the affirmative. We have provided evidence of the 'parasitic' simulacral relations of the two modalities (and later will show even the surprising 'inversion' of their relations) in order to support this proposition. Yet the implied 'violence' of this conflict is not indicative of artistic shortcoming. On the contrary, this artful grating together of two heterogeneous language games is indicative precisely of the mature Murakami's contribution to the important task of developing the sophistication of the debate around Japanese modernity from *within* what Karatani describes as the 'closed discursive space' of Japan.

This is why, amongst the many critical responses to *Nejimakidori*, Saitô's application of the psychoanalytic term 'dissociation' (although disarmingly simple) is also, at an abstract level, one of the most apposite tropes for our consideration of the text's significance for contemporary Japanese writing. Whether it be in terms of the critical undecidability of the text's genre, or the disjunctive modalities available in the reader's aesthetic construction of it as narrative, the sense that in *Nejimakidori* something is awry, out of synch, is undeniable.

Saitô points out that dissociation is a phenomenon that depends on the functioning of a phantasm (*gensô*) which can be transposed into the broader context of a fictional work (*kyokôsakuhin*). In this kind of world, some things are dissociated (*kairi sareru*) and others are repeated (*hanfuku sareru*)—the point being that some readers will take dissociation as a kind of 'mannerism' (*mannerizumu*), while others will take it as indicating simply the 'reality of repetition' (*hanfuku no riaritei*).[128] This sense of the disconnected, the disjunctive, the separate (and notwithstanding the conventional, psychopathological description of the coexistence of two or more distinct 'personalities' in the same person), can manifest as a defensive mechanism which protects against trauma and stress.

An important aspect of Saitô's description is in regard to what he describes as the loss of 'spatio-temporal continuity' (*jikanteki-kûkanteki na renzokusei*) in the mind of the individual'.[129] Here, we recall our earlier reference to Jameson's characterization of the postmodern as a kind of 'schizophrenic' construction of time, and Baudrillard's depiction of the 'schizo [who] is bereft of every scene, open to everything in spite of himself, living in the greatest confusion'.[130] On this point, we have already shown not only that the spatio-temporal logic of *Nejimakidori* assumes several forms of narrative re-telling, but also that these forms reflect a range of subjective displacements variously ordered within the overall aesthetic of the sublime.

Of all Saitô's observations on *Nejimakidori*, perhaps the one most immediately pertinent to the concluding argument of this chapter relates to nomenclature; that is, naming, and the proper noun. He reminds us of Karatani Kôjin's assertion (discussed in an earlier chapter) regarding Murakami's 'resistance' (*teiko*) to proper nouns (*koyûme*) in support of a general claim that dissociation, which can be a response to loss, manifests itself as a resistance to proper nouns.[131] It is clear that proper nouns in *Nejimakidori* keep shifting and being displaced: when Kumiko leaves the house, she loses her name and becomes the anonymous 'erotic telephone woman'; the cat (Wataya Noboru) disappears, and gets renamed Sawara upon return; when the 'prostitute of the mind', Kanô Kureta, ceases sexual engagement with Boku, she loses her name.[132]

Proceeding from the proposition that schizophrenia (*rijinbyô*) or the condition of 'the loss of the sense of reality' (*genjitsukansôshitsu*) is nothing other than the process of the 'becoming anonymous' (*tokumeika*)—the robbing of the self-image and world-image of its peculiarity (*koyûsei*) or substantiality (*kono-monosei*)—Saitô reflects on the emptying out of meaning in dissociation. In response to the question as to why dissociation entails an avoidance of peculiarity or substantiality, he concludes that the subject (*shutai*) defends itself from the wounds of external experience through 'forgetfulness' or 'being oblivious' (*bôkyaku suru*) to the world, and notes that Murakami himself, describing *Neji-makidori* in its form as a 'holy grail legend' kind of narrative, takes the task of retrieving or recuperating (*torimodosu*) 'something' as its central motif. But how does the process of dissociation bring to light what precisely it is that needs to be recuperated? And how does it relate to the graphic representation of violence, of horror, as episodes of 'extreme imagination' in this novel? Before responding to these questions, we pause to consider a further aspect of subjectivity elucidated by Kristeva, which provides a link between semiotic 'splitting' as dissociation, and the figural presentation of the abject.

As we have shown earlier, according to the Kristevan poetics of subjectivity, although the desiring subject (the subject which seeks meaning) is imagined as an existential locus of consciousness, it is only ever enacted as a *process* within language and the Symbolic. The modalities of this engagement require a synthesis—what Kristeva calls a 'condensation' or semiotic conjunction—of the components of the sign, regulated by the auditory and visual sensory modalities of the body. This conjunction shores up the subject's own imagined unity by enacting the semantic efficacy of the sign. However, when this condensed structure is threatened, ruptured or split, there arises a concomitant threat to the subject, and subsequently to the order (the Symbolic) which sustains it. Kristeva explains condensation thus:

> What is it that insures the existence of the sign, that is, of the relation that is a condensation between sound and image (on the side of word presentation) and visual image (on the side of thing presentation)? Condensation is indeed what we are dealing with, and the logic of dreams testifies to it when it brings together elements from different perception registers or when it engages in ellipses.[133]

Since all meaning is *metaphorically* inscribed within a circular system of signification and referentiality, metaphor marks the site at which the components of signification and the Oedipal order converge:

> The figure of speech known as metaphor merely actuates, within the synchronic handling of discourse, the process that, genetically and diachronically, makes up one signifying unit out of at least two (sound and sight) components. But the speaking subject enjoys the possibility of condensation because it is inscribed in the Oedipal triangle.[134]

The speaking subject is at best a tentative process which can be undermined:

> Nevertheless, when the condensation function that constitutes the sign collapses (and in that case one always discovers a collapse of the Oedipal triangulation that supports it), once the sound image/sight image solidarity is undone, such a splitting allows one to detect an attempt at direct semanticization of acoustic, tactile, motor, visual, etc., coenaesthesia. A language now manifests itself

whose complaint becomes an idiolect, and finally resolves itself through the sudden irruption of affect.[135]

This 'affect', could clearly be manifested in the form of symptoms of dissociation—of 'forgetfulness' (*bôkyaku*), the displacing of and resistance to proper nouns, and the disruption of subjectivity and spatio-temporal continuity in many of the narrative lines that we have referred to so far. And significantly, in the privileging of the register of the auditory in *Nejimakidori* (discussed in Chapter 9) we can discern a disruption of the semiotic condensation which sustains the Oedipal configuration and the order of the Symbolic. A clear instance of this occurs in the dream-scene where Cinnamon intuitively registers the 'murder' of his mother by his father.

In an eerily silent dreamscape, where 'the wind-up bird no longer cried' (*The night was so silent it almost hurt the boy's ears*),[136] the boy dreams of unearthing a freshly buried throbbing human heart which 'beat as one with his': clearly his mother's heart, the maternal heart. This heart had been buried by 'the man who looked like his father'.[137] In Cinnamon's experience of dissociation, in his feeling of abjection, not only does he feel 'beside' himself (in the sense that he had been 'put into a new container')[138] but evidence of the 'splitting' as dissolution of the Oedipal is evident from the way that he is suddenly rendered unable to utter the word 'mother':

「彼の声帯はそこにある空気を震わせることができない。まるで『お母さん』という言葉そのものが世界から消え失せてしまったみたいに。でも消えたのが言葉ではないことに少年はやがて気づく。」[139]

His vocal chords were unable to stir the air, as if the very word 'mother' had disappeared from the world. Before long, the boy realized that the word was not what had disappeared.[140]

The implication is that not only had the signifier, the quasi proper noun 'mother' disappeared, but the signified, the meaning content, the 'referent'—the actual object/image of his desire—had vanished. The splitting of the Oedipal configuration had worked in reverse, so to speak, and resulted in a crisis of the sign in which the auditory and visual registers would never again take the form of a condensation, forever separated in the lived experience of the boy's muteness in 'real' life.

Yet, paradoxically, in losing his voice—and thus the means for expressing his own *audible* language—Cinnamon becomes the 'historian', the official 'chronicler' of Nutmeg's stories of her and her father's life on the Asian continent, filling in the gaps in her memory, embellishing events, transforming and *re-writing* the stories he has heard to the point where their historical 'accuracy' is placed under serious question. Although he can speak, his writing is out of control, and this graphic incontinence undermines the Symbolic as the place where condensed 'signs' form the usual currency of exchange between 'speaking subjects'.

Just as significantly, Cinnamon's seemingly self indulgent embellishment in writing the past is clearly an ironic, indirect reference to the motivation and practices of so called 'reconstructionist' historiography. Through his writing, Cinnamon was searching for something:

> 「おそらくシナモンは自分という人間の存在理由を真剣に探しているのだ。彼はそれを自分がまだ生まれる以前に遡って探索していたに違いない。」[141]

> He was engaged in a serious search for the meaning of his own existence. And he was hoping to find it by looking into the events that had preceded his birth.[142]

In order to achieve this, however, it was necessary that his writing attempt to impose a certain sense of continuity and order on the discontinuous and chaotic 'events' which he narrated:

> 「……自分の手の届かないいくつかの過去の空白を埋める必要がある。そこで彼は物語を自分の手で作り上げることで、そのミッシング・リンクを充当しようとしたのだ。」[143]

> Cinnamon had to fill in those blank spots in the past that he could not reach with his own hands. By using those hands to make a story, he was trying to supply the missing links.[144]

and also

> 「そして物語の基本的なスタイルを、彼は母親の物語からそのまま受け継いでいた。それは事実は真実ではないかもしれないし、真実は事実ではないかもしれないということだ。」[145]

> He inherited from his mother's stories the fundamental style he used, unaltered, in his own stories: namely, the assumption that fact may not be truth, and truth may not be factual.[146]

Here, one of the most important narrative lines of the novel dealing with memory, history and events originally passed on *aurally* (it could *go on taking in changes and growing as a story does in oral transmission*[147]) from Nutmeg's father to Nutmeg, then from Nutmeg to Cinnamon, is finally transcribed onto the *Nejimakidori kuronikuru* files stored digitally as combinations of '0's and '1's in the hard disc of Cinnamon's computer, and retrievable only as written text.[148] This indirectly connotes an effective *splitting* of the condensation processes of the sign, which usually 'unite' the auditory and the visual.

As we noted earlier, according to Kristeva, following the collapse of the condensation function

> The body's inside . . . shows up in order to compensate for the collapse of the border between inside and outside.[149]

When the 'fragile container' of the skin is breached, where semen, blood, the slimy body organs and the clod of flesh 'show up' in the text of *Nejimakidori*, according to Kristeva's argument, we are witnessing an abjection which is fundamentally about reassuring a subject that is lacking its 'own and clean self'. But more than that, it is also about an overcoming of the threat of castration of the male subject:

> The abjection of those flows from within suddenly become the sole 'object' of sexual desire—a true 'ab-ject' where man, frightened, crosses over the horrors of maternal bowels and, in an immersion that enables him to avoid coming face to face with an other, spares himself the risk of castration.[150]

In short, abjection becomes the substitute for the other, and for Kristeva the 'frontiersman' who engages in it becomes a 'metaphysician who carries the experience of the impossible to the point of scatology'.[151] In *Nejimakidori*, is this metaphysician the figure of the protagonist Boku, who experiences or witnesses, directly or vicariously, just about every possible form of abjection imaginable? And if it is, are the frontiers which he approaches merely mechanisms for the avoidance of symbolic castration? Or, perhaps it is the figure of Wataya Noboru, as the perpetrator of acts of extreme violation on women who maintains an obsession with the obscene to the point of scatology? We do not require (nor would it be useful to pursue) clear-cut answers to such questions, and to further explore this would be to deviate from the main objective of this chapter, which is to explicate versions of the sublime (corporeal, historical and political) as the central aesthetic apparatuses of the main narrative lines in *Nejimakidori*.

It is useful, however, to relate the psychoanalytic reading developed so far, directly to the narrative eventuality whereby the possessor of the phallus and maintainer of the symbolic order, Wataya Noboru, is 'eliminated'. And also, to enquire as to the possible implications of this for the symbolic order, and the orders of the political in the presented world of this novel expressed in terms of some of the discursive regimes which constitute contemporary Japanese culture. Specifically, these are the regime of 'literature', regulated by the implicit critical-fictional discipline of the *bundan*, tempered by the dictates of the media-entertainment industries; and the regime of 'history', orchestrated by a complex interplay between the discourses of scholarly academia, the administration of educational curricula, and extending even to the highest levels of the judicial system.[152]

But in relation to the debate which has grown up around the problem of adequately situating *Nejimakidori* within the limits imposed by these regimes, we also note another kind of discourse: almost a hybrid, inter-discursive dialogue which operates 'outside' expected orthodoxies, taking form as a kind of psycho-analytic/psycho-political exegesis of the *Nejimakidori* text, and which revolves around the problem of the subject in Japanese modernity, and the recuperative narrative strategies entailed in stipulating/situating such a subject in terms of the categories of the political and the ethical. These strategies have been intimated in the critiques of *Nejimakidiori* offered by Yoshida and Katô as outlined above, but in concluding this chapter and fleshing out the political dimensions of the sublime, we revisit Saitô's psychoanalytic reading of the text in conjunction with further reference to Murakami's fascinating dialogue with the psychiatrist Kawai.

Firstly, however, we reiterate that the collapse of the 'Oedipal triangulation' through the splitting of the condensation function entailed in the abject presentation of the body is signified in the subversion of the 'law of the father' in the form of Wataya Noboru's demise and 'virtual murder' in Boku's dream-scene.[153] This dream is *preceded*, in simulacral fashion, by the prophetic appearance of the event of the attack in the presented, 'real' world of the novel: Boku learns of the attack he will perpetrate via the TV news,[154] and then enacts it in his dream. The distinction between 'real' and 'fictional' is dissolved here, and the usual temporal sequence of prophecy (the dream of the event followed by the occurrence of the event) is reversed.

Because Wataya Noboru is fictionally portrayed as the archetypal product of nepotism and corrupt patronage, the political rising star of the postwar Japanese system, this 'figurative' collapse and temporal inversion can be transposed onto the larger *political* and *historical* plane as connotative of, and not unrelated to the subversion of the presentation — indeed the repression — of the violence and trauma of Japan's encounter with modernity. That is, the inability *on a collective scale* (recall Durkheim's 'collective memory') to present, in terms of the na-tional-cultural memory (or the 'national-cultural-imaginary' proposed by Ivy) the contents of the abject/sublime imagination to rational understanding, albeit enacted by the provisional, elusive subject in/of Japanese modernity.

At this point it is useful to recall that Kant characterizes the experience of the sublime as 'the feeling of the unattainability of the idea by means of imagina-tion',[155] as the basis for the awareness of a contradictory, simultaneous sense of pleasure mixed with pain.[156] And it is significant that Lyotard's description of the postmodern sublime as a kind of avant-garde performative disjunction, whereby the 'impotence of the imagination . . . attests to an imagination striving to figure that which cannot be figured',[157] acknowledges that (this) 'avant-gardism is . . . present in the Kantian aesthetic of the sublime'.[158]

What seems to be a contradictory irruption of promise and threat in both the abject and the sublime is for Kristeva not surprising, because, as she argues, the two states unfold along the same experiential continuum. The admixture of pleasure/pain in the abject and the sublime are described as transformations of the appearance of the symptom as horror, and the blissful quietude of aesthetic contemplation in sublimated restraint:

> In the symptom, the abject permeates me, I become abject. Through sublima-
> tion, I keep it under control. The abject is edged with the sublime. It is not the
> same moment on the journey, but the same subject and speech bring them into
> being.[159]

And, just as in the abject,

> the sublime has no object either . . . The 'sublime' object dissolves in the rap-
> tures of a bottomless memory . . . the sublime is something added that expands
> us, overstrains us. . . . A divergence, an impossible bounding.[160]

This 'impossible bounding' is of course the double-sided coin of the pleasure and pain of the sublime: in the oscillating movement, the rising and the receding, the ebb and flow of the threat to the subject, a kind of pleasure arises—a synchronically experienced sense of liberation within constraint. And for Mura-kami's readers, perhaps a liberation from a 'self' which was awkwardly in-scribed in modern narrative in a way which never really fitted. Katô's *nai/aru* dichotomy—the trope of being and non-being—is much more apposite to the circumspect, tentative projection of 'the self' in Japanese speech and writing as the manifestation, perhaps, of no more than a necessary deictic locus, as well as the interchangeable elements of the key ontological formulation ('form is empti-ness/emptiness is form') of the *Hannya shingyô* which informs certain schools of Japanese Buddhist thought and scriptural/ritualistic performance.

We are aware that Kant integrates the seemingly contradictory nature of his aesthetic of the sublime by an appeal to a moral universality as the highest inte-grating principle, and it is also the case that Lyotard goes on to develop an im-portant enquiry into the nexus between the communicability of competing dis-courses and justice, in terms of his theory of the 'differend'. It should come as no surprise, therefore, that in our exploration of the sublime as a key aesthetic device in *Nejimakidori*, we end up with a consideration of questions of *praxis*: of ethics, justice, and the category of the political.

This shifts our focus to the politics of history, a *historical politics* and most certainly a politics of reading (very different to the ironicized politics of reading of the first trilogy)—which is exactly what Saitô is talking about, and what Mu-rakami and Kawai are gesturing towards in their long dialogue about *Nejimaki-dori*. In fact, Saitô's concluding comments on dissociation as the central trope of *Nejimakidori* unfold in a section entitled, significantly, 'The Historical Subject and Dissociative Ethics' (*Rekishiteki shutai, kairiteki rinri*), and are made in the context of a critically reflective encounter with Murakami's own dialogue with Kawai.

Saitô dismisses Ôtsuka's claim that Murakami is motivated by an impatience or irritability (*shôsô*) towards history. He suggests, instead, that whatever 'artificiality' (*sakui*) is pre-supposed in *Nejimakidori*, the motif of dissociation (*kairi*) can be regarded as being synonymous with a disease state or pathological condition (*byôjô*).[161] Noting that no other critiques of *Nejimakidori* have directly touched on the motif of dissociation, Saitô claims that in this novel, the question of *seishi* or 'authentic history' (records, chronicles, accounts) is not addressed. Rather, the question posed is: precisely how should we face up to history in ethical terms?

Saitô's response to this is illuminating. Conceding that the trauma (*gaishôsei*) and the particularity (*koyûsei*) of history should be mediated by what he terms the 'trained imagination' (*kunren sareta sôzô*), he characterizes *Nejimakidori* as an effective attempt at such mediation and then goes on to cite a crucial comment by Murakami in his dialogue with Kawai:

> 「……現代、同時代における個人というものをもし描こうとしても、……日本における個人というものの定義がすごくあいまいなのですね。ところが、歴史という縦の糸を持ってくることで、日本という国の中で生きる個人というのは、もっとわかりやすくなるのではないかという気が、なぜかしたのです。」[162]

Even if we try to depict the contemporary individual, the definition of the individual in Japan is very vague. However, by bringing along the vertical thread of history, why is it that we get the feeling that it becomes easier to understand the individual living in a country such as Japan . . ?[163]

Saitô notes that in taking up this thread of history, Murakami's method is to carefully construct a 'dissociated fictional space' (*kairishita kyokôkûkan*). The dissociation, the sense of disjunction, occurs when, after thoroughly putting into doubt the 'continuity of the world' (*sekai no renzokusei*), the narrative suddenly introduces an 'historical event' such as the Nomonhan Incident (*Nomonhan Jihen*) which is neither positioned in the present nor the past, but nevertheless assumes a 'strange reality' of its own.

It is precisely this sudden, unexpected introduction of the proper noun (*koyûme*) which strongly signifies the return of the referent which has been absent or formerly repressed. This reflects a larger desire to recuperate the referent at a much more strategically important level, and is expressed in the non-ironic use of other proper nouns such as Nihon, Manshû and so on. It is nothing other than the lost or repressed referent, in the form of the proper nouns of history, that Murakami is trying to recuperate. And the fictional presentation of the threat of dissolution, or the splitting of the subject, describes the process of an attempted recuperation—the first therapeutic steps required of the subject: the bringing to light of the contents of repressed historical memory, the reliving of its pain, and the re-instatement of the referent and the proper noun to their rightful role in a socially engaged context.

For Saitô, the fictional modality of dissociation, 'calls forth' the trauma of history and introduces a kind of 'historical materialism' (*rekishi no yuibutsuron*).

But for Murakami, the pain of the violence and trauma of history are concealed within a complicit silence, a vapid social 'correctness' apparent in contemporary Japanese society:

「僕が日本の社会を見て思うのは、痛みというか、苦痛のない正しさは意味のない正しさということです。」[164]

What comes to mind when I look at Japanese society is the meaningless correctness of a correctness without pain.

In response to this, Saitô concludes that in order to recuperate the particularity of an individual, the pain of dissociation has to be repeated, and then passed through. This applies especially to us who are living at the 'end of history', because the violence and trauma of history is detached from the foundation of any wholeness—and this is precisely why an ethicality (*rinrisei*) which can become standard or normative is required.[165] But Saitô's insightful analysis is, for our purposes, also somewhat incomplete. It finishes with a question about 'ethics' (*rinri*) which requires further exploration, and this is precisely where the momentum of the argument developed in this chapter has been heading: to a consideration, in the Conclusion, of the representational possibilities of the historical, narrated subject, within the context of the agonistic discursive regimes of contemporary Japanese culture.

In this chapter it has been argued that the main narrative lines of *Nejimakidori* are characterized by a kind of poetics of dissociation: a rupturing of our sense of the typical semantic processes made available by realist narrative, in the incessant deferral of the displaced subject/object of Boku's desire; in the rupture between history and personal/collective memory in Nutmeg's stories; and in the contradictory processes of abjection played out in various episodes depicting revulsion and horror. In all of these, we have seen in operation a form of the sublime as an aesthetic function, and it has been shown that this can operate across a range of representational modalities including the visual, the auditory, the corporeal and the historical. One aim of the Conclusion which follows, is to explore how these fictional modalities interact with other discursive regimes as forms of dispute and contestation, exemplified in Lyotard's notion of the 'differend'.

Notes

1. NDK: 2; 1; 7. WBC: 2; 1; 183.
2. Rubin, "Sekusu to rekishi to kioku—Murakami Haruki 'Nejimakidori kuronikuru'," 254-259.
3. Rubin, "Murakami Haruki," in *Modern Japanese Writers*, 239.

4. Strecher, "Magical Realism and the Search for Identity in the Fiction of Murakami Haruki," 287.

5. Ishikura, "Aratana sekaizô no kakutoku — 'Nejimakidori kuronikuru' ron," in *Murakami Haruki Sutadeizu 04* (Wakakusa Shobô, 1999), 119-151; 129,130.

6. Ishikura, "Murakami Haruki 'Nejimakidori kuronikuru' nôto," Senshû Daigaku Daigakuin, *Bunken Ronshû* (October, 1994): 1-36; 20, 21.

7. NDK 2: 6; 108-9.

8. WBC 2: 6; 230.

9. NDK 2: 11; 196.

10. WBC 2: 11; 280.

11. WBC 2: 11; 280.

12. NDK 1: 1; 9.

13. WBC 1: 1; 11.

14. NDK 1: 1; 6.

15. WBC 1: 1; 15.

16. NDK 1: 2; 57.

17. WBC 1: 2; 30.

18. Gabriele Schwab, *The Mirror and the Killer Queen: Otherness in Literary Language* (Bloomington: Indiana University Press, 1996), 171.

19. NDK 1: 1; 12.

20. WBC 1: 1; 8.

21. See Schwab, *The Mirror and the Killer Queen*, 170. Schwab is citing Marguerite Duras's *The Malady of Death*, a short story originally published in French, in 1982. See *The Malady of Death*, trans. Barbara Bray (New York: Grove, 1986).

22. Schwab, *The Mirror and the Killer Queen*, 171.

23. For episodes of ejaculation and suppressed urges of ejaculation, see for example NDK 1: 9; 189, WBC 1: 9; 103, and NDK 2: 8; 141., WBC 2: 8; 249.

24. NDK 2: 4 ; 74.

25. WBC 2: 4; 214.

26. NDK 2: 4; 73.

27. WBC 2: 4; 214.

28. NDK 3: 9; 100.

29. WBC 3: 8; 397.

30. NDK 3: 9; 100.

31. WBC 3: 8; 397.

32. See Kobayashi Masaaki, *Murakami Haruki: Tô to umi no kanata ni* (Shinwasha, 1998), 160.

33. Kobayashi, *Murakami Haruki: Tô to umi no kanata ni*, 160-61.

34. Jacques Lacan, *The Language of the Self: The Function of Language in Psychoanalysis*, trans. Anthony Wilden (New York: Dell Publishing, 1968), 63.

35. Lacan, *The Language of the Self*, 64.

36. Lacan, *The Language of the Self*, 63.

37. NDK 3: 23; 253-54.

38. WBC 3: 22; 489.

39. As shown in arguments presented above by both Ruthrof and Lacan.

40. NDK 3: 23; 264.

41. WBC 3: 22; 495.

42. NDK 3: 23; 264.

43. NDK 3: 23; 264.

44. Quoted from Buruma, *The Wages of Guilt: Memories of War in Germany and Japan*, 199.

45. Nietzsche, "The Use and Abuse of History," 61.

46. Nietzsche, "The Use and Abuse of History," 61.

47. See Karatani, "The Discursive Space of Modern Japan".

48. See Frederic Jameson, *Postmodernism, or, The Cultural Logic of Late Capitalism* (Durham: Duke University Press, 1991), 18; 25.

49. Frow, "Repetition and Forgetting," 219.

50. Frow, "Repetition and Forgetting" 219-221. Frow is referring to Pierre Nora's "Between Memory and History: *Les Lieux de Memoire*," trans. Marc Roudebush, *Representations* 26 (Spring 1989): 7.

51. NDK 3: 10; 105-129, and WBC 3: 9; 400-415.

52. NDK 3: 28; 303-327, and WBC 3: 26; 511-526.

53. NDK 3: 10; 106-8; 129-132; NDK 3: 28; 326-7, and WBC 3: 9; 401-2, 415-18; WBC 3: 26; 526.

54. NDK 3: 28; 323 and WBC 3: 26; 523.

55. NDK 3: 21; 245-6 and WBC 3; 20; 483.

56. WBC 3: 20; 482.

57. NDK 3: 10; 128.

58. WBC 3: 9; 415.

59. See Hasumi Shigehiko, "Jikan no nagarenu tôjita sekai usukimiwarui hodô no sôzôryoku," "Bungei jihyô," *Asahi Shinbun (yûkan)* (August 2, 1995).

60. Yoshida, *Murakami Haruki, tenkan suru*, 210-11.

61. NDK 3: 21; 231.

62. WBC 3: 20:474.

63. *Kenkyûsha's New Japanese-English Dictionary*, 588.

64. *Kenkyûsha's New Japanese-English Dictionary*, 290.

65. NDK 3: 15; 183, and WBC 3: 14; 447.

66. Suzumura Kazunari & Numano Mitsuyoshi, "'Nejimakidori' wa doko e tobu ka," *Bungakkai* 49, no. 10 (October 1995), 100-123; 123.

67. Barbara Foley, *Telling the Truth: The Theory and Practice of Documentary Fiction* (Ithaca: Cornell University Press, 1986), 27.

68. Nancy S. Struever, "Historical Discourse," in *Handbook of Discourse Analysis (Vol.1)*, ed. Teun A. Van Dijk (London: Academic Press Inc. Ltd, 1985), 249-271; 261-264. The first model is exemplified in Barthe's famous 1967 essay Le Discours de l'histoire; the second, in line with White's tropological analysis (1973); the third model of 'history as argument', emerged from more general initiatives in the historiography of science by Kuhn (1977), Feyerabend (1978), and Hesse (1978), and this model, writes Struever, necessarily confronted the issues of the 'distribution, exchange and reception of historical information and insight'.

69. NDK 3: 10; 117.

70. WBC 3: 9; 408.

71. NDK 3: 10; 114.

72. WBC 3: 9; 406.

73. NDK 3: 10; 116-117.

74. WBC 3: 9; 408.

75. NDK 3: 10; 133.

76. WBC 3: 9; 418. Note that the English text mistakenly translates 「七日前に」 as 'six days before'.

77. Cited in Martha J. Reineke, *Sacrificed Lives: Kristeva on Women and Violence* (Bloomington: Indiana University Press, 1997), 49.

78. Sue Vice, *Psychoanalytic Criticism: A Reader*, ed. Sue Vice (Cambridge: Polity Press, 1996), 150 - 153.Vice describes 'the semiotic' as the pre-Oedipal realm where the infant exists in as state of being defined by the 'pulsions' of the mothers body as well as its own drives.

79. Julia Kristeva, *Powers of Horror: An Essay on Abjection*, trans. Leon S. Roudiez (New York: Columbia University Press), 1982.

80. Victor Burgin, "Geometry and Abjection," in *Abjection, Melancholia and Love: The Work of Julia Krisatevai*, ed. J. Fletcher & A. Benjamin (London & New York: Routledge & Kegan Paul, 1990), 115.

81. NDK 2: 10; 156

82. WBC 2: 10; 258.

83. *Kenkyûsha's New Japanese-English Dictionary*, 1260.

84. *Kenkyûsha's New Japanese-English Dictionary*, 1181.

85. Elizabeth Grosz, *Sexual Subversions: Three French Feminists* (Sydney: Allen & Unwin, 1989), p. 50; cited in *Psychoanalytic Criticism: A Reader*, ed. Sue Vice (Cambridge: Polity Press, 1996), 152.

86. NDK 2: 7; 112.

87. WBC 2: 7; 232-3.

88. NDK 2: 7; 112.

89. WBC 2: 7; 233.

90. Horst Ruthrof, *The Body in Language* (London And New York, Cassell, 2000); especially Chapter 6, "Sign Conflict: Meaning as Heterosemiotic," 72,73. Ruthrof is quoting from Diane Ackerman, *A Natural History of the Senses* (New York: Vintage Books, 1991), 95.

91. Kristeva, *Powers of Horror*, 1-2.

92. WBC 2 13; 303.

93. NDK 2: 13; 236-237.

94. WBC 2: 13; 303-4.

95. WBC 2: 13; 303.

96. Kristeva, *Powers of Horror*, 2.

97. NDK 2: 13; 237.

98. WBC 2; 13; 304.

99. Kristeva, *Powers of Horror*, 155.

100. Kristeva, *Powers of Horror*, 155.

101. WBC 2: 13; 303.

102. WBC 1: 13; 159.

103. NDK 1: 13; 286-7

104. WBC 1: 13; 160.

105. NDK 2: 17; 326.

106. WBC 2: 16; 339-40.

107. NDK 2: 17; 326.

108. WBC 2: 16; 340. Note that the translation of this passage by Rubin is slightly adapted in the last line of the passage.

109. Gail Weiss, *Body Images: Embodiment as Intercorporeality* (New York: Routledge, 1999), 92.

110. Elizabeth Grosz, cited in Gail Weiss, *Body Images: Embodiment as Intercorporeality*, 92.

111. Kristeva, *Powers of Horror*, 53.

112. Jean Baudrillard, *The Transparency of Evil: Essays on Extreme Phenomena*, trans. James Benedict (London: Verso, 1993).

113. Stephen Snyder, "Extreme Imagination: The Fiction of Murakami Ryû," in *Oe and Beyond: Fiction in Contemporary Japan* (Honolulu: University of Hawaii Press, 1999), 199-218; 215. Snyder gives as examples of the fiction of 'extreme imagination', Murakami Ryû's *Kagiri naku tômei ni chikai burû* (1976; 1977); *Koin rokkâ beibîzu* (1980; English translation 1995), *Gofungo no sekai* (1994) and *Piasshingu* (1994).

114. See Hayao Kawai & Murakami Haruki, *Murakami Haruki, Kawai Hayao ni Ai ni Iku* (Iwanami Shoten, 1996), 76.

115. See Katô, "'Nejimakidori kuronikuru': ozomashisa to keiji," in *Murakami Haruki—ierôpêji*, 204.

116. Katô, "'Nejimakidori kuronikuru': ozomashisa to keiji," 204-5.

117. Katô, "'Nejimakidori kuronikuru': ozomashisa to keiji," 197.

118. Katô, "'Nejimakidori kuronikuru': ozomashisa to keiji," 207. Katô notes several other instances of the image of skin (*hifu*) in *Nejimakidori*. See fn. 10 on this page.

119. Katô, "'Nejimakidori kuronikuru': ozomashisa to keiji," 207-8. For example, the characters of Gotanda, in *Dansu, dansu, dansu* and Naoku, in *Noruei no mori* .

120. Katô, "'Nejimakidori kuronikuru': ozomashisa to keiji," 205.

121. Yoshida, *Murakami Haruki—tenkan suru*, 205. Yoshida cites Takeda Seiji's "Hibiki to merodei," *Gunzô*, (Sept.1995). (No page number provided).

122. *Murakami Haruki, Kawai Hayao ni ai ni iku*, Tokyo: Iwanami shoten, 1996, 173; Yoshida, *Murakami Haruki—tenkan suru*, 207.

123. *Murakami Haruki, Kawai Hayao ni ai ni iku*, 173-4.

124. Yoshida, *Murakami Haruki—tenkan suru*, 208.

125. *Murakami Haruki, Kawai Hayao ni ai ni iku*, 182.

126. *Murakami Haruki, Kawai Hayao ni ai ni iku*, 114.

127. Saitô Tamaki, "Kairi no gihô to rekishiteki gaishô," *Yurîka*, Sangatsu rinjizôkan, Sôtokushu: "Murakami Haruki o yomu," 32, 4 (March, 2000), 62-63.

128. Saitô, "Kairi no gihô to rekishiteki gaishô," 63.

129. Saitô, "Kairi no gihô to rekishiteki gaishô," 63.

130. Baudrillard, "The Ecstasy of Communication," 133.

131. Saitô, "Kairi no gihô to rekishiteki gaishô," 69.

132. Saitô, "Kairi no gihô to rekishiteki gaishô," 69.

133. Kristeva, *Powers of Horror*, 52.

134. Kristeva, *Powers of Horror*, 52.

135. Kristeva, *Powers of Horror*, 53.

136. WBC 3: 11; 423, and NDK 3: 12; 142.

137. WBC 3: 11; 423, and NDK 3: 12; 142.

138. WBC 3: 11; 425, and NDK 3: 12; 146.

139. NDK 3: 12; 146.

140. WBC 3: 11; 425.

141. NDK 3: 29; 331.

142. WBC 3: 27; 529.

143. NDK 3: 29; 331.

144. WBC 3: 27; 529.

145. NDK 3: 29; 331.

146. WBC 3: 27; 529.

147. WBC 3: 27; 529, and NDK 3: 29; 331.

148. See NDK 3: 29; 328-332, and WBC 3: 27; 528-530. Here, Boku engages in a lengthy reflection as to why Cinnamon had chosen the 'story' or 'chronicle' form—fleshing out some fragments of knowledge about his past to 'make up his own story'.

149. Kristeva, *Powers of Horror,* 53.

150. Kristeva, *Powers of Horror,* 53.

151. Kristeva, *Powers of Horror,* 54.

152. For an insightful discussion of the interplay between those discursive apparatuses which administer 'history' see "Textbook Resistance" in Ian Buruma, *The Wages of Guilt: memories of War in Germany and Japan,* 189-201.

153. NDK 3: 37; 449-455, and WBC 3: 35; 587-591

154. NDK 3: 35; 419-425, and WBC 3: 33; 570-577.

155. Kant, *The Critique of Judgement,* 119.

156. Kant, *The Critique of Judgement,* 106.

157. See Jean-Francois Lyotard, "The Sublime and the Avant-Garde," in *The Lyotard Reader,* ed. Andrew Benjamin (Oxford: Basil Blackwell, 1989), 203.

158. Lyotard, "'The Sublime and the Avant-Garde," 204.

159. Kristeva, *Powers of Horror,* 11.

160. Kristeva, *Powers of Horror,* 12.

161. Saitô, "Kairi no gihô to rekishiteki gaishô," 70.

162. *Murakami Haruki, Kawai Hayao ni ai ni iku,* 46.

163. Saitô, "Kairi no gihô to rekishiteki gaishô," 70-71; *Murakami Haruki, Kawai Hayao ni ai ni iku,* 46.

164. Saitô, "Kairi no gihô to rekishiteki gaishô," 71; *Murakami Haruki, Kawai Hayao ni ai ni iku,* 46.

165. Saitô, "Kairi no gihô to rekishiteki gaishô," 71.

Conclusion

From Simulacrum to Differend

But what proof do we have that there is a principle of compensation between genres of discourse?

Jean-Francois Lyotard,
The Differend: Phrases in Dispute[1]

The photograph comprising the entire cover of Murakami's 1998 travel-essay book *Henkyô—Kinkyô* depicts the author, dressed in sneakers and jeans, standing atop the rusting shell of a military tank girdled by sprouting weeds in a vast field of green, set against the backdrop of an azure Mongolian sky.[2] The eerily incommensurate contents of this image perfectly reflect the kinds of disjunctive modalities at the heart of the *Nejimakidori* trilogy: the distinction between personal memory and official history; the schism between the psychoanalytically determined subject and the subject of history; the division between the present and the past, between contiguous and discontinuous times; the disjunction between the familiar, presented 'landscapes' of Japan and the sublime dimensions of imagined continental Asia as other—as both promise and threat.

This photograph brings into sharp relief a problem already indicated in our analysis of the aesthetic of the sublime. The question arises as to how we are to transpose (in the context of the literary presentation of the sublime in contemporary Japanese culture) the perceived threat to the 'individual' subject onto the plane of the social and the historical, notwithstanding the fact that this very subject is said to have been so inconclusively stipulated in the discourses of Japanese modernity.

The argument throughout has insisted on the veracity of the idea that the simulacrum *is* true, because it reflects the fundamental condition of all representation. However, there are various modalities of the simulacrum, both in the trilogies of Murakami Haruki and those articulated in the array of discursive formations which constitute contemporary Japanese culture. And furthermore, the theory of the simulacrum—which describes processes of how we refer to the real, as well as *representations of* such processes—is of interest only to the extent to which it helps clarify what Barthes calls the 'second-order signifying systems' or 'myths' which constitute the important meanings entailed in the cultural forms and practices of any society.

One striking example of such a system is the so-called 'Murakami Phenomenon', evident in the simulacral typification of cultural forms in the media/marketing regimes of contemporary Japan. The discursive contexts of these forms were broadened, early in the discussion, by reference to the idea of a national-cultural imaginary constructed in terms of the philosophical paradigm of modernity. The long running debate about the nature of Japanese modernity was shown to be far from over, and it was acknowledged that uncertainty about questions of subjectivity and comparative theorization remain.

A similar indeterminacy was identified with regard to questions of periodization and the problem of situating Japanese artistic discourses globally, as well as the difficulty of precisely stipulating the generic parameters of the modern Japanese novel.

Murakami's first trilogy was described as a critique of the modern fictional orthodoxy exemplified in the paradigmatic *shishôsetsu* or 'I-novel' form. *Kaze no uta o kike* (*Hear the Wind Sing*) uses the simulacral, double-order literary strategies of parody, pastiche and metafiction as highly effective in destabilizing conventionalized reading practices, while *1973 nen no pinbôru* (*Pinball, 1973*) brilliantly deploys the trope of allegory *as* modality to interrogate the nature and limits of fictional writing. The third novel of the trilogy, *Hitsuji o meguru bôken*, (*A Wild Sheep Chase*) allegorically engages the tropes of 'landscape' (*fûkei*) at both the micro levels of the deictic and the macro scale of the national-cultural imaginary.

It has been argued that the literary-historical import of Murakami's second trilogy, *Nejimakidori* (*The Wind-up Bird Chronicle*), can be more fully appreciated by articulating the broad conditions of exteriority of the novel's publication, and understanding that its unusual narrative format is indicative of a discontinuous and disjunctive treatment of time, space and action. Furthermore, that the novel's significance as contemporary literature stems from its utilization of the aesthetic of the sublime, its deconstructive approach to history and its semiotic privileging of the auditory image over the visual in the presented worlds of the narrative. Perhaps this novel's most striking feature is its use of displaced and uncertain modalities of subjectivity in the literary construction of the aesthetic of the sublime. This presentation of the abject and the sublime—manifested in the motifs of psychoanalytic and historical dissociation—have been shown to indicate a repression of the trauma of Japan's encounter with modernity, evident in the clash of the ostensibly heterogeneous discourses of 'fiction' and 'history'.

Given these summary observations, it remains the task of this concluding chapter to more specifically interrogate how such heterogeneous discourses *interact*, enriching or curtailing meanings which are socially enacted and politically manifested in terms of determining who can speak and from which sites of enunciation. This is necessary because we have identified an aesthetic of disjunction in the complex treatment of the simulacrum in the later work which clearly indicates a development of the tropes deployed in the earlier trilogy, yet have not fully addressed the conditions within which certain discursive regimes might enter a state of contestation or dispute. Judging from the critical literature which has emerged so far, the text's radical suggestion of this contestation has not been widely discerned.

A Trajectory of Transformation

We have outlined Murakami's use of various strategies to present a critique of literary orthodoxy and ways of representing the real and, at a more abstract level, traced a change in the application of this double-order structure: there has clearly been a development, an unfolding, an increasing sophistication of the literary tropes at work in the first trilogy. The latter were characterized as the tropes of parody, pastiche, metafiction, allegory and 'landscape', and were shown to be versions of a simulacral structure which problematized relations between an 'authentic' and original discourse and its 'copy', repetition or repro-duction. In all of these, the referent was in an implied state of retreat. The real was only indicated in terms of a general modality of the de-stabilization of ref-erence.

In the second trilogy, however, the use of the simulacrum had assumed more complex proportions, for it was shown that what was at stake in *Nejimakidori* was the symbiotic, inevitable, yet problematic nexus between the discourses of 'history' and 'fiction', signified by the phantasmal 'return' of the referent. At its most abstract level, this trilogy posed certain questions. Which of these two dis-courses is prior? Which is more authentic—even more useful—in our attempts to (re)present the real? It did this by invoking the trope of the aesthetic of the sublime and therefore questioning the very basis of subject/object relations, and giving prominence to subjective reflexivity in a transcendental move which went straight to the question of the subject in/of Japanese modernity.

Unlike in the first trilogy, where the modalities of representation could be playfully and cleverly deployed without too much delving into the question of subjectivity, in the second trilogy the very foundations of the literary conven-tions of 'self' and 'world' were plunged into a state of extreme undecidability in the representation of the abject, and the threatened dissolution of the subject in the aesthetic of the sublime. This more sophisticated deployment of the structure of the simulacrum extended the boundaries of the self/world formulation (which had enabled modern Japanese naturalist fiction in the first place) to the much more indeterminate domains of the oppositions 'fiction/history', and 'subject/ object'. In doing so, Murakami significantly broadened the terms of the discus-sion of how to think about writing in terms of genre and style, and simultane-ously raised the stakes in the debate about Japanese modernity.

In the scheme of binary relations which forces us to make judgments about the value of that which is considered 'prior' and 'authentic' vis-à-vis that which is somehow derivative and 'inauthentic', we are returned to our basic models of the simulacrum and, in a sense, forced to choose what *kind* of simulacrum best describes this scheme. Based on the argument developed so far, clearly we must conclude that this is the Nietzschean and Deleuzean version of the simulacrum —of 'eternal return', of repetition and the celebration of difference—that best describes the overall work ideology of the novels under consideration.

Nevertheless, inherent in the process of what may be described as the transformation or devolution of tropes in Murakami's narratives, there is also discernible a sense of the denial and *overcoming* of the simulacrum in the violence of something unutterable and irreconcilable. We have shown that concomitant with such violence, 'fiction' and 'history' become contiguous, antagonistic and destabilized discourses and can claim legitimacy only by acknowledging the difference with themselves emerging from a process of auto-critique. Furthermore, that the subject and the object inhere only as phantasms in the differential, the trace of meaning arising from the presentation of the abject and the sublime in both of these ostensibly discrete discourses.

Extending our consideration of this development at the abstract level, we can say that the critique of orthodoxy in the first trilogy undertook a generalized destabilizing of those categories of 'self' and 'world' which had formed the basis of naturalist fiction coalescing around the 'I-novel' paradigm. Yet, in the second trilogy, the figure of the simulacrum was shown to have been put under extreme duress in the presentation of the agonistic and incommensurate discourses of 'fiction' and 'history' as being versions of the equally oppositional categories of 'subject' and 'object'. Implicit in this demonstration was the view that in more 'conventional' approaches to writing and representation, the former opposition is methodologically dependant upon the prior stipulation of the latter.

Despite the clashing, discursive grating and contestation which we have identified in the second trilogy, there is no evidence in the novels themselves to suggest that this contestation is or should be reconciled. On the contrary, the narrative does not attempt to resolve this more reified, disjunctive version of the simulacrum, but merely *presents* the terms of the battle, the confrontation, between fiction/history and subject/object. We conclude by proposing that Murakami's simulacrum used as an earlier subversive strategy, had, in the much later *Nejimakidori*, fulfilled its limits, and been transformed into a literary experimentation with what French philosopher Lyotard calls the 'differend'.

The final stage of this discussion comprises four parts. Firstly, we shall briefly define the term 'differend' and propose it as a key to better understanding the second trilogy. Secondly, the issue of the subject in/of history shall be reinterpreted in terms of its relation to forms of temporality. This will be followed by a consideration of how Murakami's use of the differend reflects or even *prefigures* what has been happening in contemporary Japanese culture *writ large*, by citing two recent and striking examples of the manifestation of the differend in ostensibly 'non-fictional' discourses. Firstly, in the form of the *Underground* books (I and II) and secondly, the *New History Textbook* controversy. It will be suggested that *Nejimakidori* stands inter-discursively in a new light in relation to other contemporary discourses in Japanese society, and that Murakami has clearly demonstrated this in his treatment of the differend in other texts.

Finally, it will be argued that the poetics of the differend are also very much evident in one of Murakami's more recent long fictional works *Umibe no kafuka* (*Kafka on the Shore*); and furthermore, that the text stands out as a kind of polemic *against* interpretation. In this intriguing work, virtually all of the tropes of the simulacrum (parody, pastiche, allegory, 'landscape' and the sublime) are arrayed in a format which is further testament to the significance of Murakami's unflagging project of cultural critique.

The Sublime as Differend

The concept of the differend is one of Jean-Francois Lyotard's most significant contributions to contemporary philosophy. It takes as a foundational given, the existence of minimal units of discourse known as 'phrases'. These phrases link together, and the question of *how* they are linked is what gives rise to politics in contemporary cultural contexts where it is commonly claimed that any master principle or universal governing rule is absent. For Lyotard, a differend arises when something that demands to be put into phrases cannot be:

> The differend is the unstable state of and instant of language wherein something which must be able to be put into phrases cannot yet be. This state includes silence, which is a negative phrase.[3]

Significantly, Lyotard recognizes the role of literature as one of the important discourses for formulating these phrases:

> What is at stake in a literature, in a philosophy, in a politics perhaps, is to bear witness to differends by finding idioms for them.[4]

This is congruous with the dilemma or double-bind of 'presenting the unpresentable' of the sublime, and reminds us of the impossible but necessary task of attempting to speak the 'unspeakable things' woven through the narratives of *Nejimakidori*. It also invokes an image of the monumental silence, the 'negative phrases' or *absence* of phrases which might have been articulated by those who felt grave injustice at the unassailable hegemony of Japanese military expansionism, implicitly and explicitly referred to in *Nejimakidori*. Murakami encapsulates this differend perfectly, and is 'bearing witness' to it in *Nejimakidori* and other texts such as the 'The Iron Graveyard of Nomonhan', when he refers to the 'meaningless' waste of human life, the 'extreme inefficiency' and 'irrationality' of the deaths at Nomonhan and in the Pacific War—the magnitude of which indicates the incomprehensibility of the sublime:

「ノモンハンで命を落とした日本軍の兵士は二万足らずだったが、太平洋戦争では実に二百万を越す戦闘員が戦死することになった。そしていちばん重要なことは……兵士たちの多くは同じようにほとんど意味を持たない死に方をしたということだった。彼らは日本という密閉された組織の中で、名もなき消耗品として、きわめて効率悪く殺されていったのだ。」⁵

Not quite twenty thousand Japanese soldiers lost their lives at Nomonhan—however, in the Pacific War, more than two million military personnel died. Yet the most important thing is that most of them died, in the same way, almost meaningless deaths. Within the tightly closed organization that is Japan, and as indistinguishable, expendable goods, they were killed with extreme inefficiency.

Notwithstanding the rhetorical force of this observation, certain questions arise. 'Meaningless' for whom? 'Inefficient' according to which criteria of efficiency? If there were meaning to be found, where would this meaning reside and who would guarantee its veracity? When Murakami suggests that this 'inefficiency' (*kôritsu no warusa*) and 'irrationality' (*higôrisei*) perhaps reflects Japan's 'Asian-ness' (*ajiasei*), he is clearly struggling to respond to such questions. Possibly this is why, like all 'pilgrims', he visits the site, the holy destination of his journey, with the aim of enacting a congruence between the mental image of the site and the act of physically viewing it.

In both *Nejimakidori* and the travel essay on Nomonhan, he is also grappling with the problem of locating the subject of history, and his differend arises from the difficulty—perhaps impossibility—of giving precise form to the terms of this struggle. It will be demonstrated later that this is why Murakami needs to invoke a transcendental narrative perspective in place of the elusive subject of history, and he needs his vertical thread, his *tate ito* as a means for what he calls 'opening up a hole in time'.

If Murakami's problem is with locating the subject, and if, as has been argued, the subject's experience of the sublime is indeed an instance of the differend, it remains to be articulated precisely how Murakami proceeds with the narrative invocation of such a differend. It is significant that Lyotard sees in the Kantian attempt to unify the heterogeneous discourses of the rational, the ethical and the aesthetic, the clearest example of the differend, and that this is crucially related to the sublime and the stipulation of the subject. As Sim notes, not only does Lyotard 'locate a differend right at the centre of sublime feeling',⁵ he vigorously contests the viability of Kant's attempt to link the discourses of the theoretical, the practical and the aesthetic. For Lyotard,

Kant's attempt at unification merely reveals the pervasive influence of the differend throughout our discourses. Kant is to be read through the differend, with the emphasis falling on any incompatibilities or aporias in his thought.[6]

It follows that in the contemporary Japanese context (and recalling Ôe's claim that Japan needs to discover its own sublime) we must consider the possibility that if there is no Japanese sublime this is probably because, quite understandably, the subject of modernity has not been adequately theorized or stipulated through an engagement with the epistemological parameters prescribed by the Kantian critical edifice.

Naturally, Lyotard's theory of the differend has attracted both supporters and critics alike. Geoffrey Bennington, for example, is one notable and enthusiastic disciple of the theory.[7] And language philosophers such as Ruthrof also acknowledge the usefulness of the concept:

> There is one set of phrases . . . which does not amount to a genre of discourse: politics. In its parasitic realization of the agonistics which exists between different genres, politics is nothing less than the linkage of the 'multiplicity of genres' itself.[8]

However, Ruthrof does take Lyotard to task for what he calls his 'realist textualism'—too much of a focus on language and purely linguistic elements which eclipses the importance of the extra-linguistic performance of the event.[9] It is clear, however, that Ruthrof's misgivings about Lyotard's theory do not necessarily apply to Murakami's presentation of the differend in *Nejimakidori*, because of (as was clearly shown in the preceding chapters) the foregrounding of the corporeal, the haptic, the auditory/visual modalities of signification which present the meaning-event as a much broader process of semiosis in this text.

With this kind of qualification in mind—and notwithstanding the definitional slipperiness of the notion—we can still find a great deal of use in the idea of the differend as we think about how to understand 'texts' and the 'events' surrounding them in the broad sense of discourses as bodies of social knowledge. Insofar as it enacts a radical crisis of re-presentation, the experience of the sublime is actually a differend which takes the terms of the simulacrum (of the original and its copy) into the liminal territory of the extreme, where meaning collapses in a violent paroxysm of incomprehension. Here, the acts of 'physical' violence figuratively depicted in *Nejimakidori* translate directly onto the experiential plane of the 'aesthetic' violence of the sublime. Lyotard writes:

> Sublime violence is like lightning. . . . It short circuits thinking with itself. . . .
> The teleological machine explodes . . . the sublime is sudden blazing, and without future.[10]

Lyotard fully appreciates the relevance of Kant's theory of the sublime in accounting for the *apparent* impossibility of representation in a 'postmodern' cultural milieu which has dispensed with any master tropes or universally applicable parameters of interpretation:

> As it is expounded and deduced in its thematic, sublime feeling is analyzed as a
> double defiance. Imagination at the limits of *what* it can present does violence
> to itself in order to present *that* it can no longer present.[11]

Under such conditions it seems that the limits of the simulacrum have in a sense been reached and even breached—and re-presentation itself appears disabled, managing only to muster a presentation of its own enervated, diminished power to signify and mean.

It is clear that the narrative of *Nejimakidori* inevitably does violence to itself in its refusal to re-present the 'contents' of history in a conventional way in order to engage in narrative denouement: it simply presents the terms of the differend and lets this presentation *speak for itself*. Undoubtedly, to admit that something can no longer be re-presented (and in terms of the simulacrum, presentation is always a *re*-presenting) is to acknowledge precisely the condition of the differend. And the horror and violence confronting the subject in *Nejimakidori* is about the differend of not being able to present the contents of the sublime and the abject to rational censure, to the order of teleology and moral resolution. Not only can some of the phrases not be found for what demands to be said, but those phrases which can (within the discursive limits of 'fiction' and 'history') are in a state of antagonism and incommensurability with one another. And as Lyotard so aptly puts it, there is no proof of any principle of *compensation* for the injustice arising out of the inability of these discourses to speak to one another. The phrases simply cannot be meaningfully linked, they cannot speak *to* or *with* one another.

In response to this dilemma, Murakami goes in search of the subject. He could not find it in the first trilogy replete with simulacral tropes, where he had to install a kind of quasi-transcendental subject/narrator in place of the literary 'self' he had abolished. Yet, his enquiry assumes a different form in the second trilogy. Murakami identifies the *possibility* of a putative subject in the very place where Lyotard tells us that Kant used to present his differend of incommensurability between the three critical discourses—that is, in the aesthetic of the sublime. In *Nejimakidori*, Murakami looks for evidence of the subject by presenting the dilemma, the pain of the sublime, and he finds his troubled, phantasmal and elusive subject (always under threat of dissolution) in the differend which arises between the discursive regimes of 'fiction' and 'history'. We shall see, indeed, that this 'subject' is none other than the possibility of articulation which corresponds to what Murakami describes as the 'warp' or 'vertical thread' (*tate ito*) of history.

In his attempt to juxtapose the discourses of 'fiction' and 'history' Murakami is confronted with the differend, and seeking to address this problem his narrative attempts to problematize time by using, paradoxically, the very device which gives rise to the differend in the first place: the aesthetic of the sublime.

This radically inventive approach goes to the heart of the debate about Japanese modernity, and in so doing, invariably engages with the issues of subjectivity and time central to the Kantian critical project.

If the violence of the sublime is, as Lyotard argues, 'without future', it is also without a past, a history. It is clear that in *Nejimakiodori*, Murakami's treatment of the subject in/of history represents a complex musing on the construction of time in modernity. Significantly, the Kantian aesthetic is characterized by Lyotard as synonymous with the postmodern concern with 'presenting the unpresentable'. This would certainly accord with a designation of Murakami's writing in *Nejimakidori* as unequivocally 'postmodern' in its tenor.[12]

'The Warp of History'—or, 'Opening a Hole in Time'

The preceding chapters have shown how the issue of subjectivity has been addressed in terms of at least three versions of the sublime: the historical, the psychoanalytic and the political. The nexus between these versions has been established by locating them within the generalized aesthetic of the Kantian critique. Notwithstanding the fact that these narrative subjectivities have been described largely at the synchronic level—as syntagmatically arrayed throughout the various narrative threads of *Nejimakidori*—it also the case that they have been articulated *diachronically*, and in an unusual way. How has this been achieved? Why is it that we can claim that in this text Murakami has proposed a new way of viewing history through fiction and vice-versa?

In *Nejimakidori*, Murakami has maintained and extended what we earlier called the transcendental narrative perspective in order to be able to cope with the subject's instantiation *in* and *through* the construction of specific temporal orders: continuous and contiguous times, discontinuous and disparate times, and the conventional division between 'the past' and 'the present'. The so-called transcendental narrative perspective has held together all of these very tentative subjectivities which were always under threat of dissolution from the sublime (through displaced sexual desire, abject horror, loss to memory, etc.) in the various stories narrated.

In a part of their discussion dealing precisely with this topic, Murakami and the psychoanalyst Kawai refer explicitly to the relationship between what they describe as the 'Japanese individual' (*Nihon teki 'ko'*) and the 'warp of history' (*rekishi toiu tateito*).[13] Significantly, we note in this dialogue the centrality of the nexus between the construction of time in modernity and the formation of subjectivity *as/in* the subject of history. Kawai accepts that the 'I' (私) of the *shishōsetsu* is very different to the Western 'ego' (given as エゴ). He is convinced, however, that Murakami has successfully used one of the central motifs in *Nejimakidori* (of the protagonist experiencing altered states of consciousness and contact with other time/space matrices after descending into a well) to evoke the possibility of a reified and 'isolated' subject as the necessary precondition for recalling to the present, historical 'events' such as the brutal Nomonhan Incident (*Nomonhan jihen*) outlined in Captain Mamiya's oral recollection.

Even more significantly, Kawai talks of the distinct sense of these narrated 'historical events' as occurring *now*, but emphasizes that this is *not* made possible by attempting to utilize the individual prescribed by 'Western individualism':

「……村上さんのお書きになったものを読んで僕が感じたのは、ノモンハンも今起こっている、すべてが今起こっているのですね。そういう受け止め方の個人があるとすれば、それは欧米の個人主義の個人とは違うと僕は思うのです。」[14]

What I felt upon reading what Murakami had written, was that the Nomonhan incident—indeed everything—was happening right now. If there is an individual perceiving things in this way, I think it is very different to the individual of Western individualism.

Murakami responds to this in an interesting way:

「僕が思ったのは、日本における個人を追求していくと、歴史に行くしかないんじゃないかという気がするのです……。」[15]

What I thought was that if one were pursuing the individual in terms of Japan, one could really turn nowhere else than to history.

Kawai claims that in contrast to history in the West where specifically dated phenomena are arrayed in a straight line, the Japanese 'feel' and 'grasp' history as an 'ill-defined lump' or 'clod' (*bakuzen toshita katamari*). He goes on to acknowledge, however, that Murakami provides a new angle (*aratana kakudo*) from which to view history, and the key to this is what Kawai calls the 'warp of history' (*rekishi toiu tate no ito*). In this idea of the 'warp' or 'vertical thread' in a weave, we see an allusion to the problem of how to 'connect' disparate times, or, put another way, the past with the future—and this brings us precisely, once again, to the questions of time, memory and subjectivity prescribed by the philosophical paradigm of modernity.

Even in the kinds of narrative perspectives opened up by Nutmeg's stories, the reader is asked to occupy a range of subject positions (some of which are contradictory) and all of which are marked by a general uncertainty. Boku's uncertainty that he can only give an 'outline', Nutmeg's unsure memory caught in the 'labyrinth between illusion and truth', the veterinarian's uncertainty and despair that he is trapped in a 'revolving door of unconnected worlds' (as well as the inherent uncertainties of many other story lines). And behind all of this we see the mute figure of Cinnamon, continuously re-writing the narratives and assigning them, as numbered 'chronicles', to cyberspace—as a kind of 'transcendental' record, a virtual inscription of the traces of subjectivity arrayed between individual, personalized memory and the abstract official history indicated by proper nouns, events, dates and statistics.

In response to the question as to how all this uncertainty and indeterminacy coheres in the narrative, clearly it is the role of the implied 'transcendental' narrative subject which overrides commonsensical limitations about how to conceive of the past and the present, and allows readers to 'enter' history as if it were *now*. All of this depends upon the subversion of the modernist construction of time, which is somehow alien to the putative forms of Japanese subjectivity. Kawai uncannily discerns this when he suggests that if there were an individual perceiving historical events as possessing the quality of 'nowness', it was certainly not the individual of 'Western individualism'. Such an 'individual'—the kind adopted through naturalism, realism and then ossified in the 'I-novel' form, as we have shown—was always somehow 'false'. This provisional 'subject' of modernity, (which, as was demonstrated in previous chapters, Murakami has been at pains to subvert) is clearly manipulated by the transcendental narrator of Murakami's fiction.

We have demonstrated the use of a transcendental structure of subjectivity in terms of a 'distanced' narratorial perspective, exemplified in the text of *Kaze* (*Hear the Wind Sing*) by the narration of history as parody, and the metafictional, self-reflexive critique of the novel form itself. We also discussed its continuation in a different form in *Pinbôru* (*1973, Pinball*) as a form of *modality* which grounds the transcendental aspect of the experience of the sublime in terms of the oscillation between epiphanic moments of great intensity, and the vacuity of the apparent *loss* to subjectivity in the ennui and nihilism of the 'postmodern' urban experience of space and time. It has also been argued that in *Hitsuji* (*A Wild Sheep Chase*), history functions in a relatively unified way, as self evident and 'archeologically' retrievable, and that if the Kantian version of the transcendental self-reflexive subject appears to operate more explicitly in *Kaze* and *Pinbôru*, it is alluded to only allegorically in *Hitsuji* as the operation of the metaphor of *fûkei* ('landscape') via the tropes of 'history', the 'national-cultural imaginary', the 'urban phantasm' and 'the phantasm of self'.

Clearly, the fundamentally 'transcendental' aspect of the narrative stance continues throughout the *Nejimakidori* trilogy as the inevitable (and by that time) conventionalized hermeneutic guidance available to readers of Murakami's fiction. The one striking difference, however, is that the previous treatment of history as parody, meta-fiction, allegory or landscape is nowhere to be found in the later trilogy. On the contrary, history has become, once again, very 'messy'. It invokes the kind of messiness—that is, the inability to adequately present the contents of the imagination to understanding—that is suggestive of what White refers to as the 'historical sublime', a notion described by Munslow as the 'inherent uncertainty of inexplicable change'.[16] Murakami himself acknowledges this 'messiness', and gestures towards the desire for clarification:

> 「もちろん僕は歴史家でもないし、歴史小説を書こうとしているわけ
> でもありません。僕のやりたかったことは、歴史というものを、ここ
> にある、この僕らの世界にそのまま、それごとひっぱりこんでくるこ
> とだったんです。もちろん僕は小説家だから、それらのものごとを小
> 説的にフィクショナイズするわけですが。」

and he continues:

> 「それはひとつの異界であるけれど、正確な意味での『異界』ではな
> い。何故ならそれは今ある僕らをもとにしたものでもあるのだから。
> それが異界であるとするなら、それは二重的、複合的な『異界』なん
> です。僕ら自身を致命的に巻き込んで、異物化していく『異界』なん
> です。僕は結局のところ、その中にいろんな登場人物を置いてみたか
> ったのだと思う。この今ある世界に時間の風穴を開けるみたいに。」

Of course I am not a historian, and I don't set out to write historical fiction. What I wanted to do was drag history as a whole, as it exists, right here into this world of ours. Bloody matters as bloody matters, things with unfathomable causes, just as they are. Although, naturally because I'm a novelist, I fictionalize those things novelistically.

This 'history' is a different world, but not a 'different world' in the precise sense of the term, because it has also brought us to our present state. If it should be a different world, then it is a double or compound 'different world'. We ourselves are fatally implicated in this alienated 'different world'. In the end, I think I wanted to place many kinds of characters in the middle of this—just like opening up an air hole in time.[17]

This reference to 'opening up a hole in time' is perhaps Murakami's most overt statement on the complicity and trickiness of thinking different historical times as contiguous and continuous. Here he is gesturing towards the kinds of issues raised by Kant's treatment of time in the *Critique of Pure Reason*, as were touched upon in an earlier chapter. The somewhat radical implication that the past is 'contained' *in*, or perhaps occluded *by* (but nevertheless somehow attendant on) the present, cannot easily be reconciled with the common sense empiricist or 'reconstructionist' approach to history. This is one instance where Murakami's inkling of the differend in his retroactive, self-reflexive critique becomes evident.

The issue of the successive treatment of time is crystallized in Kant's observation that:

In the synthesis of phenomena, the manifold of our representations is always successive. . . . But so soon as I perceive or assume, that in this succession there is a relation to a state antecedent . . . so soon do I represent something as an event, or as a thing that happens.[18]

Here, Kant is arguing that the 'common sense', 'empiricist' notion of time, causality and succession of which we are aware, points to the inevitability of recognizing the function of the temporally locatable 'event' as the basic discursive unit (and ultimately, the referent) of empiricist historiography. Yet, he is restating this point only *after* having already demonstrated (in the 'Transcendental Exposition of the Conception of Time') that our construction of the 'empirical reality of time' informs the limits—and is indeed 'the condition, of all our experience'.[19] This is based on the fundamental proposition that time *of* and *for* itself does not exist, and indeed, as he demonstrates, 'is nothing but the form of our internal intuition'.[20]

Murakami's hunch of the need to 'open up a hole in time' in a historically constructed world which is 'different' yet also 'the same' (double, compound) points implicitly to a profound dissonance, a lack, in the writing of both fiction and history in the postwar Japanese educational milieu. In this environment, the discrete disciplines of 'Japanese History' (*nihonshi*) and 'World History' (*sekaishi*) in the various school curricula, have effectively conspired to erect the edifice of a neatly packaged referentiality based on the equivalence of 'dates' and 'events', the specific contents of which are strictly monitored and approved for publication and use only under the imprimatur of the Ministry of Education.[21]

It is within such a context that Murakami's attempt to destabilize the writing of history by radically recasting the writing of fiction seems all the more significant. In bringing this discussion to a close, it is worth considering (more than two decades after the publication of the ground breaking first trilogy, and more than ten years after the publication of *Nejimakidori*) how the operation of the simulacrum and differend has emerged in more recent textual forms. Also, it is important to reflect upon what these forms may indicate for the future of 'fictional' and 'historical' discourses in Japanese culture.

Media-Event: 'Non-Fiction', the Simulacrum and the Differend

So, in the next century, there will be no more books. It takes too long to read, when success comes from gaining time. What will be called a book will be a printed object whose 'message' (its information content) and name and title will first have been broadcast by the media, a film, a newspaper interview, a television program.

Jean-Francois Lyotard, *The Differend: Phrases in Dispute*[22]

The publication in 1997 of Murakami's transcribed interviews with victims of the 1995 Tokyo subway Sarin gas attack (*chikatetsu sarin jihen*) took many by surprise. Dissatisfied with the media's trivialization of the 'event', and the simplistic application of the categories 'good' and 'evil' championed by the press, Murakami took it upon himself to let the voices of the victims 'speak for themselves'. Sixty-two people were interviewed (including doctors, railway workers and relatives)—fifty-two of whom were the hitherto largely anonymous victims, many of whom had been ostracized, ridiculed and discriminated against for having attained the status of being 'unclean' (*kegare*). They were given names, ages, birthplaces and occupations, and the chance to offer personal testimonials about the experience and its aftermath. The testimonials were given veracity by being arranged in terms of the subway lines on which the victims traveled, graphically presented in the route and station diagrams at the beginning of the text.[23]

This was a striking attempt by Murakami to confront and undermine the terms of a perceived differend, the 'negative phrase' as silence, the injustice which had emerged from the victims not being given a voice or idiom (beyond the truncated electronic media 'grab') in which to express their experience and subsequent sense of social alienation. The testimonials were tape-recorded and then transcribed as faithfully as possible by Murakami himself in order to let the victims speak in the idiom of 'normal, every day speech'—and relay their impressions (*inshô*) and recollection (*kioku*) of the 'event' which they had experienced.[24]

Perhaps even more surprising was the publication, in the following year, of interviews with some of the members of the Aum Shinrikyô religious sect ostensibly responsible for the incident. In the forward to 'Underground II' (*Yakusoku-sareta bashô de*), Murakami insists that just as he has tried to do in his fictional writing, in interviewing the Aum Shinrikyô sect followers he has attempted to facilitate the emergence of as many viewpoints as possible.[25]

This aim of establishing multiple perspectives is clearly achieved. For example, one of Aum Shinrikyô's 'rank and file believers' (*mattan no shinja*) strongly condemns the gas attack, claiming that one has to separate out the leader Asahara from the ordinary, individual believers when thinking about the issue of responsibility. He also stresses that not all the believers are criminals—and that on the contrary, there are those with very 'pure hearts' and intentions.[26] Consider also the sect member who cites as one of his reasons for searching out and joining the sect his thorough disillusionment, not only with his parents and teachers, but perhaps more significantly, with the representation of 'normal' adult life and human relations in the daily Japanese television dramas.[27]

All of this provides part of the response to the provocative question posed on the cover wrap-around of the book: 'how could these young people on a journey seeking salvation, have arrived at such a place?' The year-on-year publication of the two texts, represented a kind of large scale speech-act in progress: a set of dialogic phrases, or a dialectic, a thesis and antithesis, born of a perceived differend. And it was also productive of *new* differends emerging in the dispute about methods of representing the real, and in the inevitable sense of injustice arising, for some, from such attempts to do so.

These 'non-fiction' media-events which emerged, in simulacral fashion, largely in *response to* other media-events, were followed in 1999 by Murakami's publication of a series of short stories which returned the differend back to its 'fictional' context. In *Kami no kodomotachi wa minna odoru* (subsequently published in English as *After the Quake*), one story depicts the vanishing of a man's wife after five days of her continuous viewing of live reportage of the aftermath of the 1995 Kobe earthquake and subsequent conflagration. This is followed by his sudden departure to Hokkaido to deliver a small parcel, the contents of which remain unspecified. The story evokes an uncanny sense of stupefaction and dissociation in a world where apocalyptic images delivered by mass-media technologies live side by side with the mediocrity of daily routine, to the point where meanings collapse in an absurd cacophony of disparate messages. Here is fiction set against the narrative of a 'non-fiction' media-event, in which the 'differend of silence', the unformed phrase, has become absurdly palpable:

> 「五日のあいだ彼女は、すべての時間をテレビの前で過ごした。銀行や病院のビルが崩れ商店街が火に焼かれ、鉄道や高速道路が切断された風景を、ただ黙ってにらんでいた。ソファに深く沈み込み、唇を固く結び、小村が話しかけても返事をしなかった。首を振ったり、うなずいたりさえしなかった。自分の声が相手の耳に届いているのかいないのか、それもわからない。」 [28]

> For a period of five straight days, she spent the entire time in front of the television. In complete silence, she gazed at the scenes of crumbling banks and hospitals, blazing shopping lanes and severed railway lines and freeways. Sunk deep into the sofa, and with lips tightly sealed, even when Komura spoke to her, she failed to reply. She didn't even shake her head or nod. Komura couldn't tell if his voice was reaching his partner's ears.

Yet, perhaps the most striking example of the simultaneous play of the structure of the simulacrum with the instantiation of the differend occurred in the year 2001. In recent times, there appears to have been a shift in the operation of the signifier 'history' in the marketplace of ideas in the Japanese publishing world. We have already noted that the *seiki matsu* ('end-of-century', *fin de siècle*) concern that appeared in the titles of Japanese bookshops in the second half of the nineties was complemented by Murakami's apparent return to 'commitment', and a re-consideration of history as demonstrated in the texts of *Nejimakidori* and *Andâguraundo*.

However, the popularity of Murakami's apparent newfound historical/social concern (his entry, in other words, into the so called *shakaiha*) can also be usefully juxtaposed with a media phenomenon which can only be described as a kind of 'hyper-simulacrum'. This 'event', around the middle of the year 2001, was the meteoric rise to the top of the best-seller list of a newly published Japanese junior high school history text book entitled *Atarashii rekishi kyôkasho (New History Textbook)*.[29] Typical of schools texts of this genre, it divided its treatment of the subject into 'world' and 'Japanese' history, and apart from an unusually large number of color photographs and user-friendly format, appeared to be otherwise unremarkable.

When it was noted, however, that its reference to certain historical 'events' in controversial manner was indeed *likely to be controversial*, it was massively reprinted and marketed in a new form 'for the market' or *shihanbon* (an unusual move, since most such textbooks are not 'publicly' or commercially released) as a book that was indeed bound to become topical. Its wrap-around blurb stated 'we'd like the people to judge—this is a topical textbook!' (*kokumin ni handan moraitai—kore ga waidai no kyôkasho da!*). Sales boomed, and it reached No.1 on the non-fiction best-seller list as readers flocked to verify which aspects of it may have been controversial. In a way which confirms the extreme vacuity and semantic 'emptying out' of the Baudrillardian version of the simulacrum, the text *became its own referent*, and was consumed as a text about itself. If nothing else, this demonstrated an instance of the hyper-fetishization of the signifier 'history' in the marketing/media discourses of contemporary Japan.

Perhaps even more astonishing (and in line with the double movement of Murakami's two *Underground* texts), was the critique of *Atarshii rekishi kyôkasho* appearing soon after, entitled *Rekishi kyôkasho nani ga mondai ka (What's the Problem with the History Textbook?)*. Here, once again, was a contested speech-act wherein a contentious proposition was illuminated in the mirror-image of its critique. This critical (and in a sense 'parasitic') text soon also became a best-seller, and the 'Kinkokuniya Book Web' web-page showed the two books vying neck and neck for best selling status.[30] Containing essays by noted academics (and with highly respected Nobel Prize laureate Ôe Kenzaburo even weighing into the debate) it was clear that the appearance of this critique signaled that the controversy about 'revisionist' history, and opposition to the Education Ministry's effective control of the history curricula previously championed by Ienaga Saburô and his supporters, was entering a vast new discursive arena—even if only temporarily, and albeit at the level of a commodity related marketing phenomenon.

What do these remarkable developments in the world of publishing have to do with Murakami Haruki's narrative endeavors? It seems that whereas in *Nejimakidori*, Murakami writes fiction which somehow reads like engaged historical discourse, the *New History Textbook* (according to its critics at least) reads like fiction in the guise of history! What especially helps give rise to this impression is the plea at the outset of the book for a history education which encourages 'multiple views' (*sûôko no mikata*) and is thus considered 'with unprejudiced eyes', (*toraware no nai me de*).[31] Despite this, in the text's subsequent treatment of controversial issues involving Japan's colonial enterprises and military campaigns, it is clear that these multiple perspectives and unprejudiced approaches are all but ignored.[32] In more recent times, the textbook issue has continued to provoke cries of indignation, especially from Korea and China.

Whereas Murakami sets out to write fiction in order to evoke a more *acute sense* of history, the authorized official history textbook has been strongly criticized as being closer to 'fiction' in its highly selective interpretation of Japan's place in modern history. Is this the inevitable fate of the simulacrum-as-repetition—as a 'flipping over' to its reverse side—that Deleuze has written of?

> In the infinite movement of degraded likeness from copy to copy, we reach a point at which everything changes nature, at which copies themselves flip over into simulacra and at which, finally, resemblance or spiritual imitation gives way to repetition.[33]

Deleuze's description of this slide into undecidability—of the absurdity of attempting to distinguish the 'original' from its 'copy'—is nowhere more clearly demonstrated than in one of Murakami's most recent long novels, *Umibe no kafuka* (*Kafka on the Shore*). Not only does the differend constitute a central narrative strategy of this text, but many of the literary tropes of the simulacrum (parody, pastiche, allegory, 'landscape' and the sublime) which were deployed in earlier narratives are disjunctively arrayed in ways which are surely, at times, almost unbearable for the reader. From the US Military reports of strange events in remote Japanese mountains towards the end of 1944, to Nakata san, the illiterate gentleman who can speak with cats, conventionalized 'meanings' are virtually denied at every turn. In this novel, it would seem that the status of the referent is so thoroughly undermined as to be beyond recuperation. Nevertheless, this seeming denial of readily construable meanings is of course highly meaningful in itself. The rationale for such a claim is briefly elaborated in the following, final section of this concluding chapter.

Against Interpretation, Against Oedipus: Murakami's *Umibe no kafuka* (*Kafka On the Shore*)

> The goal is to obtain an exaggeration of the 'photo', an exaggeration of it to the point of absurdity. The photo of the father, expanded beyond all bounds, will be projected onto the geographic, historical and political *map* of the world in order to reach vast regions of it.
>
> Gilles Deleuze and Felix Guattari,
> on Kafka's 'Letter to the Father'[34]

Umibe no kafuka[35] (*Kafka on the Shore*, hereafter referred to as *Kafuka*) is a story about a fifteen-year-old boy, Tamura Kafuka, who runs away from home, finds his long lost mother, 'virtually' becomes her lover, and 'virtually' murders his father. This remarkable novel could be read as one long 'Letter to the Father' —yet not necessarily within the context of a projected act of patricide against any *particular* father. On the contrary, the image of Tamura Kafuka's estranged father is 'exaggerated' (to use the words of Deleuze and Guattari) to the 'point of absurdity', and the apparent Oedipal impulse emerging in common interpretations of Kafka's infamous 'Letter to His Father' is not, it could be argued, the central motif of this narrative. Rather, it can be said that the highly idiosyncratic method employed in this novel cleverly masks Murakami's broader project of critique.

In a description which is perfectly apposite to the narrative strategy at work in *Kafuka* (and could just as easily have been written as a description of it), Deleuze and Gauttari reject the Oedipal formula of 'interpretation' and reverse the terms of its operation. Of Kafka's letter they write:

> Deterritorializing Oedipus into the world instead of reterritorializing everything
> in Oedipus and the family. But to do this, Oedipus had to be enlarged to the
> point of absurdity, to comedy. To do this, the 'Letter to the Father' had to be
> written.[36]

It would be shortsighted and perhaps mistaken to simply seize upon on the obvious 'Oedipal' interpretation of Murakami's *Kafuka* without considering the broader perspectives which the narrative invite. Describing the novel's overall work ideology as being 'against interpretation' is prompted by the sense that apparent meanings do not readily emerge from the presentational format of so many disjunctive and discordant elements in this text.

Whether or not Murakami was aware of Kafka's letter is not important— although he does acknowledge that he did not consciously set out to create a 'Kafkaesque' world in this novel.[37] The point is that as a signifier, the proper name 'Kafka' brings into play a huge range of connotative possibilities as to how the narrative and characters are to be 'interpreted'. Certainly, Murakami is in agreement with Kafka on one point: the indeterminate, phantasmal nature of all writing, representation and interpretation; and Kafka concedes that he is not up to the task of being able to adequately re-present his feelings in writing:

> Dearest Father,
> You asked me recently why I maintain I am afraid of you. And if I now try to
> give an answer in writing it will . . . be very incomplete, because even in writ-
> ing this fear and its consequences hamper me in relation to you and because
> (anyway) the magnitude of the subject goes far beyond the scope of my mem-
> ory and power of reasoning.[38]

Undoubtedly, the magnitude of the 'subject' of *Kafuka* seems far beyond the scope of our powers of reasoning, and this impossibility of interpretation is also perhaps a function of what may be called the 'undecidability' implicit in so many of the images in this novel. On this point, the Japanese psychoanalyst Kawai offers an important insight, noting the repeated figure of the boundary (*kyo*). Beginning with the title *umibe* ('shore', 'beach') which suggests the uncertain, ever-shifting boundary between land and sea, like other of Murakami's texts, this narrative foregrounds the liminal, transitional, phantasmal or spectral pairings of life/death, good/evil, adult/child, consciousness/unconsciousness, god/human.[39]

And surely the *iriguchi* ('entrance'/'threshold') which Nakata and his unlikely young companion are searching for invokes the simultaneous enticement and threat of the liminal, in the same way that Derrida's exegesis of Plato's *pharmakon* suggests: the *pharmakon*, variously signifiying both cure *and* poison, and by implication, the possibility of both redemption *and* oblivion. Certainly, apart from its function as a key signifier of the liminal and the threshold of abjection, the 'meaning' of the *iriguchi* remains obscure to the very end of the narrative. The scenes in which Tamura Kafuka makes love to his continually transmogrifying mother-as-ghost are further, striking instances of the liminal: they position the protagonist as a true 'frontiersman' (as Kristeva puts it) daring the horror of abjection as he 'crosses over' the abyss of the maternal bowels.

Such overwhelming and starkly presented undecidability plays a crucial role in our readings of this novel, and cannot be dismissed as simply indicative of the styles of 'Magical Realism' or 'the fantastic'. Writing of the significance of undecidability in Derrida's deconstructive method, Reynolds reminds us:

> equivocation breaks open the meaning that an author seeks to impose upon their work and exposes it to alternative understandings that undermine the explicit authorial intention.[40]

Ironically, it could be argued that perhaps this observation does not apply to a text such as *Kafuka*, because as Murakami himself asserts, 'interpretations' have about as much validity as 'lies'. This is basically a rejection of the idea of a recuperable 'authorial intention' at play in the writing process. Such a claim notwithstanding, it is a matter of course that reader's enthusiastically maintain their impetus towards the construction of meaning(s). Indeed, it is reasonable to assert that Ruthrof's notion of 'sufficient semiosis' (which is generally applied to concrete, pragmatic speech situations) may be extrapolated to the discursive arena of *represented* speech-acts in the literary text. Doing so is to recognize that readers will always at least *attempt* to 'solve' the problem of interpretation by coming up with an array of possibilities informed by the socially sanctioned meanings available to their language community:

> Instead of testing truth relations in such situations, we apply the strategies of sufficient semiosis; we fantasize at high speed a variety of options and settle for pragmatic solutions.[41]

Or, perhaps we don't settle for any immediate solutions, while remaining aware that Murakami's text is offering 'interpretative' options and possibilities, not just posing riddles or puzzles.

As with other of Murakami's works, it is not just this common trope of undecidability which seemingly contradicts the high level of readership of, and interest in this novel. On the contrary, it offers, perhaps, good grounds for *explaining* such publishing success. In *Kafuka*, the entire range of versions of the simulacrum evident in earlier writings are orchestrated into one great instance or overall narrative *effect* of the differend: incommensurability at every level—and yet, a seemingly incessant striving, in the represented dialogues, to find an idiom for this symphony of dissonance.

This very striving produces one of the greatest artistic achievements of the novel: its brilliant deployment of *character as register*. In the juxtaposition and clashing of such a range of different linguistic registers, the text foregrounds the possibilities of dialogue and the representation of spoken discourse in radically new ways. Examples of such dialogues can be found in virtually every conversation in the text: between the hermaphroditic librarian Ôshima and Kafuka, between the young truck driver Yoshino and the gentlemanly Nakata san, between Kafuka and his mother, between Nakata san and the cats, between 'Colonel Sanders' and Yoshino. In such dialogues, the differend—the incommensurability of the different speech registers—continually threatens to undermine any socially cohesive nexus between the two characters. Yet, perhaps this ever present threat of the collapse of communication at the linguistic level forces alternative routes for meaning, a vying with non-linguistic modalities: 'the heart', 'love', 'the body'. Indeed, many of the characters show love and affection for one another *in spite of* their use of very different, socially prescribed idiomatic speech.

In this important sense, therefore, the significance of *Kafuka* as contemporary literature lies not merely in its apparently shocking Oedipal motif as a re-run of the well known Japanese *mazakon* ('mother complex') phenomenon and the 'absent father' syndrome. Rather (and just as Deleuze and Guattari say of Kafka's 'Letter to the Father') the implications of *Kafuka* are distinctly political, historical—a re-territorializing of the Oedipal onto the larger map of the social.

In its subversion of many established norms governing various levels of Japanese social relations (even in the post-industrial nation state) Murakami's deliberate choice of the differend as a way of opening alternative routes to socially sanctioned meanings in *Kafuka* is both shocking and refreshing. The compressed archeology of tropes in this novel is quite astounding, and begs the question: 'where to next?' Perhaps such a question is more than a little naïve, for it supposes that Murakami's oeuvre is in some way 'developing' or 'evolving'. As this discussion has shown, some dimensions of his writing (for example, narrative complexity) are evolving, while others (the use of disjunctive linguistic registers) may be said to be *devolving* away from more orthodox, prescriptive certainties of interpretation. Undoubtedly, the blending of the viewing conventions of a reality TV set with a further exploration of the juxtaposition of different speech styles in Murakami's latest long novel, *Afutâ dâku* (*After Dark*), is just as surprising as the experimentation at work in the *Kafuka* narrative.

Murakami's challenge to Japanese literary modernity represents, if anything, a disruption of momentum towards a more 'developed' form of the novel which might serve to reinforce the notions of 'truth', 'meaning' and 'identity'. The latter have been, of course, the very objects of his ongoing critique. His contribution to contemporary fiction over the last few decades, coupled with the recent developments described in this conclusion, indicate a dramatic change in the available paradigms of writing and representation, and it will be for critics to remain vigilant in their analysis of what this means for Japan's unfolding narrative of its own encounter with modernity. Summing up Murakami's engagement with this encounter as brought to light in our discussion, it is clear that the novels of his early and later trilogies (as well as his more recent work) have marked out new trajectories for literature, the significance of which will, over time, become increasingly apparent.

Notes

1. Lyotard, *The Differend: Phrases in Dispute*, 30.
2. Murakami Haruki, *Henkyô—kinkyô* (Shinchôsha, 1998).
3. Lyotard, *The Differend: Phrases in Dispute*, 13.
4. Lyotard, *The Differend: Phrases in Dispute*, 13.
5. Murakami Haruki, "Nomonhan no tetsu no hakaba," 139.
6. Stuart Sim, *Modern Cultural Theorists—Jean-Francois Lyotard* (Hertfordshire: Prentice Hall/Harvester Wheatsheaf, 1996), 100-103.
7. Geoffrey Bennington *Lyotard: Writing the Event*, Manchester: Manchester University Press, 1988.
8. Ruthrof, *Pandora and Occam: On the Limits of Language & Literature*, 122.
9. Ruthrof, *Pandora and Occam: On the Limits of Language & Literature*, 123. 10
10. See Jean-Francois Lyotard, *Lessons on the Analytic of the Sublime*, trans. Elizabeth Rottenberg, (Stanford: Stanford University Press, 1994), 54-55.
11. Lyotard, *Lessons on the Analytic of the Sublime*, 55.
12. See Jean-Francois Lyotard, 'The Sublime and the Avant-Garde', in *The Lyotard Reader*, ed. Andrew Benjamin (Oxford: Basil Blackwell, 1989), 196-211.
13. See Kawai & Murakami, *Murakami Haruki, Kawai Hayao ni ai ni iku*, 42-47.
14. Kawai & Murakami, *Murakami Haruki, Kawai Hayao ni ai ni iku*, 45.
15. Kawai & Murakami, *Murakami Haruki, Kawai Hayao ni ai ni iku*, 45-46.
16. See Alun Munslow, *Deconstructing History* (London & New York: Routledge, 1997), 146.
17. Murakami Haruki, "Meikingu obu 'Nejimakidori kuronikuru'," 288.
18. Immanuel Kant, *Critique of Pure Reason*, trans. J. M. D. Meiklejohn (London & Melbourne: Dent, 1984), 153.
19. Kant, *Critique of Pure Reason*, 51.
20. Kant, *Critique of Pure Reason*, 52.

21. The strict control of school history textbook publication has been actively challenged by Ienaga Saburô over the last few decades to little avail. See "Textbook Resistance—Japan," in Ian Buruma, *The Wages of Guilt: Memories of War in Germany and Japan,* 189-201.

22. Lyotard, *The Differend: Phrases in Dispute,* xv.

23. Murakami Haruki, *Andâguraundo* (Kodansha, 1997).

24. Murakami Haruki, *Andâguraundo,* 17. A range of Japanese critical responses to this text can be found in *Murakami Haruki Sutadeizu,* ed. Kuritsubo Ryôki & Tsuge Teruhiko (Wakakusashobô, 1999), 152-275. Of particular interest is Fukatsu Kenichirô's essay "Shôgen no 'tasha'" (194-207.), which discusses the idea of the 'other' in the act of giving of evidence, and considers problems of 'narrating the event' and Murakami's position in relation to this, as a kind of 'anti-melodrama'—all of which reflect the kinds of problems discussed by Lyotard in *The Differend.*

25. Murakami Haruki, *Yakusokusareta basho de* (Bungeishunjû, 1998). We recall that this attempt to establish multiple narrative voices is certainly evident in *Nejimakdori,* where historical 'events' are always the product of a character's 'speaking to' a sympathetic listener, rather than the fabrication of an implied omniscient narrator.

26. Murakami Haruki, *Yakusokusareta basho de,* 63.

27. Murakami Haruki, *Yakusokusareta basho de,* 26.

28. Murakami Haruki, "UFO ga Kushiro ni oriru," in *Kami no kodomotachi wa mina odoru* (Shinchôsha, 2000), 10.

29. See Nishio Kanji et. al., *Atarashii rekishi kyôkasho* (Fusosha, 2001).

30. See <http://bookweb.kinokuniya.co.jp/>(17 Jul. 2001). The web-page on July 17 2001, showed for example, the history text at number 2 of the daily 'Best Ten' with its critique at Number 3.

31. Nishio Kanji, *Atarashii rekishi kyôkasho,* 7.

32. For a detailed discussion of these issues in English, see the home page of the Centre for Research & Documentation on Japan's War Responsibility at <http://www.jca.ax.apc.org/JWRC/centre/english/>.

33. Gilles Deleuze, *Difference and Repetition,* trans. Paul Patton (London: The Athlone Press), 128.

34. Gilles Deleuze and Felix Guattari, "An Exaggerated Oedipus" in *Kafka: Toward a Minor Literature,* trans. Dana Polan, Theory and History of Literature, Volume 30 (Minneapolis: University of Minnesota Press, 1986), 10.

35. Murakami Haruki, *Umibe no kafuka,* Shinchosha, 2002.

36. Deleuze and Guattari, "An Exaggerated Oedipus," 10.

37. Murakami insists that he did not consciously set out to create a 'Kafkaesque world' in this novel. See Nomura Hiroshi, "Murakami warudo no naka no 'kafuka'—Murakami Haruki no 'Umibe no kafuka' o megutte," *Tôhoku doitsu bungaku kenkyu,* no. 47, (2003): 39-72; 41. Nomura is quoting from *Shônen no kafuka,* ed. Murakami haruki, (Shinchosha, 2003), 285. Murakami's friend, the psychiatrist Kawai Hayao, plays with the signifier Kafuka as the two Japanese words 'ka' and 'fuka' denoting the pairing, 'possible/impossible', 'able to/unable to', 'pass/fail', etc. See Kawai Hayo, "Kyôkai taiken o monogataru—Murakami Haruki 'Umibe no kafuka'," *Shincho* 99 no. 12 (December 2002): 234-242; esp. 234.

38. Franz Kafka, "Letter to His Father," trans. Ernst Kaiser and Eithne Wilkins, in *Wedding Preparations in the Country and Other Stories,* (London: Penguin, 1987), 30.

39. See Kawai , "Kyôkai taiken o monogataru," 234.

40. Jack Reynolds, "Decision" in *Understanding Derrida*, ed. Jack Reynolds and Jonathon Roffe (New York and London: Continuum, 2004), 46.

41. Ruthrof, *The Body in Language*, 147.

Bibliography

Bibliography of Works in Japanese

Aono, Satoshi. "Suteki na togibanashi." *Gunzô* 37, no. 12 (December 1982): 360-61.

Ayukawa, Shinô. "Jidai o yomu (5): Wakai sedai no kansei—Murakami Haruki: Hitsuji o meguru bôken." *Shûkan Bunshû* 24, nos. 43-46 (25 November 1982): 124-125.

Birnbaum, Alfred. "Murakami Haruki—oinaru hokotenkan." *Shinchô*, no.1 (January 1990): 266-269.

Da Buinchi. "Kaitai zensho: ninki sakka no jinsei to sakuhin." 1, no. 2 (February1996): 20-27.

Den, Kenshin. "Chûgoku no Murakami Haruki—shinsen ketsueki." *Kokubungaku* 40, 4 (March 1995):113-116.

Fujimoto-Keezing, Michael. "Naze kare wa sonna ni subarshii no ka: Murakami Haruki ga America de seikô suru ryû." trans. Okuji Hisayo. *Yurîka—sangatsu rinji zôkan* 32, no. 4 (March 2000): 68-78.

Fukami, Haruka. *Murakami Haruki no uta.* Seikyûsha, 1990.

Hasumi, Shigehiko. "Jikan no nagarenu tojita sekai usukimiwarui hodo no sôzôryoku." *Asahi Shinbun (yûkan)* (2 August 1995): 28.

Hatanaka, Yoshiki. "Murakami Haruki no namae o meguru bôken." *Sôtokushû— Murakami Haruki no sekai—Yûrika* 21, no. 8 (August 1989): 138-139.

Hatori, Tetsuya. "'Nejimakidori' no bunseki: chônôryoku no gendaiteki no imi." *Kokubungaku* 40, no. 4 (March 1995): 64-69.

Hayashi, Yoshimi. "Boku wa Nezumi de, Nezumi wa Boku de." *Shôwa bungaku kenkyû* 19, no. 7 (July 1989): 48-60.

Hioki, Shunji. "Murakami Haruki 'Nejimakidorikuronikuru' shiron." Pp. 98-118 in *Murakami Haruki sutadeizu 04.* Wakakusa Shobô, 1999.

Hirano, Yoshinobu, *Murakami Haruki to 'Saisho no otto no shinu monogatari',* Rinshobô, 2001.

Hirata, Hosea. "Amerika de yomareru Murakami Haruki." *Kokubungaku* 40, no. 4 (March1995): 100-104.

Hiromatsu, Wataru. *"Kindai no chôkoku" ron.* Kôdansha Gakujutsu Bunko, 1991.

Hisai, Tsubaki. *Nejimakidori no sagashikata.* Ota Publishing, 1994.

———. *Nonfuikshyon to karei na kyoi.* magajinhaus, 1998.

Hisai, Tsubaki and Kuwa Masato. *Zô ga heigen ni kaetta hi.* Shinchôsha, 1991.

Iguchi, Tokio. "Dentetsu toiu dekigoto—Murakami Haruki ron." *Gunzô* no. 10 (October 1983): 152-163.

Ikeda, Mutsuki. "'Buntai no nai shôsetsu' ni tsuite—'Yukiguni' no bai." Pp. 227-253 in *Buntaironkô.* Shôhakusha, 1981.

Imai, Kyoto. *Murakami Haruki—OFF no Kankaku.* Kokken Shuppan, 1990.

Imamura, Ninshi. "Bôdoriyaru shindorômu." *Tosho shinbun* 2, No. 11 (November 1983).

Ishikura, Michiko. "Fûfu no unmei II—'Nejimakidori to kayôbi no onnatachi' ron." Senshû daigaku Daigakuin *Bunkenronshû* (September 1993): 15-31.

———. "Murakami Haruki—'Nejimakidori kuronikuru' nôto". Senshû Daigaku Daigakuin *Bunkenronshû* (October 1994): 1-36.

———. et.al. "Murakami dêtabêsu." *Kokubungaku* (February1998): 182-207.

————. *Murakami Haruki sâkasudan no yukikata*, Senshû Daigaku Shuppan Kyoku, 1998.

————. "Aratana sekaizô no kakutoku—'Nejimakidori kuronikuru' ron." Pp. 119-151 in *MurakamiHaruki Sutadeizu 04*, edited by Kuritsubo Yoshiki and Tsuge Mitsuhiko. Wakakusa Shobô, 1999.

Ishimaru, Akiko. "Gendai toshi no naka no bungaku: Murakami Haruki 'Kaze no uta o Kike' o Chûshin ni." *Tôkyô Keizai Daigaku Kaishi* 190, no.1 (January 1995): 185-200.

Kamei, Hideo. "Kindai bungaku ni okeru 'katari' no imi." *Kokubungaku—kaishaku to kanshô* (April 1994): 6-13.

Kanno, Akimasa. "Ukai sakusen shindorômu—gendai shôsetsuka". Tokushû: gendai shôsetsu no hôhô teki seiha, *Kokubungaku* 33, nos. 9-12 (August 1988): 5-18.

Kanno, Shôsei et.al. "Owari no jidai—1988 nen no bungaku kaiko." *Kaien* 8, no. 1 (February 1989): 208-236.

Karatani, Kôjin. *Hihyô to posutomodan*. Fukutake Shoten, 1985.

————. "Murakami Haruki no 'fûkei'—(1)." *Kaien* (November 1989): 296-306.

————. "Murakami Haruki no 'fûkei'—(2)." *Kaien* (December 1989): 236-250.

————. *Kotoba to higeki*. Kodansha, 1993.

————. et.al. "Nijûseiki no hihyô o kangaeru." *Shinchô* (May 1996): 230-263.

Kasai, Kyoshi. "Nezumi no sôshitsu—Murakami Haruki ron." *Waseda Bungaku* 160, no. 9 (September 1989): 80-96.

Kasai, Kyoshi et.al. *Murakami Haruki o meguru bôken*. Kawade Shobôshinsha, 1991.

Katô, Kôichi. "Shinshatachi no okuri mono—Murakami haruki ron." *Gunzô* 38, no. 3 (August 1983).

Katô, Norihiro. "Natsu no jûkyû nichi kan—'Kaze no uta o kike' no dokkai." *Kokubungaku* (March 1985): 36-49.

————. "'Masaka' to 'yare yare'." *Gunzô* (July 1987): 104-127.

————. "Murakami Haruki no tatte iru basho." *Kôkoku hihyô* 158, no. 2 (February1993): 24-33.

————. ed. *Murakami Haruki—ierôpêji*. Kôchi Shuppansha, 1996.

————. "Atarashii sôshitsukan." Pp. 31-52 in *Murakami Haruki—ierôpêji*. Kôchi Shuppansha, 1996.

————. "Jidai no monogatari kara jiga no monogatari e." Pp. 54-78 in *Murakami Haruki—ierôpêji*. Kôchi Shuppansha, 1996.

————. "Ozomashisa to keiji—'Nejimakidori kuronikuru.'" Pp. 191-220 in *Murakami Haruki—ierôpêji*. Kôchi Shuppansha, 1996.

————. "Seichô to henbô o kasaneru shôsetsuka." Pp. 5-8 in *Murakam haruki ga wakaru*, Aera Mook, Asahi Shinbun Extra Report & Analysis 75, 2001.

Kawai, Hayao. "Chikatetsu sarin jiken ga oshieru koto." Pp. 174-193 in *Murakami Haruki sutadeizu—04*.Wakakusa Shobô, 1999.

————. "Kyokai taiken o monogataru—Murakami Haruki 'Umibe no kafuka'." *Shincho* 99 no.12 (December 2002): 234-242.

Kawai, Hayao & Murakami Haruki. *Murakami Haruki, Kawai Hayao ni ai ni iku*. Iwanami Shoten, 1996.

Kawamoto, Saburô. "Murakami Haruki o meguru kaidoku." *Bungakkai* 36, no. 9 (Setember 1982): 288-90.

————. "Rokujûnendai no shôchô toshite no Amerika." *Gunzô* 38, no. 2 (April 1983): 230-233.

————. "Tokubetsu intabyû—monogatari no tame no bôken". *Bungakkai* 39, no. 8 (August 1985): 49-50.

————. *Toshi no kanjusei.* Chikuma Bunko, 1988.

Kawamoto, Saburô & Murakami Haruki. "Watashi no bungaku o kataru—Interview." *Kaien* 8 (August1979): 86-94.

————. "R. Chyandorâ arui wa toshi shôsetsu ni tsuite." *Yurîka* 14, no. 3 (July 1982): 110-135.

Kawamura, Jirô. "82 Bungei jihyô." *Bungei* 21, nos. 7-9 (September 1982): 20-25.

————. "Uso rashii shinjitsu." *Kaien* 6, no. 6 (November 1987): 230-235.

Kawamura, Minato. "'Shinsekai' no owari to hâto bureiku wandârando." *Yurîka,* Sôtokushû 21, no. 8 (August 1989): 174-181.

————. "'Nejimakidori Kuronikuru' no bunseki: gendaishi toshite no monogatari—Nomonhan Jihen o megutte." *Kokubungaku* 40, no. 4 (March 1995): 57-63.

————. "Haruha kawa ni kakaru hashi—gendai toshite no monogatari." Pp. 28-38 in *Murakami Haruki sutadeizu—04.* Wakakusa Shobô, 1999.

Kawanishi, Ran & Taguchi Kenji. "Toshi o utsusu kotoba, 'boku' o kataru eizô." *Waseda Bungaku* 154, no. 3 (March 1989): 18-35.

Kazamaru, Yoshihiko. "Emputei—setto: Murakami Haruki to bokutachi no sedai." *Gunzô* 47, no. 4 (April 1992): 204-233.

————. "'Motogashisa" toiu kyôki 'Nejimakidori kuronikuru' no 'boku' to Murakami-Haruki no genzai." Pp. 62-86 in *Murakami Haruki studeizu—04.* Wakakusa Shobô, 1999.

Kim, Sokuza. "Kankoku no Murakami Haruki." *Kokubungaku* 40, no. 4 (March 1995): 116-118.

Kobayashi, Hirokazu. "Jita no enkan no chûshin." *Gunzô* 46, no. 2 (February1991): 220-256.

Kobayashi, Kyoji. *Shôsetsuden.,* Fukutake Bonko, 1988.

Koboyashi, Masaaki. *Murakami Haruki: tô to umi no kanata ni.* Moriwasha, 1998.

Kôjien. ed. Shinmura, Izura. Iwanami Shoten, 1994.

Koizumi, Kôichirô. "Murakami Haruki no sutairu—'Nejimakidori kuronikuru' o chûshin ni." *Kokubungaku* 40, no. 4 (March 1995): 27-31.

Kojima, Shinô. "'Nejimakidori kuronikuru' no kareta ido." *Shinchô* 92, no. 12 (December 1995): 57-63.

Komori, Yôichi. *Buntai toshite no monogatari.* Chikuma Shobo, 1988.

———— et.al. *Rekishi kyôkasho nani ga mondai ka.* Iwanami Shoten, 2001.

Kuritsubo, Yoshiki & Tsuge Mitsuhiko, eds. *Murakami Haruki sutadeizu,* Vol. 4. Wakakusa Shobo, 1999.

Kuroko, Kazuo. "Murakami Haruki to dôjidao no bungaku—kyôfu arui wa kiki no Monogatari." in *Murakami Haruki to dôjidai no bungaku.* Kawai Shuppan, 1990.

————. *Murakami Haruki: za rosuto wârudo* Daisan Shokan, 1993.

Maeda, Ai. "Boku to nezumi no kigoron." *Kokubungaku* (March 1985): 96-106.

————. "'Toshikûkan' kara no yomi." Pp. 46-52 in *Gendai bungaku kenkyû: jôhô to shiryô,* edited by Hasegawa Izumi. Shibundo, 1987.

————. "Kaku koto to kataru koto." Pp. 27-62 in *Bungaku tekistu nyûmon.* Chikumashobo, 1988.

————. *Kindai dokusha no seiritsu.* Iwanami Shoten, 1993.

Matsumoto, Ken'ichi. "Shudai toshite no 'toshi'" *Bungei* 21, no. 1 (January1982): 279-286.

Matsuzawa, Masahiro. *Haruki, Banana, Genichiro: jidai no kanjussei o yurasu mitsu no shigunaru.* Seikyûsha, 1989.

Miura, Masashi. *Murakami Haruki to Shibata Motoyuki no môhitotsu no amerika,* Shinshokan, 2003.

Miyoshi, Yukio. *Nihonbungaku no kindai to hankindai.* Tokyô Shuppan Kai, 1972.

——. "Kindai bungaku ni egakareta seishun." *Kokubungaku—kaishaku to kanshô* 54, no. 6 (June 1989): 6-11.

Murakami Ryû. *69 Sixty Nine.* Shûeisha, 1987.

——. "Samuzamushii jidai." *Gunzô* 5 (May 1995): 164-168.

Murakami, Ryû & Murakami Haruki. "1980 nen no tômei kankaku." *Shôsetsu gendai* 18, nos. 11-12 (December 1980): 144-158.

Maruyama, Masao. *Nihon no shisô.* Iwanami Shinsho, 1992.

Nagashima, Kyoshi. "Hitsuji o meguru bôken." *Kokubungaku kaishaku to kanshô* 54, nos. 696-699 (June 1989): 178-181.

Nakamata, Akio. *Nihon bungaku: posuto murakami no nihon bungaku,* Asahi shuppansha, 2002.

Nakamoto, Nobuyuki. "Gaikokugo kyôiku no meniyu." *Gengo* 4 (April 1995): 6-7.

Nakamura, Miharu. "'Kaze no uta o kike', '1973 nen no pinbôru', 'Hitsuji o meguru Bôken', 'Dansu, dansu, dansu', yonbusaku no sekai: enkan no sonshô to kaifuku." *Kokubungaku* 40, 4 (March 1995): 70-77.

Nakano, Osamu. "Naze Murakami Haruki genshô wa okita no ka." *Yurîka*—rinjizôkan. (June 1989): 39-45.

Nishio, Kanji et.al. *Atarashii rekishi kyôkasho.* Fusosha, 2001.

Nomura, Hiroshi. "Murakami warudo no naka no 'kafuka'—Murakami Haruki no 'Umibe no kafuka' o megutte." Pp. 39-72 in *Tohoku doitsu bungaku kenkyu,* No. 47, 2003.

Nôsaido—Tokushû: Besutoserâ saidoku 6, no. 3 (March 1996): 102-103.

Numano, Mitsuyoshi. "Murakami Haruki wa sekai no 'ima' ni tachimukau." Pp. 13-27 in *Murakami Harukisutadeizu—04,* Wakakusa Shobô, 1999.

Ôe, Kenzaburô. *Atarashii bungaku no tame ni.* Iwanami Shinsho, 1994.

——. *Manen gannen no futobôru.* Kôdansha Bungeibunko, 1994.

——. "Sekai bungaku wa Nihonbungaku tariuru ka?" Pp. 205-229 in *Aimai na Nihon no watashi.* Iwanami Shinsho, 1995.

Ôe, Kenzaburô & Yasuoka Shotarô. "Sakka to buntai." Pp. 199-229 in *Yasuoka Shotarô Taidanshû—1: Sakka to Buntai.* Yomiuri Shinbunsha, 1988.

Oka,Yasuo et.al. "Gensô bungaku sono honshitsu to hirogari." *Kokubungaku* 44, no. 10 (October 1979): 14-38.

Okamoto, Tarô. "Murakami Haruki to Itaria." *Kokubungaku* 40, no. 4 (March 1995): 120-123.

Oketani, Hideaki. *Fûkei to kioku.*Yayoi Shobô, 1989.

Ono, Yoshie. "Futatsu no JAZZ—futatsu no Amerika." *Kokubungaku* 3 (March 1985): 79-86.

Ôtsuka, Eishi. "Dankai no sedai gurafuitei." *Hon no zasshi* 13, nos. 1-3 (May 1998): 46-48.

——. "Murakami Haruki wa naze 'nazohon' o yûhatsu suru no ka." *Bungakkai* 52, no. 10 (October 1998): 238-264.

Oya,Yuki et.al. *Sutairu no bungaku shi.* Tokyodô Shuppan, 1995.

Rekishi michi: raku raku uôkingu, NHK, July, 2000.

Rubin, Jay. "Sekusu to rekishi to kioku: Murakami Haruki—Nejimakidori kuronikuru." trans. Sakai Yokuko. *Shinchô* 2 (February 1995): 254-59.

Saitô, Michiko. "'Murakami Haruki ron' kuesto." *Bungakkai* 50, no. 8 (August 1996):162-175.

Saito, Tamaki. "Kairi no gihô to rekishiteki gaishô." "Sôtokushu: Murakami Haruki o Yomu," sangatsu rinjizôkan, *Yurîka* 32, no. 4 (March 2000): 62-71.

Sakurai, Tetsuo. "'Omiire' kara no tôsô." *Chûôkôron* 98, no. 5 (October 1983): 206-213.

Sasaki, Motokazu. "Karukute keihaku narazu." *Gunzô* 34, nos. 4-6 (June 1979): 118-19.

Satô, Hiroaki. "Nakagami Kenji no buntai to eiyaku." *Yurîka* 25, no. 3 (March 1993): 113-17.

Sekii, Matsuo. "Hitsuji wa doko e kieta ka." *Kokubungaku* 30 (March 1985): 124-25.

Sengoku, Hideyo. *Airon o kakeru seinen*. Sairyûsha, 1991.

Shibata, Shôji. *Tojirarenai gûwa*. Chûsekisha, 1990.

Shimamura, Masao. "Kaze no uta o kikinagara." *Bungakkai* 12 (December 1986): 294-304.

Shimamura, Teru. "'Kuronos' to no kôso—'Nejimakidori Kuronikuru' no kôdo." Pp. 87-97 in *Murakami Haruki sutadeizu 04*, edited by Kuritsubo Ryôki & Tsuge Teruhiko. Wakakusa Shobô, 1999.

Shimizu, Yoshinori. "Sakka nezumi no shi." Tokushû—*Yurîka* (May 2000): 96-103.

Stalph, Jurgen. "Doitsu no Murakami Haruki." *Kokubungaku* 40, no. 4 (March 1995): 105-108.

Suga, Shûmi. "Gendaisei toiu shinwa." Pp. 87-98 in *Happy Jack: Nezumi no Kokoro*, edited by Takahashi Teimiko. Hokusôsha, 1991.

Suzuki, Sadami. "Kigenron no kansei: Karatani Kôjin 'Nihon kindai bungaku no kigen' hihan." Pp. 47-91 in *Gendai Nihon bungaku no shisô*. Gogatsu Shobo, 1992.

Suzumura, Kazunari. *Terefuon*. Yôsensha, 1987.

———. *Mada/sude ni*. Yôsensha, 1990.

———. *Murakami Haruki kuronikuru, 1983-1995*. Yôsensha, 1994.

———. *Murakami Haruki to neko no hanashi*, Sairyûsha, 2004.

Suzumura, Kazunari & Numano Mitsuyoshi. "'Nejimakidori' wa doko e tobu ka." *Bungakkai* 49, no.10 (October 1995): 100-123.

Takeda, Seiji. *Sekai no rinkaku*. Kokubunsha, 1987.

———. "Murakami Haruki ron—sôshitsu o oyobi yoseru mono." *Kokubungaku* no. 8 (August 1988).

———. "Ririshizumu no jôken o tou koto." *Kokubungaku* 40, no. 4 (March 1995): 32-35.

Tamaki, Kunio. "Murakami Haruki 'Hitsuji o meguru bôken' ron (1): 'toshi shôsetsu' e no shikô." Kansaigakuin Daigaku Jinbun Gakkai, *Jinbun ronkyû* 46, no. 1 (May 1996): 27-40.

———. "Murakami Haruki: 'Hitsuji o Meguru Bôken' ron (2): 'toshi shôsetsu' e no shikô." Kansaigakuin Daigaku Jinbun Gakkai, *Jinbun ronkyû* 46, no. 2 (September 1996): 2-14.

Tanaka, Minoru. "Sûchi no naka no aidenteitei." *Nihon no bungaku* 7 (June 1990): 143-171.

Tsuda, Takashi. "'Atarashii bungaku' to wa nani ka—Ôe Kenzaburô no shôsetsu riron." Pp. 7-13 in *Ashita no bungaku no hiroba e hihyô to bungaku ronsô*. Shin Nihon Shuppansha, 1988.

Tsuboi, Hideo. "Puroguramu sareta monogatari." *Kokubungaku*, (February1998): 64-72.

Tsubouchi, Shôyô. *Shôsetsushinzui*. Iwanami Bunko, 1955.

Tsuge, Teruhiko. "Sakuhin no kôzô kara—Murakami Haruki." *Kokubungaku* 35, no. 7 (July 1990): 115-126.

Ueda, Miyoji. "Yasashii Kyomukan." *Gunzô* 35, nos. 7-9 (September 1980) 298-99.

Unami, Akira. "Posutomodân saikô." Pp. 150-165 in *Han shimin no bungaku*. Hakuchisha, 1991.

Unno, Hiroshi. "Nihon Sankei." in *Fûkei gekijô: rekishishôsetsu no toporoji*. Rokyô Shuppan, 1992.

Uno, Kunikazu. "Bungaku no shûmatsu ni tsuite." *Gunzô* 34, nos. 4-6 (June 1979): 74-91.

Urazumi, Akira. *Murakami Haruki o aruku*. Sairyûsha, 2000.

Wada, Masahide. "Murakami Haruki ni okeru taishô sôshitsu no bungaku." *Waseda Bungaku* 147 (August 1988): 60-73.

Watanabe, Kazutami. "Kaze to yume to furusato." *Gunzô* 40, no. 4 (November 1985): 208-228.

Watanabe, Naomi. "'Chi' no Murakamika." Pp. 19-20 in *Kami omutsu shindorômu—Heisei Gannen e no barizôgen kuriteikku*. Kawade Shobô Shinsha, 1989.

Xu, Jinlong. "Murakami Haruki wa 'meido in chaina' no haruki teki sakuhin o umu ka." *Murakami Haruki ga wakaru*. Aera Mook, Asahi Shinbun Extra Report & Analysis, Special Number 75 (December 2001): 122-124

Yamada, Eimi. *Hizamazuite ashi o oname*. Sinchôbunko, 1988.

Yamagata, Hiroshi. "Sakusha no mokusen—Murakami Haruki no buntai." Pp. 159-162 in *Gataru kotoba, okotsu kotoba*. Kobe: Kumo Shuppansha, 1989.

Yamaguchi, Hiroshi. "Hanshizenshugi bungaku—I Natsume Sôseki." Pp. 149-176 in *Shisô to hyôgen: kindai Nihon bungaku shi no ichi sokumen*. Yûzukido, 1994.

Yasuhara, Ken. "Toriaezu no nihon bungaku hen'ai besuto 10." *Litteraire* 2 (Fall 1992): 94-95.

Yokô, Kazuhiro. *Murakami Haruki no nigenteki sekai*. Chôeisha, 1992.

———. *Murakami Haruki—kyûjûnendai: saisei no konkyô*. Daisan Shokan, 1994.

Yoshida, Haruo. *Murakami Haruki: tenkan suru*. Sairyûsha, 1997.

———. *Murakami Haruki to amerika: bôryokusei no yurai*, Sairyûsha, 2001.

Yoshida, Seiichi. *Gendaibungaku to koten*. Iwanami Shoten, 1981.

Yoshimoto, Takaaki, ed. *Kobayashi Hideo shû*. Kindai Nihonshisô Taikei, 29, 1977.

———. "Nijû seikimatsu no nihonbunka o kangaeru." in *Miedashita shakai no genkai*. Kosumo no Hon, 1992.

Yukawa, Yutaka. "Murakami Haruki Bukku." *Bungakkai* 45, no. 5 (April 1991): 35-37.

Zielinska-Elliot, Anna. "Pôrando no Murakami Haruki." *Kokubungaku* 40, no. 4 (March 1995): 109-112.

Bibliography of Works in English

Adams, Phoebe-Lou. "A Wild Sheep Chase." *The Atlantic* 264 (December 1989): 128.

Adorno, Theodor. *Aesthetic Theory*, translated by R. Hullot-Kentor. edited by Gretel Adorno and Rolf Tiedemann. Minneapolis: University of Minnesota Press, 1997.

Aizawa, Yasushi. "New Thesis." In *Anti-Foreignism and Western Learning in Early Modern Japan*, edited by Bob Tadashi Wakabayashi. Cambridge, Mass.: Harvard University Press, 1991.

Alter, Nora M. "Documentary as Simulacrum: *Tokyo-Ga*." Pp. 136-162 in *The Cinema of Wim Wenders*, edited by Roger F. Cook and Gerd Gemunden. Detroit: Wayne State University Press.

Anderson, Benedict. *Imagined Communities*. London: Verso, 1991.

Appignanesi, R., and Garratt, C. *Postmodernism for Beginners*. Cambridge: Icon Books, 1995.

Arnason, Johann. "Theory: Modernity, Postmodernity and the Japanese Experience." In *Japanese Encounters with Postmodernity*. edited by J. P. Arnason and Y. Sugimoto. London & New York: Kegan Paul International, 1995.

Barthes, Roland. *Mythologies*, translated by Annette Lavers. London: Granada, 1981.

———. *Empire of Signs*, translated by Richard Howard. London: Jonathon Cape, 1983.

Baudrillard, Jean. *For a Critique of the Political Economy of the Sign*, translated by C. Levin. New York: Telos Press, 1981.

———. *Simulations*, translated by Paul Foss, et. al. New York: Semiotext(e), 1983.

———. *The System of Objects*, translated by James Benedict. London & New York: Verso, 1986.

———. "Ballard's *Crash*," translated by Arthur B. Evans. *Science Fiction Studies* 18 (1991): 313-320.

———. "Simulacra and Science Fiction," translated by Arthur B. Evans. *Science Fiction Studies* 18 (1991), 309-13.

———. *The Transparency of Evil: Essays on Extreme Phenomena*, translated by James Benedict. London: Verso, 1993.

———. *The Gulf-War Did Not Take Place*, translated by Paul Patton. Bloomington & Indianapolis: Indian University Press, 1995.

———. *The Spirit of Terrorism*, translated by Chris Turner. London: Verso, 2003.

Benardete, Seth. *Plato's Sophist: Part II of The Being of the Beautiful*. Chicago and London: The University of Chicago Press, 1986.

———. *Plato's Statesman: Part III of The Being of the Beautiful*. Chicago and London: The University of Chicago Press, 1986.

Bennington, Geoffrey. *Lyotard: Writing the Event*. Manchester: Manchester University Press, 1988.

Bhabha, Homi. "Introduction: Narrating the Nation." In *Nation and Narration*. Edited by Homi Bhabha. London: Routledge, 1990.

Bogard, William. *The Simulation of Surveillance: Hypercontrol in Telematic Societies*. Cambridge: Cambridge University Press, 1997.

Borradori, Giovanna. *Philosophy in a Time of Terror: Dialogues with Jurgen Habermas and Jacques Derrida*. Chicago: The University of Chicago Press, 2003.

Broderick, Damien. *Reading by Starlight: Postmodern Fiction*. London: Routledge, 1995.

Burgin, Victor. "Geometry and Abjection." Pp. 104-123 in *Abjection, Melancholia and Love: The Work of Julia Kristeva*, edited by J. Fletcher and A. Benjamin. London & New York: Routledge & Kegan Paul, 1990.

Buruma, Ian. *The Wages of Guilt: Memories of War in Germany and Japan.* New York: Meridian, 1994.

Chandler, Raymond. *The Little Sister.* London: Pan Books, 1979.

————. *The Long Goodbye.* Oxford: Clio Press, 1993.

Clammer, John. "From Modernity to Postmodernity." Pp. 13-20 in *Difference and Modernity: Social Theory and Contemporary Japanese Society.* New York: Kegan Paul International, 1995.

Clifford, Gay. *The Transformations of Allegory.* London: Routledge & Kegan Paul, 1974.

Cornyetz, Nina. "Tracing Origins: Landscape and Interiority." In *Dangerous Women, Deadly Words.* Stanford: Stanford University Press, 1999.

Coulmus, Florian. "'Poison to Your Soul': Thanks and Apologies Contrastively Viewed." In *Conversational Routine: Explorations in Standardized Communication Situations and Pre-patterned Speech.* Edited by Florian Coulmus. The Hague: 1981.

Dale, Peter N. *The Myth of Japanese Uniqueness.* New York: St. Martin's Press, 1986.

Danto, Arthur. "Nietzsche's Perspectivism." Pp. 29-57 in *Nietzsche: A Collection of Critical Essays,* edited by Robert C. Solomon. New York: Anchor Books, 1973.

Deleuze, Gilles. *The Logic of Sense,* translated by Mark Lester and Charles Stivale, edited by Constantin V. Boundas. London, Athlone Press, 1990.

————. *Difference and Repetition,* translated by Paul Patton London: The Athlone Press, 1994.

Deleuze, Gilles & Guattari, Felix. "An Exaggerated Oedipus." In *Kafka: Toward a Minor Literature,* translated by Dana Polan. Theory and History of Literature, Volume 30 (Minneapolis: University of Minnesota Press, 1986)

Derrida, Jacques. *Disseminations,* translated by B. Johnson. Chicago: Chicago University Press, 1981.

————. "White Mythology: Metaphor in the Text of Philosophy." In *Margins of Philosophy,* translated by Alan Bass. Brighton: Harvester Press, 1982.

————. "Freud and the Scene of Writing." Pp. 196-231 in *Writing and Difference,* translated by Alan Bass. London: Routledge & Kegan Paul, 1981.

————. "Violence and Metaphysics: An Essay on the Thought of Emmanuel Levinas." Pp. 79-153 in *Writing and Difference,* translated by Alan Bass. London: Routledge and Kegan Paul, 1981.

————. "Aphorism Countertime." In *Derrida on the Name,* edited by Thomas Dutoit. Stanford: Stanford University Press, 1995.

Ditsky, J. M. "Review of 'A Wild Sheep Chase'." *Choice* 27, no. 2 (May 1990): 1510.

————. Review of "Hard-boiled Wonderland and the End of the World." *Choice* 29 (January 1992): 752.

Ellis, Toshiko. "Questioning Modernism and Postmodernism in Japanese Literature." Pp.140-153 in *Japanese Encounters with Postmodernity,* edited by J. P. Arnason and Y. Sugimoto. London & New York: Kegan Paul International, 1995.

Featherstone, M. and R. Burrows. *Cyberspace/Cyberbodies/Cyberpunk: Cultures of Technological Embodiment.* London: Sage Publications, 1995.

Fineman, Joel. "The Structure of Allegorical Desire." In *Allegory and Representation,* edited by Stephen J. Greenblatt. Baltimore: John Hopkins University Press, 1981.

Fisher, Susan. "An Allegory of Return: Murakami Haruki's *The Wind-Up Bird Chronicle.*" Comparative Literature Studies 37, no. 2 (2000): 155-169.

Foley, Barbara. *Telling the Truth: The Theory & Practice of Documentary Fiction.* Ithaca & London: Cornell University Press, 1986.

Foucault, Michel. *The Archeology of Knowledge,* translated by A. M. Sheridan Smith. London: Tavistock Publications, 1982.

———. *The Order of Things: An Archeology of the Human Sciences.* London: Tavistok, 1970.

Fouser, Robert. "Life Without Zero: An Interview with Miyajima Tatsuo." In *Art Asia-Pacific* 17 (1998): 49-56.

Fowler, Edward. *The Rhetoric of Fiction: Shishôsetsu in Early Twentieth-Century Japanese Fiction.* Berkeley: University of California Press, 1988.

Freud, Sigmund. *The Ego and the Id,* translated by Joan Riviere. London: The Hogarth Press, 1962.

———. "The Distinguishing Psychological Characteristics of Dreams." Pp. 112-132 in *The Interpretation of Dreams,* translated by James Strachey. Harmondsworth: Penguin, 1982.

Frow, John. "Discourse Genres." *Journal of Literary Semantics* 9, no. 2 (1980): 73-80.

———. "Tourism and the Semiotics of Nostalgia." *October* 57 (Summer 1990-91): 123-151.

———. "What Was Postmodernism." In *Time and Commodity Culture,* Oxford: Clarendon Press, 1997.

———. "Repetition and Forgetting." In *Time and Commodity Culture,* Oxford: Clarendon Press, 1997.

Fujii, James A. *Complicit Fictions: The Subject in the Modern Japanese Prose Narrative.* Berkeley and Los Angeles: University of California Press, 1993.

Gilloch, Graeme. *Myth and Metropolis: Walter Benjamin and the City.* Cambridge: Polity Press, 1996.

Goossen, Theodore W., ed. *The Oxford Book of Japanese Short Stories.* Oxford: Oxford University Press, 1997.

Grosz, Elizabeth. *Sexual Subversions: Three French Feminists.* Sydney: Allen & Unwin, 1989.

Habermas, Jurgen. "Modernity versus Postmodernity." *New German Critique* 22 (1981): 3-14.

Hall, Robert K., ed. *Kokutai no Hongi,* translated by John O. Gauntlett. Newton, Mass.: Crofton Publishing Corporation, 1974.

Halliday, M. A. K. "Spoken and Written Modes of Meaning." Pp. 55-82 in *Comprehending Oral and Written Language,* edited by Horowitz and Samuels. San Diego: Academic Press, 1987.

Harrison, Bernard. *An Introduction to the Philosophy of Language.* London: Macmillan, 1979.

Harootunian, H. D. "From Principle to Principal: Restoration and Emperorship in Japan." Pp. 221-245 in *The Uses of History: Essays in Intellectual and Social History,* edited by Hayden White. Detroit: Wayne State University Press, 1968.

———. "Visible Discourses/Invisible Ideologies." Pp. 63-92 in *Postmodernism & Japan,* edited by Miyoshi Masao and H.D. Harootunian. Durham: Duke University Press.

———. *Overcome by Modernity: History, Culture, and Community in Interwar Japan.* Princeton: Princeton University Press, 2000.

Heidegger, Martin. *The Question Concerning Technology and Other Essays,* translated by William Lovitt. New York and London: Garland Publishing Inc., 1977.

Howell, D. L. "Ainu Ethnicity and the Boundaries of the Early Modern Japanese State." *Past and Present* 142 (February1994): 69-93.

Igarashi, Yoshikuni. *Bodies of Memory: Narratives of War in Postwar Japanese Culture, 1945-1970.* Princeton: Princeton University Press, 2000.

Inoue, Ken. "Translated Literature in Japan." *The Japan Foundation Newsletter* 24, no. 1 (1996): 1-7.

Iser, Wolfgang. *The Act of Reading: A Theory of Aesthetic Response.* London: Routledge and Kegan Paul, 1978.

Ishiguro, Kazuo and Ôe, Kenzaburô. "The Novelist in Today's World: A Conversation." Pp. 163-176 in *Japan in the World,* edited by Miyoshi Masao and H. D. Harootunian. Durham: Duke University Press, 1993.

Ivy, Marilyn. "Critical Texts, Mass Artifacts: The Consumption of Knowledge." Pp. 21-46 in *Postmodernism and Japan,* edited by Miyoshi Masao and H. D. Harootunian. Durham: Duke University Press, 1989.

———. *Discourses of the Vanishing: Modernity, Phantasm, Japan.* Chicago and London: University of Chicago Press, 1995.

Iwamoto, Yoshio. "A Voice from Postmodern Japan: Haruki Murakami." *World Literature Today* 67, no. 2 (1993): 295-300.

Iyer, Pico. "Tales of the Living Dead." In "The Arts Book Review." *Time* 150, no. 18 (November 3, 1997).

Jameson, Frederic. *Marxism and Form.* Princeton: Princeton University Press, 1974.

———. *Postmodernism, or, The Cultural Logic of Late Capitalism.* Durham: Duke University Press, 1991.

Kafka, Franz. "Letter to His Father," translated by Ernst Kaiser and Eithne Wilkins, in *Wedding Preparations in the Country and Other Stories,* London: Penguin, 1987.

Kant, Immanuel. *Critique of Pure Reason,* translated by J. M. D. Meiklejohn. London: Dent, 1984.

———. *The Critique of Judgement,* translated by J. C. Meredith. London: Oxford University Press, 1957.

Karatani, Kôjin. "The Discursive Space of Modern Japan." In *Postmodernism and Japan,* edited by Miyoshi Masao and H.D. Harootunian. Durham: Duke University Press.

———. *Origins of Modern Japanese Literature,* edited by Brett de Bary, translated by Brett de Bary et. al. Durham and London: Duke University Press, 1993.

Kawakami, Chiyoko. "The Unfinished Cartography: Murakami Haruki and the Postmodern Cognitive Map." *Monumenta Nipponica* 57, no. 3 (2002): 309-337.

Keene, Donald. *The Japanese Discovery of Europe.* London: Routledge and Kegan Paul, 1952.

———, ed. *Anthology of Japanese Literature.* Hammondsworth: Penguin, 1978.

———. *Dawn to the West: Japanese literature in the Modern Era—Fiction.* New York: Henry Holt and Co., 1987.

Kelley, Theresa M. *Re-inventing Allegory.* Cambridge: Cambridge University Press, 1997.

Kellner, Douglas. *Jean Baudrillard: From Marxism to Postmodernism and Beyond.* Stanford: Stanford University Press, 1989.

———, ed. *Baudrillard: A Critical Reader.* Oxford: Blackwell Publishers, 1994.

Kokutai no Hongi—Cardinal Principals of the National Entity of Japan, edited by Robert King Hall, translated by J. O. Gauntlett. Newton, Mass.: Crofton Publishing Corporation, 1974.

Kondô, Korinne K. "Uchi no Kaisha: Company as Family?" In *Situated Meaning,* edited by Jane M. Bachnik and Charles J. Quinn, Jr. Princeton: Princeton University Press, 1994.

Koschmann, Victor. "Maruyama Masao and the Incomplete Project of Modernity." Pp. 123-41in *Postmodernism and Japan*, edited by Miyoshi Masao and H. D. Harootunian. Durham and London: Duke University Press, 1989.

———. *Revolution and Subjectivity in Postwar Japan*, Chicago: The University of Chicago Press, 1996.

Kress, Gunther. "Textual Matters: The Social Effectiveness of Style." In *Functions of Style*, edited by David Birch and Michael O'Toole. London: Pinter, 1988.

Kristeva, Julia. *Powers of Horror: An Essay on Abjection*, translated by Leon S. Roudiez. New York: Columbia University Press, 1982.

Kunikida, Doppô. "The Bonfire," translated by Jay Rubin. Pp. 31-35 in *The Oxford Book of Japanese Short Stories*, edited by W. Goossen. Oxford: Oxford University Press, 2002.

Lacan, Jacques. *The Language of the Self: The Function of Language in Psychoanalysis*, translated by Anthony Wilden. New York: Dell Publishing Co., 1968.

La Fluer, William. *The Karma of Words—Buddhism and the Literary Arts in Medieval Japan*. Berkeley & Los Angeles: University of California Press, 1983.

Layoun, Mary N. *Travels of a Genre: The Modern Novel and Ideology*. Princeton: Princeton University Press, 1990.

Lemaire, Anika. *Jacques Lacan*, translated by David Macet. London: Routledge & Kegan Paul, 1981.

Leithhauser, Brad. "A Hook Somewhere," *The New Yorker* 65 (December 4, 1989).

Liu, Lydia H. *Translingual Practice: Literature, National Culture, and Translated Modernity—China, 1900-1937*. Stanford: Stanford University Press, 1995.

Loughman, Celeste. "No Place I was Meant to Be: Contemporary Japan in the Short Fiction of Haruki Murakami."*World Literature Today* 71, no. 1 (Winter 1997): 87-94.

Lyotard, Jean-Francois. *The Postmodern Condition: A Report on Knowledge*, translated by Geoff Bennington and Brian Massumi. Minneapolis: Minnesota University Press, 1984.

———. *The Differend: Phrases in Dispute*, translated by G. Van Den Abbeele. Manchester: Manchester University Press, 1988.

———. "The Sublime and the Avant-Garde." Pp. 196-211 in *The Lyotard Reader*, edited by Andrew Benjamin. Oxford: Basil Blackwell, 1989.

———. *Lessons on the Analytic of the Sublime*, translated by Elizabeth Rottenberg. Stanford: Stanford University Press, 1994.

McHoul, A. and Grace, W. *A Foucault Prime*. Melbourne: Melbourne University Press, 1993.

Madsen, Deborah L. *Rereading Allegory: A Narrative Approach to Genre*. London: Macmillan, 1995.

Maher, John C. "The Right Stuff: Towards an Environmental Linguistics." In *Diversity in Japanese Culture and Language*, edited by John C. Maher and Gaynor MacDonald. London & New York: Kegan Paul International, 1995.

Martin, Wallace. "Points of View on Points of View." Pp. 130-135 in *Recent Theories of Narrative*. Ithica: Cornell University Press, 1987.

Matsuoka, Naomi. "Murakami Haruki and Raymond Carver: The American Scene." *Comparative Literature Studies* 30, no. 4 (1993): 423-428.

———. "Murakami Haruki and Anna Devere Smith: Truth By Interview." *Comparative Literature Studies* 39, no. 4 (2002): 305-313.

Melanowicz, Mikolaj. "Some Problems in the Theory of the Novel in Japanese Literature." In *Europe Interprets Japan*, edited by Gordon Daniels. Tenterden, England: Paul Norbury, 1984.

Miller, Laura. "Books: The Wind-up Bird Chronicle." *Salon* (November 24, 1997).
Miyoshi, Masao. *Accomplices of Silence: The Modern Japanese Novel.* Berkeley and Los Angeles: The University of California Press, 1974.
———. *Off Center: Power and Culture Relations between Japan and the United States.* Cambridge, Mass.: Harvard University Press, 1991.
Miyoshi, Masao and H. D. Harootunian, eds. *Postmodernism and Japan.* Durham: Duke University Press, 1989.
Morris-Suzuki, Tessa. *Beyond Computopia: Information, Automation and Democracy in Japan.* London & New York: Kegan Paul International, 1988.
Morton, Leith. *Modern Japanese Culture: The Insider View.* South Melbourne: Oxford University Press, 2003.
Munroe, Alexandra. *Japanese Art After 1945: Scream Against the Sky.* New York: H. N. Abrams, 1994.
Munslow, Alan. *Deconstructing History.* London & New York: Routledge, 1997.
Murakami, Fuminobu. *Postmodern, Feminist and Postcolonial Currents in Contemporary Japanese Culture: A Reading of Murakami Haruki, Yoshimoto Banana, Yoshimoto Takaaki and Karatani Kojin.* Routledge/ASAA East Asia Series. Routledge: London, 2005.
Napier, Susan. *The Fantastic in Modern Japanese Literature: The Subversion of Modernity.* London: Routledge, 1995.
———. "Ôe Kenzaburo and the Search for the Sublime at the End of the Twentieth Century." In *Ôe and Beyond: Fiction in Contemporary Japan*, edited by Stephen Snyder and Philip Gabriel. Honolulu: University of Hawaii Press, 1999.
Natsume, Sôseki. *Ten Night"s of Dream.* Tokyo: Charles E. Tuttle, 1974.
———. *The Three Cornered World,* translated by Alan Turney. London: Arena, 1984.
———. *The Miner,* translated by Jay Rubin. Tokyo: Charles E. Tuttle, 1988.
Nietzsche, Friedrich. "The Use and Abuse of History." Pp. 3-100 in *Thoughts Out of Season: Part II,* translated by Adrian Collins. Edinburgh: T. N. Foulis, 1909.
———. *Beyond Good and Evil,* translated by Walter Kaufmann. New York: Vintage Books, 1966.
Ôe, Kenzaburô. *The Silent Cry,* translated by John Bester. Tokyo: Kodansha, 1990.
Pollack, David. *The Fracture of Meaning: Japan's Synthesis of China from the Eighth through the Eighteenth Centuries.* Princeton: Princeton University Press, 1986.
Pratt, Mary Louise. "The Literary Speech Situation." In *Toward a Speech Act Theory of Literary Discourse.* Bloomington: Indiana University Press, 1977.
———. "Ideology and Speech-Act Theory." *Poetics Today* 7, no. 1 (1986): 59-72.
Quinn, Charles J. "Uchi/Soto: Tip of a Semiotic Iceberg? 'Inside' and 'Outside' Knowledge in the Grammar of Japanese." Pp. 247-294 in *Situated Meaning: Inside and Outside in Japanese Self, Society and Language,* edited by J. M. Bachnik and C. J. Quinn, Jr., Princeton: Princeton University Press, 1994.
Reineke, Martha J. *Sacrificed Lives: Kristeva on Women and Violence.* Bloomington: Indiana University Press, 1997.
Rimer, J. Thomas. *Modern Japanese Fiction and its Traditions: An Introduction.* Princeton: Princeton University Press. 1978.
Rimmon-Kenan, Shlomith. "Narration: Speech Representation." pp. 107-116 in *Contemporary Poetics.* London: Methuen, 1983.
Robins, Kevin. *Into the Image: Culture and Politics in the Field of Vision.* London and New York: Routledge, 1996.

Rosen, Stanley. *Plato's Statesman: The Web of Politics*. New Haven & London: Yale University Press, 1995.

Rubin, Jay. *Injurious to Public Morals: Writers and the Meiji State*. Seattle & London: University of Washington Press, 1984.

——. "The Other World of Haruki Murakami." *Japan Quarterly* 39, no. 4 (October/December 1992): 490-500.

——. "Murakami Haruki's Two Poor Aunts Tell Everything they Know about Sheep, Wells, Unicorns, Proust, Elephants and Magpies." In *Ōe and Beyond: Fiction in Contemporary Japan*, edited by Stephen Snyder and Philip Gabriel. Honolulu: University of Hawaii Press, 1999.

——. "Murakami Haruki." Pp. 227-243 in *Modern Japanese Writers*, edited by Jay Rubin. New York: Charles Scribner"s Sons, 2001.

——. *Haruki Murakami and the Music of Words*. London: The Harvill Press, 2002.

Ruthrof, Horst. *The Reader's Construction of Narrative*. London: Routledge & Kegan Paul, 1981.

——. "Language and the Dominance of Modality." *Language and Style: An International Journal* 21, no. 3 (1988): 315-26.

——. "Narrative and the Digital: On the Syntax of the Postmodern." *AUMLA—Journal of the Australasian Universities Language & Literature Association* 74 (November 1990): 185-200.

——. *Pandora and Occam: On the Limits of Language and Literature*. Bloomington and Indianapolis: Indiana University Press, 1992.

——. *The Body in Language*. London & New York: Cassell, 2000.

Ryckmans, Pierre. *The View from The Bridge: Aspects of Culture—The 1996 Boyer Lectures*. Sydney: ABC Books,1997.

Sakai, Naoki. *Voices of the Past: The Status of Language in Eighteenth-Century Japanese Discourse*. Ithaca: Cornell University Press, 1991.

——. "Modernity and its Critique: The Problem of Universalism and Particularism." Pp. 93-122 in *Postmodernism and Japan*, edited by Miyoshi Masao & H. D. Harootunian. Durham: Duke University Press, 1989.

Sakamoto, Rumi. "Dream of a Modern Subject: Maruyama Masao, Fukuzawa Yukichi, and 'Asia' as the Limit of Ideology Critique." *Japanese Studies* 21, no. 2 (2001): 137-153.

Sayles, Murray. "Tunnel Vision." In *The Australian Review of Books, The Australian Newspaper* (December 13, 2000): 12.

Saussure, Ferdinand de. *Course in General Linguistics* translated by Wade Baskin. London and New York: McGraw-Hill, 1966.

Schoonmaker, Sara. "Capitalism and the Code: A Critique of Baudrillard's Third Order Simulacrum." Pp.168-188 in *Baudrillard: A Critical Reader*, edited by D. Kellner. Oxford: Basil Blackwell, 1994.

Schwab, Gabriele. *The Mirror and the Killer Queen: Otherness in Literary Language*. Bloomington: Indiana University Press, 1996.

Seats, Michael. "'Differance' or 'Differend'?: Constructing Meaning Across Japanese and European Discourses on the Aesthetic." Pp. 41-68 in *Japanese Studies: Communities, Cultures, Critiques; Volume Three: Coloniality, Postcoloniality and Modernity in Japan*, edited by Vera Mackie et. al. Melbourne: Monash Asian Institute, Monash University, 2000.

Shaviro, Steven. "Film Theory and Visual Fascination." Pp. 1-79 in *The Cinematic Body*. Minneapolis: University of Minnesota Press, 1993.

Sigelman, Lee and William Jacoby. "The Not-So-Simple Art of Imitation: Pastiche, Literary Style, and Raymond Chandler." *Computers and the Humanities* 30, nos. 11-28 (1996): 11-28.

Silverman, Kaja. "The Subject." Pp. 126-193 in *The Subject of Semiotics.* New York: Oxford University Press, 1983.

———. *The Acoustic Mirror: The Female Voice in Psychoanalysis and Cinema.* Bloomington: Indiana University Press, 1988.

Sim, Stuart. *Modern Cultural Theorist —Jean-Francois Lyotard.* Hertfordshire: Prentice Hall/Harvester Wheatsheaf, 1996.

Smith, Gregory Bruce. *Nietzsche, Heidegger and the Transition to Modernity.* Chicago and London: The University of Chicago Press, 1996.

Snyder, Stephen. "Extreme Imagination: The Fiction of Murakami Ryû." Pp. 199-218 in *Oe and Beyond :Fiction in Contemporary Japan,* edited by Stephen Snyder and Philip Gabriel. Honolulu: University of Hawaii Press, 1999.

———. "Two Murakamis and Marcel Proust: Memory as Form in Contemporary Japanese Fiction." Pp. 69-83 in *In Pursuit of Contemporary East Asian Culture,* edited by Xiaobing Tang and Stephen Snyder. Boulder, Colarado: Westview Press, 1996.

Snyder, Stephen and Philip Gabriel, eds. *Oe and Beyond: Fiction in Contemporary Japan.* Honolulu: University of Hawaii Press, 1999.

Spahn, Mark and Wolfgang Hadamitzky. *Japanese Character Dictionary.* Tokyo: Nichigai Associates, 1989.

Spencer, Matthew. "Ah, So Surreal." In "The Weekend Australian Book Review." *The Weekend Australian,* (July 7-8, 2001).

Stallabrass, Julian. *Gargantua: Manufactured Mass Culture.* London: Verso, 1996.

Steiner, Henry and Ken Haas. *Cross-Cultural Design: Communicating in the Global Market Place.* London: Thames and Hudson, 1995.

Strecher, Matthew. *Hidden Texts and Nostalgic Images: The Serious Social Critique of Murakami Haruki.* Ph. D Dissertation, University of Washington, 1995.

———. "Translators Note" to Aoki Tamotsu's "Murakami Haruki and Contemporary Japan." Pp. 265-274 in *Contemporary Japan and Popular Culture,* edited by John Whittier Treat. Honolulu: University of Hawaii Press, 1996.

———. "Beyond 'pure' Literature: Mimesis, Formula, and the Postmodern in the Fiction of Murakami Haruki." *Journal of Asian Studies* 57, no. 2 (May 1998): 354-378.

———. "Magical Realism and the Search for Identity in the Fiction of Murakami Haruki." *Journal of Japanese Studies* 25, no. 2 (1999): 263-298.

———. *Dances with Sheep: The Quest for Identity in the Fiction of Murakami Haruki.* Michigan: Centre for Japanese Studies, University of Michigan Press, 2002.

———. *Haruki Murakami's The Wind-up Bird Chronicle: A Reader's Guide,* New York: Continuum, 2002.

Struever, Nancy S. "Historical Discourse." Pp. 249-271 in *Handbook of Discourse Analysis (Vol. 1),* edited by Teun A.Van Dijk. London: Academic Press Inc.1985.

Sturrock, John, ed. *Structuralism and Since.* Oxford: Oxford University Press, 1984.

Suzuki, Tomi. *Narrating the Self: Fictions of Japanese Modernity.* Stanford: Stanford University Press, 1996.

Tsubouchi, Shôyô. Extracts from "The Essence of the Novel." Pp. 100-107 in Donald Keene, *Dawn to the West.* New York: Henry Holt and Company, 1987.

Twine,Nanette. "The Genbunitchi Movement: its Origins, Development and Conclusion." *Monumenta Nipponica* 33 (Autumn 1979).

Van Dyke, Carolyn. *The Fiction of Truth: Structures of Meaning in Narrative and Dramatic Allegory.* Ithaca: Cornell University Press, 1985.

Vice, Sue, ed. *Psychoanalytic Criticism: A Reader.* Cambridge: Polity Press, 1996.

Wakabayashi, Bob Tadashi, ed. *Anti-Foreignism and Western Learning in Early Modern Japan.* Cambridge, Mass.: Harvard University Press, 1991.

Walker, Janet A. *The Japanese Novel of the Meiji Period and the Ideal of Individualism.* Princeton: Princeton University Press, 1979.

———. "On the Applicability of the term 'Novel' to Modern Non-Western Long Fiction." *Yearbook of Comparative and General Literature* 37 (1988): 47- 68.

Weiss, Gail. *Body Images: Embodiment as Intercorporeality.* New York: Routledge, 1999.

White, Hayden. *Tropics of Discourse: Essays in Cultural Criticism.* Baltimore: John Hopkins University Press, 1978.

———. *The Content of the Form: Narrative Discourse and Historical Representation.* Baltimore and London: The John Hopkins University Press, 1987.

Whittier Treat, John. "Introduction: Japanese Studies into Cultural Studies." In *Contemporary Japan and Popular Culture.* Honolulu: University of Hawaii Press, 1996.

Wilcox, Leonard. "Baudrillard, DeLillo's *White Noise* and the End of Heroic Narrative." *Contemporary Literature* 32, no. 3 (1991): 346-364.

Williams, David. *Japan: Beyond the End of History.* London and New York: Routledge, 1994.

Wilson, Michiko. "A Narrative of Simultaneity: The Football Game of the First Year of Mannen," Pp. 48-60 in *The Magical World of Ôe Kenzaburo.* New York: East Gate Books, 1986.

Yoshino, Kosaku. *Cultural Nationalism in Contemporary Japan: A Sociological Enquiry.* London: Routledge, 1992.

Young, Robert. *White Mythologies: Writing History and the West.* London & New York: Routledge, 1995.

Selected Bibliography:
Works by Murakami Haruki

Novels (*chôhen shôsetsu*)

Kaze no uta o kike. Kôdansha, 1979.
1973 nen no pinbôru. Kôdansha, 1980.
Hitsuji o meguru bôken. Kôdansha, 1982.
Sekai no owari to hâdoboirudo wandârando. Shinchôsha, 1985.
Noruei no mori. Kôdansha, 1987.
Dansu, dansu, dansu. Kôdansha, 1988.
Kokkyô no minami,taiyô no nishi. Kôdansha, 1992.
Nejimakidori kuronikuru. Shinchôsha, 1994-95.
Supûtoniku no koibito. Kôdansha, 1999.
Umibe no kafuka. Shinchosa, 2002.
Afutâ dâku, Kôdansha, 2004.

English Translations of Novels

Hear the Wind Sing. Translated by Alfred Birnbaum. Tokyo: Kodansha English Library, 1987.
Pinball, 1973. Translated by Alfred Birnbaum. Tokyo: Kodansha English Library, 1985.
A Wild Sheep Chase. Translated by Alfred Birnbaum. Tokyo & New York: Kodansha International, 1989.
Hardboiled Wonderland and the End of the World. Translated by Alfred Birnbaum. Tokyo & New York: Kodansha International, 1991.
Dansu, dansu, dansu. Translated by Alfred Birnbaum. London: Hamish Hamilton, 1994.
Norwegian Wood. Translated by Alfred Birnbaum. Tokyo: Kodansha English Library, 1989.
South of the Border, West of the Sun. Translated by Philip Gabriel. New York: Alfred A. Knopf, 1998.
The Wind-Up Bird Chronicle. Translated by Jay Rubin. London: The Harvell Press, 1997.
Kafka on the Shore. Translated by Philip Gabriel. London: Vintage Harvill, 2005.

Other Works by Murakami Haruki

Books (in alphabetical order)

Andâguraundo, 1997.
Chûgoku iki no surô bôto. Chûôkôronsha, 1983.
Henkyô—Kinkyô. Shinchôsha, 1998.
Kami no kodomotachi wa minna odoru. Shinchôsha, 2000.
Murakami Haruki zensakuhin 1979-1989, 1-8. Kôdansha, 1990-91.
Murakami Haruki, Kawai Hayao ni ai ni iku. Iwanami shoten, 1996.
Panya saishûgeki. Bungeishunjû, 1986.
Shidonî!. Bungeishunjû, 2001.
Tsukaimichi no nai fûkei. Asahi shuppansha, 1994.
TV pîpuru. Bungeishunjû, 1990.
Wakai dokusha no tame no tanpenshôsetsu an'nai. Bungeishunjû, 1997.
Yakusoku sareta basho de—Underground 2. Bungeishunjû, 1998.
Yume no sâfushitei. Asahi shinbunsha, 1998.

Essays and Interviews (in order of year of publication)

"Toshi shôsetsu no seiritsu to tenkai". *Umi,* no. 5 (May 1982):198-207.
"Kigô toshite no Amerika". *Gunzô* 38, no. 2 (April 1983): 246-250.
"Shigoto no genba kara: Nakagami kenji to no kaiwa." *Kokubungaku* (March 1985).
"Meikingu obu 'Nejimakidori Kuronikuru'". *Shinchô* 92, no. 11 (November 1995): 270-288.
Murakami Haruki rongu intabyû, *Bungakkai*, 59, no. 4 (April 2005): 172-193.

Index

About the Author

Michael Seats is a Senior Lecturer in the Division of Language Studies at City University of Hong Kong. Prior to his current appointment he held teaching and research positions in Asian Studies and Communications at Murdoch University in Western Australia, the University of Notre Dame Australia and Nagoya University of Commerce and Business in Japan. He studied Japanese language at Nanzan University in Nagoya, and has been a Visiting Research Fellow at the Institute of Comparative Culture at Sophia University in Tokyo. His research interests include comparative literature and aesthetics, contemporary Japanese literature and critical theory. He has contributed chapters and articles to books and journals in these areas. He holds degrees in English and Asian Studies, graduate qualifications in Education and a Ph.D in Comparative Literature from Murdoch University, Western Australia.